Historical Dictionary
of the
French Revolution,
1789-1799

Historical Dictionaries of French History

This five-volume series covers French history from the Revolution through the Third Republic. It provides comprehensive coverage of each era, including not only political and military history but also social, economic, and art history.

Historical Dictionary of the French Revolution, 1789-1799
Samuel F. Scott and Barry Rothaus, editors

Historical Dictionary of Napoleonic France, 1799-1815
Owen Connelly, editor

Historical Dictionary of France from the 1815 Restoration to the Second Empire
Edgar Leon Newman, editor

Historical Dictionary of the French Second Empire, 1852-1870
William E. Echard, editor

Historical Dictionary of the Third French Republic, 1870-1940
Patrick H. Hutton, editor-in-chief

Historical Dictionary of the French Revolution, 1789-1799

Edited by
SAMUEL F. SCOTT
and
BARRY ROTHAUS

Greenwood Press
Westport, Connecticut

Library of Congress Cataloging in Publication Data

Main entry under title:

Historical dictionary of the French Revolution,
  1789-1799.

  Bibliography: p.
  Includes index.
  1. France—History—Revolution, 1789-1799—
Dictionaries. I. Scott, Samuel F. II. Rothaus, Barry.
DC147.H57 1985   944.04'03'21   83-16625
ISBN 0-313-21141-8 (lib. bdg.)
ISBN 0-313-24804-4 (lib. bdg. :v.1)
ISBN 0-313-24805-2 (lib. bdg. :v.2)

Library of Congress Catalog Card Number: 83-16625
ISBN 0-313-21141-8
ISBN 0-313-24804-4 (v.1)
ISBN 0-313-24805-2 (v.2)

First published in 1985

Greenwood Press
A division of Congressional Information Service, Inc.
88 Post Road West
Westport, Connecticut 06881

Printed in the United States of America

10 9 8 7 6 5 4 3 2 1

Contents

Contributors

L. J. Abray, Scarborough College, University of Toronto, West Hill, Ontario, Canada

Thomas M. Adams, Transylvania University, Lexington, Kentucky

Effie Ambler, Wayne State University, Detroit, Michigan

Leon Apt, Iowa State University, Ames, Iowa

Eric Arnold, Jr., University of Denver, Denver, Colorado

Charles Bailey, State University of New York, College of Arts and Science at Geneseo, Geneseo, New York

Keith Baker, University of Chicago, Chicago, Illinois

H. Arnold Barton, Southern Illinois University at Carbondale, Carbondale, Illinois

Vincent W. Beach, University of Colorado, Boulder, Colorado

Georgia Robison Beale, Madison, Wisconsin

Paul H. Beik, Swarthmore College, Swarthmore, Pennsylvania

Lenard Berlanstein, University of Virginia, Charlottesville, Virginia

J.-P. Bertaud, Sorbonne, Paris, France

Richard Bienvenu, University of Missouri, Columbia, Missouri

Marc Bouloiseau, Nice, France

Ronald J. Caldwell, Jacksonville State University, Jacksonville, Alabama

Raymond L. Carol, St. John's University, Jamaica, New York

Jack Censer, George Mason University, Fairfax, Virginia

Nupur Chaudhuri, Kansas State University, Manhattan, Kansas

Clive Church, Eliot College, University of Kent, Canterbury, United Kingdom

Susan Conner, Tift College, Forsyth, Georgia

Marvin R. Cox, University of Connecticut, Storrs, Connecticut

Robert R. Crout, University of Virginia, Charlottesville, Virginia

V. M. Daline, Institute of History, Moscow, U.S.S.R.

Philip Dawson, Brooklyn College (CUNY), Brooklyn, New York

Theodore A. DiPadova, Russell Sage College, Troy, New York

William Doyle, University of York, Heslington, York, United Kingdom

Melvin Edelstein, The William Paterson College of New Jersey, Wayne, New Jersey

Elizabeth Eisenstein, University of Michigan, Ann Arbor, Michigan

David M. Epstein, University of Tulsa, Tulsa, Oklahoma

Howard V. Evans, Central Michigan University, Mount Pleasant, Michigan

Robert Forster, The Johns Hopkins University, Baltimore, Maryland

James Friguglietti, Eastern Montana College, Billings, Montana

John G. Gallaher, Southern Illinois University at Edwardsville, Edwardsville, Illinois

Clarke Garrett, Dickinson College, Carlisle, Pennsylvania

Charles A. Gliozzo, Michigan State University, East Lansing, Michigan

Jacques Godechot, Université de Toulouse-Le Mirail, Toulouse, France

Ralph W. Greenlaw, North Carolina State University at Raleigh, Raleigh, North Carolina

William D. Griffin, St. John's University, Jamaica, New York

Vivian Gruder, Queens College (CUNY), Queens, New York

James R. Harkins, Wilfrid Laurier University, Waterloo, Ontario, Canada

Robert D. Harris, University of Idaho, Moscow, Idaho

Jonathan E. Helmreich, Allegheny College, Meadville, Pennsylvania

Arthur Hertzberg, Columbia University, New York, New York

Patrice Higonnet, Harvard University, Cambridge, Massachusetts

Robert B. Holtman, Louisiana State University, Baton Rouge, Louisiana

Gerlof D. Homan, Illinois State University, Normal, Illinois

James N. Hood, Tulane University, New Orleans, Louisiana

Donald D. Horward, The Florida State University, Tallahassee, Florida

Lynn A. Hunt, University of California–Berkeley, Berkeley, California

Maurice G. Hutt, University of Sussex, Brighton, United Kingdom

Frank A. Kafker, University of Cincinnati, Cincinnati, Ohio

Thomas E. Kaiser, University of Arkansas at Little Rock, Little Rock, Arkansas

Gary Kates, Trinity University, San Antonio, Texas

Michael Kennedy, Winthrop College, Rock Hill, South Carolina

Ernest J. Knapton, Chatham, Massachusetts

James M. Laux, University of Cincinnati, Cincinnati, Ohio

Robert Legrand, Abbeville, France

Charles A. Le Guin, Portland State University, Portland, Oregon

James A. Leith, Queen's University, Kingston, Ontario, Canada

Colin Lucas, Balliol College, Oxford, United Kingdom

Jay Luvaas, Army War College, Carlisle, Pennsylvania

John Lynn, University of Illinois, Urbana-Champaign, Illinois

Martyn Lyons, The University of New South Wales, Kensington, New South Wales, Australia

Scott Lytle, University of Washington, Seattle, Washington

John P. McLaughlin, The University of Western Ontario, London, Ontario, Canada

Gordon H. McNeil, University of Arkansas, Fayetteville, Arkansas
Walter Markov, Karl-Marx-Universität, Leipzig, German Democratic Republic
Claude Mazauric, Université de Provence, Aix-en-Provence, France
Jeffrey Merrick, Barnard College, New York, New York
Andrew C. Minor, University of Missouri, Columbia, Missouri
Kate Norberg, University of California–San Diego, La Jolla, California
Alison Patrick, University of Melbourne, Parkville, Victoria, Australia
Jeremy Popkin, University of Kentucky, Lexington, Kentucky
Mary Ann Quinn, The Papers of the Marquis de Lafayette, Cornell University,
  Ithaca, New York
Clay Ramsay, Palo Alto, California
R. Barrie Rose, The University of Tasmania, Hobart, Tasmania, Australia
Steven T. Ross, Naval War College, Newport, Rhode Island
Barry Rothaus, University of Northern Colorado, Greeley, Colorado
Gail S. Rowe, University of Northern Colorado, Greeley, Colorado
Ambrose Saricks, University of Kansas, Lawrence, Kansas
Samuel F. Scott, Wayne State University, Detroit, Michigan
Monika Senkowska-Gluck, Warsaw, Poland
Joseph I. Shulim, Forest Hills, New York
Michael D. Sibalis, University of New Brunswick, Fredericktown, New Bruns-
  wick, Canada
Morris Slavin, Youngstown State University, Youngstown, Ohio
Melvin Small, Wayne State University, Detroit, Michigan
John Spears, Baltimore, Maryland
Martin S. Staum, The University of Calgary, Calgary, Alberta, Canada
Bailey Stone, University of Houston, Houston, Texas
Daniel Stone, The University of Winnipeg, Winnipeg, Manitoba, Canada
George V. Taylor, The University of North Carolina, Chapel Hill, North Carolina
Louis Trenard, Université de Lille, Lille, France
Robert Vignery, The University of Arizona, Tucson, Arizona
Michel Vovelle, Université de Provence (centre d'Aix), France
Henry S. Vyverberg, Southern Illinois University at Carbondale, Carbondale,
  Illinois

Preface

This dictionary had its inception following a series of discussions between the present coeditors. We had taught undergraduate and graduate courses in the French Revolution for over thirty years collectively, one of us at Wayne State University, the other at Wayne and at the University of Northern Colorado, and each of us had spent research time in France at various archives. As friends, we shared our teaching and research methodologies, and our professional concerns. At one point or another in every conversation we had, talk invariably turned to the lack of a single, easily obtainable, and cohesive work that would present students of the French Revolution with the basic facts and interpretations surrounding persons and events connected with that cataclysmic upheaval. Such information, we believed, would be of enormous value to students, who ordinarily would not have sufficient knowledge of the sources to know where to look for accurate data. A sophisticated work of this sort would also be of significance to mature scholars of the Revolution. Familiar as they are with the sources, they often lack the time to examine them even when the material is available in their college or university library.

We observed additionally that although comprehensive historical dictionaries exist in English for virtually every other area of world history, no equivalent historical dictionary in English—or recent work in French—existed for historians of the French Revolution—this despite the fact that much significant research and writing on the Revolution is conducted by English-speaking historians and that interest in the Revolution remains uniformly high in English-speaking universities on both sides of the Atlantic.

During early spring 1978, we met in Detroit to begin the actual planning of a historical dictionary of the French Revolution to overcome these scholarly gaps. From the beginning of our discussions, we agreed that the scope of the Revolutionary decade, the enormous impact it has had on the modern world, the sweeping reforms it engendered, and the many interpretations of its causation and progress during the decade before Napoleon was so vast and complex that if the work were to succeed, we would have to seek the aid of other specialists in specific areas of the Revolution. Consequently 165 personal letters were sent worldwide to scholars of the Revolution requesting their participation in this project. We were astonished at the number of positive responses and extremely gratified that our proposal for an English-language historical dictionary had elicited such enthusiasm from academicians. In the end we secured the agreement of over ninety historians of the French Revolution from Australia, Canada, East Germany, France, Poland, the Soviet Union, and all geographic areas of the United States to contribute articles on their specialties. This gathering together of such a galaxy of scholars for a dictionary of the French Revolution was indicative to us of the professional need for this work.

After examining innumerable reference works, texts, and monographs treating the Revolution, we selected for inclusion in the proposed dictionary some 525 separate entries germane to the history of the French Revolution. In our selection process, and the ultimate assignment of entries to our contributors, we assumed that each specialist would probably desire maximum space to develop the topics within his or her area of expertise. But as editors we also recognized that it was impossible to grant this license, for it would make the dictionary unmanageable in terms of length. While we wished to present as broad a spectrum as possible in this collaborative effort, the length of articles had to correspond with the importance of the entry in the context of the Revolutionary decade. In short, it was our view that Maximilien Robespierre merited more space than his brother, Augustin.

The choices we have made for scholarly examination may not meet with universal approbation. We believe, however, that no important element of the Revolution has been omitted. We have strived throughout this work to establish the proper balance among Revolutionary personalities, events, and constitutional developments so that every significant and representative figure and event has been examined and interpreted. Each article, moreover, has appended to it a bibliography ranging from one to seven titles. Thus, should additional research or inquiry on a specific topic be contemplated, the student or scholar would have available the most reliable sources. We have also added to every entry a list of cross-references of related entries in the dictionary so that as well rounded an analysis as possible of the subject may be presented.

In editing these interpretive essays, we refrained deliberately from imposing our own judgment on the writings of our colleagues, although we repeatedly checked factual accuracy. Every effort was made to hold to the language submitted by the authors. When necessary, however, articles were reduced in length, and sentences and paragraphs were restructured to fit the stylistic format we had adopted. In no case did we make substantive changes in the text of an entry without the permission of the author concerned. Translations from the French were done by the coeditors. We were aided significantly in translations from the German and Russian by Professors Morris Slavin and Walter Markov, each a contributor to this work, and Steven Schuyler, currently on the staff of Harvard University.

Bibliographical information was provided by the contributors to supplement each of their entries. Because this project extended over five years from inception to conclusion, with contributions being received by the coeditors throughout this period, in the summer of 1983 all authors were given the opportunity to update their bibliographies. The vast output of literature on the French Revolution during the 1978-83 period led to significant additions to almost half the entries, as well as to several textual changes occasioned by new interpretations, information, and statistical data being made available. We believe that the currency and the authoritativeness of the dictionary's bibliographies reflect our intention to make it a complete reference work. It is our hope that readers will be as pleased as we are with the care with which each specialist has selected the most relevant sources to sustain his or her work.

We acknowledge with deep appreciation the work of the ninety-six scholars whose contributions made possible *A Historical Dictionary of the French Revolution*. We are confident that their efforts will stand the test of time and that all students of the French Revolution will be grateful for this invaluable resource. We also thank Tricia Kessel, Ginny Corbin, Donna Monacelli, and Jane Hobbs for their unsung but not unappreciated typing efforts. We would be remiss, too, if we failed to recognize the support engendered for this project from Greenwood Press, which plans to publish similar historical dictionaries for nineteenth and twentieth century France. Our special thanks go to Cynthia Harris, a gentle but persuasive and persistent reference editor.

We cannot conclude these remarks without offering a paean of praise for our families whose time we stole and whose lives were made occasionally unbearable by our desire to be perfectionists. Gratefully, we thank Denise, Margie, Eric, Elizabeth, Leslie, Robert, and Timothy.

S. F. S.

B. R.

Abbreviations of Journals in References

Am. Hist. Rev.	American Historical Review
Am. J. of Psychoanalys.	American Journal of Psychoanalysis
Am. Sociol. Rev.	American Sociological Review
A.N.	Archives Nationales
Anj. hist.	Anjou historique
Ann. de Bourg.	Annales de Bourgogne
Ann. de Bret.	Annales de Bretagne
Ann. de l'Est	Annales de l'Est
Ann. de Norm.	Annales de Normandie
Ann. du pr. de Ligne	Annales du prince de Ligne
Ann.: Econ., soc., civ.	Annales: Economies, sociétés, civilisations
Ann. hist. de la Révo. française	Annales historiques de la Révolution française
Ann. Report of the Am. Hist. Assoc. 1904	Annual Report of the American Historical Association for the Year 1904
Ann. révo.	Annales révolutionnaires
A.P.	Archives parlementaires de 1787 à 1860, première série (1787–1799), ed. J. Mavidal and E. Laurent
Ass. bret.	Association bretonne
B.N.	Bibliothèque nationale
Bord. et les îles brit.	Bordeaux et les îles britanniques du XIIIe au XXe siècle
Bull. de la Comm. hist. de la Mayenne	Bulletin de la Commission historique et archéologique de la Mayenne
Bull. de la Soc. des Antiq. de Norm.	Bulletin de la Société des Antiquités de Normandie
Bull. de la Soc. hist. de l'Orne	Bulletin de la Société historique et archéologique de l'Orne
Bull. de la Soc. roy. de Vieux Liège	Bulletin de la Société royale de Vieux Liège

Bull. d'hist. écon. et soc. de la Révo.	*Bulletin d'histoire économique et sociale de la Révolution française*
Bull. of the Inst. of Hist. Res.	*Bulletin of the Institute of Historical Research*
Bull. of the J. Rylands Lib.	*Bulletin of the John Rylands Library*
Cah. d'Hist.	*Cahiers d'Histoire*
Cah. ht.-marnais	*Les Cahiers haut-marnais*
Can. Slav. Papers	*Canadian Slavonic Papers*
Ch. Hist.	*Church History*
Comp. Stud. in Soc. and Hist.	*Comparative Studies in Society and History*
Econ. Hist. Rev.	*Economic History Review*
Econ. Rev.	*Economic Review*
Eighteenth Cent. Life	*Eighteenth Century Life*
Eighteenth Cent. Stud.	*Eighteenth Century Studies*
Eng. Hist. Rev.	*English Historical Review*
Europa	*Europa: A Journal of Interdisciplinary Studies*
Eur. Stud. Rev.	*European Studies Review*
Fr. Hist. Stud.	*French Historical Studies*
Hist. bladen	*Historische bladen*
Hist. J.	*Historical Journal*
Hist. Papers, Can.	*Historical Papers, Canadian Historical Association*
Hist. Reflec.	*Historical Reflections*
Hist. Stud.	*Historical Studies (Melbourne)*
Jahr. für Gesch. Ost.	*Jahrbucher für Geschichte Osteuropas*
J. des Débats	*Journal des Débats*
J. of Mod. Hist.	*Journal of Modern History*
J. of the Hist. of Ideas	*Journal of the History of Ideas*
Mél. de. sci. relig.	*Mélanges de science religieuse*
Mém. de l'Acad. Natl. de Metz	*Mémoires de l'Académie Nationale de Metz*
Mém. de la Soc. d'Hist. de Bret.	*Mémoires de la Société d'Histoire et d'Archéologie de Bretagne*
Mém. de la Soc. éduenne	*Mémoires de la Société éduenne*
Mém. de l'Inst. hist. de Prov.	*Mémoires de l'Institut historique de Provence*
Mém. de la Soc. Archéol. de Tour.	*Mémoires de la Société Archéologique de Touraine*
Mod. Lang. Notes	*Modern Language Notes*
Nice hist.	*Nice historique*
Paris et Ile-de-Fr.	*Paris et Ile-de-France*
Past and P.	*Past and Present*
Pol. Sci. Q.	*Political Science Quarterly*
Pol. Theo.	*Political Theory*
Pro. of the Cons. on Revo. Eur.	*Proceedings of the Consortium on Revolutionary Europe, 1750–1850*

Pro. of the Roy. Mus. Assoc.	Proceedings of the Royal Musical Association
Pro. of the WSFH	Proceedings of the Western Society for French History
Pub. Opin. Q.	Public Opinion Quarterly
P.V. des A.	Procès-verbal des Anciens
P.V. des C.C.	Procès-verbal des Cinq-Cents
Rech. sov.	Recherches sovietiques
Red Riv. Val. Hist. J. of W. Hist.	Red River Valley Historical Journal of World History
Réim. de l'Ancien Moniteur	Réimpression de l'Ancien Moniteur ... depuis la réunion des Etats généraux jusqu'au Consultat, mai 1789–novembre 1799, avec des notes explicatives
Rev. de l'Anj.	La Revue de l'Anjou
Rev. de la Révo.	Revue de la Révolution
Rev. des Deux-Mondes	Revue des Deux-Mondes
Rev. des Et. hist.	Revue des Etudes historiques
Rev. des Et. Mais.	Revue des Etudes Maistriennes
Rev. des ques. hist.	Revue des questions historiques
Rev. d'hist. dipl.	Revue d'histoire diplomatique
Rev. d'hist écon. et soc.	Revue d'histoire économique et social
Rev. d'hist. litt. de la France	Revue d'histoire litteraire de la France
Rev. d'hist mod. et cont.	Revue d'histoire moderne et contemporaine
Rev. du d-h. siècle	Revue du dix-huitième siècle
Rev. hist.	Revue historique
Rev. hist. de Bord. et de la Gir.	Revue historique de Bordeaux et de la Gironde
Rev. hist. de la Révo.	Revue historique de la Révolution française
Rev. hist. de dr. franç. et etr.	Revue historique de droit français et étranger
Révo. française	La Révolution française
Stud. in Burke	Studies in Burke and His Time
Stud. in Eighteenth Cent. Cult.	Studies in Eighteenth Century Culture
Stud. on Voltaire and Eighteenth Cent.	Studies on Voltaire and the Eighteenth Century
Trans. of the Amer. Phil. Soc.	Transactions of the American Philosophical Society
USF Lang. Q.	USF Language Quarterly
Vie Judic.	La Vie Judiciaire
Wm. and Mary Q.	William and Mary Quarterly

The Dictionary

A

ABBAYE. See PRISONS.

ABONNEMENTS, lump sum payments by various corporate entities such as certain of the *pays d'états*, as well as some towns and cities and other corporate groups. See *VINGTIEME*.

ABOUKIR, BATTLE OF. See BATTLE OF ABOUKIR.

ACTES DES APOTRES, royalist newspaper, published from 2 November 1789 until October 1791. It was the work of fifteen to twenty writers, some of whom, such as F.-D. Montlosier and S. Clermont-Tonnerre, were constitutional monarchists while others, like A. Rivarol, F.-L. Suleau, and A.-B.-L.R. Mirabeau, were defenders of absolute monarchy. The founder was J.-G. Peltier who, although born in the Maine-et-Loire in 1760, had lived a long time on Santo Domingo.

The paper consisted of an introduction, written by Rivarol, which presented statements of doctrine. Satirical texts in prose or verse and songs formed the rest of the paper.

The aim of the journal was to inform the largest possible audience that the Revolution was the work of a group of troublemakers who wanted disorder and anarchy only to allow them to seize property and power. Its method was to ridicule the men and institutions of the Revolution, but the royal family was not always spared. As a satirical paper that advocated violence, the *Actes des Apôtres* had many imitators; the same tone marked a wide range of newspapers. The *Actes* enjoyed considerable success until the emigration of most of its contributors—and perhaps the cessation of royal subsidies—forced it to cease publication in the fall of 1791.

J.-P. Bertrand, *"L'Ami du Roi de* Royau, *l'Ami du Roi* de Montjoye, le *Courrier extraordinaire* de Duplais'' (diplôme d'études supérieures, University of Paris, 1959); M. Pellet,

Un Journal royaliste en 1789, les Actes des Apôtres (Paris, 1873); J. Popkin, *The Right-Wing Press in France, 1792–1800* (Chapel Hill, N.C., 1980).

J.-P. Bertaud

Related entry: MONARCHIENS.

ACTIVE CITIZEN, a person having the right to vote in the first stage of an election of legislators or administrators in the period 1789–92. The electoral laws of that period defined three degrees of entitlement to participate. The highest was to be eligible to be elected to the National Assembly. The next was to be eligible to be chosen an elector or an administrator of a department or district or municipality. The primary degree was that of active citizen, one having the right to vote in the choice of electors and in the election of municipal officials.

Differentiating between the right to vote and the ordinary civil rights (for instance, freedom from unreasonable imprisonment) was not a new idea in 1789. The use of the word *active* for this distinction, however, originated in the recommendations of E.-J. Sieyès, on 21 July 1789, for a declaration of rights. The National Assembly specified the qualifications of the active citizen in October, and they became part of the law on primary assemblies, elections, and the organization of administrative assemblies, which was completed on 22 December 1789 and ultimately became part of the Constitution of 1791.

To be an active citizen, one had to be male, older than twenty-five years of age, actually domiciled in the canton for at least one year, not in domestic service, and not bankrupt or insolvent; and one had to pay a direct tax that amounted to triple the daily wage for unskilled labor in the locality. A civic oath was required: to maintain with all one's power the constitution of the kingdom, to be faithful to the nation, the law, and the king, and to fulfill zealously and courageously the civil and political functions entrusted to one.

Official statistics, promulgated by the National Assembly on 27 May 1791, gave the number of active citizens as 4,298,360. This would have been 15.6 percent of the total population of France and about 61 percent of the males over age twenty-five, according to the population estimates by Henry and Blayo (1975).

To be eligible to be an elector or a department or district or municipal administrator, one had to be an active citizen paying an annual direct tax ten times the amount of the local daily wage. Of those eligible, a very small proportion were actually chosen as electors since the number was limited by the constitution to 1 percent of the active citizens. To be eligible to be a legislator, one had to be an active citizen paying an annual direct tax equivalent to the value of a mark (244.5 grams) of silver (the *marc d'argent*), or approximately 51 *livres*, and owning some land.

The activity of the active citizen was not limited to voting. The decree of 12 June 1790 on the organization of the National Guard obligated every active citizen to be enrolled in his local unit. A later decree, that of 6 December 1790, authorized those who were not active citizens but were already in the National Guard to remain, but new militiamen had to be active citizens.

In 1790 and 1791, the qualifications for voting and office holding were the subject of repeated objections, premised generally on the Declaration of Rights. In Paris particularly, many petty bourgeois paid no direct tax and were excluded even from the category of active citizens. After the king's attempt to flee and the massacre on the Champ de Mars, in the anxious atmosphere of August 1791 the constitution was revised in an antidemocratic sense. The eligibility requirement of the mark of silver for election to the legislature was eliminated. But the qualifications required of electors were made much more stringent. These revisions passed into the final text of the Constitution of 1791 but were intended to take effect only in 1793 and were not actually applied until 1795 under the Constitution of the Year III.

The distinction between active and other citizens was abolished by an insurrectionary movement that took shape after the decree declaring that *"la patrie est en danger"* (11 July 1792). As hundreds of National Guardsmen from Brittany, Provence, and elsewhere arrived in Paris, the Louvre section decided to admit to its National Guard unit and to its citizen meetings men who were not active citizens. Other sections followed. On the victory of the insurrection of 10 August 1792 and for three years after, the right to vote and the right to bear arms were not reserved to property owners.

L. Henry and Y. Blayo, "La population de la France de 1740 à 1860," *Population* 30, special number (November 1975); R. R. Palmer, *The Age of the Democratic Revolution*, vol. 1 (Princeton, 1959).

P. Dawson

Related entries: CHAMP DE MARS; DECLARATION OF THE RIGHTS OF MAN; PASSIVE CITIZEN; SIEYES; 10 AUGUST 1792.

AFFAIR, XYZ. See XYZ AFFAIR.

AGENTS NATIONAUX, officers of the districts and municipalities appointed under the Law of 14 Frimaire Year II (4 December 1793) to represent the national government in the local administrations. The national agents of the municipalities were to correspond directly with the administrative directories of their districts, and the national agents of the districts were to correspond directly with the Committee of Public Safety and the Committee of General Security, at Paris. All national agents were required to forward written reports at intervals of ten days. The Law of 14 Frimaire prescribed no national agents at the level of the departments because these were considered, by and large, to have compromised themselves in the federalist movement of the summer of 1793.

The *procureurs syndics* of the districts and the *procureurs* of the communes were designated *ex officio* as national agents for their administrations. Because some of those elected in November 1792 lacked either ability or Revolutionary integrity and zeal, many had to be replaced so that the position of national agent could be filled by men with the exceptional qualifications required. In the rural communes, the representatives on mission who had to replace the *procureurs* found it was sometimes necessary to appoint illiterate or nearly illiterate peasants in order to provide national agents who had a sufficient degree of Revolutionary and patriotic commitment.

The main responsibility of the national agents was to see that the national laws were enforced and the national policies set by the National Convention and its committees were carried out in the localities. For this purpose they were assigned duties of surveillance and inspection and encouraged to tour their jurisdictions looking for irregularities and overseeing the execution of the laws. In their reports, they were required to reveal all divisions, conflicts, and conspiracies, actual or suspected, that might obstruct the execution of the laws.

After the events of 9 and 10 Thermidor (27–28 July 1794), the ranks of the national agents were purged of Montagnards and other extremists, and moderates were brought in to replace those who were dismissed. The office of national agent, like nearly all other innovations of the Revolutionary government, later became a victim of the Thermidorian Reaction. The Convention suppressed it on 17 April 1795.

J. Godechot, *Les institutions de la France sous la Révolution et l'Empire*, 2d ed. (Paris, 1968); P. Mautouchet, *Le gouvernement révolutionnaire (10 août 1792-4 brumaire an IV)* (Paris, 1912).

G. V. Taylor

Related entries: FEDERALISM; LAW OF 14 FRIMAIRE; THERMIDORIAN REACTION.

AGRARIAN LAW. See PEASANTRY.

AIDES, transfer taxes. In its medieval context an *aide* was any pecuniary obligation of a vassal to his overlord paid under certain circumstances or *cas*, such as the knighting of the overlord's son or the marriage of his daughter. There are examples of the enforcement of such *aides* on peasant *censitaires* even in the eighteenth century, but by then it was an anachronism. Since the fourteenth century, the *aides* were being transformed into a royal tax on the sale of merchandise and beverages. However, as the *octrois*, a more recent tax, began to burden these same products, the *aides* became restricted to a tax on beverages, wine in particular.

The tax was exacted at each sale, each exchange, and each stopping point in transit, raising the final selling price accordingly. Estimating the precise amount of the tax was very complicated since it required measuring both the quantity and quality of the wine, cider, or brandy, while policing the trade closely in order to detect fraudulent measuring, clandestine private sales, and smuggling. More than any other tax, the *aides* involved heavy fines for fraud and constant intervention in the wine trade, including inspection of wine presses, stills, and caves, followed by appropriate documented certification. As an administrative fiscal function, the police of the wine trade was remarkably efficient for its time and had the incidental effect of protecting the consumer against short measuring and diluting. But other aspects of collection outweighed these advantages for most consumers and producers.

Understandably the *aides* were very unpopular in the wine-growing regions of the kingdom—Burgundy, Champagne, the Bordelais, and the Charente and Loire valleys. The *cahiers* of 1789 referred to the *aides* as an "atrocious *droit*" and "tyrannical tax," blaming them more for the frequency of incidence and the army of inspectors than for the actual tax rate. Here was a clear example of a tax revolt against the royal bureaucracy itself as an arbitrary intruder on the privacy of the citizenry. As the Third Estate of Nemours put it in 1789, no doubt with some exaggeration:

> The citizens are obliged to open their doors day or night to armed men ... without any way of distinguishing them from brigands ... and are obliged to entrust to them their fortune, honor, and sometimes their very life. [Quoted in M. Marion, *Dictionnaire des Institutions de la France* (Paris, 1923)]

J. Bosher, *French Finances, 1770–1795: From Business to Bureaucracy* (Cambridge, England, 1970); G. Chaussinand-Nogaret, *Les Financiers de Languedoc au XVIIIe siècle* (Paris, 1970); M. Marion, *Histoire financière de la France*, 6 vols. (Paris, 1914-1926); G. T. Matthews, *The Royal General Farms in Eighteenth Century France* (New York, 1958).

R. Forster

Related entry: *OCTROI*.

AIGUILLON, ARMAND-DESIREE DU PLESSIS-RICHELIEU D'AGE-NOIS, DUC D' (1761-1800), army officer, member of the National Assembly, and scion of a prominent and wealthy noble family. His father, Emmanuel-Armand, had a successful military career, served as governor of Brittany, and became foreign and war minister of Louis XV. Young Armand-Désirée entered military service in 1773 and rose to the rank of colonel by 1788, the year his father died and he became duke. He was elected a noble deputy to the Estates General from Agen, where his family held vast estates.

Of liberal persuasion—not surprising for a noble who grew up in a family at the center of politics—he favored the fusion of the three estates into the National Assembly and was a leader of the Breton Club. On the night of 4 August 1789, he planned to introduce a resolution at the National Assembly renouncing some noble privileges so as to forestall further peasant attacks on noble chateaux and other property. The vicomte de Noailles jumped in ahead of him, however, and offered even more generous concessions. Then Aiguillon spoke, and with more weight, for, unlike Noailles, he had considerable property to lose. Aiguillon proposed that taxes should be levied on all, according to their ability to pay; tax exemptions should be abolished for organized groups, towns, collectivities, and individuals; and feudal and seigneurial dues could be redeemed by those who owed them, at a rate to be fixed by the National Assembly. The Assembly went on to enact a number of these and other concessions.

After the night of 4 August, the duc d'Aiguillon played a small role in the Assembly's deliberations. On its dissolution, he joined the French army on the eastern frontier. He emigrated after 10 August 1792, first to London and then to Hamburg, where he lived with his friends, the Lameth brothers. He died in Hamburg in May 1800.

A. de Lameth, *Histoire de l'assemblée constituante*, 2 vols. (Paris, 1828-29); P. Kessel, *La Nuit du 4 août 1789* (Paris, 1969).

J. M. Laux

Related entries: 4 AUGUST 1789; JACOBINS; LAMETH entries.

ALEMBERT, JEAN LE ROND D' (1717-83), mathematical genius and coeditor with D. Diderot of the *Encyclopédie*; member of the French Academy and *philosophe*. See *ENCYCLOPEDIE*.

ALMANACH DU PERE GERARD, L' (1791), political pamphlet. On 19 September 1791, the Paris Jacobin club announced a contest for a pamphlet specifically written for peasants that would present the spirit and principles of the recently adopted French constitution. The Jacobins required the work to be short and in language that peasants could easily grasp. Although the idea belonged to H. Grégoire, the project reflected the club's view that the Revolution had largely been created by Parisians and that a clear understanding of the new regime's basis had to be spread throughout the countryside quickly if political stability were to be achieved. Forty-two works were entered in less than a month. A commission of five members (Grégoire, the marquis de Condorcet, F.-X. Lanthenas, E. Clavière, and E. Polverelle) studied the entries. On 23 October the club announced that the *Almanach du Père Gérard* had won the contest. This was hardly a surprise. Its author, playwright J.-M. Collot d'Herbois, was secretary of the Jacobins and one of its most outspoken members. The *Almanach* tells the story of an imaginary deputy of the Constituent Assembly (Goodman Gérard) who retires to his native Brittany in the fall of 1791. Each day the peasants of his village gather around him to discuss the new regime. These dialogues form the chapters of the pamphlet. Subjects include the nation, king, law, property, taxes, and the constitution itself. The ideology of the dialogues contains a Jacobin bias, which can be associated with the Brissotin faction in the Legislative Assembly. The Feuillants are criticized (though not by name) for supporting the *marc d'argent* and slavery in the colonies. The king is acknowledged to be the hereditary chief of the executive branch, but he is criticized for not following the wishes of the National Assembly more faithfully and for oppressing the poor during the Old Regime. Although condemned as still too royalist in the *Révolutions de France et de Brabant*, the *Almanach* was very well reviewed by the press and went through at least seven editions during its first year.

F.A. Aulard, ed., *La Société des Jacobins*, 6 vols. (Paris, 1889–97), vol. 3.

G. Kates

Related entries: CLAVIERE; COLLOT D'HERBOIS; CONDORCET; FEUIL-LANTS; GIRONDINS; GREGOIRE; *MARC D'ARGENT*; *REVOLUTIONS DE FRANCE ET DE BRABANT*.

AMALGAM, THE, reorganization of line and volunteer units of the French army into a single, uniform armed force, decreed by the National Convention on 21 February 1793. In February 1793 the Republic possessed two distinct armies, different in means of recruitment, uniform, pay, discipline, and method of promotion and advancement: the former royal army and the battalions of national volunteers. Standardizing the army would respond to both technical needs and political requirements. The creation of a single army would provide more thorough information by facilitating inspections, avoid the continued existence of skeletal units alongside excessively large battalions, allow a more efficient distribution of cadres, and permit the formation of new tactical units— the demibrigades—which the preceding campaign had shown were necessary. This would also be an opportunity to create a patriot army, for not only would the two volunteer battalions placed side by side with one regular battalion (the composition of a typical demibrigade) better learn the profession of arms, but also the volunteers would convey the Revolutionary spirit to the former army of the aristocrats. The decree of 21 February 1793 nationalized the army; volunteers and line troops would have the same equipment, the same pay, the same discipline, and leaders selected in the same way. Due to pressure from the Girondins, however, the amalgam was postponed.

Although amalgamation was applied here and there by some generals, it was not until instructions were given on 10 January 1794 that a two-year process of implementation began. The process took a number of forms, including the incorporation of conscripts, *embrigadement* or the juxtaposition of battalions, and genuine amalgamation in which soldiers of different origins were mixed at the company level. This created an incomparable tool of war and provided, under the aegis of the Jacobins who politicized the army, the means of unifying the French people, who until then had been divided by language and custom.

J.-P. Bertaud, "Notes sur le premier amalgame," *Rev. d'hist. mod. et cont.* 20 (1973) and *La Révolution armée* (Paris, 1979); S. Scott, "The Regeneration of the Line Army during the French Revolution," *J. of Mod. Hist.* 42 (1970).

J.-P. Bertaud

Related entry: DUBOIS-CRANCE.

AMAR, JEAN-BAPTISTE-ANDRE (1755–1816), terrorist, member of the Committee of General Security. He was born 11 May 1755 in Grenoble to J.

and M.-M. G. Amar, heirs of an affluent cloth merchant family. Their several rural estates provided Amar's lifelong comfortable wealth. After earning a license in law from the University of Orange, he joined the Parlement of Grenoble in 1774 as an *avocat* but showed little interest in the practice of law. In 1784 he purchased an insignificant title of nobility, treasurer of France, for 200,000 *livres*. An elegant dandy of the local aristocracy, he was tall and thin, with graceful limbs and blond hair. Although he was never a leader, he was well known as a single-mindedly dedicated worker for any cause he chose to espouse.

In November 1789 he joined the local Jacobin club and became a zealous spokesman for its causes even though he had been heretofore nonpolitical. In 1790 he was elected vice-president of the directory for the district of Grenoble and earned the reputation of a remarkably industrious and efficient administrator during his two-year term. He was elected a deputy of the Isère to the National Convention in 1792.

Immediately he won notice as a passionate spokesman of the Mountain with his ferocious attacks on the Girondins and Louis XVI. A representative on mission from March to May 1793, he arrested over 1,000 persons in the Ain and Isère. Although he executed no one, his reputation as a terrorist grew.

In the Committee of General Security to which he was elected, he was the second most important member, after M. Vadier, and was its usual spokesman in the Convention. On 3 October 1793, he made a crucial report condemning the Girondins and their sympathizers. Shortly after twenty-two imprisoned Girondins were executed and seventy-three of their defenders in the Convention were arrested. After Amar concluded a lengthy investigation of the India Company scandal, he presented reports on 16 and 19 March 1794 indicting the Dantonists and Hébertists. He used the police power of his committee to help engineer the arrests of both the Hébertists and the Dantonists. In the final phase of the Terror, Amar was at the zenith of his power, leading the acceleration of arrest orders of the committee. So successful had he been that he was elected president of the National Convention from 5 to 19 April 1794.

Amar steadfastly refused to attach himself to any leader or faction within the Mountain. He rarely attended the Jacobin club. His original dislike for M. Robespierre turned into hatred after Robespierre publicly criticized his Girondin and India Company reports and added a police bureau to the Committee of Public Safety as a rival to the Committee of General Security. Believing Robespierre to be an obstacle to the Terror, he helped lead the coup of 9 Thermidor (27 July 1794). Swept from power in the Thermidorian Reaction, he regretted his role in the coup for the remainder of his life. Arrested as a terrorist by decree of the Convention on 2 April 1795, he was imprisoned in the Hamm fortress until the general amnesty of 26 October 1795.

Amar immediately plotted a return to power and organized a group of former Montagnards to ally with G. Babeuf's Conspiracy of Equals. The Directory crushed the ill-conceived conspiracy on 10 May 1796 and arrested Amar. He was tried by the High Court of Vendôme and acquitted on 26 May 1797. From

1797 until 1807 he lived on his estates in the Isère and Mont Blanc. He spent the last years of his life in lonely obscurity in Paris studying Swedenborgianism and died in Paris, 23 December 1816, at the age of sixty-one.

Traditional historiography has repeated the Thermidorians' vengeful accusations of "le farouche" Amar, the evil engineer of his committee. Recent studies cast serious doubt on this view. Examinations of the records of the Committee of General Security show that he did not abuse his power, did not use his authority to excess, and was far from being the most active member. His release orders (653) compare favorably with his arrest orders (779) during his tenure on the committee. Amar was essentially a zealous but shortsighted administrator of government policy. By conspiring to liquidate the Dantonists, Hébertists, and Robespierrists, he unwittingly aided the destruction of his own hopes for the Revolution.

R. J. Caldwell, "André Amar and the Fall of the Mountain," *Pro. of the Cons. on Rev. Eur.* (1975); L.L.T. Gosselin (pseud. G. Lenôtre), "Le farouche Amar," *Vieilles maisons, vieux papiers,* 6ᵉ série (Paris, 1930); E. J. Walker, "André Amar and His Role in the Committee of General Security," *Historian* 23 (1961).

R. J. Caldwell

Related entries: BABEUF; CONSPIRACY OF EQUALS; GIRONDINS; GRENOBLE; 9 THERMIDOR YEAR II; THERMIDORIAN REACTION; VADIER.

AMI DES CITOYENS, L'. See TALLIEN.

AMI DU PEUPLE, L', J.-P. Marat's newspaper, which appeared from 12 September 1789 to 14 July 1793 under several titles. It is one of the most famous Revolutionary newspapers and is considered to have had a greater influence than any other paper. Without contesting this conclusion, it must be admitted that we lack any empirical evidence to prove the paper's influence. In the absence of subscription lists and lacking any systematic study of *L'ami du peuple,* we know nothing about the number of its subscribers, its daily circulation, the number of its readers, or the regional and socioprofessional composition of its subscribers. We do not even know how many, and which, Jacobin clubs were among its subscribers. One estimate of the daily circulation is 2,100. The fact that the paper lasted for nearly four years attests to its popularity. The publication of numerous counterfeit editions during periods of prolonged interruption, as well as several spurious continuations after Marat's death, is further proof of the paper's success.

Dated 12 September 1789, Marat's paper first appeared under the title *Le publiciste parisien.* On 16 September Marat renamed it *L'ami du peuple,* which continued until 21 September 1792. Reappearing on 25 September 1792 as the *Journal de la République française,* it continued under that name until 11 March 1793. Since the decree of 9 March 1793 declared the careers of deputy and journalist to be incompatible, Marat changed the title. The issues of 14–30 March appeared either as *Le publiciste de la République française* or *Observations à mes commettants*. On 1 April it reappeared under the title *Le publiciste de la République française*, lasting until 14 July 1793, the day after Marat's assassination. As a result of Marat's clandestine life, *L'ami du peuple* experienced numerous interruptions.

L'ami du peuple was a daily political journal, usually consisting of eight pages in octavo. Marat was the editor, journalist, and, at times, even the printer. The paper was directed at the Parisian popular classes. A subscription cost 12 *livres* for a quarter, or 48 *livres* for a year, but on 21 March 1791, Marat offered a 25 percent discount to 36 *livres*. *L'ami du peuple* was not cheap. Initially it was more expensive than J.-P. Brissot's daily, which cost 36 *livres* for an annual subscription. It is doubtful that the urban *menu peuple* could afford a subscription, but it was probably read to them publicly in clubs, section assemblies, at work, in cafés, or at the Palais Royal.

Marat claimed to have created *L'ami du peuple* because he had tried and failed to influence some of the most famous deputies of the Constituent Assembly. He decided to publish a newspaper to spread his views more rapidly and plead the people's cause more effectively. One of the aims of his paper was to watch over the deputies. Claiming at first to be impartial and moderate, after only two months Marat changed his tone to bitter satire and vituperation. Observing the Assembly as "the eye of the people" and judging its work like a Roman censor, the more he watched, the more he censured.

Marat's role in the Revolutionary press was that of denouncer, but without the vulgar language of J.-R. Hébert's *Père Duchesne*. Everywhere he saw traitors and plots, which he denounced to the people. Among the first to be excoriated were the Paris Commune, the Châtelet, and J. Necker. He also assailed J.-S. Bailly, H.-G. R. Mirabeau, and the marquis de Lafayette. His faith in Louis XVI endured for a while longer. Robespierre was one of the few deputies whom he admired.

Marat advocated popular insurrection and popular violence. When his early hopes for cooperation between the king and the third estate were dashed, Marat became convinced of the perversity of the supporters of the Old Regime. He believed nothing could be obtained from them except through force. He concluded that their plots could be ended only by exterminating those guilty of hatching them. Deceived by the Assembly, he called on the people to mete out justice themselves. As early as 18 September 1789, he appealed to the people to punish their enemies. Popular vengeance was only a defensive reaction to counterrevolutionary provocations and would save patriots' lives. Marat demanded popular executions, the number of heads varying from 500 to 100,000. On 17 September 1790, he argued that if 500 or 600 heads had been cut off when the Bastille was taken, the Revolution would have triumphed. But now 10,000 heads would scarcely suffice. On 18 December he demanded 5,000 or 6,000 heads. If 20,000 were needed, the people should not hesitate. On 27 May 1791, the number had risen to 50,000.

Marat was unique even among the radical journalists in his early advocacy of a dictator to crush the counterrevolution. Believing that popular insurrection could not succeed without a leader, he called on the people to pick a dictator and follow him. He demanded either a military tribune or a supreme dictator, who would serve only temporarily. He never proposed any name.

L'ami du peuple was part of the radical democratic press. Marat's contempt for the Assembly's work was based on ideology. Champion of popular sovereignty, he advocated a form of popular democracy. He rejected the distinction between passive and active citizens and opposed the *marc d'argent* qualification for deputy. Like the *sans-culottes*, he advocated the right of recall and popular referendum. He placed his faith in the people acting through electoral assemblies, patriotic clubs, or insurrection. He urged that the lot of the poor be alleviated and proposed a progressive income tax. Although the poor had the right to use force to take from the rich their superfluous wealth, he rejected equality of property. Although he regretted that the poor did not receive a larger share of the national lands, he rejected an agrarian law. Advocate of a free-market economy, Marat believed in a welfare state, not socialism. Nor was he a republican. Marat advocated a very limited monarchy. Although he lost faith in Louis XVI and even questioned the value of monarchy for France in September and November 1790, Marat did not become a republican until the Republic was proclaimed on 22 September 1792.

Disgusted with the Legislative Assembly, Marat left for London on 15 December 1791. *L'ami du peuple* ceased to appear until 12 April 1792, when Marat resumed publication with the help of the Cordeliers and financial aid from his wife. He resumed his opposition to the war, proposing to hold the royal family hostage, their lives forfeit if France was invaded. His exhortations to the troops to mutiny and massacre their perfidious generals provoked a decree of accusation (3 May 1792). Marat was forced into hiding again, only a few issues appeared between 3 May and 10 August, these appealing for action against the royal family and all traitors. He helped to incite the insurrection of 10 August 1792 by his appeal to the *fédérés* on 9 August, summoning them to hold as hostages the royal family and all perfidious deputies and public officials. Although he shared in the collective responsibility for the September Massacres (2–6 September 1792) as a member of the Commune's Comité de Surveillance, Marat's culpability has been exaggerated. On 10 August he opposed any mercy for counterrevolutionaries, and on 19 August he urged the people to kill traitors, especially the Swiss officers in the Abbaye prison; but these articles appeared before 2 September.

Elected to the Convention as a deputy from Paris, Marat changed the name of his paper to project a new image. Appearing on 25 September as the *Journal de la République française*, it carried an editorial announcing a new policy of moderation, omitting the call for a dictator. Marat had resigned himself to the Republic. The object of scathing attacks by the Girondins, Marat responded in kind. Resenting his opposition to the war and to the election of the Girondins to the Convention, they accused him of instigating the September Massacres and aspiring to be a dictator. Marat defended the Mountain, with which he allied. He urged the speedy trial and execution of Louis XVI. When some Girondins appealed for leniency toward the king, he denounced them for having sold out. Marat was accused of instigating the Parisian food riot of 25 February 1793 because that day's issue of his paper seemed to incite the people to pillage the shops and hang a few hoarders. The defection of C.-F. Dumouriez (5 April 1793) convinced Marat that the Girondins had been conspiring with that general. The deputies voted to send him before the Revolutionary Tribunal, but Marat was acquitted (24 April 1793). When the Girondins tried to move the Convention from Paris and the Commission of Twelve was established, Marat called for its suppression and supported the section petitions demanding a purge of twenty-two Girondin deputies. He played a leading role in the insurrection of 31 May–2 June 1793, urging the sections to arm while rejecting the *enragés*' demand for the dispersal of the Convention.

Marat's paper was a valuable asset in the Mountain's campaign to crush the *enragés*. Competing with the latter for the support of the *sans-culottes*, Marat tried to align the popular movement with the Mountain. Rejecting the *enragés*' economic program, he opposed the maximum and the *cours forcé* of the *assignats*, preferring to punish hoarders and withdraw *assignats* from circulation.

When C. Corday assassinated Marat on 13 July 1793, his newspaper was only a shadow of its former self. The last issue, which appeared the day after his death, called for the strengthening of the Committee of Public Safety. The efforts to continue his paper by the *enragés* and the Cordeliers proved short-lived. The void left by the disappearance of Marat's paper was filled by R. Hébert's *Père Duchesne*, which fell victim to the dictatorship Marat had demanded. No other paper played such a vital role as *L'ami du peuple* and its successors in appealing to the Parisian masses.

J. Censer, *Prelude to Power* (Baltimore, 1976); L. Gottschalk, *Jean Paul Marat* (New York, 1967); E. Hatin, *Histoire politique et littéraire de la presse en France*, 8 vols. (Paris, 1859–61).

M. Edelstein

Related entries: ACTIVE CITIZEN; CENTRAL REVOLUTIONARY COMMITTEE; CORDELIERS CLUB; HÉBERT; LAW OF THE MAXIMUM; MARAT; OCTOBER DAYS; PASSIVE CITIZEN; *PATRIOTE FRANCAIS*; SEPTEMBER MASSACRES; 10 AUGUST 1792.

AMI DU ROI (1790-92), royalist newspaper edited by abbé Royau. It was the most widely read royalist newspaper of its time, with a printing of between 4,000 and 5,000 copies. It had subscribers in all major cities and drew its readership as much from merchants and well-to-do tradesmen as from priests and nobles. It was claimed that the king read it and subsidized it.

Established on 1 June 1790, *Ami du Roi* had as its principal editor abbé Royau who, the son of a *procureur fiscal* of Pont-Labbé, taught philosophy at the

Collège of Louis-le-Grand. Royau was the brother-in-law of L.-M.-S. Fréron, the manager of *Année littéraire*, with whom he cooperated in editing this newspaper, which he transformed into a daily for the defense "of King, of God and of the Fatherland." Assisted by his brother, J. Corentin, and a professor at the Collège de Quatre Nations, E. Geoffroy, who, like him, were thoroughly familiar with the philosophy of the century, Royau very ably attacked the activity of the deputies to the Constituent Assembly.

In 1790, he recognized that injustices had existed before 1789 and that reforms were necessary; he presented the royal program of 23 June 1789 as the only acceptable plan for renewal. At the end of 1791 and in 1792, however, his attacks became more violent, and he recommended a return to the Old Regime. He incited officers to desert and presaged the armed struggle against the constitutional regime. He sought to rally the bourgeoisie by presenting the Revolution as the work of a handful of plotters ranked against proprietors. Indicted and brought before the High Court on 21 May, Royau went into hiding and died 21 June 1792.

There were two other, less influential newspapers with the same name. One was published by F.-C. Montjoye, an old friend and former collaborator of Royau; the other was a more ephemeral paper edited by a printer named Crapart, who eventually joined in partnership with Royau.

J.-P. Bertaud, "L'*Ami du Roi* de Royau, l'*Ami du Roi* de Montjoye, *le Courrier extraordinaire* de Duplais" (Diplôme d'études supérieures, University of Paris, 1959); E. Hatin, *Bibliographie historique et critique de la presse périodique française* (Paris, 1866; new ed., 1965); J. Popkin, *The Right-Wing Press in France, 1792–1800* (Chapel Hill, N.C., 1980).

J.-P. Bertaud

Related entry: COUNTERREVOLUTION.

AMIS DE LA CONSTITUTION MONARCHIQUE. See *MONARCHIENS*.

AMIS DES NOIRS, SOCIETE DES. See SOCIETE DES AMIS DES NOIRS.

AMIS DE VERITE. See CERCLE SOCIAL.

ANCIENTS, COUNCIL OF. See COUNCIL OF ANCIENTS.

ANDRE, ANTOINE-BALTHAZAR-JOSEPH D' (1759-1825), deputy of the nobility of Provence to the Estates General, constitutional monarchist, royalist agent. André (known as Dandré during the Revolution) was a *conseiller* at the parlement of Provence, was three times presiding officer of the Constituent Assembly, and served on the Constitutional Committee. After Varennes, he joined the Feuillants and worked for conservative amendments to the constitution.

Later he tried, unsuccessfully, for elective offices and conducted a business until press attacks forced him to emigrate in 1792.

In 1796-97 André made his peace with Louis XVIII, won the confidence and subsidies of the British agent W. Wickham, and played an important role in efforts to restore the monarchy in the 1797 elections. After the coup of 18 Fructidor (4 September 1797), André escaped abroad and remained in Central Europe until the Restoration. Although discredited as Louis XVIII's director of police by Napoleon's return during the Hundred Days, he retained the king's favor and the post of intendant of royal domains until his death.

W. R. Fryer, *Republic or Restoration in France? 1794–7. The Politics of French Royalism, with Particular Reference to the Activities of A.-B.-J. d'André* (Manchester, 1965); H. Mitchell, *The Underground War against Revolutionary France: The Missions of William Wickham 1794–1800* (Oxford, 1965).

P. H. Beik

Related entries: COUP OF 18 FRUCTIDOR; FEUILLANTS; VARENNES.

ANGLOMANES (1789-92), supporters of an English-style constitutional monarchy during the National Assembly and the Legislative Assembly. The *anglomanes* were deputies to the Estates General and National Assembly who sought moderate reform of monarchical institutions through collaboration of enlightened notables drawn from the clergy, the nobility, and the Third Estate. They have also been labeled Anglophiles and *monarchiens*. J.-J. Mounier, a lawyer from Grenoble, was their best-known leader. It was Mounier who led the revolt in Dauphiné in 1788 to restore the provincial estates organized on the basis of vote by head rather than by order. After June 1789 Mounier came more and more to be identified as the theoretician of his cause; the comte de Clermont-Tonnerre gained recognition as its most accomplished orator; and the comte de Virieu emerged as its bold, sometimes intemperate, man of action. Other prominent figures in the group were the bourgeois civil servant P.-V. Malouet, the lawyer N. Bergasse, the marquis de Lally-Tollendal, the bishop of Langres, the archbishop of Bordeaux, and the archbishop of Vienne. The publicist for the moderate royalist political platform was the Genevan journalist J. Mallet du Pan, editor of the *Mercure de France*.

Debates on the constitution first made the *monarchiens* aware of their common ideas about how the Revolution should proceed. Mounier was typical. It was he who proposed the Tennis Court Oath of 20 June 1789 as an act of defiance against arbitrary royal actions. Yet by the following summer, he was making it clear he was equally opposed to those who favored a radical restructuring of the French government. That apparent shift toward the defense of royal prerogatives produced a break between Mounier and J. Barnave, who had served as his lieutenant during the revolt in Dauphiné. It also brought him and his supporters into conflict with the so-called patriot party led by the abbé E.-J. Sieyès and I.-R.-G. Le Chapelier. For the most part, the *monarchiens* distrusted and avoided the notorious but popular H.-G. R. Mirabeau, although their program was in many respects similar to his. They made overtures to the marquis de Lafayette on several occasions but with no lasting results.

A majority of moderate royalists opposed, or expressed reservations about, the publication of an abstract statement of natural human rights. Mounier came out publicly in favor of such a declaration only after attempting to block it in the Committee on the Constitution. Many of his specific proposals, which closely resembled those of Lafayette, won adoption; however, he lost his campaign to prevent the completed Declaration of the Rights of Man from being published in advance of the constitution, which he thought would spell out in practical terms the duties of citizens and the limitations on their rights.

On other major constitutional issues Mounier, Virieu, and their following were more visibly united. They labored diligently but futilely to gain acceptance of a provision for a two-chamber legislature. They also threw their support behind an absolute royal veto over legislation. More than half of their fellow deputies rejected their arguments and voted for a suspensive veto, by which the king could delay but not set aside legislative acts.

The October Days, which moved the king and the Assembly from Versailles to Paris, dashed moderate royalists' hopes of reversing the Revolution's direction through parliamentary action. Consequently they turned to two other tactics. One group, headed by Malouet and Bergasse, set out to persuade at least 300 deputies to resign from the National Assembly, thereby forcing it to disband. Mounier and others returned to the provinces, confident that the people who elected them to office would support them in their opposition to the radical Parisians and leaders of the Constituent Assembly. Both tactics proved totally ineffective. Mounier and Lally-Tollendal soon joined the ranks of the *émigrés*.

Disregarding physical threats and verbal attacks, Malouet and S. Clermont-Tonnerre in Paris continued to try to stem the Revolutionary tide. In an effort to mobilize the remaining deputies favorable to his policies, Malouet organized the Club des Impartiaux in late 1789. Dedicated to reconciling Revolutionary ideals with a strong monarchy, the club limped along for a few months and then disappeared. The Society of Friends of the Monarchical Constitution, initially under the presidency of Clermont-Tonnerre took its place in late 1790. That club publicized as its program the restoration of royal executive powers under the Constitution of 1791 and made a bid for popular support by giving food and clothing to the poor people of Paris. The club maintained a precarious existence, on paper at least, until August 1792, when the king was suspended, Clermont-Tonnerre was assassinated by an infuriated crowd, and even the most courageous survivors, like Malouet, decided to emigrate. By that time the monarchy itself, in the weakened form permitted by the Constitution of 1791 and belatedly defended by A. Barnave and the Feuillant Society, was doomed.

A number of factors contributed to the failure of the *anglomanes* between 1789 and 1792. The names applied to them carried negative connotations for many Frenchmen. A passion for English institutions looked too much like the posture assumed by the ultraroyalists early in the Revolution, and the term *monarchiens* did little to clarify the misunderstanding. On the other hand, supporters of absolutism and aristocratic privilege found them as distasteful as other Revolutionaries. What is more, the rank-and-file members of the moderate royalist group were modest and unassertive men. Few of them had the stomach for fighting. They relied on strong personalities, such as Mounier and Virieu, to give them confidence in their own policies and in their ability to make them prevail. But the ablest of their leaders, if not as personally dull and uninspiring as the ex-bureaucrat Malouet, lacked the charisma and power necessary to hold them firm on every issue against the threats and outright violence from the Left. That weakness in leadership was aggravated by the early emigration of Mounier and Lally-Tollendal. Finally, the *monarchiens* failed to win the cooperation of other individuals and groups with an interest in bringing the Revolution to a moderate resolution. Louis XVI and his ministers, who had more to lose than anyone else, could not bring themselves to provide consistent leadership or positive moral support. Thus the Revolutionary party that seemed most in tune with popular sentiment as expressed in the pre-Revolutionary *cahiers*, or lists of grievances, was within three years no longer in existence as a political force in France.

F. Acomb, *Mallet du Pan (1749-1800); A Career in Political Journalism* (Durham, N.C., 1973); C. du Bus, *Stanislas de Clermont-Tonnerre et l'échec de la Révolution monarchique, 1757-1792* (Paris, 1931); J. Egret, *La Révolution des Notables; Mounier et les Monarchiens, 1789* (Paris, 1950); L. de Lanzac de Laborie, *Jean-Joseph Mounier; sa vie politique et ses écrits* (Paris, 1887); R. Vignery, "Malouet and the Failure of Constitutional Royalism," *Pro. of the WSFH # 4* (1977).

R. Vignery

Related entries: BARNAVE; CLERMONT-TONNERRE; LAFAYETTE; MALLET DU PAN; MALOUET; *MONARCHIENS*; MOUNIER; PATRIOT PARTY; SOCIETY OF 1789; SUSPENSIVE VETO; TENNIS COURT OATH.

ANNEXATION, conscious policy after 1792-93 by which the French government began to pursue a course that ultimately brought France's frontier to the Alps and gave it virtually the entire left bank of the Rhine. On 22 May 1790 the Constituent Assembly proclaimed to the world its peaceful intentions. The deputies solemnly renounced conquest and the use of force against the liberty of any other nation. Renouncing conquest did not mean, however, that Revolutionary France would refrain entirely from annexations. This course was made clear by the Assembly's response to events in Avignon and the Comtat Venaissin, two papal enclaves in the Rhône Valley, which in the spring and summer of 1790 revolted against the pope, voted to join France, and appealed to the Assembly to accept them. The deputies procrastinated for more than a year before agreeing to annexation on 14 September 1791.

Having abjured conquest, they found a new basis for annexation in the principle of self-determination. According to this principle, the peoples of the enclaves had the right to determine their political allegiance without the consent of their sovereign. The Assembly also based annexation on arguments drawn from public law. France had strong legal claims to the enclaves that its kings occasionally had invoked against the papacy, and the Assembly adduced these claims to legitimate France's title before the international community. Although they annexed Avignon and the Comtat, the deputies were not seeking to expand France. They thought the nation sufficiently large. Moreover, they adhered to the generally held idea that an expanding state opened the way for a despot because it made government too distant from the people and lessened the political influence of individual citizens. In the matter of the enclaves, the Assembly had simply responded to a fait accompli. The Assembly had not provoked rebellion in these places in order to acquire them. The deputies accepted the appeal because it was supported by a majority of the population and because the geographical location of the enclaves and the resulting close link between them and surrounding French areas made union reasonable. In short, the enclaves constituted a special case, and their annexation was not intended as the prelude to an expansionist program. The Revolution was still in its idealistic phase.

The war that began between France and Austria in April 1792, and in which Prussia, Sardinia, and some Rhenish states of the Holy Roman Empire soon joined on Austria's side, led the Revolutionaries to reverse their policy and turn expansionist. This did not occur, however, until nearly a year after the war started. Initially France aimed solely to preserve its territorial integrity and Revolutionary achievements. But to fulfill this aim and ensure future security, it decided that along the eastern frontier, it would urge the subjects of any enemy to overthrow their governments and create independent states with constitutions similar to that of France. France would proselytize these neighbors not in order to annex them but in the hope of creating a belt of sister states to protect it against a hostile Europe. Propaganda was to be a practical means to provide security for the Revolution. The Revolutionaries intended to propagandize only enemy territory, and although in a moment of enthusiasm the Convention, in its decree of 19 November 1792, promised assistance to any people seeking freedom, in fact the authorities charged with interpreting the promise rendered it virtually meaningless. Meanwhile, French armies had invaded Austrian-ruled Belgium, Liège, certain states on the left bank of the Rhine, and the Sardinian possessions of Savoy and Nice. After proclaiming that they came as liberators warring only on enemy kings and privileged orders, the French invited the people to choose a new regime. If they hoped for the adoption of a constitution modeled on theirs, the French were, nevertheless, determined on persuasion rather than coercion, and they promised to respect whatever choice the people made. In Savoy the response exceeded French hopes, for the Savoyards not only destroyed the old order but went further and freely voted to join France. On 27 November 1792 the Convention annexed Savoy on grounds of self-determination. After Nice voted for union, it was annexed on the same basis on 31 January 1793.

Other than in Savoy and Nice, the popular response was cool, and this fact, together with the development of problems in supplying and financing the Republican armies, caused the French first to force revolution on their neighbors and, shortly afterward, to annex them. If some Belgians, Liégeois, and Rhinelanders favored reforms of various degrees, a majority of the population remained attached to the Old Regime. At the same time as they heard of this disillusioning political response, the politicians in Paris learned that the armies, particularly in Belgium, were critically short of equipment and provisions. Because of the Republic's financial plight, there was insufficient specie to purchase supplies on the spot, and when the French tried to pay in *assignats*, the Belgians refused to accept this fast-depreciating Revolutionary currency. Alarmed that this situation threatened to paralyze military operations and jeopardize national security, the Convention decided to use force in occupied territories to erect regimes on which France could depend to conduct the war. This decision was embodied in the decree of 15 December 1792 which instructed the French occupation authorities to destroy existing institutions, seize the property of the former government and the church, and hold controlled elections for new governments. Supported by a small minority of local radicals, the French would effectively control the new, nominally independent states. The decree marked a turning point in Revolutionary policy. The Revolutionaries now broke the promise to respect the popular will and instead adopted coercion to refashion the occupied territories in the French image. Practical motives prompted this about-face: the new states would serve as bulwarks against foreign foes, mobilize resources for the war effort, and ease the drain on French specie through the circulation of *assignats*. Even this draconian decree proved insufficient to achieve the French objective. When the peoples of the occupied territories, charging that the decree violated their rights, successfully held up its implementation, the French decided in late January 1793 to take the short step from forced revolution to forced annexation.

On 14 February 1793 the deputy L. Carnot gave the Convention a rationale for this fresh departure. All nations, he stated, had inherent rights and interests, including the right to remain independent, and justice required each nation to respect the rights of others. Justice toward others did not, however, require a nation to compromise its own interests. Since a state need not sacrifice its safety to that of its neighbors, it could legitimately take measures of self-protection whatever the consequences for foreigners. Applying these maxims to the question of annexation, Carnot concluded that although justice required France to continue to insist on popular consent as the basis of annexations, it could waive this condition if its safety were imperiled. If the need for security justified annexations over popular opposition, it also set a limit to them. Taking up a theme sounded by Revolutionaries in preceding weeks, Carnot now equated France's security with the attainment of the natural frontiers of the Rhine and the Alps. Carnot's report served notice that in the zone between the old and the natural frontiers, which included some states still neutral, France was entitled not only to accept appeals for union but to resort to annexation by coercion.

In succeeding weeks, the Republic applied the new policy on annexations

enunciated by Carnot. French officials and their local supporters conducted plebiscites on the question of union with France in the occupied part of the left bank
of the Rhine and in most of Belgium and Liège, as well as in several neutral
places within the natural frontiers, including Rhenish states, Monaco, and part
of the Bishopric of Basel. Union was invariably approved, but in nearly every
case the use of force and chicanery made the plebiscite a mockery. The Convention agreed to annexation without debate and, although aware of the methods
used to win an affirmative vote, always alleged that union was based on popular
consent. By the spring of 1793, the deputies had shed their earlier fear that an
expanding state raised the spectre of a despot seizing power and now subscribed
to the notion that only by expanding the state could they find security. Substituting
raison d'état for self-determination, they reversed the policy of the Constituent
Assembly, violated the pledge renouncing conquest, and turned expansionist.
They cast idealism to the winds and launched a war of conquest.

The expansionist thrust was soon halted but only temporarily. An enemy
offensive in the spring of 1793 not only prevented France from attaining the
natural frontiers but recovered from it Belgium, Liège, Savoy, and much of the
occupied Rhineland. After British, Dutch, and Spaniards joined in the struggle
against France, the First Coalition was soon formed. With the Republic on the
defensive during the Terror (1793-94), the question of annexations was necessarily in abeyance, but it came again to the fore during the Thermidorian period
(1794-95) when the fortunes of war changed and the Republic seized Belgium,
Liège, and the Rhenish left bank. Would the expansionist policy of early 1793
now be renewed? Most deputies were determined to retain Savoy (retaken in
October 1793) and Nice, but opinion was divided on the desirability of incor-
porating other occupied places. Royalists, anticipating that a monarchical restoration would be facilitated if peace were made, opposed all annexations because
these would force the powers to continue the war. Some moderate republicans
were prepared to abandon Belgium, Liège, and the Rhenish territories in the
interests of achieving peace. However, most republicans, including prominent
generals, favored renewed expansion. By arguing that Belgium, Liège and the
left bank of the Rhine would secure the Republic against further foreign assaults
and ease financial burdens, these republicans reiterated the thesis that the attainment of the natural frontiers meant the salvation of the Revolution. Under
the Directory (1795-99), these divisions of opinion on the Rhine frontier persisted, and policy on annexations fluctuated according to party politics at home
and military fortunes abroad. Ultimately, however, the partisans of the natural
frontiers prevailed, largely because J.-F. Reubell, first as a member of the
Convention and later as the director with most influence on foreign policy, was
their spokesman.

Between 1795 and 1797, France forced its continental enemies to acquiesce
in its expansion. The First Coalition began to disintegrate when Prussia signed
the Treaty of Basel (April 1795). Prussia secretly agreed that if in a future
continental peace settlement, the French were given the left bank of the Rhine,

Prussia would cede its small territory there to France in return for indemnification elsewhere. The Dutch, their country revolutionized and renamed the Batavian Republic, were forced by the Treaty of the Hague (May 1795) to cede to France Maëstricht, Venloo, and a portion of territory at the mouth of the River Scheldt but were permitted to retain the Dutch part of the left bank of the Rhine. Encouraged by these concessions, the Convention reannexed Belgium and Liège in October 1795. The Austrians were brought to terms under the Directory when N. Bonaparte, after defeating them in the Italian campaigns of 1796–97, dictated peace in the Treaty of Campoformio (October 1797). In exchange for most of the Republic of Venice, Austria conceded the loss of Belgium and recognized French sovereignty over the left bank of the Rhine except for the region north of a line extending approximately from Coblentz to Venloo on the Maas. Part of this region belonged to the Prussian king, in whose possession France now agreed to leave it, and the rest belonged to various princes of the Holy Roman Empire. The treaty also stipulated that the Austrian ruler, who possessed only a small area on the ceded left bank, and other imperial princes who were to be dispossessed of their territories there, would receive compensation elsewhere in the Empire.

With the annexation of Mulhouse (a free city near the Swiss frontier) and Geneva in 1798, the expansionist program was virtually fulfilled. England remained opposed but without continental allies was unable to drive back the French to their old frontiers. Although Russia and Austria joined the British in the Second Coalition in 1799 and threatened France's acquisitions, the French repulsed the enemy and secured their grip on the annexed territories even before the Directory fell in November 1799.

In seven years of war, the Republic had annexed territory from the Mediterranean to the North Sea and brought its frontier to the Alps and, apart from a relatively small area, to the Rhine. At first France based annexation on self-determination, but it quickly reverted to the practices of the *ancien régime* and acquired territory by force combined with the classic diplomacy of exchange, compensation, and balance of power.

A. Fugier, *La Révolution française et l'Empire napoléonien* (Paris, 1954); J. Godechot, *La grande nation; l'expansion révolutionnaire de la France dans le monde de 1789 à 1799*, 2 vols. (Paris, 1956); R. Guyot, *Le Directoire et la paix de l'Europe, 1795-1799* (Paris, 1911); J. P. McLaughlin, "Ideology and Conquest: the Question of Proselytism and Expansion in the French Revolution, 1789-1793," *Hist. Papers, Can.* (1976).

J. P. McLaughlin

Related entries: ASSIGNATS; AVIGNON; CARNOT; FIRST COALITION; PROPAGANDA; REUBELL; TREATY OF BASEL; TREATY OF CAMPO-FORMIO.

ARCOLA, BATTLE OF. See BATTLE OF ARCOLA.

ARISTOCRATS. The decay during the French Revolution of aristocracy as a caste and of aristocrats as individuals was a varied process. In 1789, the political decline of the aristocracy as the second of three orders was abrupt. It was heralded in June by the determination of the Third Estate to bring into being the National Assembly. It was consecrated during the celebrated night of 4 August when the feudal system was abolished "in its entirety." It had long since been decreed when the French corporate system was forever dismantled with the passing of the Le Chapelier Law in June 1791.

The privileges of nobility were quickly rescinded in 1789–90, and on 19–23 June 1790, nobility itself was abolished, at the prompting in part of prominent liberal nobles (the marquis de Lafayette, vicomte de Noailles, baron de Menou, duc de La Rochefoucauld-Liancourt). Henceforth, the 250,000 noble-born aristocrats who lived in France became in theory the equal citizens of a constitutional monarchy organized on the principle of civic equality.

The situation of aristocrats as private persons evolved more gradually, and the bourgeois Revolutionaries were initially careful not to give nobles offense. Careful distinctions were drawn, for example, between honorific feudal dues, which were abolished without compensation, and seigneurial dues, which aristocrats theoretically were allowed to retain, though nobles who tried to collect them soon came to regret their decision. In short, until 1792, though aristocracy as a caste was everywhere pursued, aristocrats as private persons continued on as before. The *parlementaires* were compensated for their abolished offices, and the army was not purged of its noble officers.

The flight of the king to Varennes on 20 June 1791 heralded the beginning of a more difficult period for aristocrats. The Feuillants now began to make overtures to those who they thought might help them stop the Revolution—that is, to the king and the *émigrés*, most of whom at this time were aristocrats. But the drift of politics that brought the Girondins to the fore in the spring of 1792 boded ill for aristocrats. With the fall of the monarchy on 10 August 1792, matters took an abrupt turn for the worse. The penalties imposed on *émigrés* became much more severe. Their relatives at home were often threatened. Girondin propaganda made much of unity with *le peuple*, now declared the sworn enemy of nobles.

The September Massacres in 1792 soon gave the Girondins pause, but their anti-*émigré* policy and antinoble stance was now taken up by Dantonists and in early 1793 by the Mountain. Then, in the spring of 1793, all of the bourgeois factions were outstripped by the Parisian *sans-culottes* who even more vociferously demanded the expulsion of all the noble officers from the army, a policy that M. Robespierre and even J.-P. Marat were reluctant to follow. The climax of this popular agitation came with the invasion of the Convention by the Paris crowd on 5 September 1793. Soon after nobles everywhere in France were placed under a form of house arrest.

In the late fall of 1793, however, the tables suddenly turned. Popular agitation against nobles dropped off, and the *enragé* leader J. Roux even wrote on their behalf. Conversely, the Montagnard leaders, and L. Saint-Just especially, suddenly turned their hatred against nobles whom they now held to be the incarnation of corruption and, as such, the antithesis of the Republic of Virtue. On 16 April 1794, noble-born aristocrats were expelled from Paris and from some other French cities. Aristocrats who were not specifically exempted from proscription were required to give up their public office. Many nobles, like L.-N. Davoust, withdrew from the army, though it appears that some hundreds of them were still serving in the armies of the Republic in the summer of 1794.

The fall of Robespierre marked a respite, but an incomplete one. Non-noble *émigrés* were allowed to return, but aristocratic *émigrés* were specifically forbidden to do so, though many decided to come back regardless. After 1795, nobles as such continued under various disabilities, which were much aggravated after the Left-Republican coup of 18 Fructidor (September 1797). A few weeks later, nobles were deprived of their French citizenship and E.-J. Sieyès was reluctantly persuaded to give up his desire to banish them altogether. The Law of Frimaire Year VI against nobles had little effect, but in western France, it became customary to detain nobles as hostages during the war between Republican forces and counterrevolutionary bands.

N. Bonaparte's coup of 18 Brumaire, however, brought a rapid dismantling of antinoble legislation, and most of the approximately twenty thousand nobles who had left France, like the writer F.-A.-R. Chateaubriand, came home. Unsold and previously confiscated property was returned to its owners.

The Revolution was a dramatic political event for French aristocrats. Although relatively few of them were executed or killed (perhaps only 3 percent), most noble families must surely have had the experience of imprisonment and fear. French aristocrats had often been liberal in their politics before 1789. Some of them continued to be so well into the nineteenth century. But after 1800 this stance became far rarer than it had been, all the more significant for the fact that the property held by nobles during the Revolution did not appreciably decline and that nobles after the Revolution continued to exert great influence in French life. Indeed a surprising number of them became important Napoleonic officials, C.-M. Talleyrand being the most famous.

During the Revolution, the term *aristocrate* was applied very widely. Most of the people called *aristocrates* were not noble at all; they were not aristocrats in the normal sense of the word. The term had a moral and political connotation very well described by G. Babeuf's co-conspirator and chronicler, F. M. Buonarroti. In his view, *aristocrates* were individuals who exercised over others "a sovereign power or domination which belonged to the nation as a whole." In consequence, the term was often used by democrats who railed against l' *aristocratie insulaire* of Great Britain, or *l'aristocratie bourgeoise*, or, as L.-F. Sonthonax did, *l'aristocratie cutanée* of the white planters of Santo Domingo. Conversely, the term was also used by rightists to describe individuals or groups who, they thought, tyrannized the elected (and bourgeois) representatives of the nation. In this conservative view, it made sense to talk of *l'aristocratie sansculotte*, *l'aristocratie jacobine*, *l'aristocratie de la pauvreté*, and *l'aristocratie urbaine* of Paris. Only incidentally, therefore, did the term *aristocrate* refer to actual aristocrats, who were more properly, though paradoxically, described as *l'aristocratie nobiliaire*, or as A. Barnave put it, *l'aristocratie equestre*.

The social significance of the term *aristocrate* in its Revolutionary usage should not be ignored, but the fact remains that in Revolutionary rhetoric, the word had moral and political rather than social or economic value. T. Paine compared it usefully to the word *Tory* in the British colonies during the War of Independence, and his definition of the word *aristocrate* is also useful; the word, he wrote, is used to describe an enemy of the Revolution without the traditional connotation of the term.

As one might expect, the word *aristocrate* was less often employed after the heady days of 1789–94. Its counterpart, *citoyen* and *citoyenne*, survived well into the days of Bonaparte, but the word *aristocrate* was far less frequently used after 1795 than it had been in the previous six years.

H. Carré, *La Noblesse en France et l'opinion publique au 18ᵉ siècle* (Paris, 1920); R. Forster, *The Nobility of Toulouse in the Eighteenth Century* (Baltimore, 1960); J. Godechot, *La Contre-révolution* (Paris, 1961); P. Higonnet, *Class, Ideology and the Rights of Nobles during the French Revolution* (Oxford, 1981); P. de Vaissière, *Lettres d'Aristocrates* (Paris, 1907); J. Vidalenc, *Les Emigrés français* (Caen, 1963).

P. Higonnet

Related entries: BUONARROTI; FEUILLANTS; 4 AUGUST 1789; LE CHAPELIER; SEPTEMBER MASSACRES; VARENNES.

ARMEES REVOLUTIONNAIRES (1793-94), paramilitary forces organized under popular pressure to enforce policies of the Terror in the interior of France. The Revolutionary armies, organs and instruments of the Terror, should not be confused with the army of the Revolution, which was the military arm of the nation against foreign forces. The *armées révolutionnaires* had only a brief existence, at the beginning of the Year II of the Republic, at a time of great crisis in the Revolution between September 1793 and January 1794. These armies were only groups of armed civilians, more or less numerous, operating in most of the territory of the Republic to make the Revolutionary order respected. If we follow their historian, R. Cobb, the fifty-six armies he studied (not including the Parisian army) exercised their influence in most regions: the Midi, the Center, the Lyonnais, Alsace, the north, northern Lorraine, and the Loire Valley up to the estuary. The west-central region, Brittany (except for the region of Redon), the extreme east of Aquitaine, Languedoc, and eastern Franche-Comté, however, experienced only infrequent inroads by armies from neighboring regions. In contrast, the Parisian basin was completely traversed by contingents of the Parisian army, recruited among the *sans-culottes*.

The origin of the *armées révolutionnaires* dates to the spring of 1793, the dark period when the Revolution was marked by economic crisis and food shortages, dominated by military defeats on the northern and eastern frontiers, torn by social conflict and counterrevolution with insurrection in the Vendée and agitation in the south and east, and weakened by the opposition of moderates.

Consequently, committed Jacobin patriots and the *sans-culottes* of the cities deemed it necessary to impose submission to whatever the Republic required on counterrevolutionaries, conciliators, and opportunists. The majority of the Convention and the Girondin government were doing practically nothing; therefore, some people wanted to establish a coercive force in order to enforce the application of Revolutionary legal measures adopted under popular pressure between March and May 1793 and, at the same time, to emphasize the need for more rigorous measures while demonstrating the efficacy of terrorist action. The Jacobin–*sans-culotte* coup of 31 May–2 June 1793 in Paris and the period of political and military mobilization that followed favored the development of a firmer determination to reinforce the mechanism of Revolutionary terror in the countryside. Moreover, the Committee of Public Safety could hope to consolidate its authority only if it allowed this spontaneous demand for the reinforcing of Revolutionary pressure to develop and become organized. In addition, the only means of avoiding outbreaks of uncontrolled violence like what had occurred in September 1792 was to support the organization of a popular, but well-disciplined, terror. The *journée* of 4 September 1793, effected by the workers and poor artisans of Paris, imposed the creation of a Revolutionary army on the Committee of Public Safety and the Convention; demanded by the forty-eight sections of Paris, this force was established by the Convention's decree of 9 September. Thereafter, demands for the establishment of Revolutionary armies multiplied throughout the country, sometimes at the initiative of popular societies, sometimes on the proposal of representatives on mission or of local or district administrators. Of the seventy-six requests, forty-seven originated from popular societies or local authorities and twenty-nine from representatives on mission in regions experiencing crises. Thus, the *armées révolutionnaires* were born out of a fear of counterrevolution and from this fear, transformed into defensive action, was born an organized will for offensive resistance. Although an original creation of the Year II, the establishment of the *armées révolutionnaires* had its roots in the Revolutionary tradition, that of the forays of National Guardsmen or soldiers into the countryside during the autumn of 1792 in the west and around Paris, and, even before, in July and August 1792—the summer of the *patrie en danger*—when volunteers rushed to Paris and the fortresses of the east. In the same way, one can also understand how this kind of weapon was able to be turned into a counterrevolutionary army at Lyon or in Provence in the course of the federalist and royalist insurrections in June–July 1793.

The *armées révolutionnaires* had extensive terrorist functions, but their real missions were generally limited in practice. They were the more or less docile instruments of municipalities, of district administrators, or of committees of surveillance; they acted under the direction of men who served as liaisons with these bodies and, in some cases, under the direction of representatives on mission and their agents (as C. Lucas has noted in the case of the Loire). Their most important mission—especially for the Parisian army, which was charged with provisioning the capital—was making large farmers, exploiters, and *bladiers*, who speculated on inflation and sold on the black market, disgorge their produce. The armies forced observance of the maximum and the requisitioning of wheat, fodder, and other necessities. When necessary, contingents of the *armée révolutionnaire* forced rural producers to provision markets and fill the supply wagons earmarked for the armies on the frontiers. But at the same time, in the countryside and villages, the *armées révolutionnaires* echoed the ideological themes of the Parisian *sans-culottes*: social egalitarianism and a desire for direct democracy. The *armées révolutionnaires* also played a major role in the dechristianization movement, which was at the heart of the attempted cultural revolution of the Year II, marked by the more or less forced indifference of the French; thus, by requisitioning the priests' silver, by pulling down church bells, by destroying sacred objects as the "baubles of fanaticism and superstition," the *armées révolutionnaires* contributed to the disparagement of the ideas and practices of former times in the eyes of dechristianized Frenchmen. Festivals, street demonstrations, antinoble and antireligious masquerades resurrected, in their carnival-like activity, the ancient origins of pre-Tridentine popular merrymaking. This was particularly true in the departments where the armies acted most anarchically and spontaneously. The Parisian army was strictly subordinated to the Convention and acted as a kind of mobile gendarmerie. On the political level, the *armées révolutionnaires* contributed to the arrest of suspects, the enforcement of warrants, and the supervision of prisoners. In departments where serious confrontations were taking place, the *armée révolutionnaire* carried out repression by force, intimidation, and propaganda in favor of egalitarian ideas.

Generally small—most often composed of between 50 and 1,000 men spread over a number of companies and contingents—the *armées révolutionnaires* reached their greatest strength in the south where there were enthusiastic enlistments; the army of Cahors, for example, had 3,200 enlistees. The pay there was often quite high and always adequate. The leaders were elected, and democratic activity was intense; the atmosphere was civil but fraternal. Those who enlisted were often the patriotic fathers of families. They expressed themselves vigorously, without equivocation, and insisted on the familiar form of address (*tutoiement*). Besides, these old "moustaches," big eaters, heavy drinkers, and devoted billiard players were often truculent and in every way typical of the urban popular milieux that A. Soboul has studied and that constitute the basis for his sociology of *sans-culotterie*. The data for a statistical study of the *armées révolutionnaires* are very fragmentary; but on the basis of the dossiers of 481 enlistees in the Parisian and Lillois armies studied by R. Cobb, one has to draw a conclusion along these lines.

Theoretically, the armies were supposed to be maintained and paid from a tax on the rich but in practice the expense was soon charged to local finances. This contributed to making the armies insupportable, especially when their effectiveness in supplying provisions no longer seemed to be a top priority. More terrifying than effective in dealing with speculators and political opponents, vigorous and outspoken, the *armées révolutionnaires* ultimately became a source of alarm to the Revolutionary government. Linked to the Hébertist Left (notably, through General C.-P. Ronsin who commanded the Parisian army), practicing a kind of verbal one-upmanship, and frightening property owners by their proclamations and their anarchical threats to redistribute property, they finally became an obstacle to the policy of Revolutionary unity, which was central to the political strategy of the Jacobin supporters of M. Robespierre. The Law of 14 Frimaire Year II (4 December 1793), which was adopted at the end of a three-month period when the Revolutionary government was being consolidated, suppressed the *armées révolutionnaires*. This suppression played a role in the dissatisfaction of some popular elements with the dictatorship of the Committee of Public Safety that culminated in Ventôse and Germinal of the Year II.

In the final accounting, the *armées révolutionnaires* contributed to the victory of the Revolution. Described as armies of crime by their enemies, they were not in fact the instruments of unbridled violence as they are often described. They did allow the application of the policies of the Terror and in the long run helped to shake the French nation profoundly. Those who fought in their ranks subsequently participated in all the neo-Jacobin, Babouvist, and Republican activities that agitated France, more or less, until 1815.

R. C. Cobb, *Les armées révolutionnaires, instrument de la Terreur dans les départements*, 2 vols. (Paris, 1963); P. Gérard, "L'armée révolutionnaire de la Haute-Garonne," *Ann. hist. de la Révo. française* 31 (1959); A. P. Herlaut, *Le général rouge Ronsin* (Paris, 1957); C. Lucas, *The Structure of the Terror: The Example of Javogues and the Loire* (Oxford, 1973); C. Mazauric and P. Goudard, "En quel sens on peut dire que la Révolution française fut une révolution culturelle," *Europa* (December 1978); A. Soboul, *Les sans-culottes parisiens en l'an II*, 2d ed. (Paris, 1962).

C. Mazauric

Related entries: COBB; DECHRISTIANIZATION; FEDERALISM; HEBERTISTS; LAW OF 14 FRIMAIRE; LAW OF THE MAXIMUM; TERROR, THE.

ARMOIRE DE FER. Early in 1792, Louis XVI constructed a secret cabinet, or *armoire*, to safeguard his private correspondence, in a wall in the Tuileries palace, assisted by the locksmith F. Gamain (or Gamoin), who had worked for him at Versailles. Afterward Gamain was taken ill and suspected the king of poisoning him to keep the *armoire* secret.

In November 1792, when the National Convention was preparing to bring Louis to trial, Gamain revealed the existence of the *armoire*. Its contents, mostly letters received by the king, amounting to over 650 pages when printed in *Pièces imprimées d'après le décret de la Convention nationale du 5 décembre 1792, l'an II de la République* (Paris, 1793), proved largely innocuous, but it did reveal bribery of the press and dealings with various individuals, including H.-G. R. Mirabeau, the marquis de Lafayette, and J. Pétion. It did not contain evidence of actual treason to the state, for Marie Antoinette had earlier persuaded her husband to entrust the more incriminating papers to Madame Campan, according to the latter's memoirs.

While it seems doubtful that the discovery of the *armoire* materially affected the outcome of the king's trial, it strengthened the case against him and the popular demand for his punishment. It has also been a useful historical source.

H. A. Barton

Related entries: DESFIEUX; DUQUESNOY.

ARTOIS, CHARLES-PHILIPPE, COMTE D' (1757-1836), prince of the blood, brother of Louis XVI, *émigré*, and later king of France (1824–30).

Born on 9 October 1757, grandson of Louis XV and the fourth son and the fifth child of the dauphin Louis and Marie-Joséphine of Saxony, the comte d'Artois appeared to be doomed to that obscurity so often the fate of the younger sons of royalty. In retrospect it appears that the tragic deficiencies in judgment so frequently in evidence during his long life can be traced, in substantial degree, to the lack of proper education, training, and discipline during his formative years. At the age of sixteen (16 November 1773) he married fifteen-year-old Marie-Thérèse of Savoy, but even before his marriage, he had begun his career as a playboy that eventually led to his unusual relationship with Marie Antoinette, which discredited her and the monarchy.

Artois is the one on whom history has laid the greatest responsibility for the frivolity that for years characterized the queen's life. The French public, expressing itself in bawdy ballads, clearly thought that the count and Marie Antoinette were lovers. The prince's pursuit of women, intemperate drinking, addiction to gambling, and his duels, debts, and exaggerated love of hunting shocked a Paris long accustomed to excess. No complete record of Artois' debts exists, but they may have reached a total of 28 million *livres* by 1789. At last, in 1785, he began a liaison with the comtesse Louise de Polastron that continued until her death in 1805. With more stability in his private life, the count now had more time and an inclination for political affairs.

Artois became the leader of the cabal at the court of Louis XVI most interested in blocking significant institutional reform during the years immediately preceding the French Revolution. As the French financial crisis became increasingly serious, the controller general, C.-A. de Calonne, prevailed on Louis XVI to convene an Assembly of Notables to consider a comprehensive plan of reform. The Notables were organized into seven bureaus (or committees), each presided over by a prince of the blood. Artois, as chairman of the Second Bureau, was in a position to exercise some leadership. His comments during the debates within the committee furnish excellent examples of his ideas at this time. Artois insisted that property owners have the preponderant voice in the proposed assemblies because he felt the wealthy were the most enlightened. The count opposed the creation of a national assembly and indicated his lack of interest in giving Protestants civil rights or revising the criminal code.

At the second Assembly of Notables, convened in December 1788, Artois' Second Bureau rejected double representation for the Third Estate in the Estates General by a vote of sixteen to eight. The count then joined other princes of the blood in presenting a *Memorial* to Louis XVI in which they insisted that "only the separation of the orders, the right to deliberate separately, the equality of votes of the three orders" was constitutional. Artois' irresponsible conduct had set the pace for a decadent nobility whose excesses had alienated the French people and conditioned them for the upheaval to come. His excessive indulgence of the senses and his leadership of members of the nobility and clergy who opposed significant institutional changes contributed substantially to the conditions that made the Revolution possible.

The fall of the Bastille on 14 July and other developments convinced Artois that he should leave France. On the night of 16–17 July 1789, he left Versailles and headed for the Austrian Netherlands. In Brussels Marie-Christine, sister of Marie Antoinette, was vice-regent; and when she asked the comte to leave the city, he received permission to go to the court of his father-in-law, Victor-Amadeus III, in Turin. Artois behaved rather well (his wife was with him) during this period as he pleaded with European sovereigns to restore Louis XVI to full power. On 12 October 1789, the count wrote Joseph II, Holy Roman Emperor, that "the cause of the king of France is the cause of all sovereigns." But by 14 December, Louis XVI was writing Victor-Amadeus and asking him to block the plans of Artois and his entourage. Artois' old friend C.-A. de Calonne, an experienced fund raiser and politician, arrived in Turin in January 1790, took charge of *émigré* diplomacy, and negotiated desperately needed loans. He was convinced that Louis XVI could be restored to full authority only by foreign support. Efforts to goad the Holy Roman Emperor into war with France culminated in Artois' interview with Joseph's successor, Leopold II, on 17 May 1791, but Leopold made no serious commitments. He suggested that the unhappy Artois join his brother Provence at Coblentz. Victor-Amadeus of Savoy, unhappy with *émigré* intrigues, was pleased at the departure of his son-in-law and his entourage. Artois settled in Coblentz where Provence, who had fled France in June 1791, presided over a shadow government as regent and where thousands of *émigrés* had gathered. Artois became the leader of the *purs*, those *émigrés* with a blind determination to destroy every change brought by the Revolution.

Around Artois and Provence gathered the grand seigneurs of Versailles and provincial nobles, and a small *émigré* army gradually came into being. During the summer of 1791, Artois contacted W. Pitt, Frederick William II of Prussia, and the sultan of Turkey and renewed his efforts to obtain the aid of Leopold of Austria. Artois presented a grand plan: princes of the blood would issue a manifesto enumerating the crimes of the National Assembly and declaring its acts null and void. The comte de Provence was to be declared regent and was to announce to the National Assembly that a coalition of European powers had been formed to restore the Bourbons to full authority. But Leopold and Frederick William contented themselves with issuing the Declaration of Pillnitz, stating that the reestablishment of absolute monarchy in France was the concern of European rulers. Artois and Provence, fearful that Louis XVI was surrendering royal power to the Revolutionaries, reminded their brother, "You have only the usufructuary possession of your kingdom . . . and you are bound to transmit to your successors the power that you received from ycur ancestors.''

A new era began with the French declaration of war against Austria in April 1792. Nominally in command of a corps of cavalry, Artois accompanied the army of the princes that trailed after the Austrian and Prussian forces that invaded France in July 1792. But the French army muddled through to victory at Valmy (20 September 1792) and dashed Artois' hopes of a quick return to Versailles. Artois and Provence must take some of the responsibility for the threats to the Revolutionaries included in the Brunswick Manifesto, which stiffened the resolve of the Legislative Assembly to resist the invasion to the utmost. Artois (and Provence) symbolized the forces that threatened intervention in France to destroy the hard-won gains of the classes that had profited from the Revolution.

After Louis XVI's execution in January 1793, the comte de Provence declared the seven-year-old dauphin king as Louis XVII and assumed the title of regent. Artois was designated lieutenant general of the kingdom. When Louis died in 1795, Provence proclaimed himself king as Louis XVIII, and Artois became known as Monsieur in royalist circles. Artois visited Austria, Prussia, and Russia in 1793 in his search for help. Catherine II promised aid if Britain would contribute; but rebuffs by the English in the spring of 1793 left Artois idle and poverty stricken at Hamm in Westphalia where he resided with his mistress, the comtesse de Polastron.

In 1795 the English were promoting actively a plan for the invasion of western France to give support to insurgents opposing the Revolution there; and it was suggested that English troops, spearheaded by *émigrés* led by Artois, open another front against the French republicans. However, while Artois was still at Bremen, a landing at Quiberon (June 1795) by British and *émigré* troops ended in disaster. The landing force was bottled up on the peninsula by republican troops, and most members of the invading force were killed or captured. Several hundred were labeled traitors and executed, embittering royalists everywhere. The English were determined, however, and they sent the ship *Asia* to Bremen to transport Artois and his entourage to England. The count landed at Portsmouth on 7 August and demanded that the English transport him to France immediately. The English cooperated by organizing another expedition, which included some 1,500 French *émigrés* in the army of 4,000 men slated to land on the French coast to train and lead the rebels in the Vendée.

In September Artois and his entourage crossed the channel with the little invasion fleet, but communication with French royalists ashore broke down; republican forces were in the vicinity. By the time Artois indicated a readiness to land, obstacles had arisen that made an assault impractical. The English government recalled the expedition, and Artois returned to London. Yet the *chouans*, by simultaneous surprise attacks on several targets, diverted regular French troops from other fronts and kept royalist hopes alive.

In truth, Artois and his entourage were not ready to make the sacrifices inherent in a decision to debark and engage in guerrilla warfare against republican armies, which were now prepared to give special attention to the western provinces. A few months earlier, the Quiberon fiasco had provided proof that capture might mean facing a firing squad. Artois had neither military training nor experience on the battlefield, and it appeared unlikely that a man who had been so generally disliked before he left France could provide the competent and inspired leadership needed by the insurgents.

If Artois had been a truly inspirational leader with the courage and ability to carry through a project once launched, he might have thrown himself on the coast and set western France on fire in 1795. But he was not that kind of man, and the decision to return to England was correct under the circumstances. The tragic error of Artois and his advisers was to encourage F.-A. Charette de la Contrie, N. Stofflet, G. Cadoudal, L. de Frotté, and other leaders in the interior and to promise far more support than was either practical or possible to deliver.

In London, Artois was harassed by creditors who had furnished money for support of the army of the prince of Condé, and the English ministry suggested that Artois settle in Holyrood Palace in Edinburgh, Scotland, where he would be secure from legal proceedings. From there Artois (along with Provence, who was still on the Continent) continued to encourage conspiracies and excite enthusiasm by promising his presence in France, but he had missed his great opportunity in 1795. The comte was permitted to return to London in 1799 and remained in or near the city until he returned to France in 1814. The evidence is strong that Artois and the English sponsored and financed the royalist conspiracies against the life of Bonaparte in 1800 and 1804. Artois was the first of the princes to reach Paris (with the allied army) after Napoleon's downfall; and his seventeen-day tenure as lieutenant general of the kingdom before Louis XVIII arrived did not give the Restoration an auspicious beginning. During the reign of Louis XVIII (1814–24), Artois was the most extreme of the ultraroyalists and when he became king, as Charles X, in 1824 he inaugurated a program that most Frenchmen interpreted as attempts to subvert the Revolution and return to the institutions of the Old Regime. In 1830 Charles X was overthrown during the July Revolution. He lived out his years in exile and died at Gorizia (Austria) in 1836.

Archives du Ministère des Affaires Etrangères, *Fonds Bourbon*, vols. 558, 623-27, 647; *A.N.*, C[7] 11 and 34AP-3AI2; V. Beach, *Charles X of France: His Life and Times* (Boulder, Colo., 1971) and "The Count of Artois and the Coming of the French Revolution," *J. of Mod. Hist.* 30 (1958); British Museum, Windham Papers, added Mss. 37859-37868; Public Record Office, *Papiers de Calonne*, 1/124, 1/126, 1/127, 1/129, 1/131; J. Turquan and J. d'Auriac, *Monsieur comte d'Artois* (Paris, 1930).

V. Beach

Related entries: ASSEMBLY OF NOTABLES; BRUNSWICK MANIFESTO; CALONNE; CHARETTE DE LA CONTRIE; *CHOUANNERIE*; COBLENTZ; CONDE; COUNTERREVOLUTION; DECLARATION OF PILLNITZ; *EMIGRES*; MARIE-ANTOINETTE; PROVENCE; QUIBERON; VICTOR AMADEUS III.

ASSEMBLIES, PROVINCIAL. See PROVINCIAL ASSEMBLIES.

ASSEMBLY, LEGISLATIVE. See LEGISLATIVE ASSEMBLY.

ASSEMBLY, NATIONAL CONSTITUENT. See NATIONAL CONSTITUENT ASSEMBLY.

ASSEMBLY OF NOTABLES (22 February 1787–25 May 1787; 6 November 1788–12 December 1788), an advisory body of the Old Regime, including nearly 150 of the most prestigious nobles and public officials of France. The first Assembly of Notables, convened by Louis XVI to approve the last great reform program of the Bourbon monarchy, rejected unexpectedly the most important reforms, initiating the crisis leading to revolution in 1789. Historians have tended to view the Notables' opposition as a final phase of the aristocratic resurgence in the late *ancien régime*, aimed at preserving the nobility's privileges and enlarging its sphere of action. More exacting research has now modified this interpretation.

The government's program, conceived by the controller general, C.-A. de Calonne, intended to eliminate the mounting deficit through a combination of financial and institutional reform. A new land tax and provincial assemblies were the centerpieces. The land tax, holding no exemptions for nobles and clergy, would be levied in proportion to wealth and vary with annual income; assemblies, established in provinces lacking provincial institutions (estates), would assess the new tax and assist in public works and charity. Other reforms included reduction of the *taille* (tax on commoners, mainly peasants), a money payment replacing the *corvée* (peasant road service), a more equitable salt tax (*gabelle*), free internal trade in grain, and removal of tariff barriers within the national borders. The good these measures would produce, Calonne reasoned, would win the Notables' support.

The Notables did approve reforms of the *taille*, *corvée*, free trade in grain, and a single national tariff. All the other reforms, especially the land tax and provincial assemblies, they rejected, or they demanded major changes. They did not oppose these reforms merely to defend the privilege of tax exemption for nobles and clergy, which the government's program endangered; less than a handful of Notables advocated fiscal exemption; their opposition had broader scope. Close analysis of the Notables' debates and of their role in *ancien régime* society helps to explain why they opposed the royal reforms and why their example sparked broader opposition, which succeeded ultimately in undermining the monarchy and forcing it to convene an Estates General for 1789.

The Notables (144 in the first Assembly and 147 in the second), included princes of the blood, archbishops and bishops, nobles (many of them military commanders), chief judges of the sovereign courts, royal councillors, deputies of provincial estates, and heads of municipal governments. Almost all were nobles. With few exceptions they were public officials, their rank and influence, so the government expected, attracting public support for the reforms. Most of them were also landowners. Not only their noble status but their experience and outlook as public officials and their interests as landowners together or separately molded their responses to the royal program.

Although nobles, the Notables, including the ecclesiastics among them, supported fiscal equality in principle and practice. They opposed the land tax because it would increase taxes on the land, and the land was already overburdened by taxes, they argued. Their interests as landowners, rather than their privileges as seigneurs, were at stake. So, too, they opposed a tax in kind paid in produce that they could otherwise sell at rising market prices, favoring instead a money tax. Their tax revolt also led them to express political objectives by which they wed their personal interests to broader public interests in a mix with potential widespread appeal.

Public experience taught the Notables that most Frenchmen who owned or cultivated land opposed higher taxes and would support the Notables' opposition. Shock at the revelation of a deficit heightened suspicion of the crown and led the Notables to seek public control over government financial operations: annual publication of the budget, public audits of expenditures, local assessment, collection and allocation of taxes, and ultimately national consent to taxation. Controls signified a greater public role in government activities—not only in finances but also in a wide range of administration at the local level and in the nation, themes reiterated in the Notables' demands, claims, and counterproposals. They succeeded in shaping vague discontents and aspirations into concrete programs and goals that responded to the public mood and that the public could share and endorse.

With the absolute centralized monarchy as their target, the goals the Notables sought had a double guise. Public participation in government in the name of the nation would not be for all. The Notables' concern was less who would vote than who would be in government and exercise power. The provincial assemblies, they insisted, should have representation of the three orders, with up to one-half the seats assigned to nobles and clergy, thus ensuring them a strong presence and leadership, and with the Third Estate being represented by local public officials. Nobles, including clergy, and "notables" would control public affairs in the provinces and in the nation. The Notables' outrage at Calonne's appeal for public support of the royal program led them to sharpen their views. The crown must share the power of decision making, but only an assembled body of nobles and "notables," as the Assembly of Notables itself, could participate in deciding policy and making laws. A broader public should have no role in influencing policy. Public opinion should be another political instrument controlled by nobles and "notables." The wielders of power in a new France should be those of high status and those in public office.

The nation controlling and participating in government were the major themes of the first Assembly. From the spring of 1787 until the autumn of 1788, calls resounded for the convening of an Estates General and for extending the powers of provincial assemblies. Parlementary courts especially refused new or higher taxes to force the crown to yield, the government in turn attacking the courts, which further mobilized public opposition to the monarchy. Magistrates, nobles, clergy, and a broader public came together to demand an Estates General, their alliance in this period now termed the pre-revolution, ending in late 1788 with the meeting of the second Assembly of Notables.

National participation was won. The crown succumbed to financial stringency and public pressure, in August 1788 summoning an Estates General. Representation and voting in the Estates General, its organization and operation—issues that raised questions about the social basis of representation and the political effectiveness of elected institutions—became new and major controversies in late 1788. Recalled to advise on procedures for electing the Estates General, the Notables (five of their six committees or *bureaux*) supported equal representation for each order and separate deliberation and vote by order. Their decision, following a similar call by the Paris Parlement in September 1788, aimed to preserve a strong political presence of nobles and clergy in the upcoming assembly, the Notables no longer confident of the elite's ability to control public opinion and now fearful of the demographic advantage of the Third Estate. The public, perceiving the demand for separate and equal representation of the orders as a design of the first two estates to gain political predominance, opposed the Notables and magistrates, and those who supported their views among the nobles and high clergy. Most of the voices now heard in the public demanded "doubling of the Third" and "vote by head," slogans whose aims were to ensure greater influence for the Third Estate in the Estates General and success for the national body by avoiding the disputes and stalemates that, in the past, vote by order and the attendant veto by each order had produced. These issues dominated debates in 1789, until June, when the three orders merged into a National Assembly, marking the first victory of the Revolution.

P. Chevallier, ed., *Journal de l'Assemblée des Notables de 1787 par le Comte de Brienne et Etienne-Charles de Loménie de Brienne* (Paris, 1960); J. Egret, *La Pré-Révolution française, 1787-1788* (Paris, 1962), and English trans. (Chicago, 1977); A. Goodwin, "The Assembly of Notables and the *révolte nobiliaire*," *Eng. Hist. Rev.* 61 (1946); V. R. Gruder, "Class and Politics in the Pre-Revolution: The Assembly of Notables of 1787" in E. Hinrichs, et al., eds., *De l'Ancien Régime à la Révolution française, Recherches et Perspectives* (Gottingen, 1978); P. Renouvin, ed., *L'Assemblée des Notables de 1787: La Conférence du 2 mars* (Paris, 1920).

V. R. Gruder

Related entries: CALONNE; *CORVEE*; ESTATES GENERAL; FEUDALISM; *GABELLE*; NECKER; *QU'EST-CE QUE C'EST LE TIERS ETAT?*; SIEYES.

ASSIGNATS (1789–97), paper currency created after the confiscation of church lands to liquidate the national debt and bring economic stability. In 1789, the financial situation in France was alarming: receipts in August totaled 473,294,000 *livres* while expenses exceeded 531,513,000 *livres*. The abolition of certain taxes exacerbated the imbalance, and specie was scarce.

On 19 December 1789, the National Assembly took action to solve the economic crisis. To keep the government momentarily solvent, a loan of 80 million *livres* from the Caisse d'Escompte was authorized. Nationalized lands valued at 400 million *livres* were to be placed on the market, and *assignats*, redeemable in the former crown and church lands, were to be issued. Simply, the creditors of France would receive payment in *assignats*, which collectively could be used to purchase land, and the national debt would be liquidated in the process.

Specifically not legal tender, the *assignats* were to be issued in large denominations so as not to threaten the shrinking amount of metallic currency in use. They carried 5 percent interest, which was payable to the bearer of the note on the last day of the calendar year. They were to be systematically redeemed either through purchase of property or by lot over a five-year period. To oversee the issuing and redemption of the *assignats* and the surplus expected from their use, the *caisse de l'extraordinaire* was created.

There had been fierce critics of the issuance of paper currency, like P.-S. Dupont de Nemours who argued that it was an avowal of bankruptcy. Others feared depreciation of the notes and continuing economic distress. The proponents, J.-P. Brissot and H.-G. R. Mirabeau in particular, believed that the arguments against *assignats* were false because the notes were secured on real property. They turned for their support to E. Clavière's *Opinions d'un Créancier* and to the philosophy of the physiocrats—that the wealth of the county was land. The face value of the *assignat*, therefore, should remain constant. Furthermore, the redemption of the *assignats* was to be carefully monitored to avoid depreciation: 120 million in 1791, 100 million in 1792, 80 million in 1793–94, and the remainder in 1795.

From the beginning, however, there were difficulties with the *assignats*. They lacked credibility, it was argued, because the lands on which they were based were frequently encumbered with debt. To allay such fears, all outstanding liabilities were legally transferred to the government.

On 17 April 1790 interest on the *assignats* was reduced to 3 percent to encourage redemption in land. The economy, however, was not recovering at a rapid enough pace, and the National Assembly declared the *assignats* as legal tender. In the fall of 1790, the treasury reported a deficit, which would not allow the government to pay its obligations. Mirabeau's suggestion to double the issue of *assignats* to a value of 800 million was accepted. Although opponents like Dupont de Nemours and C.-M. Talleyrand railed against the measure, it set a precedent for issuing greater numbers of *assignats* without monitoring their redemption. In May 1791 the total value was set at 1,200 million, in October 1792 at 2,400 million, and in January 1793 at 3,067 million, although the number in circulation was probably 2,385 million *livres*.

Each additional issue of *assignats*, however, brought little relief to the economic crisis. Smaller denominations, printed to encourage the flow of money, only encouraged the hoarding of gold and the exportation of silver. In spite of Mirabeau's assurances, the value of *assignats* had not remained constant; those issued under Louis XVI actually carried a value 5 to 10 percent higher than those issued by later assemblies. Of greater danger, however, was the radical decline in market value compared to face value. In January 1791, 100 *livres* were valued at 91, in January 1792 at 72, in January 1793 at 51, and in July 1793 at 23 *livres*. The finance committee, particularly P.-J. Cambon, realized that the defense of the country and domestic security depended on the strength of the *assignats*.

Stringent measures, including the Law of the Maximum, were enacted in 1793 to regulate the economy and to impede transactions in specie. Merchants could not, under penalty of law, raise prices in proportion to the depreciation of paper money. In addition, laws were enacted requiring merchants to accept *assignats* at par value. Failure to do so carried a six-month prison sentence, and a second offense could carry a twenty-year term. Cambon pressed for the consolidation of the various financial agencies, demanded a forced loan from the wealthy, and amalgamated the debts in the *grand livre*. Briefly credibility returned, and the *assignats* began to regain purchasing power. The rally was short-lived, however, due to the continuing war debts, radically fluctuating money supply, and serious problems of subsistence.

On 23 December 1795, the Directory took action to regain stability. One hundred *livres* worth of *assignats* at face value were worth scarcely 60 *sous*. It was reported that a dinner for two at the Palais Royal cost 1,500 *livres*, that a pound of bread cost 50 *livres*, and that a cab ride cost 1,000 *livres*. The law of 2 Nivôse decreed that no further *assignats* could be printed, and on 9 Pluviôse, the Council of Five Hundred voted to destroy the plates. To hasten their redemption and the return to a stable currency, *mandats territoriaux* were created. The *assignats* were to be converted into *mandats* at an exchange rate of thirty to one so that no more than 800 million in *mandats* would be required to retire the *assignats* in circulation. On 21 May 1797, the *assignats* ceased to exist; they had been demonetized by the government in an effort to return to metallic currency and economic stability.

C. Gomel, *Histoire financière de la Législative et de la Convention*, 2 vols. (Paris, 1902); S. E. Harris, *The Assignats* (Cambridge, Mass., 1930); H. Higgs, "Revolutionary Finance," *The Cambridge Modern History*, vol. 8 (Cambridge, 1904); J. Lafaurie, *Les Assignats: Et les papiers-monnaies émis par l'Etat au XVIIIe siècle* (Paris, 1981); Reports of the commissioners found in the *Procès-verbaux du Comité des Finances de l'Assemblée constituante* (*Le Moniteur*).

S. P. Conner

Related entries: CAMBON; CLAVIERE; DUPONT DE NEMOURS; LAW OF THE MAXIMUM; *MANDATS TERRITORIAUX*; MIRABEAU.

ATHEISM, a materialist philosophy, denying the existence of God, held by a few *philosophes* during the Enlightenment and professed by a small elite, involved in dechristianization, during the Revolution. In the precise sense, *atheism* designates a doctrine that denies the existence of God and any principle of unity in the universe. The term has been improperly applied to stoicism, pantheism, and Spinoza's philosophy.

In the eighteenth century, J. Locke, P. Bayle, and B. Fontenelle rejected belief in the immortality of the soul and in miracles, attacked the dogma of Revelation in the name of Reason, and professed a natural religion. In a more categorical fashion, the curé J. Meslier proclaimed himself an atheist in his testament, which was publicized by F.-M. Voltaire and the baron d'Holbach. The heirs of the libertine tradition, with the exception of the atheists who were corrupt and immoral as well, scandalized people less than in the past. Generous and moral atheists, such as N. Boulanger, seemed to confuse, wrongly, superstition and religion. From the time of P. Bayle, atheism was considered merely the short-coming of some intellectuals; for the first time, an atheist, M. de Wolmar, appeared as a sympathetic hero, in the celebrated novel of the century, *La nouvelle Héloïse*.

Such indulgence favored the shift in the direction of scientific materialism, illustrated by the work of J.-G. La Mettrie: the soul is only an appendage of the body, thought a property of organic matter, and man merely a machine. The popularization of atheism in all the media was assured by P. Thiry, baron d'Holbach. He was seconded by his faithful friends, J.-A. Naigeon, C.-F. Dupuis, S. Maréchal, and J. Lalande, all of whom created more concern than they had real influence. The rationalist current indeed existed before the Revolution, but historians have tended to overestimate it. It attempted to "de-spiritualize" man, as M.-J.-A.-N. Condorcet put it; it wanted to submit all human problems to critical analysis; and it had confidence in the qualities and progress of the human spirit. The eighteenth century remained, on the whole, deist and not atheist.

The abbé Barruel, E. Burke, and J. de Maistre insist on the antireligious character of the Revolution; P.-J.-B. Buchez and A. de Tocqueville emphasize the similarity between the principles of the Gospel and Revolutionary expecta-tions. The deputies to the Estates General and to the Constituent Assembly professed a belief in the Supreme Being; they exhibited the religiosity extolled by the Savoyard vicar of J.-J. Rousseau. The measures they took, such as the Civil Constitution of the Clergy, revived Gallican and Richerist tendencies of religious toleration as a consequence of political and financial necessity. In their turn, the Girondins were bourgeois, nourished on pagan Greek and Latin culture; they despised the clergy and religious beliefs; and, for philosophical and political reasons, they engaged in a struggle against the church that gave advance notice of dechristianization. The Brissotins continued the Voltairean and Encyclopedist tradition; in September 1792 one of them had a street in Paris named after Helvétius, who, together with Holbach, represented the extremist element of the *philosophes*, the atheistic atomists. When, in December 1792, the deputy J.-L. Dupont made a profession of atheism, he provoked a scandal. Anticlericalism was more prevalent in the Revolutionary assemblies than atheism.

The political climate and the Revolutionary wars, rather than philosophical considerations, pushed the Montagnard Convention to the struggle against the nonjuring priests and to the destruction of religious symbols. The dechristianization movement began in the autumn of 1793 and the consecration of an official atheism occurred with the institution of the cult of the goddess of Reason, celebrated at Notre Dame of Paris on 10 November. It symbolized the triumph of philosophy over fanaticism. The notion of the Cult of Reason shocked certain atheists, such as J.-B. Salaville and N. Raffron-du-Trouillet. For them, Reason could not become an impersonal god; to follow Reason was to reject the divine and the transcendent; Reason was to profess atheism and to proscribe feeling and sentiment. In the Year II the apostles of Reason struggled primarily against popular superstitions. Beside symbolic Mountains they set up busts of W. Tell and of B. Franklin and trees of liberty; at Besançon a statue symbolized atheism. At these religious masquerades were foreign Revolutionary elements, such as A. Cloots and J. Pereira, who initiated violent dechristianization. Atheism affected only the Revolutionary cadres; the masses effected a transfer of religious sentiment and adapted the traditional liturgy to the temples of Reason, and venerated the Trinity of Martyrs: J.-P. Marat, L.-M. Lepelletier, and M.-J. Chalier. The Cordeliers even proposed a devotion to the Sacred Heart of Marat. In December 1793 M. Robespierre and the Committee of Public Safety condemned this as Hébertist propaganda. J.-R. Hébert himself denied that he was an atheist when he was accused of being one in December 1793, but his testimony constituted his only defense when Robespierre struck against the dechristianizers.

From that time, the Cult of the Supreme Being, with its symbolism, its hymns, and its orations, represented atheism's defeat and constituted an attempt to institute a spiritual religion based on a pantheist conception. The decree of 7 May 1794 created a cycle of celebrations, dedicated either to a particular virtue or to a benefit of nature. On 8 June 1794, during the celebration of the Supreme Being, Robespierre destroyed in flames a group of monsters that included atheism.

The Thermidorian Convention, and the Directory, proclaimed freedom of religion and the separation of church and state. The decline of morals reflected the weakening of religious beliefs; in particular, in the course of the turmoil, the family had been weakened, while civil divorce, instituted in 1791, destroyed the sacrament of marriage. The anti-Christian offensive began again, with such works as *Origine de tous les cultes* by C.-F. Dupuis, *Guerre des Dieux* by E.-D.-D. Parny, and *De l'obstination réligieuse* by P.-L. Gingnené.

The political authorities, convinced of the necessity of a religion, tried to substitute theophilanthropy for the ancient beliefs, but this religion of the elite admitted the immortality of the soul and the existence of God. National and decadal (based on the ten day *décade* into which months were divided) celebrations, inspired by N.-L. François de Neufchâteau, were intended to ensure the triumph of natural religion over revealed religions.

In reality, the Revolutionaries, both the elite and the masses, displayed religious behavior during the entire decade; they cherished the almost messianic hope of establishing a new order of universal happiness. It is possible to speak of religious transference; the republican catechisms, the hymns, the imagery appealed to virtues and great men and expressed belief in and a spiritual reverence for the immortality of the soul. To honor liberty, nature, and reason did not imply atheism.

Dechristianization, which reflected atheism to a certain degree, can be explained, according to F.-A. Aulard, as a defensive reflex against the priests who were the soul of counterrevolution; according to A. Mathiez, it was due to the desire to establish the work of the Revolution on the foundation of a new religion; according to A. Latreille, it was due to the initial weakness of the church, to marginal elements, and to the defects of the constitutional church. Atheism was of brief duration and remained an isolated and essentially elitist phenomenon.

Ann. hist. de la Révo. française 50 (1978), special number on "La déchristianisation en l'An II"; F.-A. Aulard, *Le culte de la Raison et de l'Etre suprême* (Paris, 1892); A. Cochin, *La Révolution et la libre pensée. Le socialisation de la pensée 1750-1789; Le socialisation de la personne, 1789-1793; Le socialisation des biens, 1793-1794* (Paris, 1924); J. Dulumeau, "Au sujet de la déchristianisation," *Rev. d'hist. mod. et cont.* 22 (1975); A. Latreille, *L'eglise catholique et la Révolution française,* I. *Le pontificat de Pie VI et la crise française, 1775-1799* (Paris, 1946); A. Mathiez, *Les origines des cultes révolutionnaires* (Paris, 1904) and *Le théophilanthropie et le culte décadaire* (Paris, 1904); B. Plongeron, *Conscience religieuse en Révolution* (Paris, 1969); M. Vovelle, *Religion et révolution: La déchristianisation en l'an II* (Paris, 1976).

L. Trenard

Related entries: AULARD; BURKE; CIVIL CONSTITUTION OF THE CLERGY; CLOOTS; CULT OF THE SUPREME BEING; FRANCOIS DE NEUFCHATEAU; HEBERT; MARECHAL; MATHIEZ; THEOPHILANTHROPY.

AUGUST 4, 1789. See 4 AUGUST 1789.

AUGUST 10, 1792. See 10 AUGUST 1792.

AULARD, FRANCOIS-VICTOR-ALPHONSE (1849-1928), historian, teacher, and journalist specializing in the history of the Revolution and Napoleon. Son of a professor of philosophy and secondary school inspector, Aulard received his primary education at Tours and Lons-le-Saunier before entering the Collège Sainte-Barbe and Ecole Normale Supérieure (1867-70). The Franco-Prussian War led him to join the mobile national guard of the Seine, in which he served during the siege of Paris and at the Battle of Buzenval. After the war, he became an *agrégé de lettres*, beginning a teaching career at various provincial lycées and then at the Lycée Janson de Sailly in Paris. In 1886 he became the first professor of the history of the French Revolution at the University of Paris, where he received an endowed chair five years later. He taught there until his retirement in 1922.

Originally a literary historian, he received his doctorate for a dissertation on the Italian poet G. Leopardi (1877). His interest in rhetoric led him to study the orators of the Revolution and to produce several studies of Revolutionary eloquence. Influenced by L. Gambetta, Aulard became a partisan of G.-J. Danton, whom he sought to rescue from charges of corruption and immorality. From the 1880s he devoted himself almost exclusively to the study of the Revolutionary and Napoleonic period, contributing regularly to *La Révolution française* and serving as its editor from 1887 to his death. With state subsidies and unacknowledged assistance from a team of copyists, he published numerous volumes of documents: *Recueil des Actes du Comité de Salut Public* (26 vols.; 1889-1923); *La Société des Jacobins* (6 vols.; 1889–97); *Paris pendant la Réaction Thermidorienne et sous le Directoire* (5 vols.; 1898–1902); *Paris sous le Consulat* (4 vols.; 1903–9); and *Paris sous le Premier Empire* (2 vols.; 1912–14). His other works include *Le Culte de la Raison et le Culte de l'Etre Suprême* (1893); *Histoire politique de la Révolution française* (1901); *La Révolution française et les congrégations* (1903); *Taine, historien de la Révolution française* (1907); *La Révolution française et le Régime féodal* (1919); and *Le christianisme et la Révolution française* (1925). Many of his articles were collected in his *Etudes et leçons sur la Révolution française* (9 vols.; 1898–1924). Besides his purely historical writings, Aulard contributed columns on political, religious, and education questions to a variety of newspapers and reviews, notably *La dépêche de Toulouse*, *Progrès civique*, and *Ere nouvelle*, all radical-socialist in viewpoint. He was active in the Ligue des Droits de l'Homme from its founding in 1898 and served as its vice-president from 1921 to 1928.

A.N., F[17] 22600; G. Belloni, *Aulard, Historien de la Révolution française* (Paris, 1949); *Révo. française* 81 (1928). Aulard's lecture notes are preserved at Harvard University, Ms Fr 46.

J. Friguglietti

Related entries: DANTON; MATHIEZ.

AUSTRIAN COMMITTEE (1789-92), aristocratic, monarchist, and counter-revolutionary grouping that, meeting clandestinely, attempted in vain to impose a pro-Austrian foreign policy on Louis XVI and Marie-Antoinette while advocating an internal position of monarchical absolutism. Perhaps the most significant counterrevolutionary committee during the early phases of the Revolution, the Austrian Committee (Comité autrichien) held, despite its secretiveness, quasi-official power. Although no formal evidence exists relating to its actual composition, enough circumstantial material is available to establish its likely leadership and program. The two men most often identified with the committee by contemporaries are A.-F. B. de Molleville, navy minister in 1792, and A.-M. de Montmorin, Louis XVI's minister for foreign affairs from 1787 to 1791.

The objectives of the committee were specific: to maintain and safeguard the prerogatives of the king and the royal family and to resist any encroachments by the National Assembly on these prerogatives. In foreign policy, the Austrian Committee supported the 1756 alliance with Austria, cemented as it had been in 1770 with the marriage between Marie Antoinette and the future Louis XVI.

Thus the committee advised against any rapprochement between France and England or France and Prussia even though political, diplomatic, and commercial interests might legitimately dictate such an arrangement. Additionally, the committee advocated a lenient policy toward the *émigrés* who swarmed particularly in Turin and the Rhenish principalities.

The Austrian Committee received its name not from its pro-Austrian policy but from the popular belief that the queen, *l'autrichienne*, as she had been dubbed by Madame Adélaïde as early as 1770, presided over its counsels. Parisians were persuaded that, because of her family connection with the Hapsburgs in Vienna, the queen was actively engaged in transmitting state and military information to the Austrian enemy. While correspondence from Marie Antoinette to the comte Fersen, among others, does allude to this possibility, most historians now concede that the queen's role in foreign affairs has been vastly overrated. Nevertheless, contemporary journalists like J.-P. Marat and J.-P. Brissot were quick to point their radical pens at the "perfidious intriguers and traitors" who met secretly and regularly at Saint-Cloud, Bagatelle, Auteuil, or the royal palace itself. More explicit evidence suggests that the notorious manifesto associated with the duke of Brunswick had its inception in the deliberations of the Austrian Committee, but the queen's role in this, too, is uncertain.

With all the intrigue associated with the Committee's machinations, the king's position is unclear. Without any substantiation to the contrary, Louis XVI does not appear to have been an inner member of the committee, but because of his wife's influence over him, her political desires, and those of the committee, he was led more often than not to succumb to its policies. We do know that at least once the king denied the existence of such a cabal (this in reply to a series of articles in the radical press), going so far as to institute an official inquiry. That there were no results from this investigation is probably due to the queen's involvement in the activities of the Austrian Committee.

The committee's raison d'être ceased with the royal family's imprisonment in the Temple in August 1792. Within a month, A.-M. Montmorin had been slaughtered, a victim of the September Massacres. A.-F. Bertrand de Molleville, allegedly the other chief conspirator, established a Club national in 1793. Its counterrevolutionary and monarchist goals were identical to those of the Austrian Committee, but it had limited success. More successful as an extension of the Austrian Committee was a royalist agency established in Paris in 1794 under the auspices of the comte de Provence. Supported with funds issued by Catherine the Great, this group attracted nobles and royalists and was designed to keep alive the monarchist cause. Indeed, this agency became a feeder for the much more prominent Clichy Club, which played a significant conservative role during the early period of the Directory.

A. Challamel, *Les Clubs contre-révolutionnaires: cercles, comités, sociétés, salons, réunions, cafés, restaurants et libraires* (reprint of the 1895 edition, New York, 1974).

B. Rothaus

Related entries: BERTRAND DE MOLLEVILLE; BRISSOT DE WARVILLE; BRUNSWICK MANIFESTO; CLUB DE CLICHY; MARAT; MARIE ANTOINETTE; MONTMORIN.

AVIGNON, papal enclave in the Rhône Valley annexed to France on grounds of self-determination in September 1791. Located at the confluence of the Rhône and Durance rivers, the county of Avignon, which included the city of Avignon and a few surrounding communes, had a population of about 25,000 in 1789. The county, acquired by the papacy from the ruler of Provence in 1348, was governed by the pope's representative, the vice-legate, and a municipal council controlled by the clergy, the nobility, and a few privileged bourgeois families. Abuses in the papal administration were widespread, and well before the French Revolution the industrial and commercial bourgeoisie, particularly the silk manufacturers, and members of the legal community were demanding reform in the judicial and taxation systems and a broadening of representation in the council. There was discontent as well among artisans and peasants, aggravated after 1788 by an economic crisis that led to a sharp rise in bread prices and unemployment in the silk industry, the mainstay of the county's economy. Encouraged by the first results of the Revolution in France, Avignonese Revolutionaries renewed their demands and supported them with demonstrations. By March 1790, the Revolutionaries had gained control of the municipal council. They adopted the main provisions of the constitution then being framed in France, but the pope refused to accept these. After his supporters in Avignon made an unsuccessful bid to reassert his authority by force, the Revolutionaries declared Avignon independent of the papacy and voted to join France (11 June 1790).

Many communes in the neighboring Comtat Venaissin, another papal enclave, followed Avignon's example. Ceded to the papacy by the count of Toulouse in the thirteenth century, the Venaissin contained ninety-five communes whose 125,000 residents lived largely by agriculture. Like Avignon, the Venaissin acknowledged the vice-legate as executive head, but its other governmental institutions and its laws were distinct from those of its neighbor. A movement for reform also developed in the Venaissin, but by the summer of 1790 it had divided between moderates who wanted to retain the papal headship and revolutionaries who, like the Avignonese, wanted to sever the link with Rome. After several communes voted to join France, papists and Revolutionaries engaged in civil war in which the Avignonese soon became involved.

The first appeal from the enclaves for annexation reached the Constituent Assembly in late June 1790. Although conscious that economic ties, a common language, and similar traditions made union between the peoples of the enclaves and their French neighbors attractive, the cautious Assembly debated the appeal intermittently for more than a year before replying affirmatively.

For the annexationists, who came chiefly from the Assembly's left wing, the principal argument for accepting the appeal lay in the theory of self-determination. By virtue of its right to determine its destiny, a people could declare its independence of one state and join another. The origins of this novel theory are to be found in discussions in the first year of the Revolution on the nature of French unity. The Assembly had faced challenges to its authority to legislate in certain parts of France on the grounds that the treaties by which these parts were joined to France had restricted the powers of the central government. Determined that its writ should run everywhere in the country, the Assembly had responded by reinterpreting national unity in terms of popular sovereignty, the cardinal principle of the Revolution. Each part of France, the argument ran, was joined to the rest not because of a treaty made in the past by its ruler and the French king but because its inhabitants had expressly and unconditionally willed their union with the rest of the country by participating in the election to the Estates General in 1789 and in the Festival of the Federation the next year. France was therefore one nation on the basis of popular rather than royal consent. Self-determination was the foundation of internal unity, and in 1790–91 the annex-ationists invoked the same principle in international affairs to justify the union of a foreign place to France. Transfers of territory, the annexationists insisted, must henceforth be based on popular consent, not, as hitherto, on conquest, exchange, marriage, or inheritance. The agreement of the previous ruler to such a transfer was unnecessary, since in Revolutionary theory he was merely the delegate of the sovereign people and not its master. According to this reasoning, Avignon and the Venaissin were entitled to withdraw from the papal domains and petition to join France without the pope's approval. That the enclaves had freely exercised this right, the annexationists had no doubt. Their right-wing opponents contended that union was not the will of the majority and that most voting had occurred during a civil war in which individuals were coerced into supporting union or being forced to flee for their lives. Annexation without the consent of the people, charged the spokesmen of the Right, would violate the Assembly's decree of May 1790 renouncing conquest. The annexationists denied the charge with the argument that whereas conquest meant incorporation of a territory by force, what they now proposed was simply the union of peoples by consent.

The annexationists also invoked public law to support their case. Aware of the concern in the Assembly that annexation solely on the basis of popular consent could serve as a pretext for foreign intervention in the Revolution, they reasoned that the European powers would more likely acquiesce to annexation if convinced that the French title was valid on established legal and historical grounds that the powers themselves used to justify territorial acquisitions. The French mon-archy, as heir of the former rulers of Avignon and the Venaissin, had always claimed the counties and had adduced in support arguments drawn from public law. The annexationists in the Assembly now reasserted the arguments of their monarchical predecessors, arguing that since Avignon and the Venaissin were inalienable, their cession by their rulers to the papacy in the Middle Ages was illegal and papal rule was a usurpation. Opponents of annexation insisted that the historical facts supported the pope's case and that, regardless of the legality of the cessions and the subsequent claims of the French monarchy, prescription had validated the papal title.

After lengthy debate, the Assembly, although convinced by the Left that France's legal title was sound, doubted the authenticity of the electoral verdict in favor of union rendered while civil war raged. Before accepting the appeal, the Assembly therefore decided, in May 1791, to send mediators to restore peace in the enclaves—as both warring factions there had requested—and to hold a plebiscite on union whose legitimacy could not be called in question. The mediators, supported by French troops, soon arranged a peace settlement, restored calm in the troubled areas, and then supervised a new popular consultation on union in which males over twenty-five years of age who paid a certain sum in annual direct taxation could vote. On the whole, the voting in history's first plebiscite on an annexation was conducted fairly, as spokesmen for communes that voted for the continuance of papal rule themselves testified. Of the ninety-eight communes in the two counties, seventy-one voted. With fifty-two communes voting in favor of union and nineteen against, the annexationists had a majority of thirty-three. An Assembly, chosen at the same time as voters expressed their opinion on union, confirmed the result of the plebiscite and dispatched representatives to Paris to inform the French deputies. On 14 September 1791 the Constituent Assembly, now satisfied that union was the will of the majority, declared Avignon and the Venaissin joined to France. The deputies considered self-determination the fundamental basis of union, but these realists also invoked public law in order to legitimize France's title in language understood in Europe's chancelleries. The pope, who earlier in the year had broken off diplomatic relations with France over the Assembly's religious legislation, acknowledged the loss of the enclaves only seven years later (Treaty of Tolentino, February 1797) after N. Bonaparte had invaded the Papal States in his first Italian campaign.

Annexation did not end the turbulence that had marked Avignonese public life for two years. When an antirevolutionary mob murdered a prominent municipal official, the Revolutionaries took revenge in the notorious massacre of La Glacière. On the night of 16–17 October 1791, they murdered more than sixty papists in the prisons of the Palace of the Popes and threw their bodies to the bottom of La Glacière, one of the towers of the palace. Violence flared again during the Terror. In the summer of 1793, Avignon joined in the unsuccessful federalist revolt against the Convention and the next year paid a heavy price when the Committee of Public Safety established a special tribunal, which from June to August 1794 condemned to death 332 counterrevolutionaries.

By this time, the authorities in Paris had managed to provide a permanent administrative framework for the annexed area. They had at first divided it between two neighboring departments, but in 1793 the Convention made the former enclaves the new department of the Vaucluse, with Avignon as capital. Gradually new administrative and judicial institutions were established, and the other changes the Revolution had introduced in France were extended to the Vaucluse.

J. F. André, *Histoire de la Révolution Avignonaise*, 2 vols. (Paris, 1844); A. Mathiez, *Rome et le clergé français sous la Constituante: La Constitution civile du clergé; l'affaire d'Avignon* (Paris, 1911); C. Soullier, *Histoire de la Révolution d'Avignon et du Comtat*

Venaissin en 1789 et années suivantes, 2 vols. (Paris, 1844; reprinted Marseille, 1974); S. Wambaugh, *A Monograph on Plebiscites* (New York, 1920).

J. P. McLaughlin

Related entries: ANNEXATION; FEDERALISM.

B

BABEUF, FRANCOIS-NOEL (later GRACCHUS) (1760-97), leader of the communist movement for equality during the Directory. Babeuf was born at Saint-Quentin in Picardy into a poor family. He recalled his infancy as dirty and wretched; of thirteen children in his family, only four survived. At the age of fourteen, he went to work on the construction of the Picardy canal. Although his character was molded in this setting, he managed to work his way up in life, and when he was about twenty-one years old he became a specialist in feudal law. In the course of organizing the records of feudal lords, Babeuf quickly realized that the survival of feudal dues was a great injustice. In Picardy, he had already seen that more and more poverty stricken peasants were forced to work at home in a capitalist putting-out form of manufacturing in return for minimal wages. A passionate individual, quick to become enraged, he sought to ameliorate the lot of the disinherited classes. After reading J.-J. Rousseau and G.-B. Mably, Babeuf concluded that private property—above all, landed property—was the cause of all public evil. In 1785, in letters to the secretary of the Academy of Arras, F. Dubois de Fosseux, he proposed a plan for collective farms. In 1787 he suggested that the academy conduct a contest on the theme of creating a society in which equality would exist among all members, and the land would belong to all the inhabitants; everything would be held in common. Although he was a convinced partisan of a society of perfect equality, Babeuf remained a realist and always attempted to make concrete social demands that the masses could understand as steps toward the realization of his ideal. In the fiscal crisis of the monarchy, Babeuf proposed in 1789 a plan for a tax that he justified in his *Cadastre perpétuel*.

In the spring of 1790 Babeuf led the movement against the *aides* in Picardy. The authorities ordered him arrested and transferred to prison in Paris. With J.-P. Marat's help, he was later released. While still in prison, he began to edit his *Journal de confédération*. He shared Rousseau's critical conception of representative government and declared openly his support for direct, popular democracy.

Returning to Picardy, Babeuf edited the newspaper *Correspondant picard*. On the whole, his agrarian program went beyond anything that the most radical democrats were then suggesting: the liquidation of all feudal dues without indemnity, long-term leases, confiscation of landed properties, partition of all common lands on the basis of usufruct, and finally the *loi agraire* for the redistribution of land. The fate of the wage-earning classes also attracted Babeuf's attention. During the elections for the National Convention, he proposed to the assembly of electors from the department of the Somme that there be included in the mandate for the deputies the following point: "society should assure work to all its members and set wages proportionate to the cost of all goods so that wages would be sufficient to insure the subsistence and all other needs of every family."

After the fall of the monarchy, Babeuf was elected administrator of the district of Montdidier in the Somme. Shortly afterward, however, his opponents succeeded in having him recalled and indicted by making false charges against him. Babeuf left for Paris, where, with the help of P.-S. Maréchal and P.-G. Chaumette, he became secretary of the Administration de subsistences of the Paris Commune. He became the center of the war for wheat against the landlords. He was aware that, in fact, an inventory of the available food supplies, on a national scale, was feasible at the same time as the new assessment. Meanwhile, Babeuf's enemies had succeeded in getting him condemned to twenty years of hard labor. Once again, he found himself in prison, where he remained for over six months. He was freed in July 1794, following the coup of 9 Thermidor.

As a supporter of direct, popular democracy, he found himself among M. Robespierre's adversaries at first. He united with the most extreme elements of the Parisian sections. A few weeks later, Babeuf realized the true nature of the Thermidorian revolution. In the autumn of 1794, he began to publish a newspaper, *Journal de la liberté de la presse*, which he soon renamed the *Tribun du peuple*. He began to make preparations for a new offensive by the sections against the Thermidorian Convention. He was arrested in February 1795 and sent to prison in Arras. By this time, he had defined his communist program. In his correspondence with C. Germain, as well as in his projected "Manifesto of the Plebeians," Babeuf put forward a proposal for the elimination of private property and the creation of a board of redistribution, which would be concerned with the allotment of all the products of human labor. In these plans the influence of A. Morellet, whose ideas Babeuf investigated in 1793–94, is evident.

In the fall of 1795, Babeuf was transferred to the Parisian prison of Plessis, where he met several Revolutionaries who had previously implemented the policies of the Jacobin dictatorship—F. M. Buonarroti, A.-A. Darthé, and others—who soon became his closest comrades in arms. During the uprising of 13 Vendémiaire, the prisoners in Plessis, on Babeuf's initiative, petitioned the

Convention for temporary release so that they might take up arms to stifle this counterrevolutionary revolt.

After being freed, Babeuf threw himself into the struggle against the Directory, which had replaced the Convention. He began to republish the *Tribun du peuple*, which became reasonably popular and in which he presented his "Plebeian Manifesto," affirming an openly communist program. The Babouvists tried to explore legal possibilities; at first, they joined the Pantheon Club. When this club was closed by the Directory in March 1796, Babeuf organized the "secret directory of public safety," which Buonarroti, Darthé, Maréchal, and others like them joined. They divided Paris into twelve regions, under the direction of secret agents, who had been leaders of the sectional movements. This organization had as its end the development of a new mass movement that would lead to the overthrow of the Directory. In pursuing this aim, Babeuf formulated a new political concept. He became a convinced partisan of the creation—after a successful insurrection—of the dictatorship of a provisional Revolutionary government for the establishment of a society of perfect equality.

The Babouvist organization established connections with leftist groups of Jacobins—for example, former members of the Convention—and feverishly made preparations to act. The Conspiracy of Equals, however, was exposed by one of its own members, G. Grisel. On 21 Floréal Year V (10 May 1795), Babeuf and Buonarroti were arrested in their secret headquarters, as were other participants at a later date. The High Court sat in judgment of them at Vendôme, far from Paris. The trial began on 20 February 1797 and lasted three months. In the course of the proceedings, Babeuf displayed considerable courage in defending himself and his communist ideals. On 25 May the sentences were rendered; Babeuf and Darthé received the death penalty. After sentencing, they both tried to commit suicide, but their knife wounds were not mortal. At dawn on 28 May 1797 (8 Prairial Year V), the sentence was carried out.

The testament of Babeuf is contained in his collected works, published in the Soviet Union in four volumes between 1976 and 1978. In his own words, "This precious equality . . . is my morality; it is your father's religion; it is his heritage, his faith . . . as long as men refuse to adopt this system, they will have no food, no happiness, no justice. . . . It is likely that the people of France will conduct their revolution toward this happy end of perfect equality . . . it is only then that the efforts of our Republic should cease."

V. Advielle, *Histoire de Gracchus Babeuf et du babouvisme, d' après de nombreux documents inédits*, 2 vols. (Paris, 1884); K. Bergmann, *Babeuf Gleich und Ungleich* (Cologne, 1963); J. Bruhat, *Gracchus Babeuf et les Egaux: Le premier parti communiste agissant* (Paris, 1978); F. Buonarroti, *Conspiration pour l' Egalité, dite de Babeuf* (Paris, 1828); V. M. Daline, A. Saitta, and A. Soboul, eds., *L'inventaire des manuscrits et imprimés de Babeuf* (Paris, 1966); M. Dommanget, *Sur Babeuf et le babouvisme* (Paris, 1970); R. Legrand, *Babeuf et ses compagnons de route* (Paris, 1981); R. B. Rose, *Gracchus Babeuf: The First Revolutionary Communist* (London, 1978); J. A. Scott, ed.

and trans., *The Defense of Gracchus Babeuf before the High Court of Vendôme* (New York, 1972).

V. M. Daline

Related entries: *AIDES*; BUONARROTI; CHAUMETTE; CONSPIRACY OF EQUALS; MABLY; MARAT; MARECHAL; 9 THERMIDOR YEAR II; ROUSSEAU; 13 VENDEMIAIRE YEAR IV.

BAGARRE DE NIMES, a designation calculated to minimize the violence of events during mid-June 1790 in the eighth most populous city of France, when self-styled patriots extirpated the first counterrevolutionary movement to mobilize a segment of the populace for armed combat. Throughout much of the *sénéchaussée* of Nîmes, local hierarchies had been divided for centuries by a rivalry between cultures. Grounded in geography and economics, this rivalry was most commonly defined in confessional terms. Sporadic persecution of Huguenots and royal disfavor for merchants had galvanized a tendency to associate religious dissent with participants in commerce and industry, poor as well as rich.

The urban center of Reformed faith for all of France was Nîmes. Its hinterland, most notably the Cévennes mountains to the northwest, constituted the most impregnable citadel in the entire realm for Calvinism. This area followed the lead of the city by specializing in production of goods for foreign markets, above all, silk textiles and hosiery. A contrasting pattern prevailed in the Rhône valley, the major commercial artery at the eastern extremity of territory under the jurisdiction of Nîmes. Although the Reformation had first penetrated the entire region from the east, Catholicism ultimately prevailed along the Rhône. Residents here, though living near the river, canals, and highways that served as the chief outlets for industry farther west, persisted in relatively self-sufficient agriculture, producing a wide range of crops. Throughout the *sénéchaussée* of Nîmes, as was true in all of Languedoc, exemption from the *taille* depended on legal status of land rather than on personal nobility of its proprietor. Yet in and around Nîmes, the presence of a powerful Protestant community had sensitized clerics to threats against their prerogatives. Here Catholic laymen, accustomed to dominating public affairs, felt menaced by the increasing prosperity and pretensions of merchants.

After the mid-eighteenth century, the *sénéchaussée* experienced the most spectacular burst of industrialization in France. Soon after, royal military, judicial, and administrative officials sanctioned for Calvinists both increasing de facto toleration and widened access to public office. Catholics became yet more disillusioned with the crown when, in 1787 and 1788, it seemed to favor the Reformed by providing means whereby those following that faith could marry outside the Roman church. The municipal oligarchies were shocked by royal decisions that accorded commercial interests a larger role in municipal administration, notably at Nîmes itself. Consequently, with the approval of radical nobles and a few parish priests, Catholic oligarchs appeared as eager for fundamental change as did ambitious Protestant merchants, who until recently had held scarcely a foothold in local government. By spring 1789, however, those who sought to preserve their own traditional dominion over local administration perceived mounting influence by heretics. Incipient counterrevolutionaries were terrified, for instance, by the predominant influence of J.-P. Rabaut de Saint-Etienne, a Calvinist pastor, in the assembly of the Third Estate for the *sénéchaussée* of Nîmes.

Among those working to arouse the populace against the Revolution, the chief firebrand was F. Froment. His father had recently been driven from the post of municipal registrar at Nîmes by merchants who successfully alleged that he levied too large a share of the *taille* on them. According to the younger Froment, enemies of public welfare tyrannized the city; having dominated the formation of a civilian armed force in July 1789, they maintained command over this militia and abusively extended its power. Yet in some pamphlets Froment claimed not to have recognized that the Bourbon monarchy was being undermined until 6 October when the Constituent collaborated with Parisians who thereafter held the king prisoner. Froment depicted a strong monarchy as indispensable to victory for orthodoxy, as well as for the integrity of the realm. Portraying both throne and altar as under assault, he recruited chiefly peasants to form new, exclusively Catholic companies for the militia. Parties inspired by Froment's tactics sprang up in many towns where Calvinists constituted a large minority of the population and where wealthy entrepreneurs among them had long been an object of popular grievances. Imitations of his agitation appeared as far away as Montauban, a city north of the western extremity of Languedoc.

In winter 1790, elections of new city officials encouraged Catholic militants. At Nîmes itself they clashed with regular soldiers and their noncommissioned officers early in May. At Montauban, with the connivance of the municipal officers, counterrevolutionaries had contrived for months to gain the upper hand in the militia. By a coup on 10 May, they established a virtual monopoly of armed force. The defeat of patriots at Montauban prompted those throughout the southwest to mobilize armed forces. The counterrevolutionary administration at Montauban soon felt so isolated that it released all political prisoners rather than endure a descent by militias already marching most resolutely not from nearby Toulouse but from Bordeaux. Thus, at Montauban, opponents of the Revolution effectively surrendered to patriots, who proceeded to win elections of local administrations superior to that of the city, notably that for the department, in this case, the Lot.

By contrast, Nîmes became the center of extreme strife in early June, while hosting the assembly that elected the first administrators for the department of the Gard, roughly equivalent in territory to the former *sénéchaussée* of Nîmes. In this city, counterrevolutionaries, though supported by the municipal government, were unable to gain preponderance in the governing council of the militia or to bridle it. During sessions that selected the departmental government, confrontations between armed contingents of civilians escalated. Each party accused the other of intimidating electors. While patriots consolidated their victory inside the assembly, the contest for control over the department as well as the city culminated in pitched battles through the streets of Nîmes. They began on 13 June and raged for several days. Only about 200 among Froment's backers assembled under arms. From the Protestant hinterland, thousands of militiamen marched toward Nîmes. But regular soldiers' collaboration with patriots was decisive before troops from outside arrived. The rout of Froment's partisans began when cannonades were directed against his chief stronghold. Lurid Catholic accounts stressed the cruelty of heretics plundering the faithful and torturing many before immolating up to a thousand. The few volunteers who eventually approached from Catholic zones returned home without reaching Nîmes, apparently taking at face value patriots' assurances that good order already reigned.

Thus the most extensive and brutal violence among civilians in Revolutionary France between summer 1789 and summer 1791 ended with advocates of the Constituent vanquishing municipal administrators sympathetic to counterrevolutionaries. During subsequent months, patriots extended their conquest of public power throughout most of the Gard, with the notable exception of its northern boundary with the Ardèche. Several of the leading victors of 1790 directed the short-lived participation by the Gard in the so-called federalist insurrection of 1793, which aimed to prevent dominion over France by Montagnards in the Convention. Popular myths referring to the violence that occurred in June 1790 have since fueled the local crises that developed each time the direction of government at the center became unclear. This pattern, recurring into the twentieth century, first became evident to all factions during the recrudescence of royalism which, following Thermidor, brought the first White Terror to the Gard.

J. N. Hood, "Protestant-Catholic Relations and the Roots of the First Popular Counterrevolutionary Movement in France." *J. of Mod. Hist.* 43 (June 1971), and "Revival and Mutation of Old Rivalries in Revolutionary France," *Past and Pres.* 82 (February 1979); G. Lewis, *The Second Vendée: The Continuity of Counter-revolution in the Department of the Gard, 1789–1815* (Oxford, 1978); D. Ligou, *Montauban à la fin de l'Ancien Régime et aux débuts de la Révolution. 1787–1794* (Paris, 1958).

J. N. Hood

Related entries: *BAILLIAGE; CAHIERS DE DOLEANCES*; JALES; 9 THERMIDOR YEAR II; *TAILLE*.

BAILLIAGE, a law court under the Old Regime; also the magistrates composing it, the place of its sessions, or the territory under its jurisdiction. *Bailliages* and *sénéchaussées* (the latter a synonym after about 1500 in Languedoc, Provence, and most provinces that had been Angevin fiefs in the twelfth century) were courts of ordinary civil and criminal jurisdiction. Many were seigneurial. The more important were royal, and of these almost all had authority to decide *cas royaux* and to command the attendance of clergymen and noblemen. Traditionally royal courts of this type served as the institutional framework for election of deputies to the Estates General. In 1789, they did so in seven-eighths of the circumscriptions designated for the final stage of the electoral procedure.

During the last 400 years of their history, the formal authority of the royal *bailliages* and *sénéchaussées* remained stable, but their number grew. In 1789, there were 373 with power to decide *cas royaux*. From time to time, kings had conferred additional distinctions on some. In 1552, Henri II selected fifty-eight as *présidial* courts with final authority, not subject to appeal to a parlement, in cases involving sums smaller than 250 *livres*. Later kings similarly elevated additional *bailliages* and *sénéchaussées*, so that finally 103 were *présidial* courts. In May 1788, an edict drawn up by the keeper of the seals, C.-F. Lamoignon, designated forty-one présidial courts and four other *bailliages* or *sénéchaussées*, as well as the high judicial councils of Alsace and Roussillon, to become *grands bailliages* with authority to render final judgment in most criminal cases and in civil cases involving sums up to 20,000 *livres*. The effect of this edict would have been to eviscerate the judicial functions of the parlements if it had not been withdrawn after four months.

In 1789, the electoral regulation of 24 January and subsequent rulings selected as principal *bailliages* and *sénéchaussées* the 198 such jurisdictions where the voters had the right (exercised in 1614 or acquired since then) to elect deputies directly to the Estates General. The other 154 *bailliages* and *sénéchaussées* used in the election procedure were secondary; in these, the voters only chose delegates to participate in a final election at the seat of a principal *bailliage* or *sénéchaussée*.

A. Brette, *Atlas des bailliages ou juridictions assimilées ayant formé unité electorale en 1789* (Paris, 1904) and *Recueil de documents relatifs à la convocation des Etats Généraux de 1789* vols. 3–4 (Paris, 1894–1915); P. Dawson, *Provincial Magistrates and Revolutionary Politics in France, 1789–1795* (Cambridge, Mass., 1972).

P. Dawson

Related entries: ESTATES GENERAL; PARLEMENTS.

BAILLY, JEAN-SYLVAIN (1736-93), scientist and politician. Future president of the National Assembly and mayor of Paris, Bailly was born on 15 September 1736 and reared in Paris at his father's apartments in the Louvre. As curator of the king's royal paintings, Bailly's father provided Jean-Sylvain with an excellent education and a substantial income to study the arts and literature, but Bailly was unsuccessful in his youthful efforts to become a tragedian.

During later studies under tutor N. de La Caille, Bailly was attracted to science, and he set up an observatory in the upper story of the Louvre's south gallery. Bailly then began making observations of the comets and the planets Mars and Venus. His successes brought him admission to the prestigious Académie des Sciences in 1763. In a masterful dissertation written in 1771, Bailly explored a new theory on the satellites of Jupiter. Thereafter he published the three-volume *Histoire de l'astronomie* (1781, 1785, 1787), which received scholarly acclaim. Other works, including the well-known *Histoire de l'astronomie indienne*, were less scientific and more popular. Scholars frequently rejected the inventive, speculative nature of many of these later works but continued to recognize Bailly for his talent. He was elected to the Académie française in 1783 and appointed

to the Académie des Belles-Lettres by the king. To that time, only B. le B. de
Fontenelle held the similar distinction of membership in all three academies.

Bailly also renewed his interest in writing by composing a series of eulogies
to Charles V, P. Corneille, J.-B. P. Molière, G. W. Leibnitz, and the abbé de
La Caille. Although the *Eloges* were in no way literary masterpieces, Bailly's
theory of government is revealed there. It is clear that he loved the king and
respected the institution of the monarchy, but he also believed fervently in a
meritocracy, which was neither present nor possible under an absolute monarchy.
Bailly, however, was not a political activist, and he preferred to confine his
activities to those that would bring civic benefit. He researched the theories of
F.-A. Mesmer and his disciples and unmasked them as charlatans; he reported
on conditions in the hospitals and slaughterhouses. Bailly chose not to contribute
to the *Encyclopédie*. While its goal to expand knowledge was laudable, he
believed it was too political.

In 1789, Bailly was forced to consider his position on political activity when
the Estates General was called. As a respected resident of the Feuillants district
of Paris, he was named first elector in April 1789. Soon named secretary to the
general assembly of electors, he assisted in writing the *cahiers*, which were
subsequently presented to the Estates General from Paris. On 12 May, he was
elected to the Estates General by a first-ballot vote of 173 out of 377 votes.
Somewhat unassuming, he never considered himself an orator or a true politician,
but he believed that he had been given a serious position of trust, which he could
not reject.

When the Parisian deputies made their belated entrance to the Estates General
on 3 June, the assembly named Bailly as spokesman. In that capacity, he sought
an audience with the king and later received the official notification that the Salle
des Menus Plaisirs was closed for repairs. The Third Estate retired to the tennis
court, where Bailly led the assembly in taking the oath that created the National
Assembly. Hoping to avoid violent confrontation, Bailly nonetheless remained
firm in his belief that the ''nation when assembled cannot be given orders.'' He
emerged then as the hero of 20 June and was elected the first president of the
National Assembly. On 15 July he was named mayor of Paris.

From Bailly's position in the Hôtel de Ville emerged the problems that ultimately brought his death. Too conservative for L.-C.-S. Desmoulins, Bailly was
attacked for maintaining his livery and mounted guards. J.-P. Marat said that
he plundered the state and challenged Bailly as a representative of the worst
abuses of the old venal system. Bailly chose not to defend himself against the
criticisms, preferring to spend his time administering the grain, charcoal, and
wood shipments to keep the city supplied.

Unskilled in diplomacy with the republicans, Bailly committed his fatal error
on 17 July 1791. The events began three days earlier with the second celebration
of the fête of federation, but the king's unsuccessful flight to Varennes less than
a month earlier added a somber note. Petitioners, particularly the Cordeliers,
collected on the parade ground, demonstrating their desire that a plebiscite be

held to determine the fate of the king. Allowed to believe the legality of their actions, they continued to collect in large numbers.

Early on Sunday morning, 17 July, two men were found hidden beneath the platform of the altar. Under arrest, they were lynched by people of the Gros-Caillu district of Paris. Tempers seemed on edge, and municipal authorities and the Assembly feared violence. A contingent of the National Guard and three members of the municipal government were sent to oversee the gathering. Although the commissioners maintained order on the parade ground, the crowd was not required to disband, and reports that circulated to the Hôtel de Ville gave the alarming feeling that public order was deteriorating. Caught in the middle of conflicting reports and the admonitions of the Assembly to "initiate the most secure and rigorous measures to halt these disorders," Bailly chose to declare martial law as mayor of Paris. At 6:30 P.M. accompanied by infantry and three cannons, Bailly went to the Champ de Mars. There the marquis de Lafayette had instructed the Guard simply to show force, but the crowd began to chant and appeared menacing. In the disorder brought by the appearance of the red flag, some of the unseasoned troops fired, apparently without orders but believing that summons to disband would be impossible to carry out. The casualties, according to Bailly, were a dozen deaths and a dozen wounded. Marat charged that 400 innocent casualties had been dumped unceremoniously into the Seine.

Initially the Assembly approved Bailly's actions, but criticism was soon rampant. Bailly, asserted Desmoulins and Marat, was undermining the Revolution while attempting to restore the Old Regime. Unable to quiet the criticisms, Bailly resigned on 12 November 1791. He retired to Chaillot where he hoped to return to an obscure, apolitical life.

In July 1793, Bailly was arrested and transferred to Paris to testify first in the trial of Marie Antoinette and then to stand for his own trial. The charges against Bailly were the following: having encouraged the flight of the king in 1791 and having caused the Champ de Mars massacre. Testifying before the tribunal, Bailly made it clear that he had had no complicity in the flight of the royal family and that uncontrollable circumstances had brought the bloodshed. But his own testimony from the inquiry in 1791 sealed his doom. Although he had believed the *patrie en danger*, evidence had not clearly supported his invoking martial law. On both counts Bailly was found guilty. The tribunal's actions successfully had challenged the moderates of the Revolution, and Bailly went to the guillotine on 12 November 1793.

Not content with a simple execution in the Place de la Révolution, the tribunal chose to transport Bailly to the Champ de Mars. There preceding his death, a red flag was burned symbolically to the cries and chants of the crowd.

A.N. W294, no. 235 and AF II 48; F. Arago, *Biographie de Jean-Sylvain Bailly* (Paris, 1852); F.-A. Aulard, "Bailly et l'affaire du Champ de Mars," *Révo. française* 13 (1887); J.-S. Bailly, *Mémoires de Bailly, avec une notice sur sa vie, des notes et des éclaircissemens historiques, par MM. Berville et Barrière*, 3 vols. (Paris, 1821–22); G. A.

Kelly, *Victims, Authority, and Terror: The Parallel Deaths of d'Orléans, Custine, Bailly, and Malesherbes* (Chapel Hill, N.C., 1982).

S. P. Conner

Related entries: CHAMP DE MARS "MASSACRE"; CORDELIERS CLUB; DESMOULINS; *ENCYCLOPEDIE*; LAFAYETTE; MESMER; NATIONAL GUARD; SCIENCE; TENNIS COURT OATH; VARENNES.

BAL DES VICTIMES. See *MERVEILLEUSES*.

BANALITE, seigneurial monopoly under the Old Regime. The *banalité* obliged *censitaires* to use only the seigneur's mill, oven, or wine press in the processing of their farm produce. Like most other seigneurial rights, the *banalité* implied a personal dependence. As a practical matter, few villages had enough capital to provide alternative mills, ovens, or presses, although hand mills were occasionally confiscated by seigneurial agents.

Public criticism focused especially on the mills, or more precisely on the millers who leased the mills and the right of monopoly from the seigneur. Mill rents rose sharply in the years after 1750, even more so than the price of grain, so that the millers were pressed to increase their own revenues by taking a larger percentage of each peasant's milled grain. Usually an imposing and tough person, vital to the peasant community, the miller easily became the target of village animosity, especially when he was suspected of short weighing the sacks of grain or hiding his miscalculations behind a greater skill at arithmetic. The *cahiers* register a greater hatred for the miller than for the *banalité* itself.

The *banalité* had the added disadvantage of preventing unmilled grain from leaving the local parish, which hindered grain circulation and distribution. Although the villages did not want their grain to leave the parish, especially in times of shortage, government officials promoted the movement of grain about the country. Hence, criticism of the *banalités* came from more than one source.

Banalités were abolished without indemnification in July 1793. The mills usually remained the private property of the former seigneur, now a *propriétaire* under the new regime. A monopoly and a personal dependence had been ended, but many years would pass before the average French village could afford a mill, oven, or wine press of its own.

F.-A. Aulard, *La Révolution française et le Régime féodal* (Paris, 1919); J. Q. C. Mackrell, *The Attack on Feudalism in Eighteenth-Century France* (London and Toronto, 1973); P. Sagnac and P. Caron, eds., *Les comités des droits féodaux et de la législation et l'abolition du régime seigneurial, 1789–93* (Paris, 1907).

R. Forster

Related entries: *CAHIERS DE DOLEANCES;* FEUDALISM.

BARBAROUX, CHARLES-JEAN-MARIE (1767-94), deputy to the National Convention. Barbaroux, the son of a Marseille merchant, was born on 6 March 1767. He was educated by Oratorian priests and demonstrated intelligence of the first order in his youth. By the age of twenty, he had earned a law degree, conducted numerous scientific experiments, and published learned articles in the *Journal de physique*.

During elections for the Estates General (March 1789), he drew up *cahiers* for several corporations of artisans. After the storming of the Bastille, he became involved in agitation against the Old Regime at Marseille. To avoid arrest by the counterrevolutionary provost marshal of Provence, E.-F.-A.-B. Sanchon de Bournissac, he fled to Paris in the fall of 1789, returning in December when the National Assembly stripped Bournissac of his power. In 1790 he was chosen secretary of the new municipal government. He was also one of the founders of the powerful Jacobin club of Marseille. On 31 January 1792, city officials assigned him the role of lobbyist at the Legislative Assembly. In Paris he formed a friendship with the Rolands and immersed himself in plots against Louis XVI, concocting a scheme for the establishment of a republic in the south if a planned Parisian insurrection failed. On 21 June, he sent a famous letter to Marseille requesting "six hundred men who know how to die." When a battalion of 500 Marseillais duly arrived in the capital, he helped to mastermind the overthrow of the king on 9–10 August. After the fall of the monarchy, Barbaroux rushed back to Marseille where he was welcomed as a conquering hero. On 5 September, at the electoral assembly of the Bouches-du-Rhône, he was named a deputy to the National Convention and took an oath to rid France forever of kings. In the Convention he sat with the Girondins and launched withering attacks on J.-P. Marat and M. Robespierre. Under his tutelage, a second battalion of Marseillais, which had reached Paris in October, harassed Montagnard leaders and served as a kind of praetorian guard for Roland. Barbaroux lost the support of his radical constituents when he voted (January 1793) for the appeal to the people, a Girondin ploy to delay the execution of the king by holding a national referendum to decide his fate. The club of Marseille denounced him for breaking the vow he had taken at his election and accused him of venality. When the Girondins were purged from the Convention on 2 June, he was one of twenty-nine deputies put under house arrest, but on 10 June he eluded two guards assigned to watch him. After an abortive attempt to foment a federalist uprising in Normandy, he spent nearly a year in hiding in Brittany and the Bordelais. He was finally apprehended and executed at Bordeaux on 25 June 1794.

Barbaroux's contemporaries often noted his dynamism and dashing good looks. Today he is best known for his *Memoirs* written as a fugitive in 1793-94. The sections that have survived deal mainly with the early Revolution in Provence and the events preceding the fall of the monarchy. The tone of the *Memoirs* is one of defiance rather than self-pity. Barbaroux boasted proudly that he had dedicated his life to the defense of the people and derided his political enemies.

Alfred-Chabaud, *Mémoires de Barbaroux* (Paris, 1936).

M. Kennedy

Related entries: GIRONDINS; ROLAND DE LA PLATIERE, J.-M.

BARENTIN, CHARLES-LOUIS-FRANCOIS DE PAULE DE (1738-1819), keeper of the seals. Member of a famous family of the robe nobility, Barentin joined the Parlement of Paris as counselor in 1757, advancing to advocate general in 1764. He replaced C.-G. Malesherbes as president of the Cour des Aides in 1775. A strong supporter of the magistrates in their struggle with the ministers of enlightened despotism, Barentin opposed both the Maupeou reforms of 1771 and the May Edicts of 1788. With the dismissal of C.-F. Lamoignon by the king in August 1788, Barentin replaced him as keeper of the seals.

On the matter of the convening of the Estates General, Barentin favored the coming of constitutional government but only in its most conservative form. He opposed J. Necker's doubling of the Third Estate. In the deadlocked Estates General of June 1789, Barentin strongly urged the king not to yield to the Third Estate's pretensions. In the council meeting preceding the royal session of 23 June 1789, it was Barentin who opposed Necker's conciliatory policy and who won the king over to the conservative position. With the collapse of the king's resistance to the National Assembly from 23 June to 15 July, Barentin's position in the government became untenable. He resigned as keeper of the seals on 16 July and emigrated soon after.

C.-L.-F. Barentin, *Mémoire autographe de M. de Barentin* (Paris, 1844).

R. D. Harris

Related entries: MALESHERBES; NECKER.

BARERE DE VIEUZAC, BERTRAND (1755-1841), deputy to the National Assembly and to the Convention; member of the Committee of Public Safety. Barère was born at Tarbes, near the Pyrenees, on 10 September 1755. His mother was a noblewoman, his father, a middle-class lawyer, from whom Barère inherited a small fief at Vieuzac, which permitted him to claim noble status in 1789 (though he chose not to do so). He entered law school at Toulouse at fifteen and earned his bachelor's at nineteen and master's at twenty. His father purchased for him the post of councillor at the seneschal's court at Bigorre, but Barère did not perform the functions of this post for a decade and then only briefly. He remained instead at Toulouse, where he was a successful lawyer. He also pursued the craft of writer, as he would all his life, taking part in literary contests, winning occasional prizes, and being elected to the Academy of Floral Games at Toulouse. In 1785, he entered into an unhappy marriage. Two years later, he became a member of the Masonic Grand Orient at Toulouse, though not an active one.

In his politics he was moderate, a reforming conservative. He went to Paris in May 1788 in connection with a lawsuit over the fief at Vieuzac and returned home in January 1789 more of a democrat, having shifted from his earlier support of the parlements to the view that new intermediary bodies had become necessary. He was more critical of the privileged orders and was elated by J. Necker's success with respect to doubling the Third Estate. Chosen as an elector to the assembly of the Third Estate at Bigorre, he played an important role in the task of blending the preliminary *cahiers* into a general *cahier*, and this assembly elected him deputy.

On 27 April 1789 he brought out the first issue of his *Point du jour*, one of the best and most nearly impartial of the newspapers of the day; it continued to appear until the end of the Constituent Assembly. Barère was a man of great charm, and he quickly made a place for himself in Parisian society. He was one of the circle surrounding the duke of Orléans. He joined, but rarely attended, the Jacobins, the more conservative Société de 1789, and the Abbé Fauchet's masonic Société des Amis de la Vérité.

As a deputy he was a moderate, uneasy over the attitude of the king but distrustful of the mob. The peasant insurrection during the summer of 1789 disturbed him greatly, and he praised the privileged orders for their sacrifices during the night of 4 August. He renounced his own manorial rights as seigneur of Vieuzac, and he also renounced his claim to compensation for the venal post he had held at Bigorre. He was unhappy over the October Days but bent before popular pressure and afterward praised the part played by Paris. Barère sat with the constitutionalists of the Left center, men like E.-J. Sieyès and C.-M. Talleyrand. He did not initiate legislation for institutional change but showed himself a dedicated second. He supported M. Robespierre's proposal that free Negro proprietors become citizens, as well as political rights for Jews and Protestants. On the matter of the massacre of the Champ de Mars, his paper's chief concern was to condemn the petitioners instead of the established authorities. Barère joined the Feuillants after their split from the Jacobins, and he served as their president before returning to the Jacobins in October. Yet during the reconsideration of the constitution, he stood with the democrats.

From October 1791 to January 1792, he served in Paris as judge of the court of appeals. He returned to Tarbes on personal business and then served on G.-J. Danton's judicial committee, immediately after the fall of the monarchy, in August 1792.

His department elected him to the National Convention where he was at first a member of the Plain, trying to prevent an open rupture between Girondins and Montagnards. To this end he opposed the Girondin proposal for a departmental guard, but he also condemned the anarchy of the Commune. He defended Robespierre against the charges of J.-B. Louvet but in an unflattering fashion, urging the Convention not to place pygmies on pedestals. He played a statesmanlike role in the trial of the king. He wanted the trial to be conducted with legal correctness and dignity and therefore opposed demands for a summary judgment. As president of the Convention, he personally interrogated the monarch, and he later spoke with great effectiveness against P.-V. Vergniaud's proposal that the Convention's decision should be ratified by primary assemblies. He spoke also against F.-N.-L. Buzot's request for reprieve. Throughout he voted with the Mountain, thereby breaking with his royalist past.

The odium of the treason of C. Dumouriez, whose military acumen he had earlier valued, Barère cast on the Girondins. It was due largely to Barère's efforts and those of G.-J. Danton that the Committee of Public Safety was created, and he was the first to be elected to it. There he shared responsibility for foreign policy with Danton, and he secretly sought peace negotiations with the powers, while denying such contacts when publicly challenged. With regard to the insurrectional movement against the Girondins, he sought a middle way, opposing M.-E. Guadet's motion for the reorganization of the Commune while moving the creation of the investigative Commission of Twelve. On 2 June he asked the twenty-two Girondins whose arrest was demanded to resign voluntarily. After the Girondin defeat, he reported that the cause of liberty had prevailed.

When the Committee of Public Safety was reconstructed on 10 July, he and R. Lindet were the only two members of the Dantonist committee to survive. He busied himself with foreign policy, less accommodating now than before, with naval policy, and with cultural matters, encouraging the diffusion of French and the dedication of artistic and musical efforts to the Revolutionary cause. He collaborated on police matters with Robespierre. He served the committee above all as its principal *rapporteur*. After a long discussion late at night, Barère could summarize a question rapidly and luminously, posing it so clearly that it could be easily resolved. He could also take incoherent documents and create a dramatic account from them. He did a great many reports on French victories in battle, or what passed as victories, for his chief concern was to strengthen morale. He reported on much else as well, for his knowledge was varied, he could improvise quickly, and he was always ready to leap into the breach, as he did on 5 September when conceding an extension of the Terror while retaining Committee control. He stood with Robespierre in repelling the Dantonists' challenge on 25 September, in supporting Robespierre's motion to quash the Girondins' defense, and in opposing the dechristianizers. He helped to frame the committee's policies, as well as to defend them before the Convention. The important Law of 14 Frimaire reflected his own work as a systematizer of committee procedures. Although revolted by G. Couthon's Law of 22 Prairial, he ended by supporting it. He did much to hold the committee together by his hard-working, sprightly, and affectionate character. When the committee split into factions, he took the lead in efforts to avoid a break. He remained loyal to Robespierre almost until the last. But on 8 Thermidor, after Robespierre had flayed Barère and had failed to name the deputies he intended to proscribe, Barère turned against him, preparing the decree that called for the dismissal of F. Hanriot; and on 9 Thermidor he read the report calling for the outlawry of the Robespierrists.

Barère had intended that the Terror itself should continue, and he fought to preserve the institutions of the Revolutionary government. He failed. As the Thermidorian Reaction gathered momentum, he came under attack himself, and during the insurrection of 12 Germinal, the Convention decreed his deportation to Guyana with J.-N. Billaud-Varenne and J.-M. Collot d'Herbois. He was arrested and sent to Oléron but was not transported with the others. It is not known why. He was imprisoned and then escaped, to go into hiding at Bordeaux, where he was sheltered by a wealthy merchant.

When Napoleon came to power, Barère courted him, asking for restoration of his full freedom. He obtained amnesty through J. Fouché, and Napoleon commissioned Barère to answer an attack that England's Lord Grenville had made on French policy. In October 1800, Barère was warned by his oldest friend, D. Demerville, not to attend the Opéra the following night because of some plot against Napoleon; there might be a disturbance. Barère reported this plot to General J. Lannes of Napoleon's security police, and Demerville was among those executed.

In 1803, Napoleon commissioned Barère to write regular secret reports on public opinion on whatever he thought Napoleon might wish to know. During the next four years, Barère provided more than 200 such bulletins. Toward the end of his life, Barère intended to publish them. They have disappeared. Barère also cultivated relations with Russian diplomatic agents, as well as with the Spaniard don E. Izquierdo, who reported to M. Godoy Barère's devotion to the Spanish. Napoleon dismissed Barère abruptly in 1807. He lived a marginal existence thereafter. When the Bourbons returned to power, he adopted the *fleur de lys* and, unsuccessfully, sought an interview with the new king. During the Hundred Days, he returned to Napoleon. With Fouché's aid, he was elected deputy from the Hautes-Pyrénées and tried to persuade Napoleon to provide France with a genuine constitutional regime. When Louis XVIII was restored, Barère again declared his support, as he sought permission through Fouché to remain in Paris. Matters did not work out. He went into hiding to avoid the police and finally obtained a false passport under the name of Barère de Rocqueville and left in a public coach for Belgium (March 1816).

He lived at Mons for six years and Brussels for eight. He had friends among other French exiles such as J.-L. David, who walked with him almost every day, M.-A. Baudot, M.-G.-A. Vadier, and F. M. Buonarroti. He was something of a celebrity, sought out by foreign visitors, but he lived quietly, out of politics, continuing to work on his memoirs and on other writings, including a commentary on the Psalms. He had little money, and the Belgian winters were almost too much for him. With the July Revolution, he was able to return to France. He spent two years in Paris, writing critical sketches of Parisian ways, *Le tartare à Paris*, and then returned to Tarbes for the last nine years of his very long life, during six of which he served as a member of the General Council of his department.

He sought and obtained small pensions from L. Thiers and Louis-Philippe, but his financial resources were meager. He kept up his correspondence and retained his old charm. A woman once said of him that he was "the most seductive monster I ever saw" (Gershoy, p. 383). The fact that he was successful in so many of his private relationships may explain the failure to deport him in 1795 and the relative inattention he received from the police of various regimes thereafter. He was a man who could see both sides of an issue and who sought to preserve the unity of government. He pursued the middle way. But when he was forced to choose, he chose the side of the stronger. He became a terrorist reluctantly, but he gave the Terror his lasting support.

F.-A. Aulard, *Les orateurs de la Législative et de la Convention*, vol. 2 (Paris, 1886); B. Barère, *Memoires* (Paris, 1842-44; Eng. trans., 1896); L. Gershoy, *Bertrand Barère: A Reluctant Terrorist* (Princeton, 1962); A. Kuscinski, *Dictionnaire des conventionnels* (Paris, 1916-20); E. Welvert, *Lendemains révolutionnaires* (Paris, 1907).

S. Lytle

Related entries : COMMISSION OF TWELVE; COMMITTEE OF PUBLIC SAFETY; DECHRISTIANIZATION; DUMOURIEZ; FEUILLANTS; FREE-MASONS; GIRONDINS; GREAT FEAR; JACOBINS; LAW OF 14 FRI-MAIRE; LAW OF 22 PRAIRIAL; LINDET, R; MONTAGNARDS; 9 THERMIDOR YEAR II; PLAIN; ROBESPIERRE, M.; SOCIETY OF 1789; TERROR, THE; THEORY OF REVOLUTIONARY GOVERNMENT; THER-MIDORIAN REACTION; VERGNIAUD.

BARNAVE, ANTOINE-PIERRE-JOSEPH-MARIE (1761-93), deputy to the Constituent Assembly, historian. Barnave was born in Grenoble to a nominally Protestant family of the upper bourgeoisie. His father, a lawyer at the local sovereign court, the Parlement of Dauphiné, chose a legal career for him, and in 1783 Barnave was called to the bar. He first attracted public notice in the spring of 1788 when, on the occasion of a conflict between the monarchy and the parlement, he wrote a pamphlet supporting the rebellious magistrates. That summer Barnave took part in the events that led to the Assembly at Vizille where he emerged along with J.-J. Mounier as the defender of the Third Estate. He was subsequently elected to the Estates General.

At Versailles and then Paris, Barnave quickly became one of the most prom-inent and influential members of the National Assembly. With his allies and close friends, A. Duport and A. and C. de Lameth, he led the radical faction of the Constituent Assembly in its struggle to establish a limited, constitutional monarchy. In early autumn 1789, he broke with Mounier over the composition of the new assembly, preferring a unicameral to a bicameral legislature, for fear that the upper chamber would promote the reestablishment of an aristocracy. He also championed the limiting of the king's powers in foreign and judicial affairs and even earned the reputation of a firebrand when, in July 1789, in an attempt to subdue the Assembly's discussion after the murder of Parisian intendant L.-B.-F. Bertier, he uttered the famous words, ''This blood, is it so pure that we dare not shed it?''

The year 1790 witnessed the apogee of Barnave's power and popularity. Within the Assembly, he was elected to several important committees and in March to the presidency of that body; only H.-G. R. Mirabeau rivaled him as an orator. Outside the Assembly, he enjoyed considerable influence within the Jacobin club and frequently presided over its meetings. But soon Barnave found himself challenged, not only by his traditional opponents on the Right, led by the marquis de Lafayette, but also by a new group of deputies situated to his left.

These new divisions were brought into the open during the summer of 1790 when there arose a controversy over the status of the mulattoes in France's Caribbean possessions. Barnave, as a member of the Assembly's Committee on the Colonies, argued that to enfranchise the colonies' mulattoes against the wishes of the ruling whites would drive the colonies away from France, thereby endangering its commerce and security and the Revolution itself. A group of deputies, allied with the Société des amis des noirs, among them J.-P. Brissot, abbé Grégoire, and J. Pétion, argued that to ignore the mulattoes would be a betrayal of the principles of the Revolution, in particular the Declaration of the Rights of Man. In 1790, Barnave's arguments prevailed, but within a year Brissot and his followers had persuaded the Assembly to reverse its decision and grant the mulattoes full rights.

That a powerful faction more radical than Barnave had now emerged became very evident. In May 1791, Barnave and his associates suffered a series of setbacks. Despite his opposition, the Assembly passed the rule by which no member of the Assembly could serve as a minister for two years after the legislature had terminated its session and voted the decree that made all members of the Constituent ineligible to serve in the forthcoming Legislative Assembly. So diminished was Barnave's influence at the Jacobin club that he ceased to attend its meetings. He still enjoyed enough prestige, however, to be assigned the difficult mission of accompanying the royal family back to Paris after the abortive flight that ended at Varennes.

At the time it was rumored that the spectacle of the embattled royal family touched Barnave and moved him to change his opinion of Louis XVI and the monarchy. Barnave did defend the crown more consistently in the months following Varennes and, as documents discovered at the beginning of this century have proved, he even entered into a secret correspondence with the queen. But this advocacy of the monarchy did not really represent an abrupt about-face on Barnave's part. It was circumstances, not Barnave, that had changed. With the growing power of the Brissotins and the increasing unrest among Parisians, Barnave began to fear the establishment of a republic that he deemed unsuitable to France's size and destructive to national unity. This disunity, he believed, would ultimately lead to the great European powers' defeating France and undoing all the work of the Revolution. Since no acceptable alternative to Louis XVI existed, only the king, Barnave reasoned, could save the constitutional monarchy, the constitution, and France. Consequently, he effected a reconciliation with Lafayette and his party and began writing secretly to Marie Antoinette in hope of persuading her, and through her the king, the *émigrés*, and the emperor, to accept the constitution and the Revolution. That he was unsuccessful with the queen became evident even to Barnave in the fall of 1791. In January 1792, barred from sitting in the Legislative Assembly and deprived of all influence, he retired to his home just outside Grenoble.

The next year he passed far from the political scene in study and reflection. Then, on 10 August 1792, when the king's apartments in the Tuileries were searched, a paper entitled, "A Plan of the Ministers, concerted with MM. Alexandre de Lameth and Barnave," was found among the king's possessions. Though probably little more than a proposal once presented to Louis, this paper formed in the eyes of the deputies to the Legislative Assembly proof of Barnave's involvement in a secret plot to overthrow the Assembly and the Revolution. On 15 August 1792, a warrant was issued for his arrest, and three days later he was imprisoned in Grenoble. The next few months were spent by Barnave in various prisons in Dauphiné.

At some time during this period, Barnave wrote a long essay, now known as the *Introduction to the French Revolution*. This work addressed two general subjects: the course of history and governments and the events of the Revolution itself. Although the work does cover the Revolution through 10 August 1792, the *Introduction* is neither an apology for nor an explanation of Barnave's activities, for he clearly neither intended nor expected publication. Indeed, the work was generally unknown until J. Jaurès included an analysis of it in his *Histoire socialiste de la Révolution française* (Paris, 1922). Jaurès saw in Barnave a precursor of Marxist historical materialism, for Barnave had argued that certain forms of economic activity—commerce, for example—produce certain kinds of political and social institutions, democracy, for instance.

Barnave had completed the *Introduction* by the time he was transferred to Paris to stand trial. Before the Revolutionary Tribunal, he comported himself with dignity and appeared resigned to death. He knew that his association with the Lameths, who had escaped to England, and his reconciliation with Lafayette, a deserter to the Austrians, doomed him to the guillotine. On 29 November 1793 he was executed.

E. D. Bradby, *The Life of Barnave*, 2 vols. (Oxford, 1915); J. J. Chevallier *Barnave ou les deux faces de la Révolution* (Paris, 1936); E. Chill, tr., *Power, Property and History: Barnave's Introduction to the French Revolution and Other Writings* (New York, 1971).

K. Norberg

Related entries: LAFAYETTE; MOUNIER; SELF-DENYING ORDINANCE; SOCIETE DES AMIS DES NOIRS; TRIUMVIRATE.

BARRAS, PAUL-FRANCOIS-NICOLAS, VICOMTE DE (1755-1829), terrorist and director. Born of a Provençal noble family, Barras was educated by the Carmelites. After becoming a cadet in the Languedoc Regiment at the age of sixteen, he obtained in 1775 a commission in the Regiment of Pondichéry, serving in India. Here he fought in the defense of Pondichéry against the English in 1778. He was elected in 1792 as a deputy from Var to the National Convention, taking his seat in the middle group known as the Plain and voting in January 1793 for the execution of the king.

In March 1793 Barras was sent by the Convention as a representative on mission to several of the southern departments that were in a state of unrest. At one point he despaired of what he saw and recommended abandoning the whole of Provence to the rebels. In the same year, he went with L.-M.-S. Fréron as commissioner to the Army of Italy, which undertook Toulon's recapture from British naval blockade and seizure. Here he was favorably impressed by a young captain of artillery, N. Bonaparte, who distinguished himself during the operations. After the city was regained (December 1793), Barras ruthlessly ordered the shooting of hundreds of Frenchmen who had supported the English.

In the Convention, Barras joined J.-L. Tallien, Fréron, and J. Fouché in opposing the growing despotism of M. Robespierre and on 9 Thermidor (27 July 1794) was named commandant of the armed forces of the Convention. After Robespierre's overthrow and execution, Barras was made a member of the Committee of General Security (December 1794) and the following February served as president of the Convention. F.-A. Aulard characterizes him as a Thermidorian of the Right. His last service to the Convention came with his appointment to repress the popular rising in Paris on 13 Vendémiaire (5 October 1795). He made Bonaparte, now a general, his principal subordinate, and the revolt was easily quelled.

Under the Constitution of 1795, Barras was elected to the new legislative body, which quickly made him a director, although he had barely reached the stipulated age of forty. All five directors were regicides, Barras being the only one of noble birth. He was also the only one to serve during the entire five years of the Directory—the constitution requiring one director, by the drawing of lots, to retire annually. Since the directors chose the seven ministers, whose functions were largely administrative, their authority, especially in the field of foreign affairs, was substantial. More than any of his colleagues, Barras enjoyed the magnificent directorial costume designed by J.-L. David—a gold-embroidered coat of red velvet lined with white satin and a hat with huge tricolor plumes.

Barras was one of the leading figures in the coup of 18 Fructidor (4 September 1797), which removed two directors, L. Carnot and F. Barthélemy, each suspected of royalism. Earlier, in June, he had joined his colleagues J.-F. Reubell and L.-M. La Revellière-lépeaux in urging Bonaparte to come from Italy to the aid of the Republic, but Bonaparte had refused. Following the coup, the recent election of 198 deputies was annulled, and ruthless measures were taken by military tribunals in the provinces, although only a few of the 160 death sentences imposed were in fact carried out.

Although possessing genuine ability, Barras lived a life of extreme luxury, scandalous dissipation, and unabashed greed. J. Beauharnais and T. Tallien were among his many mistresses. During the Jacobin period, Barras had learned the technique for exercising ruthless power. As the European war expanded, enormous sums could be exacted from military contractors, while the conduct of diplomacy opened yet other lucrative channels. During the Lille negotiations for peace with England in July 1797, Barras was said by Lord Malmesbury, the English representative, to have asked for £500,000. The peace with Portugal a month later is said to have brought him £400,000, and in negotiations with the Venetian Republic he is said to have received £20,000, despite which Venice disappeared as a state.

Although Barras did not play as significant a role as he claimed in arranging Bonaparte's marriage to Josephine and in making him commander in chief of the Army of Italy in 1796, he was undoubtedly important. Along with his fellow directors, Reubell and La Revellière-lépeaux, he wrote on 3 February 1797 urging Bonaparte to drive the Pope from Rome. After Fructidor, Barras engaged in a seesaw policy, playing off the threats from the Jacobin Left and the royalist Right at a time when it was apparent that the Directory could not long continue as organized. Barras in his *Mémoires* relates his distributing 185,000 francs to influence the elections of 1798 to the legislative body; and when, despite this, the outcome was a victory for the Left, he and his colleagues managed to annul 106 Jacobin choices. This was the entirely bloodless coup of 22 Floréal (11 May 1798). Barras was little affected by the coup of 30 Prairial (18 June 1799) in which the Council of Ancients and the Council of Five Hundred forced three newly elected directors to resign.

Some evidence indicates that Barras was even toying with the idea of restoring the monarchy. The Archives of the Ministry of Foreign Affairs contain a copy of a letter of 21 May 1799 written by a royalist agent, the marquis de Maisonfort, to Czar Paul I of Russia, saying that Barras had been negotiating for several months with the count of Provence about a royalist restoration. Ensuing negotiations at Hamburg suggested that Barras would be receptive to a gift of 16 million francs, a ducal title, a place in a preliminary council of regency, and ultimately the governorship of the Ile de Bourbon in the Indian Ocean. In his *Mémoires*, Barras states that he simply turned over information about such matters to his fellow directors, and this could be true.

When Bonaparte returned from Egypt in October 1799, Barras saw him in Paris on several occasions. At one of these meetings, he suggested that Bonaparte should go on to win more military laurels in the field, leaving the politicians to do their work. By this time Bonaparte had come to detest Barras, secretly calling him ''a rotten plank.'' The hastily contrived plans for the coup of Brumaire in November required the resignation of all five directors, and on the first day of the coup (9 November), this was effected. Barras remained at his apartments in the Luxembourg, where Talleyrand and Admiral E. Bruix called on him, bringing the draft of a letter of resignation. In the end, having learned of Bonaparte's success at the Tuileries, Barras signed it. When he left Paris that evening for his magnificent estate at Grosbois, he passed from history. In 1814 and 1815 he failed to get the restored Bourbons to accept his support. He died in Paris on 29 January 1829.

Barras is an extreme example of the ruthlessness, corruption, and venality that emerged during the Revolutionary period. Following his departure from public life, he worked on his *Mémoires* in which he venomously attacked those, including Josephine, with whom he had fallen out. His literary executor, R. de

Saint-Albin, edited these *Mémoires*, and whatever their distortions, they have been accepted by their modern editor as genuine.

C. d'Almeras, *Barras et son temps* (Paris, 1930); P.-F.-N. Barras, *Mémoires*, ed. G. Duruy, 4 vols. (Paris, 1895-96), Engl. tr., 4 vols. (London, 1895–96); J. P. Garnier, *Barras* (Paris, 1970); A. Meynier, *Les coups d'état du Directoire*, 3 vols. (Paris, 1928); M. J. Sydenham, *The First French Republic, 1792–1804* (Berkeley, 1974); A. Vandal, *L'avènement de Bonaparte*, 2 vols. (Paris, 1903-7); D. Woronoff, *La République bourgeoise de Thermidor à Brumaire* (Paris, 1972).

E. J. Knapton

Related entries: COUP OF 18 FRUCTIDOR YEAR V; DAVID; DIRECTORY; 9 THERMIDOR YEAR II; THERMIDORIAN REACTION; 13 VENDEMIAIRE YEAR IV.

BARTHELEMY, FRANCOIS, COMTE DE (1747-1830), diplomat and director. Born into a modest provincial family, one of fifteen children, the young Barthélemy was raised by his uncle, the abbé J.-J. Barthélemy, later famous as the author of the *Voyage du jeune Anacharsis en Grèce*. His good education and manners, as well as the protection of the duc de Choiseul, brought him into the diplomatic service. Named secretary to C. G. Vergennes, the French ambassador to Sweden, in 1768, he secured a firsthand view of political intrigue at the court of Gustavus III. During Barthélemy's stay at Stockholm, the Swedish king carried out a coup that restored royal absolutism. Promoted to first secretary of the French embassy at Vienna in 1775, he served under the baron de Breteuil. In 1784 he was named first secretary to the Court of Saint James and gained the favor of George III.

Barthélemy remained a loyal servant of his government during the early years of the Revolution and as a reward for his services was named ambassador to the Swiss Confederation at the end of 1791. The overthrow of Louis XVI in August 1792 placed Barthélemy in a difficult situation, for he felt no sympathy for the new republican regime but would be branded as an *émigré* if he deserted it. Although he did not present his new credentials to the Swiss government, he remained as the semiofficial representative of France. He assisted the Republic by encouraging trade through the neutral state at a time when Revolutionary France was cut off from overseas supplies by war and blockade. At the same time, Barthélemy protected French aristocrats and priests who had emigrated to Switzerland, while winning favor with the Swiss by looking after their interests in Paris.

After the Terror, his situation became easier, and he assumed greater authority to deal with other powers, becoming virtual minister for foreign affairs. In 1795 he acted as the French representative in peace negotiations with the Prussian emissary, baron von Hardenberg, and with him signed the Treaty of Basel in April 1795, ending the war between the two states and removing Prussia from the Allied coalition. Barthélemy arranged similar treaties with Spain in July and the Margrave of Hesse-Cassel in August. He remained in his diplomatic post under the Directory, even though he strongly disagreed with much of its foreign policy.

The victory by the royalists in the legislative elections of April 1797 led to his return to France when he was elected director two months later, replacing the republican C.-L.-F.-H. Le Tourneur. As director, Barthélemy frequently clashed with his more radical colleagues over policy, particularly with regard to peace negotiations with England, which he strongly favored. His role in government was brief, for in September 1797, with the coup of 18 Fructidor organized by the republican directors with the assistance of the army, he was arrested as a royalist conspirator.

Imprisoned briefly in the Temple, he was dispatched to the port of Rochefort and deported to the tropics of Guyana. After spending almost seven months in the prison at Sinnamary, Barthélemy escaped with five other exiles to the Dutch colony of Surinam. Traveling under British protection, first to Martinique and then to England, he was refused sanctuary in Britain on the grounds of his presumably dangerous political views. Ironically, he had been declared an *émigré* by the Directory and his property confiscated. He moved to Hamburg in August, 1799, where he observed events in France and began to write his memoirs. Returning to France not long after Napoleon's seizure of power in the coup of 18 Brumaire, Barthélemy quickly won the favor of the new ruler. He was named to the Senate in February 1800 and chevalier of the Legion of Honor for his past diplomatic services. Promoted to count of the empire in 1808, he was elevated to president of the Senate in March 1814 and in this capacity declared Napoleon deposed as emperor. Following the restoration of Louis XVIII, Barthélemy was promoted to grand officer of the Legion of Honor and after the Hundred Days was granted further honors, being named minister of state (1815) and marquis (1818). Barthélemy served in the Chamber of Peers until his death.

Mémoires de Barthélemy, 1768-1819 (Paris, 1914); *Papiers de Barthélemy, ambassadeur de France en Suisse, 1792-1797*, 6 vols. (Paris, 1886-1910).

J. Friguglietti

Related entries : COUP OF 18 FRUCTIDOR YEAR V; FIRST COALITION; GUSTAVUS III; TREATY OF BASEL.

BASEL, TREATY OF. See TREATY OF BASEL.

BASTILLE, THE, fortress-prison in Paris, seized by a crowd on 14 July 1789, a date henceforth used to mark the beginning of the French Revolution. The Bastille was constructed in 1370 to defend the entrance to Paris at the limit of the faubourg Saint-Antoine. In the eighteenth century, it was intended for use in repressing possible uprisings by the Parisians. Cannons, located on its towers, could, in fact, be leveled on the city. Furthermore, since the reign of Louis XIV, it was a state prison, a prison where the king could put away any of his subjects on the basis of a *lettre de cachet*, without trial and for an indefinite period. In 1789 the Bastille contained only seven prisoners. Nevertheless, because of the threat it presented and because of its role as a state prison, it appeared to be the symbol of royal despotism. The taking of the Bastille on 14 July 1789 constituted the first great *journée* of the French Revolution, marking the collapse of absolute monarchy and the beginning of a constitutional and democratic regime. This is why the anniversary of 14 July was chosen, from 1790, as the national holiday. Although abolished under monarchical regimes, in 1880 it once again became the national holiday of the French Republic. It has remained so since that time.

The causes of the attack on and capture of the Bastille are numerous. Some are remote and related to the general situation in France in the late 1780s; others are more immediate and are tied to Louis XVI's policy during June and July 1789, as well as to the growth of Revolutionary propaganda within the army.

Among the long-term causes, one must put in first place the general hostility of the people of France—92 percent of whom were peasants—toward the feudal regime. Feudal and seigneurial rights, still very rigorously exacted at the end of the eighteenth century—as well as the *dîmes*, paid to the church but resembling feudal rights as far as the peasants were concerned—cost farmers an average of 20 percent of their income. In addition, these dues were levied in an annoying fashion. Often the peasants refused to pay them; from this resulted lawsuits that ruined them. First, they went before a seigneurial court, which, with its bias, found against the peasants, and in an appeal, they appeared before judges, most of whom were also nobles or landlords of *seigneuries*, who were jointly liable with the accused *seigneur*. These conflicts provoked agitation that grew continually. A serious economic crisis developed in 1788–89 and aggravated matters even further. Bad weather during the summer of 1788 almost totally destroyed the harvest. The price of grain, and consequently the price of bread, instead of declining in August, as it usually did, continued to rise. In Paris in July 1789, the price of wheat reached its highest level since 1715. The number of unemployed grew considerably. Agricultural workers, without employment, rushed to the cities, notably to Paris, where they joined the laborers and artisans who were unemployed themselves. The political crisis in France, which had been latent since 1770, became worse in 1787; the royal government had been forced to convoke, for 1 May 1789, the Estates General, which had not met since 1614. The election of deputies to the Estates in March and April 1789 combined with the economic crisis to increase agitation. In Paris, on 27 April, unemployed workers attacked the wallpaper factory of Réveillon; they accused their employer of wanting to lower wages and of favoring an increase in the price of bread. The factory and its owner's home were completely ransacked. The French Guards, sent to protect them, fired on the crowd. Several hundred were killed and more wounded, so that this *journée* counts among the most bloody of the Revolution.

The Estates General met eight days later. It was paralyzed for nearly two months by a conflict between the privileged groups and the Third Estate over the forms by which they were going to vote. By order? In this case, the two privileged orders would have the majority. Or by head? Then the Third, aug-

mented by most of the parish priests and by the liberal nobles, would win. The
people of France did not understand much about this conflict over juridical
behavior, despite its importance. On 20 June the deputies of the Third, whom
some parish priests had joined, resolved the situation by proclaiming that they
represented the French nation and by constituting themselves as the National
Assembly. On 23 June the king was unable to make the Third retract this decision
and was obliged to recognize the fait accompli at least for the moment. The
same day, the king summoned troops to Paris with the intention of dissolving
the Estates General by force. But were the troops reliable? Certainly they had
acted against rioters on 27 April during the Réveillon affair. Since then, however,
they had been won over by Revolutionary propaganda, and there were many
desertions. On 24 June the French Guard refused to perform their duties and
went to fraternize with the crowd at the Palais Royal, the principal gathering
place of Parisians. Numerous incidents of the same kind took place all over
France. Nevertheless Louis XVI remained confident of the soldiers. On 11 July,
with troops gathered around Paris, the king decided to dismiss his chief administrator, J. Necker, who had supported the demands of the Third Estate. The
next day, Sunday, 12 July, this news became known at the Palais Royal. It
provoked intense emotions; the journalist L.-C.-S. Desmoulins called the people
to arms. A large demonstration spread through the streets of Paris. The Regiment
of Royal German Cavalry tried to chase demonstrators from the garden of the
Tuileries; several civilians were injured, but in the end the cavalry had to retire.
Some Swiss regiments, called to help, refused to move. During the night of 12–
13 July, the toll booths, where the *octroi* duties were collected on goods entering
Paris, were burned down and the convent of Saint-Lazare, where the proceeds
from the *dîmes*, in grain, were stored, was pillaged. On 13 July, some citizens
of Paris armed themselves spontaneously and organized patrols to restore order.
The electors (those Parisians who had elected the deputies to the Estates General)
decided to give these patrols an official status and created a bourgeois militia of
48,000 men. But it had to be armed. Where would arms and munitions be found?
Gunsmiths' shops were ransacked but provided an inadequate number of guns.
During Tuesday morning, 14 July, the news spread that many guns were stored
in the vaults of the Invalides and that there were powder and balls at the Bastille.

A huge crowd—20,000 to 30,000 people—soon went to the Invalides and
forced open its gates. At this point, there occurred a development that is essential
to understanding 14 July. A few hundred meters from the Invalides, on the
Champ de Mars, large military forces were encamped; if they had intervened,
they would have been able to prevent the taking of the Invalides. However, their
commander, P.-V. Besenval, after consulting the unit commanders, decided that
it was impossible to employ these soldiers because they were not reliable enough.
Therefore, the crowd pillaged the Invalides and seized 40,000 muskets that were
stored there, along with twelve cannons.

At the same time, other demonstrators, also very numerous, grouped before
the Bastille and demanded the 250 barrels of powder stored there. However, the

Bastille, with its walls thirty meters high, its turrets, and its cannon, was more difficult to take than the Invalides, although its garrison consisted only of thirty Swiss soldiers and eighty veterans, under the orders of the governor, B.-R. de Launey. The electors of Paris sent a deputation to the governor to demand that he yield his powder and, above all, withdraw from the towers the cannons trained on Paris. The negotiations produced no results. The crowd of demonstrators grew; new delegations came to the Bastille; but while they were negotiating, shots were exchanged between the garrison and the besiegers. The latter believed that they had been betrayed and attacked the fortress. Their efforts no doubt would have been in vain, if, at around 3:30 P.M. about sixty French Guards, commanded by a former sergeant, P.-A. Hulin, had not arrived before the Bastille with four of the cannons taken that morning from the Invalides. The cannons were trained on the gates. In order to avoid the capture of the fortress, which undoubtedly would have been followed by a massacre of the entire garrison, de Launey decided to capitulate at 5 P.M. The crowd stormed the Bastille, disarmed its defenders, freed the seven prisoners, and arrested the governor. The fighting resulted in ninety-eight killed and seventy-three wounded among the besiegers, which infuriated them. While de Launey was being conducted to the city hall, he was torn from his captors and killed. Three staff officers of the Bastille and three veterans were also killed.

The taking of the Bastille was not an isolated event; it was a development of great importance that marked the triumph of the people of Paris over the monarchy and put an end to the Old Regime. For two days the king pondered the possibilities of resisting, but the state of morale among the troops was such that he saw none. On 16 July he ordered the regiments that he had gathered to return to their garrisons, and on 17 July he himself went to Paris, where he recognized the new municipal authorities and accepted from the hands of their leader, J.-S. Bailly, the cockade that the Parisian militia had just taken, with the colors of the city of Paris, blue and red, surrounding the white of the Bourbons. Thus, at the same moment as the Bastille, the symbol of the Old Regime, was about to disappear, the new national flag, the symbol of the Revolution and the new regime, appeared.

F. Braesch, *1789, l'année cruciale* (Paris, 1941); P. Chauvet, *L'Insurrection parisienne et la prise de la Bastille* (Paris, 1946); J. Godechot, *The Taking of the Bastille, July 14th, 1789* (New York, 1970); G. Lefebvre, *The Coming of the French Revolution* (New York, 1970); J. Mistler, *Le 14 juillet* (Paris, 1963).

J. Godechot

Related entries: BAILLY; BESENVAL; DESMOULINS; FEUDALISM; LAUNEY; *LETTRE DE CACHET*; NECKER; REVEILLON RIOT; TENNIS COURT OATH.

BATAVIAN REPUBLIC (1795-1801), Revolutionary regime established in the Netherlands during the era of the French National Convention and changed into the so-called Batavian Commonwealth in September 1801 at the insistence of First Consul N. Bonaparte. The once-famous Republic of the Seven United Provinces born during the Eighty Years' War with Spain (1568–1648) was only a shadow of its former greatness during the late eighteenth century. It had reached its peak of diplomatic, economic, and cultural influence during the seventeenth century when it participated in the European wars against Louis XIV, acquired a colonial empire, controlled much of the world's carrying trade, and produced numerous famous artists and scientists.

After the War of the Spanish Succession (1702-14) the Dutch Republic began an era of political, economic, and diplomatic decline and followed Britain in its foreign policy. The two stadtholders of this period, William IV (1747–51) and William V (1766–95), were weak-willed individuals who failed to provide strong leadership while political opposition and criticism mounted. Two factions demanded political and other changes during the latter part of the eighteenth century. The reactionaries demanded a curtailment of the stadtholder's prerogatives, if not the abolition of the stadtholderate. Another faction demanded democratization and modernization of the political structure. The latter were led by Baron J. D. van der Capellen (1741-84) who wrote in 1781 his famous *Aan het volk van Nederland* [*To the people of the Netherlands*]. Together these two factions formed the opposition called the patriotic movement or party. Their agitation became more intense after the disastrous war with Britain (1780–83) caused by the Dutch Republic's inability and unwillingness to enforce an embargo against the American revolutionaries. The patriots' attempt to seize power in 1787 failed, however, and many of them fled to France. They would return with the French Revolutionary armies in 1795.

The National Convention declared war on Britain and the Dutch stadtholder in February 1793. French troops did not invade Dutch territories until the winter of 1794–95 when the major rivers were frozen. The government of William V fled to England, and the so-called Batavian Republic was proclaimed amid considerable popular enthusiasm. The price of French liberation was rather high and dampened much of the initial welcome given the French armies. By the Treaty of the Hague (May 1795), the Dutch had to pay some 100 million florins to the bankrupt French government, cede certain frontier areas, accept a French garrison in Flushing, maintain a French army of 25,000 on Dutch territory, and conclude an offensive and defensive treaty with the French Republic. Subsequently the Netherlands became to all practical purposes a French satellite and in 1810 part of Napoleon's empire until 1813.

Meanwhile, efforts had been made to revolutionize the political structure of the old Dutch republic. In the spring of 1796, a National Convention was elected to draft a new constitution and to effect other reforms. Two factions, the so-called unitarians and the federalists, were sharply divided over the future political structure. The federalists advocated a reform of the old federal structure of the now-defunct Dutch Republic, while the unitarians supported the idea of a unitarian state in which old provincial rivalries and jealousies, which had undermined and weakened the Republic in the seventeenth and eighteenth centuries, would have no place. After lengthy debates, the Convention finally accepted a proposal that did not create a truly unitarian state but retained many of the old provincial prerogatives. It was rejected in a national referendum in August 1797, after which a second National Assembly was chosen. The outcome of the election did not satisfy many of the unitarians, who proposed to the French ambassador F.-J.-M. Noël and the French commander P. de Beurnonville that the National Convention be purged. This purge took place on 22 January 1797 when some twenty-two federalists were removed from the Convention.

A new constitutional proposal was accepted in April 1798 that provided for political and administrative unity. The former semiautonomous provinces were to be replaced by eight departments. The legislature, to be chosen by universal male suffrage, would be comprised of the First and Second Chamber. The executive would consist, like the French counterpart, of five directors chosen by the legislature.

Instead of dissolving itself after its task had been completed, the second National Convention declared itself to be the new legislature and elected an executive. This action triggered a new purge, which was effected by the former Patriot General H. Daendels, who struck on 12 June 1798, with the approval of the French Directory, when he removed various members of the legislature and the executive. Subsequently elections were held, and a new legislature and executive were chosen. Thus after three years of discussion and two purges, the Dutch finally had a new constitutional system that had the blessings of the French government.

But France remained unhappy over its Dutch ally. The Dutch fleet was badly mauled at Camperdown on 11 October 1797, and two years later an Anglo-Russian force invaded the province of North Holland but was repulsed with French assistance later in the same year.

First Consul Bonaparte demanded a more compliant and less democratic regime. He refused to lessen the military obligations imposed by the Treaty of the Hague and demanded a revision of the Batavian constitution. Public sentiment also seemed to favor political changes and a return to a less democratic and more decentralized political system after years of instability and confusion. But the Dutch legislature refused to yield to Bonaparte's pressure, and it was not until September 1801, after a purge of the executive and a closing of the legislature, that a new constitution could be adopted. This document of October 1801 created the so-called Batavian Commonwealth or *Staatsbewind*, as it is more commonly known. It provided for a weak one-house legislature and a twelve-men executive and returned some of the powers to the former provinces. At Napoleon's command, the Batavian Commonwealth received another constitution in 1805, which provided for the regime of Councillor Pensionary R. J. Schimmelpennink, whose administration would be terminated by the French emperor in May 1806 when he placed his brother Louis on the throne of the newly proclaimed Kingdom of Holland.

In spite of the failure of the Dutch revolution and a return to some former patterns of political behavior, important achievements had been made during the time of the Batavian Republic.The Dutch had their first democratic experiment on which they could draw in later years; equality before the law was established; church and state were separated; and the once-famous East India Company was dissolved, its properties and possessions going to the nation.

H. T. Colenbrander, ed., *Gedenkstukken der algemeene geschiedenis van Nederland van 1795 te 1840*, vols. 1-3 (The Hague, 1905-22); H. T. Colenbrander, *De Bataafsche Republiek* (Amsterdam, 1908); Simon Schama, *Patriots and Liberators, Revolution in the Netherlands, 1795-1813* (New York, 1977); Gerlof D. Homan, *Nederland in de Napoleontische tijd* (Haarlem, 1978): R. R. Palmer, "Much in Little. The Dutch Revolution of 1795," *J. of Mod. Hist.* 26 (1954).

G. D. Homan

Related entry: WILLIAM V.

BATTLE OF ABOUKIR   (1799), French defeat of Turkish expedition to Egypt. The French army had been in Egypt for more than a year and was in control of the lower and middle Nile regions when a Turkish flotilla, supported by British warships under Commodore S. Smith, landed approximately 15,000 men at Aboukir on 15 July 1799. The Turks, under the command of Mustafa Pasha, came ashore unopposed, massacred the 300 French defenders of the village of Aboukir, and laid siege to the fort at the end of the peninsula. The fort, which was unprepared for a siege, surrendered after three days, and the Turkish army settled down behind a hastily but well-prepared defensive position.

General N. Bonaparte, in Cairo, received the news of the enemy landing, and he immediately gathered all available troops and marched to the sea. Reaching Aboukir on 24 July, Bonaparte ordered an attack on the Turkish position for the following morning. The French force at Aboukir numbered only 10,000 men but had the advantage of including 1,000 well-mounted cavalrymen. At dawn on 25 July, the French attacked the Turkish position, which extended across the peninsula and was supported by Turkish gunboats off shore. At noon General J. Murat led the French cavalry in a charge that broke through the enemy defenses and reached the fort at the tip of the peninsula. As the French infantry followed the cavalry, the Turkish army fled. Within an hour, the victory was complete; Mustafa Pasha was taken prisoner, and Turkish losses were extremely heavy. Fort Aboukir held out until 2 August, at which time all military operations came to an end. The failure of this Turkish expedition left Bonaparte firmly in control of Egypt and enabled him to turn over command of the army to General J. Kléber and return to France.

J. Christopher Herold, *Bonaparte in Egypt* (New York, 1962); C. E. de la Jonquière, *L'Expedition d' Egypte, 1798–1801*, vol. 5 (Paris, 1899–1907); Jean Thiry, *Bonaparte en Egypte* (Paris, 1973).

J. G. Gallaher

Related entries: EGYPTIAN EXPEDITION; KLEBER; MURAT.

BATTLE OF ARCOLA (15-17 November 1796), between the Army of Italy commanded by N. Bonaparte and the Austrian forces under General J. Alvintzi, who had been ordered to relieve the blockaded fortress of Mantua. In an effort to defeat Alvintzi's 28,000-man army before he was reinforced by a second army of 20,000 commanded by General P. Davidovich advancing down the Adige, Napoleon resolved to attack at once. Preliminary operations resulted in French failures at Segonzano (2 November) and Caldeiro (12 November), so Napoleon moved to cut Alvintzi's communications at Villanova, seize his supply train, and prevent a union of the two Austrian armies. On 14 November, Generals A. Masséna and C. Augereau crossed the Adige at Ronco and the following morning attacked the Croat regiments defending Arcola, but they were repulsed from the wooden bridge over the Alpone. Two more assaults were made on the bridge, but Augereau was unable to clear it.

Napoleon arrived and ordered another attack. Leading a column across the bridge, he was turned back, and his horse was forced into the nearby swamps; he was saved from capture only by the most vigorous efforts of his staff. Finally General J. Guieu seized Arcola from the rear, but Alvintzi's troops escaped through the Villanova defile. That night the French were inadvertently withdrawn from the village of Arcola, and two days of hard fighting and a *ruse de guerre* by trumpeters in the rear of the Austrians were needed to recapture the village and bridge. In the three-day battle, the Austrians lost 7,000 men and 11 guns, while the French casualties numbered over 4,500. In concrete results, the Austrian forces had been unable to relieve Mantua, Alvintzi's army was defeated and driven back to Montebello, and Napoleon reoccupied Verona. He wrote to L. Carnot, minister of war, that "never had a battlefield been more vigorously contested."

G. J. Fabry, *Histoire de l'armée d'Italie, 1796-1797*, 3 vols. (Paris, 1900–1901); W. G. Jackson, *Attack in the West* (London, 1953); R. W. Phipps, *The Armies of the First French Republic and the Rise of the Marshals of Napoleon I*, 5 vols. (Oxford, 1926-39).

D. D. Horward

Related entries: BONAPARTE, N.; MASSENA.

BATTLE OF FLEURUS (26 June 1794), in which the French decisively defeated Austrian forces along the Sambre River and assured the conquest of the Austrian Netherlands. For the French troops along the Sambre River, Charleroi was the prime objective of the 1794 spring campaign. Under the overall command of General J.-C. Pichegru, units of the *Armée du nord* and its subsidiary, the *Armée des Ardennes*, crossed the river three times in May and early June but were beaten back each time. Marching at the head of 50,000 troops detached from the *Armée de la Moselle*, General J.-B. Jourdan finally joined these units along the Sambre. This new collection of armies, with a field force of some 75,000 combatants, was placed under Jourdan's command on 8 June and received the designation *Armée de Sambre-et-Meuse* on 13 June. After one more unsuccessful attempt to cross the Sambre and lay siege to Charleroi, the *Sambre-et-Meuse* succeeded on 18 June.

The threat to Charleroi prompted a major Austrian thrust. The prince of Saxe-Coburg, who commanded Austrian forces in the Netherlands, marshaled 52,000 men against Jourdan. Believing that Coburg's army numbered 90,000, Jourdan decided to stand on the defensive and entrenched the bulk of his army in a great semicircle covering the besieging forces.

Coburg divided his force into five columns and directed them in a concentric attack on Jourdan's lines. The battle itself began about 3 A.M. and continued into the evening. Since Coburg's columns were not closely coordinated with each other, Fleurus developed more as several isolated battles than as one great battle. On the French left, the Austrians were beaten back. In the center, early Austrian success was frustrated finally by a counterattack late in the day. On the French right, victory seemed to be within grasp of the Austrians. The division on the extreme right was thrown back, some of it recrossing the Sambre. But its neighbor, commanded by General F.-J. Lefebvre, a future marshal, fought with exceptional tenacity. By evening the Austrian menace on the French right was also beaten back. Fleurus was an extremely hard-fought battle. Later Marshal Soult called it the most desperate fighting that he had ever seen.

Coburg could have reopened the struggle the next day, but he chose to withdraw, a withdrawal that continued until all of the Austrian Netherlands was in French hands. It may be that before the Battle of Fleurus, the Austrian high command had lost the will to hold the southern Netherlands. The emperor, who had come to join his armies earlier in the spring, returned home before Fleurus, and his parting may have been a judgment on the fate of the Netherlands.

To the extent that the Terror was a response to the military crisis of 1793, the victories of Tourcoing (17-18 May 1794) and Fleurus contributed to its collapse by eliminating much of its raison d'être. Brussels fell to the French on 10 July; the Austrian Netherlands was completely in French hands before the end of the year, and Holland fell by the spring of 1795.

V. Dupuis, *Les opérations militaires sur la Sambre en 1794: La bataille de Fleurus* (Paris, 1907); R. W. Phipps, *The Armies of the First French Republic and the Rise of the Marshals of Napoleon the First*, vol. 2 (London, 1929).

J. A. Lynn

Related entries: BATTLE OF TOURCOING; JOURDAN; PICHEGRU; ROBESPIERRE, M.; TERROR, THE.

BATTLE OF HONDSCHOOTE (6-8 September 1793), in which the *Armée du nord* defeated an Anglo-Hanoverian army and broke the siege of Dunkirk. In the late summer of 1793, the Allies split their forces, which were threatening the French Republic's northern frontier. The duke of York led his 35,000 troops north in order to besiege Dunkirk, and the Austrians moved south. On orders from the Committee of Public Safety, General J.-N. Houchard, in command of the *Armée du nord*, marched against York with 45,000 men. Houchard muddled the campaign; his own mediocrity and his fear of the guillotine made him cautious and indecisive. Finally resolving on a simple, direct advance on Dunkirk, he divided his army into six columns and drove them across a front of thirty-five kilometers.

The movements of these six columns, however, were uncoordinated. On 6 September they collided with elements of the Hanoverian force of 16,000, which was covering the besieging troops under York's direct command. Fighting climaxed two days later in a clumsy but successful assault on the Hanoverian positions at Hondschoote. The difficult ground forced the French to disperse in swarms of skirmishers. After this hard-won victory, Houchard let slip the chance to cut off York's retreat, thereby denying the French a decisive victory. Houchard's delay condemned him to the fate he most feared. He was arrested, tried, and guillotined.

V. Dupuis, *La Campagne de 1793 à l'Armée du nord et des Ardennes*, vol. 1 (Paris, 1906); R. W. Phipps, *The Armies of the First French Republic and the Rise of the Marshals of Napoleon the First*, vol. 1 (London, 1926).

J. A. Lynn

Related entry: FIRST COALITION.

BATTLE OF JEMAPPES (6 November 1792), in which French troops were successful in defeating the main enemy troops defending the Austrian Netherlands and consequently opened this territory to French invasion and ultimate occupation. General C. Dumouriez had long been intent on French conquest of the Austrian Netherlands, but the Prussian invasion of France had called him away from the northern frontier. After Valmy, he was able to win the government over to his plans. Concentrating his main forces at Valenciennes in late October, he finally began to advance on Mons during the first days of November.

His opponent, Duke Albert of Saxe-Teschen, dispersed his forces along the border with France so that he had only 14,000 men at Mons to resist Dumouriez on the morning of 6 November. The fortifications of Mons were in such disrepair that Duke Albert did not rely on them. Instead he established a defensive line along a ridge of high ground that ran through the village of Jemappes, near Mons. The Austrians buttressed their positions with a series of six redoubts and awaited the French attack. Dumouriez marshaled about 40,000 men, including 10,000 under General L.-A. d'Harville, who that morning had linked up with Dumouriez' main force. Harville's men were of crucial importance to the original plan of battle sketched by Dumouriez. Stationed to the right of Dumouriez' main army, they were to maneuver against the exposed Austrian flank. However, the troops under Harville were inexperienced volunteers of 1792, and this made him reluctant to engage the Austrians; consequently, he stood off from the Austrian left, neither outflanking it nor assaulting it, a course of action allowed him by the confused and ambiguous orders issued by Dumouriez. This inaction reduced the main attack to a brutal frontal assault by Dumouriez' battalions.

After an extensive but largely ineffective cannonade, the French battalions of the center deployed into columns and swept up the hill. They were met by intense fire, and for the next two hours the fighting was vicious and costly for each side. Although the assault was neither well conceived nor well coordinated, the French troops displayed great courage and resolve. Dumouriez and his staff, notably the future King Louis-Philippe, rallied troops and pressed the attack by conspicuous heroics. Meanwhile, on the extreme left of the French line, a less dramatic but highly effective improvised flanking attack was being led by General J.-H. Ferrand de la Caussade at the head of six battalions. The French succeeded in driving the Austrians from the village of Jemappes at about 2 P.M., after which the entire Austrian line dissolved. The exhausted French troops did not pursue the retreating Austrians, who immediately abandoned Mons in their flight.

The strategic consequences of the battle were great and immediate; it left the Austrian Netherlands exposed to French occupation. French success seemed so complete that the *patrie* was declared to be no longer in danger, and many volunteers returned home, seriously weakening the army. This exodus and disorganization made possible the reconquest of the Netherlands by the Austrians in March 1793. The battle had an emotional impact as well; it was the first major battle won by the French infantry in the open field. It was a victory of patriotic élan, not of skill; and it justified, therefore, the new citizen army of the Revolution. The historian A. Chuquet calls it "toute héroïque, toute populaire."

A. Chuquet, *Jemappes et la conquête de la Belgique (1792-1793)* (Paris, 1890); C. de La Jonquière, *La bataille de Jemappes* (Paris, 1902); R. W. Phipps, *The Armies of the First French Republic and the Rise of the Marshals of Napoleon the First*, vol. 1 (London, 1926).

J. A. Lynn

Related entries: BATTLE OF VALMY; DUMOURIEZ.

BATTLE OF LODI (10 May 1796), between the Army of Italy commanded by N. Bonaparte and the Austrian army under General J. Beaulieu. To outflank the Austrian army defending Lombardy, Napoleon crossed the Po at Piacenza and advanced to Lodi, where he hoped to open the road to Milan and western Lombardy, as well as bring the Austrian army to battle. The village and bridge of Lodi were defended by Austrian General K. Sebottendorf with a rear guard of 8,500 men and 14 cannons. Lodi was seized by the French, and the Austrians retreated across the 170-yard wooden bridge over the Adda River before cutting two of its spans. While a French cavalry detachment crossed the Adda at the Mozanica ford to outflank and divert the Austrians, Generals A. Masséna and A. Berthier led an assault of 1,000 volunteers across the bridge, but they were turned back by heavy fire. Again, Masséna attacked the bridge. Supported by General J. Cervoni, he climbed down the broken span into the water and led his men ashore, driving the Austrians before them. The Austrians lost 2,000 men and 14 cannons; French casualties totaled 1,000. As a result of the Battle of Lodi, the French occupied western Lombardy and the capital of Milan. It was at Lodi that Napoleon, in reconnoitering the enemy and directing the battle, demonstrated his personal courage and won the respect of his men as the "little corporal."

G. J. Fabry, *Histoire de l'armée d'Italie, 1796-1797*, 3 vols. (Paris, 1900–01); R. W. Phipps, *The Armies of the First French Republic and the Rise of the Marshals of Napoleon I*, 5 vols. (Oxford, 1926-39); S. Wilkinson, *The Rise of General Bonaparte* (Oxford, 1930).   *D. Horward*

Related entries: BONAPARTE, N.; MASSENA.

BATTLE OF NEERWINDEN (18 March 1793), which occurred east of Tirlement, Belgium; Austrian defeat of the French enabled Austria briefly to regain control of the southern Netherlands. In March 1793 a veteran Austrian army under the duke of Coburg invaded French-held Belgium and forced the Convention's raw troops to retreat west. General C. Dumouriez hastily returned from a campaign in Holland and counterattacked. French foot soldiers outnumbered the Austrians; the reverse was true in cavalry. The French fought honorably in Neerwinden and other villages but were overwhelmed in open areas. In retreat, many contingents deserted, leaving an easy path for Austrian advance.

This battle demonstrates the lack of suitability of eighteenth-century military tactics for an untrained army. Evident also are the skills of General C. Mack, staff officer to Coburg, and of the young Archduke Charles, who commanded the grenadiers; the victory gained the latter attention and launched an illustrious career. The defeat may have further stimulated thoughts of deserting the French cause in the mind of Dumouriez, who was aware of the harshness with which the National Convention treated its generals and was at odds with some of its leaders. He shortly did desert, in fact, to the Austrians.

A. Chuquet, *La trahison de Dumouriez* (Paris, 1891); T. A. Dodge, *Napoleon*, 4 vols. (Boston, 1904); R. W. Phipps, *The Armies of the First French Republic and the Rise of the Marshals of Napoleon the First*, vol. 1 (London, 1926).

J. E. Helmreich

Related entries: BELGIUM; DUMOURIEZ; MIRANDA.

BATTLE OF RIVOLI (14 January 1797), final major battle in Napoleon Bonaparte's first Italian campaign. In the spring of 1796, Bonaparte took command of the Army of Italy. His mission was to tie down Austrian troops stationed in Piedmont and Lombardy and prevent them from reinforcing Austrian units in southern Germany, where the French planned to launch their main blow. The campaign, however, took a different turn. French forces in Germany were unsuccessful, and the Austrians ultimately drove them back to the Rhine. On the other hand, Napoleon attained spectacular victories in Italy.

After crossing the Alps, Bonaparte drove Piedmont out of the war and quickly penetrated into the north Italian plain. Milan soon fell, and the French pushed on, surrounding a large Austrian force in Mantua. Napoleon wanted to take Mantua and advance into southern Austria, but first he had to drive off the Austrian expedition coming south from Germany. He defeated the Austrians at

Bassano and Arcola, but in January 1797 the Austrians launched a two-pronged attack toward Mantua. Ignoring the weaker of the two forces, Napoleon concentrated his divisions against the larger Hapsburg contingent and defeated it at Rivoli on 14 January. He then rushed back and dealt with the remaining Austrian force near Padua.

The Austrians had thus failed to relieve Mantua, and the starving garrison capitulated early in February. The elimination of Mantua enabled the French to advance without a threat to their flanks and rear and set the stage for the final assault against the Hapsburg crown lands.

G. Fabry, *Histoire de l'armée d'Italie, 1796–1797*, 3 vols. (Paris, 1900-01); F. Grazioli, *La battaglia di Rivoli, 14–15 gennaio 1797* (Florence, 1925); W. Jackson, *Attack in the West; Napoleon's First Campaign Re-read Today* (London, 1953).

S. T. Ross

Related entries: BONAPARTE, N.; FIRST COALITION; TREATY OF CAMPOFORMIO.

BATTLE OF THE NILE (1 August 1798), British naval victory contributing to the defeat of Napoleon's Egyptian expedition. At the end of 1797, France was at peace with all of the major European powers with the exception of England. The Directory desired a policy designed to force England to make peace before London could create a new coalition. The directors were faced with two strategic choices. The first was the risky but potentially decisive method of a cross-channel invasion. The other alternative was an indirect approach involving French maritime attacks on British colonies. If successful, such assaults would reduce Britain's trade and make it financially impossible for Britain to continue the war.

The Directory at first decided to try the direct approach. N. Bonaparte received command of the Army of England and began to gather transports in the channel ports. The French could not, however, find sufficient shipping to support the cross-channel idea, and in March 1798 Paris adopted the indirect colonial strategy. The Directory ordered Bonaparte to seize Egypt for use as an advanced base for an attack on Great Britain's holdings in India. After occupying Egypt, Napoleon was to send troops to French-held islands in the Indian Ocean via the Red Sea. France would form an alliance with Mysore and, together with that state, would strike at the British. A basic ingredient for success was the ability to maintain a line of communications with metropolitan France. Since the British had withdrawn their warships from the Mediterranean in 1796, Paris assumed that a force operating in Egypt could obtain equipment and reinforcements without interference.

The first phase of the operation went well. In May a force of 32,000 men sailed from Toulon. Bonaparte occupied Malta against feeble resistance and landed successfully in Egypt. Leaving his fleet anchored in Aboukir Bay, he moved promptly to crush the Mamelukes and occupy the country. Meanwhile the British were seeking to counter the French strategy. On learning of the Toulon expedition, the cabinet assumed that it would strike at Naples, Portugal, or Ireland. Only H. Dundas guessed its true destination. W. Pitt decided finally to send a fleet to the Mediterranean to frustrate French designs, whatever they were, and also to encourage Austria and the Italian princes to resume the war with the Republic.

Led by H. Nelson, the fleet entered the Mediterranean, only to find that the Toulon fleet had sailed. Nelson set off eastward, guessing that the French were going to strike at India by way of Egypt. He reached Alexandria before the French and left Egyptian waters to continue his search. He then returned to the Egyptian coast at the end of July and on 1 August found the French fleet anchored across Aboukir Bay. In the ensuing engagement, the British won a decisive victory. Only two of thirteen French ships-of-the-line escaped capture or destruction, and the French lost over 8,900 men while the British suffered fewer than 900 casualties. The Army of the East was isolated in Egypt, and the Battle of the Nile encouraged other powers to take up arms against the French Republic. Encouraged by Nelson's triumph, the Ottoman Empire concluded an alliance with Russia and declared war on France. England and Russia also formed an alliance, and Russia and Austria agreed to go to war against France. By the spring of 1799, the Second Coalition was organized and prepared to resume hostilities.

In India the British crushed Mysore, thus ending French hopes of finding a powerful Indian ally. Bonaparte held Egypt but suffered a defeat at Acre in 1799 when he tried to invade Syria. He later left his army and returned to France where he led the Brumaire coup. His army in Egypt, commanded by J.-B. Kléber and then J.-F. Menou, held out until 1801 when it surrendered to the British.

Thus the Battle of the Nile reversed the strategic situation. In 1798 France was at peace on the Continent and England was isolated. In 1799 it was the French who were isolated and Great Britain was once again leading a coalition against the republic.

F. Charles-Roux, *L'Angleterre et l'expédition française en Egypte*, 2 vols. (Cairo, 1925), and *Les origines de l'expédition française en Egypte* (Paris, 1910); P. G. Elgood, *Bonaparte's Adventure in Egypt* (Oxford, 1931); J. H. Rose, "The Political Reactions of Bonaparte's Eastern Expedition," *Eng. Hist. Rev.* 44 (1929).

S. T. Ross

Related entries: BONAPARTE, N.; COUP OF 18 BRUMAIRE; DIRECTORY; EGYPTIAN EXPEDITION; KLEBER; MENOU; PITT; SECOND COALITION; SIEYES; TALLEYRAND.

BATTLE OF TOURCOING (17-18 May 1794), in which the French defeated a major Anglo-Austrian offensive in Flanders. The early spring of 1794 witnessed a series of minor battles along the French northern frontier. Swelled by troops conscripted in 1793, the *Armée du nord* under General J.-C. Pichegru was ineffective at first, but in early May, the French seized Menin and Courtrai. The Allies then sought to crush the two divisions occupying these towns by encircling them with six converging columns, totaling 73,000 troops. In Pichegru's absence, General J. Souham was left in command of the threatened sector. As the noose tightened, Souham shifted the 60,000 men under his command so as to defeat the menacing columns in detail. Holding off the largest column with only one French brigade, he concentrated on two of the weaker columns. The hardest fighting occurred on 18 May at Courtrai and around Tourcoing. By nightfall, the Allies were stalled or in retreat.

This French victory was impressive and important. It was the first great battle in which the French defeated a numerically superior force by intelligent maneuver and skillful tactics. The battle raised French morale and shook the Allied high command; it was clear that the French were no longer awkward and ineffective. Tourcoing did much to prepare the way for Fleurus a month later.

H. Coutanceau and H. Leplus, *La Campagne de 1794 à l'Armée du nord*, part II, vol. 2 (Paris, 1908); R. W. Phipps, *The Armies of the First French Republic and the Rise of the Marshals of Napoleon the First*, vol. 1 (London, 1926).

J. A. Lynn

Related entries: BATTLE OF FLEURUS; PICHEGRU.

BATTLE OF VALMY (20 September 1792), in which the French army halted the first invasion of France and turned back foreign and *émigré* forces. After capturing the fortresses of Longwy (23 August) and Verdun (2 September), the Allied armies under the duke of Brunswick moved into the Argonne Forest. In order to protect Paris, C. Dumouriez's army left Sedan, and F.-C. de Kellermann's marched from Metz. When the two French forces made contact with each other, they numbered over 50,000 troops, both line troops and national volunteers; Brunswick's Prussian army, which included King Frederick William II, contained slightly fewer than 35,000 men.

After some preliminary disagreements over strategy, Kellermann occupied the heights of Valmy while Dumouriez took up positions to his rear, with the French forces facing toward Paris and the Prussians closer to the capital. The Prussians opened the combat at 7 A.M. with an artillery barrage, followed by an infantry attack around noon. Although the French cannon were outnumbered approximately three to two, expert gunnery forced the Prussians to retire amid cries of *Vive la Nation!* and to the strains of the "*Ça ira*." Subsequently the French mounted a counterattack of their own, which also failed. When a second Prussian attack was repulsed, the combat drew to a close by 8 P.M.

After the battle, Dumouriez initiated peace talks with the Prussians, but with the news that a Republic had been declared (22 September 1792), negotiations collapsed. Suffering from a lack of supplies, harsh weather, and dysentery, the Prussian forces began to retreat at the beginning of October, a retreat that Dumouriez did nothing to hamper.

According to J. W. von Goethe, a witness to the battle, this struggle marked the beginning of a new era in history. Indeed, despite the small number of casualties (about 300 Prussian and fewer than 200 French), Valmy was a critical engagement. It provided the first evidence that the French army had recovered from the immense strains and defections that had plagued it since 1789. It proved that regular troops and National Guardsmen, recently called to active service, could operate effectively together. The use of Revolutionary slogans and music by the French gave the battle a peculiarly political character. Furthermore, "the cannonade of Valmy" presaged the importance of massed artillery in combat. Finally, Valmy saved not only Paris but the Revolution and possibly France itself from impending defeat.

J. P. Bertaud, *Valmy: La démocratie en armes* (Paris, 1970); A. Chuquet, *Valmy* (Paris, 1887).

S. F. Scott

Related entries: BRUNSWICK; DUMOURIEZ; *EMIGRES*; KELLERMANN.

BATTLE OF WATTIGNIES (17 October 1793), in which the French army defeated the Austrians. The small village of Wattignies, since the day of the battle called Wattignies-la-Victoire, is located nine kilometers south of Maubeuge in northern France. There occurred the famous victory over the Austrians by the French republican General J.-B. Jourdan. At age thirty a divisional commander, Jourdan on 22 September 1793 led the *Armée du nord* and the *Armée des Ardennes*, composed of only 18,000 men; with the arrival of reinforcements he could muster 50,000 combatants. On 23 September the Austrians under the command of count Clairfayt and the prince of Coburg besieged Maubeuge, where 20,000 French troops were entrenched. On 8 October L. Carnot joined Jourdan at Guise, and on the morning of the fifteenth Jourdan attacked the Austrians on their flanks. That evening Carnot held a council of war where it was decided to weaken the French left and center and concentrate the offensive on the right wing. Jourdan's troops moved in the early morning of 16 October while a thick fog covered the deeply forested countryside and meadows, themselves criss-crossed by rows of hedges, thus permitting three French columns that had left from nearby villages to regroup before the Wattignies plateau. The French, attacking to the martial air of the "*Marseillaise*," threw the numerically superior Austrians into disarray. On 17 October, their line broken, Clairfayt and Coburg retreated toward Mons, thus raising the siege of Maubeuge.

A. Chuquet, *Les guerres de la Révolution*, vol. 4 (Paris, 1890).

R. Legrand

Related entry: JOURDAN.

BATTLE OF ZURICH (25 September-5 October 1799), decisive conflict between the Army of Helvetia, commanded by A. Masséna, and the Austro-Russian army, commanded by A. Suvórov. After the armies of the Second Coalition had driven the French out of Italy and Germany, the Allies planned to invade France through Switzerland and overthrow the French Republic. Russian General I. Rimski-Korsakov, with a force of 27,000 men at Zurich, supported by an Austrian army of 22,000 men under General D. Hötze, posted along the Linth, planned to invade France as soon as Suvórov arrived from Italy with some 30,000 reinforcements. However, Austrian minister F. Thugut, hoping to extend the Hapsburg lands, repositioned an army under Archduke Charles, thereby exposing Suvórov's army during its proposed invasion of France. The French government, recognizing this strategic error, reinforced Masséna with men and supplies for a counteroffensive. On 25 September, Masséna attacked with some 80,000 men. Feinting an attack along the Rhine so that Korsakov would shift and divide his forces, Masséna struck with his main force at Dietikon, driving the Russians behind the city walls. Simultaneously, the Austrian force was attacked by General N. Soult and driven back from the Linth so they could not reinforce the beleaguered Russians. On 26 September the battle was renewed, and Korsakov's army was cut to pieces, evacuating Zurich with the loss of 2,000 dead and 5,000 captured. After Hötze's troops were forced across the Rhine with 5,000 casualties, Masséna turned against Suvórov's army advancing through the Saint Gothard Pass toward Zurich. The Russians were delayed at Devil's Bridge by General C. Lecourbe, while Masséna moved to concentrate his forces in the surrounding mountains. As the French attacked, Suvórov fought his way through Klonthal Pass and along the Linth River to Germany with the loss of his baggage train, guns, and 5,000 men. The Battle of Zurich was a brilliant tactical and strategical victory for Masséna and his subordinates, as well as the Directory government. Not only were the Russians and Austrians defeated, but France was spared from invasion and the Second Coalition began to disintegrate.

E. Gachot, *Les campagnes d'Helvétie (1799)* (Paris, 1904); L. Hennequin, *Zurich, Masséna en Suisse* (Nancy, 1911); J. B. F. Koch, *Mémoires de Masséna rédigés d'après les documents qu'il a laissés*, 7 vols. (Paris, 1848-50); S. Ross, *Quest for Victory, French Military Strategy, 1792–1799* (New York, 1973).

D. D. Horward

Related entries: MASSENA; SECOND COALITION; SURVOROV-RYMNIKSKII.

BATZ, JEAN-PIERRE, BARON DE (1754-1822), royalist conspirator. A military officer and financial speculator before 1789, Batz represented the nobility of Nérac and d'Albret in the Estates General. He is alleged to have drawn up a plan for financing the government debt without the consent of the Estates as part of the plot that led to the dismissal of Necker on 11 July 1789. He served on several minor committees in the National Assembly and participated in the right-wing deputies' protest against its actions when it dissolved in 1791. Batz subsequently emigrated but returned to Paris during Louis XVI's trial and, together with the Spanish ambassador, plotted to bribe Convention deputies to vote for acquittal. When that failed, he planned to rescue the king on his way to the scaffold and later conspired to liberate Marie Antoinette from the Temple prison. He is primarily associated, however, with the complex scandal over the Compagnie des Indes, in which a number of Convention deputies, notably F. Chabot, C. Bazire, J. Delaunay, J. Julien de Tculouse, and P.-F. Fabre d'Eglantine, were also involved. M. Robespierre apparently believed that Batz had master-minded this complex manipulation of the Compagnie des Indes' stock as a way of discrediting the Convention and dividing its members. The deputies involved were arrested, but Batz, apparently protected by friends in the police, escaped. A disparate collection of suspects were tried and executed as participants in the *conspiration de Batz* (17 June 1794), although many of them had little or no connection with him. After Thermidor, Batz took part in the counterrevolutionary movement of 13 Vendémiaire Year IV and was briefly arrested afterward but released without trial. He lived quietly under Napoleon and the Restoration.

A. de Lestapis, *La 'Conspiration de Batz'* (Paris, 1969).

J. Popkin

Related entries: CHABOT; FABRE; JULIEN.

BEAUMARCHAIS, PIERRE-AUGUSTIN CARON DE (1732-99), author, financier. Son of a Parisian watchmaker, Pierre-Augustin Caron first gained wide attention by inventing what became the standard escapement mechanism for watches. This invention and his personal charm gave him entrée to the royal court, where he met the wealthy woman who became his first wife. It was from a small property of hers that he took the name Beaumarchais. Although he frequented literary circles in Paris, he never would enter the *philosophe* group of liberals and reformers. After his wife's death, he became a music teacher and confidant of the royal princesses and protégé of the financier J. Pâris-Duverney. Buying an office that conferred nobility, he also became extremely wealthy from commerce and finance. A sojourn in Spain (1764-66), undertaken for business and family reasons, later would furnish background for his two most famous plays.

In 1770, Beaumarchais lost through death his second wife and the aged Pâris-Duverney. The entanglement of the affairs of the latter and of Beaumarchais and the enmity of Pâris-Duverney's principal heir led to lengthy lawsuits and a skillful published memoir by Beaumarchais enlisting public sympathy for his cause. This memoir and others are considered in quality second only to the Figaro plays among Beaumarchais' writings. Louis XV and XVI each commissioned him (1774) to perform secret missions abroad for the surveillance and destruction of tracts allegedly libelous to royalty.

Le barbier de Séville was performed first at the Comédie française in February 1775. A lively situation comedy, it details the successful machinations of the valet-barber Figaro in arranging the marriage of the count of Almaviva to Rosine, the ward of the elderly Doctor Bartholo. The play sought not to preach but to amuse; its most subversive line was perhaps Figaro's observation that "a great [noble] does us enough good when he does us no harm."

From 1776 until formal French intervention in the American Revolution, Beaumarchais engaged, with royal consent, in a clandestine arms traffic aiding the revolutionaries. Sincerely caught up in the current enthusiasm for the American cause, Beaumarchais eventually lost money in the affair. A public performance of *Le mariage de Figaro*, largely finished in 1778, was delayed by royal disapproval until 1784, when it enjoyed immense success. In this sparkling comedy, character is more subtly developed than in the *Barbier*, as Figaro and his intended bride, Suzanne, together with the countess Rosine, foil the count's lustful designs on Suzanne. Here criticism of the nobility, of miscarriages of justice, and even of the low legal position of women extends much further than anything in the *Barbier*, though never as intrusive polemicism.

In the late 1780s Beaumarchais remarried a second time and presided over the project of editing and publishing F.-M. Voltaire's works. Although seldom politically active in the early Revolutionary period, Beaumarchais did help prepare a petition to the National Assembly that resulted in a decree (13 January 1791) recognizing the rights of authors to their plays. He gained popular enmity, however, by his flamboyantly luxurious new mansion in the working-class district of the faubourg Saint-Antoine. Denounced in the Assembly for allegedly hoarding weapons, he was imprisoned briefly (1792) but was released through the efforts of his mistress. Later that year he went abroad in an unsuccessful attempt to buy muskets in Holland. His position with the government remained unstable, as he was both a suspect and an agent of the Committee of Public Safety. Declared an *émigré* (1794), he went into exile in Germany. In 1796 the Directory authorized his return to France.

Beaumarchais was essentially a man of the Old Regime and used that regime most effectively for his own economic and literary success. He demanded no basic social reforms and indeed defended the nobility as intermediary between king and people, and thus as a guarantee against despotism. In the course of demanding justice for himself, however, he espoused the cause of equal justice for all. Beyond this, his personal views on government seem not to have gone beyond the modern reformism of C. de Montesquieu. Despite occasional protestations of Revolutionary fervor in the 1789–94 period, he was never a true Revolutionary by temperament or philosophy. Nevertheless, his mockery of aristocrats, real or fictional, and his appeals for justice against the established system did make him a symbolic and influential figure in the disintegration of the Old Regime.

P.-A. Caron de Beaumarchais, *Oeuvres complètes*, ed. E. Fournier (Paris, 1876); R. de L. C. Castries, duc de, *Figaro ou la vie de Beaumarchais* (Paris, 1972); G. Lemaitre, *Beaumarchais* (New York, 1949).

H. S. Vyverberg

Related entries: COMMITTEE OF PUBLIC SAFETY; MONTESQUIEU; THEATER.

BEES, ORDER OF. See ILLUMINATI.

BELGIUM, territory formed of possessions and dependencies of the Hapsburg emperor, conquered and annexed by France in 1792 and 1793, retaken by Austria, reconquered in 1794, and incorporated into France from 1795 to Napoleon's fall in 1814. In the eighteenth century the country that forms today's Belgium was divided into two parts. The Austrian Low Countries were a fragment of the former Burgundian state, which had achieved great prosperity at the end of the fifteenth century under Charles the Bold. After this duke's death, the Low Countries passed to the Emperor Charles V and then to the kings of Spain, his successors. In 1714 they were ceded to the head of the Hapsburg house, that is, the German emperor. The second part was the Bishopric of Liège, which since the Middle Ages had formed a dependent principality of the German Empire.

The two regions were divided linguistically. If the Bishopric of Liège was almost entirely French speaking, in the Austrian Low Countries the area north of a line going from Mouscron (near Tourcoing), passing by Brussels, and ending at Visé, on the Meuse, was inhabited by a population speaking Flemish, a German dialect. South of this line the Walloons spoke French. French, however, was also the language of the aristocracy, the bourgeoisie, and the administration; Flemish was spoken only by the peasants and workers, a large proportion of whom were illiterate. Flemings and Walloons were both ardently Catholic, which placed them in opposition to the inhabitants of the northern Low Countries, or the United Provinces, the majority of whom were Protestant.

At the end of the eighteenth century, the Austrian Low Countries and the Bishopric of Liège were won to the Enlightenment. The press there was freer than in France and Masonic lodges were numerous. The American War for Independence (1778–83), and the revolution in the United Provinces that followed immediately (1783–87) had profound repercussions in the Austrian Low Countries and the Bishopric of Liège. People there began to talk about independence and to evoke old urban and provincial institutions, which were viewed as proofs of former independence that had nearly disappeared. The sovereign of the Low Countries, the Emperor Joseph II, saw these archaic institutions as incompatible with the modernization of the country that he felt was indispensable. Joseph wanted to develop industry and commerce in Belgium. The privileges of cities and corporations created obstacles. He therefore decided to suppress the corporations and establish free trade in grain. Discontent among the mass of the population was profound. Religious toleration that the emperor instituted at the same time was insufficient to win over the Voltairean bourgeoisie of the cities, who reproached the sovereign for not according political liberty for Belgium. Eventually the entire population united against Joseph II; nevertheless he remained obstinate in pursuing his reforms. In 1787, ignoring Belgian traditions, he overthrew all judicial and administrative institutions of the country and divided it into new circumscriptions, administered by intendants responsible to the government in Vienna. Opposition grew. Newspapers denounced the violation of Belgium's rights, which Joseph II had bound himself to respect by the charter of the *joyeuse entrée*. Riots broke out. The revolutionaries adopted the Brabantine cockade, black, yellow, and red. The emperor responded forcefully, annulling the *joyeuse entrée* on 7 January 1789. The Austrian Low Countries rose up and expelled Austrian garrisons in the autumn of 1789.

At the same time, in the principality of Liège, the inhabitants revolted against the prince-bishop whom they reproached for governing arbitrarily. The Liégeois patriots, however, did not unite with those of the Low Countries. Furthermore, the latter wasted no time in dividing among themselves. Some, the statists, wanted simply to maintain the old regime. They had as their leader the barrister H. Van der Noot. The others, led by J.-F. Vonck, gained their support from the artisans and peasants, to whom they addressed themselves in Flemish. They had been profoundly influenced by the American Revolution. The declaration of independence of the province of Flanders, which they drew up, bore a striking resemblance to the Declaration of Independence of the United States, and the Act of Union of the Belgian Provinces, which they had voted, reproduced certain passages of the American Articles of Confederation almost word for word.

But the statists refused to cooperate in more liberal reforms. Joseph II had died in February 1790, and his brother and successor, Leopold II, appeared more accommodating. The statists negotiated with him and let Austrian troops reoccupy the Low Countries, while German contingents restored the prince-bishop of Liège to power. The most ardent of the Belgian and Liégeois patriots, the Vonckists, crossed the southern frontier and joined, in Revolutionary France, those Dutch patriots who had been refugees there since 1787. Henceforth they put all their hopes in a war that would allow the French Revolutionaries to move into Belgium and help them establish a liberal and independent state there.

In April 1792 war broke out between Austria and Prussia, on one side, and France, on the other. At first the Austrians and Prussians enjoyed some successes. But after the battles of Valmy (20 September 1792) and Jemappes (6 November), French troops entered Belgium and occupied the Austrian Low Countries, as well as the Bishopric of Liège. Their general, C. Dumouriez, at the insistence of Belgian patriots who followed the army, intended to make Belgium an independent state. At Paris, however, the government and the National Convention wanted to profit from the victories to give France its natural frontiers—the Rhine, the Alps, and the Pyrenees—thus requiring the annexation of Belgium to France. The French government ordered that the population be consulted about its desires. But there was no general referendum, only local plebiscites, under pressure from French troops. These favored annexation, and from 1 to 30 March 1793 fifteen decrees annexed Belgium to France, bit by bit. Meanwhile the Austrians had retaken the offensive, had beaten Dumouriez' troops at Neerwinden (18 March 1793), and reoccupied all of Belgium. He would defect to the Austrians shortly thereafter. Fifteen months later, the French armies attacked anew, won a victory over the Austrians at Fleurus (26 June 1794), and reestablished themselves in Belgium.

The Committee of Public Safety, which henceforth directed the policy of France, did not favor the independence of Belgium. It wanted to annex it but was divided over the extent of the territories to be united with France. L. Carnot believed it was necessary to give France secure and easily defended frontiers; he therefore proposed to annex only southern Belgium, where the population spoke French, with the two fortresses of Anvers and Namur defending the crossings of the Scheldt, the Sambre, and the Meuse. On the other hand, under the influence of the deputy L.-F.-R. Portiez de l'Oise and of the commercial bourgeoisie, the majority of the committee declared itself in favor of annexing all of Belgium. Furthermore, commissioners of the Republic were already traversing Belgium and introducing French laws and (paper) money there. Finally, some days before adjourning, on 1 October 1795, the Convention voted the annexation to France of all Belgium, including, beyond that, some territories (Dutch Flanders, Maestricht, and Venloo) that the United Provinces had ceded to France by the Treaty of the Hague on 16 May 1795.

This enlarged Belgium was divided into nine departments. The deputies E. Pérès-Lagesse and Portiez de l'Oise, and later the Commissioner L.-G. Bouteville-Dumetz, were charged with introducing all French laws and institutions in Belgium. Without doubt, the Belgians would have preferred independence to annexation, but the patriots realized that they were neither strong enough nor numerous enough to defend Belgian independence and that French support was indispensable. In addition, by becoming an integral part of French territory, Belgium was exempted from the war contributions and requisitions that had weighed heavily on it since Fleurus, when French occupation forces treated it as a conquered country. Also, the annexation to France did not at first provoke significant opposition and was even felt as a relief. The language question did not arise. The governing classes spoke French, and among the popular classes, who used Flemish, those who knew how to read and write were few. In the departments where the Dutch language was dominant, laws, decrees, and regulations were published in both languages, but French was made obligatory in official acts. In fact, it was not the language problem that provoked opposition but rather religious policy and the obligation to military service.

During the elections of the Year V (1797), the first in which Belgians participated, those dissatisfied with the antireligious policy of the Directory voted for conservatives. At Paris, the republicans correctly attributed this vote to the influence of priests. They demanded from the latter oaths of submission and obedience to the laws of the Republic and then of hatred to royalty and anarchy. More than 800 Belgian priests and religious figures who refused the oath were arrested, with 350 of them being interned on the islands of Ré and Oléron. Discontent became general and openly manifested itself when the Directory decided in 1798 that the law on obligatory and universal conscription would apply to Belgium. Young peasants, especially from the regions of Gand and Anvers, revolted in October (as the Vendéans had done in France in 1793). The urban conscripts did not support them. The National Guard and the regular troops pursued the insurgents. Nevertheless the insurrection spread to Luxembourg and did not subside until December 1798. The repression was severe; at Malines forty-one insurgents were shot by firing squads. The Directory ordered the mass deportation of all the Belgian clergy (over 9,000 priests), but most escaped arrest.

The Consulate produced appeasement. The Concordat concluded between France and Pope Pius VII allowed the return of the priests and the normal resumption of Catholic worship. The Belgian economy developed. Belgian industries, particularly metallurgy and textiles, profited more from the annexation to France than did French industries. Indeed, the more advanced Belgian industries could produce at low cost a greater quantity of merchandise that was exported to France and competed with French products. Thus, Belgium was one of the most prosperous regions of the French Empire, and until 1811 this prosperity made people forget conscription and the mortality due to war, which was the same there as in the departments of old France (2.23 percent of the population). But beginning in 1812, the number of men refusing to report for induction increased, all the more so as the clergy, upset by the religious policy of Napoleon (who was keeping the pope prisoner at Savona), preached insubordination and desertion. Thus, in 1814 most Belgians applauded the fall of Napoleon and warmly welcomed the Allied troops. They quickly became disappointed with them as requisitions, plundering, and violence recalled the French occupation of 1793. The Belgians also wanted independence, but in the treaties of Vienna they were united nevertheless with the Kingdom of the Low Countries, a union that lasted only fifteen years. The independence of Belgium was, in fact, gained in 1830, and then it had to be protected by neutrality guaranteed by the great European powers. The invasions of 1914 and 1940 showed how illusory this guarantee was. Meanwhile, the opposition between Flemings and Walloons in Belgium continued to grow. Belgium, born of the Revolution, has not always enjoyed stability.

J. Cathelin, *La vie quotidienne en Belgique sous le régime français* (Paris, 1967); R. Darquenne, *Histoire économique du département de Jemappes* (Mons, 1965); R. Devleeshouwer, *L'Arrondissement du Brabant sous l'occupation française, 1794–1795* (Bruxelles, 1964); J. Godechot, *La grande nation* (Paris, 1956); P. Harsin, *La révolution liègeoise en 1789* (Bruxelles, 1954); S. Tassier, *Les démocrates belges de 1789* (Bruxelles, 1930): Y. Vanden Berghe, *Jacobijnen en Traditionalisten, De reacties van de Bruggelingen in de Revolutietijd, 1780-1794* (Bruxelles, 1972).

J. Godechot

Related entries: BATTLE OF FLEURUS; BATTLE OF JEMAPPES; BATTLE OF NEERWINDEN; DUMOURIEZ; ENLIGHTENMENT; JOSEPH II; JOURDAN LAW; VALMY; VONCK.

BERNADOTTE, JEAN-BAPTISTE-JULES (1763-1844), marshal of France, king of Sweden and Norway. The son of a lawyer of Pau, young Bernadotte left his position as a junior clerk and joined the Royal Marines when his father died in 1780. Serving in various locations in Corsica and Dauphiné, he rose to the rank of sergeant major by 1788. He supported the Revolution and during his wartime service along the Rhine began to rise rapidly in rank—second lieutenant April 1792, captain July 1793, lieutenant colonel August 1793, colonel April

1794, major general October 1794. These promotions rewarded his courage, discipline, and prudence and gave evidence to the popularity he enjoyed among his men and fellow officers. He was a protégé of General J.-B. Kléber.

In January 1797 the Directory sent Bernadotte with 20,000 men to Italy to reinforce N. Bonaparte. Bernadotte admired Bonaparte's knowledge and skill but believed he did not receive from him the consideration that he deserved. Bernadotte accepted appointment as ambassador to Vienna in January 1798, curious to test himself in diplomacy. He soon grew to dislike this position, asked to be relieved, and then caused an incident by raising the French tricolor outside his embassy (a very rare practice in this period). The ensuing riot led Bernadotte to leave Vienna in April 1798. Back in Paris, he married D. Clary, sister of J. Bonaparte's wife.

After some commands on the German frontier, Bernadotte was named minister of war by the Directory in July 1799. His efficient action in this capacity helped stem the advances of the Second Coalition, but E.-J. Sieyès and two other directors dismissed him in September 1799. Bernadotte refused to support Bonaparte's coup of 18 Brumaire, being concerned about the threat to republican institutions and the personal risk involved, but he did not oppose it either, because many of his friends and his new wife were in Bonaparte's camp. This episode demonstrates his frequent indecision in moments of major crisis.

Bernadotte soon received important posts under the First Consul—councillor of state and commander of the Army of the West—and from the emperor—marshal, prince and duke of Ponte Corvo, and various army commands. In August 1810, the Swedish Diet elected Bernadotte crown prince of Sweden, a decision reluctantly approved by Napoleon. Bernadotte actually directed Swedish policy and decided in 1812 that the better choice was to support Russia rather than France. He led a Swedish army against the French in northern Germany in 1813 and then forced Denmark to yield Norway to Sweden. Bernadotte toyed with the idea of succeeding Napoleon as head of French affairs, but the Norwegian complication and his lack of boldness put this prize beyond his grasp. He became King Charles John XIV of Sweden and Norway in 1818 on the death of Charles XIII. He died in 1844 after an increasingly conservative reign.

D. P. Barton, *Bernadotte*, 3 vols. (London, 1914–25); G. Girod de L'Ain, *Bernadotte* (Paris, 1968); T. T. Hojer, *Bernadotte, Maréchal de France* (Paris, 1943).

J. M. Laux

Related entries: KLEBER; SECOND COALITION; SIEYES.

BERNIS, FRANCOIS-JOACHIM DE PIERRE DE (1715–94), cardinal, ambassador. Born into an ancient noble family of Languedoc, Bernis, as a younger son, was destined for the church. He attended the Parisian collège of Louis-le-Grand but subsequently made a name for himself as a society poet in the salons of the capital and was elected to the French Academy in 1744. Befriended by Madame de Pompadour, he began his diplomatic career in 1752 as ambassador to Venice. He negotiated the Austrian alliance of 1756 and served as secretary of state for foreign affairs in 1757-58. Named a cardinal in 1758, Bernis was appointed archbishop of Albi in 1764 and ambassador to Rome in 1769. In the latter capacity he played an important role in the conclaves that elected Popes Clement XIV and Pius VI and in the suppression of the Jesuits (1773).

As a proponent of divine right monarchy, the hierarchy of estates, and ecclesiastical privileges, Bernis opposed the Revolution from the beginning. Having declined to preside over the clergy in the Estates General, the cardinal remained in Rome, where he had the difficult task of dissuading the pope from breaking openly with the National Assembly over the suppression of annates, tithes, and religious orders, the promulgation of the Civil Constitution of the Clergy, the sale of church property, and the annexation of Avignon. His protests against these measures were ignored in Paris. Since Bernis added a qualifying clause concerning his religious obligations in subscribing to the constitutional oath required by the decree of 17 November 1790, he was relieved of his ambassadorship as well as his archbishopric in March 1791. A year later his name was inscribed in the list of *émigrés*, and the family estate of Saint-Marcel was pillaged. Bernis welcomed French expatriates to Rome, most notably the aunts of Louis XVI, but he refrained from active involvement in the *émigré* cause, and his influence at the papal court was eclipsed in the last years of his life by that of the more belligerent Cardinal Maury. He died on 3 November 1794 and was buried in the French church of Saint-Louis, where he had staged a memorial service for Louis XVI a year earlier.

F. Masson, *Le cardinal de Bernis depuis son ministère 1758–1794; la suppression des jésuites, le schisme constitutionnel* (Paris, 1884); A. Mathiez, *Rome et le clergé français sous la Constituante: la constitution civile du clergé, l'affaire d'Avignon* (Paris, 1911); J. Sudreau, *Un cardinal diplomate: François-Joachim de Pierre de Bernis* (Paris, 1969).

J. W. Merrick

Related entry: CIVIL CONSTITUTION OF THE CLERGY.

BERTHOLLET, CLAUDE-LOUIS (1748–1822), chemist, discoverer of the bleaching properties of chlorine. See SCIENCE.

BERTIER DE SAUVIGNY, LOUIS-BENIGNE-FRANCOIS (1737–89), intendant. Officially *adjoint* to his father, Louis-Jean, intendant of Paris, in 1768, "François" assumed his full duties in 1771 and took the title in 1776. Active in royal councils, he also supervised a royal network of beggars' prisons, the *dépôts de mendicité*, from 1767 to 1787. He reformed the *taille* of the *généralité* of Paris according to a new land survey. Opposed to A.-R.-J. Turgot's policies on the grain trade, he won the favor of Louis XVI by swiftly repressing the *guerre des farines* in 1775. Two years later, he was named *surintendant de la maison de la Reine*. In July 1789, posters in the Palais Royal denounced Bertier as a famine-monger. Responsible for provisioning royal troops around Paris, Bertier had papers relating to grain supplies in his portfolio when he was arrested by authorities at Compiègne. He was sent, on 22 July, with an escort to answer to the electors of the city of Paris. Taunts, signs, and threats greeted him. The head of his father-in-law, J.-F. Foulon, was held up to him on a pike. Dissatisfied with the electors' intention of keeping Bertier at the Abbaye pending trial, members of the crowd slaughtered him before the Hôtel de Ville.

T. M. Adams, "A Reconsideration of Bertier de Sauvigny, Last Intendant of Paris," *Proc. of the WSFH* (1977); G. de Bertier de Sauvigny, *Le comte Ferdinand de Bertier et l'énigme de la congrégation* (Paris, 1948); H. Dinet, "La grande peur en Hurepoix," *Mémoires de la Fédération des Sociétés historiques et archéologiques de Paris et de l'Ile-de-France*, vols. 18–19 (1970) and sequel vols. 23–24 (1972).

T. M. Adams

Related entry: BASTILLE.

BERTRAND DE MOLLEVILLE, ANTOINE-FRANCOIS, MARQUIS DE
(1744-1818), royalist, historian. After legal studies in his native city of Toulouse, Molleville became intendant in Brittany in 1784, where he aroused some animosity for having participated in the dissolution of the parlement at Rennes. In October 1791 he was named minister of the navy at a time when ministers found it difficult to govern under the new constitutional monarchy. Louis XVI had offered him the post because of his reputation as an efficient administrator and supporter of the monarchy. Bertrand de Molleville turned down the offer at first, fearing to compromise the monarch in a ministry composed of men with attitudes he opposed. Reassured by a personal note from the king, he accepted.

He is said to have quarreled with L. de Narbonne-Lara, which was one of the causes of the latter's resignation in March 1792. He had several disputes with the Assembly's Committee on the Navy and encountered sharp opposition from the Brest deputies, who remembered his actions in Brittany. One of the disagreements was over the number of officers who had left the navy because of threats, mutiny, and physical attacks. Bertrand de Molleville could not stop the emigration of officers; under the circumstances, he was somewhat sympathetic to their situation. Although the king supported him, it was obvious that his presence in the ministry was embarrassing to the monarch, and he resigned in March 1792. G. Morris, in *A Diary of the French Revolution*, mentions meeting Bertrand de Molleville frequently during this period.

The former minister continued serving Louis by operating a kind of secret service that maintained surveillance over the extreme Jacobin leaders. According to P. Gaxotte, Bertrand de Molleville had persuaded Louis that the political activity of the Revolutionary leaders could be checked by bribery and was put in charge of large sums to be distributed for this purpose. Among those apparently involved in such bribery were P.-F. Fabre d'Eglantine, A.-J. Santerre, E.-J. Sieyès, and P.-V. Vergniaud.

On the night of 9 August, he advised Louis to stand firm, and after the fateful tenth of August, he engaged in plans for the flight of the king. When these came to naught, Bertrand de Molleville was hidden in a garret on rue Aubry-le-Boucher in Paris by a surgeon, a long-time friend. He escaped from Paris and reached England in October. While exiled there, he wrote several political and historical works, including his *Annals of the French Revolution*, published in English before it appeared in French. It was long regarded as a primary source on Revolutionary events, even though it favored the monarchy, and was used by many first-generation historians. Also in England he had exchanges with C. J. Fox, claiming Fox had misquoted him in Parliament, and with J. Mallet du Pan over aspects of certain activities of Louis XVI. Bertrand de Molleville returned to France in 1814 and found little favor with the Restoration, being accused of siding with critics of Louis XVIII. He died in Paris in 1818.

H. Ben-Israel, *English Historians on the French Revolution* (Cambridge, 1968).

R. L. Carol

Related entries: AUSTRIAN COMMITTEE; FABRE; FOX; GAXOTTE; MALLET DU PAN; MONTMORIN DE SAINT-HEREM; NARBONNE-LARA; SANTERRE.

BESENVAL, PIERRE-VICTOR, BARON DE (1722–91), lieutenant general who commanded troops in Paris in the summer of 1789. Born in Switzerland, Besenval entered French service in the Swiss Guard as a boy. For almost sixty years he served the king with more bravery than talent or good judgment. He frequented court circles and reputedly exercised political influence over Marie Antoinette. He was assigned to protect grain convoys to Paris in 1788–89 and to maintain law and order in the capital in April 1789. Having failed, he fled in panic after the fall of the Bastille but was arrested en route to Switzerland. The Paris municipal authorities charged him with conspiracy and *lèse-nation* for his role in the events of July. In the face of enraged public opinion, the Châtelet acquitted Besenval in January 1790. He lived undisturbed in retirement until his death on 2 June 1791.

A.N., BB[30] 82 and BB[30] 161; P. V. Besenval, *Mémoires du Baron de Besenval*, 2 vols. (Paris, 1821).

M. D. Sibalis

Related entry: BASTILLE.

BICETRE. See PRISONS.

BIENS NATIONAUX, properties confiscated from the crown, the church, *émigrés*, and suspects, and, in most cases, subsequently offered for sale by the nation. The sale of *biens nationaux* is an issue of immense interest and value for historians of the French Revolution. It is also a complicated issue to research and evaluate, and, despite its importance, there are few studies that satisfactorily encompass and address it. For the social historian, the *biens nationaux* provide a litmus of the social nature of the Revolution. If the economic basis of rural power changed during the Revolutionary period, the confiscation and sale of *biens nationaux* will be in large measure the key to this change.

The *biens nationaux* are also of interest for what they illustrate of the process of revolution. From the history of the sales, one can learn of the levels and stages in which the Revolution was administered, of the depth to which it penetrated, and of the enthusiasm, indifference, or hostility that it generated or with which it was embraced. Chronology is a crucial and complicating element in the study of *biens nationaux*, for decisions were not enacted uniformly, and there were several simultaneous and overlapping chronologies of sales and payments. The *biens nationaux* can also serve as a measure not so much of attachment as of alienation or disaffection from the main ideological currents of the Revolution.

The legislative history of the *biens nationaux* is elaborately detailed, particularly in its later stages, but it may be traced in three major periods or modes of sale. The *biens nationaux* came into existence by legislative decree in November and December 1789 when the Constituent Assembly declared the property of the church at the disposition of the nation. This confiscation was a fiscal expedient, designed to restore state finances. On 19 December the Assembly announced the emission of 400 million *livres* in *assignats*, based on the sale of church and crown properties. In June and July 1790, all *biens nationaux* except forests and certain royal residences were offered for sale.

The Law of 14–17 May 1790 established the mode of sale for these nationalized church and crown properties, known as *biens nationaux* of first origin. Ecclesiastical property had been placed under the administration of the departments and districts in April 1790, and municipalities could request authority to sell properties within their territory. Properties were to be sold by bid, and if individual bids collectively matched the bid on the whole unit, the property would go to the greatest number of bidders. This system of bidding theoretically favored the small bidder but in practice favored the rich. In some cases peasants associated in bidding for a unit of property and then divided it after adjudication. Revolutionary authorities disapproved of this sort of concurrence and formally prohibited it in April 1793. In some other cases, peasants interpreted the transfer to the municipality of administrative authority over *biens nationaux* as giving them rights over the land and discretion concerning the way the land would be sold and to whom. The payment schedule set forth in the May 1790 law stipulated an initial payment of from 12 to 30 percent, depending on the type of property, with the rest of the bid to be paid in twelve annual payments at 5 percent interest. Purchasers were required to honor current leases on the properties they acquired, which limited the attractiveness of certain properties for peasant purchasers.

Social concerns never outweighed the fiscal motivations in the sale of *biens nationaux* of first origin. The confiscation of the property—and the successions—of *émigrés*, the deported, and the condemned, which began in early 1792, created a new class of *biens nationaux*—of second origin. The Law of 3 June–25 July 1793 declared new motives and a new mode of sale for these properties. The salient difference from the 1790 regime was that the properties were to be as divided as possible (by the decree of 14 August into units of between two and four hectares). Bidding would be done at one time and lot by lot, and payment was due in ten annual terms beginning with the month of sale. Any citizen could request the division and sale of sequestered property. In addition, the law specified that communes lacking common lands ought to reserve a sufficient portion of the sequestered property within their territory to be able to lease an arpent of land to each landless household; the provision was soon (13 September) changed to include only the landless poor, who were enabled to purchase land in twenty annual payments without interest. There were very few cases where either provision was applied. In November and December 1793 (2 Frimaire and 4 Nivôse Year II), the mode of sale created by the Law of 3 June was extended to all *biens nationaux*.

The sale of *émigré* property was inspired by political and social motives. From the social perspective, the 1793 legislation must be viewed in conjunction with the laws of the same period calling for the division of *biens communaux*. Through these legislative programs, the Convention proposed the broadest possible distribution of property as the formula for revitalizing the nation. The sale of *émigré* lands was also a weapon for fixing allegiance to the Revolution and guaranteeing its survival; it would strengthen its popular base of support and weaken at once the internal and external position of its enemies. J. Michelet's dictum that "Jacobins became purchasers, and purchasers, Jacobins" has its heuristic value; yet expropriations viewed as unjust could alienate rather than convert.

The third mode of sale marks an abrupt departure from earlier dispositions and goals. Beginning in late May and June 1795 (10–15 Prairial Year III), the state's aim in the sale of *biens nationaux* seems to have been to liquidate the *biens nationaux* and salvage its finances by obtaining quick sale and quick payment. The laws of Prairial abolished the system of bidding and allowed one to purchase *biens nationaux* simply by offering to pay the estimated price in *assignats* taken at face value with no account for inflation or for monetary depreciation. Subsequent legislation reestablished at least in part the system of bidding and at last required adjustment for the *assignat*'s depreciation. In March 1796 (28 Ventôse Year IV), the Directory, having abandoned the *assignat*, issued *mandats territoriaux*, which could be exchanged for their value in *biens nationaux*. Sales were henceforth transacted at the departmental level, and the payment schedule was accelerated so that full payment was due within three months. In November 1796 (16 Brumaire Year V), bidding and estimation according to the system of 1790 was reestablished. One-half payment was due in the first six months and the rest within four years; subsequent and frequent modifications adjusted exchange rates for payments. The volume of sales and speculation increased greatly under this legislative regime, but the profit the state drew from these sales was wholly inadequate to the real value of property sold. Sales continued under the Consulate and Empire but on a greatly reduced scale. The state paid closer attention to its own interest in the sale and attempted to recoup its losses by pursuing those persons who had defaulted or were delinquent in their payments.

The sale of *biens nationaux* halted with the Restoration. The Concordat guaranteed the Revolutionary confiscation and sale of church property, and the law of 5–6 December 1814 maintained all other previous sales of *biens nationaux*, though unsold property or payments still owing from sales would be returned to the original owners. On 27 April 1825, the law known as the Indemnity of the Milliard provided for the final dismantling and guarantee of the *biens nationaux* by establishing a fund to indemnify in slight measure those persons and their families and heirs whose property was confiscated under the laws concerning the *émigrés*.

The legislative history of the *biens nationaux* presents but the ideal framework of the sales. One must recast the molds to assess the fiscal, social, political, and ideological significance of the sales. The sales were not a fiscal windfall for the nation, yet they kept the Revolutionary government solvent. A fiscal accounting of the *biens nationaux* must deal in multiple chronologies and study bids in comparison not only to the estimated value of a property (and the strength of that estimation) but also to the price actually paid. Owing to inflation, it was the period during which payment was made much more than the period of sale that determined the costs and profits of sale to state and citizen. For the first sales, adjudications often exceeded the estimations, and to pay the price within these first few years was to pay a price bearing some relation to the estimated value of the property. For later sales, adjudications were often less competitive. Estimates and payments for all sales were made with no account (until very late) for monetary depreciation.

Judgment of the social consequences of the sale of *biens nationaux* focuses on the victory claims of peasant or bourgeois. By blunt assessment, the *biens nationaux* were the Revolution's bounty to the bourgeoisie, who had the wealth and at times the ambition to outbid the peasantry. But several factors shade this view. *Biens nationaux* included urban as well as rural property; the location, extent, type, and quality of property available affected the competition for it. Estimates of the peasants' success make little sense on a global basis, though many studies indicate that the sales were often a peasant victory. In some areas there were few or no *biens nationaux*. Similarly, châteaux were of little interest to the peasantry, whereas curés' plots could be highly contested. Competition with urban investors or more wealthy rural inhabitants often precluded the mass of the peasantry from obtaining much land. The example of the Sarthe suggests that peasant success was greatest in areas where the quality of the land was so poor as to discourage bourgeois investment. Peasants did at times succeed, however, in controlling sales, *à main-forte* or by *mauvais gré* if necessary, or in associating for collective price-fixing or purchases. In general, the peasants who benefited from the sales were those who already possessed material standing in the rural community. Finally, from the peasant's perspective, the division of landholding units that followed many of the sales could be more important than his own accession to landownership, for it meant greater opportunity of leasing small units of land.

Political and ideological considerations also affected the sales of *biens na-*

tionaux. War and invasion made all property but especially the *biens nationaux* insecure, and sales were delayed and purchases inhibited in border areas such as the Nord. That the state might nationalize church property as needed raised few objections, though the church was at times successful in threatening purchasers with anathema. The case of Alsace suggests that ideological objections did not always result in total (and resentful) abstention from purchases. In some Catholic regions, particularly heavy purchases suggest an effort to keep coveted church lands out of Protestant hands. The confiscation of *émigré* lands seemed less secure and often less justified, and sales fluctuated with the fortunes and distance of war. In general terms, personal interest dictated the purchase of *biens nationaux*. Politics became an issue when personal interest or investment was blocked or threatened.

Peasant participation in the sales tended to be heaviest in the early years of the Revolution. Yet *biens nationaux* were often more popular when purchased from a second party. Resales should not be viewed strictly from the point of speculation. The intermediate transaction in some cases produced an ideological cleansing of the purchase. It also tended to divide property, making it more accessible to the poorer peasantry. Particularly in the later period, when sales were conducted on the departmental level, brokers could serve an important function in reoffering the sales on a local level. The social consequences of the sale of *biens nationaux* can be realized only through an examination of resales that ventures well into the nineteenth century.

P. Bois, *Paysans de l'Ouest: Des structures économiques et sociales aux options politiques depuis l'époque révolutionnaire dans la Sarthe; (Le Mans, 1960);* M. Bouliseau, *Etude de l'émigration et de la vente des biens des émigrés (1792-1830); Instruction, sources, bibliographie, législation, tableaux* (Paris, 1963); P. Caron and E. Desprez, eds., *Recueil des textes législatifs et administratifs concernant les biens nationaux*, 3 vols. (Paris, 1926-1944); G. Lefebvre, "La Vente des biens nationaux," *Etudes sur la Révolution française* (Paris, 1954) (article first published 1928); M. Marion, *La Vente des biens nationaux pendant la révolution avec étude spéciale des ventes dans les départements de la Gironde et du Cher* (Paris, 1908); R. Marx, *La Révolution et les classes sociales en Basse-Alsace: Structures agraires et vente des biens nationaux* (Paris, 1974).

M. A. Quinn

Related entries: ASSIGNATS; NATIONAL CONSTITUENT ASSEMBLY; PEASANTRY.

BILLAUD-VARENNE, JACQUES-NICOLAS (1762-1819), radical political leader and member of the Committee of Public Safety. Born Jacques-Nicolas Billaud at La Rochelle in 1762, the son of an attorney to the presidial court, he studied law at Poitiers after schooling at the collège of Harcourt in Paris and became an attorney in 1778. On returning to La Rochelle, he produced an unsuccessful comedy, *La femme comme il n'y en a plus*, taught at the Oratorian school of Juilly, and was dismissed for trying to present his opera, *Morgan*. In 1785 he was admitted to the bar in Paris; the following year he married A.

Doyen, the illegitimate daughter of a farmer-general, and added the name *Varenne* to his own.

A partisan of the new ideas from 1787 on, he kept company with G.-J. Danton and wrote, anonymously, several works, including *The Despotism of the Ministers of France Combatted by the Rights of the Nation* (Amsterdam, 1789), which was seized by the police. He joined the Jacobin club very early and from 1790 figured among the most ardent patriot orators. After the king's flight, he proposed, in vain, an examination of the advantages of republican government. More welcome at the Cordeliers Club, he published the essence of his ideas in *Acephocracy, or Federative Government*, which led to proceedings against him and forced him into hiding for some time. Subsequently he published *The Elements of Republicanism*. He became secretary and later vice-president of the Jacobin club. He was named a member of the Insurrectionary Commune of 10 August (1792) and became the substitute for its *procureur*, P.-L. Manuel.

Elected deputy for Paris to the Convention on 7 September, he voted for the death of the king without delay. He sat with the Mountain and took an active part in the struggle against the Girondins. He was sent to the Breton coast by the Convention and with his colleague, J. Sevestre, contributed to the pacification of that region. Returning to Paris, on 2 June 1793 he called for a decree of indictment against twenty-nine Girondin deputies. On 1 August he was charged with a new mission to the department of the Nord and proceeded to arrest numerous suspects. Elected president of the Convention on 5 September, he improved the efficiency of the Revolutionary Tribunal and supported the death sentence for Marie Antoinette, the former queen. The following day, 6 September, along with J.-M. Collot d'Herbois, he joined the Committee of Public Safety, where both were especially responsible for correspondence with the representatives on mission, with the established authorities, and with the popular societies. This immense but obscure task (for which French archives still preserve the evidence) suited the authoritarian temperament, rigorous principles, and methodical spirit of Billaud. In the collective work of the committee, these efforts assured the unity of action and centralization required by the Revolutionary government and the Terror. On 25 Pluviôse Year II (17 February 1794) he went to Saint-Mâlo to supervise an expedition being prepared against the island of Jersey.

During Year II he presented numerous reports on domestic conditions to the Convention, in the name of his colleagues, and frequently spoke from the rostrum of the Jacobins where he supported the social aspirations of the *sans-culottes*. He contributed to the indictments against P. Egalité (the former duc d'Orléans), G.-J. Danton, the Hébertists, and subsequently M. Robespierre, whom he had supported until the end of Prairial but whom he violently attacked in Thermidor for his intransigence and for the actions he took without the committee's concurrence.

He retired from the committee on 15 Fructidor Year II (1 September 1794) but courageously continued to show his solidarity with his terrorist colleagues;

he disdainfully denied the calumnies against them and published his own justification in *Response of Billaud to Personal Charges against Him*. He was denounced before the Convention on several occasions by the deputy L. Lecointre; and the Convention ordered his arrest on 12 Ventôse Year III (2 March 1795), along with that of other former members of the Committees of Public Safety and General Security. Condemned to deportation with B. Barère and Collot d'Herbois, he embarked for Guyana with the latter on 7 Prairial Year III (26 May 1795). He was imprisoned at Cayenne together with convicts and later, despite his precarious health, banished to Sinnamary where he lived in almost total isolation. His suspicious personality led him to refuse the amnesty offered by N. Bonaparte after the coup of 18 Brumaire. At Cayenne he acquired the little estate of Darvilliers, which he worked himself. His wife, whom he loved deeply, had promised to share exile with him, but she remained in France, obtained a divorce, and married an Englishman named Johnson. In 1816 he sold his land and went first to New York and then to Santo Domingo; there he was welcomed by President Sabès (called Petion), the founder of the Republic of Haiti, whose secretary he became and who accorded him a pension. He died on 13 June 1819 at Port-au-Prince.

A. Begis, ed., *Mémoires inédits et correspondance accompagnés de notes biographiques sur Billaud-Varenne et Collot d'Herbois* (Paris, 1893); J. Guilaine, *Billaud-Varenne, l'ascète de la Révolution, 1756–1819* (Paris, 1969).

M. Bouloiseau

Related entries: COMMITTEE OF PUBLIC SAFETY; REPRESENTATIVES ON MISSION; REVOLUTIONARY TRIBUNAL; TERROR, THE.

BIRON, ARMAND-LOUIS DE GONTAUT, DUC DE (1747-94), general. Biron was born to an influential and wealthy family: His father, a general, was the marquis de Montferrant and duc de Gontaut; his father's older brother was the duc de Biron, a marshal of France; and his mother's sister was the wife of the duc de Choiseul. Until 1788 Biron was known as the duc de Lauzun. As a young man, he was most renowned for his loves and dissipations. In 1776 he sold his estates in exchange for a yearly rent of 80,000 *livres*, but the buyer went bankrupt in a few years, and Biron was left penniless. An essay he wrote on the military state of England and its empire caught the eye of the government, and in 1778 he was placed in charge of an expedition to the West African coast, where he seized the fort at Cape Blanc. On his return to France, he sailed with J.-B. Rochambeau to America in 1780. Returning to France in 1783, he commanded the Lauzun Hussars and rose to the rank of *maréchal de camp* (major general).

Biron's checkered past and brash manners made him unpopular at court; in fact, the queen refused to deal with him, and he drifted into the party surrounding the duc d'Orléans. In 1789, Biron was elected a representative of the nobility to the Estates General, where he sat as a liberal noble. Immediately after the flight of the king in June 1791, Biron was appointed once again to serve with

Rochambeau along the French northern frontier. In the company of C.-M. Talleyrand, he went on a diplomatic mission to England late in 1791. There he was arrested for debt. With his release, Biron returned to the *Armée du nord* where he was permitted a fairly independent command under Rochambeau. In 1792, he urged C.-F. Dumouriez, then minister of war, to pursue an aggressive strategy, and on 28 April Biron led his own troops in an advance on Mons. However, on 30 April his men panicked before Mons and fled back to Valenciennes. On Rochambeau's resignation, Biron was offered command of the *Nord*, but he declined. In June 1791, much of the *Nord* was transferred to the *Armée du Rhin*. Biron was among those who went, and on 21 July he was promoted to command of the *Rhin*. His most notable action as commander was to send A.-P. Custine on a raid to Speyer. Custine performed so well that he replaced Biron as chief of the *Armée du Rhin* on 7 November.

Biron soon found himself commander of still another army when he was given the *Armée d'Italie* on 16 December. There, as before, he complained of the inadequacies and inefficiencies of the army administration then in the hands of the minister of war and the representatives on mission. His complaints only grew when he was once more transferred, this time to the *Armée des Côtes de La Rochelle*, organized to fight in the Vendée. He was raised to this command in April 1793 but did not arrive until 28 May. His forces retook Saumur, but nonetheless his days were numbered. He continued to quarrel with agents of the central government. Representatives on mission claimed a lack of vigor in persecuting royalists, and shifts in the Committee of Public Safety led to his recall in midsummer. On 11 July 1793 he was arrested. Biron stood before the Revolutionary Tribunal on 31 December and went to the scaffold the following day.

It was more Biron's connections and his birth that doomed him than any real failure. He suffered from his Orleanist ties and his Girondist associations. At a time when all aristocrats were under suspicion, Biron was bound to suffer. He was not just a noble; he was a *ci-devant* duke. The man who replaced him in command, J.-A. Rossignol, was not a man of great skill, but he was a *sans-culotte*.

A. L. Biron, *Memoirs of the Duc de Lauzun* (New York, 1928); R. W. Phipps, *The Armies of the First French Republic and the Rise of the Marshals of Napoleon the First*, 5 vols. (London, 1926-39).

J. A. Lynn

Related entries: CUSTINE, DUMOURIEZ; ROCHAMBEAU.

BOISSY D'ANGLAS, FRANCOIS-ANTOINE, COMTE DE (1756-1826), deputy to the National Assembly, National Convention, and Council of Five Hundred. Son of a Protestant doctor from Grimaudier (Ardèche), Boissy d'Anglas studied law and joined the Paris bar before the Revolution. He purchased the office of *maître d'hotel* to Monsieur, the future Louis XVIII, and belonged to several literary academies. Despite this successful social ascent, he supported the Revolution and represented the Third Estate of Annonay in the Estates

General. In the National Assembly, he defended the storming of the Bastille and the *journées* of 5–6 October 1789 but was not prominent in major debates. He denounced counterrevolutionary movements in his native region but defended the monarchical constitution of 1791 against republican critics. When the National Assembly dissolved, he was elected *procureur-général-syndic* of his native Ardèche department.

Returned to Paris as a Convention deputy in September 1792, he went on mission to Lyon to calm bread riots there. In the crucial months from December 1792 to June 1793, he voted with the Gironde, opposing the execution of the king and favoring the impeachment of J.-P. Marat, but his friend H. Voulland, a member of the Committee of General Security, protected him from arrest after 31 May 1793. Boissy sat with the relatively silent deputies of the Plain during the Jacobin dictatorship, flattering M. Robespierre in at least one speech. He was nonetheless influential and was one of the key moderate deputies with whom the Thermidorian plotters bargained to win the Plain's support.

After Thermidor, Boissy d'Anglas emerged as a leading spokesman for the coalition of moderates and former Montagnards who controlled the Convention. He delivered major reports in the winter of 1794-95 expressing the Thermidorian majority's determination to restore social order and to seek peace on the basis of France's natural frontiers. He also announced the lifting of restrictions against Catholic worship and served as spokesman for the economic campaign against the Parisian *sans-culottes*, supporting the closing of government workshops and, as head of the *comité des subsistances*, announcing cuts in the bread ration. He presided over the stormy Convention sessions of 12 Germinal Year III and 1 Prairial Year III; his refusal to yield the chair to the insurgents during the latter riot made him a national hero.

Both A.-C. Thibaudeau and L.-M. La Revellière-lépeaux, who served with him on the Committee of Eleven that drafted the Constitution of 1795, described him as a monarchist but not a partisan of an outright return to the Old Regime. Boissy later informed Louis XVIII that he would not support a restoration without strong constitutional guarantees. When the death of Louis XVI's son (1795) ruled out a Convention-controlled regency, Boissy served as chief spokesman in presenting the moderate republican constitution. Voters in the 1795 elections, forced to choose two-thirds of the deputies to the new councils from the *conventionnels*, gave Boissy an overwhelming endorsement; he was elected by seventy-seven departments. He advocated a compromise with the right-wing movement in the Paris sections in Vendémiaire Year IV, and some of his former Thermidorian allies accused him of supporting it, but he was allowed to take his seat in the Council of Five Hundred.

From the beginning of the Directory to the coup of 18 Fructidor Year V, Boissy remained a leading right-wing spokesman in the councils, but he was overshadowed by both more determined monarchists and more consistent moderates. He spoke against press restrictions, urged repeal of laws denying regular trials to *émigrés*, and was on the councils' committee to investigate the threatening addresses from the armies that foreshadowed Fructidor. He was one of the deputies listed for arrest in the Fructidor coup, but Madame de Staël had warned him in advance, and he escaped to England. After 18 Brumaire Year VIII, he returned and sat in the Tribunate and Senate. He was named to the Chamber of Peers in 1814, accepted a mission to the Midi during the Hundred Days, was readmitted to the Chamber of Peers in the Second Restoration, and was a prominent liberal spokesman there until his death in 1826. Sincerely dedicated to a narrow, socially conservative liberalism, Boissy d'Anglas served any regime that promised to uphold the "principles of 1789" and nothing more. Thermidor brought him to unexpected national prominence, but he lacked real political skills and was more of a figurehead than a leader.

A.N. series 175 AP (Boissy d'Anglas papers); Boissy d'Anglas, *Quelques idées sur la liberté, la révolution, le gouvernement républicain, et la constitution française* (n.p., 1792); A.-C. Thibaudeau, *Mémoires sur la Convention et le Directoire* (Paris, 1824).

J. Popkin

Related entries: COUNCIL OF FIVE HUNDRED; COUP OF 18 FRUCTIDOR YEAR V; TWO-THIRDS LAW.

BONAPARTE, JOSEPH (1768–1844), king of Naples (1806–08) and king of Spain (1808–13), which dignities he attained, despite fairly limited talents and a likable character, essentially because of his younger brother's patronage and requirements after the coup of 18 Brumaire (November 1799). Rather independent in adolescence, Joseph decided not to enter the church with his Uncle Fesch, preferring law as a preparation for public life in his native Corsica. The Bonaparte clan had rallied to the French when the latter occupied the island (1768) but managed, briefly, to work alongside P. Paoli when that exiled patriot leader returned (1790). Joseph's career in the Conseil Supérieur and then on the Departmental Directory in Corsica (1791) ended, however, in the family's flight to France when, in June 1793, open conflict broke between Paolists and the government in Paris.

Republican, anti-Paolist, with good contacts in Paris, Joseph's two immediate objectives were attainable: a good job as *commissaire des guerres* (September 1793) and a major role in an expedition to Corsica. Abortive attempts to seize the island in June 1794 and February 1795 were followed by success in October 1796, and for six months, Joseph ruled the southern half of the island. His competence and political reliability, in addition to his connection with the brilliant commander in Italy, undoubtedly earned him the embassy at Rome, where his clandestine role helped prepare the ground for an armed incursion and the proclamation of the Republic (15 February 1798).

While his brother was in Egypt, Joseph served as a deputy for Corsica in the Council of Five Hundred, and he continued to serve the Bonapartes' interests by keeping open and extending links with politicians and soldiers, by watching Josephine, and also, on Napoleon's return from Egypt, by watching his brother-in-law J.-B. Bernadotte. At the same time, he indulged his own interests by writing a romantic novel, *Moïna*, and by purchasing and embellishing the Morte-fontaine estate. The coup of Brumaire was partly planned there, Joseph on that day helping neutralize Bernadotte and, it would seem, using his political connections and skills to counter possible opponents and to rally the doubting. After Brumaire, his star soared and fell with that of his exacting benefactor-brother. Although Joseph and his heirs were not to succeed the Emperor Napoleon, the Kingdom of Italy was offered to him, and an army was provided to take and keep Naples, if he so chose—which he did; and two years later, in 1808, he was transferred to Madrid. Always obedient in the end, even if he allowed himself verbal opposition, he remained in that impossible post, king in name only, until the final defeat at Vittoria (21 August 1813). Placed in charge of the defense of Paris in 1814, he served again in the Hundred Days, escaping to settle in the United States (1815–32 and 1837–39), in England (1832–36 and 1839–40), and in Tuscany, where he died 28 July 1844, followed by his wife, Julie, eight months later.

A.N., *Archives de J. Bonaparte, roi de Naples puis d'Espagne: inventaire* (Paris, 1982); J. Bonaparte, *Mémoires et correspondance politique du Roi Joseph, annotés et mis en ordre par A. du Casse*, 10 vols. (Paris, 1853–54); O. Connelly, *The Gentle Bonaparte: A Biography of Joseph, Napoleon's Elder Brother* (New York, 1968); G. Girod de l'Ain, *Joseph Bonaparte, le roi malgré lui* (Paris, 1970); F. Masson, *Napoléon et sa famille*, 13 vols., 2d ed. (Paris, 1927); and J. Tulard, *Bibliographie critique des mémoires sur le Consulat et l'Empire* (Paris, 1971).

M. G. Hutt

Related entries: BERNADOTTE; BONAPARTE, N., ROMAN REPUBLIC.

BONAPARTE, LUCIEN (1775-1840), younger brother of Napoleon and favorite son of the widowed Letizia. Intelligent and headstrong, Lucien Bonaparte early had a desire to play a public role; this later was replaced by the determination to live the private life of a scholarly gentleman when it became clear that subordination to his overbearing elder brother was, otherwise, the price. After school at Brienne and a switch, at his desire, to prepare for the priesthood, Lucien plunged into politics in 1789. A *patriote*, it was his denunciation of P. Paoli that precipitated the open conflict on Corsica in which the unprepared Bonaparte faction lost out; and as a zealous republican, he was arrested briefly as a terrorist after Thermidor (27-28 July 1794), the anti-Robespierrist putsch.

Helped by Napoleon into a position as *commissaire des guerres*, he was soon in dispute with his brother over marriages in the family—not least that with Josephine—and when, after some time back in Corsica, he was invited to join the expedition to Egypt, he decided not to indulge his archeological interests but instead to lead an active political role as a deputy for Corsica in the Council of Five Hundred. One of the active plotters of Brumaire (November 1799), he also played a crucial role in the operation of the coup. As president of the Five Hundred, he parried awkward questions on the eighteenth and saved the situation on the next day when, first, he held up a motion to outlaw Napoleon and then, the meeting having escaped his control, he rallied the wavering troops outside and led them to clear the chamber. Rewarded with the ministry of the interior, Lucien soon gave his brother sufficient reasons, in his eyes, to move him to the Madrid embassy, where A. Jouberthon completed Lucien's reasons for choosing to live henceforth a private life since his now-imperial brother was unrelentingly hostile to an unsuitable marriage whose issue might inherit the throne.

Lucien retired to live near Rome and, when political pressures on him mounted, sailed for the United States, was captured en route, and interned on a country estate near London (1811–14). In the Hundred Days, however, Lucien returned to his brother's side but was only briefly interned after Waterloo (16 June 1815) before resuming his life as prince of Canino (a papal title) in Frascati, collecting Etruscan vases, writing epic poetry, and assembling material for what became the start of his memoirs.

L. Bonaparte, *Mémoires*, vol. 1 (no more published; London, 1836); H.-F.-T. Jung, *Lucien Bonaparte et ses Mémoires*, 3 vols. (Paris, 1882); F. Masson, *Napoléon et sa famille*, 9th ed., 13 vols. (Paris, 1927); F. Pietri, *Lucien Bonaparte* (Paris, 1939); J. Tulard, *Bibliographie critique des Mémoires sur le Consulat et l'Empire* (Paris, 1971).

M. G. Hutt

Related entries: BONAPARTE, J.; BONAPARTE, N.; COUP OF 18 BRUMAIRE; EGYPTIAN EXPEDITION; 9 THERMIDOR YEAR II.

BONAPARTE, NAPOLEON (1769-1821), general, first consul, emperor of the French. Napoleon Bonaparte was born on 15 August 1769 at Ajaccio, Corsica, a year after the island had passed from Genoese to French rule. His dilettante father, Count C. Bonaparte, was a member of the lesser Corsican nobility. His mother, L. Ramolino, a woman of strong character and great beauty, had little formal education. At the age of nine, Bonaparte won a seat at the royal school of Brienne, where sons of impoverished nobles were given military training. Before going, he spent several months in Autun, learning to substitute French for his Corsican dialect.

After five years at Brienne, Bonaparte went to the celebrated Ecole militaire in Paris where, in 1785, he was commissioned after one year instead of the usual two or three. Having excelled in mathematics, he was posted at the age of sixteen to the artillery Regiment de La Fère, one of the best of its kind. From 1785 to 1789 he carried out his normal duties, including further artillery training.

Surviving notebooks show that Bonaparte studied the new military treatises, which sought to transform strategy and tactics by stressing quickness of maneuver and massed firepower. He read, superficially, some of the *philosophes*, had a passing enthusiasm for J.-J. Rousseau, and considered writing a history of Corsica, which he visited twice between 1785 and 1789. A few youthful essays actually were printed.

In August 1789 Bonaparte swore the new oath of allegiance to the nation, refusing to emigrate. Now stationed at Auxerre, he joined the local Jacobin club and in 1793 published a dialogue, *Le Souper de Beaucaire*, which championed the Jacobins against the Girondins. In June 1793 he joined the forces seeking to recapture the anti-Jacobin ports of Toulon and Marseille, which had welcomed an English and Spanish fleet. His outstanding artillery work led to his promotion to general of brigade in February 1794, following which he became an operational planner for the intended campaign against the Austrians in northern Italy. He was imprisoned briefly after M. Robespierre's fall in Thermidor, but after political confusion and a temporary loss of rank, he regained his place and was appointed by P. Barras as artillery commander to suppress the rightist Vendémiaire rising in Paris (October 1795) against the new constitution.

Chance led him at this time to meet J. de Beauharnais, six years his senior and widow of a former viscount guillotined during the Terror. Letters show how passionately he flung himself into an affair, which culminated on 9 March 1796 in a hasty civil marriage. Two days later, he left to assume his new duties as commander in chief of the Army of Italy. He was twenty-six.

The campaign of 1796 was intended to drive the Austrians from Italy. Bonaparte put into effect his ideas of strategy and tactics: better firepower based on new weapons, constant mobility, and the use of the famous *ordre mixte*, columns for approach and a combination of column and line for the final attack. Above all, Bonaparte insisted on execution.

Within a few weeks of his arrival, Bonaparte had driven Piedmont from the Coalition and wheeled against the Austrians, crossing the Adda River at Lodi and occupying Milan on 14 May. In a series of famous battles, he drove the enemy completely out of Lombardy and then pushed toward Trieste. By the end of March 1797, he was in the Julian Alps, within a hundred miles of Vienna, causing the Austrians to sign the Preliminaries of Leoben (18 April 1797). War was beginning to pay for itself, since huge quantities of specie and art treasures were sent to France.

In October 1796 Bonaparte had announced the creation of the Cispadane Republic out of papal lands south of the Po River. In June 1797 Genoese territories were reorganized into a new Ligurian Republic. Over the next three months, Bonaparte formed the Cisalpine Republic by adding the Duchy of Milan and some Venetian and Piedmontese territory to the Cispadane. Earlier, the Directory had created the Batavian Republic out of the former Netherlands (January 1795). These and subsequent sister republics were given institutions similar to those in France, with the addition of powerful French authority exercised from above.

In this exhilarating period, Bonaparte forced Austria to sign the Treaty of Campoformio (27 October 1797). Austria recognized the Cisalpine Republic, ceded the Austrian Netherlands (Belgium) to France, and agreed to support French claims to the left bank of the Rhine against its German possessors. The Hapsburg Empire also agreed to end the Venetian Republic, taking some of its mainland possessions, and was promised the Archbishopric of Salzburg. The Ionian Islands in the Adriatic were to be French, a significant clue to Bonaparte's growing eastern dreams.

Bonaparte chose to remain in Italy during the coup of Fructidor (September 1797) because he felt that the time was not yet right. He wished profoundly to terminate the war with England, the sole remaining member of the First Coalition, but on returning to France, he quickly determined that an invasion of the British Isles was then impossible. He turned instead to a project that had long fascinated him, a descent on Egypt. C.-M. Talleyrand as foreign minister supported him, and the directors quickly accepted his plan.

Four hundred ships with 38,000 troops and 150 scholars and artists left Toulon in May 1798 and safely reached Alexandria. Napoleon won the Battle of the Pyramids (21 July) but lost his fleet to Lord H. Nelson at the mouth of the Nile (1-2 August). A French invasion of Syria failed, and Turkey entered the war. The meager news from France told of growing political unrest, military victories on the part of the newly formed Second Coalition, and Josephine's continued infidelities. After defeating the Turks in the land battle of Aboukir (25 July 1799), Bonaparte left Egypt in August with four small ships and about 400 men, safely eluding the British fleet. He landed at Fréjus on 8 October and enjoyed a triumphal passage to Paris, where he arrived a week later.

The coup of Brumaire (9–10 November 1799) made Bonaparte the political master of France. A hastily organized conspiracy headed by E.-J. Sieyès, Talleyrand, J. Fouché, and L. Bonaparte and supported by a display of military strength overthrew the Directory government. The quickly drafted Constitution of the Year VIII (1799) replaced that of 1795. Bonaparte, with enormous powers, was the first of the three consuls. A Senate, Tribunate, Legislative Body, and Council of State were created, and local institutions were fitted into a highly centralized structure. Proclaimed on 25 December 1799, the constitution was overwhelmingly ratified two months later in a national plebiscite.

As first consul, Bonaparte sought peace abroad and order at home. He contemptuously rejected a Bourbon plea to return and was quickly rebuffed in the peace overtures he made to Britain and Austria. It took his victory at Marengo in northern Italy (June 1800) and J. Moreau's at Hohenlinden in southern Germany (December 1800) to force Austria to sign the Treaty of Lunéville (February 1801). After the other allies quickly withdrew, England had little choice but to sign the Treaty of Amiens (March 1802), bringing peace to the Continent. Since France had annexed Savoy, Belgium, and the Rhineland and had established several client states in northern Italy, the Revolutionary goal of the natural frontiers had been exceeded.

In domestic matters, political order, financial stability, and industrial growth were primary concerns. The first draft of a civil code, completed in December 1800, would be followed by the famous law codes of the imperial years. Huge numbers of royalists had their names stricken from the *émigré* lists kept by the police. The Bank of France, a powerful stabilizing influence, was created as early as January 1800. The Concordat with the papacy (July 1801) asserted Catholicism to be the religion of the majority of the French, with clerical salaries paid by the state and bishops nominated by the first consul and consecrated by the pope. Impressive building programs appeared on the drawing boards. Public education was enlarged, centralized, and disciplined, and the Legion of Honor was a means of recognizing all kinds of public ability. Less benign was the police system and the rigorous censorship. In 1802 Bonaparte became sole consul for life, with power to name his successor, and in May 1804 the Senate decreed an emperorship hereditary in the direct male line of Napoleon. The imperial years saw a continued growth in industry and agriculture. The continental system, beginning in November 1806, was intended to bar the goods of England and its colonies from entering the Continent. It failed and contributed to Napoleon's downfall.

Napoleon's continued meddling in Europe caused England to renew hostilities in May 1803, with Russia and Austria joining this Third Coalition in 1805. Although the Battle of Trafalgar (October 1805) gave England control of the seas, Austria's defeats at Ulm and Austerlitz (October and December 1805) forced it to sign the Treaty of Pressburg within weeks. Prussia, belatedly joining the war, was defeated at Jena and Friedland (October 1806 and June 1807) and with Russia was obliged to sign the Peace of Tilsit (July 1807).

Such spectacular successes led Napoleon to undertake a sweeping reorganization of central Europe. The Holy Roman Empire was brought to an end in August 1806, its former ruler becoming simply emperor of Austria. The Confederation of the Rhine (July 1806) combined sixteen states of western Germany into a French-dominated structure, with Napoleon's brother Jerome as king of the newly created Westphalia, while his brother-in-law J. Murat became grand duke of Berg. His brother Louis became king of Holland in June 1806. Prussia lost substantial territory, some of it going to the Grand Duchy of Warsaw, created in July 1807 from Polish territory. A Kingdom of Italy with Napoleon as titular head appeared in the northern part of the peninsula in 1805. In the south, Murat in 1808 succeeded J. Bonaparte as king of Naples, Joseph becoming, in name at least, king of Spain. Eventually the actual frontiers of the French Empire were extended to include a coastal strip of Italy reaching to Rome; in similar fashion, a northern extension reached through Belgium and Holland to touch the Baltic.

Austria unwisely joined the Fourth Coalition in March 1809, only to be defeated at Wagram in July. In a calculated diplomatic move, Napoleon, having divorced Josephine, who had given him no heir, married the young Marie-Louise, daughter of Emperor Francis (April 1810). Peace, however, was still unsure, for Czar Alexander I of Russia, deeply resenting the continental system, was also developing a religious sense of his European mission against Napoleon. Thus in June 1812, the latter led one of his largest armies into Russia. His catastrophic losses brought into existence the Fifth Coalition. The great French defeat at Leipzig (October 1813) enabled the allies to cross Germany and in the spring of 1814 to campaign on French soil. The duke of Wellington, meanwhile having cleared Spain, where rebellion had been in process since 1807, entered France from the south. J. Bonaparte's surrender of Paris led to Napoleon's abdication (4 April 1814) and the return of the Bourbons. After a year's exile at Elba, he returned in March 1815 for the vain effort of the Hundred Days. The Congress of Vienna declared him an outlaw, and Waterloo (18 June 1815) ended his hopes. The Bourbons returned again, and the Second Treaty of Paris (November 1815) restored France to its ancient limits. Although Napoleon had sought asylum in England, its government sent him as a prisoner to St. Helena, where on 5 May 1821 he died.

A. Fugier, *Napoléon et l'Italie* (Paris, 1947); J. C. Herold, *The Mind of Napoleon, A Selection from His Written and Spoken Words* (New York, 1955), and *Napoleon in Egypt* (New York, 1962); J. E. Howard, ed., *The Letters and Documents of Napoleon*, vol. 1, 1769–1802 (London, 1961); G. Lefebvre, *The French Revolution from 1793 to 1799* (New York, 1964); F. M. H. Markham, *Napoleon* (London, 1963); A. Vandal, *L'Avènement de Bonaparte*, 2 vols. (Paris, 1902-05).

E. J. Knapton

Related entries: BARRAS; BATAVIAN REPUBLIC; BELGIUM; CISALPINE REPUBLIC; CISPADANE REPUBLIC; CONSTITUTION OF 1799; COUP OF 18 BRUMAIRE; COUP OF 18 FRUCTIDOR YEAR V; DIRECTORY; FEDERALISM; FIRST COALITION; FOUCHE; GUIBERT; JOSEPHINE; LIGURIAN REPUBLIC; PRELIMINARIES OF LEOBEN; SECOND COALITION; SIEYES; 13 VENDEMIAIRE YEAR IV; TREATY OF CAMPOFORMIO.

BONNEVILLE, NICOLAS DE. See *BOUCHE DE FER*.

BOSC, LOUIS-AUGUSTIN-GUILLAUME (1759-1828), naturalist, administrator, academician. Destined at an early age for a military career—his mother's father and brothers were generals—Bosc was sent to the Collège de Dijon to learn mathematics while his father's glass manufacturing enterprises kept the family in Burgundy. At school he developed a great interest for examining plants and animals, a pursuit doubtless favored by the long tradition in medicine on his father's side. By the time that Louis completed his preparatory studies, however, his father's financial reverses had precluded further schooling in either the martial arts or natural history.

In 1777 his father settled Louis as clerk in the controller general's offices in Paris and acquired for himself a charge as *Médecin du Roi*. Father and son together moved into scientific circles of the capital, where the father had made friends twenty years before, when, just after receiving his medical degree at Hardenwyck in Holland, he had come to Paris to learn physics and chemistry and how to apply their principles to glass making. Very soon Louis discovered that a job was no obstacle to his interests in natural history. Before the year was out, he left the controller's office and became a secretary to the baron d'Ogny, intendant of the post office. While he won the confidence of his employer at work, he used what leisure he had to follow courses at the Jardin du Roi, botany with A.-L. de Jussieu and agronomy with A. Thoüin.

Slowly Bosc's circle enlarged. At botany lectures, he met J.-M. Roland de la Platière and his wife, M. Phlipon. Scientists traveling through Paris often visited the Jardin du Roi, and he was sometimes included in their conversation and entertainment. As he was given increased responsibility at postal head-quarters, a valued perquisite of his position, the franking of mail, led to his helping maintain communications between naturalists in France and those of other countries. Meantime, as early as 1784 (the same year his father died; his mother had died when he was two years old, and his father had remarried), he began to publish articles, the first a description of a new genus of cochineal, appearing in the abbé Rozier's *Journal de physique*. In March 1788 he was included in the first group of foreign members chosen by the newly founded Linnean Society of London, and within the year he helped P.-M.-A. Broussonet launch a Société Linnéenne in Paris. Short-lived, this group's dissolution was followed in 1790 by the formation of the Société d'histoire naturelle; again Bosc was active as an officer and contributed numerous articles to the bulletin that the organization began publishing.

With minimal censorship at the collège de Dijon, Louis had very early ac-quainted himself with the century's philosophical works. His own Calvinist background, as well, predisposed him to anticlericalism, even when he was tempted as an adolescent to take holy orders for the pure pleasure of reading and having a garden of his own. A decade's exposure in Paris to the intellectual currents of the 1780s conditioned him to look for political and social change. Titles should disappear, of course: he dropped the particle from his name and notified the Linnean Society in London (24 July 1790) to relist him as Louis Bosc. For the rest of his life, he signed simply BOSC. A member of the Société des Amis de la Constitution, he followed its transition to the Jacobins and gladly agreed to work as one of its secretaries, deploying his familiarity with the postal system on behalf of its correspondence with provincial branches as naturally as he was helping scientists keep in touch with one another.

During the Legislative Assembly, with Roland as minister of the interior, Bosc was called on to help reorganize the mail service and was named one of its five central administrators, with *messageries* as his specialty. Because his competence and connections were respected, he soon came to represent the entire board in its liaison with the ministry. Even with Roland out of the ministry and the Convention in place, Bosc continued in his office. Involved by the May–June 1793 proscriptions, he persisted unscathed until September, when he finally resigned and made himself as inconspicuous as possible at the priory of Sainte Radegonde, a small house in the forest of Montmorency owned by J.-H. Bancal des Issarts There he contrived to shelter temporarily a series of proscribed friends, among them Roland and L.-M. La Revellière-lépeaux, future member of the Directory. At high risk to himself, he visited Madame Roland in prison, receiving from her the second version of her memoirs, the first having been destroyed.

After Thermidor, Bosc returned to Paris, where he was appointed guardian of the surviving Roland daughter. He had hoped to return to the postal service but refused to take as colleagues men who had contributed to the death of his friends and under whose prodding, he declared, he had countenanced the first violation of the secrecy of the mails of his entire career. Despairing of being able to dislodge these persons from mail personnel, he eked out an existence by writing for scientific publications, most notably for the agricultural sections of C.-J. Panckouke's *Encyclopédie*. In 1795 he saw through publication the first edition of Madame Roland's *Appel à l'impartial posterité*.

Falling deeply in love with the fourteen-year-old E. Roland yet aware that it was unacceptable for him at thirty-seven to marry his minor ward, he decided to travel to the United States and obtained a passport to go privately as a naturalist, not, however, without a promise by the director La Revellière-lépeaux to appoint him consul at some American city as soon as possible. He embarked on the American ship *Eliza* in August 1796 and arrived at Charleston, South Carolina, in October, only to find that he and A. Michaux, with whom he had expected to stay until the consular appointment reached him, had passed somewhere in mid-Atlantic, set on opposite courses. The appointments, when they did come, as vice-consul at Wilmington, North Carolina, in 1797, and then as consul at New York in 1798, availed him only a modest salary for about a year because the lively nursing of grievances between France and the United States prevented his obtaining an exequatur. Disappointed, he spent two years in and near Charleston on field trips, collecting specimens and writing descriptions of Carolina flora and fauna, greatly improving his own expertise and adding to French knowledge of the American scene.

Returning to France by way of Spain late in 1798, Bosc was named by the Directory almost immediately to a political mission in the south of France and then for a time served as administrator of the hospices of Paris. In 1799 he married a cousin, S. Bosc; to this marriage four daughters and one son were born.

Dating from the Consulate, he wrote and edited articles, single volumes, and series on scientific and agricultural matters. In 1803 he was appointed inspector of gardens and nurseries at Versailles and in 1805 inspector general of nurseries. On the death of A. Thoüin in 1824, Bosc, as of 1825, succeeded him as professor at the Muséum d'histoire naturelle.

On 11 August 1806 Bosc was elected a member of the Classe des sciences physiques et mathématiques of the Institut de France. At the reorganization of the Institut in 1816, he was named to the Académie des sciences, Section d'économie rurale, in which he continued until his death. He was buried in a private cemetery in the forest of Montmorency. His eulogy was pronounced by G. Cuvier on 15 June 1829 at a meeting of the Académie des sciences. Long before then, he had been honored by membership in a score of learned societies in France and over Europe. A marble bust by D. d'Angers is preserved at Soudon in Maine-et-Loire, property where Bosc's daughter Floralie went to live. Twin portraits in oil are hung, one at Salidieu in the Vendée and the other in the Muséum d'histoire naturelle in Paris. Bosc papers are to be found in Paris at the Muséum national d'histoire naturelle, the Bibliothèque and Archives of the

Institut de France, and Bibliothèque municipale, as well as at the Bibliothèque universitaire et publique of Geneva.

G. R. Beale, "Bosc and the Exequator," *Prologue* (U.S. Archives) (Fall 1978); C. Perroud, "Le Roman d'un Girondin," *Rev. du d.-h. siècle* 2 (1914) and 3 (1915–16); A. Rey, *Le naturaliste Bosc et les Girondins à Saint-Prix* (Paris, 1882).

G. R. Beale

Related entries: LA REVELLIERE-LEPAUX; ROLAND DE LA PLATIERE, J.-M.; SCIENCE.

BOUCHE DE FER (1790-91), journal and organ of the Cercle Social, edited by N. de Bonneville, a Parisian intellectual. The primary function of the *Bouche de fer* was to reprint the minutes of Cercle Social meetings and discuss issues relevant to the club's concerns. Worthy of special mention are C. Fauchet's weekly commentaries on J.-J. Rousseau's *Social Contract*, many of E. Palm's feminist writings, speeches by M.-J.-A.-N. Condorcet on political matters, a debate over F.-M. Voltaire's place among the Revolutionary patriarchs, and a letter by Madame Roland advocating inheritance law reform. During the spring of 1791, the journal reprinted many documents from the burgeoning democratic movement, including several Cordeliers Club petitions.

The *Bouche de fer* was published thrice weekly from October 1790 to 22 June 1791, when it became daily, until its suppression on 28 July 1791. The subscription price (9 *livres* per quarter) was tied to the club's membership; whoever subscribed to the journal also received a membership card. In this way, the *Bouche de fer* allowed the Cercle Social to develop a national following. The title of the journal comes from a specific Cercle Social procedure whereby citizens were urged to drop all types of notices into a box shaped in the form of a lion's head and located at Cercle Social headquarters (4 rue Théâtre-Français—today the rue Odéon). The Cercle Social would publish these notices, giving the press a democratic quality. While such a practice may have been tried during the early days of the club, it was certainly not in use after 1791.

A. Mathiez, "Sur le titre du journal *La Bouche de fer*," *Ann. révo.* 9 (1917); A. Soderhjelm, *Le Régime de la presse pendant la Révolution française*, reprint ed. (Geneva, 1971).

G. Kates

Related entries: CERCLE SOCIAL; CONDORCET; CORDELIERS CLUB.

BOUILLE, FRANCOIS-CLAUDE-AMOUR, MARQUIS DE (1739-1800), a general who began his military career in the Seven Years War, fought brilliantly in the West Indies during the American Revolution, and is best known for his role in the repression of the Nancy mutiny and in the attempted flight of Louis XVI during the French Revolution. Bouillé was born on 19 November 1739 at the chateau of Cluzel in Auvergne into an ancient aristocratic family. Orphaned at the age of eight, he was raised by an uncle who was a bishop with extensive connections at court. Bouillé entered the army before he turned fifteen and commanded his own company by the age of seventeen. He fought gallantly during the Seven Years War, was wounded and later captured, and was selected to carry back to Versailles captured battle flags, a mission that led to his promotion to the rank of colonel in 1761.

After the war, Bouillé's regiment was sent to the French West Indies. In 1768 he was appointed governor of Guadeloupe and two years later named brigadier general. He returned to France and life at court in 1771. As the likelihood of war with England increased, in 1777 he was made governor general of the Leeward Islands. Following France's entry into the American Revolution, Bouillé led a series of successful amphibious operations against English-held islands in the Caribbean: Dominica in 1778, Tobago and St. Eustatius in 1781, and St. Kitts in 1782. These victories, so welcome after the humiliations of the Seven Years War, won for Bouillé promotions to major general (October 1778) and subsequently to lieutenant general (May 1782) and widespread military renown in Europe. He returned to Europe after peace came in 1783. He traveled widely and was warmly welcomed by high society in England, Holland, Prussia, and Austria for both his military reputation and his connections at the French court.

When France's financial and political crises deepened in the late 1780s, Bouillé showed himself a staunch monarchist by defending the prerogatives of the king in the Assembly of Notables in 1787 and again in 1788. In 1789 he was appointed military commandant of the Trois-Evêchés, and the next year his command was extended to include the provinces of Alsace, Lorraine, and Franche-Comté as well, thus putting nearly half of the regular army under his orders. He accepted the new political changes only reluctantly; it took a personal letter from Louis XVI to exact from Bouillé the oath of loyalty to the new constitution required of all officers. He was also alarmed by the disintegration of discipline within the army. In the spring and again in the summer of 1790, Bouillé was forced to deal with mutinous troops at his own headquarters in Metz.

This wave of insubordination reached its climax at Nancy in August 1790. The garrison of this city mutinied en masse, took their officers into custody, and forced the distribution of money from unit funds. Faced with the possibility of the complete collapse of the standing army, the National Assembly authorized Bouillé to restore discipline among the troops at Nancy. He led an army of almost 4,500 men, with a large proportion of foreign mercenaries in the service of France, against the garrison. After bitter fighting, on 31 August Bouillé entered Nancy and initiated a series of repressive measures, including the execution of twenty-three mutineers, long sentences to the galleys for forty-one men, and scores of lesser punishments. For his actions at Nancy, Bouillé was vilified by patriots and his name identified with counterrevolution.

Indeed, Bouillé did oppose the Revolution and had considered emigrating from France for some time, but he felt that he could not desert the king. Bouillé's dilemma was resolved when Louis XVI finally decided to take the step advocated by many since the beginning of the Revolution and flee Paris. The king had been consulting Bouillé on this decision since October 1790, and they ultimately agreed that Louis should leave the Tuileries secretly on 20 June 1791 and, together with his family, go to Montmédy, where he would rally forces loyal to him and repress the Revolution. Bouillé took charge of providing reliable military escorts for the royal family at various stages along their route. From its inception the plan was badly bungled; the fugitives left Paris well behind schedule and consistently failed to arrive at rendezvous on time. When the king reached the small town of Varennes around midnight on 21 June, he was recognized and arrested. By the time Bouillé was informed of this and had gathered a force to lead from Montmédy to Varennes, it was too late; Louis XVI was on his way back to Paris under a large escort of National Guardsmen. Bouillé's path was now clear. After writing a letter to the Assembly warning the deputies not to harm the king, Bouillé emigrated.

During the following months, Bouillé was very active throughout Europe, attempting to organize intervention in France that would restore the monarchy to full power. He visited Coblentz, where the princes were gathering an army of émigrés to invade France. He went to Russia where he received from Catherine II the promise of 36,000 troops for such a venture. He prepared to take command of a Swedish army to lead against France, but this plan collapsed when King Gustavus Adolphus III was assassinated in March 1792. War came the following month, and Bouillé served with the Army of Condé during the ill-fated campaign of 1792.

His hopes to restore Louis XVI to power were dashed by the ignominious defeat and retreat of the foreign and émigré armies in the latter part of 1792 and destroyed entirely with the king's execution in January 1793. Bouillé retired to England where he would remain, except for a two-year visit to the West Indies, for the remainder of his life. He died in London on 14 November 1800, five days short of his sixty-first birthday.

W. C. Baldwin, "The Beginnings of the Revolution and the Mutiny of the Royal Garrison in Nancy: *L'Affaire de Nancy*, 1790" (Ph.D. diss., University of Michigan, 1973); A. de Bouillé, *Varennes et la dernière chance de Louis XVI* (Lyon, 1969); F.-C.-A. de Bouillé, *Mémoires du Marquis de Bouillé* (Paris, 1821); R. de Bouillé, *Essai sur la vie du marquis de Bouillé* (Paris, 1853).

S. F. Scott

Related entries: ASSEMBLY OF NOTABLES; COBLENTZ; CONDE; COUN-TERREVOLUTION; MALOUET; MUTINY OF NANCY; VARENNES.

BOURDON, FRANCOIS-LOUIS (1758-98), politician. Known as Bourdon de l'Oise, he is not to be confused with Léonard Bourdon. Born at Rouy-le-Petit (Picardie), he acquired the office of *procureur* in the Parlement of Paris in 1783. His role in the agitation among the law clerks and officials in Paris in 1789 opened a career as a minor Parisian militant during the early Revolution. He participated actively in the agitation leading to 10 August 1792. His admission to the National Convention resulted from a confusion. The electors of the Oise nominated ''Bourdon, substitute procureur at Paris and one of the conquerors of the Bastille.'' There ensued an abuse-laden public wrangle between him and L. Bourdon as to which of them this meant. The dispute was resolved by L. Bourdon's election by the Loiret, and Bourdon took the seat for the Oise.

Bourdon's political attitudes in the Convention are often hard to define. Their ambiguity was perhaps heightened by a drinking problem, which frequently brought him inebriated to the evening sittings. He was given to passionate denunciation, excessive drama, and tenacious personal vindictiveness. He remained silent, however, during the purge of the factions, played a minor role on 8–9 Thermidor, and was relatively inconspicuous during the insurrections of the Year III. J.-R. Hébert once accused him of having been a Brissotin. This seems to be only invective. Certainly Bourdon launched bitter attacks on Girondist leaders after his return from a mission to supervise recruitment in the Orne (March–mid-May 1793). In the autumn and winter of 1793, he emerged as a leading figure in the moderate offensive against the Hébertist radicals. However, Bourdon was probably not a Dantonist in any strict sense of the term. He apparently quarreled with G.-J. Danton over the latter's financial dealings and several times disparaged him during the early months of Year II when Danton's friends were coming to prominence. His connections were more with P. Philippeaux, P.-F. Fabre d'Eglantine, and possibly L.-C.-S. Desmoulins. Despite his relations with corrupt deputies, there is little evidence that he was particularly corrupt at this stage, although he was later involved with dubious dealings in national lands under the Directory. At the same time, he seems to have been close to the radical J. Billaud-Varenne with whom he shared a common hatred of M. Robespierre during the months before 9 Thermidor and to whom he remained loyal for some time after.

Bourdon's political activity during the autumn and winter of 1793 primarily concerned a private vendetta against the radical minister of war, J.-B.-N. Bouchotte. This began soon after Bourdon was recalled on 28 August from a mission against the Vendée rebels. Against the orders of the Committee of Public Safety, he had suspended the radical General J.-A. Rossignol, who was Bouchotte's protégé. Bourdon proceeded to attack repeatedly Bouchotte, together with his protégés in the War Office and the army, on pretexts provided by the parlous state of military supplies, the financial confusion, and the nonpayment of stipends to soldiers' families. Since Bouchotte and his protégés formed a kind of military wing to the Cordeliers group, Bourdon's campaign necessarily made him a prominent associate of the Dantonists in the struggle with the Hébertists in the months of Frimaire and Nivôse. It was Bourdon who obtained the arrest of C.-P. Ronsin and F.-N. Vincent on 27 Frimaire (17 December), which is seen as the first major Dantonist success and which brought Hébert to seek his exclusion from the Jacobin club on 1 Nivôse (21 December). Although Robespierre steered the Jacobins away from expelling him on 21 Nivôse (10 January 1794), Bourdon's campaign irritated him. This was partly because of Robespierre's antifaction stance and because he preferred to defend the ministry rather than see the war effort disrupted; above all, enmity ensued because Bourdon jeopardized the structure of government. In order to get at Bouchotte, he made several attempts to destroy the ministerial system altogether, and, on 22 Frimaire (12 December), he almost succeeded in getting the membership of the Committee of Public Safety renewed.

Although Bourdon escaped inclusion in the purge of the factions, he was clearly vulnerable. He therefore attempted to postpone the debate on the text that became the 22 Prairial Law, streamlining the Revolutionary Tribunal, and then attempted, on 23 Prairial (11 June 1794), to deprive the government committees of the power to send deputies to the Tribunal. An exchange between Bourdon and Robespierre in the Convention the next day made it clear that Robespierre considered him to be one of the surviving faction leaders whom Robespierre was denouncing. Such evident danger brought Bourdon into the plotting that preceded 9 Thermidor. J. Fouché remembered him as one of his most energetic allies. His inclination to see issues in personal terms was revealed again by his desire to stab Robespierre in the Convention, perhaps in conscious imitation of Brutus's murder of Caesar. However, although Bourdon opened the criticism of Robespierre's speech in the Convention on 8 Thermidor by a prudently worded plea against its publication, the real attack was mounted by M.-G.-A. Vadier, P.-J. Cambon, and J.-N. Billaud-Varenne. On 9 Thermidor, he intervened, almost as a footnote, only after B. Barère's crucial speech had demonstrated Robespierre's isolation.

Bourdon's evolution during the Thermidorian Reaction typified the moderates' slide into reaction under the pressure of events. During Thermidor and Fructidor, he attempted to preserve the strong government associated with the Terror while reforming those aspects that appeared arbitrary or democratic. Thus, he argued against the renewal of the committees of government as endangering the war effort and insisted, in the debate on a new committee structure, that strong government was essential for internal security and military success. His comments on the reform of the Revolutionary Tribunal and on the problem of arrested suspects sought to distinguish between arbitrary actions and patriotically correct behavior. It was he who imposed consideration of the accused's intentions by the Tribunal and initiated an inquiry into the reasons for each suspect's arrest. Whatever the practical consequences of such proposals, they aimed at rendering repression less indiscriminate but not less real. In Fructidor, he denounced J.-L. Tallien as wishing to end all arrests of suspects and attacked J.-S. Rovère's vendetta against E.-C. Maignet as initiating endless denunciations against deputies. This did not prevent him from actively promoting the rapid release of suspects. He was therefore clearly not allied to the extreme reactionaries around Tallien, L.-M.-S. Fréron and L. Lecointre at this stage. He was an exponent of a middle way policy of a reformed and regulated Revolutionary government. His membership on the Committee of General Security from 15 Fructidor Year II to 15 Nivôse Year III and again from 15 Pluviôse to 15 Ventôse (1 September 1794-4 January 1795 and 3 February–5 March) coincided with the period in which the committee tried to hold the line against unbridled grass-roots reaction. Finally, he revealed his antidemocratic instincts by moving the suppression of the 40 *sols* indemnity to *sans-culottes* attending sectional assemblies and by opposing a motion to distribute national lands to soldiers and the poor.

The combination of Jacobin resistance and popular agitation moved him to reaction. Although on 3 Complémentaire Year II (19 September), he insisted that turbulent elements on both sides should be repressed, he spoke against the radical Electoral Club in mid-Vendémiaire Year III (early October) and by mid-Brumaire (early November), was siding with Tallien in denunciations of the Jacobin club. By mid-Ventôse (early March 1795), he was saying that bread line disturbances were the work of Robespierrist agitators. Silent during the invasions of the Convention in the *journées* of the Germinal and Prairial, Bourdon was remarkably vindictive in his denunciations of Montagnard deputies after each of the risings. He was personally responsible for the arrest of seven of them and, in alliance with J.-B. Clauzel, conducted the campaign that sent seven Montagnards to the Military Commission after the Prairial conflict. His old hatred of Bouchotte also resurfaced on 5 Prairial (24 May 1795) when he obtained the arrest of Bouchotte and some of his Year II associates. However, Bourdon's time of greatest influence had been the two months after 9 Thermidor. He became less voluble and less significant as Year III wore on. He sat in the Council of Five Hundred during the First Directory as one of the additional deputies appointed by the Convention to meet the requirements of the Two-thirds Law. He became increasingly identified with the Right, at whose service he placed his talent for personal vituperation in the Year V by his attacks on the Directory's colonial policy. He was not a royalist but rather an anti-Jacobin. He may have been close to L. Carnot; J. Mallet du Pan classified him as a constitutional republican of the Thibaudeau type, concerned to reduce the power of the Directory. Arrested after the Directory's coup of 18 Fructidor Year V (4 September 1797), he was deported to Guyana, where he died.

N. Hampson, *Danton* (London, 1978); A. P. Herlaut, *Le Colonel Bouchotte*, 2 vols. (Paris, 1946).

C. Lucas

Related entries: BILLAUD-VARENNE; CORDELIERS CLUB; DANTON; FABRE; GIRONDINS; HEBERTISTS; INDULGENTS; LAW OF 22 PRAIRIAL; 9 THERMIDOR YEAR II; TALLIEN; 10 AUGUST 1792; VENDEE.

BOURGEOISIE, collective noun that was applied before, during, and after the French Revolution to various social categories. The root is *bourgeois*, a singular or plural noun applicable to any person or persons falling under these categories. Inherent in these words are ambiguities that cause misunderstanding, confusion, and disagreement in the study of the Revolution. Accordingly, whoever uses them should adopt definitions and adhere consistently to them, and any reader who encounters them without definition should determine from the context what they are intended to mean and whether they are used uniformly in that sense.

Samples of usage that historians have collected show that before the Revolution, *bourgeoisie* and *bourgeois* were used in ways that overlapped, clashed with one another, and varied from region to region. Generally all who lived in towns, whatever their economic or social condition, were called bourgeois. Often, however, that term was reserved for the wealthier and more prestigious townsmen, to the exclusion of the others. At La Rochelle, every ship owner was called a bourgeois, even though he lived in the country. In some towns, only merchants and masters of predominantly commercial guilds were called bourgeois, and in others anyone who employed one or more clerks or workmen was a bourgeois. Peasants called the urban landlords from whom they rented farms, *métairies*, fields, meadows, houses, or other property bourgeois, often with hostility. Conversely, in the tax rolls of Bigorre and Upper Languedoc, only the most important rural proprietors were called bourgeois, even though they lived in the country.

The word *bourgeois* also conveyed stereotypes, both favorable and unfavorable. People spoke respectfully of bourgeois as non-nobles who were wealthy and independent, enjoyed economic and physical security, were not obliged to work with their hands or solicit trade, and showed forethought and prudence in managing their wealth, even if it was mediocre. But bourgeois were also described as calculating, avaricious, exploitive, crude, uncultivated, and possessed of wealth they had acquired in demeaning or dishonest ways. Aristocratic contempt for bourgeois was a constant source of bourgeois resentment. Even when a bourgeois fulfilled his fantasies and became noble, it might take years or even decades for other nobles to recognize his family as such. A famous example of aristocratic ridicule of bourgeois was Molière's comedy, *Le bourgeois gentilhomme* (1670), in which an enriched merchant hires a tutor to teach him the manners and learning of gentlemen, with hilarious results. To some extent the bourgeois themselves accepted this aristocratic contempt and internalized it. The mother of the boy who later became the abbé de Choisy reminded him often that the only nobility that counted was the military nobility, and since his own recent forebears, although noble, were men of law, administrative officers, and state councillors, he was, after all, only a bourgeois.

Before the Revolution, *bourgeois* had two further meanings, those of the bourgeois living nobly and the privileged municipal bourgeoisie, both of which had legal significance. A bourgeois living nobly was a commoner *vivant noblement sur ses revenus*, or living, as nobles traditionally had, on income from land, urban property, annuities, or venal office, without practicing a profession or trade. We now call such persons *rentiers*. Many bourgeois living nobly were retired persons who, abandoning their vocations, had invested their savings in properties and annuities that yielded a reliable income. Others belonged to respected families who over some generations had acquired enough capital to live nobly on investments; it was not unknown for some of them to own *seigneuries*.

Whatever their origins, the bourgeois living nobly were taxed as a group for the *vingtième d'industrie*. In the political structure of the town, they comprised a political category, among several others, with uniform rights of representation and eligibility for municipal office. In the elections for the Estates General of 1789, in cities where occupational bodies met separately to elect the city assembly of the Third Estate, the bourgeois living nobly had an electoral assembly of their own, although it sometimes happened (as at Reims) that other individuals for whom no place could be found in the vocational categories were dumped into the bourgeois assembly, thereby diluting and denaturing it. During the Revolution, the bourgeois living nobly ceased to be described in the documents as bourgeois and came to be known instead as *propriétaires* (owners of property), a term that confirms their traditional differentiation from the professionals and merchants.

The privileged municipal bourgeoisie consisted of all those who enjoyed the *droit de bourgeoisie*, the "rights of the city," which municipalities granted to families that met local criteria on such considerations as length of residence, tax contributions, philanthropy, and adherence to the established religion, which was Roman Catholic. On meeting such requirements, a family was inscribed in the local *livre de bourgeoisie*, or "register of the bourgeoisie," and acquired privileges, some of which could be financially valuable. A bourgeois of Paris, for example, had the right to bring the wine produced from his vineyards into the city without paying the *octroi*, or municipal tariff. A bourgeois of Bordeaux could bring his wine into the town at the beginning of the annual market; all others had to keep theirs outside until the bourgeois had profited from the high prices of the first sales. In many towns, someone who enjoyed the *droit de bourgeoisie* was exempt from certain taxes or paid a low rate on others. Generally the *droit de bourgeoisie* conferred eligibility for election to the senior council of the town, from which representatives of shopkeepers' and artisans' guilds were excluded.

These privileged municipal bourgeoisies included most, if not all, resident nobles. This admixture came about for two reasons. First, many noble families had obtained nobility by buying offices that conferred noble status; once ennobled, they retained the municipal privileges they had previously enjoyed. Second, a noble family, on first taking residence in a town, would make a point of acquiring bourgeois privileges because they were worth having. In most cities that offered the *droit de bourgeoisie*, therefore, the privileged municipal bourgeoisie was a compound of nobles and wealthy commoners who were accustomed to bearing collectively the social and political responsibilities of the community and profiting from their status. That is why, during the elections of 1789 at Paris, many nobles insisted that as bourgeois of Paris, they had the right to sit in electoral assemblies of the Third Estate. As one of them put it, according to A. Cobban (1964), "There is no noble, whatever his rank, who is not accustomed to hear himself called Bourgeois of Paris, and there is none who could be offended to find himself sitting beside a member of the Third Estate judged worthy of its confidence.''

To some extent the Revolution reduced the semantic confusion inherent in *bourgeoisie* and *bourgeois*. When the National Assembly (1789–91) established civil and fiscal equality and abolished the urban legal categories in which privileges had been codified, it made the concepts of the bourgeois living nobly and the privileged municipal bourgeoisie nonfunctional so that they disappeared from use. But the other old usages of these words survived Revolutionary change. People still thought of bourgeois as townsmen, or well-to-do townsmen, or employers, and used the old stereotypes to which *bourgeois* was attached. Peasants continued to speak of urban landlords as bourgeois. And Revolutionary leaders like M. Robespierre in 1794 used *bourgeois* to refer to wealthy people, commoners or former nobles, who cared more for their property than for the Revolution or its principles, were reluctant to make contributions to the poor, and opposed or were expected to oppose the Convention's measures for redistributing wealth through confiscations, taxes, and the decrees of Ventôse (February and March 1794).

Our modern concept of the bourgeoisie as a social class born of capitalism and fundamentally capitalist in wealth, function, attitudes, values, and goals seems not to have been publicly articulated during the French Revolution, and there is no evidence that it counted in the social and political consciousness of that struggle. Although the Revolutionary A.-J. Barnave (1761–93) wrote in 1792 that the revolution of the Third Estate against the old order was generated by the development of commerce and industry, his essay to that effect was not published unil 1843, and no other eighteenth-century expression of this idea, or of any that approximated it, has been put forward. The concept of a capitalist revolutionary bourgeoisie appears rather to have emerged in socialist writings of the 1840s in Western Europe and is generally ascribed to K. Marx. Historians who call the French Revolution a bourgeois revolution imply that it was one in which a capitalist bourgeoisie overthrew a feudal aristocracy and the social system it dominated, then reconstructed the state, the society, and the culture according to capitalist interests and values, opening the way for the Industrial Revolution and the expansion of capitalism on a global scale. Historians who have followed this tradition include J. Jaurès, A. Mathiez, G. Lefebvre, and A. Soboul. All assume that the economic unity of the bourgeoisie in the relations of capitalism gives it a sense of social community and a political cohesion that makes it, under certain conditions, a revolutionary class. Soboul has called this interpretation the classic interpretation of the French Revolution, but since it was never fully articulated until the years 1901–4, when Jaurès published the first four volumes of his *Histoire socialiste*, there is some opposition among scholars to calling it classic. All would agree, however, that it has inspired many historians, including some of great distinction, and that in the Soviet world and even in France it is the dominant interpretation of the history of the French Revolution.

Since 1962 this view of the bourgeoisie and of its role in the French Revolution has been under scholarly attack in Great Britain, the United States, Canada, France, and the German Federal Republic. The evidence put forward against it is massive and decisive. Some of that evidence, paradoxically, was developed by Marxist historians who expected it to support the Marxist interpretation. The main negations of the concept of a bourgeoisie that was capitalist, non-noble, and revolutionary are the following:

1. That the capitalist bourgeoisie was in large part nonbourgeois since it included by definition the noble entrepreneurs who outweighed non-noble entrepreneurs in mining, canals, finance, and the metallurgical industries, and the ennobled bankers and merchants who continued in business while they and their families were being assimilated to the aristocracy.

2. That the capitalist bourgeoisie excluded most of the well-to-do commoners we usually call the middle class because only a minority of the middle class was capitalist, and the majority had the same kinds of noncapitalist wealth (land, urban property, annuities, venal offices, and occasionally *seigneuries*) as most of the nobles.

3. That the Revolutionary leadership, which took shape in the Estates General of 1789 and the National Assembly of 1789–91, had little to do with capitalism since it consisted mainly of legal practitioners and other professionals, intellectuals, nobles, and clerics, who far outnumbered the merchants and bankers in their midst.

4. That the Chambers of Commerce, which were the publicly constituted agencies of the capitalist bourgeoisie, took no Revolutionary initiatives, remained indifferent to the Revolutionary ideology, distrusted its economic liberalism, and concentrated on dissuading the National Assembly from taking measures that would harm business interests, such as the abolition of black slavery in the French West Indies.

5. That the concept of a capitalist bourgeoisie counted for nothing in the social consciousness of the Old Regime because the categories with which the French identified themselves before the Revolution were orders, ranks, and corporate bodies fixed by law and tradition rather than social classes determined by productive relationships.

In these and other ways the accumulated evidence makes it impossible to identify the political bourgeoisie of the Revolution with the social bourgeoisie of the Old Regime or to identify either with the economic bourgeoisie of pre-Revolutionary capitalism. The discrepancies that dissociate these concepts from one another are not small, eccentric divergences lost in the aggregates; they are large incongruities. Consequently, the theory embodied in the notion of a bourgeoisie that was simultaneously capitalist, non-noble, and Revolutionary describes neither the society of the Old Regime nor the origin and development of the Revolution. Its persistence in the face of the evidence mobilized against it since 1962 and the failure to substantiate it with evidence since that time cannot be accounted for on scholarly or scientific grounds.

The conclusion is that students of the French Revolution need to understand the semantic multiplicity of the word *bourgeoisie* so that when they meet it in the evidence or in the histories of the Revolution, they will interpret it critically and exactly. They should also be aware that it is freighted with too many ambiguities to serve in research as a general analytical tool or operational category.

A. Cobban, *The Social Interpretation of the French Revolution* (Cambridge, England, 1964); W. Doyle, *Origins of the French Revolution* (London and New York, 1980); G. Ellis, "The 'Marxist Interpretation' of the French Revolution," *Eng. Hist. Rev.* 93 (April 1978); F. Furet, *Penser la Révolution française* (Paris, 1978); P. Goubert, *The Ancien Régime*, vol. 1, trans. S. Cox (New York, 1973); R. Mousnier, *Les institutions de la France sous la monarchie absolue, 1598–1789* (Paris, 1974); G. V. Taylor, "Noncapitalist Wealth and the Origins of the French Revolution," *Am. Hist. Rev.* 79 (1967).

G. V. Taylor

Related entries: JAURES; MATHIEZ; LEFEBVRE; NATIONAL CONSTITUENT ASSEMBLY; *OCTROI*; *RENTE*; SOBOUL; VENTOSE DECREES.

BRETEUIL, LOUIS-AUGUSTE LE TONNELIER, BARON DE (1730-1807), diplomat and minister of state. Trained for the profession of arms, Breteuil gravitated into the diplomatic service. From 1758 to 1783 he served the French government at several posts: Cologne, Saint Petersburg, Stockholm, Vienna, and Naples. In 1778, at the Congress of Teschen, he helped mediate the brief war between Prussia and Austria. He returned to France in 1783 to become minister of state in charge of the king's domestic household, a post that gave him administrative responsibility for the department of Paris. He became known for his reform of penal institutions and hospitals, for restricting the use of *lettres de cachet*, and for clearing the hovels from bridges that spanned the Seine. Outspoken and abrasive, Breteuil was a staunch supporter of the absolute monarchy and called for energetic measures against the Parlement of Paris in 1788 and against the Third Estate in 1789. Louis XVI held him in great respect and appointed him chief minister when J. Necker was dismissed on 11 July 1789. But the storming of the Bastille and the recall of Necker to the ministry meant the end of Breteuil's career in the government. He emigrated to Soleure, where he received full powers from Louis XVI to negotiate with the courts of Europe on behalf of the French monarchy. But this power was revoked after 1790, and the leadership of the emigration passed to the princes.

"Breteuil," in *Biographie universelle*, ed. J.-Fr. Michaud, vol. 5 (Graz, 1966; rep. of 1854 ed.); G. Fagniez, *La politique de Vergennes et la diplomatie de Breteuil, 1774–1784* (Paris, 1922); J. Flammermont, *Négotiations secrètes de Louis XVI et du baron de Breteuil avec la Cour de Berlin, 1791–1792* (Paris, 1889); R.-M. Rampelberg, *Le ministre de la maison du roi, 1783–1787: Baron de Breteuil* (Paris, 1975).

R. D. Harris

Related entries: BASTILLE; COUNTERREVOLUTION; *EMIGRES*.

BRETON CLUB. See JACOBINS.

BRISSOT DE WARVILLE, JACQUES-PIERRE (1754–93), Girondist and writer. Before the French Revolution, Brissot was an aspiring *philosophe* who had published several books advocating various political and humanitarian reforms. But his books did not sell well, and since he had paid the printing costs himself, he was constantly in debt. By 1782 he had spent two months in the Bastille. His desperate financial condition drove him to spy for the Paris police, who gave him some money and allowed his works to circulate in France in exchange for information about other clandestine books and writers. Brissot was finally rescued from poverty by some wealthy friends, including financier E. Clavière, who sent him to the United States in 1788 as their financial agent.

When Brissot returned from America in the spring of 1789, the pre-Revolution had already begun. Like many other radical writers, Brissot saw the crisis as a unique opportunity to further his revolutionary ideals of a democratic society and to raise his own status within that new regime. During the spring of 1789, he was elected president of his electoral district in Paris, and in the summer he was elected to the Paris Communal Assembly.

In August 1789 Brissot wrote a constitution for Paris, the Plan de municipalité, which after several revisions and stages became the model for the municipal constitution passed by the National Assembly in 1790. The Plan expressed Brissot's belief in representative democracy. It divided Paris into three parts: sixty districts that had electoral and administrative responsibilities but little legislative power; the Communal Assembly, composed of representatives from the districts; and the Town Council, composed of the mayor and his assistants. The Plan vested real political power in the Communal Assembly. Mayor J.-S. Bailly and the districts, led by the Cordeliers, immediately attacked the Plan and tried to impose their own models. Bailly wanted a hierarchical municipal government that was enlightened and efficient but antidemocratic. The Cordeliers objected to Brissot's Plan for the opposite reason—that it was not democratic enough.

The Paris municipal revolution of 1789–90 was largely a struggle between factions representing these viewpoints. Brissot became one of the leaders of a group in the provisional Communal Assembly, fighting for a municipal system based on representative democracy. His supporters included the marquis de Condorcet, C. Fauchet, J.-P. Garran-Coulon, J.-H. Bancal des Issarts, and N. de Bonneville. These were the first Brissotins, and it is no coincidence that all of them became leading Girondins during 1792–93.

At the same time, Brissot further enhanced his reputation and his financial position by starting a newspaper, the *Patriote français*. This four-page, in-folio daily gave brief and well-written accounts of international, national, and local news and included a book review and entertainment listings in each issue. Among the paper's regular contributors were Madame Roland and F. Lanthenas, two of Brissot's closest allies. Brissot used the newspaper to further the cause of representative democracy, as well as his career and the careers of his friends. Of the hundreds of newspapers begun during this period, the *Patriote français* became one of the most popular in the nation.

Brissot was not reelected to the Communal Assembly in August 1790 and spent the next year channeling his political energies through various clubs, including the Jacobins, the Cercle Social, and, most important, the Société des Amis des Noirs. Brissot founded this last club in 1788, and by the outbreak of the Revolution it had 140 members, including Condorcet, Clavière, marquis de Lafayette, H.-G. R. Mirabeau, E.-J. Sieyès, J. Pétion, and abbé Grégoire. The Amis des Noirs lobbied for an immediate end to the slave trade and for a gradual end to slavery itself. While the group was highly visible among the patriots, it was not very effective in achieving its goals. In 1790, the Constituent Assembly voted to continue slavery in the West Indian colonies, and slavery was not abolished officially until 1793. One reason for the ineffectiveness of the Amis des Noirs was that Brissot and his friends used idealistic moral arguments instead of basing their case against slavery on economic grounds. Nonetheless, Brissot's role in the club furthered his reputation as a zealous patriot and publicist.

Brissot's response to Louis XVI's flight to Varennes is still a subject of controversy among historians. There is no doubt that Brissot played an important role in the campaign to overthrow the king following 21 June 1791, but many of his activities were performed privately, among friends. He was a master of behind-the-scenes political intrigue. Clearly Brissot wanted to leave himself room to maneuver during the unprecedented crisis. His *Patriote français* shrewdly praised republican groups and their petitions without itself advocating the overthrow of the monarchy. But such ambiguity made him vulnerable to his enemies, who accused him of supporting the duc d'Orléans' monarchical ambitions, a charge that was to reappear in 1793. Despite these accusations, Brissot's friends publicly defended his patriotism, and his popularity increased during the summer of 1791.

During the first two years of the Revolution, then, Brissot had made his reputation as a journalist, clubbist, and local political activist. But all along he had aspired to greater power and badly wanted to become a member of the national legislature. That opportunity finally came in September 1791 when Brissot won election as Paris' twelfth deputy to the Legislative Assembly. Brissot made the most of this new opportunity. Within months he became one of the nation's most important politicians and the leader of the Girondins. This period marked the zenith of Brissot's political career.

The Girondins were not a political party; they were a group of friends and like-minded individuals who met in clubs and salons but did not necessarily vote as a bloc inside the Assembly. Nevertheless, they shared some distinct political positions, including a belief in representative democracy, support for the Civil Constitution of the Clergy, and the need for a political economy established along laissez-faire principles. The core of the Girondins came from two distinct groups: a group of Paris-based politicians who had become friendly with Brissot during the municipal revolution, among whom were Fauchet, Condorcet, Garran-

Coulon, and J. Godard, and a group of extraordinary orators from the Department of the Gironde, including A. Gensonné, J.-A. Grangeneuve, M.-E. Guadet, and P.-V. Vergniaud.

At first the Legislative Assembly was dominated by another faction, the Feuillants, and the Girondins were a minority. But during the fall of 1791, Brissot and his friends effectively used the issue of a war with Austria to increase their power. In an important speech made to the Jacobins on 15 December 1791, Brissot listed three essential reasons for going to war: to rally the people around a patriotic cause, to purge Europe of despotism, and to test the king's loyalty. Although some Jacobins, including M. Robespierre, objected to the speech, the Girondins successfully exploited the issue and dramatically increased their popularity in the Legislative Assembly. By 1792 this policy had been so successful that the Feuillants had lost practically all power, and the king's ministers were threatened with impeachment.

The Girondins were rewarded for these efforts in March 1792 when Louis XVI dismissed his Feuillant ministers and accepted a ministry that included E. Clavière and J.-M. Roland, two ministers hand-picked by Brissot. Now that Brissot and his friends controlled the Legislative Assembly and the ministry, they were able to pass a declaration of war against Austria on 20 April 1792. When the first campaigns went poorly, several deputies blamed the Girondins for mismanaging the war. Brissot and his friends, in turn, blamed the defeats on the king's half-hearted support of the Revolution. On 10 June 1792 Louis XVI dismissed the Girondin ministers for publicly accusing him of disloyalty.

During the weeks preceding the 10 August 1792 overthrow of the monarchy, Brissot supported the republicans but stopped short of advocating a republic himself. He wanted to pressure the king into accepting the Girondins back into the ministry on their terms. Brissot believed that if the Girondins could force the king to restore them, they could then isolate the king, thereby effectively diminishing his power without a new revolution.

What Brissot misunderstood, or at least underestimated, was the power of the Parisian *sans-culottes*. Brissot hoped to use the *sans-culottes* to intimidate the king, but he never took them seriously as a political force. After 10 August 1792, tensions between Girondins and *sans-culottes* grew. Although the Girondins dominated the executive branch, they in fact owed their new control of the executive branch to the *sans-culottes*, who had risen against the king. But the *sans-culottes* dissented from many Girondin positions; they wanted wage and price controls, a more forcefully managed war, and a renunciation of the Civil Constitution of the Clergy. During the weeks following 10 August, the *sans-culottes* were led by a group of municipal politicians in the Paris Commune and a group of national deputies known as the Montagnards, led by Robespierre.

Until September 1792 there were several efforts made to reconcile Brissot and Robespierre, and their respective allies. But the September Massacres intensified the rivalry between the two groups and cut off any further communication between them. Although Brissot and his friends were easily elected to the National

Convention, only one Girondin was elected from Paris, the center of the *sans-culotte* movement.

The struggle between the Girondins and the Montagnards soon reached the Jacobins, and on 10 October 1792 Brissot was expelled from the club because of his opposition to the Paris Commune. In his reply, *A tous les républicains de France sur la Société des Jacobins de Paris*, Brissot accused his adversaries of being anarchists and of dividing the Republic so that Paris would dominate the rest of the nation.

Brissot's position inside the Convention did not slip until the trial of Louis XVI. The Montagnards used the trial against the Girondins in precisely the same way that the Girondins had used the war issue against the Feuillants one year earlier. The Montagnards were united in their call for the king's head, and they organized a persuasive propaganda campaign that labeled the Girondins as monarchists. Brissot and his allies were divided on what to do with the king after he had been found guilty. Some wanted to imprison him; others wanted to exile him; still others wanted to execute him. Brissot himself stated that he would support regicide but only after it had been approved by the people in a nationwide referendum.

By the time Louis XVI was executed, Brissot's influence had been seriously eroded. During the spring of 1793, a number of factors, including a deteriorating economy, counterrevolution in the Vendée, defeats in battle and C. Dumouriez's treason, and a failed attempt to impeach J.-P. Marat contributed to the decline of the Girondins' power.

Brissot's political career finally came to an end on 31 May 1793, when Parisians invaded the Convention, demanding the arrest of all Girondins. On 2 June the Convention heeded this request and ordered the arrest of Brissot and twenty-nine other Girondins. Brissot fled to the provinces but was discovered in Moulins, posing as a Swiss merchant. He was returned to Paris on 22 June and sat in prison for five months, where he composed his memoirs and prepared his defense. His trial was an excellent demonstration of Montagnard propaganda, and Brissot was found guilty within a week. On 31 October 1793 he died on the scaffold.

Brissot's rise from an impoverished and little-known writer to one of the most important politicians in Revolutionary France is remarkable. He deserves praise for his commitment to liberty and political equality, for his abolitionist and humanitarian causes, and for his political talents in leading the Girondins. But despite these attributes, Brissot made some major mistakes, which limited his effectiveness as a statesman. He rose to national prominence by advocating a war with Austria, a policy that proved disastrous for the Revolution. His rigid economic doctrines prevented him from understanding the aspirations and power of the Parisian *sans-culottes*. His war created a national emergency that required solutions too radical for his social and economic policies.

J. P. Brissot de Warville, *Correspondance et papiers*, C. Perroud, ed. (Paris, 1912) and *Mémoires*, ed. C. Perroud, 2 vols. (Paris, 1910); R. Darnton, *The Literary Under-*

ground of the Old Regime (Cambridge, Mass., 1982); E. Ellery, *Brissot de Warville: A Study in the History of the French Revolution* (New York, 1915; repr. 1970); C. Perroud, ed., *Lettres de Mme. Roland*, 2 vols. (Paris, 1900–1902); D. P. Resnick, "The Société des Amis des Noirs and the Abolition of Slavery," *Fr. Hist. Stud.* 7 (1972); M. J. Sydenham, *The Girondins* (London, 1961).

G. Kates

Related entries: BAILLY; CIVIL CONSTITUTION OF THE CLERGY; CORDELIERS CLUB; DUMOURIEZ; FEUILLANTS; GENSONNE; GIRONDINS; GUADET; ROBESPIERRE, M.; SEPTEMBER MASSACRES; SOCIETE DES AMIS DES NOIRS; VARENNES; VENDEE; VERGNIAUD.

BRISSOTINS. See GIRONDINS.

BROGLIE, VICTOR-FRANCOIS, DUC DE (1718–1804), general, minister of war. The duc de Broglie was born to a noble family of Italian origin that had entered French service in the mid-seventeenth century. Above all, the Broglie family followed a military vocation; both the father and grandfather of Victor-François had been awarded marshal's batons. Victor-François saw his first military action before he reached the age of fifteen. At sixteen he commanded a company of cavalry. After campaigning with his father and M. de Saxe, Broglie was promoted to general in 1743, to *maréchal de camp* in 1745, and to lieutenant general in 1748.

The Seven Years War brought him both personal triumph and disgrace. Broglie handled French cavalry well enough at Rossbach to escape that French disaster with his reputation intact. The next campaign brought him further honors. His victory over the duke of Brunswick at Bergen won him the highest praise from Louis XV and from the Holy Roman Emperor. In December 1759 he became a marshal of France. The field instructions he drafted for the campaign of 1760 constituted a watershed in the development of the combat division, later to be perfected under the Revolution. However, in July 1761 he met defeat at Filingshausen, probably through the prince de Soubise's failure to support him adequately. Broglie now fell victim to his own brusque and maladroit personality. The duc de Choiseul, French foreign minister, had always regarded the Broglie family with extreme disdain, whereas the prince de Soubise enjoyed great favor at court. By *lettre de cachet*, Broglie was exiled to his Normandy estate in February 1762.

The exile was not permanent. Welcomed back at court, he was appointed governor of the Trois-Evêchés in 1771. Then, with French involvement in the American Revolution, he received command of the French army concentrated in Normandy against England. There, at Vaussieux, he conducted tactical experiments important to the development of the French army. By 1789, the marshal was a crucial military adviser to Louis XVI. The imperious and abrupt septuagenarian urged Louis to take strong measures against the rising threat of disorder. Louis finally turned to him and appointed him minister of war when J. Necker fell on 11 July. Yet once in a position to march against Paris with the troops he had concentrated around Versailles, Marshal Broglie had to report that his men were unreliable and that he could not even guarantee the king's safety should the king decide to flee Versailles.

The frustrated marshal emigrated shortly after the fall of the Bastille and joined L. Condé's forces. Broglie fought his last military campaign as commander of a corps of *émigrés* in 1792. Later Broglie received the title of marshal from the czar. When Napoleon recreated the marshalate, he invited Broglie to return to France, but the old aristocrat chose to end his days as an *émigré* in Germany, dying at Munster in 1804. His son, the liberal noble C.-L.-V. Broglie, had preceded him in death, going to the scaffold in 1794.

J. de La Varende, *Les Broglies* (Paris, 1950).

J. A. Lynn

Related entries: CONDE; COUNTERREVOLUTION; *EMIGRES*; GUIBERT; NECKER.

BRUMAIRE, COUP OF 18. See COUP OF 18 BRUMAIRE.

BRUNSWICK, KARL WILHELM FERDINAND, DUKE OF (1735–1806), German general, born in Wolfenbuttel. Well educated, widely traveled, and a man of broad cultural interests, he first served in the Seven Years War, becoming a Prussian field marshal. He succeeded his father as duke of Brunswick in 1780 and earned a reputation as a model enlightened ruler. In 1787 he commanded the Prussian army that occupied the United Netherlands to suppress the Dutch patriot movement.

Early in 1792, he was offered command of the French army, but at the onset of the War of the First Coalition in April, he accepted command of the Prussian and Austrian forces. Despite his known liberal sympathies, his name was given to the threatening manifesto of the coalition powers in July 1792. His invasion of France was turned back at Valmy on 20 September 1792. He resigned his command in 1794 and returned to his duchy. In 1806, urged by Queen Louise of Prussia, he took command of the Prussian army against Napoleon but was badly defeated and mortally wounded at Auerstädt on 14 October. He died near Hamburg on 10 November 1806.

Allgemeine deutsch Biographie, vol. 15 (Leipzig, 1875–1912); K. Heidrich, *Preussen im Kampfe gegen die französische Revolution bis zur zweiten Teilung Polens* (Stuttgart and Berlin, 1908).

H. A. Barton

Related entries: BATTLE OF VALMY; BRUNSWICK MANIFESTO; FIRST COALITION.

BRUNSWICK MANIFESTO, declaration issued on 25 July 1792 in the name of the duke of Brunswick, commander of the Prussian and Austrian forces then preparing to invade France following the outbreak of the War of the First Coalition (1792-97) in April, on behalf of the allied monarchs. This declaration proclaimed that the allies were invading France to suppress anarchy and restore the king's authority. Peaceful citizens were guaranteed protection, but those who bore arms against the allies would be treated "according to the rigor of the laws of war, and their houses demolished or burned." Public authorities were to be accountable for peace and order within their districts, and the city of Paris was held specifically responsible for the safety of the royal family, on pain of "military punishment and total destruction."

The manifesto was well precedented in the diplomatic usage of the eighteenth century and was the culmination of numerous competing but basically similar projects for such a declaration emanating from the *émigrés*, the Tuileries, and the foreign courts ever since 1789. In the form adopted, it was prepared by the Belgian marquis de Limon, secretly commissioned by the Swedish count A. von Fersen, who was in close contact with Marie Antoinette.

News of the manifesto reached Paris by 28 July, where it aroused a patriotic furor largely credited with having precipitated the storming of the Tuileries palace and the overthrow of the French monarchy on 10 August 1792.

H. A. Barton, "The Origins of the Brunswick Manifesto," *Fr. Hist. Stud.* 5 (1967); J. H. Stewart, ed., *A Documentary Survey of the French Revolution* (New York, 1951).

H. A. Barton

Related entries: BRUNSWICK; *EMIGRES*; FERSEN; FIRST COALITION; 10 AUGUST 1792.

BUONARROTI, FILIPPO MICHELE   (also PHILIPPE) (1763-1837), Babouvist leader, anti-Metternich conspirator. As a Jacobin agent and Babouvist leader who became a cosmopolitan conspirator during the Metternich era, Buonarroti served as a prototype for nineteenth-century professional revolutionaries, such as A. Blanqui and M. Bakunin. He also provided a link between eighteenth- and nineteenth-century radical movements.

He was born in Pisa into a family of Tuscan patricians, descended from Michelangelo's brother. After receiving a law degree from the University of Pisa and securing the patronage of the Austrian grand duke, he seemed destined to become a Florentine magistrate—a career his son, Cosimo, pursued successfully. But his conversion to the doctrines of J.-J. Rousseau made him an enemy of the Hapsburg regime. As an anticlerical Freemason and radical journalist, he was soon at odds with the authorities. In October 1789 he left Italy, permanently abandoning family and fortune, in order to serve the French Revolutionary cause. He went first to Corsica where he worked as a Jacobin agent and made friends with the Bonapartes while opposing P. Paoli's anglophile policy. He also made secret missions to Italy, accompanied military expeditions to Saint-Pierre and Toulon, and was naturalized as a French citizen by a decree of 27 May 1793 during a visit to Paris where he met M. Robespierre. In April 1794 he was made national commissioner of Oneglia and tried to enforce Jacobin legislation in that part of French-occupied Italy despite local resistance.

Arrested for his Robespierrist activities after Thermidor, he was imprisoned in Plessis where he met and joined forces with F.-N. Babeuf. On being released in 1795, he served the Directory as an unofficial adviser on Italian affairs even while joining in the Babouvist plot against the government. Arrested with his co-conspirators on 8 May 1796, he was condemned to captivity in a fortress near Cherbourg.

After Napoleon's rise, his situation was eased, thanks to his friendship with the Bonapartes. In 1806 he went to Geneva where, under police supervision, he eked out a living teaching music and Italian. His clandestine activities included contacting the Carbonari in northern Italy and recruiting agents for his own cosmopolitan secret society, the Sublimes Maîtres Parfaits. After Waterloo, he tried, through this society, to infiltrate and control the various underground movements of resistance to Metternich and the Bourbons. His plans were discovered when one of his agents, A. Andryane, was captured by Metternich's police in 1823. After a year in hiding, he fled to Brussels, where he recruited new agents for his reorganized secret society, the Monde, and resumed contact with exiled officials of the First Republic, such as B. Barère and M.-G.-A. Vadier. Stimulated by their arguments about the Revolution, he wrote his two-volume chronicle, interwoven with documents, defending Robespierre's policy, tracing the history of the Babeuf plot, and expounding its ideology.

First published in Brussels in 1828, then in Paris in 1830, and in an English translation (by the Chartist B. O'Brien) in 1836, the *Conspiration pour l'égalité dite de Babeuf* appeared thereafter in several French abridgements and was translated into German, Italian, and Russian (under Communist auspices) in the twentieth century. By making Robespierre and his colleagues appear as conscious architects of a communist republic, based on blueprints provided by Rousseau, G. Mably, and A. Morellet, it injected a spirit of revolutionary messianism into continental socialism, founded a long-lived historiographical school, and created a martyrology that inspired many of the future men of 1848.

Returning to Paris after the July Revolution, Buonarroti participated actively in the left-wing opposition to the Orleanists by working, in close collaboration with C. Teste and V. d'Argenson, through such organizations as the Charbonnerie Reformée and the Société des Droits de l'Homme. With his two associates, he directed a steady stream of propaganda, supporting republican and socialist movements. Outside France, he was deeply involved in Italian affairs, dominating various secret societies in northern Italy and precipitating a schism with G. Mazzini. He also gained a following among Belgian radicals and English Chartists. His funeral was an occasion for a Parisian demonstration when he died, in 1837, since he had helped to perpetuate as well as reshape the Jacobin heritage.

With his death, his conspiratorial network collapsed and his reputation (which owed much both to the romantic ethos and his personal magnetism) rapidly diminished. After the fall of the Second Republic discredited the men of 1848, who had revered him as the patriarch of revolution, his name was forgotten for almost a century. Since the 1930s, however, he has become the focal figure for a variety of scholarly controversies involving pre-Marxian socialism, the role of French Jacobinism in the Risorgimento, the real or mythic nature of cosmopolitan conspiracy in Metternich's Europe, French Revolutionary historiography, and the origins of a totalitarian left.

P. Buonarroti, *Conspiration pour l'Egalité dite de Babeuf*, 2 vols. (Paris, 1957); E. Eisenstein, *The First Professional Revolutionary: F. M. Buonarroti* (Cambridge, Mass., 1959); A. Galente Garrone, *Buonarroti e Babeuf* (Turin, 1948); P. Onnis, *F. Buonarroti e Àltri Studi* (Rome, 1971); A. Saitta, *Filippo Buonarroti*, 2 vols. (Rome, 1951).

E. Eisenstein

Related entries: BABEUF; CONSPIRACY OF EQUALS; GENERAL WILL; 9 THERMIDOR YEAR II; ROBESPIERRE, M.; ROUSSEAU.

BUREAU DE POLICE GENERALE, a key administrative section of the Committee of Public Safety, which played a major role in the events leading up to the fall of M. Robespierre. Although in the constitutional theory of the Terror, police matters were under the purview of the Committee of General Security, the great expansion of the numbers of local elected magistrates and officials and their tendency to what was seen as torpor and moderation led the Committee of Public Safety to seek to extend central power over the administrative apparatus. The objective was to exercise stricter control over the administration and to purge the apparatus as part of a general systematization of the Terror. The military surveillants used by P.-G. Gateau were a forerunner of this process. Hence a decree of the Committee of Public Safety on 27 Germinal Year II established *le bureau de surveillance administrative et de police générale* as a new section of the committee's own administrative apparatus. It was probably intended to complement the action of the Committee of General Security rather than to rival it; and L. Saint-Just at least tried to limit friction both by seeking to divert some affairs from the *bureau* to the Committee of General Security, and by permitting the Executive Commission for Civil Administration, Police, and Courts to execute its decision. However, Robespierre did not take the same stance and papers were sent to him in his retreat at M. Duplay's early in Messidor. The *bureau* thus became for many people nothing more than part of the Robespierrist-dominated state secret police. It did contain a spy service, including M.-A. Jullian in Bordeaux, J. Garnerin in Alsace, P.-C. Pottofeux in Troyes, and P. Guerin and H. Roussevile in Paris. Hence a legend, dating from the autumn of 1794, made the *bureau* the tool of the triumvirate, although this was not so, particularly after 15 Messidor when it was at last properly organized. Decisions taken by the three were in fact confirmed by the full committee.

Even so, it was resented by the group hostile to Robespierre on the Committee of General Security, and one recent authority claims that it did more than anything else to embitter relations between the two committees in the period before Thermidor. It was indeed one of the factors that led many people to support the overthrow of Robespierre. As a result, it probably did more to unleash boundary conflicts than it did to censure dubious or career-minded officials. Before Thermidor it dealt with some 3,777 affairs, producing 464 decisions of which 250 were arrests and 50 were liberations; 295 of these concerned officials. The number of decisions taken was actually far fewer than those taken by the Committee of General Security, even though it was the *bureau* that came to be regarded as responsible for stepping up the Terror.

At its height the *bureau* consisted of four divisions arranged on a largely geographical basis together with a central bureau. Its staff rose from eighteen in Floréal to over fifty by Thermidor, when it represented just under 10 percent of the Committee of Public Safety's total administrative staff. Its secretary in chief was A. Lejeune, an invalid soldier and protégé of Saint-Just who had previously worked in the Foreign Affairs Commission. He himself claimed that he used his post to help victims of the Terror rather than to prosecute them and hence incurred the hostility of Robespierre and Saint-Just. The *bureau* was wound up on 27 Thermidor, having failed to control the army of officials or to increase governmental centralization. Its historical image has thus been more of a political than an administrative one.

C. H. Church, *Revolution and Red Tape* (Oxford, 1981); J. P. Gros, *Sainte-Just, sa politique et ses missions* (Paris, 1976); A. Ording, *Le Bureau de Police du Comité de Salut Public* (Oslo, 1930).

C. Church

Related entries: COMMITTEE OF GENERAL SECURITY; COMMITTEE OF PUBLIC SAFETY; 9 THERMIDOR YEAR II; ROBESPIERRE, M.

BURKE, EDMUND (1729-97), member of Parliament and political theorist. One of the most prominent and eloquent British statesmen of his time, Burke tolled the bell of counterrevolution long before the movement had begun to take form. For decades a forceful opponent of the expansion of royal power, Burke molded the same language and conceptual apparatus of traditional Whiggism that he had used to support American resistance to British colonial policy into a powerful argument against the French Revolution.

Burke was born in Dublin, the son of a middle-class Protestant father and a Catholic mother. He received his education at Trinity College, where he composed an influential work on aesthetics that was published with revisions in 1757 under the title, *A Philosophical Inquiry into the Origins of our Ideas on the Sublime and the Beautiful*. Shortly after graduation in 1749, Burke began legal training at the Middle Temple, but his interest in literature led him to abandon his legal education. Publication of various political works—most notably *The Vindication of Natural Society* in 1756—opened the door to powerful political circles. Following a stint as secretary to W. Hamilton and then to the marquis of Rockingham, Burke ran successfully for Parliament, which he entered in 1766 under Rockingham's auspices. A master stylist of the English language, Burke was made a spokesman of the Rockingham faction, though he was never fully accepted within it. His capacity for work was prodigious. When warming to a cause, he made every effort to inquire into its background; few could match his understanding of the intricacies of American history or the Warren Hastings case. But the passionate nature of his stands eventually won him the scorn of younger members of Parliament and put great strain on his political alliances, leaving his political effectiveness considerably reduced in an age when personal relationships were at the core of the political process. Although at the end of his career, the turn of events brought many converts to his crusade against the French Revolution, Burke had ceased to exercise much political influence in Parliament, and he retired in 1794 alienated from some who had been his closest associates.

That Burke should so early and so passionately take up the cause of counterrevolution in his later years has long been thought by many, including some of his contemporaries, to constitute a betrayal of his Whig principles, but recently the balance of scholarly opinion has tipped in favor of Burke's own claim that his opposition to the French Revolution was consistent with his earlier ideas. Certainly fundamental themes reappear throughout his speeches and writings. Again and again Burke emphasized that social institutions are at least as much the product of history as they are of human reason and that no purely theoretical construct alone can be used to determine social or political policy. Never did Burke advocate major social or political changes that would have meant departure from traditional practice in any abrupt or violent way. Such principles allowed him to take what might appear to be politically progressive positions on, for example, the American colonies—where he argued against attempts to force them to pay higher taxes and to interfere more directly in their internal affairs— and the relationship between the king and Parliament—where he argued for reducing royal intervention in parliamentary affairs. Yet his grounds for taking these positions were strongly traditionalist. Burke rested his case for the colonies on the contention that current British colonial policy was violating the historically acquired right of colonial self-rule and his case for an independent Parliament on the notion that Parliament had a historic right to defend English liberties. Burke remained a strong opponent of parliamentary reform, in particular of any reform that would have made representation less virtual and more direct.

It seems hardly inconsistent with his earlier positions, therefore, that when the French Revolution exploded in 1789, Burke should, after an initial period of suspended judgment, come to abhor a movement that had interrupted established procedures of government with the threat and use of mob violence. For the next seven years Burke made the counterrevolution a central focus of his public life. Perceiving in the French Revolution a threat not merely to England but to civilization itself, Burke brought together his previously acquired knowledge of French society and the information he received from French exiles in Britain—most notably C.-A. de Calonne—to produce a steady stream of pamphlets and speeches warning Europe of the dangers of the Revolution to society. Although British public opinion was slow to respond to his admonitions and W. Pitt was reluctant to lead the kind of crusade Burke was preaching, his counterrevolutionary writings were widely read and debated in his own time and long into the following centuries.

Most thorough and remarkably successful (many thousands of copies were sold within a few months of publication, and the work was quickly translated into French, German, and Italian) was Burke's seminal *Reflections on the Revolution in France*, the first of his major counterrevolutionary writings. The work was composed in response to inquiries made in late 1789 by a young acquaintance, C. DePont, concerning Burke's view of the latest events unfolding in France. By this time Burke had arrived at the profoundly hostile stance he maintained until the end of his life, and his passions on the subject had recently been kindled by a sermon given by a Dr. R. Price, "A Discourse on the Love of Country," at the Revolution Society on 4 November. Price perceived in the French Revolution the coming of a new glorious age of reform throughout Europe, which would complete in England the unfinished business of the Revolution of 1688, including the reform of Parliament and the disestablishment of the Anglican church; the society had not only heard Price out but had also sent its congratulations to the National Assembly in Paris for its defense of human rights and its reorganization of government. As its full title indicates, Burke's *Reflections on the Revolution in France and on the Proceedings in Certain Societies in London Relative to that Event: in a Letter Intended to Have Been Sent to a Gentleman in Paris* was transformed from a personal reply to a private letter into a public examination of the claims of the Revolution's supporters. Working for nearly a year on the project, Burke published the work in November 1790.

The first half of the *Reflections* was intended to show that the Revolution was unnecessary and dangerous, the second half that it was riddled with internal contradictions. In demonstrating that the Revolution was unnecessary, Burke did not deny that the Old Regime needed reform. But his central point was that the Old Regime was slowly remedying its ills within the structure of traditional institutions. There were clear signs, Burke thought, that economic progress was being made and that, as absolute monarchy was falling of its own weight, liberty was increasingly secure. Making virtually no mention of the economic plight of the peasants and artisans, Burke charged an unholy alliance of new monied interests and atheistic *philosophes* with having fomented a revolutionary movement that threatened to uproot traditional government, the church, and the hierarchy of privilege. To Burke, the Revolutionaries' doctrines of rights were meaningless in that they were conceived without reference to the needs of society; the Revolutionaries' social theories were misleading in that they distracted men from considering the practical requirements of governance; and the Revolutionaries' celebration of change was destructive of that healthy regard for tradition that in normal times imposed restraint on impulsive behavior. Burke was not opposing rights, theory, or change per se but what he regarded as the Revolutionaries' esteem for rights disconnected from duties, theory unconditioned by practice, and change unguided by experience. The Revolution, he warned, was destroying the best of the Old World; loud and brash, it was opening the flood-gates of cheap commercialism and social anarchy. "The age of chivalry is gone," he sighed. "That of sophisters, economists, and calculators has succeeded, and the glory of Europe is extinguished forever."

In the concluding part of the work, Burke reviewed the reforms of the National Assembly. As a whole he regarded them as an unmitigated disaster, describing them as inconsistent, unwise, and unjust. For all their commitment to the principle of equality, Burke contended, the Revolutionaries had produced a plan of government that was essentially inequitable. The policies of property confiscation, he charged, violated fundamental human rights; the new fiscal measures were bound to fail; and discipline in the army had been subverted by the widespread challenge to the notion of authority. In the end, Burke predicted, the Republic was fated to fall into the hands of a military ruler.

Burke's *Reflections* played a crucial role in the argument over the French Revolution. It prompted numerous responses, among them T. Paine's *Rights of Man* in 1792. But it was also a major source of inspiration to countless counterrevolutionary writers. Claims regarding the abstract nature of the Revolutionaries' doctrines and those of the *philosophes*, the supposed threat to organic social relationships posed by the Revolution, and the destruction caused by the Revolution would be heard again and again in the writings of the counterrevolution and in the works of later historians sympathetic to its message. That these claims should remain a source of controversy in the twentieth century is due in no small part to Burke's eloquent statement of them barely a year after the fall of the Bastille.

G. W. Chapman, *Edmund Burke—The Practical Imagination* (Cambridge, Mass., 1967); C. B. Cone, *Burke and the Nature of Politics*, 2 vols. (Lexington, Ky., 1957, 1964); I. Kramnick, *The Rage of Edmund Burke: Portrait of an Ambivalent Conservative* (New York, 1977); P. J. Stanlis, *Edmund Burke and the Natural Law* (Ann Arbor, 1958); B. T. Wilkins, *The Problem of Burke's Political Philosophy* (Oxford, 1967).

                                                                  T. E. Kaiser

Related entries: CALONNE; COUNTERREVOLUTION; PAINE; PITT.

BUZOT, FRANCOIS-NICOLAS-LEONARD (1760-94), Girondist. Son of a provincial *procureur*, Buzot became a prominent lawyer in Evreux before the Revolution and married the daughter of a manufacturer. He gained election to the Estates General and joined the radical camp, favoring abolition of feudal privileges and full powers for the Assembly. The flight to Varennes made Buzot a republican; but, returning to Evreux in 1791, he limited his activities to the presidency of the local Criminal Tribunal. Elected to the National Convention in 1792, Buzot associated with Girondist deputies in denouncing the September Massacres and accusing M. Robespierre of conspiring to create a dictatorship. To offset the growing support of Paris for the Jacobins, he advocated creating a departmental guard, drawn from all over France, to protect the Convention. Buzot also alienated the Jacobins by wishing to submit the case against Louis

XVI to the people instead of deciding it in the Convention; personally, he favored the death penalty.

Named a member of the Committee of Public Safety and General Defense, Buzot was denounced by J.-P. Marat and the Paris sections in 1793 for complicity in C. Dumouriez' defection. He was one of the twenty-two Girondist deputies arrested on 2 June but escaped to Evreux before moving to Caen where he observed the federalist revolt as a nonparticipant. After its collapse, Buzot fled to Brittany and Bordeaux with other Girondins. Eventually he attempted to escape France by sea but was identified and fled overland with J. Pétion. The two apparently shot themselves, and their bodies, partially eaten by wolves, were found in the woods. Jacobin authorities later punished those who had given him shelter. Buzot's house in Evreux was demolished and in its place was erected a pyramid with an abusive inscription. The inscription was removed after Thermidor.

In hiding, Buzot wrote memoirs in which he denounced the Jacobins. He also argued that federalism was appropriate for large countries like the United States but not for France. He wished to maintain a proper balance between Paris and the provinces.

F. Buzot, *Mémoires inédits* (Paris, 1866); J. Herissay, *Un Girondin, François Buzot* (Paris, 1907).

D. Stone

Related entries: DUMOURIEZ; ESTATES GENERAL; FEDERALISM; GIRONDINS.

C

CABARRUS, FRANCOIS, COMTE DE (1752-1810), banker. Born at Bayonne into a rich shipping and trading family established in this city, at Bordeaux,
and in Spain, Cabarrus was sent to learn the business with a French correspondent
at Saragossa. Appointed director of a soap factory near Madrid in 1773, he
became friendly with G.-M. Jovellanos and was patronized by P.-R. Camponanes
and P.-A.-J. Olavide. On his advice during the American Revolution, the Spanish
treasury solved its cash-flow problems by a scheme of interest-yielding bearer
bonds functioning as short-term money. In 1782, he was instrumental in the
creation of the Saint-Charles Bank, of which he became the director. This bank
operated as a paying institution for the royal treasury at a discount of 4 percent
and a commission of 1/6 of 1 percent. Its profits attracted considerable speculation
in its shares, especially among Parisian financiers who employed H.-G. R.
Mirabeau in an unsuccessful pamphlet war to depreciate their market value.
From the bank's profits, he established the Philippines Company with a monopoly
of Spanish Pacific trade in 1785 and shortly afterward became a member of the
Council of Finance. He fell out of favor and was imprisoned from mid-1790 to
late 1792. Indemnified on his release by a pension and the title of count, he
became a focal point for French *émigrés* in Spain. In 1796, he was appointed
ambassador to the negotiations preparing peace with France and, the next year,
plenipotentiary to the Rastadt Congress (November 1797–May 1798). Nominated
Spanish ambassador to France, he was rejected by the Directory, ostensibly on
the grounds of his French nationality but more probably for his connections with
the royalist Clichyens. He was therefore given the embassy at the Hague. In
1808, he initially supported Ferdinand VII as king of Spain, but in July he
became J. Bonaparte's minister of finance. His historical importance is as one
of the Spanish *afrancescados*. As far as the French Revolution is concerned, his
main claim to fame is as the father of T. Cabarrus.

M. Ferrus, *Madame Tallien à Bordeaux pendant la Terreur* (Bordeaux, 1933); H. Mirabeau, *De la Banque d'Espagne, dite de Saint-Charles* (1785); J. M. de Toreno, *Histoire du soulèvement, de la guerre et de la Révolution d'Espagne* (Paris, 1836).

C. Lucas

Related entries: CABARRUS, J.-M.-I.-T.; CLUB DE CLICHY.

CABARRUS, JEANNE-MARIE-IGNACE-THERESE (signing herself THERESIA) (1773-1835), a leader of society during the Thermidorian Reaction and the Directory, whose extravagance has been used to typify the period. Born at Caravanchel de Arriba (Spain), the daughter of F. Cabarrus, she entered Parisian society in 1785 and in 1788 married J.-J. de Fontenay, *conseiller* at the Parlement of Paris, who acquired the title of marquis in 1789. It was a marriage of considerable wealth on both sides. All contemporary accounts agree that she was an outstanding beauty and also remarkably promiscuous. Divorced in April 1793, she went to stay with her relatives at Bordeaux. It is not clear whether she was in fact arrested there during the Terror, as legend would have it. However, she did catch the eye of J.-L. Tallien, representative on mission in the city, and established a public liaison with him. Although the Thermidorians later attributed the mildness of Tallien's and C.-A. Ysabeau's policies there to her influence over the former, it is probable that these moderate Montagnards needed little such encouragement. However, her salon certainly became an established route by which relatives of suspects could contact Tallien. His liaison with her was a factor in the mounting governmental criticism of Tallien in the spring of 1794. This relationship with a wealthy ex-marquise and daughter of the banker of the king of Spain was particularly well suited to M. Robespierre's standard foreign corruption plot thesis. When she came to Paris following Tallien, Robespierre wrote her arrest warrant on 3 Prairial (22 May). There can be no substance to the legend that Tallien participated in the overthrow of Robespierre to save her from the guillotine. He had better reasons for this action, and indeed she was not released until several days later. However, he did subsequently abandon another mistress and marry Thérésia on 6 Nivôse Year III (26 December 1794).

It was during the Thermidorian Reaction that she achieved prominence. Her direct political influence was negligible, however, and her later claims in this respect must be dismissed. But she did become a symbol of Thermidorian attitudes and values. Her beauty and predisposition to indulgence made her the idol of the *jeunesse dorée* (militant reactionary youths) who called her Notre-Dame de Thermidor. Her salon of La Chaumière became the center of a lavishly self-indulgent and affected Thermidorian high society, frequented by such morally questionable political figures as L.-M.-S. Fréron and P. Barras, and by artistic and literary personalities such as the younger D.-J. Garat, A.-C. Vernet, and J.-S. Duplessis-Bertaux. She launched the new fashions of Greek costumes, diaphanous clothing, and hair styles *à la victime*.

Under the Directory, her salon remained a meeting place for influential and wealthy society. Its moral laxity seemed to typify one element of the Directorial political world. She herself drifted away from Tallien and in early 1796 became the mistress of the banker G.-J. Ouvrard. She lost all influence with the rise of Napoleon, who even forbade her erstwhile friend Josephine to see her. Divorced from Tallien in 1802, she married F. Riquet, comte de Caraman and prince de Chimay, in 1805.

J. Castelnau, *Madame Tallien* (Paris, 1938); M. Ferrus, *Madame Tallien à Bordeaux pendant la Terreur* (Bordeaux, 1933); A. Houssaye, *Notre-Dame de Thermidor* (Paris, 1866).

C. Lucas

Related entries: CABARRUS, F.; *JEUNESSE DOREE*; REPRESENTATIVES ON MISSION; TALLIEN; YSABEAU.

CADOUDAL, GEORGES (1769-1804). See *CHOUANNERIE*; VENDEE.

CAEN, chief city in Normandy and center of the federalist revolt in 1793. A substantial city of some 35,000 inhabitants, Caen marketed Normandy's rich agricultural produce and housed a prosperous textile manufactory. As the *intendant's* residence, Caen contained law courts and the university; after 1789, it became the capital of the department of Calvados. As a major communications hub, the city enjoyed strategic importance. A substantial Protestant community lived there.

Caen enthusiastically welcomed the early years of the Revolution but objected to the growing independence of the Paris Commune, which organized the *journée* of 10 August and tolerated the September Massacres. Publicists in Caen viewed J.-P. Marat as an anarchist leading the mob to interfere with duly elected representatives. A series of public addresses from the departmental authorities to the National Convention testified to Caen's growing dissatisfaction with the course of the Revolution. The popular societies of Caen, formed in 1789 by local artisans to combat royalists and revived in 1792, agreed fully with the merchants who dominated local government, and Caen's Jacobin society severed its connection with the Jacobins of Paris.

A joint meeting of city, district, and departmental officials to discuss the growing tension between Girondists and Jacobins in the spring of 1793 dispatched a delegation to Paris to ask the National Convention to restrain the Paris Commune. The delegation reached Paris on 2 June only to find the Girondist deputies under arrest and the Commune in control of the governmental apparatus. Their account of Parisian developments after their return helped inspire the formation of a departmental army to march on Paris and restore the National Convention to its pre-May state; Calvados acted together with the department of the Eure, whose activities the delegation had observed during their return. The representatives on mission, C.-G. Romme and C.-A. Prieur de la Côte-d'Or, were arrested; all funds were placed under local control; and General L.-F. Wimpffen, commander of the Army of the Côtes de Cherbourg, agreed to assume command of the departmental army. Commissioners were dispatched to all neighboring departments, a move that led to the formation of the Central Assembly of Resistance to Oppression on 30 June; Bretons joined the Normans in that Assembly.

Despite enthusiasm, action was tentative. Wimpffen moved his headquarters to Caen only in early July. After an initial success in recruiting when the entire popular society of Carabots volunteered as a group, enlistments fell off; part of the trouble lay with the failure of the departmental authorities to support the families of volunteers. The Assembly suspended food shipments to Paris, causing great concern; this was probably done more to supply local markets than to starve the Commune. The 1793 Constitution circulated in Caen despite a ban.

The military effort was unsuccessful, almost farcical. A parade in Caen on 7 July elicited only seventeen additional recruits; however, C. Corday watched it and left for Paris two days later to take matters into her own hands. On 13 July, some 2,000 Norman and Breton volunteers encountered a small Parisian force at Brécourt and fled ignominiously after a brief and almost bloodless skirmish. Little effort was made to rally them or to form new detachments. The Bretons retreated westward in good order, accompanied by the Central Assembly and some of the Girondist deputies. Local officials in Caen now retracted their resistance to Parisian authority, and the sections ratified the new constitution on 25 July. Submission to Paris was spurred by demonstrations of women clamoring for food. The department released Romme and Prieur from captivity. Republican forces entered Caen on 2 August; and R. Lindet, assigned the responsibility for rehabilitating Normandy, arrived the following day. There were few arrests and no executions.

A. Goodwin, "The Federalist Movement in Caen during the French Revolution," *Bull. of the J. Rylands Lib.* 42 (1960); J. Gralle, "Le Fédéralisme (Eure et Calvados)," *Bull. de la Soc. des Antiq. de Norm.* 55 (1961); F. Vaultier, *Souvenirs de l'insurrection normande dite du fédéralisme en 1793* (Caen, 1858).

D. Stone

Related entries: FEDERALISM; INTENDANTS; NATIONAL CONVENTION; PRIEUR DE LA COTE-D'OR; ROMME; SEPTEMBER MASSACRES; 10 AUGUST 1792; WIMPFFEN.

CAHIERS DE DOLEANCES, literally copybooks of complaints, grievances, or troubles, drafted in the assemblies that elected each deputy to the Estates General of France, beginning with those of 1484. This article deals exclusively with those *cahiers* of 1789 written for the last Estates General, between February and April of that year.

In principle the *cahiers* were intended to serve as instructions or authorizations that the voters gave the representatives they elected to the Estates General, and for that reason each was to be accompanied by a formal mandate instructing the representative how to vote or what measures to initiate on behalf of his constituents. Without the *cahier* and the mandate, the representative theoretically could be held to have no authority at all. During 1789, in fact, some deputies professed that they were not empowered to act on certain issues, and some asked their constituents for additional instructions or powers. But after the major issues of 1789 were settled, the mandates were of little subsequent importance.

In form and content, most of the *cahiers* went beyond instructing the deputies. Although some were drafted as instructions, most were written as pleas or petitions to the king or to the Estates General, as statements of the assemblies' recommendations or desires, or as descriptions of the hardships and injustices from which the writers believed they suffered. Some *cahiers* included carefully written programs of political, social, and economic change and went so far as to direct the deputy to vote for no financial relief for the crown until it had agreed to some of the changes specified in the *cahier*. At the other extreme were *cahiers* written by apolitical groups concerned entirely with local economic or legal problems and unaware of (or disinterested in) the prospect of change on a national or even regional scale.

The *cahiers* are therefore enormously varied. They lack the consistency they might have had if the government had issued detailed instructions on how they should be drawn up, or if it had confronted the assemblies with questionnaires that presented the issues and the possible solutions and asked the assemblies to express their preferences among the solutions. The instructions the government gave were, in fact, unrestrictive and open-ended. They said nothing about the structure and content of the *cahiers*, requiring only that they be written, that the drafting committees work on them without interruption or delay, and that they empower the deputies to act on behalf of the voters as a group. As for questionnaires, the only ones distributed in 1789 were issued by the Intermediate Commission of the Provincial Estates of the Dauphiné before the royal government had sent guidelines for electoral procedures; they were therefore illegal, and the responses to them had no standing. Besides, the Dauphiné questionnaire was mainly a request for information rather than for ideas of reform or instructions for deputies, and the replies, accordingly, are of less interest than we would wish if we are studying political programs or ideological values. And so, because the government's call for *cahiers* was unrestrictive, the *cahiers* it produced were extremely heterogeneous in content.

Each of the several thousand *cahiers* of 1789 reflects the knowledge and thought of the electoral assembly that drew it up and can be profitably interpreted only if the social identity of that assembly is kept in mind. The regulations that directed how the assemblies were to be constituted, who was to attend them, and what use would be made of their *cahiers* were prepared early in 1789 by the royal government, and those regulations recognized a variety of systems and authorized many exceptions, especially as concerned the Third Estate.

Concerning the types of *cahiers* written in 1789, there are three fundamental observations to be made. First, the basic electoral district was the jurisdiction of a royal court called in some regions a *bailliage* and in others a *sénéchaussée*, but there were also principalities, governments, *prévôtés*, royal jurisdictions, intendancies, *vigueries*, counties, and baronnies; for convenience we call all these circumscriptions *bailliages*. Second, in the overwhelming majority of cases, each *cahier* emanates from a group belonging to one of the three estates. Most of the exceptions are supplemental *cahiers* written in common session by members of the electoral assemblies of all three estates in *bailliages* that elected deputies directly to the Estates General. But all these common *cahiers* were prepared after the assembly of each order had completed its own *cahier*, and few are of much interest. Third, in every *bailliage* each order had its own pattern of convening its people, writing *cahiers*, and electing deputies. Especially in the Third Estate, the elections were hierarchical and indirect. Subject to many exceptions and irregularities, the electoral process may be described as follows.

In the elections of the clergy, members of cathedral chapters and monastic institutions and ecclesiastics without offices met in preliminary assemblies to choose deputies to the *bailliage* assembly of their order. In the *bailliage* assembly of the clergy, these deputies met with all the curates and with the bishop (if there was one in the *bailliage*). All *bailliage* assemblies of the clergy wrote *cahiers*, but some of the preliminary assemblies did not. In the elections of the Second Estate, all nobles could attend the *bailliage* assembly of their order, and there were for them no preliminary assemblies. In general, therefore, only one noble *cahier* was written in any *bailliage* unless there was a sharp division of opinion as a result of which the outvoted minority wrote a dissenting *cahier*. The elections of the Third Estate involved four kinds of preliminary assemblies and *cahiers*: (1) those of country parishes and small towns, (2) those of urban guilds of shopkeepers and artisans, (3) the corporate professional bodies of the upper Third Estate in 142 towns and cities named in a *règlement général* of 24 January 1789, and (4) town assemblies composed of deputies chosen by the guilds and corporate bodies in those 142 towns and cities. In the *bailliage* assemblies of the Third Estate, representatives of the parishes and small towns met with those elected by the town and city assemblies, but in order to keep the *bailliage* assemblies at a manageable size and avoid having the urban deputies excessively outnumbered, the deputies of the parishes and small towns chose a fourth of their number to sit in the *bailliage* assemblies. All of these preliminary assemblies of the Third Estate were expected to write *cahiers*. In practice, however, in some of the 142 towns listed in the general regulations, the guilds and corporations failed to meet, and they consequently produced no *cahiers*.

A further complication in the elections of the Third Estate and, accordingly, in the status of its various *cahiers* is that the *bailliage* assemblies of that order were of three kinds: secondary *bailliages*, principal *bailliages*, and *bailliages* without subdivisions. In a secondary *bailliage*, the *bailliage* assembly wrote a *cahier* and elected deputies to the assembly of a principal *bailliage*. In a principal *bailliage*, the electoral assembly wrote a *cahier* and elected deputies to the Estates General. A *bailliage* without subdivisions was one whose members were chosen directly by its parishes and towns rather than by secondary *bailliages*, of which, in fact, it had none, and which elected deputies to the Estates General. Added to these distinctions were others that it would be too cumbersome to explore here. The late B. Hyslop found in the electoral patterns of the Third Estate *bailliages* seven distinct systems of convocation, plus a large number of authorized exceptions. Anyone who plans to do research in the *cahiers* should carefully read the first part of her *Guide to the General Cahiers of 1789*, in which these complexities are fully explained.

Hyslop gave special significance to what she called general *cahiers*, those written by the electoral assemblies of all three orders that elected deputies directly to the Estates General. According to her tabulations, 615 such *cahiers* must have been written—194 by the clergy, 182 by the nobility, 213 by the Third Estate, 18 by joint assemblies of the three orders, and 8 by joint assemblies of two orders—and 523 of them have survived. She emphasized that the assemblies of all *bailliages* were expected to embody in their *cahiers* all the demands put forward by the preliminary assemblies of their jurisdictions and that the *bailliage* assemblies that elected directly to the Estates General ought to reflect more fully than those of any other groups the state of opinion in the country at large. Accordingly, she focused her work on the general *cahiers*, and others have tended to follow her example. With this approach, however, there are two serious disadvantages. First, in practice many general *cahiers* did not embody all demands put forward in their *bailliages*, and in some places their omissions became the object of complaint. Second, those who in the Third Estate drafted the *cahier* of a principal *bailliage* had participated in drafting, discussing, or revising the *cahiers* of two or three subordinate assemblies and in the process had become more ideologically aware and politically aggressive than the peasants, the urban artisans and shopkeepers, and even the wealthy merchants and professionals of the towns. They had received, in other words, much more of a Revolutionary education than those who attended only preliminary assemblies and who, once those assemblies adjourned, returned to work. In the aggregate their *cahiers* are more heavily directed by political and ideological values than those written in the preliminary assemblies, as quantitative analysis has established. When one reads the *cahiers* of peasants, guildsmen, and townsmen of the upper Third Estate, it is impossible to envision or predict the Revolution that was to come only a few weeks after they were written. However, the general *cahiers* point to the Revolutionary thought and program the National Assembly formulated in the summer of 1789. But this is to say that the general *cahiers* reflect the thought and knowledge of the most thoroughly politicized minority, which had not yet been learned or accepted by the rest of France, and that they are not as representative of the national state of opinion as Hyslop thought. So the state of public opinion of 1789 must be determined through study of the preliminary *cahiers* as well as the general *cahiers*.

The social and cultural categories under which the *cahiers* of 1789 were written enable us to compare opinion in one order with opinion in the other two, or in the Third Estate to isolate the opinion of peasant communities from that of the shopkeepers and artisans of the guilds or the professional people of the upper Third Estate. One may study the opinions of specific vocations or professions in France as a whole, or compare urban opinion with rural opinion, or compare opinion in some regions with that in others, as, for example, in contrasting opinion in zones where the Great Fear of 1789 was intense with that of the zones in which it was unimportant, so as to obtain clues to the causes of that rural unrest. By analyzing vocabulary, concepts, and patterns of thought, it is possible to identify pre-Revolutionary thought systems and value systems in the *cahiers* and to weigh the importance or unimportance of Enlightenment thought, or traditional thought, or religious thought in these documents and in the minds of those who wrote them. The method of such investigations must be quantitative; otherwise they will be impressionistic and inconclusive. It must embody valid procedures of sampling and content analysis. It must establish not only which ideas and demands are expressed in the *cahiers* but which are absent or occur only rarely. Research of this kind has been applied to the *cahiers* only recently, but the results indicate that there is no doubt of its feasibility and importance.

G. Chaussinand-Nogaret, *La noblesse au XVIIIe siècle: De la féodalité aux lumières* (Paris, 1976); B. F. Hyslop, "French Gild Opinion in 1789," *Am. Hist. Rev.* 44 (1939), *French Nationalism in 1789 according to the General Cahiers* (New York, 1934), *A Guide to the General Cahiers of 1789, with the texts of Unedited Cahiers*, 2d ed. (New York, 1968), *Répertoire critique des cahiers de doléances pour les Etats Généraux de 1789* (Paris, 1933), and *Supplément au répertoire critique des cahiers de doléances pour les Etats Généraux de 1789* (Paris, 1952); G. V. Taylor, "Revolutionary and Nonrevolutionary Content in the *Cahiers* of 1789: an Interim Report," *Fr. Hist. Stud.* 7 (1972).

G. V. Taylor

Related entries: ARISTOCRATS; *BAILLIAGE*; BOURGEOISIE; ESTATES GENERAL; FEUDALISM; PEASANTRY.

"CA IRA," the most notorious of the Revolution's songs. It is inevitably associated with popular violence and hatred of the aristocracy because a refrain added to the original version called for the hanging of aristocrats from lamp posts. When it first appeared during the preparations for the Fête de la Fédération (14 July 1790), however, "*Ça ira*" was a gay and hopeful song. The words were composed by a street singer named Ladré who borrowed a vigorous and bouncy contredanse tune, "*Le carillon national.*" The very first words "Ah, ça ira"—"Ah, it will succeed," or more idiomatically, "Ah, we'll make it"—announce the song's celebration of patriotism, national unity, and a light-hearted determination to vanquish the enemies of France and of the Revolution.

"*Ça ira*" was an immediate popular success. In addition to the violent anti-aristocratic refrain, other variants appeared spontaneously, including a royalist parody that demanded the death of democrats and deputies.

Although the "*Marseillaise*" became the most favored of patriotic songs, "*Ça ira*" was almost as popular and was included in the official programs of many Revolutionary festivals. It managed in fact to survive the Thermidorian Reaction. In 1796 the Directory ordered it sung daily at theatrical performances. It was performed as late as 1799.

P. Barbier and F. Vernillat, *Histoire de France par les chansons*, vol. 4 (Paris, 1957); P. Constant, *Les Hymnes et chansons de la Révolution française* (Paris, 1905).

R. Bienvenu

Related entries: MUSIC; ROUGET DE LISLE.

CALENDAR OF THE FRENCH REPUBLIC (22 September 1792–31 December 1805), an attempt to establish a Republican calendar more rational, secular, and harmonious with nature than the Gregorian. It was the most radical calendar reform in modern history. The National Convention, on motion of J.-N. Billaud-Varenne, decided on 22 September 1792, the date of the proclamation that France was a Republic, that a new calendar in keeping with the new status was necessary. It entrusted the work to its Committee of Public Instruction, whose president, C.-G. Romme, became the chief architect of the new calendar. He sought the advice of some outstanding members of the Academy of Sciences. Both the Egyptian calendar and the *Almanach des honnêtes gens* (1788) of P.-S. Maréchal strongly influenced the committee. The committee reported on 20 September 1793 to the Convention, which adopted the new calendar on 5 October, retroactive to 22 September 1792. The definitive decree of 24 November 1793 (4 Frimaire Year II) incorporated various changes of name.

The years were to be numbered—with Roman numerals, because of the classical influence—as of the republican era, implying that the birth of the Republic surpassed in importance the birth of Christ. At first the Revolutionaries wanted the Gregorian and republican years to coincide: a decree of 2 January 1793 provided that Year II began on 1 January. On official documents, Year I lasted only through 1792, but in the fall of 1793, the starting date of the years was changed to the autumnal equinox (symbolizing equality). Since the autumnal equinox varied from 22 to 24 September, a concordance with the Gregorian calendar became a necessity.

The year was divided into twelve equal months of thirty days each. Initially the months and days were also to be numbered, but the poet P.-F. Fabre d'Eglantine was charged with drawing up a better nomenclature. The Law of 24 November 1793 decreed that the months were to be named in keeping with the concept of natural, universal seasons or phenomena, but the names really applied to the region of Paris. To show the seasons, the months of autumn all ended in *-aire*, of winter in *-ôse*, of spring in *-al*, and of summer in *-or*. In order, the months were Vendémiaire (vintage), Brumaire (fog), and Frimaire (frost); Nivôse (snow), Pluviôse (rain), and Ventôse (wind); Germinal (budding), Floréal (flowering), and Prairial (meadows); and Messidor (harvest), Thermidor (heat), and Fructidor (fruit).

The extra days necessary to make the calendar year coincide more nearly with the solar year at first were called complementary days. The definitive law, however, provided that they be known as *sansculottides* (another example of the importance of symbolism in the calendar), named Virtue, Genius, Work, Opinion, and Reward. On 7 Fructidor Year III, a less leftist Convention abolished the name *sansculottides* in favor of a return to *complementary days*. Every fourth year, in which a sixth extra day was needed, was called a *sextile*. The period between sextile years was a *franciade*, and the sixth extra day, the "Day of the Revolution," celebrated Republican games. It fell in the Years III, VII, and XI.

The rationalism of the calendar was to be shown especially in the application of the decimal system. Each month was divided into three *décades* (which, unlike weeks, divided the months exactly), each day into ten hours, each hour into one hundred decimal minutes, and each minute into a hundred decimal seconds. (Very few clocks were manufactured according to the new specifications.) The days were named after the ordinal numbers— *primidi, duodi*, up to *décadi*—so as to replace a qualitative with a quantitative designation.

Fabre d'Eglantine's proposal that the calendar should glorify agriculture was incorporated into a decree of 24 October 1793. Each *quintidi* was to be named after an animal, bird, or fish that could help or charm man; each *décadi* received the name of an agricultural implement. All the other days were named after grains, fields, trees, roots, flowers, fruits, or plants so as to eliminate saints' days. Only the *décadi* were to be days of rest.

The calendar experiment failed for many reasons. It was a reform effected by a zealous few, not one demanded by the populace in general. The fact that only France adopted the calendar hampered its international political and commercial relations. People resented having only every tenth rather than every seventh day as a day of rest. In April 1802 N. Bonaparte decreed that Sunday would be the day state employees did not work. On 21 December 1802 the official newspaper, the *Moniteur*, started using double dates, for the Christian and republican eras. Religious feeling was stronger than the reformers realized. Napoleon's reconciliation with the Roman Catholic church meant that the republican calendar was doomed. A *senatus consultum*, proposed on 2 September and passed 9 September 1805, officially suppressed the republican calendar as of 1 January 1806. Its only revival was by the Paris Commune in 1871.

G. G. Andrews, "Making the Revolutionary Calendar," *Am. Hist. Rev.* 36 (1931); J. W. Ekrutt, *Der Kalendar im Wandel der Zeiten* (Stuttgart, 1972); J. H. Stewart, ed., *A Documentary Survey of the French Revolution* (New York, 1951); E. Zerubavel, "The French Republican Calendar: A Case Study in the Sociology of Time," *Am. Sociol. Rev.* 43 (1977).

R. B. Holtman

Related entries: FABRE; MARECHAL; ROMME.

CALONNE, CHARLES-ALEXANDRE DE (1734-1802), controller general of Finances, intendant, *émigré* and counterrevolutionary. Calonne was born at Douai on 20 January 1734, the son of the first president of the Parlement of Flanders. Trained in law, he was a brilliant student who held a number of administrative posts at the local level before he was appointed Maître des requêtes au conseil d'état du roi in 1765.

While still procurer general of Flanders, Calonne was asked to resolve the controversy that had developed between officials of the central government and the Parlement of Brittany. When he made the decision to support royal authority in what essentially was a struggle between the central power at Versailles and the parlement, which was posing as the protector of local privileges and liberties, the Paris Parlement was deeply offended.

He became intendant at Metz (1766) and Lille (1778), and his efforts to promote industrial and commercial growth in these intendancies met with considerable success. In 1783, as a protégé of the comte d'Artois, Marie Antoinette, and C.-G. Vergennes, he was appointed controller general of finance and became Louis XVI's chief minister. Calonne's propensity for paying the debts of Artois and the queen, providing pensions for court favorites, and presenting less than candid reports to Louis XVI and others relative to the financial affairs of France made him vulnerable to attack by his critics. But he instituted a pump-priming operation that was the beginning of the modernization process in French economic life. He built roads and bridges, established lower and more uniform import duties, and labored to remove obstacles to internal trade. Subsidies were provided by the government for the modernization of the mining, porcelain, glass, cotton, iron, and steel industries. Calonne expanded the use of paper money, abolished government wage scales, and discussed the possibility of establishing a national bank. Harbor improvements, new canals, improved marketplaces, and new public buildings also were the result of the controller general's efforts to stimulate business activity. But there was a problem: stabilization of the economic structure could not be achieved until the nobility and clergy paid their share of direct taxes.

Calonne financed his projects with loans that totaled over 650,000,000 *livres* by 1786. At wit's end as to how to resolve the financial crisis, he recommended to Louis XVI a comprehensive plan of reform. The king finally agreed to summon an Assembly of Notables in an effort to head off impending bankruptcy. At the first sitting of the Notables on 22 February 1787, Calonne explained that the special privileges of certain social classes, corporations, and localities must end. He recommended that a land tax, based on ability to pay, be collected from all proprietors, nobility, clergy, and Third Estate alike. Among other things, the controller general recommended the abolition of internal customs duties, the creation of provincial assemblies where they did not already exist (in the *pays d'élection*), the removal of most restrictions on the movement of grain within France, the reform of the *gabelle* and the *corveé*, and a new stamp tax that would fall most heavily on the wealthy. Calonne presented a significant and well-integrated program of reform in 1787, which must be considered the precursor of the more radical changes of the Revolutionary era. But the strong opposition of the parlements and protests from the most articulate and able members of the higher clergy resulted in his dismissal as controller general in April 1787. On 24 May Louis XVI sent the Notables home. For three months, the first Assembly of the Notables had debated the proposals submitted by Calonne, but in the end it declared itself incompetent to advise the king on fiscal matters. However, Calonne had set in motion forces that triggered debate and controversy and set the stage for the radical changes of 1789 and after.

Calonne was no revolutionary; he was not seeking limitations on kingly authority or trying to establish a parliamentary system, and he was not seeking to establish freedom of profession, which would have ended the monopoly of office holding by the nobility and clergy. Neither was he trying to abolish feudalism nor did he intend to establish the principle of equality before the law. In reality he was working to inaugurate a significant program of limited administrative and economic reforms (mostly in the tax structure) in order to save France from bankruptcy and preserve his job as controller general. Calonne was able, energetic, imaginative, and ambitious, but certain defects of character made him controversial and distrusted by reactionary and progressive alike.

After his dismissal as controller general, Calonne went into exile in England, remaining there until he joined the *émigré* princes in 1790 on the Continent. Outside France he was a bitter and persistent critic of reforms instituted by the National Assembly, and he published some twenty works in which he defended his policies as controller general, analyzed the Revolution, and became a prime mover in the counterrevolution. In November 1790 Calonne joined the comte d'Artois in Turin and finally settled with the *émigrés* at Coblentz where he served as a kind of first minister of the shadow government of the exiles. For some two years, he guided *émigré* diplomacy and negotiated desperately needed loans for the exiles. He warned European monarchs that the French Revolution was not only a tragedy for the French but a threat to their thrones and the institutions on which they depended for support.

The ex–controller general returned to Great Britain after the defeat of the Austrian, Prussian, and *émigré* forces in the fall of 1792 and continued his writing. He published *Tableau de l'Europe en Novembre 1795*, in which he wrote that he could visualize no restoration unless the power of the king was regulated and tempered by fundamental laws fixed and established in constitutional fashion and incorporated in a solemn code. Calonne had moved successively from the progressive posture of his years as controller general to the role as first minister of the counterrevolution and then to a constitutionalism that was most unwelcome to the more extreme monarchists.

He was a lover and collector of good art with a taste for luxury; when impoverished, Calonne sold 360 of his paintings at auction in March 1795. After the peace of Amiens, he returned to France and offered his services to Napoleon. Rejected, he died in October 1802. Calonne had left his papers in England, and his son claimed them. However, the English foreign office persuaded him to sell these important documents to the British government for 500 pounds. There are 4,000 pieces from 1 to 50 pages in length and a typescript catalog (289 pages). The *Papiers de Calonne* constitute one of the major sources for any study of the emigration.

A. Goodwin, "Calonne, the Assembly of French Notables of 1787 and the Origins of the *révolte nobiliaire*," *Eng. Hist. Rev.* 61 (1946); R. Lacour-Gayet, *Calonne: financier, reformateur, contre-révolutionnaire, 1734-1802* (Paris, 1963); Public Record Office, *Papiers de Calonne*; W. Pugh, "Calonne's New Deal," *J. of Mod. Hist.*, 11 (1939).

V. W. Beach

Related entries: ARISTOCRATS; ARTOIS; ASSEMBLY OF NOTABLES; COBLENTZ; *CORVEE*; COUNTERREVOLUTION; *EMIGRES; GABELLE*.

CAMBACERES, JEAN-JACQUES-REGIS DE (1753-1824), Duc de Parme, French statesman, second consul, and archchancellor of the empire. Born at Montpellier 15 October 1753 into a family of the nobility of the robe, as early as 1771 he succeeded his father as councillor in the Court of Accounts, *Aides*, and Finances at Montpellier. He drew up the *cahier* of the nobility of his *sénéchaussée*. When his election to the Estates General was annulled, he became president of the criminal court of the Hérault. In 1792 this department elected him to the National Convention, where he followed a circumspect policy. He voted for the death of Louis XVI but wanted the penalty imposed only after hostilities had ended. Initially a partisan of the Girondins, he abandoned them on 31 May and 2 June 1793, and only when victory was certain did he join the enemies of M. Robespierre in 1794.

In the Convention he proposed the establishment of the Revolutionary Tribunal. On 26 March 1795 he became a member of the Committee of Public Safety. As a member, he signed the decree dismissing N. Bonaparte from the army for refusing to accept the Vendéan command in 1795; as its president, responsible especially for foreign affairs, he helped effect peace with Spain. He proposed plans for a civil code, and was given the charge, with P.-A. Merlin de Douai, of preparing a definitive codification of all laws. Although nothing came of this charge, Cambacérès played a leading role in formulating the civil code of Bonaparte, presiding over half of the sessions of the Council of State at which it was discussed. His work on the code, including the proposal of a jury in civil cases, was his main contribution during the Consulate.

Having great influence after 9 Thermidor, Cambacérès cooperated in drafting the Constitution of the Year III. Elected to the Council of Five Hundred, he failed reelection in 1797, and his election from Paris in 1798 was annulled. In June 1799 he became minister of justice, and he joined E.-J. Sieyès and P. Barras in forcing the resignation of J. Bernadotte as minister of war in 1799. In the coup of 18-19 Brumaire he played a discreet part, which won him nomination as second consul.

In this capacity and also as archchancellor of the Empire, Cambacérès presided over the Senate and the Council of State. In 1804 he was one of a council of five, plus Bonaparte, that decided the duc d'Enghien should be abducted. His advice to Napoleon was important in the selection of judicial personnel. Napoleon selected him as one of two men to draft a constitution for the Kingdom of Westphalia. In 1808 he was named duke of Parma. When Napoleon was on campaign in 1814, Cambacérès served virtually as regent, though his unpublished letters to Napoleon (recently discovered) show that the emperor kept a rather tight rein and that Cambacérès was no vice-emperor.

Although Cambacérès had voted in the Senate for Napoleon's deposition in 1814, during the Hundred Days Napoleon insisted that he again be minister of justice and archchancellor, presiding over the Imperial Chamber of Peers. A charter member of the Institute in 1795, in the second restoration he was expelled from it and exiled from France as a relapsed regicide. After two years in Brussels and Amsterdam, Cambacérès was readmitted to France in May 1818 with all his political and civil rights. He died on 8 March 1824 at Paris, eight days after suffering a stroke.

Through his legal practice and his appointments, Cambacérès became very wealthy. He was often a target of ridicule because of his love of decorations and his gourmet tastes. He was a valuable adviser to Napoleon, a man of broad experience, a consummate juriconsult. He did not strongly oppose the adoption of policies he disapproved of and advised against.

F. Papillard, *Cambacérès* (Paris, 1961); J. Thiry, *Jean-Jacques-Régis de Cambacérès, Archichancelier de l'Empire* (Paris, 1935); J. Tulard, "Preface" to Cambacérès' *Lettres inédites à Napoléon 1802-1814* (Paris, 1973).

R. B. Holtman

Related entries: BARRAS; CONSTITUTION OF 1795; COMMITTEE OF PUBLIC SAFETY; COUNCIL OF FIVE HUNDRED; MERLIN DE DOUAI; REVOLUTIONARY TRIBUNAL; *SENECHAUSSEE*; SIEYES.

CAMBON, PIERRE-JOSEPH (1756-1820), the member of the Legislative Assembly and the Convention most responsible for the finances of the Revolution. Cambon was born on 10 June 1756 into a family of textile merchants in Montpellier. His father, who retired from business in 1785 with a fortune estimated at 385,000 *livres*, was a leader of the local Third Estate in the political activity of 1788–89. Pierre-Joseph was elected a member of the Montpellier municipality in 1790 and was a founder of the town's *Société des amis de l'Egalité*. He was among the first purchasers of *biens nationaux* in an uncertain local climate and a strong partisan of the Constitutional clergy. After Louis XVI's flight to Varennes, Cambon presided over a meeting of his club that drafted a petition urging the Constituent Assembly to proclaim a Republic.

In September 1791 Cambon was elected a member of the Legislative Assembly for the Hérault; he joined the Jacobin club in Paris the same month. His conduct in the Assembly was that of a constitutionalist of the Left; no republicanism was apparent in his statements. He fought the proposed weakening of the civic oath for priests and showed a distrust of the church that would soon broaden into anticlericalism. When the Girondins began to promote war in December 1791, Cambon was convinced that this policy would consolidate the Revolution.

Cambon's financial abilities surfaced early in the Legislative Assembly. Throughout his career, he steadfastly pursued two goals: the unification of national finances and the careful management of the *assignat*, which he sought to align securely on the real value and actual sale of the *biens nationaux*. In November 1791 Cambon urged the unification of the Assembly's several finance committees and proposed that the creation of *assignats* be limited to a lower figure. In May 1792 he offered the first sound estimate of the national debt. At this time also he first announced his project of a *Grand Livre*, a single account book for all monies owed by the state to its creditors.

In the days before the *journée* of 10 August 1792, Cambon showed a scrupulous attachment to the 1791 constitution. However, he was not discomforted by the proclamation of a Republic, and his own tone in the following weeks clearly grew more radical. On 26 August he declared that if men of property would not defend the Revolution, they should disarm themselves and arm the *sans-culottes*; in the same month he proposed the deportation of nonjuring priests to Guyana in an outburst that most of the Assembly found inhumane.

Cambon was elected to sit in the Convention in September 1792, was named to the finance committee, and remained its virtual head until April 1795. From the beginning of the Convention, he sought to inspire confidence in the *assignat* by demonstrating the substantial wealth of the *biens nationaux*. He now insisted on the abolition of a variety of special funds in order to make the treasury the center of all receipts and expenses. He instituted the printing of monthly general Treasury accounts. Supporter of the annexation of Belgium, increasingly the enemy of C. Dumouriez, he moved ever further from the Girondins; an unhesitant regicide, he took a dim view of the first measures of the Terror and obtained immunity for treasury officials from the new Revolutionary Tribunal.

A strong centralist, Cambon was among the originators of the idea of a nine-member Committee of Public Safety and of the unlimited charter of representatives on mission over their assigned departments. Yet the rising struggle between Girondins and Montagnards disturbed him deeply; he preferred to ascribe it all to egoism, and in the Convention he often announced military news to disrupt a heated debate. Infuriated by the insurrection of 2 June 1793, he accepted the power of the Paris popular movement with the greatest reluctance and was not reelected to the second Committee of Public Safety, which charged him to supervise the treasury on its behalf.

Cambon's financial achievements during the Year II deserve to be regarded as an integral part of the Terror. The stress of the national emergency gave him the chance to unify the old royal debts with the new republican ones in the single index of the *Grand Livre*. With the two debts indistinguishable, the creditors of France could not easily divide into Revolutionary and counterrevolutionary camps. Cambon also insisted on taxing not only land but chattel property. When this tax increased the reluctance of *rentiers* to file their titles for the *Grand Livre*, he persuaded the Convention to decree their arrest. In his regulation of the *dette viagère* (state debts to private creditors payable in annuities), he altered the terms of some debts to a degree that disquieted the Committee of Public Safety. Cambon created two war taxes, the *emprunt volontaire* and the *emprunt forcé*, that bore

many resemblances to the modern tax on revenue, including a progressive schedule. He urged and obtained the suppression of the Old Regime financial companies like the Compagnie des Indes and the Caisse d'Escompte when he believed
their operations were weakening the *assignat*. He sought, but did not get, the
outright confiscation of private hoards of metal currency and the imposition of
a limit that would force rich legatees to give way to poor ones in inheritance
law. Defender of free commerce though he was, there were few measures Cambon shrank from when he believed the soundness of the *assignat* to be at stake.

Yet Cambon's views remained distinct from the social tendencies inherent in
the ideas of M. Robespierre and L. Saint-Just. Cambon despised the maximum,
though he knew that to combat it would be futile. He strongly opposed the
sequestration of property held in France by citizens of hostile nations and fought
every project that assumed the French economy could stand alone in the world.

This philosophical opposition made him a natural target for Robespierre's
speech to the Convention of 8 Thermidor Year II (26 July 1794), when Robespierre declared that the nation's financial system was run by *fripons* (rogues).
Cambon's vigorous self-defense broke the spell that Robespierre's vague accusations had cast on the Convention and helped to prepare his fall on the next
day. Yet Cambon made a poor Thermidorian. From autumn 1794 on, public
and private attacks on his reputation multiplied until on 3 April 1795 he was
excluded from the Convention when he refused to resign from the finance committee. Half-implicated by his enemies in the *journées* of Germinal and Prairial,
he was outlawed until the amnesty of 4 Brumaire Year IV.

Cambon retired to Montpellier, where he held local office during the Directory.
N. Bonaparte hoped to include him in the government of the Consulate, but
Cambon refused as a republican. He kept to private life until 1815, when he
was again elected deputy for the Hérault under the Hundred Days' regime. The
Restoration exiled Cambon as a regicide; he died in Belgium on 15 February
1820.

He was one of the creative figures of the Revolution, an inventor of much of
the modern state's financial apparatus. His policies and his rigor in pursuing
them were perceived by his contemporaries as an aspect of the Terror. He
represents the Terror's most bourgeois side and shows its filiation to the financial
development of the modern state.

F. Bornarel, *Cambon et la Révolution française* (Paris, 1905); G. Saumade, "Cambon
et sa famille, acquéreurs de biens nationaux," *Ann. hist. de la Révo. française* 16 (1939).

C. Ramsay

Related entries: BIENS NATIONAUX; COMMITTEE OF PUBLIC SAFETY;
DUMOURIEZ; LAW OF THE MAXIMUM; 10 AUGUST 1792; TERROR,
THE; VARENNES.

CAMPOFORMIO, TREATY OF. See TREATY OF CAMPOFORMIO.

CAPITATION, head tax. As one of the first efforts to extend direct taxation
to the privileged in French society, the government of Louis XIV established a

universal head tax in 1695. The entire population of the kingdom was divided into twenty-two classes according to occupation. The classification is an interesting example of the perceived rankings of wealth at the end of the seventeenth century. The fiscal hierarchy ranged from the princes of the blood and the farmers general paying 2,000 *livres* tax to soldiers and day laborers paying 1 *livre*. This method of assessment was abandoned in subsequent years in favor of a fixed sum assigned to each tax district (*généralité*), making it possible for those provinces with local estates (the *pay d'états*) to negotiate with the royal treasury and reduce their share.

Despite repeated royal efforts in the course of the eighteenth century to enforce the *capitation* on the *non-taillables* (those who did not pay the regular direct tax, the *taille*), the privileged groups or corps, the nobility in particular, were usually able to reduce their *capitation* to less than 2 percent of their incomes. They did this by flagrantly falsifying their income declarations, by direct intimidation of tax collectors, and by formal protests in the courts. The parlements transformed tax protests of this kind into a constitutional issue. The commoners of the Third Estate, on the other hand, were subjected to ever larger quotas of the *capitation* as the privileged orders, including many *bourgeois de ville*, evaded their share. Thus for the defenseless majority of French taxpayers, the *capitation* became a supplement to the *taille*, and a substantial one, as the government receipts show. True, the royal government had established the principle of universal taxation, but with the implicit understanding that the privileged would make only a token payment and retain separate tax rolls. The *capitation noble* must not be confused with the *capitation* for commoners.

At the end of the Seven Years War, the royal government made still another effort to enforce the *capitation* on the *non-taillables*, doubling the rates on the privileged and tripling them for all office-holders. In the latter case the government even employed the modern devise of withholding tax on incomes (*gages*). But results were meager. Like the *vingtième* tax of 1750, which was intended to levy a 5 percent land tax on every French household, the *capitation* could not be adequately enforced until it was equitably assessed. Most tax assessments on real estate (the *cadastres*) had not been revised for generations and were shamelessly manipulated to favor the rich, the well born, and the influential in every village and town of the kingdom. Reassessment was an enormous administrative task. This was the work of the Revolution.

J. F. Bosher, *French Finances, 1770–1795: From Business to Bureaucracy* (Cambridge, England, 1970); G. Chaussinand-Nogaret, *Les financiers de Languedoc au XVIIIe siècle* (Paris, 1970); M. Marion, *Histoire financière de la France*, 6 vols. (Paris, 1914-26) and *Les impôts directs sous l'ancien régime* (Paris, 1912); G. T. Matthews, *The Royal General Farms in Eighteenth Century France* (New York, 1958).

R. Forster

Related entries: FARMERS GENERAL; *TAILLE; VINGTIEME.*

CARMAGNOLE, Revolutionary song. The author of the lyrics and the composer of the music are unknown, but J. Tiersot argues persuasively that the tune is based on a folk song that accompanied a dance called the *carmagnole* associated with the laborers who came to Provence each fall from the area around Carmagnola in Piedmont to work in the grape and olive harvests. The dance and a version of the song may have been brought north by the Marseillais National Guardsmen in the summer of 1792. The words of the Revolutionary lyrics refer specifically to the events in Paris between 10 August 1792 and the incarceration of the king and queen in the Temple three days later. Newspapers report that the song, known variously as *Madame Véto* and *Dansons la Carmagnole*, enjoyed wide popularity in Paris through the Terror, and there are reports of its having been danced and sung in anti-Jacobin demonstrations in 1795. It was prohibited by Napoleon. The dancing and singing of the *Carmagnole* is represented, with scant historical accuracy, in a Soviet ballet, *The Flames of Paris*.

A. Cox, *Die Musik der Französischen Revolution zur Funktionsbestimmung von Lied und Hymne* (Munich, 1978); C. Pierre, *Les Hymnes et chansons de la Révolution* (Paris, 1904); J. Tiersot, *Les Fêtes et les chants de la Révolution française* (Paris, 1908).

C. *Garrett*

Related entries: MUSIC; 10 AUGUST 1792.

CARMES. See PRISONS.

CARNOT, LAZARE-NICOLAS-MARGUERITE (1753-1823), politician, military man, savant, the Organizer of Victory in Year II. Carnot was born 13 May 1753 at Nolay, Burgundy; his father was an *avocat en parlement*, a royal notary, and a local judge. Although of bourgeois origin, Carnot was allowed to enter the royal school for military engineers at Mézières in 1770 through the influence of the duc d'Aumont. Commissioned a lieutenant in the Corps of Engineers in 1773, for the next few years of garrison duty Carnot divided his time between technical studies and Enlightenment literature. He joined a number of provincial academies, including that of Arras where M. Robespierre was a member. Among his publications during this period were *Essai sur les machines* (1783), *Eloge de Vauban* (1784), and *Mémoire...au sujet des Places fortes* (1788). The military intellectual, however, found both his professional and personal life frustrated by his common origins; he could not be promoted above the rank of captain and was refused the hand of a petty aristocrat's daughter.

A confirmed opponent of the Old Regime by principle and personal experience, Carnot played a minor political role during the Constituent Assembly. In September 1789 he wrote to the assembly urging reform of the Corps of Engineers, and the following April in another letter he advised the Assembly to use church property to pay public debts but opposed its sale. On 17 May 1791 he married M. du Pont, twelve years his junior. His only direct involvement in politics was confined to the city of Saint-Omer and the department of the Pas-de-Calais where he followed the lead of his younger brother, known as Carnot-Feulint.

Both brothers were elected to the Legislative Assembly as deputies for the Pas-de-Calais in 1791. Although the elder Carnot increasingly identified with the Left in the Assembly, he did not join the Paris Jacobin Club. He served on a number of legislative committees and was particularly active in discussions of military issues, for example, concerning passive obedience and the arming of citizens with pikes. Following the overthrow of the monarchy on 10 August 1792, he was selected as a representative of the Assembly to the Army of the Rhine in order to ensure its acceptance of the new political situation. Thus, when Carnot was elected to the National Convention in September 1792, he was prepared for the duties he would undertake during the most critical phase of the Revolution.

In the Convention, Carnot sat with the Mountain and, while still not a Jacobin, espoused many of its policies, among them, public assistance to the poor, progressive taxes, and a system of national education. On the fate of Louis XVI, he voted for death without postponement. On the other hand, in questions involving annexations and natural frontiers, he supported the expansionist policies of the Girondins. Meanwhile, he served as a representative on mission, to the Pyrenees (September 1792–January 1793) and to the Army of the North (March–August 1793). In the course of the latter mission he uncovered the treason of General C. Dumouriez, ordered his arrest, and rallied opposition to the general that forced him to flee to the Austrians.

On his return from the north, Carnot joined the Committee of Public Safety in mid-August. Together with R. Lindet and C.-A. Prieur de la Côte-d'Or, he took charge of military affairs, especially matters of personnel and strategy. For the next eleven months, Carnot participated in the frantic and herculean tasks arising from civil and foreign war that confronted this governing body. In addition to dealing with counterrevolution in the Vendée and federalist revolts throughout much of the country, Carnot had to raise, train, arm, equip, transport, and maintain an army approaching a million men. He had to draw officers for this army from men who were both professionally competent and politically reliable. Moreover, there were problems of strategy and tactics, discipline and morale. His success earned him acclaim as the Organizer of Victory. This and his growing disagreement with the Robespierrist elements of the Committee helped him to survive the purge of 9 Thermidor Year II, and he continued to serve on the committee periodically until March 1795.

Eight months later, Carnot became one of the original five executives of the new government, the Directory. In this capacity, he continued to supervise military affairs; among his appointments was General N. Bonaparte to the command of the Army of Italy. In May 1796 Carnot helped crush the Babeuf conspiracy. In the face of the growing royalist threat of 1797, he remained devoted to the Republic, but at the same time he was unwilling to violate the constitution in order to preserve it. This attitude sealed Carnot's fate during the coup of 18 Fructidor, and he was forced to flee to Geneva to escape arrest.

Carnot returned to France with other political exiles under the amnesty granted by the new first consul on 24 December 1799 and served as minister of war from April to October 1800. Elected to the Tribunate in March 1802, he cast the lone dissenting vote in that body against the life consulate later that year and against the Empire in 1804. His opposition to Napoleon, however, went no further than this, and he remained in the Tribunate until its dissolution in 1807 when he retired to private life. In the crisis of 1814, Carnot rallied to Napoleon and directed the defense of Antwerp against the allies until after the first abdication. Subsequently he pleaded with Louis XVIII for constitutional government. During the Hundred Days, he accepted Napoleon's promises of liberalization and served as minister of the interior. Proscribed under the second Restoration, he went into exile at Magdeburg, where he died on 2 August 1823.

H. Carnot, *Mémoires sur Lazare Carnot*, 2 vols. (Paris, 1907); E. Charavay, ed., *Correspondance générale de Carnot*, 4 vols. (Paris, 1892–1907); H. Dupre, *Lazare Carnot: Republican Patriot* (Oxford, Ohio, 1940); M. Reinhard, *Le Grand Carnot*, 2 vols. (Paris, 1950 and 1952); S. Watson, *Carnot* (London, 1954).

S. F. Scott

Related entries: ANNEXATION; COMMITTEE OF PUBLIC SAFETY; COUP OF 18 FRUCTIDOR YEAR V; DIRECTORY; DUMOURIEZ.

CARRA, JEAN-LOUIS (1742-93), editor and *conventionnel*. Carra was born on 9 March 1742 into the household of a minor official at Pont-de-Veyle (Ain). While still a student at the Jesuit collège of Mâcon (1758), he was accused of theft and imprisoned for two-and-a-half years. Whether guilty or innocent (as he always claimed), he was emotionally scarred by this incident.

We have no information about his activities in the period immediately following his release. From 1768, when he resurfaced, until 1785 when he became a clerk at the Royal Library in Paris, he drifted from job to job, invariably quarreling with his employers. He served one unhappy year (1775-76) as secretary to the Hospodar of Moldavia. Fashioning himself to be a *philosophe*, Carra authored a bewildering variety of poems, philosophic essays, scientific treatises, romantic novels, histories, and translations in the two decades before 1789. Like J.-P. Marat, he attributed his failure to receive a pension or recognition from the intellectual establishment to persecution and intrigue.

With the advent of the Revolution, he flung himself into Parisian politics. In 1787-88, he dashed off works vilifying the finance minister, C.-A. de Calonne, and the former police lieutenant, J.-B. Lenoir. He was a founder of the Society of the Friends of the Blacks, an abolitionist organization established on 19 February 1788. In 1789 he published a number of radical pamphlets of which the best-known was the *Orateur des Etats-Généraux*. His meteoric rise to national prominence commenced with the foundation of the *Annales patriotiques et littéraires* (3 October 1789). As the principal editor of this daily newspaper and a highly visible member of the Paris Jacobins, he had an incalculable impact on the departmental Jacobin clubs. An analysis of club records has shown that no other paper exceeded the *Annales* in popularity prior to 1792.

As a journalist, Carra's consuming passion was foreign affairs. He was an ardent partisan of an offensive war against Austria in late 1791 and such an enthusiastic admirer of Frederick William II and the duke of Brunswick that his enemies accused him of being a Prussian agent. No firm evidence exists to support this assertion, but on one occasion he apparently accepted a bribe of 333 *florins* from rebels in the Austrian Netherlands.

After Louis XVI's attempted flight in 1791, Carra became a vociferous critic of the king. In July 1792, he joined a secret committee plotting to overthrow the monarchy. And on the night of 9–10 August, he visited the federalist battalion from Marseille prior to its successful attack on the Tuileries Palace. Carra reached the zenith of his popularity in late 1792. In August–September, he was elected as a deputy to the National Convention by eight departments, a total nearly twice that of any other man.

During the Convention, Carra was a representative on mission to the Army of the North and Center (September-November 1792) and the Vendée and Deux-Sèvres departments (March–June 1793). He was arrested on 3 August 1793 and guillotined three months later, 31 October 1793, along with the Girondins. Because of the circumstances of his death and his past friendship with J. Pétion and J.-P. Brissot, historians have traditionally categorized Carra as a Girondin. Close study of his career and the contents of the *Annales* in 1792–93, however, casts doubt on this interpretation. Carra voted with the Montagnards on many issues, including the death of the king. And the *Annales* maintained a precarious neutrality in the party strife, antagonizing both Girondins and Montagnards.

M. L. Kennedy, "L'Oracle des Jacobins des départements; Jean-Louis Carra et ses *Annales patriotiques*," *Actes du Colloque Girondins et Montagnards* (Paris, 1980); P. Montarlot, "Carra: Les députés de Saône-et-Loire aux assemblées de la Révolution," *Mém. de la Soc. éduenne* 33 (1905).

M. Kennedy

Related entries: BRUNSWICK; CALONNE; FREDERICK WILLIAM II; GIRONDINS.

CARRIER, JEAN-BAPTISTE (1756-94), terrorist. Carrier was born at Yolet (Cantal), on 16 March 1756 to J. Carrier, a well-to-do tenant farmer, and his wife M. Puex. He was a clerk in a law office for five or six years, until 1779 when he became a *praticien*, or minor judicial official. After studying in Paris, he settled in Aurillac to practice law in 1785 and to become a *procureur* of the *bailliage*.

Carrier enthusiastically joined the Revolutionaries and became an increasingly prominent radical orator. On 5 September 1792, he was elected the fifth deputy of the Cantal to the National Convention. He joined the Montagnards and, although quiet at first, gradually emerged as a frequent spokesman for radical ideas. He voted for the immediate execution of Louis XVI and against any appeal, promoted the establishment of the Revolutionary Tribunal, and supported the coup of 31 May, which overthrew the Girondins.

Carrier's significance in the Revolution derives mainly from his missions in 1793–94. On 12 July 1793 he was sent as representative on mission to Normandy and on 14 August to Brittany to counteract pro-Girondist movements there. In October he was directed to the Army of the West, which was engaged in a difficult guerilla war with the Vendéan rebels. Taking residence in Nantes, he decided that the best way to protect the city and aid the army was to accelerate the Terror.

Faced with the combined forces of counterrevolutionary nobles, refractory priests, and Vendéan peasants fighting, and sometimes defeating, the national army near Nantes, Carrier ordered extreme measures. With bulging, disease-ridden prisons that lacked food, he either approved or ordered mass executions of the imprisoned suspects without trials. In the notorious *noyades*, he loaded especially equipped barges with hundreds of suspects and drowned them by flooding the barges in the Loire River, a practice he called ''vertical deportation.'' By this method he executed 2,000 to 3,000 priests and Vendéans in December 1793–January 1794. He also ordered mass executions of suspects by firing squads. The exact number of victims is impossible to know, but some estimates range as high as 10,000. In time, the increasing violence and menacing intolerance of moderates led to the local Jacobins' appeal to Paris for his recall. Prompted by M. Robespierre, the Committee of Public Safety ordered his return to Paris on 8 February 1794.

Returning to Paris under attack, he defended his recent work, continued his violent orations, and sided with J.-M. Collot d'Herbois and J.-R. Hébert. Believing that Robespierre intended to send him before the Revolutionary Tribunal, he helped organize the conspiracy that overthrew the Incorruptible on 9 Thermidor Year II (27 July 1794).

Inundated by denunciations against Carrier, the Convention established a commission to investigate his conduct. On 22–24 October he testified in lengthy and impassioned appeals that he was only carrying out orders of the Committee of Public Safety. On 11 November he was placed under arrest by a near-unanimous vote and sent to the Revolutionary Tribunal. Always haughty and coldly dignified, he was convicted of crimes of terrorism. Still stoical, he went to the guillotine on 16 December 1794, in the place de Grève amid a large crowd.

Carrier's proconsulate at Nantes remains a matter of debate. Numerous contemporary enemies in Nantes and Paris denounced him in scathing terms as a criminally insane dictator who, reveling in unlimited power, lived by grisly murder orgies on one hand and bizarre sex orgies on the other. This view of terror gone mad has been repeated by many historians, not all of whom come from the conservative tradition. The standard biography by M. Fleury is also critical. Yet some writers have challenged these claims of atrocities. Carrier's grand-niece, E.-H. Carrier, in *Correspondence of Jean-Baptiste Carrier* (London, 1920), strongly defended him as a good and decent man. A. Gernoux, in *Carrier-le-maudit* (Nantes, 1935), sought to rehabilitate him by examining the sources of the stories of atrocities. A. Lallié, *J.-B. Carrier* (Paris, 1910), maintained that the system of government, rather than Carrier personally, was at fault. Most important, G. Martin described him as an unexceptional terrorist in an exceptional situation and emphasized his constructive work, Generally his defenders maintain that the huge numbers of mass murders were great exaggerations, enlarged by time, and that Carrier did no more than any other effective representative on mission would have done in the same situation. Despite these defenders, Carrier's reputation remains as an unjustly harsh terrorist.

M. Fleury, *Carrier à Nantes* (Paris, 1897); G. Martin, *Carrier et sa mission à Nantes* (Paris, 1924).

R. J. Caldwell

Related entries: BAILLIAGE; 9 THERMIDOR YEAR II; *NOYADES DE NANTES*; REVOLUTIONARY TRIBUNAL.

CARTES DE CIVISME. See CERTIFICATES OF CIVISM.

CATHERINE II ALEKSEEVNA (born SOPHIE AUGUSTE FRIEDERIKE, Prinzessin von Anhalt-Zerbst) (1729-96), empress of Russia. Daughter of an impoverished German petty prince, Catherine was summoned to St. Petersburg at fourteen to marry the graceless heir presumptive to the Russian autocracy. She attained sole power following a coup against her husband, Peter III, in 1762, soon after his accession to the throne. During her long reign, she supervised rapid territorial growth of the Russian Empire at the expense of Poland and Turkey, traditional enemies of Russia and allies of France. She was in full charge of foreign policy at all times. Internally, she attempted to systematize and render more efficient a bureaucratized corporate state structure inherited from her predecessors, especially Peter I. Present-day historiography of the period is concerned chiefly with the personnel and actual functioning of the bureaucracy, the relationship of nobility to bureaucracy, and the possibly autonomous nature of the eighteenth-century absolutist state. No adequate biography of Empress Catherine has been completed.

Although she received little formal education, Catherine read widely as an adult; her statecraft was profoundly influenced by Montesquieu, Blackstone, Beccaria, and others. In her own abundant writings (legislative materials, letters, essays, drama), she represented her rule as a reign of enlightenment that was bringing political liberty (*gosudarstvannaia vol'nost'*) to a servile people. She often spoke of her republican spirit. She corresponded extensively with select *philosophes* such as F.-M. Voltaire, D. Diderot, and Baron Grimm, each of whom accepted her as an intellectual peer and praised her enlightened government. Noting Catherine's failure to emancipate the serfs, share power with representative bodies, or replace the corporate social structure with a society of autonomously functioning individual citizens, many pre-Revolutionary and most Soviet historians have judged her a hypocritical despot and her correspondents' dupes. Western historical opinion usually holds that she began to rule with progressive intentions but took fright and abandoned them when confronted by the Pugachev Rebellion and the American and French revolutions. Recent efforts to understand her vocabulary within the context of Western and Central European political thought during her own formative years show that her claims to enlightened and republican absolutism were constant throughout the reign and fully justified in the eyes of contemporaries by implementation of the rule of law ("republican" monarchy) and active state intervention (*état policé*) to foster education and cultural development, agricultural-commercial prosperity, and religious tolerance. (That so many of her efforts bore so little fruit derives from the nature of Russian society, not from her intentions.) By the end of Catherine's life, political terminology and assumptions were undergoing rapid change, but her framework of discourse, formed in the middle third of the century, made it impossible for her to reach an understanding of the politics of any stage of the French Revolution. (She denied to all participants the name *republican*.)

For several years prior to 1789, France and Russia had been moving toward rapprochement based on common opposition to the growth of English power. Although Catherine opposed the French Revolution consistently from the first seditious usurpation of royal prerogative, she also opposed plans current among the allies of the First Coalition to partition France. Only an undivided France under strong monarchical absolutism could act as counterweight to Britain and Prussia. Even before conclusion (January 1792) of an exhausting war with Turkey, which had precluded other military efforts, Catherine attempted to organize a royal crusade against Revolutionary France; but the deaths of her confederates, the rulers of Sweden and Austria, thwarted this plan. Catherine early recognized the comte de Provence as regent of France and from 1795 as King Louis XVIII. In the spring of 1793, her elaborate plan to arrange invasion of France by an *émigré* army, to be formed in the Channel Islands under command of the comte d'Artois, died for lack of English support. Two proposals to place Russian armies at the disposal of England (spring 1793, late 1793–94) collapsed on the refusal of England to subsidize the Russian troops (although at the same time subsidizing Prussia). Despite evidence that England's chief interest lay in prolonging conflict and seizing French colonies, Catherine repeatedly sought to cooperate with the British against the Revolutionary threat. Thus she ceased all commerce with France, to the detriment of customs revenues (March 1793). She sent a Russian squadron to enlarge the blockade fleet, despite combat with Poland (June 1795). In January 1795 Russia took the initiative that led to restructuring the anti-French coalition after the Prussian defection. Serious Russian plans for military intervention at that time were impeded first by a French-inspired revolutionary nationalist uprising in Poland (resulting in the final partition of that country) and then by the death of the empress (November 1796).

D. M. Griffiths, "Catherine II: the Republican Empress," *Jahr für Gesch. Ost.* 21 (1973); C. Larivière, *Catherine II et la Révolution française d'après des nouveaux documents* (Paris, 1895); J. W. Marcum, "Catherine II and the French Revolution: A Reappraisal," *Can. Slav. Papers*, 16 (1974).

E. Ambler

Related entries: ARTOIS; FIRST COALITION; GUSTAVUS III; JOSEPH II.

CAZALES, JACQUES-ANTOINE-MARIE DE   161

CAZALES, JACQUES-ANTOINE-MARIE DE (1758-1805), noble deputy
to the Estates General, talented orator of the rightist opposition in the National
Assembly, royalist *émigré* and counterrevolutionist. Son of a *conseiller* at the
Parlement of Toulouse, Cazalès in 1789 was thirty-one, an army captain, largely
self-educated, who emerged as an eloquent speaker in the meetings of the noble
deputies at Versailles. A believer in reform through traditional representation by
estates, he opposed verification in common of the powers of the deputies, and
when Louis XVI, after the failure of the royal session on 23 June, ordered the
representatives of the three estates to meet together, Cazalès left Versailles for
Toulouse. Forced to return and resume his duties as a deputy, he proved to be
a formidable debater, one of the few articulate defenders of the aristocratic
traditionalism that had been so strong on the eve of the Revolution. His inter-
ventions illustrate both the tactical necessities of a losing cause and the contours
of a political and social philosophy that during the Revolutionary years tended
to be eroded toward either intransigent absolutism or the Anglophile views of
such men as J.-J. Mounier, P.-V. Malouet, and J. Mallet du Pan.

Cazalès was appreciated by contemporaries for his courage and forthrightness.
He and A. Barnave, political opponents who fought a duel in August 1790 in
which Cazalès was slightly wounded, liked and respected each other. Having
failed to preserve the Estates General, Cazalès tried to safeguard the powers of
the crown against what he took to be the National Assembly's pretensions to
sovereignty. In so doing, he acknowledged the sovereignty of the nation and
argued that the king's executive powers and equal share in the legislative power
had the sanction of the people's consent through the centuries. Whatever the
National Assembly did in the way of constitutional legislation would have to be
ratified by the nation. Cazalès rejected divine right of kings while defending the
clergy's mission and authority as divinely sanctioned and denying the Assembly's
right to reorganize the Church. His arguments in the National Assembly anticipated those of later counterrevolutionary theorists who were to identify the
general will with traditional institutions historically evolved. He was less a
theorist than a practical tactician looking toward the replacement of the National
Assembly by another body meeting away from Parisian influences.

Cazalès denied the existence of an oppressive feudal aristocracy, arguing that
the monarchy had long since overcome such people and declaring his allegiance
to equality before the law, which he viewed in a manner that could not have
shocked many of his listeners. Property, justified by its origin in labor and its
role in the founding of societies, was also an important measure of political
competence. Upon its correct social distribution by inheritance laws depended
the preservation of families, moral standards, and patriotism. Cazalès was an
admirer of the English, whom he described as ''profound in the science of
liberty'' (Cazalès, 1821). Although it is not possible to distinguish with certainty
his fundamental beliefs from his tactical proposals, the behavior of Cazalès in
the National Assembly suggests social realism and political moderation aimed
at halting the Revolution at a point where the aristocracy still had, or could

recover, an important part in a representative system. This posture, less and less tolerated in *émigré* circles, and perhaps also the newness and relative insignificance of his title, help account for the cool reception Cazalès received when he experimented briefly with emigration after the king's arrest at Varennes, but he went abroad again after 10 August 1792 and served in the *émigré* army of the princes. When Louis XVI was placed on trial, Cazalès demanded permission to return to France and take part in the king's defense. When refused a safe conduct, he published *Défense de Louis XVI* (s.l., 1793). After serving the comte de Provence, the future Louis XVIII, on several missions, Cazalès settled in England. In 1803 his name was removed from the list of *émigrés*. Although he refused offers from Napoleon, he returned to spend his last years in southwestern France.

F.-A. Aulard, ''Cazalès,'' *La Grande Encyclopédie. Inventaire raisonné des sciences, des lettres et des arts. Sous la direction de M. Berthelot et al.*, vol. 9 (Paris, n.d.); J.-A.-M. de Cazalès, *Discours et opinions de Cazalès, précédés d'une notice historique sur la vie. Par M. Chare; suivis de la défense de Louis XVI par Cazalès* (Paris, 1821); R. d'Amat, ''Cazalès,'' *Dictionnaire de biographie française, sous la direction de M. Prevost et Roman d'Amat*, vol. 8 (Paris, 1959).

P. H. Beik

Related entries: ANGLOMANES; EMIGRES; PROVENCE.

CENS, seigneurial due. A fixed, annual payment, the *cens* was the basic feudal rent, supposed to derive from an original concession of property by the lord, and marking the lord's *directe* or overlordship over all tenures of non-noble property in the seigneurie. The *cens* was usually a money payment; it was perpetual and could not be alienated, redeemed, or divided. The *cens* was generally an insignificant fee by the end of the Old Regime owing to monetary devaluation and inflation, but for more recent contracts and for those measured in kind, payments were more onerous. The amount of the *cens* varied greatly even within seigneuries. In many cases, a land rent attuned to market values was demanded along with a nominally low *cens*. Property that owed the *cens* usually was also subject to the payment of *lods et ventes* when it was sold or transferred out of the line of succession. This was a heavy fee, usually one-twelfth of the purchase price of the property.

The *cens* was important to the seigneur for its political and honorific value since it was a perpetual acknowledgment of the subordination of the tenants to the lord. Because of its symbolic importance, the *cens* is a good vehicle for assessing the nature of the Revolutionary attack on the so-called feudal order.

The Revolutionary (and post-Revolutionary) history of the *cens* is marked by the attempt to distinguish between those seigneurial dues based on a concession of property and therefore redeemable and those based on servitude and distinctions of persons and to be abolished without indemnity, Although the National Assembly in its decrees of 4–11 August 1789 is said to have destroyed the feudal regime, perpetual landed rents such as the *cens* were not destroyed but declared redeemable, and their collection was to continue until redemption. This judgment was repeated by the decrees of 15–28 March 1790, which further emphasized that all seigneurial dues such as the *cens* were presumed to derive from a concession of property unless the tenant could prove the contrary. The decrees of 3–9 May 1790 stipulated the rules for redemption of seigneurial dues: the *cens* could not be redeemed by individual tenants but had to be purchased for the whole territory on which it was levied, and annual dues such as the *cens* could not be redeemed apart from the transfer fees (the *droits casuels*, such as the *lods et ventes*). The decrees of 18 June–6 July 1792 declared that *droits casuels* were abolished except in cases where a title could be produced proving that the fees derived from a concession of property. On 20–22 August 1792 the Legislative Assembly provided for individual and separate redemption of seigneurial rights. This regulation was emphatically repeated by the decrees of 25–28 August 1792, which abolished outright any seigneurial due that could not be supported by a formal title proving the concession of property. Finally, on 17–18 July 1793, the Convention discarded all of its earlier distinctions, abolished all seigneurial dues without indemnity, and decreed the burning of all seigneurial titles. It did stipulate, however, that purely landed rents with no taint of feudality were maintained. It was this last provision that complicated post-Revolutionary adjudications of properties and tenures, for the seigneurial and the landed elements were often highly imbricated, and Restoration courts were no more willing than the early Revolutionaries to throw out one with the other.

Revolutionary decrees concerning the *cens* must be considered in the light of actual rural experience. Unrest in the countryside and the refusal to pay seigneurial dues prompted the first renunciation by the National Assembly. Later decrees were in large part recognition after the fact that the peasantry had taken the proclamation of a seigneurial regime "entirely destroyed" at its face value and refused to redeem or even to pay the seigneurial dues demanded of them.

M. Garaud, *La Révolution et la propriété foncière* (Paris, 1958); P. Sagnac and P. Caron, eds., *Les Comités des droits féodaux et de législation et l'abolition du régime seigneurial (1789-1793)* (Paris, 1907); A. Soboul, "Survivances 'féodales' dans la société rurale française au XIXe. siècle," *Ann.: Econ., soc., civ.*, 23 (1968).

M. A. Quinn

Related entries: FEUDALISM; 4 AUGUST 1789.

CENTRAL REVOLUTIONARY COMMITTEE, Parisian representatives who organized the overthrow of the Girondins on 2 June 1793. From the opening of the National Convention on 21 September 1792 until 31 May 1793, the Girondins dominated the French government. An ill-defined faction of *conventionnels* who rallied around the deputies J.-P. Brissot, F.-N.-L. Buzot, J.-M. Roland, and P.-V. Vergniaud, they formed a minority of the assembly as did their radical opponents, the Montagnards. These two factions vied for dominance over the nebulous majority of deputies called the Plain.

Although they held sway in the Convention, the Girondins gradually developed a mutual enmity with the Parisian masses, the *sans-culottes*. The Parisians assailed the Girondin government for its inability to deal with rising prices and food scarcities, for the military reverses in Belgium and the Rhineland, the treason of the Girondin ally C. Dumouriez, the outbreak of the rebellion in the Vendée, and the spreading antigovernment troubles across France. By March 1793, the masses sharply denounced the Girondins as traitors and allied with the Montagnards who became their champions in the Convention. As talk of a purge of the Convention swept the streets of Paris, various committees met intermittently at the Evêché (archbishop's palace) to discuss actions against the Girondins.

The Girondins struck forcefully against their enemies, apparently expecting to eliminate at least the most popular leaders. The Convention reduced the Mountain by sending its leaders on missions to the departments. It arrested the violent J.-P. Marat, a popular agitator and archenemy of the Girondins, and sent him before the Revolutionary Tribunal. At the same time, a majority of the Parisian sections presented a petition to the Convention calling for the arrest of twenty-two leading Girondins.

The fatal confrontation between the Girondins and the *sans-culottes* came in late May. On 21 May the Convention created the Commission of Twelve, all Girondins, with the purpose of examining the hostile assemblies of Paris. The Convention passed numerous decrees suppressing or limiting local meetings and arresting several radical leaders, most notably J.-R. Hébert and C.-E. Dobsen, president of section Cité. On 27 May the Montagnards riposted by pushing through the Convention a decree abolishing the week-old commission and releasing Hébert and Dobsen.

When the Girondins managed to reinstate the commission the next day, 28 May, the crisis reached a breaking point. Encouraged by the Montagnards, the Cité section appealed to all other sections of Paris to send representatives to the Evêché for the purpose of planning an insurrection against the Girondins. On 29 May, a crowd of men chosen from thirty-three sections assembled in the Great Hall of the Evêché. Twenty-seven of those sections, a bare majority of all the sections of Paris, had sent their representatives with unlimited power, a fact that allowed the assembly to claim the legal right of issuing decrees in the name of the people of Paris. While the large assembly met, nine men from it gathered in an adjoining room and called themselves the Revolutionary Committee. They were Dobsen, the president, J.-F. Varlet, A. Simon, M. Wendling, A.-M. Guzman, L.-F. Bonhonmet, F.-L. Fournerot, C.-H. Laurent, and a section leader by the name of Mitois. Led by Dobsen and Varlet, the group of militant but little-known radicals formed the nucleus of what was to become the Central Revolutionary Committee.

On the next day, 30 May, the two groups reassembled at the Evêché. In the Great Hall popular orators harangued while the committee of nine declared itself permanent and insurrectionary. On the same day, the department government summoned a general meeting of all the Parisian sections to be held the following day at the Jacobins. The committee proceeded to issue orders for insurrection. Meeting into the early hours of the morning, they ordered the closing of the city gates, the sounding of the tocsin, and the firing of the alarm cannon, all to signal the beginning of the insurrection.

At 6:30 the next morning, 31 May, the committee traveled to the meeting hall of the municipal government, the Conseil général of the Commune of Paris, which was still in session. There, Dobsen acted out a scene that had been prearranged with the Conseil. He announced that the people of Paris had established a new revolutionary council and that all previously constituted authorities were annulled. He then declared that the former Conseil was reinstated in power. Now properly ''revolutionary,'' the Conseil recognized the committee and raised its number to ten. This charade supposedly legitimized the roles of the Conseil and the committee in the upcoming insurrection.

A similar scene was acted at the Jacobins where Wendling met with the assembly called by the department. This assembly added eleven men to the committee, including L.-M. Auvray, M. Bouin, J.-N. Dunouy, J.-B. Loys, A. C. Rousselin, and J.-M. Seguy. At 2:30 P.M. the commune conseil added five names to the committee: M.-F. Cailleux, B. Duroure, J.-H. Hassenfratz, J.-B. Marino, and C.-L. Perdry. With twenty-six members, representing most Parisian social classes and neighborhoods, the Central Revolutionary Committee was completed.

The committee had begun to act even before its number finalized. Earlier the same day it had named F. Hanriot as commander of the National Guard of Paris, had promised 40 *sous* a day for workers who remained under arms, and had begun the firing of the alarm cannon at about noon. It had also sent a delegation to the National Convention to announce that the people were in rebellion against counterrevolutionaries. The Convention politely and firmly dismissed this scarcely veiled threat.

With its organization completed, the committee prepared for action. At about 3:30 P.M. it drew up a list of fourteen demands to present to the Convention, the first of which was the arrest of the twenty-two already named Girondins. Immediately after, committee members led a group into the Convention hall bearing the demands. The Convention responded by decreeing a few of the demands, including the abolition of the Commission of Twelve and approval of the 40 *sous* wage. Yet it refused to order any arrests.

The next day, Saturday, 1 June, the committee called for massive crowds in the streets and planned a final initiative against the Girondins. It composed a new list of demands, including the arrest of twenty-odd Girondins, while it sounded the alarm and provisioned the swelling crowds around the Convention hall. By evening the armed citizens had surrounded the hall, but by then the assembly had adjourned for the day. Nevertheless, the committee made its demands to the remaining deputies who sent the list to the Committee of Public Safety for a report within three days. Once again, however, the Convention had rejected the committee.

The next day, 2 June, brought the conclusion of the crisis. By 4:00 A.M. the

Central Revolutionary Committee was already making its final plans. It sent an order to Hanriot directing him to surround the Convention with enough armed men to seize the Girondin leaders in case the Convention once again refused to decree their arrest. On the sound of alarm, thousands of armed men and women converged on the Convention hall and completely surrounded it with well-stocked cannons. At 10:00 A.M. the Convention opened its session for the business of the day. About four hours later the president of the committee led a delegation into the hall and read the demand for the Girondins' arrest. For the third time in three days, the Convention disposed of the demand by sending it to the Committee of Public Safety for a report. The enraged committee men stormed out of the hall waving their fists and shouting "to arms!" Soon thereafter, B. Barère reported for the Committee of Public Safety the proposal that the Girondin leaders voluntarily resign their posts. Some Girondins stoicly resigned, but others indignantly refused.

At about 5:00 P.M. the Convention tried to lift the siege by passing a decree ordering the removal of the armed force. The deputies walked out as a group to confront their besiegers with the decree, but the crowd forced them back. Confused, helpless, and finally exhausted, the *conventionnels* returned to their benches and decreed the arrest of twenty-nine Girondin deputies. The Central Revolutionary Committee promptly sent a congratulatory message, hailing the saviors of the Republic.

The removal of the Girondins made the Mountain dominant in the Convention and turned the Revolution toward the Terror. Having accomplished its original aim, the Central Revolutionary Committee no longer had a raison d'être. The commune and department governments resumed their normal roles. Since the Montagnards no longer had a use for the committee, they reduced its power. It ceased to exist by mid-June.

L. Mortimer-Ternaux, *Histoire de la Terreur, 1792–1794*. vol. 7 (Paris, 1869); G. Pariset, *Histoire de France contemporaine*, vol. 2 (Paris, 1920); P. Saint-Claire Deville, *La Commune de l'an II* (Paris, 1946); A. Tuetey, *Répertoire général des sources manuscrites de l'histoire de Paris pendant la Révolution*, vol. 9 (Paris, 1910); H. Wallon, *La Révolution du 31 mai et le fédéralisme en 1793*, 2 vols. (Paris, 1886).

R. J. Caldwell

Related entries: BRISSOT; COMMISSION OF TWELVE; GIRONDINS; HEBERT; ROLAND DE LA PLATIERE, J.-M.; *SANS-CULOTTES*; VARLET.

CERCLE SOCIAL (1790-93), club and publishing company. Although begun by a small group of Parisian intellectuals and municipal leaders in early 1790, the Cercle social first gained fame when it opened its club (technically known as the Confederation of the Friends of Truth) in October 1790. The purpose of the club was to reinterpret Enlightenment thought in the wake of the Revolution. Each of its weekly meetings was led by the abbé C. Fauchet, who analyzed a portion of J.-J. Rousseau's *Social Contract*. The club also developed radical notions concerning the rights of women and the poor and vigorously supported the Civil Constitution of the Clergy. With an unusually high membership of over 5,000, the club posed a threat to more moderate groups. The Jacobins attacked the Cercle social in their *Journal des amis de la constitution* and warned affiliated societies to avoid any relationship with the club. After Fauchet left Paris in April 1791 for the bishopric of Calvados, the Cercle social became increasingly involved in the burgeoning democratic movement. It was instrumental in organizing the republican campaign following the king's flight to Varennes. While the club was suppressed immediately after the "massacre" at the Champ de Mars, the publishing company expanded its activities. Between 1790 and 1793, the Cercle social published more than 180 pamphlets and journals, including the *Bouche de fer, Sentinelle*, and the *Chronique du mois*. The Cercle social became an important organ for the Girondins, and the Roland government secretly subsidized several of its publications. The Cercle social was closed when the Girondins fell in June 1793.

V. Alexeev-Popov, "Le Cercle Social (1790-1791)," *Rech. sov.*, no. 4 (1956); R. B. Rose, "Socialism and the French Revolution: The Cercle Social and the *Enragés*," *Bull. of the J. Rylands Lib.* 41 (1958-59). Many Cercle social publications have been reprinted in the microfiche collection *Nicolas de Bonneville et le Cercle Social, 1787-1800* (Montrouge, 1976).

G. Kates

Related entries: *BOUCHE DE FER*; CHAMP DE MARS "MASSACRE."

CERTIFICATES OF CIVISM (1793-95), documents required of citizens, attesting to their conduct during the Revolution. The obligation of carrying certificates of civism was established as one of the police and surveillance measures whose enforcement was imposed as much by internal struggles as by the state of war. The first measure of this sort dated to the Law of 11 August 1792, which allocated to departments, districts, and communes powers of police and general security. This gave birth to the Committees of Surveillance (later called Revolutionary Committees). Legislation, originally aimed at foreigners, was intensified and systematized by the Law of 21 March 1793, which imposed on all communes the establishment of these committees that, together with the General Councils of the communes, were charged with demanding certificates of civism from foreigners. When such people possessed neither property nor proof of useful activity, they were required to furnish an affidavit signed by six citizens who had lived in the locality more than a year and a security deposit that could be as much as half their total wealth.

Ultimately, it was the Law of Suspects of 17 September 1793 that made the obligation of carrying certificates of civism a general one, insofar as all citizens who could not produce them were liable to arrest under the general category of suspects. It was not without confusion and some reallocations of authority that this practice was established; the problem of certificates of civism assumed a considerable role in collective life, especially in the cities, as the debates of the sections testify to.

What conditions were required to obtain a certificate of civism? This issue was constantly discussed in 1793–94, and the arbitrary quality that always affected the criteria for issuing them continuously poisoned these debates. The most popular and committed elements of the *sans-culotte* movement always demanded that certificates of civism be refused to certain categories, ex-nobles and priests, and sometimes to merchants and entrepreneurs. This demand, which continued until the spring of 1794, was never accepted officially. Perhaps the criterion for a certificate most frequently demanded was that required by the ministry of war of its personnel, evidence certifying that the individual "has continually served the Revolution since 14 July 1789, that since this time he has never deviated from its principles" and that he has never given in to the temptations of "Feuillantism or federalism."

The authority to issue these certificates changed successively, according to circumstances. At first it was the municipal authorities and the section assemblies who controlled this operation; but the Law of 20 September 1793, by putting the Revolutionary Committees over them, gave evidence of the government's desire to control this essential function through these more docile organs. However, this power was disputed, especially at Paris during the winter of 1793–94, when P.-G. Chaumette demanded the return of certificates of civism to the authority of the Commune, but this claim failed in the face of the Committee of General Security's rejection. The full power of the Revolutionary Committees was far from absolute; at Paris they progressively surrendered their authority, not to the section assemblies but rather to the popular societies of the sections, which consolidated this prerogative in their hands during the spring of 1794— not without accusations that they abused this authority by their arbitrary and annoying refusals to issue certificates. In any case, in the campaign waged against the section societies, beginning in Germinal Year II, the problem of the certificates of civism weighed heavily in the evidence of their bad reputation, despite their denials of wrongdoing.

During the Thermidorian period, a law of 13 Vendémiaire Year III transferred to the Civil Committees of sections (the heirs of the Revolutionary Committees) the issuance of certificates of civism, a formidable prerogative that provided them with an effective weapon in the anti-Terrorist repression of Year III. The certificates had not disappeared with the regime of the Terror, but they tended to be confounded with security cards (*cartes de sûrété*), the registers of which were maintained by the municipalities during the period of the Directory. Following the freeing of suspects, the cards lost their special significance as stakes in the urban political struggle in which they had been the central issue in Year II.

A. P. Herlaut, "Les Certificats de civisme," *Ann. hist. de la Révo. française* 15 (1938); A. Soboul, *Les Sans-culottes parisiens en l'an II*, 2d ed. (Paris, 1962).

M. Vovelle

Related entries: CHAUMETTE; COMMITTEES OF SURVEILLANCE; LAW OF SUSPECTS; SECTIONS.

CHABOT, FRANCOIS (1756-94), a Capuchin monk turned Revolutionary, among the first clerics to swear the oath to the Civil Constitution of the Clergy. Chabot was something of a prodigy, having entered the collège of Rodez at age eleven. On graduation he began advancing progressive ideas both verbally and in writing. His bishop forbade him to preach, but this did not prevent him from moving to the Left politically when the Revolution began. In 1790 he founded a Jacobin club in Rodez and shortly after was elected deputy from the department of the Cher-et-Loire to the Legislative Assembly and, after the fall of the monarchy, to the National Convention. He held a position on the Left, as may be seen by his radical ideas in such publications as his *Projet d'act constitutif des Français* (1793), his reply to J.-P. Brissot in his letter "François Chabot à Jean-Pierre Brissot" (1793?), and his *Discours prononcé par François Chabot. . .* (14 June 1793).

Chabot is linked indelibly to the notorious affair of the Indies Company, which A. Mathiez (1920) declared was "the key to the political proceedings of the Terror." There is little question that he accepted money for favors to his banker friends, among whom were S. and J. Frey (nés Schonfeld), Austrian Jews converted to both Christianity and the Revolution. He was betrothed to their sixteen-year-old sister, Léopoldine. Despite the fact that the Freys had contributed generously to the Jacobins and the younger brother had been wounded in the attack on the Tuileries on 10 August 1792, Chabot's betrothal was a political error, coming at a time when all foreigners were suspect. Moreover, as a former member of the Committee of General Security, Chabot had done favors for other bankers and speculators and was linked to the counterrevolutionary schemes of baron de Batz, a royalist intriguer. The Hébertists in fact had suspected him of corruption even before he became involved in the Indies Company affair. After accepting a bribe of 100,000 *livres* to make advantageous modifications in the liquidation of the Indies Company, he became frightened and tried vainly to convince both M. Robespierre and the Committee of General Security that his role was that of a patriot who was ferreting out the plots of enemies of the Republic. He was executed together with the Dantonists on 5 April 1794.

J.-M.-J. de Bonald, *François Chabot membre de la Convention (1756-1794)* (Paris, 1908); A. Mathiez, *Un Procès de corruption sous la Terreur, l'affaire de la Compagnie des Indes* (Paris, 1920); A. Mathiez, ed., *François Chabot réprésentant du peuple à ses concitoyens qui sont les juges de sa vie politique* (Paris, 1913).

M. Slavin

Related entries: BATZ; COMMITTEE OF GENERAL SECURITY; JULIEN; 10 AUGUST 1792.

CHAMPART, seigneurial tax. One of the annual charges levied by a seigneur against cultivated land or other income-producing property in his seigneurie, the *champart* consisted of a fraction of the produce or income of the property on which it was paid and was often characterized as a seigneurial tithe, comparable to the tithe of the church, which was assessed in the same way.

The rate of the *champart* varied from place to place. So did the name. When payable on cultivated land, as R. Mousnier has found, it might have been called *champart, terrage, agrier, agrière,* or *tasque*; when payable on vineyards, it might have been called *complant, terceau, vignage,* or *querpot.* In Poitou a *champart* paid on meadows was called a *herbaux,* and in the Nivernais a *champart* on the total income of a leasehold was called *bordelage.* The *champart* on a house would be called *hostise,* or *fouage,* or *festage.* But whatever it might be called and whether paid in money or in kind, the *champart* remained a charge on the income derived from property within a seigneurie.

In the legislation of 4–11 August 1789, the National Assembly abolished all *champarts* on condition that those obliged to pay them reimburse their seigneurs for the capitalized value at a rate fixed by the Assembly and that they continue to pay them until they had provided the reimbursement. Most peasant communities, however, refused to pay the reimbursement or the *champart,* which was finally abolished along with all other feudal dues by the National Convention on 17 July 1793, whether the reimbursement had been paid or not.

P. Caron, ed., *La suppression des droits féodaux: Instruction, recueil de textes et notes* (a *fascicule* of the *Bull. d'hist. écon. de la Révo.* 1920-21, pp. 1-230); R. Mousnier, *Les institutions de France sous la monarchie absolue, 1598-1789:* vol. 1 (Paris, 1974); P. Sagnac, *La législation civile de la Révolution française* (Paris, 1898).

G. V. Taylor

Related entries: FEUDALISM; 4 AUGUST 1789; PEASANTRY.

CHAMP DE MARS "MASSACRE" (17 July 1791), republican demonstration in Paris during which several persons were killed by National Guard troops commanded by the marquis de Lafayette. This demonstration marked a major split within the Third Estate between democratic republicans and constitutional monarchists. Before 1791 Parisian activists generally supported the efforts of the Constituent Assembly, adopting a wait-and-see attitude. Only a small group of radical municipal politicians and journalists associated with the Cordeliers Club doubted the intentions of the national leaders. But during early 1791, the Cordeliers were able to convince an increasingly large segment of Parisian public opinion that the Constituent Assembly wanted to end the Revolution by establishing a new aristocracy of wealth in place of the old nobility. By May 1791 the Cordeliers' view was shared by several popular clubs and the movement focused on three specific issues: the necessity of collective petitions, concern for the unemployed, and revocation of the *marc d'argent.*

On 10 May the Constituent Assembly debated a bill outlawing petitions from any corporate group, including club, parish, or governmental agency. In the future, only petitions from individual active citizens would be heard by the government. Supporters of the bill argued that the measure was consistent with the Revolution's attempt to deny authority to corporations and place all political power in the hands of individual citizens. But there was more to it than that. Petitions were one of the most important political weapons used by popular clubs to pressure the municipal, departmental, and national leaders. Without collective petitions, the debates at the various clubs would seem impotent. M. Robespierre, F.-N.-L. Buzot, and H.-B. Grégoire realized that the true purpose of the bill was to undermine the clubs, and they attacked it as a violation of the Declaration of the Rights of Man. Their views were ignored and the decree was easily passed.

Parisian radicals reacted angrily in their clubs and newspapers. The Cercle social pushed aside all routine business and devoted four consecutive meetings to the matter. Speakers rejected the view that the collective petition was a holdover from the Old Regime, arguing that it provided a necessary check on the power of governmental leaders. They noted how the collective petition served to articulate the views of women and the urban poor and attacked the legislature for trying to exclude the disenfranchised masses. On 10 June the Cercle social passed a resolution claiming that the decree attacked the sovereignty of the nation. The club urged all citizens to demand its revocation.

Meanwhile Parisian wage earners were also becoming increasingly disenchanted with the government. Unemployment had been rising in Paris at a disturbing rate. In January 1791, 24,000 laborers had been employed in the public workshops, the last stop before unemployment. By June the number had risen to 31,000. The laborers naturally looked to the government for help, but they were quickly disappointed. On 8 May Paris mayor J.-S. Bailly announced the closure of the Bastille workshop (which had employed 800 laborers), and in June the Constituent Assembly supported his action by decreeing the general closure of the public workshops. The wage earners responded to the crisis by forming groups that could lobby for better social legislation. One important organization was the Point central des arts et métiers. Its leaders claimed that every worker had a right to a job; if he could not attain one in the private sector, the government was obligated to provide him with one. The Point central urged the Constituent Assembly to develop a comprehensive national public works program. Moreover, the radical clubbists provided the necessary political leadership for the laborers' campaign. The Point central met at the headquarters of the Cercle social, and that club published its important 28 June petition. The Cordeliers offered to have its secretaries sign the petition for any laborer who did not know how to write.

The Point central, Cordeliers, and Cercle social all became members of the Comité central des diverses sociétés fraternelles, established in May by the Cordeliers' journalist F. Robert. Composed of at least ten other clubs, the Comité central was a kind of federal assembly of Parisian radicalism. It demanded that the Revolution not be slowed until the completion of a democratic state. Its leaders argued that this could be accomplished only when all citizens were eligible for public office. But nineteen months earlier, the Constituent Assembly had passed a decree limiting eligibility for national office to those men who paid a direct tax of at least fifty days' wages, known as the *marc d'argent*. Although the radicals had never supported the *marc d'argent*, recent events allowed the Comité central to attack the measure as the first step in the creation of a new aristocracy that ignored the aspirations of the laboring classes. In Comité central meetings, speakers claimed that those citizens without property would be more oppressed under the new regime than under the old. A petition of 17 June warned the Constituent Assembly that it was leading the nation to the brink of civil war.

The king's flight to Varennes played into the hands of the radicals by transforming their cause into a united republican movement. The Cordeliers were the first to act. On 21 June, only hours after hearing of the king's flight, the club passed a resolution calling for the establishment of a republic. This declaration was published by the Cercle social as a poster and was posted on walls throughout the capital. Three days later, a crowd of 30,000 met at the Place Vendôme to demand a trial of the king. On 26 June the *Bouche de fer* (a democratic daily) called for a plebiscite through which the people could abolish the monarchy. On 1 July the marquis de Condorcet publicized his recent conversion to republicanism in the first issue of his new journal, *Le républicain*. On 11 July the Comité central sent a petition to the Constituent Assembly demanding the establishment of a republic.

The leaders of the Constituent Assembly and the municipality were far more concerned about this democratic threat than about the king's behavior. They believed that they could control Louis but worried that the democrats would undermine the foundations of the new regime. Thus the king's flight changed these constitutional monarchists into a party of reactionaries. Its leaders demanded the restoration of law and order at any price. They were willing to forgive the king for all his mistakes in order to suppress the democratic movement.

The political crisis reached a climax in mid-July. On the evening of 15 July, the Cercle social drew up a petition scolding the Constituent Assembly for taking no action on a trial of Louis XVI. After the meeting, a huge group (one journalist estimated 4,000) took the petition to the Jacobin club. They arrived at 11:00 P.M. to find that most of the conservative members had already gone home. The remaining group decided to write their own petition. C. de Laclos, G.-J. Danton, A.-F. Sergent, F. Lanthenas, and J.-P. Brissot were appointed to a committee for this purpose. By 11:00 the following morning (16 July), they had presented the petition to the Jacobins and had obtained some signatures. But the vast majority of Jacobins were so offended by the radical nature of the petition that they seceded from the club and immediately established their own club at the convent of the Feuillants. The Cordeliers Club also met on the morning of 16 July and instructed its members to gather that afternoon at the Champ de Mars to sign the Jacobin petition. Around noon Danton arrived at the Champ de Mars to read the petition to a crowd of 200 to 400 people. The petition demanded that the Constituent Assembly interpret the king's flight as an abdication and provide for his replacement by all constitutional means. Many listeners in the audience were offended by this last phrase, claiming that the word *constitutional* was but a ruse to pave the way for the duc d'Orléans to obtain the throne. They urged the demonstrators to reject the petition and accept nothing short of a genuine republican declaration. In the face of such opposition, Danton agreed to take the petition back to the Jacobins and asked the crowd to return the following day to sign a corrected version.

Meanwhile, the Constituent Assembly tried to use its powers to end the crisis. First, it declared that the 25 June suspension of the king would remain in effect until he accepted the new constitution. This amounted to a virtual reinstatement of the king and a complete rejection of the radicals' demands. Neither a trial nor even a serious investigation of the king's behavior would be made. Second, the Assembly gave the Paris municipal government full authority to maintain law and order, a clear warning to the democrats that the Assembly would no longer tolerate its activities.

The Jacobins debated the suppression of the *constitutional* phrase during its evening session on 16 July. After heated discussion the club voted to withdraw the petition altogether, fearing that the Constituent Assembly's pronouncement on the king had made it illegal.

The next day (17 July) thousands of Parisians from all parts of the capital flocked to the Champ de Mars to sign the revised Jacobin petition. The crowd included a cross-section of the Parisian laboring classes: craftsmen, tradesmen, wage earners, and domestic servants. At 12:00 a deputy from the Jacobins told the demonstrators that the Jacobins had disavowed all petitions because of the Constituent Assembly's ruling. But the crowd was now under the leadership of the Cordeliers Club. Robert drew up a new petition, which called for the abdication of the king and his replacement by a new executive council. The crowd had finally received a thoroughly republican petition. But its victory was short-lived. Earlier in the day, before most of the demonstrators had arrived, two individuals had been discovered hiding under the speaker's platform. The crowd suspected that they were going to sabotage the demonstration, so it killed the two men, hanging them from a window by a rope. J.-S. Bailly used the murder as a pretext to declare martial law, meaning that all demonstrations were illegal. Lafayette, the commander of the Paris National Guard, took his men to the Champ de Mars to break up the republican demonstration. When he arrived in the afternoon, he found some 50,000 demonstrators, 6,000 of whom had already signed the petition. Lafayette ordered the crowd to disperse. What happened next is not clear. Some may have tried to leave peacefully, but the Champ de Mars was surrounded by iron gates with few exits. Others apparently began stoning the troops. At some point, the excited troops began firing; when it was over, between thirteen (Bailly's estimate) and fifty (Robert's estimate) Parisians had been killed. Such was the "massacre" at the Champ de Mars.

Encouraged by the Constituent Assembly, municipal authorities began a general repression of the democratic movement. Some 200 activists were arrested in the sections, including J.-R. Hébert, F.-N. Vincent, A. F. Momoro, and E. Palm. Robert and L.-C.-S. Desmoulins went into hiding in Paris, while Danton fled to England. The *Bouche de fer* ceased publication, the Cordeliers did not meet until August, and the Cercle social permanently closed its club. But compared to later reprisals, the repression was actually quite mild. Both the radicals and the Feuillants wanted to avoid civil war. By October most of the clubs had reopened, and the presses were back in operation.

The fundamental conflict of the "massacre" was not really between monarchy and republicanism but rather between popular democracy and parliamentary government dominated by a new elite. To what extent would the new regime accommodate the political desires and economic needs of the urban laboring classes? During the spring and summer of 1791, the laborers came to feel betrayed by the king and the Constituent Assembly. The "massacre" sharpened the conflict within the Third Estate between radicals, who demanded full political rights for the laborers, and Feuillants, who wanted an end to the Revolution. It revealed that the Feuillants were willing to use force to thwart the democratic movement. The radicals could achieve their aims only through renewed violence.

F. Braesch, "Les petitions du Champ de Mars," *Rev. hist.* 143 (1923); J. Censer, *Prelude to Power: The Parisian Radical Press, 1789–91* (Baltimore, 1976); A. Mathiez, *Le Club des Cordeliers pendant la crise de Varennes et le massacre du Champ de Mars* (Paris, 1910); M. Reinhard, *La chute de la royauté* (Paris, 1969); G. Rudé, *The Crowd in the French Revolution* (New York, 1959).

G. Kates

Related entries: ACTIVE CITIZEN; BAILLY; *BOUCHE DE FER*; CERCLE SOCIAL; CORDELIERS CLUB; FEUILLANTS; *MARC D'ARGENT*; JACOBINS; VARENNES.

CHAMPION DE CICE, JEROME-MARIE (1735-1810), archbishop, deputy to the Constituent Assembly. Born in Rennes 3 September 1735, Champion de Cicé became one of the most respected members of the clergy and rose easily into its upper ranks. He became an *agent general* of the clergy in 1765, bishop of Rodez in 1770, and archbishop of Bordeaux in 1781. Worldly and personally ambitious, he was nevertheless conscientious in his clerical duties and an active participant in the affairs of the Bordeaux region. He came to champion not only the rights of the clergy but also the needs of the common people for change. His advocacy of reform increasingly isolated him from the majority of his colleagues in the upper clergy. This circumstance was especially evident during the sessions of the Assembly of Notables in 1787 and 1788 in which he was a participant. His voice then and later was raised in support of moderate, well-planned changes in government and social structure.

After the summons for an Estates General went forth in 1788, Champion de Cicé saw the need for its reorganization if any worthwhile reform was to be accomplished. He joined with other prominent individuals in the so-called patriotic party to arouse support for reorganization. Not surprisingly, he became one of the deputies of the First Estate in the Estates General and was able to work for change from within. On 22 June 1789, he was one of the 149 clerics who gave their support to the Third Estate and thereby helped to transform the Estates General into the National Assembly.

Once the gateway to change was thrown open, Champion de Cicé faced the dilemma of most moderates: how to effect needed reform without encouraging changes that would be too radical. The disorders of the summer of 1789 were especially disturbing and led to rather ambivalent actions on the part of Champion de Cicé. He presented to the Assembly the basic draft of the document that later became the famous Declaration of the Rights of Man and of the Citizen, although the original was condensed and given a more radical turn during the debate on it. At the same time he accepted from Louis XVI appointment to the ministry as keeper of the seals, a position in which he might be able to advise the king. In general his advice and actions were cautious, thereby arousing dissatisfaction from Right and Left—the usual fate of moderate reformers. He advised delay on the acceptance of the 4 August and later decrees and thereby unwittingly helped precipitate the demonstrations of 5–6 October, though he was not the only one who so advised the king. Regarding the confiscation of church land and, later, the Civil Constitution of the Clergy, he advocated acceptance by Louis and hoped for approval of the latter by the pope. Such approval did not come, but by that time (March–April 1791), Champion de Cicé was no longer in the ministry.Although he had done his best to maintain a middle course and was proud of his ministry, events moved too fast for his cautious approach. On 21 October 1790 he offered his resignation to Louis but actually left only a month later. Meanwhile on 10 November G.-J. Danton had vigorously denounced the ministry in the name of the forty-eight Paris sections. Clearly the Revolution was proceeding too far beyond his control or influence. He eventually emigrated.

He did not return to France until the Napoleonic amnesty of 1801. Soon after, under the Concordat, he was named archbishop of Aix, where he served quietly until his death on 10 August 1810. In 1808 he had been honored by being named count of the Empire.

J.-M. Champion de Cicé, *Mandement et instruction pastorale . . . qui ordonne des prières publiques, pour demander au ciel l'heureux succès des Etats-généraux du royaume, convoqués par le roi* (1789) and *Rapport fait . . . au nom du comité choisi . . . pour rédiger un projet de constitution* (27 juillet 1789); M. Prevost in *Dictionnaire de biographie française*, vol. 8 (Paris, 1959); L. Lévy-Schneider, *L'Application du Concordat par un prelat d'ancien régime, Mgr Champion de Cicé, archevêque d'Aix et d'Arles (1802-1810)* (Paris, 1921).

A. Saricks

Related entries: CIVIL CONSTITUTION OF THE CLERGY; ESTATES GENERAL; PATRIOT PARTY.

CHAMPIONNET, JEAN-ETIENNE (1762-1800). See PARTHENOPEAN REPUBLIC; SECOND COALITION.

CHAPPE, CLAUDE (1763-1805), engineer and physicist. Chappe was the nephew of the astronomer J. Chappe d'Auteroche; he took a serious interest in science from his earliest years and contributed several noteworthy articles to the *Journal de physique*. He is best known for his invention of the optical telegraph, which was widely used in France until it was superseded by the electrical telegraph. The basic idea was not new, since there were antecedents as early as classical times, but he was the first to work out a simple system that was easy to employ. His device consisted of an upright post with a traverse bar fixed across the top, at the ends of which were attached two smaller arms on pivots. The position of the arms represented certain letters. By setting up a series of such machines, each visible to the next one, messages could be conveyed rapidly. The Legislative Assembly adopted his invention in 1792, and it was first used the following year to transmit news to the Convention of the recapture of Condé from the Austrians. The Assembly made Chappe *ingénieur—télégraphe* and commissioned him to set up other lines, but soon the originality of his invention was challenged by others. Although the government maintained him in his post, he became despondent and committed suicide. His elder brother, Ignace-Urbain-Jean, who had helped perfect the device, continued his work along with a younger brother and in 1824 published *Histoire de la télégraphie*.

F. Gautier, *Centenaire de la Télégraphie: L'Oeuvre de C. Chappe* (Paris, 1893); E. Jacquez, *Claude Chappe* (Paris, 1893).

J. A. Leith

Related entry: SCIENCE.

CHARETTE DE LA CONTRIE, FRANCOIS-ATHANASE (1763-96), royalist commander in Bas-Poitou. In 1790 the chevalier resigned from the navy in which he had served through the American Revolution and emigrated, briefly, to Coblentz. Tough, energetic, and a good woodsman, he was precisely of that type of local, traditional gentry to whom some bands looked for leadership in the March 1793 rising in the Vendée, and his courage and resourcefulness made him a splendid captain well suited to conduct guerrilla-type warfare in the marshy and wooded countryside of Bas-Poitou. Despite a certain sense of strategy, he usually operated independently; this resulted from his character as much as from the republican dispositions aimed at denying him the coast and contact with the insurrection in the *bocage* to his east.

In 1793, however, involved in an assault on Machecoul (20 June), he established some degree of military order on the peasant cohorts, thus confirming his ascendancy over other *chefs* in the area, and then he led them to help in the abortive attacks on Nantes (28-29 June) and on Luçon (14 August). Thereafter, apart from a prolonged raid into the Mauges (December 1793), he held to and/ or was kept pinned in, the zone in which he was the unchallenged *chef*.

Needing aid, wanting a Bourbon prince to come to the Vendée, he sent a messenger to England after taking Noirmoutier (October 1793). In response he received glowing commendations and, from Louis XVIII, appointment as supreme commander of the Catholic and royalist forces in western France; that, though, was not until the summer of 1795, which is when he finally began to receive money and arms. The great bulk of all British aid, however, went to Quiberon, while from the Yeu expedition Charette and his thousand followers derived little material benefit and failed in their hopes that the comte d'Artois would land to head a unified royalist army.

Under growing military pressure, in the winter of 1794–95, Charette had begun to cooperate with N. Stofflet's forces in southern Anjou, an alliance split first by Republican sorties and then by the chevalier's unilateral conclusion of a treaty at La Jaunaye (17 February 1795) by which the private exercise of Catholicism was to be permitted, indemnities for war damage granted, and the core of his forces to be maintained in being, ready to fight again. Charette's forces then decupled to around 20,000, when the news came of the Quiberon landing. That disastrous event intensified Charette's contempt for J.-G. Puisaye and the *chouans*, which in turn improved his standing in the eyes of pure royalists, for whom he seemed, after H. du Vergier La Rochejaquelin's death, the perfect representation of the *preux chevalier français*. Republican stories and history focused on the undoubted cruelty he could show and on his ruthlessness; and folklore concentrated on the common touch and the bravery of a *chef* who roughed it with his men and the red scarves which were the only insignia to distinguish him from the rest of that band of cavalry that formed the spearhead of his assaults on *bleu* detachments, patriot *bourgs*, or food-supply convoys.

Refusing a chance to emigrate (February 1796), Charette was surrounded and hunted down. His capture and execution (29 March) finally guaranteed his place in the nineteenth-century clerico-royalist pantheon.

R. Bittard des Portes, *Charette et la guerre de Vendée* (Paris, 1902); G. Lenôtre (pseud. L. Gosselin), *M. de Charette, le roi de Vendée* (Paris, 1924); J. B. Russon, "Essai sur le portrait moral de Charette," *Ass. bret.* 70 (1961); M. de Saint Pierre, *Monsieur de Charette, chevalier du Roi* (Paris, 1977).

M. G. Hutt

Related entries: ARTOIS; *CHOUANNERIE*; LA ROCHEJAQUELIN; PUISAYE; QUIBERON; VENDEE.

CHARLES IV (1742-1819), king of Spain. Born in Naples 11 November 1742, Charles IV married his first cousin, Maria Luisa of Parma, and succeeded to the Spanish throne in 1788. Of mediocre ability, he was dominated by his wife and her lover, M. Godoy, throughout his reign. After the execution of Louis XVI (21 January 1793), he joined the forces of the First Coalition in war against the French Republic. Following several military defeats in the province of Roussillon, the expulsion of his Spanish troops from Toulon, and the French invasion of Catalonia, he supported Godoy in ending the war by the Treaty of Basel (22 July 1795). An alliance was formed with France at the first Treaty of San Ildefonso (19 August 1796), and Spain declared war on England. This was augmented by a later treaty in which Charles IV exchanged Louisiana for Italian territory destined for his son-in-law. Spain subsequently joined France in the

War of Oranges against Portugal, and the area of Olivenza was annexed to Spain by the Treaty of Badajoz (6 June 1801).

Between 1801 and 1808, Charles IV was an obedient supporter of Napoleon, reflecting French political, economic, and military policies. He thwarted a conspiracy by his son, Ferdinand, in October 1807, to oust Godoy, but the following year, as French troops began to occupy northeastern Spain, revolt erupted at Aranjuez, and he was duped into abdicating in favor of Ferdinand VII (19 March 1808). On reflection, Charles IV withdrew his abdication decree and traveled to Bayonne in France to seek Napoleon's support for his restoration. Meanwhile, Ferdinand, also seeking Napoleon's recognition and a possible Bonaparte princess, traveled to Bayonne, only to be forced to recognize his father. Charles IV promptly renounced his crown in favor of Napoleon, who placed his brother Joseph on the throne. With an annual pension of 6 million *livres*, Charles IV retired with his wife, Godoy, and a small cortege to Compiègne and then Marseille before settling in Rome (1812), where he lived until his death (20 January 1819).

The philosophy of Charles IV was that of a country gentleman rather than a king. He delegated authority to Godoy and directed his attention to personal interests. He was unprepared and incapable of ruling, and the decline of Spain during his reign clearly reflected this fact.

M. Godoy, *Cuenta dada de su política ó sean Memoiras crítica...*, 6 vols. (Madrid, 1836–42); J. Gómez de Arteche y Moro, *Reinaldo de Carlos IV*, 3 vols. (Madrid, 1896); A. Savine, *L'abdication de Bayonne d'après les documents d'archives et les mémoires* (Paris, 1908).

D. D. Horward

Related entries: FIRST COALITION; TREATY OF BASEL.

CHATELET, notoriously harsh Parisian jail. Before the Revolution, the Châtelet was the main civil and criminal court of Paris below the parlement, and it maintained prisons to house debtors and those accused of crimes who were awaiting trial and judgment. Until 1780, there were two prisons, the Petit and the Grand Châtelet, situated at the north end of the pont au Change and famous for their crowded and unsanitary conditions. By the declaration of 30 August 1780, J. Necker authorized the construction of a new prison at the Hôtel de la Force to replace the older ones of Fort l'Evêque and the Petit Châtelet, and by 1783 both of the latter had been demolished. From 1782, all debtors were sent to La Force and the Châtelet housed exclusively those awaiting criminal trial or judgment. The declaration of 30 August had also abolished underground dungeons, one of the most notorious features of both Châtelet prisons; but in 1783 the English penal reformer J. Howard was shown eight dungeons of eleven feet by seven in the Grand Châtelet. In four of them he saw 16 prisoners, two in irons with straw for their beds. Howard counted in the entire prison in May 1783 305 inmates, of whom 47 were housed in rooms, 16 in dungeons, and 33 in infirmaries. The remainder slept on straw in general areas of confinement. In

May 1790 the National Assembly was informed that there were 350 prisoners in the Grand Châtelet.

The inmates of this prison were reputed to be particularly dangerous, and when the Parisian crowd began to force open the prisons on 13 July 1789, it refused to attack the Châtelet for fear of those it might set free. Rumors of the attacks, however, reached the prisoners, who rioted in an attempt to escape. They failed, but not before four had been fatally shot and another twenty wounded.

The court of the Châtelet, after a brief period of Revolutionary glory as the court judging the new offense of *lèse-nation*, was abolished by the law of 25 August 1790, and ceased to function on 24 January 1791. The prison remained, however, fulfilling much of the same functions as before for the new district tribunals of Paris. In this capacity it contained 269 prisoners on 2 September 1792 when the massacre of priests and suspects began at the Abbaye prison south of the Seine. When, that evening, the attention of the crowds turned to other prisons north of the river, the Châtelet was one of the first to be attacked, and that night between 215 and 220 prisoners were killed there. All were criminals or debtors, giving little ground for political suspicion, but no doubt the reputation of the Châtelet for housing dangerous elements was enough to justify purging them in the eyes of the frightened and suspicious popular tribunal that was established, as in other prisons, to conduct the executions.

P. Caron, *Les Massacres de septembre* (Paris, 1935); J. Howard, *The State of Prisons*, 3d ed. (London, 1784); A. Wills, *Crime and Punishment in Revolutionary Paris* (Westport, Conn., 1981).

W. Doyle

Related Entries: PRISONS; SEPTEMBER 1792 MASSACRES.

CHAUMETTE, PIERRE-GASPARD (ANAXAGORAS), (1763-94), dechristianizer and *procureur* of the Paris Commune. Chaumette was an apostle of atheism who made the Cult of Reason his deity. His life was a testimonial that the dechristianization movement was a significant phenomenon of the Revolution. He shunned his Christian name, Pierre-Gaspard, and preferred the name of the irreligious Greek philosopher Anaxagoras. While he was an editor of *Les Révolutions de Paris* and a writer for the *Chronique de Paris*, these newspapers became significant organs in promoting his anti-Christian policies. He established a *réligion laïque* whose commandments would emphasize morality, goodness, duty, and patriotism. Influenced by J.-J. Rousseau's ideas of human dignity and men of nature, Chaumette implemented these in his political and religious philosophy.

With the outbreak of the Revolution, Chaumette found a sense of identity and emerged as one of the most influential leaders of the lower middle class. His Revolutionary baptism began on 17 July 1791 on the Champ de Mars when he organized a popular movement to draft a petition supporting the dethronement of Louis XVI. This event, which led to the unfortunate "massacre" of Champ de Mars, was a significant step toward a united movement against the monarchy.

Its ultimate downfall came when Chaumette, as a principal organizer of the Paris sections and of the insurrectional Commune, was responsible for the successful attack on the Tuileries, on 10 August 1792.

As president and later elected *procureur* of the Commune, Chaumette was a major figure in Parisian political and religious movements in 1793. It was under his leadership and that of J.-R. Hébert (assistant *procureur* of the Commune) that the pleas of the insurrectionists of 4–5 September 1793 for severe measures against hoarders and political suspects were heeded by the Convention. It enacted the Law of the General Maximum (price-wage controls) and established a Revolutionary army as an instrument of the Terror to ensure grain and meat provisions to Paris.

In alliance with the Hébertists, the Commune under Chaumette's direction initiated an intensified dechristianization campaign. In August–September 1792, the Commune had established a secularization program and *le culte de la patrie*. Secularization measures included the oppression of religious orders and the closing of their premises; removal of valuable objects, including bells, from churches and religious residences; termination of church control of public welfare, parish registers, and education; and recognition of divorce. Chaumette's religious policy was to disestablish the constitutional church and to foster a *culte de la patrie*, which created altars to the nation. This cult was a forerunner of the Cult of Reason whose chief promoter was Chaumette.

On 10 November 1793, the Commune formally inaugurated the Cult of Reason by taking control of Notre Dame and transforming it into a Temple of Reason. This event was commemorated by a Festival of Reason at Notre Dame, primarily organized by Chaumette. The Commune's actions provoked numerous festivals of Reason in the Paris sections and in the provinces, accompanied by mock religious ceremonies and vandalism in the churches. Chaumette was also instrumental in fostering a dechristianization policy in the provinces. On his arrival in his birthplace of Nevers on 18 September 1793 to visit his mother who was ill, he urged the local representative on mission, J. Fouché, to promote dechristianization. Subsequently Fouché embarked on a radical anti-Christian policy in the department of the Nièvre and in Moulins where there were spoliation of the churches, attempts to end celibacy, and secular practices in place of Christian worship. Dechristianization was at its height in 1793, and the establishment of the Cult of Reason marked a triumph for Chaumette's *réligion laïque*.

Dechristianization was to lose its impact in 1794 under the attacks of M. Robespierre and the establishment of the Cult of the Supreme Being, which adhered to the existence of God as well as to the doctrine of the immortality of the soul. Extreme dechristianization was anathema to Robespierre whose deistic beliefs and political realism launched an assault on Chaumette and the dechristianizers. Chaumette was denounced as a corrupter of morality whose atheistic policies discredited France. Accused as an aristocrat and traitor to the Republic, Chaumette was guillotined on 13 April 1794.

A.N. dossiers T604 and W345; F.-A. Aulard, *Mémoires de Chaumette sur la Révolution du 10 août 1792* (Paris, 1893); F. Braesch, ed., *Papiers de Chaumette* (Paris, 1908).

C. Gliozzo

Related entries: ATHEISM; CHAMP DE MARS "MASSACRE"; *CHRO-NIQUE DE PARIS*; CLOOTS; CULT OF REASON; CULT OF THE SUPREME BEING; DECHRISTIANIZATION; FOUCHE; HEBERT; LAW OF THE MAXIMUM; TERROR, THE.

CHENIER, ANDRE-MARIE (1762-94), poet. Born in Constantinople, raised in Carcassonne and Paris, Chénier, with his brother Marie-Joseph, attended the progressive, upper class Collège de Navarre. He had determined at sixteen to be a poet but realized he could never earn a living at it. He was serving in the French embassy in London when, on hearing of the outbreak of the Revolution, he returned to Paris and began writing political tracts. He believed that he and other artists were called to serve as moral legislators. Active in the anti-Jacobin Société de 1789, Chénier became increasingly disenchanted with developments, and in his *Avis au peuple français* (15 August 1790) he bitterly denounced the roles of the Paris crowd and the political clubs. Although never a counterrevolutionary, Chénier broke with most of his former political allies, including the marquis de Condorcet and his brother Marie-Joseph. In his 1791 *Ode au Jeu de Paume*, one of very few of his poems published in his lifetime, Chénier called on the genuine people to resist the rabble and the "hangman-orators."

His continued vehement attacks on the Jacobins forced him to go into hiding in the summer of 1792. Two years later, he was arrested in Paris, and on 25 July 1794 he was guillotined.

His significance in the Revolution is problematic. He was neither the dangerous counterrevolutionary portrayed by some historians nor the advocate of any viable political program. He knew ancient Rome and an idealized America better than he knew French realities. He embodies especially poignantly the idealism and innocence of the last generation of intellectuals of the French Enlightenment.

F. Henry, "Vertu de la Révolution française," *USF Lang. Q.* 12 (1973); F. Scarfe, *André Chénier* (Oxford, 1965); R. Smernoff, *André Chénier* (Boston, 1977).

C. Garrett

Related entries: CONDORCET; SOCIETY OF 1789.

CHENIER, JOSEPH-MARIE (1764-1811), poet and playwright. Chénier's pre-Revolutionary efforts were not well received, but in December 1789 his play *Charles IX* created a sensation. In attacking absolute monarchy and clericalism while extolling Henry IV as the patriot king, it precisely fit the mood of the times. By the end of 1790, Chénier's reputation as playwright, political pamphleteer, and writer of lyrics for patriotic songs was securely established.

A festival on 11 July 1791 celebrating F.-M. Voltaire's interment in Paris, on which Marie-Joseph Chénier (as he was known) collaborated with other leading artists including J.-L. David, established the pattern for the Revolutionary festivals of the next several years. He was active in the Cordeliers Club and the Paris Commune as well. Elected to the National Convention, he continued to write plays and songs, served on the Committee of Public Instruction, and was especially active in efforts to create a Revolutionary religion. By 1794 he had drawn the ire of M. Robespierre, who prevented Chénier's songs from being used for the festival of the Supreme Being. His 1794 song *"La Chant du Départ,"* however, surpassed even the *"Marseillaise"* in popularity.

After Thermidor, Chénier wrote relatively little, but he continued to be politically active through Napoleon's consulate and then served in several minor administrative posts.

A. J. Bingham, *Marie-Joseph Chénier* (New York, 1939); D. L. Dowd, *Pageant Master of the Republic: Jacques-Louis David and the French Revolution* (Rpt., Freeport N.Y., 1969); J. Vier, "Marie-Joseph Chénier (1764-1811)," in *Les fêtes de la Révolution: Colloque de Clermont-Ferrand* (Paris, 1977).

C. Garrett

Related entries: CORDELIERS CLUB; DAVID; 9 THERMIDOR YEAR II; PARIS COMMUNE; ROBESPIERRE, M.

CHERUBINI, LUIGI (1760-1842). See MUSIC.

CHOUANNERIE, sporadic and persistent unrest, especially in northwestern France, escalating into civil strife and, in the circumstances of the 1790s, into anti-Republican insurrection. The name probably derived from *chat-huant*, screech-owl, a nocturnal creature, the imitation of whose cry could serve as a guiding signal in wooded and hilly terrain within the rectangle of Lorient, Le Mans, and Saint-Brieuc.

No more than in the Vendeé was the violence the achievement of agitating priests and plotting noblemen. Catholic faith was important to its participants, and nobles, more especially *émigrés*, attempted to use it to break the Republic; but its origins are to be sought in strains within peasant society, rifts opening, overt conflict erupting, when the events of the Revolution added to existing pressures (for example, the way local government reform or sales of church and *émigré* property favored certain interest groups) and when the Revolution failed, against expectation, to remedy long-standing ills. Certainly it appears that disappointment (and later *chouannerie*) was especially strong in areas where land reform legislation failed to alleviate that hardship that in the 1780s had replaced the relative prosperity of the past two decades. Many farmers in the parcellized lands of central Brittany rented their 6 to 8 hectares holdings or, in the southwest of the province, held them by the *domaine congéable*, the five- to nine-year leasing system; neither system was reformed, whereas those who owned land benefited from the abolition of tithes and seigneurial dues (August 1789, July 1793). Some of the latter were owner-occupiers in the countryside where, away from the coasts, some three-quarters of the population lived scattered in hamlets or on isolated farmsteads, but much of the land was owned by nonfarmers who, in upper Brittany, lived in the towns or who, as in the western Maine, lived in the villages that dotted that particular area. Such owners constituted one type of target for *chouan* bands; local officials and constitutional priests were another.

In the Maine, the Finistère, and eastern Normandy, fairly clearly defined zones soon became apparent as conflicts escalated between 1791 and 1793; to the east of Le Mans, Brest, and Argentan, *patriotes* were in the ascendant and "troubles" (the official word) endemic in the western Maine and southwestern Normandy. The coastal areas of the Morbihan, Côtes-du-Nord, and the Ille-et-Vilaine also tended to be *patriote*, but inland in the *bocage* and on the uplands, a confused patchwork persisted, *patriote* Guard-maintaining communes interspersed with *chouan*-tendency parishes. Save in the immediate area of the towns, this confused situation was not clarified, as it was in the Vendée, in the course of 1793; no "White" base area came into existence, no armies coalesced, despite the efforts of J.-G. Puisaye. Bands, consisting of permanent cadres, on occasion could call out thousands of (ill-armed) peasants, but such *rassemblements* operated only locally and were easily dispersed by disciplined troops. Such activity, though, proved almost impossible to quell save when, as in the spring of 1796, the northwest was flooded with troops or when, as between the Babeuf conspiracy and the coup of 18 Fructidor (May 1796–September 1797) the government pursued a conciliatory line, suspended the enforcement of penal laws against refractory priests, and included even *chefs de bande* in its offers of amnesty.

That no clarifying polarization by area did occur in the summer of 1793 was largely because the authorities rapidly took effective action to check the insurrection prompted by the attempt to levy troops, and although some small towns were overrun, none was retained and no large ones were captured. Even when nascent columns had been dispersed, bands could hold out in the *bocage*, where the inhabitants' attitudes plus the terrain both worked for them—but where, it transpired, they could, save on the one occasion (Quiberon in June–July 1795), be held at a safe distance from the Republic's naval depots at Lorient, Brest, and Saint-Malo.

The earliest *chouan* bands appeared in the lower Maine in the spring of 1792, one *chef* being J. Cottereau known as "Jean Chouan." Many *chouan chefs* were, like him, *roturiers*, though in the Côtes-du-Nord and the eastern Ille-et-Vilaine, C. Bras de Forges, chevalier de Boishardy, and the brothers Picquet du Boisguy were the leading *chefs*, as G. Cadoudal, with J. Guillemot, were, from early 1795, dominant in the Morbihan and the vicomte L. de Frotté dominant in southwestern Normandy. An *émigré* sent to organize that area in spring 1795, Frotté can be taken to represent the efforts made by royalists to capture for their cause the *chouannerie* and by Puisaye who sent him to prepare the ground before Quiberon. After the failure of that expedition, the British were able to put ashore only limited supplies in the Morbihan and a few hundred *émigré* volunteers on the northern coast (spring 1796), whereas L. Hoche was able, after quelling the Vendée, to bring thousands of troops north of the Loire.

In 1797–98 sporadic local violence again erupted as troops were withdrawn, and although Brittany, like the Vendée, was exempted from the *loi Jourdan* (5

September 1798), the conscription issue plus a renascent anticlerical Jacobinism after 18 Fructidor, a lack of troops in that area, and encouragement from the comte d'Artois and the Second Coalition's leader, England, led to another—and this time partly concerted—rising in the autumn of 1799. On this occasion, with Frotté, P.-D. La Prévalaye, and A.-C. Picquet du Boisguy, P.-L. G. Châtillon, M.-P. Scépeaux, and L.-A.-V. Bourmont commanding Normandy, upper Brittany, Anjou, and the Maine, Cadoudal was the only non-*émigré*, non-noble leader, and the numbers mobilized were fewer than in 1793. Nevertheless the rising came at a dangerous time for the Republic and, briefly, appeared threatening. The British landed supplies in the Morbihan, and although in Normandy and upper Brittany the *chouans* were checked, farther south and west they captured, albeit only momentarily, Le Mans, Nantes, and La Roche-Bernard (15, 20, 26 October). The government, now under N. Bonaparte, employed a blend of ruthlessness and conciliation, the former symbolized by Frotté's murder (18 February 1800), the latter by an amnesty and, in 1801, the Concordat; but even though *rassemblements* ceased, a sort of anti-"Blue" banditry persisted alongside vendettas and plain armed robbery, and there was always the chance that *chefs* like Cadoudal and Guillemot could, supported by London, rekindle an insurrection, cut communications with Brest, or even deliver Belle-Ile to the English. After 1805, with these two *chefs* and many others dead, the security forces were by and large dominant save in the heavily wooded interior of the Morbihan, but *patriotes* still lived threatened lives, and there were still *chefs* to call "Whites" to arms in 1815. Despite this last effort the tone and image of *chouannerie* was such that royalists then and in their nineteenth-century histories did not enthuse over it or its *chefs*, but it remained the case that *chouan*-saturated areas tended subsequently to show on electoral maps as anti-Republican—that is, (in "Blue" terminology) priest-ridden, obstinately attached to locality (not *la patrie*), ignorantly, and, if challenged, violently, attached to their traditional (understand backward) ways.

P. Bois, *Paysans de l'Ouest: des structures économiques et sociales aux options politiques depuis l'époque révolutionnaire dans la Sarthe* (Le Mans, 1960); G. de Cadoudal, *Georges Cadoudal et la Chouannerie* (Paris, 1887); J. Le Falher, *Le Royaume de Bignan* (Hennebont, 1913); J. Godechot, *The Counter-Revolution, Doctrine and Action, 1789-1804* (London, 1972), pt. 2; L. de la Sicotière, *Louis de Frotté et les insurrections normandes*; T. Lemas, *Un District breton [Fougères] pendant les guerres de l'Ouest et de la Chouannerie, 1793-1800* (Paris, 1894); D. Sutherland, *The Chouans: The Social Origins of Popular Counterrevolution in Upper-Brittany, 1770-96* (Oxford, 1981).

M. G. Hutt

Related entries: HOCHE; JOURDAN LAW; PUISAYE; QUIBERON; SECOND COALITION; VENDEE.

CHRONIQUE DE PARIS, daily newspaper published from 24 August 1789 to 25 August 1793. Founded by A.-L. Millin and J.-F. Noël, the *Chronique de*

Paris featured regular contributions from such well-known writers as the marquis de Condorcet, C. Villette, and J.-P. Rabaut Saint-Etienne. During its first two years, the *Chronique* was primarily a literary review of Parisian cultural life. While the paper contained daily reports of municipal and national assemblies, they were quite brief, and most issues were dominated by book reviews, analyses of operas and plays, and stock market quotations. During the Legislative Assembly, the *Chronique* devoted more space to political news and became associated with the Girondins. From 17 November 1791 until 9 March 1793, Condorcet contributed daily articles on the activities of the Legislative Assembly and Convention. During the night of 9–10 March 1793, the *Chronique's* presses were destroyed by *sans-culotte* activists, but after four days the paper was back in circulation under a different press. After the Girondins were expelled from the Convention during 31 May–2 June 1793, the editors announced that the paper would soon cease publication.

   H. Deslaux, *Condorcet journalist (1790-1794)* (Paris, 1931).

G. Kates

Related entries: CONDORCET; GIRONDINS; RABAUT SAINT-ETIENNE.

CIRCULAR, PADUA. See LEOPOLD II.

CISALPINE REPUBLIC (1797–99 and 1800–02), created by N. Bonaparte with the support of Italian revolutionaries and the principal sister republic in Italy during the French occupation, it served as a model for other French-dominated republics in Italy and, for some Italians, heralded the eventual union of all Italy.

   The origins of the Cisalpine Republic must be seen against the background of France's Italian policy and the maneuvering of Italian revolutionaries. After defeating Austria and its Italian allies in the spring of 1796, Bonaparte occupied Piedmont, the duchies of Milan, Mantua, Modena, and Parma, and part of the Papal States. His later occupation of much of Venetia left him master of the Po Valley. Italian revolutionaries—drawn largely from the middle class but including liberal nobles and ecclesiastics—saw in this situation the opportunity to oust existing governments and establish republics after the French model. Revolutionaries in Milan and other occupied places seized government offices and appealed to the French for assistance. The French Directory did not intend to revolutionize the Italian states. It planned to exploit them to help finance the war and then use them as diplomatic pawns in a future peace settlement in which Austria, in return for suitable territorial compensation, would recognize French conquests elsewhere in Europe. Bonaparte, however, had more ambitious plans than these. He hoped to create in part of northern Italy a republic that would serve as a personal political base, and to this end he supported certain Italian revolutionaries while ignoring others. The Directory, increasingly dependent on its successful commander, eventually accepted his policy. At the end of 1796, Bonaparte encouraged revolutionaries in occupied territories south of the Po

River to proclaim the Cispadane Republic, but the following year he envisaged a larger political entity than this. He joined the Cispadane with the Austrian possessions of Milan and Mantua, the Valtellina (a region indirectly linked with the Swiss Confederation), and western Venetia to form the independent Cisalpine Republic. Milan became the capital of the new state whose population was some 3.5 million. Swept away by the armies of the Second Coalition in 1799, the Cisalpine Republic was resurrected by the French after they returned the next year. It survived under different designations until the collapse of the Napoleonic Empire.

The Cisalpine Republic was independent in name only since the French provided its two constitutions and controlled its political life. With the French Constitution of 1795 as a model, Bonaparte, advised by a committee of native revolutionaries, drew up the first Cisalpine constitution of July 1797. It provided for a legislature of two chambers and an executive composed of five directors chosen by the legislature. Although nearly all adult males had the franchise, the indirect electoral system meant that only men of some means were chosen as legislators. Deeming this safeguard insufficient against the influence of the masses, the French government instructed Bonaparte not to implement the electoral system for at least a year but instead to appoint the Cisalpine Republic's first directors and legislators. When even the appointed legislators proved too independent, the French carried out a series of purges to remove opponents. In September 1798, disturbed by the radical leanings of some revolutionaries in Milan, the French introduced a second constitution that further restricted the franchise and strengthened the executive at the expense of the legislature. Before this, in February 1798, France's grip had been tightened when the two republics signed a treaty that required the Cisalpine to maintain a force of 22,000 men under French command, subsidize a French army of 25,000 men, and, in conformity with the Directory's plan to weaken Britain and strengthen France through economic measures, exclude British imports and limit customs duties on French goods to 6 percent.

Notwithstanding their resentment at the vassal status to which their republic was reduced, Italian revolutionaries welcomed the French because they brought the principles of their Revolution to Italy. The idea of equality was introduced in the decisions to abolish nobility and open careers to talent. A wide measure of press freedom and a judicial system designed to protect citizens against the arbitrary actions of government affirmed the belief in the principle of individual liberty. The abolition of torture reflected the humanitarian impulse of the age. The desire for a rational system of administration led to the division of the country into units of local government (called, as in France, departments), which were roughly equal in size and through which laws could be uniformly applied. Economic reforms included the abolition of the privileged guilds, the inefficient tax structure and feudal regulations that impeded the transfer of land, and the elimination of tariff barriers made the Cisalpine an economic unit, thereby stimulating the circulation of goods. Measures illustrating the drift toward secularism in the Cisalpine were the confiscation of church lands, the suppression of religious orders, the institution of civil marriage, the substitution of state-supported schools for those of the church, and the introduction of religious toleration. If the masses, for whom subsistence and land shortages were the chief grievances, were largely indifferent to a program that offered them little, the middle-class revolutionaries saw it inaugurating a modern society that responded to their aspirations and gave them political leadership.

An additional objective of the more radical of these revolutionaries was to convince the French to unify Italy. There were about a dozen states in the peninsula before 1796, and the idea of uniting them in a single Italian state had been developing in enlightened circles since the middle of the eighteenth century. The radicals in Milan, encouraged by like-minded individuals who gathered there from other places in the peninsula, hoped that the formation of the Cisalpine Republic was the first step toward unity. The French directors, however, would not sanction unification, partly because it was promoted by what they considered to be a minority of Italian extremists linked with Jacobins in France whom the directors wanted to curb and partly because unification conflicted with France's international interests. The directors accepted Bonaparte's Cisalpine Republic and later agreed to the transformation of other Italian states into sister republics in its image; but the directors considered them as places to be exploited and never intended to form them into a united republic that one day could pose a threat to France. Moreover, the directors approved the Treaty of Campoformio in which Bonaparte, who negotiated it in 1797, not only left Italy divided but sacrificed one Italian state, Venice, to Austria in exchange for recognition of the French conquest of Belgium and most of the Rhenish left bank. The aspirations of Italian radicals were sacrificed to French interests, and unity was postponed for sixty years. The Cisalpine Republic nevertheless indirectly contributed to the ultimate unity of Italy. By joining together parts of states hitherto divided, by partially breaking down the old spirit of particularism, and by habituating men from different regions to work together in a common enterprise, the Cisalpine strengthened the belief that the unity of the entire peninsula was a realizable project.

J. Godechot, *La grande nation; l'expansion révolutionnaire de la France dans le monde de 1789 à 1799*, 2 vols. (Paris, 1956); R. R. Palmer, *The Age of the Democratic Revolution*, vol. 2 (Princeton, 1964).

J. P. McLaughlin

Related entries: CISPADANE REPUBLIC; CONSTITUTION OF 1795; DIRECTORY; SECOND COALITION; TREATY OF CAMPOFORMIO.

CISPADANE REPUBLIC (1796-97), first sister republic created during the French occupation of the Italian peninsula between 1796 and 1799. N. Bonaparte's invasion of northern Italy in the spring of 1796 gave hope to Italian revolutionaries that they might transform their states into republics modeled on Revolutionary France. There were revolts in several cities, including Bologna and Ferrara, in the northern part of the Papal States, and in Modena and Reggio in the adjoining Duchy of Modena. In these cities, all south of the Po River, revolutionaries feared that continued political decentralization and especially the spirit of municipalism, so characteristic of the Italian states, would permit the ruling oligarchies to maintain the status quo. For this reason, representatives of the four cities, after first forming a league (October 1796) to defend themselves against counterrevolutionaries, decided, at the urging of Bonaparte, to transform the Duchy of Modena and the northern part of the Papal States into a unitary state as the sole way to overcome resistance from privileged groups and implement reform. An assembly, elected on a broad franchise and composed largely of middle-class representatives, met at Reggio in December 1796 and proclaimed the Cispadane Republic. To emphasize the centralized character of the union, the revolutionaries termed the new state ''one and indivisible,'' in imitation of the French Republic.

The following March, the assembly, meeting now in Modena, promulgated a constitution, which the voters subsequently endorsed by plebiscite. The constitution—the only one during the 1790s to be framed by Italians elected for that purpose—closely resembled the French Constitution of 1795. The Cispadane constitution separated legislative and executive functions. It provided for a bicameral legislature chosen by a system of indirect election, which gave effective political power to the propertied classes and favored the towns where republicanism was more pronounced than in rural districts. Executive functions were to be exercised by three directors chosen by the legislature. The constitution affirmed the principles of popular sovereignty and equality of taxation, guaranteed property, and prohibited distinctions based on birth. Unlike the French, however, the framers of the Cispadane constitution made Catholicism the state religion and limited the right of public worship by non-Catholics and the Jewish community.

Although it was the first place in Italy to proclaim French Revolutionary principles, the Cispadane Republic was too short-lived to have great influence. In June 1797, only three months after its constitution was promulgated, Bonaparte joined the Cispadane with territories north of the Po River to form the Cisalpine Republic; and it was through the latter that the French Revolutionaries introduced their ideas to the Italian peninsula.

J. Godechot, *La grande nation; l'expansion révolutionnaire de la France dans le monde de 1789 à 1799*, 2 vols. (Paris, 1956). R. R. Palmer, *The Age of the Democratic Revolution*, vol. 2 (Princeton, 1964).

J. P. McLaughlin

Related entries: CISALPINE REPUBLIC; CONSTITUTION OF 1795.

CISRHENANE REPUBLIC, a sister republic in the Rhineland that was projected in 1797 but never realized. At the end of 1794, following the victory at Fleurus, French armies had moved into the feudal territories of the Holy Roman Empire on the west (or left) bank of the Rhine River, bypassing the fortifications of Mainz. Unlike Belgium, which had been quickly annexed by the French Republic, the status of the Rhineland remained undetermined for a long time, even after Prussia had secretly recognized it as a French sphere of influence by the Treaty of Basel (5 April 1795). Most of the local rulers, both lay and ecclesiastical, had fled, yet neither the Thermidorian Convention nor the first Directory decided on the fate of the region. Each government treated the Rhineland as a foreign country under military occupation, and only the administrative system was changed; in other words, they made no attempt to export the French Revolution there.

Despite the lack of French support, local patriots, among them J. B. Geich, F. Hanf, and M. Biergans, did establish republican clubs and newspapers in some of the larger cities in 1795 and advocated separation from the Empire and cooperation with the moderate, post-Thermidorian French Republic. The arguments of this minority of intellectuals and bourgeois were based on economic and ideological, rather than nationalist, considerations. Meanwhile in Paris, refugees from Mainz were lobbying in vain for the incorporation of the area into France or its establishment as a sister republic.

The situation changed in 1797. After the preliminary peace of Leoben (18 April), the Directory, at the urging of L. Carnot, advised General L. Hoche to refrain from creating French departments on the left bank of the Rhine and recommended instead a sister republic, modeled on the Cisalpine and Batavian republics. Hoche, a warm partisan of this solution, ordered the Intermediary Commission in Bonn, the administrative center for the occupied area, to encourage the movement of the Cisrhenans. This group, which included J. N. Becker, J. Görres, J. J. Haan, J. B. Hetzrodt, F. von Lassaulx, M. Metternich, C. Sommer, J. J. Stammel, M. Venedey, and H. Wyttenbach, had joined forces in June, established themselves at Bonn, and swore to "live and die free."

Beginning on 5 September 1797, the Cisrhenans disassociated themselves from the rest of Germany and launched their campaign for a sister republic. This movement became general on 15 September when the Intermediary Commission announced the abolition of tithes and feudal obligations for every commune that planted a liberty tree. A Central Bureau for the embryonic Cisrhenane Confederation was established in Bonn, with district headquarters in Cologne, Coblentz, and Neuss. In October the Central Bureau issued "A Protest of the Cisrhenane Confederation against the Appeal of the Elector Maximilian Franz." Republican bodies replaced the local government in some towns, and people began to wear a green cockade, the symbol of the new state.

The Cisrhenans, however, were soon frustrated by changing circumstances. Their patron, Hoche, died at Wetzlar on 19 September, and the earlier coup of 18 Fructidor (4 September) in Paris presaged a shift in the German policy of the Directory. J.-F. Reubell, who replaced Carnot as director, was an uncompromising advocate of the Rhine as the natural frontier of France, a policy that meant direct annexation of the region. In addition, the Treaty of Campoformio, signed with Austria on 17 October, allowed France to dispose of the left bank of the Rhine south of Cologne as it wished. In November, F.-J. Rudler, an Alsatian, was sent as commissioner general to the Rhine in order to organize the area into four departments of France and to establish French institutions there. On the whole, the Cisrhenans complied with the decision, although many preferred the status of sister republic, and they supported incorporation with petitions, which were signed by one-fifth of the electorate (57,000 out of 260,000 eligible voters).

Even afterward, some of the militant Cisrhenans (who never numbered more than 2,000) debated the issue until 1800 when Bonaparte squashed all discussion. In 1801 the Treaty of Lunéville provided for international recognition of the annexation. The majority of the former Cisrhenans served both the Consulate and the Empire, although a few like Görres (1776-1848), who would have a long and outstanding political career, broke not only with France but the idea of revolution in general.

S. S. Biro, *The German Policy of Revolutionary France, 1792–1797*, 2 vols. (Cambridge, Mass., 1957); J. Droz, *La Pensée politique et morale des Cisrhénans* (Paris, 1940); J. Görres, *Gesammelte Schriften*, ed. M. Braubach, vol. 1 (Bonn, 1928); J. Hansen, *Quellen zur Geschicte das Rheinlandes im Zeitalter der Franzosischen Revolution, 1780-1801*, 4 vols. (Bonn, 1931–38); and P. Sagnac, *Le Rhin français pendant la Révolution et l'Empire* (Paris, 1917).

W. Markov

Related entries: BATAVIAN REPUBLIC; BATTLE OF FLEURUS; CISALPINE REPUBLIC; CARNOT; COUP OF 18 FRUCTIDOR YEAR V; PRELIMINARIES OF LEOBEN; REUBELL; TREATY OF BASEL; TREATY OF CAMPOFORMIO.

CITIZEN, ACTIVE. See ACTIVE CITIZEN.

CITIZEN, PASSIVE. See PASSIVE CITIZEN.

CIVISM, CERTIFICATES OF. See CERTIFICATES OF CIVISM.

CIVIL CONSTITUTION OF THE CLERGY (12 July 1790), legislation passed by the National Assembly to reorganize and restructure the Roman Catholic church in France. There was nearly universal agreement in 1789 that France's anticipated political renovation would also include reform of the structure of the church. Church and state were closely intertwined at every level, and the promised revolution was to be a national moral regeneration as well. It was thus in a mood of hopeful anticipation that the National Assembly, in the aftermath of its abolition of privilege on the night of 4 August 1789, appointed an ecclesiastical committee to reorganize the French church on the basis of the newly proclaimed social and political principles. It is now generally agreed that the committee members were sincere Catholics, although some of them had been influenced by Jansenist criticisms of the eighteenth-century papacy and by the Gallican tradition of administrative autonomy for the church in France.

The product of the committee's labors was presented to the National Assembly at the end of May 1790. It was called a civil constitution because its authors insisted that it affected only the earthly or temporal status of the clergy and not the church's spiritual and eternal dimension, which was in the care of the papacy.

After two weeks of acrimonious debate, the Civil Constitution was passed on 12 July. The long document completely reorganized the ecclesiastical structure. The dioceses were reduced in number from 135 to 83, one for each department. The bishops were to be elected, like other departmental officers, by the tax-paying citizens. Since the church's property had been nationalized in December 1789, the clergy was now to be salaried, and it was to perform its services without charge.

The Civil Constitution's supporters insisted they had simply suppressed the flagrant abuses and inequities of the Old Regime church, thus making possible one that was administratively effective and morally and spiritually regenerated. Its opponents replied that the Civil Constitution went beyond legitimate reforms to usurp powers that belonged to the pope. Pius VI, however, made no public statement of his own views. Always circumspect, he seems to have hoped that Louis XVI and the French bishops would prevent its being implemented, thus avoiding a confrontation with the National Assembly by opposing it or encouraging other Catholic governments to do as the French had done by acceding to it.

In the next several months, as the clergy awaited guidance from Rome, the situation of the church became urgent. The maintenance of its religious services and its educational and welfare institutions—and the sale of its property—depended on carrying out the reorganization. In the provinces, there were anticlerical demonstrations and demands that the church be brought into conformity with the National Assembly's wishes. It was in a mood of impatience, but also with the belief that bishops and pope would yield in order to avoid schism, that the National Assembly, on 27 November, decreed that all clergy in public service must take an oath to support the Civil Constitution. Having received no guidance from Rome, Louis XVI on 26 December gave the decree his reluctant sanction.

The number of clergy who refused to take the oath, thus excluding themselves from the state church, was considerably higher than the Assembly had anticipated. Only seven bishops took the oath, and none of them was distinguished for piety. Among the lower clergy, the percentage of those who refused the oath (the so-called refractory or nonjuring clergy) varied widely from region to region. Acceptance or rejection of the oath coincided broadly with earlier patterns of religious indifference or fervor. Recent local studies suggest that practical realities were also a factor. In Dauphiné, for example, where nine-tenths of the parish clergy took the oath, the Civil Constitution provided higher salaries, a pension system, and a voice in diocesan decisions, all of which they had demanded for years. On the other hand, in the west many parish clergy had enjoyed higher incomes under the Old Regime than they would under the new, and there the great majority of clergy rejected the oath. Local studies also show that the clergy were often guided by the attitudes of their parishioners toward the Civil Constitution.

C.-M. Talleyrand's final act as a bishop, in March 1791, was to consecrate new bishops for the state church, thus assuring that it would maintain the apostolic succession. Shortly after, Pius VI at last declared himself. In two briefs, he roundly denounced the Civil Constitution, stated that it was based on heretical principles, voided the elections of the new bishops, and threatened clergy who participated in the now schismatic church with excommunication.

For the next three years, harassed on the one side by those faithful to the pope's position and on the other by Revolutionaries seeking to extirpate Christianity in France, the schismatic church persisted. It went into a sort of limbo when on 21 February 1795 the National Convention separated church and state. In 1801, Napoleon's Concordat with Pius VII made possible the reunion of the remaining schismatic clergy with Rome, but a remnant, including the constitutional church's ablest and most eloquent proponent, H. Grégoire, refused to return.

Few if any of the National Assembly's actions had the historic impact of the Civil Constitution of the Clergy. It led to a tragic polarization between religion and revolution and produced attitudes that have colored French thought and politics to the present day.

O. Chadwick, *The Popes and European Revolution* (Oxford, 1981); A. Latreille, *L'Eglise catholique et la Révolution française*, 2d ed. (Paris, 1970); J. McManners, *The French Revolution and the Church* (New York, 1969); B. Plongeron, *Les Reguliers de Paris devant le serment constitutionnel* (Paris, 1964); T. Tackett, *Priest and Parish in Eighteenth Century France* (Princeton, 1977).

C. Garrett

Related entries: 4 AUGUST 1789; GREGOIRE; PIUS VI.

CLAVIERE, ETIENNE (1735-93), financier and cabinet minister. J. Calvin and J.-J. Rousseau suggest continuing links between France and Geneva. The French Revolutionary figure who maintained the tradition was Etienne Clavière, born in Geneva on 27 January 1735. In the second half of the eighteenth century, Geneva was a school for politics and a financial and business center, an environment that had its impact on Clavière. He was active in political movements and debates focusing on the nature of government; he was expelled from Geneva in 1782 during disturbances that resulted from political activities in which he had been involved. By the time of his expulsion, Clavière, who made his livelihood as a banker, had made a reputation for himself in the business community as a financial expert. Taking refuge in Paris, he continued his career in banking, using funds he had carried out of Geneva. Parisian financiers viewed him as something of a genius and learned much from him about the workings of the stock market; stock-jobbing and speculation on public funds had been practiced in Paris with little success or assurance before Clavière's tutelage.

Two men, H.-G.R. Mirabeau and J.-P. Brissot, became closely associated with Clavière after he settled in Paris. He and Mirabeau formed a close alliance since Mirabeau needed a circumspect adviser, especially someone financially adroit. He welcomed Clavière as a collaborator on various projects, found him useful in attacking J. Necker, and paid homage to him in the National Assembly. Mirabeau was a useful front for Clavière's ideas, and one important result of their collaboration may have been the idea of *assignats*. E. Dumont, Clavière's friend and fellow Genevan, in his *Souvenirs* assigns to Clavière the role of instigator of the *assignats*.

As a young man, Brissot had visited Clavière in Geneva, and their friendship flourished subsequently. They collaborated on a number of pamphlets dealing with financial subjects, and they founded the Société Gallo-Américaine, which sought profit in Franco-American relations and resulted in a book, *De la France et des États-Unis* (1787), in which the principles for such profit were laid down.

Clavière was quick to approve of the Revolution when it commenced, and his friends regarded his support as useful. He and Brissot worked together for various Revolutionary journals and societies, among them the *Patriote français* and the Jacobins. Brissot acknowledged his friend by including him in his partisan plans and praising him in print and in the Legislative Assembly. It was undoubtedly Brissot who arranged Clavière's appointment to the ministry of finance at the time of the formation of the Girondist government in March 1792. It was an appointment that was generally well considered since Clavière was politically sound, financially experienced, and widely considered to rival Necker in expert knowledge and abilities.

Clavière's ministry was characterized by his steady Girondist partisanship and by a crisis resulting from his blunt dismissal of the director of posts. He sided with J.-M. Roland against C. Dumouriez, supported the controversial letter to the king, and was dismissed, along with Roland and J. Servan, on 13 June as a result of that letter. As one of the patriot ministers, he was recalled after the monarchy was overthrown on 10 August, becoming yet again financial minister, in the Provisional Executive Council.

As the Girondist-Montagnard struggle for power emerged in the months after the proclamation of the Republic, Clavière remained courageously at his post and loyal to his friends and came increasingly under siege from M. Robespierre and his faction. One of the first targets of the 31 May–2 June 1793 insurrection, which marked the victory of the Montagnard faction, Clavière was arrested and imprisoned on 2 June and indicted seven days later. Kept in suspense for six months, he was finally shown his jury and witness list on the eve of his trial. Recognizing on the list only the names of radicals from whom he could expect little mercy and no hope for release, he preferred suicide to the scaffold. On the night of 8–9 December 1793, he stabbed himself in the chest; two days after his death, his wife poisoned herself.

Clavière was suspected, even by some of his political associates, of being cunning and artful, yet he could be blunt and hot tempered. Madame Roland found him to be irascible, opinionated, caviling and difficult, though she admitted he was an active and hard worker. He was clearly a solid and loyal Girondist partisan, a team worker with desirable expertise, who served his friends to the best of his ability and who shared their fate.

J. Benetruy, *L'Atelier de Mirabeau: Quatre proscrits genèvois* (Geneva, 1962); E. Clavière, *Opinions d'un créancier de l'Etat sur quelques matières de finance importantes dans le moment actuel* (London, 1789); E. Clavière and J.-P. Brissot, *De la France et des Etats-Unis, ou de l'importance de la Révolution de l'Amérique pour le bonheur de la France* (London, 1787); P.-E.-L. Dumont, *Souvenirs sur Mirabeau et sur les deux premières Assemblées législatives* (Paris, 1951); C. Perroud, "Une amie de Madame Roland: Souvenirs inédits de Sophie Grandchamp," *Révo. française* 37 (1899).

C. A. Le Guin

Related entries: ASSIGNATS; BRISSOT; DUMOURIEZ; DUMONT; MIRABEAU; NECKER, ROLAND DE LA PLATIERE, J.-M.; SERVAN DE

CLERGY, JURING. See CIVIL CONSTITUTION OF THE CLERGY.

CLERGY, NONJURING. See CIVIL CONSTITUTION OF THE CLERGY.

CLERGY, REFRACTORY. See CIVIL CONSTITUTION OF THE CLERGY.

CLERMONT-TONNERRE, STANISLAS, COMTE DE (1757-92), Anglophile, deputy to the Estates General and National Assembly. The grandson of an illustrious marshal of France, Clermont-Tonnerre decided to pursue a military career when he was fifteen. In 1789 he was thirty-two years old, a cavalry colonel scheduled to assume command of his own regiment, an aspiring diplomat with influential connections, and deputy-elect to the Estates General representing the nobility of Paris. In the early months of the Estates General, he championed the reformist cause and helped break the deadlock over organization by leading forty-seven aristocrats to join the Third Estate on 25 June.

In the months that followed royal recognition of the National Assembly, Clermont-Tonnerre distinguished himself as one of its most eloquent orators. His early popularity led to his appointment as a member of the Committee on the Constitution and election as president of the Assembly on 17 August and again on 14 September 1789. As an admirer of English institutions, he soon became identified with the so-called *anglomanes*, or *monarchiens*, who counted among their number J.-J. Mounier, P.-V. Malouet, T.-G. Lally-Tollendal, and the comte de Virieu. Although he was not present in the Assembly on the night of 4 August, he later stated his disapproval of the abolition of seigneurial rights. In the constitutional debates he expressed reservations about the Declaration of the Rights of Man, supported creation of a two-chamber legislative body, and advocated absolute royal veto power over legislation. The positions he took on these issues and his condemnation of spreading disorder in the nation quickly eroded his popularity. The October Days of 1789 and the subsequent transfer of the royal family and the Assembly from Versailles to Paris shocked and disillusioned him. Yet unlike Mounier and other moderates who left to fight the Revolution from the provinces or from outside France, he stayed on to campaign for the kind of constitutional monarchy in which he believed.

Early 1790 found Clermont-Tonnerre associated with Malouet in the short-lived Club des Impartiaux and engaged in verbal duels with members of the patriot party, whom he regarded as determined to dismantle completely the political and social structure of the Old Regime. In late 1790, again in collaboration with Malouet, he founded the Society of Friends of the Monarchical Constitution of 1791. Already widely regarded in Paris as a traitor to the Revolution, Clermont-Tonnerre came under even heavier fire as president of the Club Monarchique. A. Barnave denounced him for trying to buy the support of sans-culottes when his club distributed bread to poor Parisians. Others condemned him for opposing the annexation of Avignon, for supporting propertied interests against the blacks in the colonies, and for allegedly encouraging the king to flee from Paris on 20 June 1791. By the end of the National Assembly, the Society of Friends of the Monarchical Constitution had disbanded and its cause seemed hopeless.

When the Legislative Assembly convened, only Clermont-Tonnerre, Malouet, and a few other monarchiens remained in France. On 10 August 1792 they were prime targets for the antiroyalist crowds that filled the streets of Paris. Warned in time, Malouet escaped to England. Clermont-Tonnerre was not so fortunate. Arrested, released, then wounded in the head while trying to speak to a hostile crowd, he fled to the house of a friend. His assassins found him there and hurled him to his death from a fifth-story window.

Although he was more charismatic, courageous, and tragic than most of his political allies, he was nevertheless quite representative of the early Revolutionary moderate royalists. He readily sacrificed his initial popularity on the twin altars of political principle and public order without winning in turn the esteem or cooperation of the extreme royalists. By holding firm to his middle course between royalist reactionaries and Revolutionary extremists he proved his personal integrity but also his political naïveté.

C. du Bus, *Stanislas de Clermont-Tonnerre et l'échec de la Révolution monarchique, 1757-1792* (Paris, 1931); A. Challamel, *Les Clubs contre-révolutionnaires; cercles, comités, sociétés, salons, réunions, cafés, restaurants et librairies* (Paris, 1895); J. Egret, *La Révolution des Notables; Mounier et les Monarchiens, 1789* (Paris, 1950).

R. Vignery

Related entries: ANGLOMANES; AVIGNON; MALOUET; OCTOBER DAYS; SOCIETY OF 1789.

CLICHY, CLUB DE. See CLUB DE CLICHY.

CLOOTS, JEAN-BAPTISTE (ANACHARSIS) (1755-94), dechristianizer, Jacobin, and *conventionnel*. In the complex and turbulent religious history of the French Revolution, Anacharsis Cloots emerges as an avowed atheist and a leading protagonist of dechristianization. Born in 1755 to a wealthy Prussian family, Cloots became an ardent Francophile who donated major portions of his fortune to the Revolution. In an act of religious intolerance in October 1790, he substituted the Greek name *Anacharsis* for his Christian name, *Jean-Baptiste*.

In his major anti-Christian works published during the Revolution, *L'Orateur du genre humain ou dépêche du Prussien Cloots au Prussien Hertzberg* (Paris, 1791), *La République universelle ou addresse aux tyrannicides* (Paris, 1792), and *Bases constitutionelles de la république du genre humain* (Paris, 1793), Cloots substituted mankind for God, calling it *le Peuple-Dieu*. Cloots' church was a republic of mankind with Reason serving as its guide. He proposed a civil religion in which fathers of families would replace salaried priests and guarantee the civil rights of man. His republic of mankind meant a confederation of individuals in which all members would have the same rights and interests. As a contributor to the newspapers, *La Chronique de Paris* and *Le Batave* (the organ of the exiles), Cloots wrote articles depicting themes of revolution in conservative neighboring countries. Recognition came to him in August 1792 when he was declared a French citizen, and in September 1792, he represented the department of the Oise in the National Convention, where he voted for the death of Louis XVI in the name of mankind.

Since Cloots had a deep hatred for Christianity, which he considered incompatible with liberty, it is not surprising that he should be one of the chief promoters of a new religion, the Cult of Reason, in the autumn of 1793. The National Convention had already gone far in attacking Christianity by instituting a new calendar that abolished Sundays and saints' days. Cloots wanted to go much further. On the evening of 6 November, he, the deputy L. Bourdon, and the Portuguese-born J. Pereira visited J.-B. Gobel, the bishop of Paris. Under pressure from them, the bishop agreed to resign his ecclesiastical position. His public renunciation had an important impact. Throughout France many clerics renounced their priesthood, often under pressure from local patriots. The *déprêtisations* were a prelude to the establishment of the Cult of Reason. *Sociétés populaires* were established in each section of Paris to propagate the Cult of Reason, and Cloots was sent to the suburbs by the Paris Commune to preach the new faith. The Paris Commune on 10 November 1793, under the direction of its *procureur*, P.-G. Chaumette and J.-R. Hébert (assistant *procureur* and editor of *Le Père Duchesne*), formally inaugurated the Cult of Reason by taking control of Notre Dame cathedral and transforming it into a Temple of Reason. Cloots was an ardent supporter of Hébert's anti-Christian articles and policies.

The celebration of the Cult of Reason marked the triumph of Cloots' crusade for a rational religion, but it also prepared the way for his downfall. Rigorous anti-Christian feelings and public displays such as Festivals of Reason throughout Paris and in the provinces angered members of the Convention who had remained deists or who recognized the dangers of insulting the religion still professed by a majority of Frenchmen. Most important of these deputies was M. Robespierre who attacked Cloots and the Hébertists in speeches delivered before the Jacobin club on 21 November and 12 December 1793. Robespierre, who believed that atheism was allied with the foreign enemies of the Republic, denounced Cloots as a traitor and belittled him for his association with Bishop Gobel. Cloots was dismissed from the Jacobin club despite his recent election to its presidency. Prevented from speaking to the Jacobins, the stunned Cloots soon replied to the accusations hurled at him by writing two pamphlets, *Appel au genre humain* (Paris, 1793) and *Instruction public. Spectacles* (Paris, 1793). His abiding faith in the people to save him failed. Cloots found himself an outcast, and on 25 December 1793, he and T. Paine were expelled from the Convention.

Cloots died as he had lived. On the day of his execution, 24 March 1794, he preached a sermon on atheism to the prisoners who accompanied him to the guillotine. Taking this act and his religious views in retrospect, it is no wonder that Cloots has been called the personal enemy of Jesus Christ and the orator of mankind.

G. Avenel, *Anacharsis Cloots, L'Orateur du genre humain*, 2 vols. (Paris, 1865 rpt. in 1 vol., Paris, 1976); H. Baulig, "Anacharsis Cloots avant la Révolution," "Anacharsis Cloots journaliste et théoricien," "Anacharsis Cloots conventionnel," *Révo. française* 41 (1901); A. Cloots, *Oeuvres*, 3 vols. (Munich, 1980).

C. A. Gliozzo

Related entries: BOURDON; CALENDAR OF THE FRENCH REPUBLIC; CHAUMETTE; *CHRONIQUE DE PARIS*; CULT OF REASON; DECHRISTIANIZATION; GOBEL; HEBERT; PAINE.

CLUB DE CLICHY right-wing political grouping, 1794-97. The group that came to be known as the Club de Clichy was a loose association of deputies, newspapermen, and political agitators, most of whom held strong counterrevolutionary sentiments. The group grew out of an earlier association that brought together some of the deputies who had carried out the coup of 9 Thermidor Year II with some of the moderate *conventionnels* who had been imprisoned during the Terror. As the group grew in size during the winter of 1794-95, it had trouble finding a suitable place to meet, and finally accepted the invitation of the deputy J. Gérard-Desrivières to meet in a house that he owned on the rue de Clichy. After the closing of the Jacobin club in November 1794, the danger of a left-wing movement that had united the Thermidorians, moderate Republicans, and counterrevolutionaries in the club faded, and the more pro-republican members soon dropped out. The group continued to meet several times a week during the last months of the Convention, but little is known about its activities in this period.

The failure of the Vendémiaire insurrection and the installation of the Directory inaugurated a new period in the club's existence. A number of deputies from the *nouveau tiers* of men who had not sat in the Convention played a leading role in the organization. This group included moderates like J.-G. Siméon, M. Dumas, and G.-A. Tronçon Ducoudray, who hoped to guide the Directory toward a policy of social conservatism, and more aggressive counterrevolutionaries like R.-G. Lémerer and J.-P. Imbert-Colomès, who aimed at a monarchical restoration. The membership continued to include a number of right-wing former *conventionnels*, such as P.-F. Henri-Larivière and F.-A. Boissy d'Anglas. It had close contacts with a number of the successful right-wing newspapers that sprang up after Thermidor, including the *Nouvelles politiques*, the *Éclair*, the *Véridique*, and the *Messager du soir*. Although the club membership as a whole was not royalist, Louis XVIII's agents had contacts with several leading members, but even those most sympathetic to a restoration, such as Lémerer, advised the Pretender that he could not count on the club's support unless he committed himself to substantial constitutional safeguards.

With the arrival of the new *tiers* of deputies elected in 1797, the Club de Clichy seemed poised to dominate the councils. Its activists put strong pressure on the new deputies to attend the meetings, and total attendance rose to about 300, which was still short of a majority of the 750 in the two councils. The growth of the club, however, soon led to important political divisions among its members. The more intransigent monarchists formed a subgroup of some eighty members and met at the home of J.-L. Gibert-Desmolières, a leading right-wing deputy, to prepare for the Clichy sessions. A moderate subgroup led by members of the M. Dumas circle also formed a separate faction and tried to prevent the Clichy group as a whole from forcing a confrontation with the Directory. The club did manage to unite behind F. Barthélemy as a candidate for the vacant seat on the Directory and placed its members in charge of the two councils, but it soon demonstrated that it was not a well-disciplined party capable of enacting an agreed-on program. Despite the efforts of A.-B.-J. d'André, the royalist agent who had organized a scheme to restore the monarchy by electoral means, individual club members continued to launch uncoordinated initiatives, such as J.-V. Dumolard's controversial protest against N. Bonaparte's occupation of Venice, which hardened republican resistance and irritated many moderate deputies. Nor was the club successful in enacting several key features of its legislative program in the months before the coup of 18 Fructidor Year V. The Council of Five Hundred voted against abolishing the oath of loyalty to the Republic required of Catholic priests, and the Council of Ancients rejected a scheme to deprive the Directory of control over the treasury. Behind the scenes, the factions within the club pursued divergent policies. The moderate group threatened to pull out of the club altogether, and its members negotiated actively with the directors L. Carnot and P. Barras in an effort to reach an agreement on policy that would have enabled them to support the government publicly, a move that would have undoubtedly split the Club de Clichy completely.

In addition to its internal weaknesses, which were aired extensively in the press, the Club de Clichy came under increasing attack as a royalist association from republicans reacting to their election defeat in 1797. The directors had agents in the organization and were well informed about its internal problems, but they found it useful to call it a menacing, subversive group and tar all its members with the royalist brush. At the same time, the club came under attack from the extreme Right. Royalist pamphleteers accused the members of being more concerned in retaining their comfortable deputies' seats than in bringing back the king.

With the collapse of negotiations between the Clichy Club moderates and the Directory, the three republican directors Barras, J.-F. Reubell, and L.-M. La Revellière-lépeaux began moving openly toward a coup to silence the opposition in the councils. The dismissal of the three ministers closest to the Clichy Club at the end of Messidor Year V and Barras' abortive coup attempt drove the Clichy factions back together temporarily. Club members controlled the two councils' committees of inspectors, which tried to prepare resistance to any coup, but the club remained paralyzed by internal disagreements over tactics and took no effective action to ward off attack. The Club de Clichy officially dissolved itself in response to the Law of 7 Thermidor Year V banning political gatherings, which right-wing deputies had supported as a weapon against the republican groups that the Directory encouraged for its own support, but in fact the Clichy group continued to meet until the coup. The proscription of a number of its leading members and the purge of right-wing deputies elected in 1797 broke up the group, although some former members remained in the councils.

Like the earlier Club des Feuillants, the Club de Clichy was an attempt to use the organizational tactics pioneered by the Revolutionary movements in the interests of conservatism. Despite strong support in the national electorate, among the deputies, and in the press, the Club de Clichy proved incapable of surmounting its own internal divisions, in particular, the split between those members who wanted a restored monarchy and those who feared the effects of a genuine counterrevolution. As a result, even as republican propaganda portrayed the Clichyens as having virtually accomplished a counterrevolution, the club was on the point of disintegrating internally, and it was unable even to organize resistance to a determined attack by the Directory.

A. Challamel, *Les clubs contre-révolutionnaires* (Paris, 1895); A. Delarue, *Histoire du dix-huit fructidor* (Paris, 1821); Mathieu Dumas, *Souvenirs du lieutenant general comte Mathieu Dumas* (Paris, 1839); W. Fryer, *Republic or Restoration in France? 1794-97* (Manchester, 1965); A. C. Thibaudeau, *Memoires sur la Convention et le Directoire* (Paris, 1824).

J. Popkin

Related entries: ANDRE; BARRAS; BARTHELEMY; BOISSY D'ANGLAS; CARNOT; COUP OF 18 FRUCTIDOR YEAR V; FEUILLANTS; LA REVELLIERE-LEPEAUX; REUBELL; 13 VENDEMIAIRE YEAR IV.

CLUB NATIONAL. See AUSTRIAN COMMITTEE.

COALITION, FIRST. See FIRST COALITION.

COALITION, SECOND. See SECOND COALITION.

COBB, RICHARD CHARLES (1917-   ), historian. Perhaps the most significant living English French Revolutionist, Cobb is certainly the most individualist
historian working in the field today. He belongs to no school. A youthful admiration for A. Mathiez and association with post-1945 French Marxist scholars
have left him undogmatic; despite interests similar to the *Annalistes*, he has not
joined that movement and has been critical of its penchant for quantification as
a substitute for overall interpretation. Cobb's history is concerned with the tan-
gible, not the abstract, the human, not the ideological.

Three features inform all his works: a delight in research, a passionate but
not indiscriminate love of France, and a compassionate concern with human
relationships. Very early he found research and the acquisition of material exciting in its own right. His enthusiasm for investigation resembles that of a
detective; it deflected him into many unexpected and often peripheral subjects,
which became ends in themselves. His curiosity and his commitment to research
are evident in the topical and geographical range of such works as *Les armées
révolutionnaires des départements du Midi* (1955) and *Death in Paris, 1795–
1801* (1978).

Cobb's devotion to France began when he was a teenager, and he has spent
much of his adult life in France, both before and after World War II. He chose
to work in French history because he liked being in France. He approaches
French history in the light of his experience in France; for him the two are
inseparable. French became a second language for him, and he preferred it for
his first books, notably the two-volume *Les armées révolutionnaires: Instruments
de la Terreur* (1961–63) and *Terreur et subsistances, 1793–95* (1965). History
cannot be disassociated from language for Cobb, who acknowledges that he does
not say the same thing in French as in English. There is a distinct difference
between those of his books published in French and those published in English.

For Cobb, history is not a matter of academic theories. It is not a science,
even a human science. It is concerned with human beings; it is their story. Cobb's
empathy for his fellow man, his concrete curiosity about them, in conjunction
with a breadth and diversity of research, have resulted in a steady flow of articles
and books. Such works as *The Police and the People* (1970), *Paris and Its
Provinces* (1975), and *The Streets of Paris* (1980) suggest as broad a view of
the human comedy as Balzac's.

Cobb is currently (1985) professor of modern history at Oxford University.
   R. Cobb, *A Second Identity* (London, 1969) and *Reactions to the French Revolution*
(London, 1972).

C. A. Le Guin

Related entry: MATHIEZ.

COBBAN, ALFRED BERT CARTER (1901-68), historian. At the time of
his death, Cobban was professor of French history at University College, London,

a post he had held since 1953, the culmination of a long and distinguished academic career. Educated at Cambridge, he taught at the University of New-castle-upon-Tyne before he moved to London in 1937. After World War II, he served as visiting professor at several American universities, including Chicago, Harvard, and Johns Hopkins. During the forty years of his academic career, he was mentor to a number of younger historians who have distinguished themselves in French history; these students and an impressive list of books perpetuate Cobban's reputation as a leading authority on eighteenth-century France.

Cobban's bibliography contains a variety of works—scholarly monographs, general histories, critical and speculative works, collections of essays. His earliest books, *Edmund Burke and the Revolt against the Eighteenth Century* (1929) and *Rousseau and the Modern State* (1934), deal with ideological dimensions of the eighteenth century. These early works reveal what was to become a characteristic Cobban trait: the use of historical insight to expose clichés that result from ideological or antihistorical interpretations.

Books of more topical concern—*Dictatorship: Its History and Theory* (1939) and *National Self-Determination* (1948)—appeared around the time of World War II. In them Cobban continued to hold a firm balance between historical fact and ideology, producing a commonsense analysis of the origins and development of concepts of dictatorship and self-determination of peoples.

It was after the war that Cobban's publications began to suggest that his interest and expertise in eighteenth-century French history had focused on the Revolution. This concentration was inaugurated with the concise Historical Association pamphlet, *Causes of the French Revolution* (1946); in 1950 came *The Debate on the French Revolution*; in 1955, his professorial inaugural lecture, *The Myth of the French Revolution*, appeared in print; in 1964 came his Wiles lectures, *The Social Interpretation of the French Revolution*, the quintessence of Cobban's Revolutionary historiography; and finally, in the year of his death, a collection of fifteen of his articles and shorter pieces, *Aspects of the French Revolution* (1968), was compiled. These works mark a progressive distillation of Cobban's study of the French Revolution; they reveal his strengths as a historian and are among his most important works. In them Cobban takes issue with those who treat the Revolution in terms of preconceived ideas or who do not transcend generalizations and theories based on the circumstances of later times. For Cobban, the Revolution must be understood in terms of a broad eighteenth-century context, especially in terms of clear historical understanding of the century's social aspects and of the changes underway before Revolution broke out in 1789. Cobban's judgment is based on long reflection about the broad bases of Revolutionary history, especially those relating to social structure and the change and direction of social movement. His interpretation is a vigorous challenge to the sociological-ideological conclusions of leftist historiography, but he is concerned with more than attacking a school of interpretation. He suggests replacement for that which he criticizes, supplying a fresh and affirmative restatement and reversal of older points of view.

Toward the conclusion of his career, Cobban turned from his concentration on the French Revolution yet again to a more generalized look at the eighteenth century, in such works as *In Search of Humanity* (1960), a look at the impact of the Enlightenment on modern history, and *Eighteenth Century Europe and the Age of Enlightenment* (1961). He showed himself a first-class archival researcher in *Ambassadors and Secret Agents* (1954) and a synthesizer of masterly erudition and wit in his three-volume *History of Modern France* (1957-65), the product of a learned, critical, and urbane historical mind, and perhaps his most representative work.

A. Cobban, *The Myth of the French Revolution* (London, 1955), *The Social Interpretation of the French Revolution* (Cambridge, 1954), and *A History of Modern France*, 3 vols. (London 1957-65).

C. A. Le Guin

Related entries: LEFEBVRE; SOBOUL.

COBLENTZ (or COBLENCE), small fortified city at the confluence of the Rhine and Moselle rivers, which became a center of the counterrevolution. Coblentz was the old residence of the elector of Trier, one of the three archbishops who had the privilege of participating in the election of the Holy Roman Emperor. From 1790, it became one of the most important rallying points of French *émigrés* who were trying to assemble forces to intervene against the Revolution of 1789 in order to reestablish the absolute monarchy of the Old Regime. The princes, the brothers of Louis XVI, established their headquarters and council there. A daily routine was organized around the comte de Provence, the comte d'Artois, the duc de Bourbon, and, later, the prince de Condé. Along with C.-A. de Calonne and M.-A. Bombelles, the princes waged a diplomatic campaign at foreign courts to procure subsidies and to support an army. Temporary cantonments were set up in the outskirts of town, including one at Thal, and in the nearby woods. At first the city benefited from the irresponsible expenditures of these high-born personalities. Subsequently the number of *émigrés* grew until, at the end of September 1791, it reached 863 noblemen (out of 2,283 nobles in Rhenish towns), of all ages and ranks, including officers, members of the parlements, and the high clergy; and to these could be added the soldiers and noncommissioned officers of the royal army, women, and children. Many of these quickly were disillusioned and returned to France after being frightened by the measures taken against their families and properties. The military men remained and fought alongside the troops of the coalition. As a result, Coblentz became for patriots a den of traitors, of conspirators, and of royalists, and its very name symbolized the counterrevolution.

When General F.-S. Marceau seized the city on 2 Brumaire Year III (24 October 1794), its inhabitants scattered and left behind a large quantity of goods. The Rhenish areas were then divided into four departments that were put under military occupation until their official incorporation into France on 18 Ventôse Year IX (9 March 1801). From the beginning of the Year IX (September 1800),

French laws and institutions had been implemented there. Coblentz became the capital of the department of the Rhin-et-Moselle and remained so until 1814.

M. Bouloiseau, "Des listes originales de nobles français émigrés," *Bull. d'hist. écon. et soc. de la Révo.* (Paris, 1965); H. Chassagne, *Coblence* (Paris, 1939); R. Dufraisse, "Les Emigrés des régions rhénanes et leurs biens," *Bull. d'hist. écon. et soc. de la Révo.* (Paris, 1964); P. de Vaissière, *A Coblence, ou les émigrés français dans les pays rhénanes de 1789 à 1792* (Paris, 1924).

M. Bouloiseau

Related entries: ARTOIS; CALONNE; CONDE; COUNTERREVOLUTION; DECLARATION OF PILLNITZ; *EMIGRES.*

COLLOT D'HERBOIS, JEAN-MARIE (1749-96), terrorist, member of the Committee of Public Safety. Collot d'Herbois was born on 19 June 1749 in Paris to G.-J. Collot, a goldsmith, and his wife J.-A. Hanner. At about the age of twenty, he became an actor and joined a touring troupe. For the next twenty years he traveled about France, Holland, and Switzerland performing on the stage and writing plays. His political opinions in these years were strongly royalist. All of his plays, which were mildly successful but mediocre comedies and romantic dramas, lauded royalty, aristocracy, and the institutions of the Old Regime: *Lucie*, 1772; *Le bon Angevin*, 1775; *Le seigneur d'Anjou*, 1776; *Le nouveau Nostradamus*, 1777; *L'amant loup-garou*, 1777; *Le paysan magistrat*, 1777; *Les français à Grenade*, 1779; and *La fête dauphine*, 1780. In 1787 he became the director of a theater in Lyon where he assumed the stage name of d'Herbois. In 1789 he briefly directed a theater in Geneva before moving to Paris.

At the outbreak of the Revolution, Collot abandoned his royalist opinions in favor of the popular view in Paris, constitutional monarchy. His last plays, written between 1789 and 1792, praised the new Revolutionary ideals, constitutional monarchy, and patriotism: *L'inconnu*, 1789; *La journée de Louis XII*, 1790; *Famille patriote*, 1790; *Le procès de Socrate*, 1790; *Portefeuilles*, 1791; and *L'aîné et le cadet*, 1792. These now-forgotten plays enjoyed enormous popularity with the public and established Collot as a leading Revolutionary playwright.

In 1791 Collot began his political career by publishing the *Almanach du père Gérard*, his first political pamphlet. It won first prize in a contest held by the Jacobins for a patriotic almanac to educate the public on the new constitution. He also emerged as a popular orator in Paris, drawing on his years of theatrical experience to formulate an exciting, dramatic, and flamboyant oratorical style. In 1792 his successful crusade in defense of the Swiss soldiers of Châteauvieux established him as one of the most influential popular spokesmen in Paris.

In the summer of 1792 Collot modified his political opinions again and embraced the radical demands of the Parisian masses. For the rest of his life, he was recognized widely as one of the most extreme Revolutionary leaders. On 10 August he joined the new insurrectional Commune of Paris and helped lead the coup that overthrew the monarchy. Some writers have averred, without convincing evidence, that he was a leading instigator of the September Massacres. He presided over the electoral assembly of Paris, which met on 3 September to elect deputies to the National Convention, and was one of the first to be chosen by the assembly.

In the Convention, Collot was a leader of a small but influential faction, the left wing of the Mountain. During the first session on 21 September 1792, he demanded the decree abolishing the monarchy and declaring the Republic. It passed unanimously. On 14 November he, C.-A. Goupilleau, and M.-D. Lasource were sent on mission to Nice to investigate complaints of pillaging by the Army of the Var. Returning to Paris in time to vote in the trial of Louis XVI, he declared for immediate death and against all appeals. On 9 March 1793, the Convention directed Collot and G. Laplanche to the departments of the Nièvre and Loiret where Collot ordered mass arrests of all priests and religious individuals who were suspected of opposing the government. Shortly after his return to Paris, he was elected president of the National Convention, serving from 13 to 27 June.

In the spiraling crisis of 1793, extreme radicals in Paris pressured the Convention to arrest the Girondin leaders and to adopt harsher economic measures. Collot and his closest ally, J.-N. Billaud-Varenne, championed the radicals' cause in the Convention and brought passage on 27 July of the famous law that required the death penalty for food speculators. On 1 August the Convention sent him on mission to the Oise and Aisne. Even though he was absent, extremist forces coerced the Convention on 8 September to elect Collot and Billaud to the most powerful government committee, the Committee of Public Safety. The two formed the left wing of the committee, constantly demanding more extreme measures and often opposing the relatively more moderate policies of the committee leader, M. Robespierre.

Collot's fame as a violent terrorist rests mainly on his mission to Lyon in November and December 1793. After government forces had defeated the federalist revolt there, the Convention decreed ''the city of Lyon shall be destroyed'' and directed Collot and J. Fouché (30 October) to reestablish the Revolutionary order in Lyon. Supported by an army contingent, they organized mass executions of bourgeois prisoners, killing many of them by tying them in bunches and firing on them with cannons and muskets. Between November 1793 and February 1794, 1,667 prisoners were executed in Lyon. Barraged by complaints from Lyon about his cruelty, the Committee of Public Safety recalled Collot in December.

On his return, he made a successful attack on these accusations in the Convention (21 December) while the deputies responded with praise and applause. After the executions of the leading Hébertists, Collot demanded and achieved the arrest of the Dantonists, who were also executed. On 3 Prairial Year II (22 May 1794) he narrowly escaped assassination when a royalist, H. Ladmiral, fired a pistol at him.

Collot was a leading organizer of the conspiracy to overthrow Robespierre. By May 1794 his long-standing opposition had evolved into outright hostility to Robespierre, who had criticized his mission to Lyon, liquidated his Hébertist allies, complained of his dechristianization demands, and then menaced J. Fouché, Collot's colleague at Lyon. The meetings of the Committee of Public Safety degenerated into violent quarrels of Collot and Billaud against Robespierre. On 1 Thermidor (19 July) the anti-Robespierrists managed to elect Collot president of the Convention. He presided over parts of the session of 9 Thermidor (27 July) and played a major role in the defeat and arrest of the Robespierrists.

Much to his dismay, Collot was swept away by the Thermidorian Reaction. On 15 Fructidor (30 August), he left the Committee of Public Safety at the expiration of his term. The Thermidorian leaders now singled him out for attack as one of the cruelest terrorists. On 12 Vendémiaire Year III (3 October 1794), A.-M. Legendre made such a stirring attack on Collot, Billaud, and B. Barère as accomplices of Robespierre that the Convention established a commission on 7 Nivôse (27 December) to examine their conduct. The Convention voted a decree of accusation on 12 Ventôse Year IV (2 March 1795) and heard Collot defend himself in a dramatic and eloquent appeal on 5 Germinal (25 March). During the radical-inspired uprising of 12 Germinal (1 April), the Convention suspended the hearing and decreed the deportation of Collot, Billaud, and Barère to Guyana, the "dry guillotine."

In Guyana Collot began moving to inspire the blacks to rebel and attack the whites. The authorities then incarcerated him in the Sinnamary fort, where he soon fell ill with yellow fever. While he was being transported to the hospital, he called for something to drink to quench his terrible thirst. His attendants mistakenly gave him a bottle of rum instead of water. With one swallow, he fell into horrible sufferings and died on arriving at the hospital, 20 Prairial Year IV (8 June 1796). He was forty-five years old.

Robespierre once called Collot the "trumpet of the Revolution." More accurately, he was the trumpet of the radical poor of Paris. As an experienced professional actor, he was a remarkably effective popular orator. However, his agitation for harsher economic measures against property owners, his demands for dechristianization, his use, or abuse, of the terror at Lyon, and his alliance with *enragés* and Hébertists made him too extremist for most other Revolutionaries, particularly Robespierre. When the moderates gained power in Thermidor, he was one of the first to be removed from power.

A. Begis, *Billaud-Varenne, membre du Comité de salut public; mémoires inédits et correspondance accompagnés de notices biographiques sur Billaud-Varenne et Collot d'Herbois* (Paris, 1893); V. Fournel, "Les comédiens révolutionnaires. Collot d'Herbois, acteur et auteur dramatique," *Le Correspondant* 172 (1893); M. Fuchs, "Collot d'Herbois comédien," *Révo. française* 79 (1926); H. Lebasteur, "Collot d'Herbois et la société lyonnaise," *Ann. du pr. de Ligne* (1920); R. R. Palmer, *Twelve Who Ruled: The Year of the Terror in the French Revolution* (Princeton, 1941).

R. J. Caldwell

Related entries: ALMANACH DU PERE GERARD, L'; BILLAUD-VARENNE; COMMITEE OF PUBLIC SAFETY; DECHRISTIANIZATION; FEDERAL-ISM; FOUCHE; HEBERTISTS; INDULGENTS; *NOYADES DE NANTES*; SEP-TEMBER 1792 MASSACRES; THERMIDORIAN REACTION.

COMITE AUTRICHIEN. See AUSTRIAN COMMITTEE.

COMMISSION OF TWELVE (21 May 1793–2 June 1793), committee of inquiry formed by the National Convention and abolished by demand of insurrectionary Paris. Composed largely of Girondins, the commission sought to break the power of the Paris Commune and to suppress radicalism in the sections. Its provocations triggered the *journées* of 31 May and 2 June and brought about the fall of the Girondins.

When the news of military reverses and of the treason of C. Dumouriez arrived in March 1793, the Parisian popular movement began to call for the expulsion of some Girondins from the Convention. The rising in the Vendée heightened the sense of emergency and threw the Girondins' incompetence to direct the war into sharp relief. The Girondins met attacks by moving to discredit the Mountain while their command of the Convention's majority still held. J.-P. Marat, the most vulnerable of the leaders of the Mountain, was impeached, only to be acquitted by the Revolutionary Tribunal of Paris. On 15 April, thirty-three of the forty-eight sections of Paris petitioned for the expulsion of twenty-two Girondin deputies. The Montagnards perceived that an alliance now with the sections was a worthwhile risk; as the minority in the Convention, they needed external support to defeat the Girondins' efforts to divide and isolate them. On 20 April, the Mountain first supported the sections' demands for price controls on food. On 1 May the Convention, surrounded by 6,000 demonstrators from the faubourg Saint-Antoine, consented to decree a maximum on grain. This incident aggravated the Convention's prickliness over Parisian leverage, and it was in this atmosphere that the Commission of Twelve was framed.

On 18 May M.-E. Guadet renewed an earlier proposal that a shadow Convention composed of the representatives' substitutes sit at Bourges; if the Convention at Paris was overwhelmed by force, the Bourges Convention was to hold its legitimacy in trust. Guadet also urged the dissolution of the Paris Commune; the section presidents could administer the city in its place. B. Barère, seeking middle ground between Girondins and Montagnards, proposed instead that a Commission of Twelve be created to inquire into the Parisian situation, and this idea won the Convention's approval.

Fewer than 200 deputies were present to vote for members of the commission on 20 May. The twelve selected were F. Bergoeing, C.-A. Bertrand de l'Hodiesnière, J. Boilleau d'Ausson, J.-B. Boyer-Fonfrède, J.-F. Gardien, J.-A. Gommaire, G. de Kervélegan, P.-F.-J. Henri-Larivière, E. Mollevaut, J.-P. Rabaut Saint-Etienne, F.-J. Saint-Martin Valogne, and L.-F.-S. Viger. All were drawn from the Girondin group or from the Plain.

The commission began by questioning J.-N. Pache, mayor of Paris, and D.-J. Garat, minister of the interior. It ordered the sections to surrender their minutes to the commission and to close their meetings at 10 P.M. On 24 May J.-R. Hébert (*procureur* of the Paris Commune and author of the popular news sheet *Père Duchesne*), J.-F. Varlet (an *enragé* agitator), and J.-B. Marino (a municipal officer who had counseled the kidnapping of the twenty-two Girondins) were arrested. To the protesting deputation from the Commune that appeared the next day, the Girondin M. Isnard, president of the Convention, threatened to punish any insurrection against the Convention by annihilating Paris. The foolhardiness of this remark can hardly be overstated; it proved the surest inducement to an immediate rising before military reinforcements could be summoned.

On 26 May the commission attacked the local surveillance committees, an institution then only three months old. The commission suppressed the committee of the Unité section; it forbade surveillance committees to call themselves *comités révolutionnaires*; it invited the ministry of the interior to investigate them. When 16 Paris sections protested, the Convention referred them to the commission. The commission then arrested C.-E. Dobsen (president of the Cité section, which had refused to surrender its minutes) and urged moderate sections to arm themselves against the radical sections.

27 May was a day of tumult in the Convention. In the spectators' galleries, *sans-culotte* militants confronted 200 armed men from the moderate Butte des Moulins section. The Mountain sought to bring the continued existence of the commission to a vote; the president Isnard resisted for several hours. After midnight the deputies present dwindled until the Mountain succeeded in passing the dissolution of the commission and the release of its prisoners.

On the following day, the Girondins returned in force and mustered enough of the Convention's center to reinstate the Commission of Twelve by 279 to 238 votes. The Mountain—and the gallery—refused to accept this decision. The attempts by Rabaut to read the commission's report were howled down, and the Convention was forced again to accept the release of the commission's prisoners.

On 31 May, with insurrection impending, the Mountain moved once more that the commission be abolished. Instead the Convention voted for an investigation of the rising visibly in progress. The immense crowd that surrounded the Convention in the afternoon and evening was able to force the Convention to suppress the commission again, but no more. The hesitations of many sections and the reluctance to use force against the national legislature gave the *journée* of 31 May an ambiguous result; the Convention still refused to arrest any of its own number. On 2 June 80,000 men of the Paris National Guard forced the Convention to decree the arrest of twenty-nine deputies, including ten members of the Commission of Twelve.

The Commission of Twelve was the concluding chapter in the Girondins' resistance to the Parisian popular movement. Bitterly opposed to *sans-culotte* participation in any aspect of government or national defense, by May the Girondins had only two alternatives: they could establish an alternate center of power beyond the reach of Paris or try to suppress the city's radical political life. By creating the Commission of Twelve, they embarked on the second course, and they approached it in a juridical and unrealistic fashion. The Girondins did have support in Paris from the *muscadins*, young clerks and shop assistants who were the social predecessors of the reactionary *jeunesse dorée* of Year III. The *muscadins* presented a threat sufficient for the Commune to bring out the National Guard against them in May. Had the Commission of Twelve temporized with some sections while *muscadins* took hold in others, the threat of insurrection might have been neutralized. Then a purge of the sections, prepared by confiscation of their minutes, arrest of Commune leaders, and similar measures, might have succeeded. Instead the commission proceeded on the fundamental Girondin assumption that the Convention could, if necessary, defend itself with armed forces called from the departments—hence the threats of Isnard. The federalist effort to rally the provinces against Paris after 2 June proved a failure. The activities of the Commission of Twelve were only a last symptom of the Girondins' inability to make common cause with social classes below their own.

A. Soboul, "Girondins et Montagnards," *Actes du Colloque "Girondins et Montagnards"* (Paris, 1980); M. Sydenham, *The Girondins* (London, 1961); H. Wallon, *La Révolution du 31 mai et le fédéralisme en 1793* (Paris, 1886).

C. Ramsay

Related entries: FEDERALISM; GIRONDINS; HEBERT; *JEUNESSE DOREE*; *JOURNEES REVOLUTIONNAIRES*; *MUSCADINS*; SECTIONS; VARLET; VENDEE.

COMMITTEE, AUSTRIAN. See AUSTRIAN COMMITTEE.

COMMITTEE, CENTRAL REVOLUTIONARY. See CENTRAL REVOLUTIONARY COMMITTEE.

COMMITTEE OF DUPORT. See COMMITTEE OF THIRTY.

COMMITTEE OF GENERAL DEFENSE (*Comité de défense générale*) (January-April 1793), an attempt by the National Convention to provide for organization of the Republic's war effort. The first Committee of General Defense (1 January 1793) emerged almost without debate as the last of a series of proposals from the deputy A. Kersaint in anticipation of a maritime war with Great Britain. Such discussion as there was (J.-P. Rouyer and J.-P. Rabaut Saint-Etienne supported it, C. Charlier and J.-A. Thuriot opposed it) suggests a Girondin maneuver. It was composed of three members from each of the committees of war, finance, colonies, commerce, diplomacy, the navy, and the constitution.

The total membership of these committees seems to have included the contending factions in roughly equal numbers, but Montagnard strength was concentrated in the large war and finance committees, whereas the Girondins had a majority on a number of the smaller ones; moreover, the large and strongly Montagnard general security committee was excluded, despite its apparent relevance, and the small, strongly Girondin constitution committee was included, despite its tenuous connection with preparations for war. This should have given the Gironde a chance to take the initiative.

This committee, however, was a failure and the Girondin move self-defeating. In the circumstances and the atmosphere of January–February 1793, it would have been impolitic to suggest private sessions, which would best have served the committee's nominal purpose. Its public sessions became disorderly and polemical, and its members apparently gave priority to the business of their parent committees, a revealing choice for J.-P. Brissot, whose *comité diplomatique* was rapidly disintegrating. As the war crisis deepened, B. Barère suggested a reconstruction, which was carried out on 25 March.

The reorganized committee was now elected from the Convention at large, and its twenty-five members drew heavily on both the factions, with a slight Montagnard majority. B. Barère, E.-J. Sieyès, M.-E. Guadet, and A. Gensonné were still members; Brissot was not. It was renamed the *comité de défense générale et de salut public* (Committee of General Defense and Public Safety), and it included six men, in addition to Barère, who served later on the more famous Committee of Public Safety: G.-J. Danton, L.-B. Guyton-Morveau, J.-F. Delmas, J.-J. Bréard, M. Robespierre, and P.-L. Prieur de la Marne. But it was only a stop-gap. It was still too large, there was still no provision for privacy, it had no funds at its disposal, and despite the careful stipulations concerning regular reports to the Convention, significant details—such as the size of the majority needed for a decision—were left surprisingly vague. Nor was it realistic to hope for the smooth functioning of a group with F.-N.-L. Buzot, M. Isnard, C.-J.-M. Barbaroux, and P.-V. Vergniaud at one end of the table and M. Robespierre, P.-F. Fabre d'Eglantine, L.-C.-S. Desmoulins, and Prieur at the other. Less than two weeks later, at Isnard's instigation, there was yet another committee: small (nine members), united, with a precise term of office, some sketchy but effective working rules, and a budget to be spent at its own discretion: the first Committee of Public Safety *tout court*. Before 1795, no Girondin was ever elected to this. But Barère was. He was the only deputy to serve continuously from 1 January 1793 until Fructidor Year II.

L. Cahen and R. Guyot, *L'oeuvre legislative de la Révolution* (Paris, 1913); M. J. Sydenham, *The Girondins* (London, 1961).

A. Patrick

Related entries: COMMITTEE OF PUBLIC SAFETY; GIRONDINS; MONTAGNARDS.

COMMITTEE OF GENERAL SECURITY (*Comité de sûreté générale*) (1792–95), one of the two famous committees of the Terror, the longest-lived of the National Convention's executive committees. The Convention decided at its first full session, 21 September 1792, to maintain provisionally the committee structures of the Legislative Assembly until they could be replaced. Since twenty-three members of the Legislative's *comité de surveillance* were sitting in the Convention, these deputies continued their former duties until on 17 October a new *comité de sûreté générale et de surveillance* of thirty members (including fourteen of the twenty-three) was elected. This Convention committee, varying in size from time to time, had a continuous existence until the Convention itself dissolved in 1795. Despite this precedence and continuity and despite its work, which demanded a more general perspective than that of the other committees devised in 1792, the committee did not evolve further and was eventually overshadowed by the Committee of Public Safety, created in April 1793, but both its personnel and its activities were of considerable significance, not least because of the share of some of its members in the intrigues leading to the fall of M. Robespierre in 1794.

During its first months, the political orientation of the committee attracted pointed comment. The twenty-three members of the original *comité de surveillance*, who were nearly all to become deeply involved in the disputes of 1793, included a strong Montagnard majority; eight were or became Jacobins, and ten were open Montagnards or close fellow-travelers. Three belonged to the loose inner group of the Gironde; only two were to stay with the Plain. These proportions were transferred after 17 October to the new committee, despite its enlargement; this had twenty-two Montagnards of various kinds. There was much complaint from the Gironde, and on 3 January 1793, when half the membership was due to be routinely replaced, C.-J.-M. Barbaroux demanded a complete reorganization. Then there was a Girondin coup as temporary as it was striking. The fifteen new members chosen on 9 January included six of Barbaroux's friends and associates, four of their future sympathizers, four deputies from the Plain, and a solitary Montagnard. Not surprisingly, the announcement of the election-result produced an uproar in which J.-P. Marat took a leading part. Precisely how the coup had been achieved, it would be interesting to know, for it proved an aberration. On 21 January another election was held, the committee's members were reduced to twelve, and all of those chosen twelve days earlier were eliminated. There were now eleven Montagnards, including seven Jacobins, and one Girondin, and all twelve had approved unswervingly the execution of Louis XVI, which had taken place that day. The political victory symbolized by this election was maintained until early 1795.

From 21 January 1793, there were four main phases in the history of the committee: the consolidation of its membership and the expansion of its duties (January–October 1793); its growing bureaucratization, under the formal control of the Committee of Public Safety, and the increasing estrangement of its leading members from Robespierre (October 1793–9 Thermidor Year II); the restriction of its powers and its domination by ex-Montagnard Thermidorians (Thermidor Year II–Germinal Year III); and the dwindling of the ex-Montagnards on the committee (though they remained a very substantial minority) until they were outnumbered by the total of surviving Girondins plus men from the Plain. At no point after Thermidor did the Plain succeed in taking over the committee or play a really significant role on it; throughout its lifetime, it was heavily dominated by men who had opted for one or the other of the contending factions of 1793.

Unstable membership in 1793 was related to the committee's business (police and security), in conjunction with a rule, usually but not invariably enforced, that anyone going on mission should be deemed to have resigned. Since a number of members did go on mission, there was a continual shuffling in and out, with new members being added every month to fill the gaps. In addition, there was a flavor of political intrigue about some of the elections. F. Chabot was not perhaps a highly desirable member of any committee, least of all this one, but by September 1793, apart from an absence on mission in the spring, he had served almost continuously since October 1792. It took two elections (10 and 14 September) and five days of sustained effort in the Convention before J.-B. Drouet and N.-S. Maure managed to dislodge him along with J. Julien and C. Basire, to the relief of many deputies who did not much like what they suspected about his behavior.

The committee that emerged by Brumaire Year II (November 1793) functioned almost unchanged, under the general direction of the Committee of Public Safety (CPS) until Thermidor. It had fourteen members—M.-G.-A. Vadier, E.-J. Panis, P.-F.-J. Le Bas, J.-L. David, J. Guffroy, L. de Lavicomterie, J.-B.-A. Amar, P. Rühl, H. Voulland, M. Bayle, J.-N. Barbeau-Dubarran, G.-M. Jagot, J.-A. Louis (Bas-Rhin) and E. Lacoste—who were reduced to twelve when first Panis and later Guffroy resigned. Its membership was noticeably older than that of the more famous committee, had less legislative experience, and was occupationally more varied. Its seven lawyers worked alongside an artist (David), a bookkeeper (Moise Bayle), a doctor, a civil servant, a landowner, a journalist, and one colleague whose pre-1789 occupation does not appear. Five members were ex-deputies, five came from departmental and one from district office, and three had been simply political activists. At the end of 1793 the average age was about forty-four, as against thirty-seven for the CPS. The CPS had only one man (R. Lindet) over forty-five; the Committee of General Security (CGS) had four over fifty, of whom three (Vadier, Rühl, and Guffroy) were notably short-tempered. As in the CPS, personalities differed: in religious outlook (Vadier's vitriolic Voltaireanism, Rühl's Protestantism), in temperament (Amar's cold savagery, Louis's gentleness, Rühl's generosity), and in political attitude (David admired Robespierre, whom Lavicomterie feared and Vadier came to detest).

Since the committee neither chose nor controlled anyone on mission and its own members were not often away after late 1793, it had only limited responsibility for the great episodes of provincial Terror, though it did in general organize what happened in Paris. Its work included much routine and related to passports, arrests, and imprisonments, as well as to trials and executions. It drew on the revolutionary committees of the provinces, who by the Law of Suspects (17 September) were supposed to report arrests directly to it. Down to late 1793, the CGS and the CPS, drawn equally from the Convention, were uneasily independent. The 14 Frimaire (4 December) decree finally established CPS control, although CGS activities remained separate.

As the government of the Terror took shape, the CGS began a systematic organization of its tasks. After an attempt on 17 September to divide these into categories (inquiries, arrests, and passports; correspondence; reports), it was decided that the Republic itself should be divided into four regions, with one group of deputies responsible for each. This system was maintained into 1794. By Germinal, when the ministries were abolished, the paperwork of the CGS was clearly enormous, and a new decree (20 Germinal) gave the committee a staff of well over 100, with a budget of 385,800 *livres*. Revealingly, there was a special bureau of sixteen officials to handle (and, it was hoped, to dispose of) arrears of business.

In the spring of 1794, relations between the two great committees, never easy, became subject to complex antagonisms. The Law of 22 Prairial and Robespierre's new police bureau were both presented to the Convention without prior consultation with the CGS, whose jurisdiction was obviously affected. But much more than institutional jealousy was involved; there was also the matter of the purpose of the new policies and the individuals against whom they might be directed. Amar and Vadier especially had reason for both political and personal apprehension since they bitterly disliked Robespierre's religious program, and the new legislation offered deputies no protection from indictment. Dating from Danton's death, confusion and fear produced in the Convention a baffling fog of intrigue, amid which Robespierre's precise intentions remain unknown. The countermoves of the CGS—the attempt to discredit Robespierre through C. Théot's pathetic delusions, the conspicuous execution of C. Renault and other parricides, the repellent escalation of Terror, for which Robespierre bears no responsibility—do the committee little credit, but they suggest desperation as well as lack of scruple.

During the events of Thermidor, in which Amar and Vadier were deeply involved, the CGS, like the CPS, was divided. Lebas killed himself, and David said later that he owed his own life to Barère, who had warned him to stay home from the Convention. Jagot and Lavicomterie were dropped from the reconstructed committee of 14 Thermidor, but the other eight were reelected.

After Fructidor and another election, which only Amar, Louis, and Barbeau-Dubarran survived, the committee limped on, still in a sense a Jacobin body (eleven of its sixteen members could then have claimed club allegiance) but hastily repudiating awkward associations. It had recovered its independence, but its powers were restricted, the Jacobin network of provincial committees was unavailable, and a quarter of its membership now changed every month in rotation. By Vendémiaire all its pre-Thermidor members had disappeared. In Ventôse (March 1795) the first election of a surviving Girondin was a pointer to the future. After the Germinal rising, Amar was arrested and Vadier condemned (*in absentia*) to deportation. Then came the rising of 1 Floréal. On 10 Floréal, Rühl committed suicide in prison, and by the end of the month, every living member of the CGS of the Terror, except Louis who was successfully defended by Pierret, was either in hiding or under arrest. Historians have taken little note of their 1795 successors, who indeed are not very interesting; the CGS does not figure largely in accounts of the White Terror. In the committee's last incarnation (15 Vendémiaire Year IV), its only well-known member was P. Barras.

R. Bienvenu, *The Ninth of Thermidor* (Oxford, 1968); L. Cahen and R. Guyot, *L'oeuvre législative de la Révolution* (Paris, 1913); J. Guillaume, *Etudes révolutionnaires*, 2ᵉ série (Paris, 1909); N. Hampson, *The Life and Opinions of Maximilien Robespierre* (London, 1974); A. Kuscinski, *Dictionnaire des conventionnels* (Paris, 1916–20); G. Lefebvre, *The Thermidorians and the Directory*, tr. R. Baldick (New York, 1964).

A. Patrick

Related entries: AMAR; BARBAROUX; CHABOT; COMMITTEE OF PUBLIC SAFETY; DROUET; GIRONDINS; LAW OF 14 FRIMAIRE; LAW OF SUSPECTS; LAW OF 22 PRAIRIAL; MONTAGNARDS; 9 THERMIDOR YEAR II; PLAIN, THE; VADIER.

COMMITTEE OF PUBLIC SAFETY (1793-95), provisional committee of the Revolutionary government, born of the tragic circumstances in which France struggled in 1793; it came to an end when the war was won. The Committee's history is linked intimately with that of the Jacobin Republic. Yet its establishment was difficult; of all the major Revolutionary creations, it was the slowest to be realized. After the fall of the monarchy on 10 August 1792, there was still hesitation to break with the sacrosanct principle of separation of powers, as extolled by Montesquieu. To unite legislative and executive power in the same hands made no sense to the bourgeois regime that had elaborated the Constitution of 1791. Still, the Convention, once elected, had constituent authority and, until the new document that it was authorized to draw up was completed, it had to legislate, administer, and judge at the same time. Only reluctantly it resolved to do so, while defending itself on the basis of necessity.

On 15 August, before dissolving itself, the Legislative Assembly transferred the powers of the deposed king to a provisional Executive Council composed of ministers chosen from outside the Assembly. The heavy burden of administration, its complexity, and its slowness could not respond to the demands of conducting a war that since April 1792 had resulted only in French reverses. At the least, it was necessary to centralize the services that coordinated military and diplomatic operations and to provide them with a common direction. This was accomplished on 1 January 1793 by the creation of the Committee of General Defense by the Girondin-dominated Convention; this committee's twenty-four members were selected from among deputies who composed seven of its normal working committees. In theory, its role consisted of assisting the ministers and, with them, deciding on urgent military measures. Very quickly its inefficiency became evident. Nevertheless, there had been established the principle of confiding very extensive decision-making power to a delegation of elected representatives of the sovereign people. Thus, the levy of 300,000 men, voted on 24 February 1793, was the work of representatives sent on mission by the Assembly, and the Committee of General Defense itself, on 18 March, proposed the establishment of a smaller committee of public safety in which Girondins and Montagnards would sit together.

On 28 March, it was formally named the Committee of Public Safety. Still, the twenty-five deputies chosen were, in the majority, moderates and Girondins. M. Robespierre, who was selected, declined on the grounds that the country could not be saved in this fashion. B. Barère agreed. What was necessary was a restricted *comité d'exécution* that would be collectively responsible to the Assembly and to which the ministers would be subordinated. On the evening of 6 April, after much hesitation the Convention made its decision and named the nine members who would compose this committee.

The First Committee of Public Safety, 7 April–10 July 1793, began its sessions 7 April in the Pavillon de Flore; on it were such specialists as the financier P.-J. Cambon, the jurist J.-B. Treilhard, the chemist L.-B. Guyton-Morveau, as well as J.-F. Delmas and J.-J. Bréard. Its sponsor, Barère, had been elected first, followed by G.-J. Danton and his friend, C. Delacroix (of the Eure-et-Loire). All were moderates; all were patriots. The personality of Danton dominated them and his compromises with the traitor C. Dumouriez discredited the entire committee from its beginnings. Conscious of the dangers that threatened the Revolution, the committee's members divided its tasks and imposed an enormous work load on themselves. The members had been elected for one month, but the Convention prolonged their term on 11 May. They opposed Minister J.-B. Bouchotte on the issues of General A.-P. Custine and the attempts at negotiations inspired by Danton. Moreover, on all fronts the French armies continued to retreat. The Convention sent to the armies representatives who enjoyed unlimited powers and who were chosen from among the Montagnard deputies. The committee gave them its support, but in the political struggle, the Girondins were losing ground, and their plan for a constitution was poorly greeted. Eliminated from the Assembly after 31 May, the Girondins left their place to the Mountain, which pressed to reorganize the committee and introduce into it Jacobin members, including G. Couthon and L. Saint-Just. While its efforts were recognized, its mistakes were denounced. The institution itself was good, but it was necessary to confide it to true Revolutionaries. Danton and his friends were ousted on 10 July. The ''Great Committee'' was about to be born.

The Great Committee of Public Safety, 10 July 1793–27 July 1794. Two more months were required before the selection of the team of twelve members who would govern the country and conduct the war: Barère, R. Lindet, A. Jeanbon Saint-André, G. Couthon, C.-A. Prieur (de la Côte-d'Or), P.-L. Prieur (de la Marne), L. Carnot, M. Robespierre, L.-A.-L. de Saint-Just, J.-N. Billaud-Varenne, J.-M. Collot d'Herbois, and M.-J. Hérault de Sechelles (until his arrest on 18 March 1794). They distributed tasks among themselves: some concerned themselves with military affairs, the navy, provisions, transport, diplomacy; others with correspondence with representatives on mission; still others with relations with the Assembly, which reelected them each month. The Convention accorded them its confidence without interruption until Thermidor. One is still amazed by the working power of these men and the great number of decisions they had to make every day. The very number of decisions prohibited deliberations in common, but their power was collegial and no member dreamed of evading his responsibilities. In addition, the committee considered itself interdependent with the Convention; the committee acted in the name of the Convention and thereby in the name of the nation as a whole. It did not rule, it served. Undoubtedly, agreement among its members did not always prevail, but a single objective guided them: victory over all enemies of the Revolution. The Law of 14 Frimaire Year II (4 December 1793), the real charter of the Revolutionary government, recognized its preeminence, and the Terror furnished its coercive force.

The ministers and constituted authorities obeyed this nerve center. On 12 Germinal (2 April 1794), the former were replaced by executive commissions directly dependent on its bureaus, and the latter were regenerated by the *scrutin épuratoire*. All citizens had to give proof of their *civisme*, their patriotism, and their Jacobin spirit. Robespierre exercised surveillance over the essential unity, by persuasion or by coercion. Opponents were arrested and executed: J.-R. Hébert along with the leaders of the Cordeliers Club on 4 Germinal; Danton together with Desmoulins and "corrupted" deputies on 15 Germinal. The conduct of military operations was henceforth firmly managed by Carnot, Saint-Just, and the representatives to the armies. The judicious choice of young and enthusiastic generals corresponded to the ardor of the troops, now unified by the Amalgam and the *embrigadement*. Saint-André took charge of reinforcing the defenses of ports and of increasing the number of ships. Prieur (de la Côte-d'Or), aided by many scientists, including J.-A. Chaptal, J.-H. Hassenfratz, and A.-T. Vandermonde, greatly increased the production of war industries, while Lindet requisitioned essential materials for the armies and towns. This was the price of repulsing the foreign invasion and repressing internal disturbances. Then Revolutionary France crossed its frontiers, establishing itself in Belgium after the victory of Fleurus (26 June 1794), in the Rhineland, Piedmont, and Catalonia. But with the victories, public opinion wanted a relaxation of the strict economic controls and an end to the excesses of the Great Terror. The *sans-culottes* also wanted social measures in favor of the "little people" and the establishment of direct democracy. At last, a majority of the Convention and the committee itself split. Thermidor was the consequence.

The Thermidorian Committee, 28 July 1794–4 November 1795. The elimination of the Robespierrists did not entail the end of the Revolutionary government, but its institutions were reorganized. Hatred of the dictatorship and fear captured the Convention, which divided governmental authority among the Committees of Public Safety, General Security, and Legislation, while it endowed the other twelve committees of the Convention with the power of execution. The Committee of Public Safety concerned itself only with the conduct of the war and diplomacy. The number of its employees was reduced, and the collegial character of its decisions was reinforced. Above all, the continual reappointment of its members, which had ensured continuity of operation in the Year II, ended; henceforth its personnel changed each month. In the course of the year, sixty-eight deputies passed through the committee, unknowns for the most part and moderates, while the last terrorists were eliminated; E.-J. Sieyès, F.-A. Boissy d'Anglas, and J.-J. Cambacérès dominated the group and even Carnot gave up his place on 15 Ventôse Year II. Furthermore, the task of the committee, which retained the right to requisition, was singularly complicated by the abolition of the maximum and the monetary inflation. The events of Germinal and growing anarchy precipitated the end of the Revolutionary government. Negotiations with Prussia, Spain, and Holland took place, and peace was signed at Basel and the Hague in May and July 1795. A new constitution, voted on 5 Fructidor Year III (22 August 1795), put the finishing touches on the paralysis of the committee, which disappeared 13 Brumaire Year IV (4 November 1795).

F.-A. Aulard, ed., *Recueil des Actes du Comité de salut public*, 28 vols. (Paris, 1889–1951); M. Bouloiseau, ed., *Tables et supplément* to previous source, 6 vols. (Paris, 1955-80); M. Bouloiseau, *Le Comité de salut public*, 3d ed. (Paris, 1980); E. Charvay, ed., *Correspondance générale de Carnot*, 4 vols. (Paris, 1892-1907); R. R. Palmer, *Twelve Who Ruled: The Year of the Terror in the French Revolution* (Princeton, N.J., 1941).

M. Bouloiseau

Related entries: AMALGAM, THE; BARERE; BILLAUD-VARENNE; CAMBON; CARNOT; COLLOT D'HERBOIS; COMMITTEE OF GENERAL DEFENSE; COMMITTEE OF GENERAL SECURITY; COUTHON; DANTON; DUMOURIEZ; HERAULT DE SECHELLES; LAW OF 14 FRIMAIRE; *LEVEE EN MASSE*; LINDET, R.-T.; 9 THERMIDOR YEAR II; PRIEUR DE LA COTE-D'OR; PRIEUR "DE LA MARNE"; ROBESPIERRE, M.; SAINT-ANDRE; SAINT-JUST; *SCRUTIN EPURATOIRE*; TERROR, THE; TREILHARD.

COMMITTEE OF THIRTY, a club that played a leadership role in articulating the aims of the patriot party or liberal movement for the Third Estate in the winter and spring of 1788–89. The Committee of Thirty was the most powerful of the liberal clubs that sprang up in the fall and winter of 1788–89. It was more commonly known at the time as the committee of Duport because its meetings were usually held at the Parisian home of A. Duport, a member of the Paris Parlement. The name by which the club is known today is due largely to the historian A. Chérest who derived it from a reference to the Committee of Thirty by the comte de La Marck. The membership, which required unanimous consent for admittance, consisted of a mixture of liberal nobles, such as the marquis de Lafayette, the marquis de Condorcet, and the comte de Mirabeau, clerics such as C.-M. Talleyrand and the abbé Sieyès, and magistrates and members of the legal profession like Duport, D. d'Eprémesnil, and G.-J.-B. Target. The meetings of the club were usually held on Sundays, Tuesdays, and Fridays from five to ten in the evening.

The major function of the Committee of Thirty was to serve as a pressure and propaganda organization for the aims of the patriot party, a loose coalition of liberal aristocrats and bourgeois. The committee wrote, financed, published, and distributed political pamphlets advocating the cause of the Third Estate. The most famous of these was *What Is The Third Estate?* by the abbé Sieyès. In addition, the club established liaisons with other societies, sent agents into the provinces, and maintained an active correspondence with local groups.

Encouraged by the club's agents and pamphlets, the Third Estate had their municipalities overwhelm the government with a flood of petitions on the composition and voting procedures of the forthcoming Estates General. The Committee of Thirty was pressing the government to adopt doubling, wherein the Third Estate at the Estates General would have as many deputies as the other two combined, and to sanction vote by head, or individual deputies, rather than by units so that the liberals rather than the conservative aristocracy could control that body. A partial victory was won when the government in its "Result of the Council" on 27 December 1788 granted doubling but said nothing on the key issue of voting procedures. On 5 December 1788, the Paris Parlement, in a vain attempt to regain its popularity, reversed its previous opposition to doubling.

Despite strains within the membership, especially over whether the *parlementaires* were exercising too conservative an influence, the committee held together and plunged into the elections to the Estates General, which were held in the spring of 1789. The electoral regulations of 24 January 1789 allowed each electoral assembly to draw up a *cahier de doléances* (list of grievances and goals). The club wrote, published, and disseminated model *cahiers* and supported various candidates.

A model *cahier* that the club circulated in Paris contained many of the features found in those of the Third Estate. In addition to a general statement that all power was derived from the people and an expression of loyalty to the monarchy, the *cahier* included proposals for periodic meetings of the Estates General in which there would be vote by head, for consent of the governed to all legislation including taxes, and for such basic rights as equality before the law, freedom of speech and the press, and freedom from arbitrary arrest. Although the committee apparently was disbanded after the elections, many of its members served as deputies in the National Assembly and played a significant role in the Revolution.

The scanty evidence precludes a precise statement about the influence and historical significance of the Committee of Thirty. Historians are in general agreement that it was the most active of the various clubs and did exercise a leadership role in the patriot party. The club articulated and disseminated the views of the liberal reformers, helped to stimulate public discussion of the issues, and provided model platforms for the elections to the Estates General. Thus the Committee of Thirty was both a product of and a catalyst for the times.

L. Gottschalk and M. Maddox, *Lafayette in the French Revolution: Through the October Days* (Chicago, 1969); C. A. McClelland, "The Lameths and Lafayette: The Politics of Moderation in the French Revolution, 1789-1791" (Ph.D. dissertation, University of California at Berkeley, 1942); G. Michon, *Essai sur l'histoire de parti feuillant, Adrien Duport* (Paris, 1924).

D. M. Epstein

Related entries: DU PORT; PATRIOT PARTY; *QU'EST-CE QUE C'EST LE TIERS ETAT?*; "RESULT OF THE COUNCIL"; SIEYES.

COMMITTEES OF SURVEILLANCE (1792-95), local Revolutionary organizations established under popular pressure for the supervision, arrest, and punishment of suspects that were gradually brought under the control of the central government. The process of institutionalization of the committees of Revolutionary surveillance followed a pattern; their origin, like that of all the major institutional creations of the democratic Revolution, is to be found in the nearly spontaneous movement of Revolutionary defense, when the primary means for waging the struggle were established, in the course of the summer of 1792. With the national and social crisis of the spring of 1793, the creation of structures that had not been organized to last but that seemed to be effective received new impetus. Thus, the committees of Revolutionary surveillance multiplied, and the law that generalized the experience confirmed their existence. Soon with the Jacobin consolidation of power, beginning in November 1793, the committees of surveillance became essential instruments of government and the machinery of Revolutionary centralization. Subsequently they would contribute in some way to the derevolution (F.-N. Babeuf's term) that followed Thermidor.

At the origin of the initiatives that resulted in the establishment of committees of surveillance was the defensive reaction of the popular leaders of the Revolution who were sensitive to the fear that spread among the masses in the face of the threats of military defeat and counterrevolution. In order to reduce this anxiety and to create the conditions for resistance and, later, for victory, the Revolutionary militants little by little succeeded in substituting practical initiatives capable of uniting around them the *sans-culottes* and the inhabitants of towns and villages in place of passiveness and the tendency to draw back. In establishing the committees, they were inspired by models of organization inherited from the first years of the Revolution when clubs and assemblies of citizens multiplied. By channeling this punitive will, as G. Lefebvre calls it, of the popular masses, these structures transformed popular, anarchical violence into legal and formalized political terror, a genuine instrument of power in the service of the Jacobin government.

In the midst of the war and invasion, the Law of 11 August 1792 confided the general security of the Republic to local and departmental administrations. This law, in fact, responded to a pressing demand from the masses, from Jacobin organizations, or from primary assemblies that grouped together the most politicized patriots regardless of wealth. From this arose the celebrated Committee of Surveillance of the Commune of Paris, which has been held responsible for the September 1792 Massacres, when in fact all it did was supervise and provide leadership for this great wave of bloody outbursts inspired by the fears of Parisians at the beginning of September 1792. However, under different forms this also took place at essentially the same time in Toulouse, Montauban, Caen and Rouen, Auxerre, and Châlon-sur-Saône. Subsequently these committees became less active with the victories of the autumn of 1792 and the election of the Convention; most disappeared or performed only residual activities. With the resumption of Revolutionary activity due to the king's trial, royalist propaganda, the economic crisis, and foreign problems, there was renewed talk of Revolutionary vigilance. At Rouen, for example, the royalist demonstration called the Rougemare on 11 and 12 January 1793 seemed to be the result of the weakness of the moderate municipal authorities. It was to combat this weakness that the Jacobins of the city imposed the establishment of a committee of surveillance in February. In Paris, starting in January 1793, the committee of the sections, meeting at the bishop's palace, planned the organization of surveillance committees for each section. The same vigilance, organized against nobles, refractory clergy, and foreigners, appeared in the Ardèche where counterrevolution seemed to threaten. J. Godechot has shown how a bureau of surveillance was created at Nancy on 3 March and how this decision served as a model. The initiative came from popular societies and municipal administrations; but in order not to be surpassed by mass Revolutionary pressures, as in August 1792, the departmental administrations took the lead as quickly as possible. For example, right after the city of Rouen established its committee, the department of the Seine-Inférieure created a departmental committee. In about thirty departments, committees of this sort, consisting of between six and twelve members, were set up as agencies of surveillance to control, and if necessary incarcerate, foreigners and persons known to be hostile to the democratic Republic. Defeats in Belgium and the insurrection in the Vendée added to fear of the aristocracy and at the same time to the demand for firm measures of coercion against internal enemies.

The Law of 21 March 1793 attempted to respond to this expectation; while legalizing existing practices, however, it wanted to restrict its execution to a single authority over all foreigners in France. Besides, in order to justify itself, the law used as a pretext the poor treatment suffered by the French in Spain. In fact, the law established a logic that ultimately led to general surveillance throughout the country. This anticipated the establishment of a committee of surveillance, consisting of twelve citizens elected by an electorate corresponding to 10 percent of the population, in every commune or, in the large cities, every section. Eventually, there should have been nearly 38,000 committees of surveillance. In fact, there was nothing like this. Many communes refrained from creating them, ignoring the law or deciding to take a great deal of time before submitting to its requirements. In the Seine-Inférieure there were only nine committees established by June 1793; there would be 290 the following year. In addition, to assemble a hundred electors out of a thousand eligible inhabitants seemed to be a gamble in such uncertain times, so popular societies or municipal or district administrators took on themselves the designation of members of the surveillance committees.

The instruments of political vigilance, so hastily installed and confided to an elite of lawyers or government officials, were incapable of surmounting the mass of perils. In the midst of being organized when the federalist movement erupted, most often they were paralyzed, bitterly divided, or inactive. Some even went over to the side of opponents, as at Nîmes and Bordeaux, or even to the side of the royalists, as at Lyon. The departmental committees, in the majority, sided with the anti-Parisian insurrection. In early June, the Convention contemplated suppressing the surveillance committees but finally resolved to destroy only those that had allied with the federalist insurrection or the enemy. This decision was the work of the Montagnard representatives on mission in the countryside who wanted to reinforce the committees of surveillance and regenerate, in a Revolutionary sense, those that had given in to weakness. As a result, the Law of Suspects of 17 September 1793, passed under pressure from the *sans-culottes*, did not hesitate to expand the powers of the surveillance committees and to regularize their role. They were charged with arresting suspects under the terms of the law, imprisoning other citizens provided the reasons were specified, delivering certificates of civicism, which were really internal passports, sealing any papers seized, and establishing lists of persons incarcerated to be transmitted to the Committee of General Security. The decree of 14 Frimaire Year II (4 December 1793) put the surveillance committees, like all other institutions of the Terror, under the control of national agents in each district and defined their function within the framework of a system of government that made the Committee of Public Safety the preeminent organ. In Paris, from September 1793, these committees, "freed from the tutelage of general assemblies and gradually escaping that of the Commune" (in the words of A. M. Soboul, 1962), had tended to control the entire life of the sections. After the decree of 14 Frimaire, the Revolutionary committees became part of the machinery of the government, directly subordinated to it. Furthermore, all the departmental committees were suppressed at the end of Frimaire Year II, except the Paris committee, which survived until the summer.

What types of men composed the committees of surveillance? At the beginning, lawyers, government officials, property owners living from their income, and merchants were dominant— for example, at Montauban, Nancy, and Le Havre. Later, with the summer and popular pressure, new committee members began to come from more modest backgrounds: artisans, old clothes dealers, shoemakers, wigmakers, and even journeymen and workers. In the sections of Paris, in contrast to the civil committees where bourgeois and the well-to-do, who could fulfill their mandate and at the same time survive by practicing their professions or by living off their income, were dominant (73.8 percent of the members), most of the Revolutionary committees had a very popular membership (63.8 percent were artisans or small shopkeepers, 9.9 percent were workers, and the rest were people of talent, actors, journalists, men generally without an inheritance). Because of this it was necessary to allot them a payment of 5 *livres* per day, the result of the Convention's decision of 18 Brumaire Year II. Thus, from militants these committee members became, little by little, functionaries under the orders of the Committee of Public Safety and transmitted their reports to the national agent and to the Committee of Public Safety, from whom came their directives.

The terrorist activity of the committees of surveillance, whose emblem generally consisted of an eye and compass or level, varied from one place to another in intensity and effectiveness. Each committee regulated its own organization and hours under the control of a representative on mission and later a national agent. Activity resulted, above all, from the initiative of the members of each committee. At Nantes, at the doorway to the insurgent Vendée, the bourgeois who composed the committee acted with extreme violence: 4,000 to 5,000 arrests, thousands drowned, shot, guillotined. It was the same or nearly the same at Lyon (renamed Ville Affranchie), Nîmes, Avignon, and elsewhere. However, at Nancy and Rouen, there were only a few hundred arrests and a few dozen suspects detained. In Paris, the effort was more persistent and methodical than violent. The truth is that in France the committees of surveillance took charge of between 300,000 and 800,000 suspects, according to different estimates— that is, between 1 percent and 4 percent of the population. Aside from some spectacular incidents, it appears that generally the Revolutionary committees acted with order and considerable probity, controlled the movement of persons and expression of opinions in a routine fashion by using checks and considerable circumspection, and supervised the application of economic regulations and of the laws. They often tried to implement the Ventôse decrees but were quite quickly paralyzed by the contradictions of the social policy of the Robespierrists. In the cities, where their control was better assured by government agents and patriotic opinion, the committees restricted abuses and the inevitable tendency to different kinds of peculation; but in the countryside, where committees fell into the hands of clans or families, they served to settle personal accounts, to cover up the designs of real swindlers, or rather to legalize a Revolutionary iconoclasm for which the churches paid the price.

The rapid dismantling of the Revolutionary government after 9 Thermidor was decisive for the committees of surveillance. The Law of 7 Fructidor (24 August 1794) abolished them in towns of fewer than 8,000 inhabitants unless they were district capitals. At Paris their number was reduced to one committee for each *arrondissement* of four sections, and their members were required to know how to read and write; these measures allowed the expulsion of the most humble *sans-culottes*. The Thermidorian Committee of General Security exercised over the committees a meddling and contradictory authority that paralyzed them. In the spring of the Year III, the committees in cities of fewer than 50,000 inhabitants were suppressed, and the remaining committees of surveillance were forbidden to use the term Revolutionary. The Constitution of Year III suppressed them entirely; by then they were merely groups of police keeping an eye on dealers in illegal goods, refractory clergy, and former "terrorists and drinkers of blood." Their political role as organs of the Revolution had been over for more than a year. In Year II, however, they had fulfilled the task expected of them.

M. Bouloiseau, *Le Comité de salut public du Havre-Marat* (Rouen, 1935); H. Calvet, *Un instrument de la Terreur à Paris, le Comité de surveillance du département de Paris* (Paris, 1941); J. Godechot, "Le Comité de surveillance révolutionnaire de Nancy (2 avril 1791-1er Germinal an III)" in *Regards sur l'époque révolutionnaire* (Toulouse, 1980); C. Mazauric, *Sur la Révolution française, contribution à l'histoire de la Révolution bourgeoise* (Paris, 1970); P. Rousset, "Les origines du Comité de surveillance de Montauban," *Ann. hist. de la Révo. française* 24 (1952); J. B. Sirich, *The Revolutionary Committees in the Departments of France* (Cambridge, Mass., 1943); A. Soboul, *Les sans-culottes parisiens en l'an II*, 2d ed. (Paris, 1962).

C. Mazauric

Related entries: COUNTERREVOLUTION; COMMITTEE OF GENERAL SECURITY; COMMITTEE OF PUBLIC SAFETY; FEDERALISM; LAW OF 14 FRIMAIRE; LAW OF SUSPECTS; SEPTEMBER 1792 MASSACRES; TERROR, THE; VENDEE; VENTOSE DECREES.

COMPAGNIE DES INDES (Company of the Indies), trading company. The Company of the Indies was the most important trading organization of eighteenth-century France. Its policies and activities were intertwined with royal finances and colonial ambitions. As a target of free trade advocates, the company was a source of frustration to provincial merchants and served to weaken loyalty to the absolute monarchy.

The company had its origins in the plans of J. Law to transform public finances under the regency. Along with his bank, the company was a foundation of the audacious Law system. In August 1717, Law received approval for his Company of the West, which had a monopoly on the trade with Louisiana. He soon combined this one with the languishing companies of Senegal, East India, Africa, Santo Domingo, and China. By 1720, the company had virtual control over French colonial trade. However, Law destined this undertaking to be far more than just a commercial venture. As part of his effort to establish the circulation of paper money, the Company of the Indies received the privilege of coinage in July 1719, and several months later, it replaced the farmers general as the tax collector of France.

Law soon lost control of his grandiose scheme to speculators. Shares in the company, with face values of 5,000 *livres*, sold for 15,000 *livres* in January 1720. Since the prospects of the company could not support such prices, a loss of confidence was inevitable. Law fled France in December, and the privileges of the company were suspended.

The company was reestablished in 1723 with commercial monopolies over India, Africa, the Barbary Coast, and Louisiana. It had some forty vessels and capital of 137 million *livres*. It embarked on organizing the settlement of several thousand colonists in Louisiana. One or two ships a year visited Canton. As many as thirty visited India before the Seven Years War. Although, in principle, the company had a monopoly over trade with Santo Domingo, the planters there successfully resisted this privilege and broke the will of the company to enforce it.

The ventures of the company in India took them well beyond commercial considerations. B. Dumas, who began his governorship of the company in India in 1735, was among the first Europeans to exploit the internal political situation. He befriended the nabob of Carnatic and participated in local disputes. His successor in 1740, J.-F. Dupleix, carried the policy further. He leased 2,000 French troops to native rulers and established an important clientele among them. The goal of Dupleix seems to have been to raise money from political revenues for use in commerce. The company directors in Paris were increasingly anxious about war with England and, wishing only commercial profits, recalled Dupleix to France in 1754.

Despite the military setbacks French colonies suffered in the Seven Years War, the trade of the company flourished after the peace. Confidence in the company, however, did not flourish. Provincial merchants outside its chief port, Lorient, had long been jealous of its monopolies. Public officials, influenced by physiocratic thought, soon joined the denunciations. As early as 1755, the intendant of commerce, V. de Gournay, produced a brochure arguing that the company was injurious to the state. As the fifty-year franchise of the company came to term in 1769, criticism became more forceful, and the crown permitted the privileges to expire.

The eagerly anticipated experiment with free trade during the 1770s was not fully satisfactory. Only about twenty-one vessels a year departed for the Indies. Many thought that French markets were not being adequately supplied. The minister of commerce, C.-G. Vergennes, worried about the lack of a strong French presence in India while British strength grew. Ultimately, Parisian banking interests, with the aid of C.-A. de Calonne, were able to procure the reestablishment of the company, with a monopoly over trade beyond the Cape of Good Hope, much to the chagrin of most merchants.

At the outbreak of the Revolution, the advocates of free trade were once again in control. The Constituent Assembly opened commerce to all in the spring of 1790. It did not, however, liquidate the India Company itself. The company took revenge on the Republic of Virtue in 1793 by sowing corruption. Certain prominent Jacobins enriched themselves by extorting from private businesses, the Indies Company included. When all stock companies were abolished in August 1793, P.-F. Fabre d'Eglantine used his position on the liquidation committee to gain a fortune for himself. To divert suspicion, he charged the Hébertists with participation in a foreign plot, and this resulted in the Committee of Public

Safety's turning on its most radical supporters. Fabre and others eventually lost their lives for the fortunes they made at the expense of the company.

W. Dagleish, *The Company of the Indies in the Days of Dupleix* (Easton, Pa., 1933); E. Levasseur, *Histoire de commerce de la France*, 2 vols. (Paris, 1911); A. Mathiez, *Un procès de corruption sous la Terreur: l'affaire de la Compagnie des Indes* (Paris, 1920); A. Morellet, *Mémoire sur la situation actuelle de la Compagnie des Indes* (Paris, 1769); F. Nussbaum, "The Formation of the New East India Company of Calonne,"*Am. Hist. Rev.* 37 (1933); H. Weber, *La Compagnie française des Indes* (Paris, 1904).

L. Berlanstein

Related entries: CALONNE; CHABOT; COMMITTEE OF PUBLIC SAFETY; FABRE D'EGLANTINE; FARMERS-GENERAL; HEBERTISTS.

COMPANIES OF JESUS, counterrevolutionary terrorist gangs that operated in the Lyon region in 1795. From February until July 1795, assassinations occurred almost daily; 120 died in one prison massacre. The bodies were often dumped in the Rhône or Saône rivers. After the Convention suspended the powers of the municipal administration and replaced the representatives on mission, order was restored, but rumors of the Companies of Jesus persisted, and there was a brief recrudescence of terrorism in 1797.

There is some debate among historians whether the companies were an actual organization or a name given by republicans to bands of toughs bent on personal vengeance. On the basis of archival police reports, G. Lewis holds that they were indeed organized and were partially directed and funded by agents of the British government and the royalist *émigrés*. While local grievances and personal vendettas certainly played a part, he concludes that the violence perpetrated by the Companies of Jesus in Lyon, by the Companies of the Sun in Provence, and by the roving bands recruited in the Gard by the long-time counterrevolutionary activist D. Allier were indeed, as ex-Jacobins contended at the time, politically inspired and coordinated by royalists.

J. Godechot, *The Counter-Revolution* (New York, 1971); G. Lewis, *The Second Vendée* (Oxford, 1978); M. Lyons, *France under the Directory* (New York, 1975).

C. Garrett

Related entries: COMPANIES OF THE SUN; COUNTERREVOLUTION; DIRECTORY; *EMIGRES*; LYON; THERMIDORIAN REACTION; WHITE TERROR.

COMPANIES OF THE SUN, counterrevolutionary terrorist gangs that operated throughout Provence, mainly in 1795. Several representatives on mission actually encouraged the wave of assassinations that led to several hundred deaths in the region by disarming and rounding up ex-Jacobins, encouraging the royalists' takeover of the National Guard, and looking aside when killings occurred. There were prison massacres in Toulon, Marseille, and Tarascon, and few if any communes were spared the violence. The Jacobins responded in kind, killing returning *émigrés* and briefly seizing control of Toulon. They were routed by an army consisting of Companies of the Sun and royalist National Guardsmen.

The pattern of violence persisted after 1795, in part because the directors (especially L. Carnot) were led by the Babeuf conspiracy to fear the Jacobins more than the royalists. While personal vengeance, thuggery, and economic distress after the terrible winter of 1794–95 all fostered the violence perpetrated by the Companies of the Sun, police reports indicate that their activities were in part orchestrated by British and royalist political agents.

J. Godechot, *The Counter-Revolution* (New York, 1971); G. Lewis, *The Second Vendée* (Oxford, 1978); M. Lyons, *France under the Directory* (New York, 1975).

C. Garrett

Related entries: BABEUF; COMPANIES OF JESUS; CONSPIRACY OF THE EQUALS: COUNTERREVOLUTION: DIRECTORY; *EMIGRES*; MARSEILLE; THERMIDORIAN REACTION; TOULON; WHITE TERROR.

COMPANY OF THE INDIES. See COMPAGNIE DES INDES.

COMPTE-RENDU (February 1781), the first published account of the royal finances of the French monarchy for a fiscal year. It was a customary practice for the finance ministers of the *ancien régime* to submit to the king each year a statement on his finances. These *comptes-rendus* varied considerably in the form of statement used and the data presented. Some finance ministers were more methodical about these reports than others. The abbé Terray, A.-R.-J. Turgot, J. Necker, and E.-C. de Loménie de Brienne made up the most systematic and complete reports. But the most famous *compte-rendu* of the *ancien régime* was that presented by J. Necker, director general of finances, to the king in January 1781 and published a month later. It was an astounding success with the book-buying public, which indicated a keen interest in the fiscal affairs of the royal government.

It has been said that finances was the Achilles heel of the French monarchy of the *ancien régime*. Eighteenth-century warfare and diplomacy required money on a scale that exceeded by far the annual taxing abilities of the governments. These wars became wars of credit, and the British government seemed to have dramatically unlocked this weapon. The importance of Necker in the reform era preceding the Revolution is that he sought to introduce British methods of public credit to France. Among these was the publicity given to the royal finances so that creditors would have exact knowledge of the government's income and obligations. Necker was unique among the finance ministers of the *ancien régime* in coming from a background of private banking rather than from the usual magistrate class. Therefore he understood the problems of public credit from the viewpoint of the lender. The purpose of the publication of the *compte-rendu* in 1781 was not only to reveal the revenue and expenditures of the government but to explain to the king, the ministers, and the public the reforms in fiscal policy that were necessary in order to raise these enormous sums.

There has been much misunderstanding about this first published account of the royal finances. It was limited to the regular or "ordinary" revenue and expenditure for the year and did not include money raised by loans or expenditures that were deemed "extraordinary," of which war expenditures were the greatest proportion. Necker's *compte-rendu* of 1781 showed a surplus of 10 million *livres* of ordinary revenue over ordinary expenditures, enough to finance the loans necessary for the campaign of 1781. He included as ordinary expenditures the interest charges on all loans and, with some exceptions, the amortization costs of the public debt. If the ordinary accounts were balanced, Necker believed that the credit posture of the government was sound. If the ordinary expenditures should exceed the ordinary revenue, then it was necessary to balance the expenditures by raising revenue through taxes or reducing expenditures by economy. Necker preferred the second method rather than raising taxes since he thought the existing tax system was too inequitable to permit surtaxes on it.

The *compte-rendu* of 1781 was violently attacked by Necker's enemies, among whom was C.-A. de Calonne, comptroller-general from 1783 to 1787. To explain the enormous deficit between ordinary revenue and expenditure in 1787, Calonne alleged before the Assembly of Notables that the *compte-rendu* of 1781 was inaccurate by as much as 70 million *livres* when compared to documents he called *comptes effectifs*. But he declined to present these documents to the Assembly of Notables when asked to do so. In his refutation of Calonne, Necker pointed out that the *compte effectif* was simply the money received by a department in the calendar year and had nothing to do with what was allocated to a fiscal year. Thus, the *compte effectif* indicated only 29 million *livres* were received during the calendar year 1781 from the department of the royal domain and forests. But according to contract with the financiers, 42 million would be collected eventually for the fiscal year 1781. Necker insisted that there was nothing speculative or contingent about the ordinary revenue and expenditures and that an accurate knowledge of them was the starting point of any fiscal policy.

C.-A. de Calonne, *Réponse de M. de Calonne à l'écrit de M. Necker, publié en avril 1787* (London, 1788); J. Necker, *Compte rendu au Roi*, vol. 2 of *Oeuvres complètes* (Paris, 1820-21); R. D. Harris, *Necker, Reform Statesman of the Ancien Régime* (Berkeley, 1979).

R. D. Harris

Related entries: ASSEMBLY OF NOTABLES; CALONNE; NECKER.

COMTAT VENAISSIN. See AVIGNON.

CONCIERGERIE. See PRISONS.

CONDE, LOUIS-JOSEPH DE BOURBON, PRINCE DE (1736-1818), cousin of the king, Old Regime general and royal governor, central figure in the counterrevolution. The Condé branch of the Bourbon family dated from an uncle of

Henri IV. One of its members was Louis II, known as "le Grand Condé" (1621–86), soldier, courtier, and sometime rebel of the reigns of Louis XIII and Louis XIV. In the early eighteenth century, a descendant, the duc de Bourbon (1692–1740), presided over the regent's council and served briefly as Louis XV's principal minister. His son, L.-J. de Bourbon, prince de Condé, inherited his father's considerable wealth, which included the beautiful estate of Chantilly, and various offices, among them that of grand master of the king's household.

At eighteen he was appointed governor of Burgundy, a post he held until the Revolution. As lieutenant general, Condé served with distinction in the Seven Years War. In the quarrels between the crown's officials and the parlements, he supported the crown but opposed the Maupeou court reform of 1771 and was briefly exiled to Chantilly. When the tension between the crown and the aristocracy reached new heights between 1787 and 1789, Condé presided over the fourth bureau of the first Assembly of Notables and with his grandson, the duc d'Enghien, over the fourth bureau of the second Assembly of Notables; in this role he collaborated with the majority, which acknowledged the need for reforms while refusing to endorse the government's methods. At the close of the second Assembly of Notables, Condé helped compose the *Mémoire des princes*, which defended the rights of the first two orders as part of France's historic constitution and linked those prerogatives to property rights in general; the clergy and nobles would give up their pecuniary privileges out of consideration for the citizens of the Third Estate, but the latter must limit themselves to tax reforms or face resistance.

Condé and his son and grandson emigrated soon after 14 July 1789. Always associated with the highest *émigré* councils, Condé stayed for a time at Turin with Louis XVI's youngest brother, the comte d'Artois, and later established himself as head of a small *émigré* army in the Rhineland. Artois and his older brother, the comte de Provence, the future Louis XVIII, lived nearby at Coblentz, where they presided over an *émigré* court and collected an army of their own. Both the Condé army and the army of the princes were supported by Austria and other European powers. Both, as symbols of counterrevolution, aroused fears and tensions within France. Condé's proclamations helped to provoke Revolutionary legislation against *émigrés* and nonjuring priests; eventually he himself was outlawed and his properties were sequestered.

Like Artois and Provence, Condé was consistent in his support of pure royalism, which disdained compromises such as those hoped for by the Anglophile *monarchiens* and by the *constitutionnels* identified with the Constitution of 1791. With the succeeding phases of the Revolution, pure royalism gained strength even among many former moderates who were driven into emigration. This tendency was paralleled by a movement in the opposite direction, toward constitutional monarchy or moderate republicanism, but while it is impossible to quantify such shifts, it is clear that compromise proposals fared better in the interior than in leading *émigré* circles. Initially the militancy of the *émigrés* was a threat to the projects and safety of Louis XVI and Marie Antoinette. This militancy continued to dash the hopes of the moderate royalists, as on the occasion of J. Mallet du Pan's mission in 1792 and the subsequent Brunswick Manifesto. After Thermidor, divisions between pure royalists and moderates handicapped attempts to forestall and later to alter the Directory — for example, on the occasions of 13 Vendémiaire (5 October 1795) and 18 Fructidor (4 September 1797). Moreover, Condé and the princes never enjoyed the full support of the Austrian and Prussian courts, where dynastic and territorial aims were more important than aid to the French royal family and aristocracy.

After the failure of the 1792 campaign, the army of the princes disintegrated for lack of financial and political support. Condé's army saw little action, but he was able to keep it in being; he, his son, and his grandson entered Alsace with the Austrians in the campaign of 1793. Condé came to suspect the Viennese court of designs on Alsace, and by 1795 he was relying mainly on the English, with whose aid there was to be a grand combined operation: an Anglo-French invasion of Brittany, local uprisings there and in the Vendée, another invasion from across the Rhine by Condé's army, the defection of the republican General J.-C. Pichegru and his army to the royalist cause, and a triumphant entry into Paris. The Quiberon disaster in July 1795 and the Vendémiaire failure in Paris three months later were among the disappointments that eroded this project. Supported by funds from the British agent W. Wickham, Condé continued lengthy negotiations with Pichegru, who in 1797 was elected to the Council of Five Hundred and became its president. Royalists in that year were looking toward an overthrow of the Directory from within France; some hoped for peaceful change within the provisions of the 1795 constitution, while others envisaged additional help from Condé's army and Pichegru's influence with the military. But with the Directory's Fructidor coup against the legislature, the weaknesses of the counterrevolution were again apparent. Louis XVIII's public refusal, of which Condé approved, to offer any concessions that might weaken absolutism or the privileges of the aristocracy was matched by the confusion and indecisiveness of the moderate legislative majority. Moreover, although the British supported French royalist efforts, there was no concerted plan by the great powers. Austria, battered by Napoleon, was about to make peace with France (Campoformio, 17 October 1797).

Italy and central Europe were becoming territories in which Louis XVIII and Condé were unwelcome. In 1798 both were forced to take refuge in the Russia of Czar Paul I, who provided Louis XVIII with a residence and a pension in Courland (present-day Latvian SSR) and supported Condé's army in the Ukraine while their leader visited St. Petersburg. In 1799 Condé and his troops returned to Central Europe to take part in the War of the Second Coalition. This last stand having failed, Condé's army was disbanded.

Condé in 1801 went to England, where in 1807 Louis XVIII also settled. At the Restoration, Condé returned to France, shared the king's displacement during the Hundred Days, and resumed the office of grand master of the king's household. His grandson, the duc d'Enghien, had been lost to him in 1804 when

Napoleon had had him seized at his residence in Baden and taken to the fortress-prison of Vincennes, to the east of Paris, where he was charged with treason and executed. With Condé's own death in 1818, his son, Louis-Henri-Joseph, d'Enghien's father, became the last living prince of the Condé line. In August 1830, he was found hanged in his château at Saint-Leu. The cause remained a mystery.

J. Egret, *La Pré-révolution française (1787–1788)* (Paris, 1962); W. R. Fryer, *Republic or Restoration in France? 1794–7: The Politics of French Royalism, with Particular Reference to the Activities of A.-B.-J. d'André* (Manchester, 1965); J. Godechot, *La Contre-révolution, doctrine et action, 1789–1804* (Paris, 1961); *La Grande encyclopédie*, vol. 6 (Paris, 1973); A. Martin, "Condé (Louis-Joseph)," *Dictionnaire de biographie française sous la direction de Roman d'Amat*, vol. 9 (Paris, 1961); H. Mitchell, *The Underground War against Revolutionary France: The Missions of William Wickham, 1794-1800* (Oxford, 1965).

P. H. Beik

Related entries: ARTOIS, ASSEMBLY OF NOTABLES; BRUNSWICK MANIFESTO; COBLENTZ; COUNTERREVOLUTION; COUP OF 18 FRUCTIDOR YEAR V; *EMIGRES*; *MONARCHIENS*; PICHEGRU; PROVENCE; QUIBERON; SECOND COALITION; 13 VENDEMIARE YEAR IV; TREATY OF CAMPOFORMIO.

CONDORCET, MARIE-JEAN-ANTOINE-NICOLAS CARITAT, MARQUIS DE

(1743-94), academician, *philosophe*, Revolutionary. The most influential among the generation of the *philosophes* who lived to confront the French Revolution and one of the most encyclopedic thinkers of the entire Enlightenment, Condorcet was born in Ribemont, Picardy, on 17 September 1743. His father, a military officer who died shortly after, came from an old noble family established in the Dauphiné since the sixteenth century; his mother was the daughter of a *président trésorier de France* in the generality of Soissons. Educated by the Jesuits at Reims, he went on to receive an unusually advanced scientific education at the collège of Navarre in Paris. His early scientific papers, devoted to mathematical problems important for the development of Newtonian physics, established his reputation as a mathematician and earned the respect of J. d'Alembert, who became his patron, mentor, and close friend. Admitted to the Academy of Sciences in 1769, he was encouraged by d'Alembert to publish a volume of academic *éloges* in 1772 in order to demonstrate his suitability to become secretary of that body. Partly on that basis but principally as a result of d'Alembert's intrigues, he was named assistant secretary of the academy in 1773 and became its permanent secretary in 1776. From that date until the academy's suppression in 1793, he served as the principal spokesman for organized science in France. His experience in this capacity strengthened his belief in the constant progress of scientific knowledge and in its power to transform social life, a view well stated in the reception speech he gave on his admission to the French Academy in 1782.

Introduced by d'Alembert into the salon of J. de Lespinasse, where he met many of the *philosophes* and the members of the Parisian elite who favored their enlightened ideas, Condorcet embraced the cause of enlightenment with passionate conviction. Accompanying d'Alembert on a visit to F.-M. Voltaire at Ferney in 1770, he entered into close correspondence with the sage of the *philosophe* movement, whose biographer and editor he later became. His anonymous *Lettres d'un théologien à l'auteur des trois siècles* (1774) was a bitterly subversive defense of the principles of enlightenment and reform. It was to be followed in the next fifteen years by many other pamphlets devoted to the cause of enlightened humanitarianism, including such issues as the reform of criminal justice, the institution of civil rights for Protestants, and the abolition of slavery.

Condorcet's intellectual interests and convictions were also profoundly influenced by his friendship with A.-R.-J. Turgot, the former intendant of the Limousin who became controller general shortly after the accession of Louis XVI. Embracing Turgot's vision of a social order transformed by the mobilization of scientific knowledge and the determined exercise of monarchical authority in accordance with rational principles (a philosophy that found one of its clearest expositions in his *Vie de M. Turgot* in 1786), Condorcet gave his passionate support to the controller general during the two years of his reforming ministry. Organizing the application of scientific expertise to technical problems (such as weights and measures and canal building), he also pressed for a wide range of social reforms (such as abolition of the *corvées* and suppression of seigneurial dues). In defense of Turgot's reintroduction of free trade in grain (which prompted widespread grain riots in 1775), he published a series of scathing polemics elaborating the principles of laissez-faire economics in broadly physiocratic terms.

Turgot's fall from power left his younger friend angry and frustrated. Returning to his mathematical interests, he seized on a new field: the calculus of probabilities, to which he devoted important articles in the *Encyclopédie méthodique* and the volumes of the Academy of Sciences. His most substantial philosophical work, the *Essai sur l'application de l'analyse à la probabilité des décisions rendues à la pluralité des voix* (1785), sought to apply the calculus of probabilities to the theory of representation and decision making. It constitutes the clearest expression of his probabilistic philosophy and of his conviction that the application of this calculus to social affairs could rationalize social action and extend individual choice.

Thus on the eve of the French Revolution, Condorcet was one of the most powerful and influential intellectual figures of the Old Regime. With his marriage in 1786 to S. de Grouchy, a brilliant young woman who shared his liberal views and strengthened his feminist convictions, the Condorcet salon became the gathering place for many of the most liberal representatives of the Parisian elite. Condorcet followed closely the constitutional debate in the infant American republic, and his writings on these questions played an important part in bringing their significance before the French public. He also gave strong support to the reforms proposed in France by controller general C.-A. de Calonne and by his successor, E.-C. Loménie de Brienne, particularly to their proposals for the institution of provincial assemblies. Regarding the creation of such provincial assemblies and their gradual evolution toward a national assembly as infinitely preferable to the immediate calling of the antiquated and unrepresentative Estates General, he repudiated the demand for this body in 1788 as the turbulently reactionary clamor of the privileged classes in defense of their interests. As part of this campaign, he developed a comprehensive program for detailed consti- tutional change in his *Essai sur la constitution et les fonctions des assemblées provinciales*, published at the end of 1788.

By the time this work appeared, however, Loménie de Brienne had been forced from office and the convocation of the Estates General announced. Fearful of the consequences of an ill-prepared assembly, Condorcet played an active part in the Society of Thirty, which circulated model *cahiers* and worked for the election of liberal deputies. He participated in the electoral assembly of the nobility of Mantes (where he was the principal author of a very liberal *cahier*) and of Paris, but in neither was he elected to represent his fellow nobles at the Estates General. Not until after the fall of the Bastille had triggered the collapse of city government in the capital did he win elective office, as a member of the new Paris municipal assembly. He played a conspicuous part in the efforts of that assembly to maintain order in the troubled period after the October Days, and he was one of the principal founders of the Society of 1789, the club inaugurated early in 1790 to mobilize the influence of the moderate Parisian elite on behalf of stability, order, and the peaceful consolidation of the achievements of 1789.

Condorcet broke with his closest associates within this moderate group (the marquis de Lafayette, L.-A. La Rochefoucauld-d'Enville, F.-A. La Rochefou- cauld-Liancourt, P.-S. Dupont de Nemours) in June 1791 over the issue of the king's flight to Varennes and the subsequent "massacre" at the Champ de Mars (17 July 1791). Engaging with new allies, J.-P. Brissot and T. Paine, he de- manded the abolition of the monarchy and the institution of a republican con- stitution. Elected as one of the Parisian representatives to the Legislative Assembly, he joined with the Brissotins in campaigning against the irresponsible exercise of the royal veto and the policies of untrustworthy ministers and in pressing for war against Austria. Ironically, the declaration of war on 20 April 1792 inter- rupted the presentation of the report drafted by Condorcet on behalf of the assembly's Committee on Public Instruction. Never adopted in the form he proposed, this plan for public instruction shaped the Revolutionary debates on education in powerful ways and found substantial expression in the educational system eventually adopted in 1795. It combined a broad system of elementary instruction, as the condition of true equality among citizens, with a hierarchical system of advanced instruction to maximize the sum of knowledge and ability available to society as a whole.

In the weeks following the popular demonstration of 20 June 1792, Condorcet played a leading part in the politics of the Legislative Assembly. With the

Brissotins, he tried to use the growing threat of popular disorder to force the king to submit to the will of the assembly and force the assembly to curtail the king's power. When that policy failed, he found himself a reluctant witness to the revolution of 10 August 1792, which overthrew the monarchy by direct popular insurrection. Recognizing this insurrection and the Paris Commune that it created as a serious threat to the principles of representative government, Condorcet spent the last weeks of the Legislative Assembly in fruitless efforts to shore up its authority.

He was elected now to the Convention, this time representing the Aisne. When the king was brought to trial, Condorcet voted to find him guilty but against punishment by death. On 15 February 1793, he presented his constitutional plan to the Convention on behalf of its constitutional committee. Complicated in its arguments and provisions, this plan was conceived as a scientific solution to the problem Condorcet regarded as central to Revolutionary politics: that of making representative government rational and responsible to the people while preventing a minority from usurping the power to act in the name of all. Supported by Brissot and his associates, the plan fell hostage to the struggles between the Girondins and the Jacobins to control the assembly. Their power secured through the expulsion of the leading Girondins from the Convention by popular insurrection on 2 June 1793, the Jacobins plundered Condorcet's plan to produce their own constitution, which was quickly approved. To these events, Condorcet replied with pamphlets protesting the expulsion of the Girondins and ridiculing the adoption of the Jacobin constitution. Denounced for this latter action on 8 July 1793, he disappeared before he could be arrested.

Hiding in Paris near the Luxembourg Gardens, Condorcet found consolation for his political failures in a project he had long contemplated, a comprehensive historical demonstration of the nature and course of human progress. The hasty introduction to that unfinished study, published posthumously as *Esquisse d'un tableau historique des progrès de l'esprit humain* (1795), immediately became his most influential work, regarded by friends and critics alike as the philosophical testament of the eighteenth century. Abandoning his hiding place toward the end of March 1794, Condorcet sought refuge on the outskirts of Paris, where he was arrested and imprisoned at Bourg-Egalité (Bourg-la-Reine). He died after two days' captivity on 29 March 1794.

K. M. Baker, *Condorcet. From Natural Philosophy to Social Mathematics* (Chicago, 1975); K. M. Baker, ed., *Condorcet: Selected Writings* (Indianapolis, 1976); L. Cahen, *Condorcet et la Révolution française* (Paris, 1904); M.-J.-A.-N.C. Condorcet, *Sketch for a Historical Picture of the Progress of the Human Mind*, intro. S. Hampshire (London, 1955); A. Condorcet-O'Connor and F. Arago, eds., *Oeuvres de Condorcet*, 12 vols. (Paris, 1847–49); O. H. Prior, ed., *Condorcet, Esquisse d'un tableau historique* (Paris, 1933 [1970]); R. Reichardt, *Reform und Revolution bei Condorcet* (Bonn, 1973).

K. Baker

Related entries: BASTILLE; CALONNE; CHAMP DE MARS "MASSACRE"; COMMITTEE OF THIRTY; CONSTITUTION OF 1793; EDUCATION; ENLIGHTENMENT; LAFAYETTE; LOMENIE DE BRIENNE; OCTOBER DAYS; SCIENCE; SOCIETY OF 1789; 10 AUGUST 1792.

CONSPIRACY OF EQUALS (1796-97), a radical plot to overthrow the Directory. This affair has been called the last episode of the French Revolution. It has been seen as a tentative step toward a socialist state and has been interpreted as an extreme reaction by traditional classes against an advancing capitalism. In either view, the conspiracy itself is very much a chapter of the French Revolution and can be explained only through the experiences of that Revolution. Within those experiences there are two major ingredients: the conspirators who had worked their way through the Revolution on the cutting edge of a social democratic front and the cruel conditions and narrowing political alternatives of Thermidorian France.

There are a variety of dates scattered along the route of the conspiracy as its participants came together, singly and in groups, in the political clubs of Paris and in the political communities of the prisons following the mass arrests of the Germinal and Prairial riots in the spring of 1795. The final associations of the conspirators were made in Le Plessis prison in the fall of 1795; the direct steps toward their conspiracy came in the initial months of the Directory after these prisoners were released by the general amnesty of 26 October. That winter France experienced its worst privations of the Revolution, for which the Thermidorians had no workable solutions. Economic controls had been abandoned, the paper currency had collapsed, and commerce stagnated. Popular resistance to such conditions, which had abounded in France the previous year, had been largely stifled. For the first time in the Revolution, the Paris police recorded cases of starvation.

It is not surprising that voices surfaced demanding extreme remedies to extreme conditions. It was G. Babeuf in his *Tribun du peuple*, the newspaper that he revived in November after his release from prison, who offered the most uncompromising attack on the Thermidorians and the boldest alternative to the existing conditions. In the pages of his newspaper and in additional public correspondence, Babeuf spelled out the communist convictions most of the conspirators had shared in Le Plessis. The exact details of the proposed communist state and society were never completed; these details and their historical and intellectual sources are still debated. At the center of this communist society was an absolute equality of goods and labor. This equality, *le bonheur commun*, necessitated the disestablishment of all private property and the creation of an administrative system to direct the activities of production and distribution for the entire society. It was Babeuf's voice more than any other that tried to get the message to a *sans-culotte* force that had once more to be aroused to action.

His associates in the winter months of 1795–96 directly participated in a variety of unsuccessful efforts to reorganize a coherent popular political force. In particular the Club panthéon provided a forum for these radical voices. This club began in November as a society of moderate democrats loyal to the Directory, but its membership took a turn to the left after the appearance on 30 November of the thirty-fifth issue of the *Tribun du peuple*, which carried the *Manifeste des plébéiens*. The *Manifeste* was not a careful, coherent, precise testament for the new society; it was a vigorous and animated presentation of the egalitarian ideals of the proposed society, alongside the failures of the bourgeois capitalism at work in the Revolutionary settlement of 1795. It rallied sympathetic but somewhat disparate radical forces who came to dominate the Club Panthéon; however, when the size and radical character of the club appeared a threat later in February 1796, the government shut it down.

This initiative by the Directory, which took away an important public forum, forced the democratic opposition in early 1796 to accept the defeat of their political hopes or to organize a revolt. A number who had been meeting at the home of J.-B.-A. Amar, a former member of the Committee of General Security, accepted the necessity of revolt. However, these talks came to nothing as the gap between the ex-Montagnards and the Equals could not be bridged. In late March, Babeuf finally entered directly into the conspiratorial ranks. Along with S. Maréchal, P.-A. Antonelle, and F. Le Pelletier, he formed an Insurrectionary Committee, which was soon joined by A.-A. Darthé, C. Germain, P. Buonarroti, and F.-A. Debon. By 8 April the central leadership of the conspiracy was completed.

The Revolutionary ideology of the conspiracy has been the subject of considerable controversy. The ultimate purpose of the planned insurrection was the communist society espoused by Babeuf in his *Tribun*, whose principles had largely been accepted in Le Plessis. The exact nature of that society, the essential meaning of *le bonheur commun*, probably varied somewhat from conspirator to conspirator. From early April to their arrest in mid-May, the basic principles and justifications for the society were posted and printed in numerous handbills, posters, and newspapers. Still, at the time of their arrest the details of this society existed in very unfinished form. When Babeuf and Buonarroti were captured at their central headquarters on 10 May, the police took possession of their papers, including a great variety of drafts and outlines of projected decrees, which played a part in the later trial. We can most coherently approach the structure of that projected society in Buonarroti's history of the conspiracy and the accompanying evidence published with it. Considering the experience and the perceptions of the formulators of these rough drafts, it is understandable that the administrative emphasis is on the distribution of commodities rather than on their production and on the public title of property rather than on any ambitious collective organization of the means of production. As in Babeuf's public writings, the organizing social purpose is an absolute equality of goods and labor. But it is less the details of the projected society than the necessary details of the conspiracy and insurrection that have won an important historical place for the Equals.

Tied fatally to a reawakening of the popular forces in Paris, the insurrection never had a real chance of success. Babeuf recognized the passiveness of those forces. In fact, it is that awareness which pushed him to the necessary revolutionary strategy of a popular dictatorship in the initial transfer of power. It is ironic that it is in this popular dictatorship that a number of historians have found the greatest originality of the Equals and the chief legacy of the conspiracy to later generations of social democratic conspirators. For the ardently democratic

Babeuf, it was an unpleasant concession to the conditions of 1796 and to the special logic that each revolution created for itself, but a concession that was to last only a few months. Tactically, for the insurrection itself, the Insurrectionary Committee had begun to build through its agents, assigned to each of the twelve Paris arrondissements and the several military camps in and around Paris, a secret network that would propagandize, recruit, and prepare to direct the uprising. Revived in Buonarroti's history a generation later, it became the conspiratorial model for nineteenth-century Europe.

In fact, neither the tactics nor the strategy had much potential in 1796. There did exist an audience for Babeuf's egalitarian preachments, but it was not available to the conspiracy as an insurrectionary force. If anything, the real life of the conspiracy began on 10 May when its leaders and its archives were swept up by the police after being betrayed by a double agent, a Captain Grisel. The Directory elected to make their trial a great public trial of high treason before a high court set up in the former abbey of the small provincial town of Vendôme. The state took ten months to prepare its case, but in the end it bungled its execution. In a trial that dragged on for three months, the prosecution lost the initiative, and the state found itself on trial. Greatly hampered by their wish to protect the less compromised of the defendants, the conspirators ultimately tried to deny the existence of the conspiracy but at the same time justify the legitimacy of one. Their success is seen in the failure of the state to prove a conspiracy and the acquittal of fifty-six of the accused. It is, as well, witnessed by the martyrdom of the seven who were accused and convicted not of conspiracy but of the public demand for the return to the Constitution of 1793. Five of them were deported; Babeuf and the silent, intransigent Darthé were executed.

Their execution was carried out on 27 May 1797 after Babeuf's final defense, which had lasted four days, in which he offered his last public testament to his communist society. In death and martyrdom, he left behind a legacy of social democracy and revolutionary planning that Buonarroti revived in 1828. It became an essential beginning, partly myth, partly fact, of a socialist heritage in the nineteenth century. In Babeuf and in the Conspiracy of Equals, which bears his name, historians have found the first purposeful political attempt to achieve a social organization of absolute equality inspired by a materialistic philosophy framed within a historical perception of a profound class warfare.

V. Advielle, *Histoire de Gracchus Babeuf et du Babouvisme, d'après des nombreux documents inédits*, 2 vols. (Paris, 1884); P. Buonarroti, *Conjuration pour l'Egalité dite de Babeuf* (Paris, 1957); M. Dommanget, *Sur Babeuf et la conjuration des égaux* (Paris, 1970); C. Mazauric, *Babeuf et la Conspiration pour l'égalité* (Paris, 1962); R. B. Rose, *Gracchus Babeuf, the First Revolutionary Communist* (Stanford, Calif., 1978); D. Thomson, *The Babeuf Plot: the Making of a Republican Legend* (London, 1947); K. D. Tønnesson, *Le défaite des sans-culottes. Mouvement populaire et réaction bourgeois en l'an III* (Paris, 1959).

J. R. Harkins

Related entries: AMAR; BABEUF; BUONARROTI; DIRECTORY; MARECHAL; THERMIDORIAN REACTION.

"CONSPIRATION DE BATZ." See BATZ.

CONSTITUENT ASSEMBLY. See NATIONAL CONSTITUENT ASSEMBLY.

CONSTITUTION OF 1791, the first written constitution in France and one of the earliest in the world. Drawn up by the National Assembly between 6 July 1789 and 3 September 1791 and accepted by Louis XVI on 13 September 1791, this constitution was overthrown by the insurrection of 10 August 1792. It defined the citizenry and its rights, organized the different branches of government, and imposed general limits on certain kinds of governmental action.

The constitution begins with the Declaration of the Rights of Man and of the Citizen, followed by title I, which restates some fundamental provisions drawn from that declaration, from the decree of 4 August 1789, and from decrees relative to church land and to election of parish and episcopal clergy. Title II describes how citizenship is acquired and lost, stating incidentally that the law considers marriage only as a civil contract; and it specifies the territorial sub-divisions of the kingdom: departments, districts, cantons, and communes. The last parts of the document limit particular types of activity carried on by the government. Title IV regulates the armed forces; title V, taxes; title VI, relations with foreign governments. Title VII ostensibly provides for constitutional amend-ment but actually renders it impossibly slow and difficult, since it would extend over at least four years and two months, punctuated by three nationwide elections, and it could not begin until March 1797.

The central part of the constitution, title III, is much the longest, having 171 articles. Its chapters are: 1. The National Legislative Assembly; 2. The Royalty, the Regency, and the Ministers; 3. The Exercise of the Legislative Power; 4. The Exercise of the Executive Power; 5. The Judicial Power.

As a whole, it elaborately fulfills the requirement that the separation of powers must be defined in order for a constitution to exist (Declaration of Rights, article 16). The legislative power is delegated to the Legislative Assembly, a continuing body that the king cannot dissolve. All of its 745 seats are in one chamber and are to be filled every two years by indirect elections. First, all registered voters, who are called active citizens, meet in local primary assemblies and choose 1 percent of their number as electors, then these meet and elect the representatives. The executive power is delegated to the king, and the position of king is delegated hereditarily to Louis XVI and his line of descent from male to male in order of primogeniture. The legislature and the king are interdependent, their relations finely balanced. The king can neither adopt nor propose a decree but (with a few important exceptions) can block it with a veto, which can be overridden, but only by a subsequent legislature. The king's person is "inviolable and sacred," but his orders must be countersigned by a minister who is justiciable for any "offense against the national security or the constitution." The legislature can neither select nor remove a minister but can vote an indictment against a minister, which the king cannot veto. The annual sum for the king's salary and expenses, called the civil list, is to be fixed by the legislature at the beginning of each reign. (It was set at 25 million *livres* plus domanial revenues amounting to about 1.09 million *livres* on 9 June 1790.) War can be declared only after the king's formal proposal and the legislature's decree sanctioned, in turn, by him. The first words in a declaration of war were required to be: "From the king of the French, in the name of the Nation. ..." The legislature and the king were each to exercise a distinct authority over public administration within the kingdom as well. The administrators of departments and districts were elected not as representatives but as agents acting under the king's oversight and subject to his annulment of acts contrary to law or to his orders, while the legislature alone would make the rules and define the modes of administrative action.

The legislative and the executive branches are expected to act on each other and sometimes to act jointly. In contrast, the constitution separates administrative action and judicial action in order to subject each to fixed rules. Judicial authority can be exercised only by elected judges. Judges cannot order or prohibit any administrative action and cannot summon any administrator to appear before them; to do so would infringe on the executive branch. They can neither make laws nor suspend the execution of laws. They are expected to decide each case in accordance with preexisting law and, where the law is silent or obscure, the legislature is to make good the deficiency. In such a perspective, there could be neither authority nor occasion for a court to rule on the constitutionality of an administrative or legislative act. In reality the government consists of two principal branches: the legislative and the executive, and a lesser branch, the judicial.

The constitution describes citizens' rights not only in the Declaration of Rights and Title I but in other articles as well. Titles II and III, chapter 1, give the right to elect municipal officials and legislative representatives. Title III, chapter 5, sets forth important rights of defendants. On the other hand, the same chapter limits freedom of the press by allowing prosecution of those who have published writings that "deliberately provoked readers to disobey the law, revile the constituted authorities or resist their acts."

All of the provisions in the constitution are not in logical order, partly because the text was not drafted continuously from title I through title VII. It resulted from an intricate process of enactment, selection, revision, and rearrangement. The National Assembly's committee on the constitution took the main responsibility throughout, but its methods evolved and twice its membership was modified. During the summer of 1789, under J.-J. Mounier's leadership, the committee proposed a small number of basic constitutional principles for adoption. The idea was to begin building by placing the cornerstones. (Some of these are visible in the final text—for instance, title III, chapter 2, section 1, articles 1–3.) On 10 and 11 September 1789, the National Assembly voted that the new legislature would not have two houses, only one, and that the royal veto could be overridden. Four of the eight members, including Mounier, resigned from the committee; of the new members, J.-G. Thouret and J.-N. Démeunier played important roles.

The committee began to propose one comprehensive law after another to create or reshape an institution: municipalities (adoption completed 14 December 1789), territorial subdivisions of the kingdom (16 February 1790), the clergy (12 July 1790), the judiciary (16 August 1790), the legislature (13 June 1791), and others. From each completed law, the committee selected a few articles deemed fundamental and permanent to be incorporated in the constitution. To make these selections, the committee was enlarged on 23 September 1790 to fifteen members. Many constitutional articles had been accumulated in this way when, on 20 June 1791, Louis XVI departed from Paris, leaving behind a declaration written in his own hand and addressed to all French people; it denounced as unworkable the plan of government wrought by the National Assembly, the essential objection being that the king was deprived of too much power. The royal family was stopped and brought back. At the suggestion of Thouret and others, the National Assembly decided to suspend the king, complete the constitution, and obtain his acceptance and oath to maintain it; new articles were added specifying the actions that would be taken as equivalent to abdication (title III, chapter 2, section 1, articles 5–8). The accumulated constitutional provisions were rearranged in their present order, and Thouret read them to the National Assembly on 5 August 1791. Final revisions occupied the remainder of that month.

The Constitution of 1791 is an interpretation of the political past of France and a diagnosis of its misfortunes, as well as a prescription. The constitution also preserves in many details the reflection of conditions and events during the period when it was being written. In both these ways it grew out of the political history of France.

P. Bastid, *Sieyès et sa pensée*, 2d ed. (Paris, 1970); P. Duclos, *La Notion de constitution dans l'oeuvre de l'Assemblée constituante de 1789* (Paris, 1932); J. Egret, *La Révolution des notables. Mounier et les monarchiens. 1789* (Paris, 1950); L. Gottschalk and M. Maddox, *Lafayette in the French Revolution* (Chicago, 1969-74); J. H. Stewart, *A Documentary Survey of the French Revolution* (New York, 1951).

P. Dawson

Related entries: ACTIVE CITIZEN; CIVIL CONSTITUTION OF THE CLERGY; JUSTICE; LEGISLATIVE ASSEMBLY; MOUNIER; NATIONAL CONSTITUENT ASSEMBLY; SELF-DENYING ORDINANCE; SUSPENSIVE VETO; 10 AUGUST 1792; VARENNES.

CONSTITUTION OF 1793, Jacobin constitution for the French Republic, ratified by the Convention on 24 June 1793, approved nationally in a referendum of primary assemblies but never put into effect; it was first overridden by the emergency regime of Year II and then abrogated by the Convention in the conservative reaction of Year III. The Convention was elected in the summer of 1792 to draft a republican constitution that would replace the monarchical one of 1791. A number of projects were submitted, of which the most influential was the marquis de Condorcet's (reported on 15 February 1793). The trial of the king overshadowed deliberation on the constitution during the winter. The

Girondins slowed the pace of discussion while seeking to avoid the king's condemnation. After the execution of Louis XVI on 21 January, however, the Girondins pressed for early completion. Many Montagnard deputies were absent raising the *levée en masse* in the departments, and demonstrations of support there for the Girondins made the Mountain fear, and the Girondins expect, a Girondin victory in the elections that would follow the ratification of a constitution.

But after the insurrection of 31 May and the arrest of leading Girondins, both factions reversed their tactics. Now the Montagnards were ready for a constitution that would bear their own stamp while the Girondins sought to postpone the consolidation of the Mountain's victory. On 2 June (the day of the Girondin arrests) the Convention voted to debate the constitution each afternoon until agreement was reached. M.-J. Hérault de Séchelles presented a version on 10 June, which was accepted with some modifications on 24 June.

The Convention presented the new constitution to France along with a succession of social measures: the sale of confiscated *émigré* property in small parcels (3 June), the equal division of commons (10 June), and the abolition of seigneurial rights without compensation (17 July). The democratic language of the constitution was displayed in the context of these Revolutionary laws that abridged hitherto sacrosanct property rights. Hence the constitution could mobilize the egalitarian aspirations of the popular movement while it legitimized Jacobin domination of the Convention.

As literature, the 1793 constitution has an extraordinary power, which found immediate recognition when Hérault de Séchelles read the draft on 10 June. Hérault (who was responsible for the wording of the text) had hit on a style that imitated Lycurgus and contrasted boldly with eighteenth-century rhetoric. B. Barère likened it to the Roman Republic's twelve tables, and M. Robespierre extolled the constitutional project's virtues for France's friends.

The 1793 constitution outlines the workings of direct male universal suffrage on the scale of a modern state. In its scheme, the population elects one representative to the National Assembly for every 40,000 inhabitants. The representatives' constituencies do not correspond to the departments. The people also elect their municipal officers and justices of the peace, but for the administration of districts and departments, they select the members of electoral colleges, who then vote for district and department officials. Consequently, the department is denied the political advantage of any directly elected representatives.

The difference in roles allowed the department is the essential distinction between the project of Condorcet and that of the Jacobins. This followed from the nature of support for the two factions: the Girondins were supported by officials in many departmental administrations; the Jacobins were rooted in the town societies that corresponded with them, received their packets, and sought to keep their municipalities aligned with the Jacobins' course.

The constitution makes the primary assembly of 200 to 600 voters the cell of French political life. The vote is not only the birthright of the Frenchman but of any adult foreigner who has lived in France from his own labor for over a year (article 4). It is the primary assemblies that vote directly for representatives to the National Assembly, municipal officers, and justices of the peace.

The 1793 constitution identifies the people, rather than the nation, as the source of sovereignty. Thus it explicitly makes the modern justification for representative democracy, although this should not be misread as the Convention's approval of direct democracy.

Although much of Condorcet's project remained to contribute elements of a framework, its direction was sharply revised. Condorcet meant the executive council (essentially a council of ministers) to be elected directly by the nation. Only half its members, as opposed to all the National Assembly, were to be renewed each year. The Montagnard project firmly subordinated the executive council to the Assembly, which would select its members from a list of candidates provided by the electoral colleges of the departments (articles 62–64). The Girondins had tried and failed to introduce a measure of bicameralism into the future Assembly; the Mountain rejected bicameralism conclusively. The Girondins had proposed a system of referendums by which the primary assemblies of a department could force the National Assembly to deliberate a petition. The Mountain stopped short of rejecting referendums but bounded them with conditions that made their exercise difficult, perhaps impossible. All of these changes reinforced the authority of the National Assembly and the finality of its decisions.

The constitution divides acts of the Assembly into decrees and laws (articles 54–55). Decrees include affairs of war, welfare, and general security, and for them the Assembly's sole authority suffices. Laws include civil, criminal, and financial legislation and are open to referendum. But the conditions for a referendum are extreme: one-tenth of the primary assemblies in a bare majority of departments must request it within forty days of the law's enactment. These requirements would have stretched the capacity of eighteenth-century communication to its limits. Thus the notion of the referendum is kept, while the Assembly is defended against its use.

The Assembly chooses an executive council of twenty-four members from a list of candidates, one for each of the eighty-three departments. The council negotiates treaties to be ratified by the legislature, and it names and supervises executive agents of the republic whose duties are defined by the legislature (articles 65–69).

The defense of the Republic is declared to be the duty of the whole population (article 107), and all Frenchmen are to be trained in the use of arms. By the constitution, the army has no supreme commander; the legislature and the executive council retain this function (article 110). The constitution proclaims solidarity with all free peoples and forbids peacemaking with an enemy occupying French territory (articles 118, 121).

The concept of balance of powers plays no part in the 1793 constitution, and this absence is not exclusively Jacobin. Condorcet also rejected the idea that class interests are ineradicable and must be represented and muted by a set of interlocking institutions. He preferred to think that great legislation could display a public interest recognizable by every class as common to all. The deputies of the Mountain went a step further: they believed that all power must be concentrated in the Assembly and all legitimacy in the masses who elected it.

This refusal of balance of powers is illustrated by the fate of Condorcet's idea of a national grand jury, which Hérault de Séchelles took up again in his report of 10 June. This body, composed of one individual elected annually from each department, was to be the citizen's recourse against oppression by the legislature. This check on the Assembly's power was rejected by the Convention. By refusing an institutional counterweight, the Convention chose to rely on the direct popular expression of social tension to redirect the government, and the emphasis on the people's right to insurrection was made even stronger in the revised Declaration of the Rights of Man and the Citizen that accompanied the constitution.

The Convention printed and dispatched the new constitution at once, with the intent of obtaining the consent of the primary assemblies by 10 August, the first anniversary of the monarchy's fall. The primary assemblies' response was widely, though not unanimously, favorable. Over 100,000 voters put conditions on their approval; they demanded the liberation of the twenty-two imprisoned Girondin deputies or the dissolution of the Convention with immediate elections. Over 4 million abstained, and some probably voted for the constitution in the hope of turning out Montagnard deputies in the elections to follow. In Paris an opposition of the Left found voice in J. Roux, who wanted the constitution to carry a deeper social content. Nevertheless, the vote of 1,801,918 yes against 11,610 no did more than simply consolidate the position of the Mountain; it rebuffed local federalist movements and anchored the central authority of the legislature for months to come.

The constitution was duly inaugurated in Paris on 10 August in an immense festival designed by J.-L. David. The deputies of the Convention, eighty-three venerable pike-bearing elders from all the departments, and the people of Paris walked in procession through a series of stations that symbolized the turning points of the Revolution. The elders bound their pikes into a fasces of unity and deposited it, with the new constitution, in an ark of cedar that was borne back to the hall of the Convention. The dangerous road of republican government had been chosen.

Now the Convention had acquitted itself of its original duty and was free to act as an emergency regime. From 11 August the constitution was a closed subject. Robespierre indicated that the constitution was not for immediate application in a session of the Jacobin club on the evening of 11 August. The constitution was not officially set aside until 10 October 1793, when the Convention declared the French government to be Revolutionary until the peace. The indiscipline of the Terror's various organs demanded some type of statute, and from September 1793 to July 1794 the legal development of institutions passed through the consolidation of the emergency regime. After the fall of Robespierre, the newly dominant Right in the Convention planned to constrain the constitution of 1793 with a body of organic laws. The attempted insurrections of 12 Germinal and 1 Prairial (1 April and 20 May 1795) inclined the Convention toward the project of an entirely new constitution.

The Constitution of the Year III pushed the 1793 constitution into republican mythology, where its attractiveness continued to grow throughout the nineteenth century. Taken up as a battle cry in the *journée* of 1 Prairial ("Bread and the constitution of 1793"), it inspired the revolutionaries of 1848, passed into the ideological armory of the Third Republic, and was exalted by the socialist leader and historian J. Jaurès. Perhaps such a reputation is undeserved for an untried instrument, drafted in haste for a tactical purpose. Yet the extension of suffrage and the evolution of representative institutions over the nineteenth century inevitably lent prestige to the early Jacobin conception that foreshadowed them.

Later debate over the constitution of 1793 has focused largely on the question of whether it could have worked had it gone into effect in peacetime. Jaurès insisted that it could. But the negative judgement of A. Mathiez has been generally retained by historians of all persuasions since 1930. He argued that a nation of citizens could have been formed only by decades of education and that in this sense the 1793 constitution was premature, although he added that its requirement of annual elections would have made the best school for citizenship.

A further, and less frequently asked, question is whether the constitution's makers ever intended it to work. The eloquent silence that ensued after 10 August in the Convention on the subject of the constitution and the ease with which it was shelved in October strongly suggest its solely tactical place in the Revolution. And yet if the constitution was only a gesture, the gesture must be allowed a more than tactical meaning. The constitution was an absolute declaration of republicanism, without nuance or hesitiation. In this the constitution completed the work of the regicide. The regicide had implicated all the deputies who had voted for it; the whole nation was implicated by the referendum on the constitution. Half document, half battle standard, it was to show an unusual capacity to embody democratic values to succeeding generations.

A. P., 2d ed., vols. 64–70 (Paris, 1879–1913); J. Godechot, *Les institutions de la France sous la Révolution et l'Empire* (Paris, 1968); P. Kropotkin, *La grande Révolution, 1789–1793* (Paris, 1909); A. Mathiez, "La Constitution de 1793," *Girondins et Montagnards* (Paris, 1930); M. Troper, *La séparation des pouvoirs et l'histoire constitutionnelle française* (Paris, 1973).

C. Ramsay

Related entries: CONDORCET; DAVID; GIRONDINS; HERAULT DE SECHELLES; JACOBINS; JAURES; LAW OF 14 FRIMAIRE; *LEVEE EN MASSE*; MATHIEZ; ROUX.

CONSTITUTION OF 1795, the third of France's Revolutionary constitutions, in effect under the Directory. The Constitution of the Year III (1795) was a reaction to the never-implemented democratic Jacobin Constitution of 1793. It represented the last act of the National Convention, being completed in September. Wishing to preserve the essential gains of the Revolution, its framers sought above all to establish order and gave considerable authority to the executive branch. They diluted the power of the electorate and took great care to prevent one strong man from seizing the reins of authority. Its principal framer was P. Daunou, a former Girondin and legal scholar.

The constitution began with a Declaration of Rights and Duties. The former were stated to be liberty, equality, security, and property. The latter were epitomized in the statement that every citizen owed his services to *la patrie*. For the first time, France was to have a bicameral legislature. This, the Legislative Body, was to have 750 members chosen in two stages by limited, indirect suffrage based on residence and direct taxes. Active citizens comprised every man born and domiciled in France and twenty-one years of age, with further provisions to include also certain men of foreign birth. Meeting in cantonal assemblies, they were to choose electors numbering about 30,000. The latter had to be at least twenty-five years old and pay substantially more taxes than did the primary voters. Meeting in their departmental gatherings, the electors were first to choose the 250 members of the Council of Ancients, or Elders, who were to be at least forty years old and either married or widowed (a stipulation designed against the selection of priests). Then they were to choose the members of the Council of Five Hundred, with a minimum age of thirty. One-third of each body was to be renewed annually. The duty of the Council of Five Hundred was to propose laws (this, in the expression of one of the drafters, represented imagination); then the Council of Ancients would vote on them (their action representing reason).

The constitution further provided for an Executive Directory of five men, each of whom was to be at least forty years old, chosen by the Council of Ancients from a list of fifty members of the entire Legislative Body and submitted to the Ancients by the Five Hundred. For the first five years, one director, chosen by lot, was to retire annually. The constitution declared that the directors were to provide, according to law, for the external and internal security of the Republic. They had substantial executive powers, which were divided functionally. To avoid the danger of the emergence of a single strong leader, they were to preside, in turn, for a period of three months. They were to appoint the generals and the seven ministers, the latter having merely administrative duties and never sitting as a single body. The directors could communicate with the Legislative Body only by messages, with the predictable consequence of dangerous divergences between the two branches. Every year the directors were required to take an oath of hatred toward royalty and anarchy, the latter term presumably meaning the prospect of universal suffrage and popular democracy.

The judicial arrangements set up earlier in the Revolution remained more or less unchanged, as did the administration of local government through the departments, cantons, and communes. Somewhat similar to the way in which the directors were chosen, five commissioners of the treasury were to be appointed by the Council of Ancients from a list provided by the Five Hundred. These had a very substantial authority in levying taxes and directing the spending of funds.

Primary schools were required for all parts of France. Schools superior to the primary schools were authorized, with at least one for every two of the eighty-nine departments. For the entire Republic, a National Institute was authorized. The armed forces were to consist of a Resident National Guard composed of all the citizens and sons of citizens capable of bearing arms and a National Guard on active service constituted by voluntary enlistment and, in case of need, by the method determined by law. War could be declared only by decree of the Legislative Body on the proposal of the Executive Directory.

The amending process vividly revealed the fears of the constitution's designers. Amendments to the constitution must be submitted three times by the Ancients to the Council of Five Hundred at intervals of three years. This would entail a minimum waiting time of six years. Then a specially elected body of men, at least forty years old and married or widowed, would consider the amendment. They were to sit at least one hundred kilometers from Paris, and their decisions would have to be accepted or rejected by a plebiscite in the primary assemblies throughout France. It is hardly surprising that the amending procedure was never attempted.

In its final article, the constitution was entrusted to "the fidelity of the Legislative Body, the Executive Directory, the administrators, and the judges; to the vigilance of the fathers of families, to wives and mothers; to the affection of young citizens and to the courage of all Frenchmen." When submitted to a plebiscite, it was accepted by a vote of 1,057,000 to 50,000, an overwhelming endorsement in the narrow sense, yet expressing the wishes of only about one-fifth of the eligible primary voters. A supplemental decree, not actually a part of the constitution, stipulated that two-thirds of the original 750 members of the two councils must be drawn from the membership of the Convention. When this provision was submitted to a plebiscite, the meager vote showed only 205,498 in favor and 108,784 against. The rising of 13 Vendémiaire (5 October 1795), put down by N. Bonaparte, was in essence a protest against the two-thirds decree.

The tripartite system of legislative, executive, and judicial power that remained headless boded ill for the future. Yet whatever its defects, the Constitution of 1795 provided the structure under which France operated for four years, and recent historical judgments on the work of the Directory can find much on the favorable side. Moreover, the constitution provided a model for those in the sister republics being established outside France's borders. Since the constitution was almost impossible to amend, it is not surprising that there were at least nineteen violations of its provisions, brought about by intrigue and accepted with relative indifference. The coups of Fructidor (1797), Floréal (1798), and Prairial (1799) were all arbitrary acts, and by the great coup of Brumaire (November 1799) General Bonaparte threw the entire constitution into discard.

P.-J. Buchez and P.-C. Roux, *Histoire parlementaire de la Révolution française*, 40 vols. (Paris, 1834–38), vol. 36; M. Deslandres, *Histoire constitutionnelle de la France de 1789 à 1815*, vol. 1 (Paris, 1932); L. Duguit and H. Monnier, *Les constitutions et les principales lois politiques de la France depuis 1789*, 6th ed. (Paris, 1943); J. Godechot, *Les institutions de la France sous la Révolution et l'Empire* (Paris, 1951); J. H. Stewart, *A Documentary Survey of the French Revolution* (New York, 1951, reissued 1965).

E. J. Knapton

Related entries: CONSTITUTION OF 1793; COUNCIL OF ANCIENTS; COUNCIL OF FIVE HUNDRED; COUP OF 18 BRUMAIRE; COUP OF 18 FRUCTIDOR YEAR V; COUP OF 30 PRAIRIAL YEAR VII; COUP OF 22 FLOREAL YEAR VI; DIRECTORY; 13 VENDEMIAIRE YEAR IV; TWO-THIRDS LAW.

CONSTITUTION OF 1799, the fourth of France's Revolutionary constitutions and the charter of the Consular period (1799-1804). N. Bonaparte's essential purpose in the coup of 18 Brumaire (9–10 November 1799) had been to overthrow the Directory and drastically remodel the Constitution of 1795 under which it had operated. With his success at Saint-Cloud on the second day of the coup, he moved quickly to have the Council of Ancients and the Council of Five Hundred each set up a committee of twenty-five to work with the new Provisional Consuls (N. Bonaparte, E.-J. Sieyès, and P.-R. Ducos) to accomplish the necessary organic changes.

Work on a new constitutional draft began in Paris immediately after Brumaire, the committees being pushed hard by Bonaparte. Sieyès made it clear that he intended to press his own ideas, many of which were acceptable. Two, however, soon met Bonaparte's opposition: one envisaged a grand elector, to be named by a proposed new Senate and living in great splendor at Versailles; the second provided that the grand elector should nominate two consuls, one for domestic and one for military and diplomatic affairs. Bonaparte declared contemptuously that if he were to become grand elector, he would be living at Versailles like a fatted pig; if only a consul, he could be removed by the grand elector.

In the end, the fifty members of the two committees were summoned to regular evening meetings with the three provisional consuls. P. Daunou, the chief framer of the Constitution of 1795, was ordered to prepare a complete draft from these discussions. When this was done, Bonaparte went through it at the meetings, page by page and night by night, instructing Daunou to insert the changes he desired. Working rapidly, the group finished its labors on 12 December 1799. Since the names of the three new consuls were to be inserted in the constitution, Bonaparte instructed each member to deposit his choices in a vase. Then, fearing the outcome, he suddenly asked Sieyès to make three nominations. Sieyès, having been overruled on many aspects of the new constitution, had little choice but to propose three names that he knew Bonaparte wished—Bonaparte, J.-J. Cambacérès, and C.-F. Lebrun, the last two being solid, distinguished figures. These were accepted, and Bonaparte threw the unopened ballots into the fire.

Its ninety-five succinct articles make the Constitution of 1799 shorter than its three predecessors. It contained no declaration of rights and no provision for amendment. Sieyès' concept of a grand elector vanished, as did his idea of "absorption" back into the new Senate of major office-holders who had proved unsatisfactory. In many respects, however, the structural ideas of Sieyès remained.

All Frenchmen, twenty-one years of age, born or resident in France, and enrolled for one year on a communal register, were citizens. Within each communal district the voters, meeting locally, chose one-tenth of their number to make up the communal list. Those chosen met in departmental centers to make up the departmental lists. These members in turn chose another one-tenth making up the national list. These successive reductions meant a shift from approximately 6 million voters to 600,000, from this to 60,000, and from this to 6,000. Members who were to serve in the central legislative bodies were to be chosen from this final list and lesser officials from the departmental and communal lists. The concept of popular suffrage in the democratic sense had thus been destroyed.

A complex scheme of central government was created. The Conservative Senate (Sénat Conservateur), a key feature, was not a lawmaking body. It was to have eventually eighty members appointed for life. The former provisional consuls, Sieyès and Ducos, were to be its first members, and they, along with the new consuls, Cambacérès and Lebrun, were to select twenty-nine more senators. These then co-opted an equal number. Two members were to be added annually by the Senate until the total of eighty had been reached. The Senate was to choose from the national list the members of the Tribunate and Legislative Body, as well as the future consuls and other high officials. It also had duties resembling those of a supreme court in that it was to sustain or annul all acts referred to it by the Tribunate or the government as supposedly unconstitutional.

Legislation was in the hands of the two assemblies. The Tribunate, composed of 100 members at least twenty-five years of age and renewed annually by one-fifth, was to consider proposed laws submitted to it by the consuls. It could discuss and accept them or return them to the consuls, but it could not amend them. The Legislative Body (Corps Législatif) had 300 members at least thirty years of age and was also to be renewed annually by one-fifth. It received proposals from the Tribunate, sometimes directly from the three consuls, and then had to vote without discussion. A substantial number of members from earlier Revolutionary assemblies appeared in both bodies.

A strikingly new feature, the Council of State, had a name reminiscent of the ancien régime. It was mentioned only briefly in the constitution; details regarding it were set forth in a special ordinance of 26 December 1799. Its twenty-nine original members were appointed by the first consul, who painstakingly chose able men of every political persuasion. The Council of State was divided into five sections: war, navy, finance, legislation, and domestic affairs. Since Bonaparte soon joined in its remarkably free discussions, it approximated the collective mind of a cabinet, although the ministers themselves never met as a body. It drafted laws and decrees, drew up administrative ordinances, interpreted statutes, and even came to have some appellate jurisdiction as a court.

The executive authority of the three consuls best exemplifies Sieyès' famous dictum that confidence should come from below and power from above. Bonaparte, Cambacérès, and Lebrun were named as consuls in the constitution; the first two were appointed for ten years and Lebrun for five. Very special authority was given to the first consul, who promulgated laws, appointed and dismissed members of the Council of State, ministers, ambassadors, officers of the army and navy, the principal members of local administrations, civil and criminal judges, and other legal officials. The consuls proposed laws to the Tribunate, supervised receipts and expenditures, provided for internal security, declared war, and made treaties of peace and alliance. The famous article 42 made clear Bonaparte's preeminent power; it provided that the second and third consuls should have a consultative voice and could register any objections, "after which the decision of the First Consul shall suffice."

In the judicial realm, the first consul appointed civil and criminal judges. The members of the Court of Cassation (a supreme court of appeals) were chosen by the Senate. Only local justices of the peace continued to be elected, and juries were authorized only in criminal cases.

Arrangements for local government were presented briefly. In essence there was a pyramidical structure, with the 40,000 villages, towns, and cities at the base. Above these were the 398 communal *arrondissements* defined in the Organic Law of 17 February 1800. The departments now numbered 98. Prefects, subprefects, and members of the departmental councils were appointed by the first consul. Only in villages and smaller towns were mayors and local councils still elected. The constitution was proclaimed on Christmas Day 1799 and was submitted to a plebiscite nearly two months later. This resulted in 3,011,007 votes in favor and only 1,526 against.

Although a Paris newspaper answered its own question as to what was in the constitution, by stating simply "Bonaparte," the role of Sieyès should not be ignored. J. Bourdon's scholarly study of the Constitution of 1799 declares it to be one of the legends of Brumaire that Bonaparte simply swept away Sieyès' unworkable scheme and dictated his own. With some major exceptions, much of Sieyès' structural plan remained, and for some time as president of the Senate he exercised considerable power. Moreover, he was chief among the revisionists seeking to move France in the direction of bourgeois domination, and this domination was to prevail throughout the greater part of the nineteenth century. The Constitution of 1799 was amended in 1802 to make Bonaparte sole consul for life; it was replaced in 1804 by the Imperial Constitution of the Year XII.

P. Bastid, *Sieyès et sa pensée* (Paris, 1939, rev. ed. 1970); J. Bourdon, *La Constitution de l'An VIII* (Paris, 1941); M. Deslandres, *Histoire constitutionnelle de la France de 1789 à 1815*, vol. 1 (Paris, 1932); L. Duguit and H. Monnier, *Les constitutions et les principales lois politiques de la France depuis 1789*, 6th ed. (Paris, 1943); J. Godechot, *Les institutions de la France sous la Révolution et l'Empire* (Paris, 1951); F.-A.-T. Hélie, ed., *Les constitutions de la France* (Paris, 1880); J. H. Stewart, *A Documentary Survey of the French Revolution* (New York, 1951, reissued 1965).

E. J. Knapton

Related entries: BONAPARTE, L.; BONAPARTE, N.; CAMBACERES; COUP OF 18 BRUMAIRE; LEBRUN; SIEYES.

CONVENTION, NATIONAL. See NATIONAL CONVENTION.

CORDAY D'ARMANS, MARIE-ANNE-CHARLOTTE (1768-93), assassin of J.-P. Marat. Charlotte Corday came from a petty noble family in Calvados and acquired republican sentiments from reading Plutarch, J.-J. Rousseau, and the abbé Raynal at a convent school in Caen. In April 1793, she decided to visit Paris for family reasons, but the federalist revolt turned her journey to other purposes. The arrival in Caen of exiled Girondist deputies from Paris convinced her that the Mountain was destroying the work of the Revolution. Evidence suggests that early in July she decided to kill Marat, whom she considered most responsible for this destruction; and she was confirmed in her decision by the unsuccessful review of federalist troops on 7 July. She traveled to Paris where she gained access to Marat on 13 July by promising him news of the Norman revolt; they conversed while he was bathing to treat a skin ailment. When Marat said that the federalists would lose their heads on the scaffold, Corday pulled out a butcher knife and stabbed him fatally. At her trial before the Revolutionary Tribunal, she explained her views on tyrannicide and denied any links to other federalists. She was guillotined on 17 July. Her beauty and simplicity made her an appealing figure to many enemies of the Mountain, as well as to political sympathizers. J.-L. David later painted the assassination scene.

J. Shearing, *The Angel of Assassination* (London, 1935); C. Vatel, *Charlotte de Corday et les Girondins* (Paris, 1864–72).

D. Stone

Related entries: CAEN; FEDERALISM; GIRONDINS; MARAT; REVOLU-TIONARY TRIBUNAL.

CORDELIERS CLUB (1790–95), a Parisian political society whose influence over the militant Revolutionaries of the capital's sections and popular societies rivaled and sometimes challenged that of the Jacobin club between 1790 and 1794. The Cordeliers club was founded as the Société des amis des droits de l'homme et du citoyen (its formally correct title) during April 1790. Its first meeting place was a room (probably the library) of the former Franciscan or "Cordelier" monastery in the rue des Cordeliers, on the Left Bank. Together with the premises, the club acquired the monks' nickname, which it retained even though for most of its existence it met elsewhere. In May 1791 the club was expelled from the monastery by the Paris municipal administration. After some vicissitudes it then settled, on 18 May, in the hôtel de Genlis in the rue Dauphine, quite close, in a building formerly occupied by the Musée, a literary and scientific society. There the club disposed of a suite of four rooms; the meeting hall was on the ground floor looking out on the Lelièvre gardens.

The initiative for the club's foundation came chiefly from the citizens of the Cordeliers district, which, under the leadership of G.-J. Danton, J.-P. Marat, and L.-C.-S. Desmoulins, had taken the lead in democratic agitation in Paris during 1789 and 1790. The reorganization of the Parisian municipal government in 1790, which the Cordeliers district had opposed, threatened to deprive the Cordeliers militants of their political base by merging the district in the newly formed Théâtre-Français section, and the formation of the club was, in part, a defensive reaction.

The Cordeliers club subsequently turned the tables by establishing an unshakable domination over the sections, to such effect that one of the club's members, the journalist N. de Bonneville, described its membership as being composed of the section's elite. While drawing most of its membership from the immediate *quartier*, the club was open to all, attracted members from all parts of Paris, and like the Jacobins, established correspondence with other popular societies in the provinces. Danton, although prominent in both district and section affairs, rarely spoke at or visited the club. It was not a Dantonist political fief but an arena in which many different individuals and tendencies competed for support.

The first recorded president, in April 1790, was J.-P. Dufourny de Villiers, the city engineer of Paris and a former president of the adjacent Mathurins district. Others who occupied the presidency during 1791 included (most frequently) the Avignonnais lawyer, L.-F. Peyre, F. Lawalle l'Ecuyer, A.-S. Boucher de Saint-Sauveur, and a lawyer named Colin (or Collin). Among the earliest secretaries were the journalists J.-A. Dulaure, A.-F. Momoro, and J. Rutledge.

In its first public manifesto, printed in the *Moniteur* on 4 May 1790, the Cordeliers club stressed particularly its intention to act as a watchdog against the abuse of power by public authorities and "every kind of attaint on the rights of man." The club symbolically adopted the eye of vigilance as its device. An indication of the intellectual inspiration of the founders may be gleaned from a contemporary description of the furnishings of the meeting room: a wall plaque of the Declaration of the Rights of Man, surmounted by crossed daggers, and plaster busts of Brutus, William Tell, Mirabeau, Helvétius, and J.-J. Rousseau. Each session began with a joint recital of the Declaration.

An observer found about three-hundred persons of both sexes present at one of the early meetings. Active membership generally appears to have been of this order; one of the club's petitions, presented on 12 July 1791, was supported by the signatures of 381 members.

The monthly subscription of 2 *sous* was low; passive citizens were admitted; and some accounts misleadingly emphasize the comparative poverty of members. A. Mathiez's conclusion was that "*bourgeois* and men in easy circumstances" exercised a preponderant influence, and this accords with the evidence. Twenty-four of the twenty-five second-degree electors of the Théâtre-Français section in 1791 were members of the club. They included seven lawyers, three journalists, three printers, and two artists, as well as seven merchants and master tradesmen. Other notable members at that time included the wholesale butcher A.-M. Legendre and A.-J. Santerre, the brewer of the faubourg Saint-Antoine. Membership seems to have been particularly attractive to journalists, among them L.-C.-S. Desmoulins (*Révolutions de France et de Brabant*), N. de Bonneville

(*Bouche de fer*, Cercle social), Dulaure (*Thermomètre du jour*), L.-M.-S. Fréron (*Orateur du peuple*), P.-F.-J. Robert (*Mercure national*), and J. Rutledge (*Le Creuset*). For a time Momoro published the club's own proceedings as the *Journal du club des Cordeliers*.

Women were admitted to the sessions, contributed to discussions, and even made motions, although there is no evidence that they served on the bureau. On 30 June 1791 a Mademoiselle Lemaure, described as "one of the ladies who most assiduously attend the session" (Mathiez, p. 66), was delegated to take a gift of clothing to R. Audu, the imprisoned organizer of the women's march to Versailles in October 1789, whom the club had taken under its protection. In July, however, the number of entry cards for women was formally restricted to sixty.

In general the Cordeliers sessions were regularly concerned, as promised, with Revolutionary vigilance: denunciations, investigations, visits to imprisoned patriots, appeals to the Jacobin club, subscriptions for the families of victims of oppression, the defense of victimized patriots. The club also intervened more positively and deliberately in Revolutionary politics.

Its first major campaign, mounted in late 1790 and early 1791, was to support the foundation of a network of popular societies in various parts of Paris. By May 1791 at least nine such societies existed; there would ultimately be more than a score. Many of the founders were members of the Cordeliers club: among them, for example, Santerre (Ennemis de despotisme), P. Degrouhette (Société fraternelle), A.-F. Sergent (Société populaire des halles), J.-C.-H. Mehée-Latouche (Société des carmes), C.-F.-J.-J.-M. Concedieu (Nomophiles), J.-L. Vachard (Société des indigens) and Robert, who organized a central federation of the societies, with its headquarters at the Cordeliers.

During the summer of 1791, the Cordeliers club and the popular societies mounted an unsuccessful campaign for a democratic revision of the new French constitution through the introduction of virtual universal suffrage and the abandonment of the wealth qualifications for public office. Guided, in part, by Rousseau's friend and disciple, the former marquis René de Girardin, the club also pressed for the introduction of such elements of direct democracy as strict electoral mandates, the recall of deputies, and direct popular legislation by referendum. After Louis XVI's flight to Varennes in June 1791, this campaign merged with that for the suspension or deposition of the king. On 24 June 1791, delegates of the Cordeliers club, representing an organized crowd of demonstrators estimated to be 30,000 strong, presented a petition to the National Assembly. The movement culminated in the great demonstration on the Champ de Mars of 17 July, which the club helped to organize, and the resultant "massacre," or dispersal of the crowd, by the National Guard.

In the repression that followed, many prominent club members were arrested or fled the capital, and attendance at meetings was reduced to as few as a dozen. Recovery from this setback was hampered by a schism in the club in November 1791, when one group, led by P.-G. Chaumette, seceded and founded another

Société des amis des droits de l'homme in the rue de la Vieille Monnaie, Bonne Nouvelle section, on the Right Bank.

The Cordeliers club had been restored to vigor again by the summer of 1792, when it played a prominent part, together with the popular societies and the sections, in the agitation that led to the overthrow of the monarchy on 10 August 1792. On 15 July 1792, the Cordeliers club launched the crucial demands for the suspension of Louis and the calling of a National Convention to redraft the constitution. On 30 July the Théâtre-Français section, presided over by Danton, and two other Cordeliers, Chaumette and Momoro, took the lead in throwing section meetings open to passive citizens.

The influence of the club continued to be felt in the struggle for control of Paris in 1793. During the attempted rising against the Girondin ministry on 9–10 March, 2,000 insurgents were said to have gathered at one point at the Cordeliers club. During the summer, the members came under the influence of the *enragés*, supporting, during May and June, their campaigns against food hoarding and currency speculation and for a purge of nobles from the armies and of moderates from the Convention. As a consequence, the club earned the displeasure of M. Robespierre, who was anxious to consolidate the Montagnard victory of 2 June, and on 30 June, it suffered the first of a series of purges that ultimately weakened it disastrously. On this occasion the *enragé* leaders J. Roux and J.-T.-V. Leclerc were expelled at the instigation of a delegation from the Jacobin club.

By September 1793, the dominating influence was that of the ultra-Revolutionary followers of J.-R. Hébert, the editor of *Père Duchesne*, and of F.-N. Vincent, secretary of the war ministry. The club now began to challenge the growing centralization of power by the Montagnard-Jacobin alliance, putting forward demands for economic and political terror and for social legislation similar to those canvassed by the *enragés* earlier in the year.

In the factional in-fighting of this period, the club was weakened by the expulsion of several veteran members, and notably of Dufourny, the founder, and Chaumette, now procureur of the Paris Commune, who had been responsible for rallying the members after the Champ de Mars affair. Such other stalwarts as Danton and Desmoulins had long since abandoned the sessions.

Finally, in the crisis of Ventôse Year II (March 1794), the Robespierrist Committee of Public Safety moved against the Hébertists. The remaining cadres of the Cordeliers club, Hébert, Vincent, and Momoro included, were arrested, charged with conspiracy to overthrow the Convention, and executed. Demoralized, the club made abject submission to the Jacobin club, purged itself yet again, and seriously debated closing its doors. Nevertheless, a few members continued to meet together at least until March or April 1795; the Cordeliers thus survived the Jacobins by several months. In this final period, the leading spirit was a Jacobin functionary (a juror on the Revolutionary Tribunal), J.-E. Brochet, who was elected president soon after the overthrow of Robespierre in July 1794.

The club was now only a ghost of its former self. An observer noted no more than fifteen men and women in attendance during three sessions held during December 1794. On one occasion, the members separated without saying or doing anything; on the other two, some spoke out against the Thermidorian regime, referring to themselves ironically as *buveurs de sang*, the description given by contemporaries to inveterate and blood-thirsty terrorists.

G. Lenôtre, *Paris révolutionnaire* (Paris, 1908); A Mathiez, *Le Club des Cordeliers pendant la crise de Varennes et le massacre de Champ de Mars* (Paris, 1910); R. B. Rose, *The Making of the Sans-Culottes* (Manchester, 1983); A. Soboul, *Les sans-culottes parisiens en l'an II: Mouvement populaire et gouvernement révolutionnaire, 2 juin 1793-9 thermidor an II* (Paris, 1958); K. Tønnesson, *La Défaite des sans-culottes: Mouvement populaire et réaction bourgeoise en l'an III* (Oslo and Paris, 1959).

R. B. Rose

Related entries: CHAMP DE MARS "MASSACRE"; CHAUMETTE; DANTON; DESMOULINS; *ENRAGES*; FRERON; HEBERT; JACOBINS; LECLERC; MARAT; MOMORO; ROUX; SECTIONS; VARENNES.

CORVEE, unpaid labor service under the Old Regime. In eighteenth-century France there were two kinds of *corvées*: royal *corvées*, requiring unpaid labor services on the royal roads, and seigneurial *corvées*, requiring labor services for the seigneur. The royal *corvées* were newer and much more burdensome. Instituted around 1730 by certain royal intendants, such as Orry at Soissons, the royal *corvée* varied greatly from one administrative district to another in the number of days (and other conditions) of labor required of each *corvéable*. Like the royal *taille*, the *corvée* was essentially a peasant's obligation; nobles, ecclesiastics, their household servants, the residents of towns, as well as country school teachers, postmasters, and even shepherds, were exempt.

Partly because the *corvée* was new and very onerous at harvest time, popular resistance was widespread. By 1750, the *corvée* was a subject for public debate. Even the parlements, which usually defended seigneurial rights, frequently remonstrated against the abuses of the royal *corvée*. By 1760, many royal intendants began to commute the royal *corvée* into a money tax on the local parishes, thus distributing the burden more equitably. In 1776, the controller general, A.-R.-J. Turgot, went a step further and transformed the *corvée* into a regular tax borne by every French family, even the privileged. Although Turgot's reform failed, largely due to the resistance of the privileged, the substitution of a money payment—with fiscal privileges retained, to be sure—had become common practice by 1789. The royal *corvée* was finally abolished in 1789, though there were some public improvers in the early nineteenth century who still believed the only way to save the roads was to reinstitute the royal *corvée*.

The seigneurial *corvée*, though generally condemned in the *cahiers* of 1789, was much less onerous than its royal counterpart. Limited by law to a maximum of twelve days, the seigneurial *corvée* rarely claimed more than four days per year in practice. Like other seigneurial rights, the *corvée* was increasingly criticized by publicists and reformers as a vestige of an older servitude, and was abolished by the Revolution. Thereafter, a landlord's demand for labor services was based on a modern contract or lease.

F.-A. Aulard, *La Révolution française et le régime féodal* (Paris, 1919); S. Herbert, *The Fall of Feudalism in France* (London, 1921); J. Q. C. Mackrell, *The Attack on Feudalism in Eighteenth Century France* (London and Toronto, 1973).

R. Forster

Related entries: ASSEMBLY OF NOTABLES; FEUDALISM; INTENDANTS.

"COUNCIL, RESULT OF THE." See "RESULT OF THE COUNCIL."

COUNCIL OF ANCIENTS (1795-99), upper house of the legislature established by the Constitution of the Year III (1795). This house was composed of 250 deputies, who were required to be at least forty years of age, married or widowed, and resident for at least fifteen years within the territory of the Republic. The deputies were elected for three-year terms, with one-third of the membership renewable each year. Resolutions passed by the Council of Five Hundred could not become law unless approved by the Ancients. On the other hand, the upper house could not initiate or amend laws, though it did have the sole right of fixing the location of the legislature. The significance of this power became apparent on 18 Brumaire Year VIII (9 November 1799) when the Ancients readily agreed to move the legislature to Saint-Cloud, outside Paris. The move much facilitated N. Bonaparte's coup d'état.

The division of the legislature into two chambers represented a significant departure from previous arrangements: all the preceding legislatures consisted of a single assembly. The framers of the Constitution of 1795 aimed to prevent a recurrence of Jacobin dictatorship, which had been organized by special committees of deputies from within the National Convention. The Council of Ancients was expected to act as a brake on any such attempt. Moreover, it was assumed that the smaller number of deputies in the Ancients (half as many as in the other house) would be conducive to orderly and deliberate proceedings; most political leaders thought that large assemblies encouraged demagoguery and political instability.

When they proposed the establishment of a second legislative chamber, the members of the Constitutional Commission specifically differentiated it from a Senate or House of Lords. The Ancients were elected in exactly the same fashion and for the same term as the members of the Council of Five Hundred. The two councils followed the same procedures; for example, each council elected a new president every month. All legislators were paid the same salaries, housed at the expense of the Republic, and reimbursed for office expenses. These arrangements were designed to prevent the emergence of a new aristocracy from within the Council of Ancients. The two houses were separate yet virtually equal, and neither was allowed to intervene in the affairs of the other.

The belief that legislative, judicial, and executive powers should be clearly separated informed the major provisions of the Constitution of 1795. To this end, deputies could not hold other positions in government. Each of the councils disposed of its own special guard of 1,500 men as protection against interference from either the public or the other branches of government. Nevertheless, the separation of powers was only partial in theory and rarely maintained in practice. The Council of Ancients chose the five directors of the Executive Directory from nominations made by the Council of Five Hundred. Every year the Five Hundred presented a new list of ten names for the position that fell vacant; as a consequence, the legislature shaped the nature of executive power.

Even more serious, however, was the interference of the Executive Directory in the operation of the legislature. The most notorious example of this intrusion was the coup d'état mounted by the three moderate directors against the councils in September 1797. After a rightist landslide in the elections of that year, the directors P. Barras, L.-M. La Revellière-lépeaux, and J.-F. Reubell ordered troops under their command to invest the meeting rooms of the two councils. After the soldiers had arrested many supposed royalist deputies, the majority of the deputies remaining in the councils agreed to ratify the patently illegal action of the directors. The other two directors and several deputies were sentenced to deportation, and the elections of forty-nine departments were annulled. Less than a year later, the two councils worked with the Executive Directory to exclude scores of recently elected leftist deputies. In both instances, the Council of Ancients failed to uphold the constitutional arrangement and thus cooperated with the Council of Five Hundred and ultimately with the Executive Directory in undermining the legal foundation of the liberal Republican regime.

The Council of Ancients never managed to establish a distinct identity for itself within the directorial government. Its constitutional position was weak from the start; because it could not initiate legislation and because it resembled in every other way the Council of Five Hundred, the Ancients could function only as a truncated half of the legislative body. Moreover, since one-third of the deputies were up for reelection every year, the composition of the Ancients shifted dramatically in a relatively short period of time. The frequent elections and repeated pressure from the Executive Directory effectively prevented the establishment of regular parties within either council. Despite the weaknesses written into the constitutional arrangement, the introduction of a second house did promote the regularization of parliamentary discipline. The sessions of both councils after 1795 were much more orderly and predictable than those of the single chambers that preceded them. The Council of Ancients scrupulously respected the independence and autonomy of the Five Hundred.

The Council of Ancients did not survive the coup that it had facilitated on 9 November 1799. At Saint-Cloud on 10 November, the Five Hundred actively opposed Bonaparte when he appeared before them. The Ancients were more submissive; after troops loyal to Bonaparte had ejected the opposition from the lower house, the remaining deputies voted the abolition of the Directory, its replacement with a three-man executive, and the establishment of provisional commissions chosen from the two councils. These men helped write the new constitution of the Consulate.

M. Deslandres, *Histoire constitutionnelle de la France de 1789 à 1870*, vol. 1, (Paris, 1932); G. Dodu, *Le parlementarisme et les parlementaires sous la Révolution, 1789–1799* (Paris, 1911); J. Godechot, *Les institutions de la France sous la Révolution et l'Empire* (Paris, 1968); *J. des Débats; P.V. des A.*, 49 vols.

L. A. Hunt

Related entries: CONSTITUTION OF 1795; COUNCIL OF FIVE HUNDRED; COUP OF 18 BRUMAIRE; COUP OF 18 FRUCTIDOR YEAR V; COUP OF 30 PRAIRIAL YEAR VII; COUP OF 22 FLOREAL YEAR VI; DIRECTORY; TWO-THIRDS LAW.

COUNCIL OF FIVE HUNDRED (1795-99), lower house of the legislature established by the Constitution of 1795. It was composed, as its name suggests, of five hundred deputies, who were required to be at least thirty years old on election (until the Year VIII the age minimum was set at twenty-five) and resident for at least ten years within the territory of the Republic. Like the Ancients of the upper house, the Five Hundred were elected for three-year terms, with one-third of the membership renewable each year. No deputy could hold office for more than six consecutive years. Only the Council of Five Hundred could initiate legislation, but no law was definitive until passed by the Council of Ancients. In most other ways, the two councils were alike: all the deputies were elected by a two-stage process in which the final choice was made by electors who had to be substantial property owners; deputies were remunerated identically; and the internal procedures of the two councils were much the same.

The annual elections of new deputies to the two councils made possible continual shifts in political composition. Since the Council of Five Hundred initiated legislation, changes in its membership were more readily apparent than in the Council of Ancients. Moreover, since younger men (under forty) could be elected only to the Five Hundred, political newcomers were more likely to be found in the ranks of the lower house. In order to ensure continuity, the National Convention passed a special decree on 5 Fructidor Year III (22 August 1795) requiring the electoral assemblies of 1795 to choose two-thirds of the members of the new councils from among the deputies to the National Convention. This holding action stabilized the membership for only one year, however, and it bought that year at the cost of dubious constitutional tinkering, which compromised the legitimacy of the new regime from the start. Royalists dominated the elections of the Year V (1797); then the resurgent Jacobins did well in the elections of the Year VI (1798). After each of these unfavorable elections, the supporters of the Directorial regime in the councils worked with the Executive Directory either to arrest or exclude first the rightists and then the leftists. These coups exacerbated the constitutional crisis of confidence inaugurated by the Two-thirds Law of 1795.

The stability of the legislative councils was essential to the survival of the directorial regime. The constitutional arrangement of 1795 succeeded in fostering greater attention to parliamentary procedure within the councils. The parades of petitioners that had so encumbered the meetings of the National Convention were formally prohibited, and public attendance was limited to one-half the membership of the councils. Even in the large Council of Five Hundred, discussions were generally orderly and disciplined in comparison with those of its predecessor.

Nevertheless, many factors worked against parliamentary stability. Annual elections not only raised the spectre of decisive changes in political composition, they also diverted the deputies' energy and attention away from matters before the legislature. Consolidation of the regime at the top had to take second place to electioneering and thus to patronage relations. Deputies swarmed to the salons of the directors and the bureaus of the ministers in the hope of placing their followers at home in local positions of political and pecuniary importance. During the elections, local political groups, as well as agents of the central government, made every attempt to manipulate the results to their advantage, and when such preparations failed, rival groups resorted to secession from the electoral assemblies. The councils themselves made the final choice in such cases.

Although the deputies and local political factions recognized the significance of elections and did everything possible to influence them, the formation of national political parties was stymied during the Directory. Both on the Right and the Left, political clubs proliferated whenever they were officially tolerated, but as soon as either the Right or the Left seemed on the verge of establishing an effective national party, their leaders and organizations were squelched. Personal patronage networks were allowed; ideologically based electoral organizations were not. Rather than forming a center party to protect its own interests, the majority in the councils worked with the Executive Directory to nip in the bud any kind of party organization. The failure to form a center party further undermined parliamentary stability; the deputies turned instead to intrigue and extraconstitutional coups as the means of holding together republican government.

The deputies in the councils and the members of the Executive Directory shared many political attitudes, but the constitutional arrangement of 1795 did not facilitate regular cooperation between them. The directors chose the ministers who served them, but the ministers had no responsibility to the councils. And just as the directors could intervene only in an extraconstitutional fashion in the affairs of the councils, so too the councils could not change the composition of the Directory without resorting to extraordinary tactics. In June 1799 the councils forced the resignation of two directors by threatening to indict them.

After the elections of 1799, the Left seemed to dominate the Council of Five Hundred. This shift frightened the center deputies in both councils and made them increasingly receptive to demands for constitutional revision. The coup d'état of 18 Brumaire was planned by a group of so-called revisionists led by E.-J. Sieyès, who was then a director. The final destruction of the Council of Five Hundred was plotted and then pushed through by the president it had elected at the end of October 1799, L. Bonaparte. When his brother, Napoleon, appeared before the Five Hundred on 10 November 1799, he was shouted down by defiant deputies. As president, Lucien ordered the troops outside to clear the chamber; the rump of the two councils then deprived many leading Jacobins of their seats and elected provisional commissions to direct the transition to a new government. The Council of Five Hundred had resisted this last coup of the Directorial regime, but its members did not have the unity of purpose and base of support necessary to carry resistance beyond the chamber itself.

G. Dodu, *Le parlementarisme et les parlementaires sous la Révolution, 1789–1799* (Paris, 1911); L. Hunt, D. Lansky, and P. Hanson, "The Failure of the Liberal Republic in France, 1795–1799: The Road to Brumaire," *J. of Mod. Hist.* 51 (1979); *J. des Débats*; *P. V. des C.C.*; J.-R. Suratteau, *Les Elections de l'an VI et le "coup d' état du 22 floréal" (11 mai 1798)* (Paris, 1971).

L. A. Hunt

Related entries: BABEUF; CONSTITUTION OF 1795; COUNCIL OF ANCIENTS; COUP OF 18 BRUMAIRE; COUP OF 18 FRUCTIDOR YEAR V; COUP OF 30 PRAIRIAL YEAR VII; COUP OF 22 FLOREAL YEAR VI; DIRECTORY; SIEYES; TWO-THIRDS LAW.

COUNTERREVOLUTION, a movement, consisting of both doctrine and action, aimed at combating the French Revolution and revolution in general. The counterrevolution began at the same time as the Revolution; from its origin, adversaries of revolution resolved to oppose it. The reaction extended beyond France—to America, the United Provinces, Geneva, and Belgium—and was not limited to the period extending from 1789 to 1804. In each case, however, loyalists were opposed to those men who wished to sever the ties of traditional authority and government. The situation was the same in France where, from 1789, some of the deputies to the Estates General, notably those from the nobility and upper clergy, tried to prevent any change.

Were these counterrevolutionaries acting on the basis of some doctrine? It appears not. They were quite simply attached to the old institutions that benefited them and guaranteed their privileges. Without doubt, they could appeal to C. Montesquieu, who, in the *Spirit of the Laws*, had praised limited monarchy, the division of the nation into three orders, and the maintenance of the feudal regime whose suppression he would accept only for redemption payments. But on the whole, they simply preferred to retain the regime that existed in France in 1789 and which had been described and justified by the royal historiographer, J.-N. Moreau, in several works, especially in a huge treatise of twenty-three volumes entitled *Principles of Moral, Political and Public Law Drawn from the History of Our Monarchy*. Louis XVI drew inspiration from this for the program of reforms that he presented to the Estates General on 23 June 1789 and that, for twenty-five years, would constitute the maximum concessions that he, and later the pretender, Louis XVIII, would extend to the "revolutionaries": maintenance of the three separate orders and of the privileges of the first two, the possibility

of redemption fees for seigneurial rights, the participation of the clergy in rehabilitating state finances while keeping the tithe, fiscal equality, individual
liberty, and freedom of the press.

This program was not based on any theoretical consideration. In fact, it was
not until the publication of *Reflections on the Revolution in France* by the
Englishman E. Burke in November 1790 that counterrevolutionary ideas found
a philosophical justification. This work consists of two parts. The first is a virulent
pamphlet against the French Revolution of 1789, which Burke finds totally
different from the English Revolution of 1688. This first part, arbitrary and filled
with errors, has scarcely any validity. In contrast, the second part is a doctrinal
exposition of counterrevolutionary ideas, and it has found an immense response
in the world. Burke's general idea is that institutions constructed on a blank slate
are unendurable. Burke combats with all his energy ideas that he considers
utopian and that form the foundation of revolutionary doctrine. He does not
believe that a secular state is viable; he does not think that reason and scientific
development will permit unlimited progress for humanity or could provide man
with happiness on earth. Burke does not know what liberty means in the abstract;
for him, there is the liberty of the honest man and the liberty of the escaped
thief, and the latter is harmful. He criticizes the use of the word *nature* by the
members of the Constituent Assembly. These people believe, as do J. Locke
and J.-J. Rousseau, that everything that is inherent in human nature, at all times
and in all places, is natural. In contrast, Burke argues that what is the result of
a long historical development, of ancient custom, is natural. He gives great
weight to precedents, which are the result of history, and criticizes the rationalist
philosophy that combats them. Burke's doctrine was coherent, it responded to
the aspirations of counterrevolutionaries, and it enjoyed immense success. His
book was immediately translated into French, then into German in 1791, and
later into Italian. It was welcomed in the United States by the Federalists who
represented conservative opinion. It could not, however, be introduced into
Spain; the Inquisition feared that it would acquaint Spaniards with the Revolution.

It was only in 1796 that there appeared the first French work on counterrevolutionary doctrine: J. de Maistre's *Considerations on France*. The author, a
Savoyard, showed that the Revolution that had broken out in France was the
consequence of the moral and religious decadence that had marked all of Europe
during the eighteenth century. To combat the Revolution, then, morality and
religion had to be restored. Maistre believed that it would be inadequate to
restore the old regimes as they existed prior to 1789; it was necessary to construct
a new regime, essentially based on obedience to the will of God. For this reason,
he has been described as a theocrat. In the same period, another Frenchman, L.
de Bonald, anonymously published a similar work, entitled *Theory of Political
and Religious Power in Civil Society, Demonstrated by Reason and History*.
This is an austere, heavy work, much more difficult to read than Maistre's
Considerations. But it too is a book that considers religion the cornerstone of
the state and wants the creation of a theocratic regime. ''God,'' writes Bonald,

"is the author of all States; man can provide nothing for man except through God and owes nothing to man only to God." According to Bonald, the Revolution arose out of the Reformation. To fight the Revolution, it was necessary to fight the Reformation and to oppose religious pluralism. Bonald, as Burke and Maistre, condemns written constitutions and declarations of rights. For him, man has no rights; he has only duties. The Revolution should conclude with a Declaration of the Rights of God that will annul the Declaration of the Rights of Man. Then a "royal monarchy, absolute and hereditary," would be reestablished, formed at its base by millions of subjects, at its apex by the king, and between the two by "intermediary bodies," consisting of ministers, courts of justice, and municipal governments.

The opponents of the Revolution did not await the publication of these theories to act. Since they perceived that they were an unorganized minority, their first move was to leave France and go to foreign countries hostile to the Revolution in order to form armed bands that, together with foreign troops, could invade France and destroy the Revolution, as had been done in Geneva in 1782, in the United Provinces in 1787, and in Belgium in 1790. Emigration began right after 14 July 1789 when the king's brother, the comte d'Artois, left France to go to Turin. Emigration grew after the failure of the king's attempted flight on 21 June 1791 and reached a peak during the winter of 1791–92. It abated after France's declaration of war on Austria and Prussia on 20 April 1792 but did not stop until 1802. The total number of *émigrés* can be estimated at approximately 150,000. They were, in major part nobles, and military and naval officers. However, entire families left France, and in 1793 more than 20,000 peasants abandoned Alsace to follow the retreating Austrian army.

From the end of 1791, the military *émigrés* formed small armies on the banks of the Rhine, the "army of the princes" at Coblentz, the "Black Legion" of A.-B.-L. R. Mirabeau-Tonneau (the brother of the great orator) in Baden, the army of the prince de Condé between the two. In April 1792 these troops joined the Prussian army when it opened its offensive against France, but they were placed in the rearguard, since the general in command, the duke of Brunswick, had little confidence in them. After the Prussian defeat at Valmy (20 September 1792), the *émigrés* were forced to retreat. The Prussians and Austrians held them responsible for their repulse, for, contrary to the promises of the *émigrés*, no insurrection had developed in France. The duke of Brunswick and the Holy Roman Emperor demanded the dispersion of the *émigré* troops. Alone, the army of Condé survived and did not disappear until 1802. Counterrevolutionary action led from abroad had failed.

Consequently, it was necessary to consider uprisings within France, but for these to occur at the most propitious time and place and be coordinated with action by foreign troops, it was indispensable to be well informed on the situation in France. It is for this that intelligence networks were created. The English agents, F. Drake in Italy and later in Germany and W. Wickham in Switzerland, collected information, transmitted in what was apparently commercial correspondence with messages between the lines written in invisible ink. An *émigré*, the comte d'Antraigues, collected and synthesized this information and communicated it to British agents and to other governments involved in the struggle against France. However, the coordination between the counterrevolutionary insurrections and foreign aid was never perfect.

The first great insurrection took place in the Vendée in March 1793. It was provoked by a mass levy of men for the army. Under the Old Regime, the Vendéans had never submitted to the recruitment of royal militia with good grace. This sentiment was mobilized on the spot; the Vendéans were loath to leave their homes. In 1789 they showed themselves to be partisans of the Revolution, but the religious reorganization had upset them. Furthermore, they were certain that the Revolution benefited the urban bourgeois much more than the peasants. Finally, the nobles, many of whom had not emigrated, and the refractory priests had, since 1791, devoted their efforts to active counterrevolutionary propaganda in the Vendée and in Anjou. The peasants of these regions rose en masse on 11 March 1793, the day for the drawing of lots for volunteers. They quickly formed a "Catholic and Royal Army," a huge and disorganized mass of over 10,000 men, which many women and even children joined. This army pushed forward to seize a port from which the English and *émigrés* could support them, but it failed before Nantes, Les Sables d'Olonne, and later Granville (14 November). The army then fell back in disorder; it was attacked by regular troops who had come from Mainz and defeated at Le Mans (12 December) and at Savenay (23 December). The Vendéan insurrection, which lasted nine months, failed miserably. It was prolonged, however, for a long time in Brittany in the form of a guerrilla struggle by the *chouans*. In the spring of 1795, at a time when reaction in France was growing after M. Robespierre's fall, one of the *chouan* leaders, J.-G. Puisaye, believed that circumstances were favorable to a new counterrevolutionary offensive. From the British government he obtained a commitment that a fleet would land a corps of *émigrés* in Brittany, which would subsequently be supported by English troops. The landing took place on the Quiberon peninsula at the end of June. However, the great Vendéan uprising, anticipated by Puisaye, did not occur, and the English did not disembark their infantry. The 4,500 *émigrés* were soon encircled by the Republican troops of General L.-L. Hoche and had to capitulate. Seven hundred and forty-eight *émigrés* were shot by virtue of laws voted by the Convention. This was a disaster for the royalists. Nevertheless, the *chouan* movement persisted until 1804, and there were even sporadic recurrences during Napoleon's return from Elba in 1815 and in 1830 after Louis-Philippe ascended the throne of France.

The Vendéan insurrection could have been very dangerous to the Revolution if it had been coordinated with federalist uprisings that took place at the same time, but the two movements remained completely independent. The federalist revolt was provoked by the *coup de force* of the Jacobin Commune of Paris, which, on 2 June 1793, forced the Convention to arrest twenty-nine Girondin deputies or federalists, deputies who rejected the dictatorship of Paris over France and wanted to reduce the capital to "one eighty-third of its influence" (since France was divided into eighty-three departments). The Girondin deputies who were able to escape arrest gathered at Caen in Normandy and, with a small force, attempted to march on Paris, but they were defeated on 13 July at Pacy-sur-Eure. Yet in many departments the elected councils and sometimes the clubs were shocked at the arrest of the Girondins and demanded the meeting of a new Convention in a provincial city, such as Bourges or Grenoble. The revolt was particularly violent in southeastern France, at Lyon, Nîmes, Marseille, and Toulon. Toward mid-June there was fear of an insurrection of the entire Midi against Paris. The inhabitants of Nîmes even proposed the creation of a federal republic of the Midi, but the southern departments could not unite. Bordeaux and the Gironde could not effect a junction with the federalists of Montpellier, Nîmes, and Marseille because of the attitude of Montauban and Toulouse which proclaimed their fidelity to the Montagnard Convention. Avignon and Nîmes were occupied by troops of the Convention at the end of July, Marseille on 25 August, and Lyon, after a long siege, on 9 October. At Lyon the federalists, who at first opposed not the Revolution but only the Montagnards (the most radical Jacobins), ended up allying with the royalists. At Toulon, they appealed for help to the English and Spanish fleets and even recognized as king the young Louis XVII, then a prisoner at Paris in the tower of the Temple. Toulon, however, was taken thanks to the skill of a young artillery commander, N. Bonaparte, on 18 December 1793; with the fall of this port, the greatest threat to the Revolution since 1789 disappeared.

Under the Directory, the counterrevolutionaries attempted to coordinate their efforts better. In 1799, while English, Austrian, Russian, and Turkish troops were attacking French forces from the Texel in northern Holland to Calabria in southern Italy, counterrevolutionary insurrections broke out everywhere in the rear of the French armies, but they were poorly synchronized. In Calabria the insurrection began in May, in Tuscany in June; but it was, above all, the advance of A. Suvórov's Russian troops that forced the French to evacuate Italy. In Holland an uprising began at the time of an Anglo-Russian landing at the end of August, but it was soon checked by General G.-M.-A. Brune's troops, and the force that landed found no assistance from the populace and had to capitulate on 19 October. Within France, an attack against Toulouse, organized by armed royalist bands on 5 August, failed. The insurgents were thoroughly beaten at Montréjeau on 20 August; many were captured, although some succeeded in escaping to Spain. An attack on Bordeaux was scheduled to take place at the same time, but it was late, and the failure at Toulouse discouraged the royalists of the Gironde. Some uprisings broke out in the Vendée, in Brittany, and in Maine but not until October; Nantes was even occupied by the royalists during the night of 20–21 October and Saint-Brieuc on 25 October. The royalists were, however, unable to maintain control anywhere. The coup d'état of 18 Brumaire (9 November), Bonaparte's advent as head of the government, the victories that he won in Italy in June 1800, and then the restoration of peace put an end to counterrevolutionary attempts. These, however, began again when the war recommenced in 1803. The royalists then thought they could seize power by assassinating Bonaparte. They counted on a *chouan* leader, G. Cadoudal, and on two former generals of the Republic, J.-C. Pichegru, who had rallied to the royalists in 1795, and J.-V. Moreau, who was well disposed to them. But, trapped by the police, Moreau, Pichegru, and finally Cadoudal were arrested. Cadoudal was condemned to death and executed; Pichegru committed suicide in prison; and Moreau was condemned to exile in the United States (he would return from there in 1813, join the Allies, and be killed by a French bullet at the Battle of Dresden). Bonaparte, however, was of the opinion that these men were only confederates and that the plot had been organized by a member of the Bourbon family. Indeed, one of them, the duc d'Enghien, was living in Baden, near the French frontier; Bonaparte believed, on the basis of inaccurate information, that he was the organizer of the scheme. He had him carried off, thereby violating neutral territory, transferred to the Château of Vincennes, tried during the night, condemned to death, and shot immediately. Other royalist leaders were also executed or imprisoned. These harsh actions put an end to counterrevolutionary plots. Henceforth, royalist agitation took on a more disguised and secret form. It fully manifested itself only in 1814 at the defeat of Napoleon's troops.

P. Beik, *The French Revolution Seen from the Right* (Philadelphia, 1946); J. Chaumié, *Le Réseau d'Antraigues et la Contre-Révolution* (Paris, 1965); W. Fryer, *Republic or Restoration in France? 1794-1797* (Manchester, 1965); J. Godechot, *The Counter-Revolution: Doctrine and Action 1789–1804* (New York, 1971); H.-J. Le Sage, *De la Bretagne à la Silésie: Mémoires d'exil (1791-1800)* (Paris, 1983); H. Mitchell, *The Underground War against Revolutionary France: The Missions of William Wickham, 1794 -1800* (Oxford, 1965); J. Popkin, *The Right-Wing Press in France, 1792-1800* (Chapel Hill, N.C., 1980); E. Vingtrinier, *La Contre-Révolution* (Paris, 1924).

J. Godechot

Related entries: BELGIUM; BURKE; *CHOUANNERIE*; COBLENTZ; CONDE; *EMIGRES*; *ESPRIT DES LOIS, L'*; FEDERALISM; HOCHE; LOUIS XVII; MONTESQUIEU; PUISAYE; QUIBERON; VENDEE; VONCK; WICKHAM.

COUP OF 18 BRUMAIRE (9–10 November 1799), Napoleon Bonaparte's forceful action resulting in the overthrow of the government of the Directory and in constitutional changes that made him master of France. By this almost bloodless coup, N. Bonaparte turned from his spectacular career on the battlefield, terminating the Directory and assuming unchallengeable political control.

Although the Directory had done much substantial work, it was threatened by acute political divisions and uncertain leadership. During its four years, it had experienced three lesser coups (Fructidor, Floréal, and Prairial), as well as other less important violations of the constitution. On the eve of the coup of Fructidor (September 1797), the three directors involved had written to Bonaparte in Italy, urging him to join them in Paris, but he had refused, believing that the time was not yet right. In the ensuing two years, the picture changed; and the Egyptian campaign of 1798–99 gave Bonaparte added luster. By 1799 many French leaders, chiefly P. Barras, J. Fouché, E.-J. Sieyès, and C.-M. Talleyrand, were seeking a victorious general—not necessarily Bonaparte—to reestablish order. When Bonaparte received scattered reports from France in the late summer of 1799 of alarming French defeats at the hands of the Second Coalition, he decided to return from Egypt, leaving his army behind. Accompanied by about 400 of his most trusted men, he safely eluded British naval forces in the Mediterranean and on 8 October reached the southern coast of France.

When Bonaparte arrived at Paris (16 October 1799) he was welcomed as the inevitable choice by the conspirators. A scheme was quickly thrown together in secret at his home. This involved summoning a meeting of the Council of Ancients and the Council of Five Hundred on 9 November under the pretext of a Jacobin plot. The Ancients would appoint Bonaparte commander of the troops in Paris (which was illegal) and order the transfer of the two councils on the following day to the palace of Saint-Cloud (which was legal), away from the possible turmoils of Paris. The five directors would be made to resign, leaving the way clear for the necessary constitutional changes.

With the aid of Napoleon's brother Lucien, it was arranged for the president of the Council of Ancients to send formal summons to those members deemed sympathetic, requiring them to attend an early morning meeting on 9 November at the Tuileries. There the decrees authorizing the transfer of the two councils to Saint-Cloud and giving Bonaparte his military command were quickly enacted, following which a formal delegation was sent to Bonaparte's house inviting him to attend. He rode with a military cortege to the Tuileries where he made his address. He vowed stern punishment to all who might threaten the Republic, thanked his generals, and declared that France would have a Republic founded on true liberty, equality, and national representation; this was greeted with loud cheers. The Council of Five Hundred, of which Lucien—fortuitously as events proceeded—was president met around noon. Lucien informed them of the decrees passed by the Council of Ancients, and then, having no power to act, he adjourned the session. The three directors (Sieyès, P.-R. Ducos, and Barras) who were in the plot submitted their resignations, while the unwilling L.-J. Gohier and J.-F. Moulin were held under guard at the Luxembourg until they accepted the inevitable and yielded their posts.

At Saint-Cloud on 10 November, hasty preparations were made to seat the two councils, while large bodies of troops were assembled in the courtyard outside the palace. Bonaparte first appeared before the Council of Ancients, which had met at noon in the Gallery of Apollo. In a rambling speech with strong military overtones, he declared that the Directory as a body of five no longer existed and that constitutional changes must be made. He encountered some hostile criticisms from those members who had not been summoned on the previous day, and his secretary, L.-A.-F. Bourrienne, eventually persuaded him to leave.

Bonaparte then went to the Council of Five Hundred, sitting in the Orangerie. Here he met violent opposition from the Jacobin deputies, some of whom actually threatened him, and in the uproar he was dragged, half-fainting, by his soldiers from the hall. In his nervousness he had scratched his face, drawing blood, thus giving rise to the celebrated legend that he had been threatened by assassins. Lucien soon adjourned the tumultuous session and joined his brother outside. The two addressed the troops, and then Napoleon, hearing the continued uproar, ordered a file of grenadiers with fixed bayonets to enter the Orangerie and clear the hall. This they did, some of the deputies escaping through the windows and casting aside their red togas as they fled into the dusk.

Later in the evening some of the Five Hundred, perhaps sixty, were rounded up and voted to accept Sieyès, Ducos, and Bonaparte as provisional consuls with authority to undertake the work of constitutional revision. After the Council of Ancients, still in session, had agreed, a committee of twenty-five from each council was authorized to participate in the work. The legislature was to be adjourned for six weeks, and sixty-one specified Jacobin members were formally excluded from it. By the narrowest of margins, the coup of Brumaire had succeeded.

Within several weeks, a new constitution was created at the Tuileries. Highly skillful propaganda in newspapers, pamphlets, and posters brought public opinion into line. The three provisional consuls and the two committees worked daily for long hours at their task. It is one of the legends of Brumaire that the over-elaborate and in some respects unworkable proposals of Sieyès were ruthlessly cast aside by Bonaparte. Actually much of Sieyès' structural plan remained, tempered, to be sure, by the insistent demands of Bonaparte. Still another legend of Brumaire is that the coup came about because of the imminent danger of military disaster abroad. In fact the military situation had been transformed by other generals before Bonaparte returned from Egypt. The Constitution of the Year VIII was completed in six weeks and proclaimed on 25 December 1799. It was accepted overwhelmingly by plebiscite the following February.

The coup of Brumaire made possible Bonaparte's four years of authoritarian rule under the consulate and led to an even stronger imperial rule after 1804. France became more rigorously centralized than ever it had been before. Popular voting was so diluted through three successive stages that the voice of the people became a mere whisper. As first consul, Bonaparte had far greater powers than those of his two colleagues. He directly influenced appointments to the Senate and less directly to the two law-making structures, the Tribunate and the Legislative Body. He appointed and presided over a Council of State, approximating a cabinet, drawn from a wide spectrum of political views. All high officials were directly chosen and removed by him. Even so, since sixty-six members of former Revolutionary bodies sat originally in the Tribunate and 277 in the Legislative Body (about four-fifths of the total), Bonaparte could, in this sense at least, claim to be maintaining the link with the Revolutionary years.

F. Bessand-Massenet, *Le 18 Brumaire* (Paris, 1965); L. Bonaparte, *La Révolution de*

Brumaire (Paris, 1845); F. Grousset, *Les origines d'une dynastie. Le coup d'état de Brumaire* (Paris, 1869); A. Meynier, *Le Dix-huit Brumaire, an VIII* (Paris, 1928); J. Thiry, *Le coup d'état du 18 Brumaire* (Paris, 1947); A. Vandal, *L'avènement de Bonaparte*, 2 vols. (Paris, 1903-5).

E. J. Knapton

Related entries: BONAPARTE, N.; COUP OF 18 FRUCTIDOR YEAR V; COUP OF 30 PRAIRIAL YEAR VII; COUP OF 22 FLOREAL YEAR VI; DIRECTORY; EGYPTIAN EXPEDITION; SECOND COALITION; SIEYES; TALLEYRAND.

COUP OF 18 FRUCTIDOR YEAR V (4 September 1797), Republican coup d'état. On 18 Fructidor Year V, the three directors, P. Barras, J.-F. Reubell, and L.-M. La Revellière-lépeaux, supported by the army, expelled their two moderate colleagues, L. Carnot and F. Barthélemy from the Directory and purged the legislative councils of right-wing deputies. This coup ended a period of acute political tension resulting from the right-wing victory in the April 1797 legislative elections. The directors had interpreted the election results as a vote for royalism and considered using force to quash them immediately but could not agree among themselves and finally let the new deputies take their seats. The resulting right-wing majority did elect a monarchist sympathizer, Barthélemy, to the Directory, but neither he nor the newly elected deputies proved very effective.

Nevertheless, the prospect of another right-wing election victory in 1798 worried the loyal republican directors. Carnot, the most moderate of them, proposed enlisting legislative support by compromising with the important group of moderate deputies, thereby breaking up the right-wing majority. He had Barthélemy's support, and for a while the moderate deputies thought they had won over Barras as well. In fact, however, by the end of June 1797, Barras had agreed with the two remaining directors, Reubell and La Revellière-lépeaux, to reject any compromise with the moderates. Apparently acting on his own, Barras arranged with L. Hoche, commander of the Army of the Sambre and Meuse, to send troops toward Paris at the beginning of July 1797, even before Carnot brought the split in the Directory into the open on 14 July 1797 by proposing a reshuffling of the ministers to satisfy the moderates in the councils. Barras surprised him by voting with Reubell and La Revellière-lépeaux to dismiss the moderates' favorite ministers instead, thereby giving the first public indication of the pending crisis.

On 16 July 1797, the just-dismissed war minister, C. Petiet, informed the councils that Hoche's troops had violated the constitutional limits around Paris. Reubell and La Revellière-lépeaux refused to support Barras' hasty coup attempt, however, and Barras did not defend Hoche when the other directors chastised him for his illegal action. In fact, however, his troops remained a key part of the coup plan; they were sent on a march route that kept them close to the capital for an extended period. The three militant directors, dubbed the *triumvirs* in the press, also began systematic preparations for a second coup attempt. They en-

couraged a revival of neo-Jacobin agitation in Paris and the provinces and replaced many right-wing local government officials with trusted republicans.
Soldiers in most army units were encouraged to draft addresses affirming their
militant republicanism and openly threatening the right-wing deputies; in turn,
provincial republican clubs sent congratulations to the troops. Rather than relying
on a popular movement, however, the *triumvirs* intended to use the army for
their coup. They infiltrated soldiers into Paris surreptitiously. N. Bonaparte,
whose independent policy in Italy had been strongly criticized in the councils,
dispatched a loyal subordinate, General P.-F.-C. Augereau, to command them.
Within the world of Parisian political intrigue, the *triumvirs* had the support of
the republican deputies, mostly ex-*conventionnels*, and of intellectual leaders
like Madame de Staël, who urged strong measures against the Right and revision
of the Constitution.

While the three republican directors organized their coup, the right-wing deputies in the councils failed to agree on countermeasures. They had hoped that
Carnot would join them in a firm stand against any violation of the constitution,
but he had been effectively paralyzed when Barras showed him documents,
obtained when Bonaparte occupied Venice, proving that General J.-C. Pichegru,
one of the most prominent and popular of the right-wing deputies, had had
treasonous contacts with the royalists in 1795. Pichegru himself was involved
in secret negotiations with Barras and offered no leadership to the right-wing
deputies either. The councils appointed committees to investigate Barras' abortive
coup attempt but were frustrated by Carnot's refusal to help them expose it.
Their efforts to create a counterweight to the army by reviving the moribund
National Guard and reorganizing the *gendarmerie* were also unsuccessful. The
widely read right-wing newspapers that had flourished after the 1797 elections
reported the troop movements and urged strong measures against the *triumvirs*,
but when the councils failed to act at once, the press served to publicize the
deputies' indecisiveness, cooling any general public support for them. Behind
the scenes, Carnot and some of the moderate deputies continued efforts to work
out a compromise solution to the political crisis. As a result, the moderate
deputies like A.-C. Thibaudeau kept the councils from taking any firm action
even though the *triumvirs* showed no signs of backing down. Around mid-
August, a rash of street scuffles between troops and civilian supporters of the
councils raised tension to a peak, but despite rumors, nothing occurred.

After a brief lull when Augereau succeeded in halting the street clashes, tension
mounted again when La Revellière-lépeaux replaced Carnot as president of the
Directory. His two menacing speeches on 10 Fructidor Year V convinced most
right-wing deputies that there was no hope of compromise, and they drew up a
last-ditch plan to convoke the councils in permanent session, denounce the
directors' plot, and impeach them. In case of an armed clash, they counted on
support from their Legislative Guard, which in fact had been won over to the
Directory's side, and on an irregular force of royalists organized by A.-B.-J.
d'André, an agent of Louis XVIII. The three *triumvirs* had agents at the right-

wing deputies' planning sessions in the quarters of the councils' Committees of Inspectors, which were virtually open meetings anyhow; and in any event, the deputies continued to postpone action from one day to the next, hoping to gain more support and get clearer proof of their opponents' plans. Although several deputies learned that the coup was finally set for the night of 17–18 Fructidor, their leaders let both chambers adjourn on the afternoon of the seventeenth, leaving only a few members of the Committees of Inspectors on watch. The right-wing newspapers were also taken by surprise.

Just before midnight on 17 Fructidor, the *triumvirs* closeted themselves in the Luxembourg and launched their blow. Carnot escaped arrest, but Barthélemy was caught. Augereau, with almost 20,000 troops under his command, quickly surrounded the councils' chambers in the Tuileries and arrested several leading right-wing deputies. The commander of the legislature's guard, J.-P. Ramel, surrendered without a fight and his troops went over to the Directory. Wall posters, prepared secretly in advance, justified the coup as a defense against a royalist conspiracy and printed documents exposed Pichegru's treason. There was no resistance to the coup, either in Paris or the provinces, but no spontaneous support for it was allowed either: a group of *sans-culotte* militants who gathered in Paris was quickly dispersed. The victors claimed that the coup had been completely bloodless, but a well-informed German source asserted that Augereau's troops had killed a couple of suspected royalists.

To complete their coup, the *triumvirs* summoned reliable republican deputies from the two councils to meet at the Odéon Theater and the School of Medicine nearby. Troops dispersed other deputies who tried to draw up a protest against the coup. The rump councils passed a set of emergency laws authorizing the arrest and deportation of Carnot, Barthélemy, fifty-three deputies and several other right-wing politicians, and the suppression of more than thirty right-wing newspapers. These *fructidorisées* were all accused of participating in a royalist conspiracy. In fact, the list was an amalgam including a minority of genuine royalists and an assortment of moderates. No evidence was ever produced linking most of the victims to any specific conspiracy. Most of those proscribed escaped, but Barthélemy and a number of prominent deputies were shipped to Guyana.

In addition to these proscriptions, the laws passed on 19 Fructidor Year V expelled *émigrés* who had been provisionally readmitted to France, reinstated harsh measures against refractory priests, and gave the Directory power to ban newspapers at will. They also nullified the election results from fifty-three departments and reversed earlier decisions in two disputed elections, thereby purging the councils of most right-wing deputies. The coup thus gave the republican directors a free hand to deal with counterrevolutionary opposition. It also had consequences outside of France. A series of similar coups in the French-dominated sister republics brought their policies in line with the new course, at the price of demonstrating these governments' subservience to Paris. The Directory broke off peace negotiations with England, but the defeat of the French moderates convinced Austria that it had to agree to French terms in the treaty of Campoformio.

Although there is general agreement among recent historians that there was no coherent royalist conspiracy involving all, or even a majority, of the politicians marked for arrest in the coup, and that some, like Carnot, were not royalists at all, most scholars, including A. Meynier, G. Lefebvre, and A. Soboul, have continued to justify the events of Fructidor as a necessary measure of republican defense; M. Sydenham has recently offered a contrary viewpoint. Local studies show that it did not help the Directory root out opposition in firmly counterrevolutionary areas like the Ardèche. There is general agreement, however, that the Fructidor coup was fatal to the constitutional experiment launched in 1795. It abolished the electorate's theoretical control over the government and gave the executive greatly expanded powers, setting a precedent for an authoritarian, pseudo-constitutional regime that foreshadowed N. Bonaparte. The coup, carried out against the representatives of the conservative notables without the support of the lower classes, also left the Directory isolated from all possible sources of political support within the electoral system and made it dependent on the generals and the armies, thus preparing the way for Napoleon's coup in 1799.

C. Ballot, *Le coup d'etat du 18 fructidor An V* (Paris, 1906); W. R. Fryer, *Republic or Restoration in France?* (Manchester, 1965); A. Meynier, *Les coups d'etat du Directoire* (Paris, 1927); V. Pierre, *Le 18 fructidor* (Paris, 1893); J. Popkin, *The Right-wing Press in France, 1792–1800* (Chapel Hill, N.C., 1980); M. Reinhard, *Le grand Carnot*, 2 vols. (Paris, 1952); M. Sydenham, *The First French Republic* (Berkeley, 1973).

J. Popkin

Related entries: ANDRE; BARRAS; BARTHELEMY; CARNOT; LA REVELLIERE-LEPEAUX; PICHEGRU; REUBELL; TREATY OF CAMPOFORMIO.

COUP OF 30 PRAIRIAL YEAR VII (18 June 1799), successful attempt by the Council of Ancients and the Council of Five Hundred to purge the Directory of several of its members, thereby reversing the trend of executive domination over the legislature as seen in the coups of Fructidor Year V and Floréal Year VI.

The legislative elections of 7 Floréal Year VII (26 April 1799) had returned a republican majority to the two chambers, as in the elections held a year earlier. The directors wanted to annul these elections as they had on 22 Floréal Year VI (18 May 1798), but this time the rumor of a potential coup led the two councils to offer open resistance. On 17 Prairial (5 June) the Council of Five Hundred demanded an accounting of the Republic's foreign and domestic situation from the directors, who failed to respond. On 28 Prairial, the Five Hundred reiterated its demand and declared itself in permanent session until the directors presented a response; the Council of Ancients adopted the same posture as the lower house.

With the executive board paralyzed by indecision and internal division, the gauntlet of challenge was assumed in the Five Hundred by a deputy named G. Bergasse de Laziroule, who declared that the election of J.-B. Treilhard a year earlier to the Directory was illegal. Treilhard was ineligible for the office, Bergasse asserted, since less than a year had elapsed between his leaving the Council of Five Hundred in 1797 and his subsequent election to the executive board in 1798. (In fact, there were but four days in question.) While constitutionally accurate in his claim, Bergasse had ignored the fact that the time discrepancy had been discussed, and discounted, in the debate surrounding Treilhard's nomination. Despite the efforts of L.-M. La Revellière-lépeaux, a director, to dissuade him, Treilhard resigned immediately. He was replaced by L.-B. Gohier, a former minister of justice, on 29 Prairial.

On the same day, the directors finally responded to the demand of the Five Hundred. In their written reply, the directors allowed that the apparent collapse of internal order (revival of the *chouannerie*, appearance of the right-wing Companies of Jesus, deterioration of the currency) and the recent military reversals were a consequence of the government's lack of sound money. Despite this explanation, the deputies renewed their attack. La Revellière-lépeaux and P.-A. Merlin de Douai, two directors disliked because of their antilegislative stance, were now accused of treason and malfeasance in office. With no support from either the abbé Sieyès, elected to the Directory on 20 Floréal (16 May 1799) to replace the retiring J.-B. Reubell, or the unprincipled P. Barras, who affected indifference to politics except insofar as a crisis might impinge on him directly, the two threatened directors resigned on 30 Prairial. Merlin was replaced by the regicide P.-R. Ducos, while La Revellière-lépeaux saw his seat taken by the obscure General J.-F. Moulin. The Directory was now composed of Barras, Sieyès, Gohier, Moulin, and R. Ducos, of whom the most important was the anti-Directory mole, Sieyès.

Technically the events of 30 Prairial were not a coup d'état. The army, used so effectively in Fructidor for example, had not been called in. Neither La Revellière-lépeaux nor Merlin de Douai were indicted for their actions in office (though this had been a real threat). But the legislature had extended its authority over the executive branch of government, and the appointment of such figures as R. Lindet to the Ministry of Finance is reflective of this legislative intrusion in the affairs of state. One must not forget, however, that while the events of Prairial changed the personnel of the government to suit the councils, the government itself remained unweakened; the Directory lost none of its constitutionally established authority.

What occurred principally on 30 Prairial is that the legislative victims of Fructidor (1797) and Floréal (1798) had taken revenge on the Directory. In the two earlier coups, the directors had treaded only the barest constitutional line in removing allegedly hostile deputies from the legislative councils. In Prairial, it was the legislature that had purged the Directory. It had, unwittingly to be sure, created a political crisis of the first magnitude, which ultimately served as a death knell for the Directory. As M. Lyons (1975), a recent writer on the Directory, declares, "With the departure of Reubell, and the resignations of La Revellière-lépeaux and Merlin de Douai, whose staunch Republicanism was never in doubt, the last flicker of hope of saving the régime died." Sieyès, whose known disenchantment with the Constitution of the Year III (1795) had been well advertised, was now the commanding influence among the directors. The road was paved for the last agony of the Republic: 18 Brumaire.

G. Lefebvre, *The Directory*, trans. R. Baldick (London, 1964); R. Guyot, "Du Directoire au Consulat: les transitions," *Rev. hist.* 111 (1912); M. Lyons, *France under the Directory* (Cambridge, 1975); A. Meynier, *Le 22 floréal an VI et le trente prairial an VII* (Paris, 1928); I. Woloch, *Jacobin Legacy: The Democratic Movement under the Directory* (Princeton, 1970); D. Woronoff, *La République bourgeoisie de Thermidor à Brumaire, 1794–1799* (Paris, 1972).

B. Rothaus

Related entries: BARRAS; COUP OF 18 BRUMAIRE; COUP OF 18 FRUCTIDOR YEAR V; COUP OF 22 FLOREAL YEAR VI; DIRECTORY; GOHIER; LA REVELLIERE-LEPEAUX; MERLIN DE DOUAI; MOULIN; REUBELL; SIEYES; TRIELHARD.

COUP OF 22 FLOREAL YEAR VI (11 May 1798), nullification of the election of a large number of Jacobin deputies to the legislative councils of the Directory. After the coup of 18 Fructidor Year V (5 September 1797), preparations for the elections of the Year VI became a major preoccupation of the Directory. At stake were some 437 legislative seats, including 236 held by former *conventionnels* (the perpetuals, as they had been dubbed in Vendémiaire Year III). On 12 Pluviôse Year VI (31 January 1798), the legislature arrogated to itself the right to verify the credentials of the deputies to be elected that spring. This amounted to the incumbent members of the two councils having the legal authority to purge the newly elected deputies if they wished.

The Pluviôse decision was made with the understanding that in the forthcoming elections, only the revived Jacobin party could benefit. Royalist sympathizers and aristocrats either would not vote or had been disenfranchised as a consequence of the Fructidorian repression. The neo-Jacobins, meanwhile, had created extensive political organizations to support them in their campaigns for the legislative seats. Moreover, it was certain that the Jacobins held administrative support from members of the Republic's administration. The directors, particularly L.-M. La Revellière-lépeaux, P.-A. Merlin de Douai, and P. Barras, were little more desirous of having a majority of alleged social levelers in their midst now than they were a year earlier in having moderates and royalists in control.

Plans were carefully laid by the directors to control the elections. Anti-Directorial officials were dismissed from office, several towns were placed in a state of siege, and inspectors were dispatched, overtly to investigate the application of the road tolls but actually to instruct and bribe electoral commissioners. Perhaps the directors' most flagrant ploy was to permit the increase of the number of *scissions* (secessions). Instigated by P.-A. Merlin de Douai, these *scissions* permitted the Directory to validate only those electoral assemblies producing deputies most amenable to Directorial policies. Thus, for example, as A. Soboul (1975) observes, "While the left-dominated electoral assembly in Paris was in session at the Oratoire, the government encouraged the establishment of another assembly of 212 'seceders' out of 609 at the Institut.'' This procedure was not uncommon throughout other areas of France as well. In any case, the election returns should not have alarmed the middle-of-the-roaders in the government, but the Directory was intent on having a majority it could easily control. This meant that the political power of the government—the directors and the two councils and their supplicants—was to be thrown behind the seceders. The validation of their election was demanded. Under great pressure from the directors, a majority of deputies in each of the councils was forced to accept the directors' list of deputies to be excluded.

By the Law of 22 Floréal Year VI (11 May 1798), elections in eight departments where there had been no secession were nullified; elections in nineteen departments where secession had occurred were validated; and sixty elected judges and administrators were summarily dismissed. Overall, 106 deputies were, in G. Lefebvre's words, "floréalized." One hundred ninety-one government candidates obtained seats in one or the other of the two legislative councils.

The Directory now held a majority in the councils, but its dubious extralegal policies at the elections served to discredit further a regime that had used the army in Fructidor to nullify the elections of the Year V. For the second time in the space of a year, the executive branch of government had bent the legislature to its will, and it was only a matter of time before the executive-legislative antagonism would again appear. The so-called coup of 30 Prairial Year VII (18 June 1799) would be the legislature's response to both Fructidor and Floréal.

G. Lefebvre, *The Directory*, trans. R. Baldick (London, 1964) and *The French Revolution from 1793 to 1799*, trans. J. H. Stewart and J. Friguglietti (London, 1964); M. Lyons, *France under the Directory* (Cambridge, 1975); A. Meynier, *Le 22 floréal an VI et le trente prairial an VII* (Paris, 1928); A. Soboul, *The French Revolution, 1787–1799: From the Storming of the Bastille to Napoleon*, trans. A. Forrest and C. Jones (New York, 1975); J.-R. Suratteau, *Les élections de l'an VI et le coup d'état du 22 floréal* (Paris, 1964); I. Woloch, *Jacobin Legacy: The Democratic Movement under the Directory* (Princeton, 1970); D. Woronoff, *La République bourgeoisie de Thermidor à Brumaire, 1794–1799* (Paris, 1972).

B. Rothaus

Related entries: DIRECTORY; COUP OF 18 FRUCTIDOR YEAR V; COUP OF 30 PRAIRIAL YEAR VII; MERLIN DE DOUAI.

COUTHON, GEORGES-AUGUSTE (1755-94), member of the Committee of Public Safety. The son of a notary, Couthon was born in the Auvergne in the town of Orcet on 22 December 1755 and was educated as a lawyer. After he opened his practice in Clermont-Ferrand, he became known as a benevolent and compassionate champion of the poor, to whom he donated his services, and as a progressive and enlightened participant in the town's intellectual life.

He began to acquire political experience in 1787 as a legal consultant to the provincial assembly of Auvergne. By the beginning of the Revolution, he had become a member of Clermont-Ferrand's governing body and a proponent of constitutional monarchy, a position he argued in his work, *L'aristocrate converti*. He attempted to stand for election to the Estates General but was declared not to have met residency requirements.

Deprived of the chance to further the Revolution at the center of France, Couthon devoted himself to Revolutionary politics at home. He became a Free-mason in 1790 and helped establish a patriotic society that soon became an affiliate of the Jacobin club of Paris. The department of the Puy-de-Dôme elected Couthon to the Legislative Assembly on 9 September 1791. When he arrived in Paris to take office, Couthon was already partially disabled and had to walk with a cane. His disease—probably meningitis—would by 1793 cripple him com-pletely and make it necessary for him to use a wheelchair or be carried about.

Couthon's maiden speech in the Legislative Assembly on 5 October 1791 was a vigorous attack on what he considered the sycophantic deference of the protocol followed by the Assembly when the king attended its sessions. Yet despite the radical tone of this first speech, Couthon remained a constitutional monarchist and failed to distinguish himself as a leader of left-wing opinion within the Assembly. He did become a popular and influential member of the Jacobin club, over which he presided in November and December 1791.

Couthon supported ardently the bellicose policy of J.-P. Brissot and the Gi-rondins, and he welcomed war when it came. At the end of May 1792 he characterized the royal palace as a foyer of conspiracy against the French people. He did not, however, take part in the developments that led to the overthrow of the monarchy because he left Paris in July in an attempt to recover his health at the baths at Saint-Amand in the Nord. He was there when the Tuileries was attacked on 10 August. He greeted the monarchy's fall with joy, but when he returned to Paris at the end of August, he took an equivocal position on the September 1792 Massacres in his letters to his constituents.

The department of the Puy-de-Dôme elected Couthon to the National Con-vention on 6 September 1792. Faced by the growing antagonism between the Girondins and the Mountain, he vacillated and at first attempted to reconcile the two factions. By the end of October 1792, however, he decisively allied himself with M. Robespierre, to whose policies he was to remain faithful to the end.

At the end of November 1792, Couthon was sent on mission to the Loir-et-Cher to quell disorders caused by food shortages and the breakdown of the grain trade. He accomplished his task without resort to force or intimidation by ap-pealing to the patriotism of all and by assuring farmers, merchants, and consumers that their interests would be protected. On his return to Paris, Couthon came to the conclusion that the king must be executed. In his 26 December speech to the Convention, he argued that the Convention's mandate gave it the power to decide the king's fate, and, in a pamphlet against referring the decision to the electorate, he introduced the theory that the Convention was not merely a leg-islative body but a Revolutionary assembly that could take whatever measures it thought necessary for the general security, including the execution of the former monarch. Couthon voted for Louis' execution.

Couthon was sent on his second mission in March 1793 to oversee the annexation of the principality of Salm and its incorporation into the department of the Vosges. During the spring of 1793, he played a leading role in the Mountain's struggle for power with the Girondins, attacking the latter with increasing vehemence. When the Convention was prevented from leaving its meeting place by masses of armed men on 2 June and forced to retreat ignominiously, it was Couthon who boldly announced that the Convention was in fact free and then successively moved that the Girondin deputies be arrested. On 10 July 1793 Couthon was elected to the Committee of Public Safety.

The high point of Couthon's Revolutionary career began at the end of August 1793 when he was ordered on mission to his native Puy-de-Dôme to secure its faltering allegiance to the Convention and to bring the siege of Lyon to a speedy conclusion. He found a difficult situation. Departmental officials were supporting the Lyonnais rebels. The harvest was poor and the department plagued by disorders. He nevertheless declared a *levée en masse* on 2 September and managed to raise a force, which he dispatched to join the Convention's troops before Lyon. Couthon himself remained in Clermont-Ferrand where, in a series of energetic measures, he replicated in miniature the kind of total mobilization of resources that was to enable the Revolutionary government at Paris to defeat its domestic and foreign enemies. Before departing for Lyon at the end of September, Couthon organized armament production, requisitioned supplies and equipment, and fixed prices.

Lyon, already weakened, fell to the Convention's forces on 9 October, and Couthon began to conduct a stern but relatively restrained punishment of the Lyonnais, attempting to preserve some due process in the trials and execution of rebels. He could not, however, bring himself to carry through the Convention's decree ordering the complete destruction of the city and requested to be relieved of his mission at Lyon.

Before going back to Paris, Couthon returned in triumph to the Puy-de-Dôme and issued another series of decrees designed to complete the Revolutionary transformation of the department. He requisitioned grain, ordered a capital levy on the rich, and undertook a radical program of dechristianization, apparently unaware that his colleagues on the Committee of Public Safety had denounced such attacks on the church as anti-Revolutionary.

From November 1793 to 9 Thermidor, Couthon's role was almost entirely one of seconding Robespierre's policies and of sharing his fears, his vision of a virtuous republic, and, ultimately, his fate. The progress of his crippling disease accelerated, attacking his upper body, and Couthon was often absent from the Convention and the meetings of the Committee of Public Safety, instead devoting his energy to the Jacobin club. On 20 January 1794 at the Jacobins, Couthon successfully proposed that all kings be declared guilty of crimes against the human race ex officio. At the Convention a few days later, he proposed the decrees that called for the expropriation of suspects, and in February he moved the Ventôse decrees organizing, at least on paper, the distribution of the confiscated property.

Despite his reputation for mildness, Couthon was caught up in the increasingly paranoid fear of counterrevolutionary conspiracy and assassination. Even after he wholeheartedly and effectively collaborated with Robespierre in the destruction of the Hébertists and the Dantonists (March and April 1794), he insisted that more extermination was necessary. And it was Couthon who proposed and then carried the Law of 22 Prairial (10 June 1794), which streamlined the Revolutionary Tribunal's procedure, extended the categories of capital crimes against the Revolution, and deprived the accused of any defense whatever.

As the conspiracy to overthrow Robespierre began to develop both in the Convention and in the Committee of Public Safety itself, Couthon apparently decided to triumph or fall with his friend. Twice ordered away on mission by the Committee of Public Safety, he managed to ignore their commands and was thus in Paris for the tumultuous session at the Convention on 9 Thermidor (27 July 1794) when Robespierre's enemies engineered an arrest decree. Couthon's demand to be included was immediately granted, and he was imprisoned at the De la Bourbe prison. Released by the sympathetic municipal government, he returned home but later that night joined Robespierre at the Hôtel de Ville and was there when the troops sent to arrest them arrived.

Since Robespierre, G.-A. Couthon, L. Saint-Just, and those accused with them had been declared outlaws, it was only necessary to have their identity verified before they could be executed. Couthon's end on 28 July 1794 was made grotesquely painful by the executioner's unsuccessful attempts to straighten out his twisted and withered body on the guillotine's plank.

G. Bruun, "The Evolution of a Terrorist: Georges Auguste Couthon," *J. of Mod. Hist.* 2 (1930); F. Mège, ed., *Documents inédits sur la Révolution française: Correspondance de Georges Couthon* (Paris, 1872), *Le Puy-de-Dôme en 1793 et le pro-consulat de Couthon* (Paris, 1877), and *Nouveaux documents sur Georges Couthon* (Clermont-Ferrand, 1899); R. R. Palmer, *Twelve Who Ruled: The Year of the Terror in the French Revolution* (Princeton, N.J., 1970).

R. Bienvenu

Related entries: BRISSOT; COMMITTEE OF PUBLIC SAFETY; DECHRISTIANIZATION; GIRONDINS; LAW OF 22 PRAIRIAL; 9 THERMIDOR YEAR II; ROBESPIERRE, M.; SAINT-JUST; SEPTEMBER 1792 MASSACRES; 10 AUGUST 1792; VENTOSE DECREES.

CULTE DECADAIRE. See THEOPHILANTHROPY.

CULT OF REASON (1793–94), Revolutionary attempt by local groups and authorities to replace traditional Christianity with a civic religion; eventually disowned by the central government. The Cult of Reason emerged in the autumn of 1793 as part of the dechristianization movement then getting underway in

Paris and the provinces. Its most dramatic expression was the ceremony on 10 November in the former cathedral of Notre Dame, which was converted into a Temple of Reason. The movement had diverse roots, some going back into the Enlightenment, others growing gradually in the first five years of the Revolution, and still others appearing as the Revolution entered the radical phase known as the Terror, in the Year II of the French Republic.

The Enlightenment had seen many of the *philosophes* attacking not only the power of the church but many of the basic tenets of the Christian religion. F.-M. Voltaire, the best-known intellectual in eighteenth-century France, had waged a long campaign in poems, plays, essays, dialogues, encyclopedia articles, and other genres against the historic fanaticism of the church and the alleged unreasonable dogmas of Christianity and other revealed religions. His war cry had been *écrasez l'infâme*, "crush the infamous thing." He did not publicly reject belief in a Creator or an afterlife, beliefs he thought provided a foundation for morality, but he advocated getting rid of other dogmas and the power of the clergy. J.-J. Rousseau advocated a more sentimental expression of religion, but he too wanted a drastically simplified faith. The civic religion he proposed in the *Social Contract* would have consisted simply of belief in God, the immortality of the soul, and the sanctity of the laws. Other *philosophes* had gone further. D. Diderot advocated a materialistic view of the universe, giving matter a sort of vital potential. The baron d'Holbach campaigned for outright atheism.

In addition to this inherited mélange of anti-Christian ideas, the Cult of Reason was also a product of the failure of the Civil Constitution of the Clergy, the reform of the church carried through by the Constituent Assembly. The Civil Constitution had made the dioceses coincide with the new departments, had provided for popular election of both the higher and lower clergy, and had made the church dependent on state support since its lands had been confiscated and its tithe abolished. The Revolutionaries had hoped to make the church the moral branch of the government, but more than half the clergy had refused to swear obedience to this Civil Constitution and Pope Pius VI had condemned it and the Revolution. The nonjuring or refractory clergy were driven into a counterrevolutionary position. To eradicate this threat, the Legislative Assembly, and then the Convention, had passed increasingly harsh legislation against refractory priests. The sight of priests hunted down, condemned, and exiled or executed prepared the way for an attack on the whole church, including the Constitutional clergy.

Dechristianization and the Cult of Reason was also the product of the inner momentum for change that the Revolution built up. The Revolution had rejected in turn the privileges of the Old Regime, the existence of a legally hierarchical social structure, and then the monarchy itself. As one institution or custom after another was repudiated, radicals called everything into question—traditional measurements, linguistic terms from the Old Regime, plays featuring kings or nobles, even playing cards with effigies of kings, queens, and valets. This obsession to reject everything associated with the old society naturally extended to the church, which had been deeply enmeshed in the feudal and monarchical system, which taught dogmas resting on tradition rather than reason, and whose head was still a prince with territories of his own. Moreover, many of the constitutional clergy lamented the overthrow and execution of the king. As the Revolution reached its crescendo, radicals demanded a new cult uncontaminated by the past.

Meanwhile in the festivals and pageants of the Revolution, the ingredients for a cult such as that of Reason had gradually emerged. At first some of these components had existed alongside the rituals of the church, as in the great Festival of Federation in July 1790 in which the clergy, the Mass, and the *Te Deum* had played an important role. In the procession transporting the remains of Voltaire to the Pantheon in July 1791, however, the clergy were conspicuously absent. By the autumn of 1793, all the makings of a substitute civic religion were present. There were dogmas—the Rights of Man and the republican constitution; there were rituals—processions through the streets, civic oaths, and communal feasts; there were symbols—Phrygian bonnets, tricolor cockades, levels of equality, and fasces; and there were sacred architectural structures—civic altars, triumphal arches, and commemorative columns. During the Festival of Unity and Indivisibility on 10 August 1793, the procession had stopped at stations decorated with temporary architectural constructions and sculptures reminiscent of the Stations of the Cross. Moreover the Revolution now had its martyrs: L.-M. Lepelletier, M.-J. Chalier, and J.-P. Marat, who were treated like saints.

Finally, the immediate circumstances of the autumn of 1793 produced a charged atmosphere that bred radicalism. The king had been overthrown and executed, and the new republican constitution had been completed and proclaimed, but the country was menaced by foreign invasion, counterrevolutionary insurrection, especially in the Vendée, and economic dislocation and serious inflation. The situation seemed to demand extreme measures that would finally rid France of its enemies, eradicate remnants of the Old Regime, and make the Republic secure. In this electrified situation, there were leaders anxious to show their Revolutionary zeal by leading an attack on Christianity and by promoting a new cult. The leaders included some men close to G.-J. Danton, such as P.-F. Fabre d'Eglantine, C. Basire, and J.-A. Thuriot, and also some Paris radicals such as P.-G. Chaumette, F. Desfieux, and J. Pereira.

All of these developments culminated in a series of anti-Christian manifestations, including the Cult of Reason. In the provinces in October and November 1793, representatives on mission such as J. Fouché, A. Dumont, and G. Laplanche sponsored anti-Christian ceremonies, destroyed religious symbols, forbade clerical attire in public, and pressed priests to abandon their calling. In Paris, P.-G. Chaumette and other members of the Commune staged a festival in Notre Dame and converted it into a Temple of Reason. A symbolic mountain was erected in the choir surmounted by a Temple of Philosophy decorated with busts of philosophers and benefactors of humanity. On a rock burned the flame of Truth. A choir of young girls, dressed in white, sang a hymn to Reason, musicians from the opera and National Guard provided accompaniment, and an actress in a tricolor robe played the role of Liberty.

This Cult of Reason that appeared at Notre Dame was imitated in various forms in the sections of Paris and in the provinces. In Bordeaux, in the southwest, the Parisian architect A. Brogniart designed a triumphal arch decorated with the inscription "To Reason," which may have been a prop for a theatrical production or a festival. He also drew up plans to convert the cathedral of Saint-André into a Temple of Reason with a huge symbolic mountain crowned with a statue of Liberty in the apse. The plan included a spiral path to carry participants in Revolutionary liturgies up to the summit to pay tribute to the statue and then to descend, proceed through the nave, and out onto the street again. Far to the north in Lille, a local architect named Verly drew similar plans to transform the church of Saint-Laurent into a temple. Once again there was to be a symbolic mountain, this time rising against a backdrop of thunder and lightning. On the slopes there were to be monuments to Revolutionary martyrs. The focal point was to be a civic altar and a statue of Liberty. The municipality spent considerable money, and local artisans toiled for months to carry out this transformation.

The Cult of Reason alarmed M. Robespierre and other members of the Revolutionary government. Their suspicions were aroused by the fact that the cult was promoted mainly by two groups, the Dantonists and spokesmen for the *sans-culottes* of the sections, who attacked each other as counterrevolutionaries. The members of the ruling dictatorship feared that extreme acts of some of the dechristianizers would repel those who still clung to traditional beliefs. The leaders of the government feared that extreme attacks on Christianity would also discredit the new Republic in the eyes of foreign states, especially those which were still neutral. Above all, Robespierre and his associates suspected that the chief advocates of the cult were atheists whose rejection of belief in the Almighty and immortality of the soul would undermine the moral foundation of the Republic. Atheism was a common charge against the Hébertists who were purged in March 1794 and the so-called Dantonists who were executed in April.

The leaders of the Revolutionary government shared the desire to destroy the church and Christianity, but they favored less provocative methods and a Revolutionary cult that would include belief in God. Robespierre elicited a decree from the Convention reaffirming religious freedom. The correspondence of the Committee of Public Safety shows repeated attempts throughout the Terror to moderate the extreme anti-Christian acts of some of the representatives on mission to the provinces. The disapproval of the committee did moderate the Cult of Reason. For instance, in the autumn of 1793, the authorities in Lille spoke of the converted church of Saint-Laurent as the "Temple of Reason," but soon they usually called it the "Temple of Morality" and finally simply "the Temple."

Robespierre's proposal in May for a cycle of festivals starting with a Festival of the Supreme Being was an attempt to create a Revolutionary cult that would replace Christianity but would emphasize belief in God and the immortality of the soul. His cult, like that of Reason, was to have a simple creed, was to center on the fatherland, and was to be free from any priesthood, but it was too mystical for extremists and too radical for traditionalists. In any case, the great Festival of the Supreme Being in June was followed by the overthrow of Robespierre and his principal supporters in July. However, the effort to create a civic cult to replace Christianity did not end with the Thermidorian Reaction. Under the Directory, government leaders once again promoted a cycle of civic ceremonies on the anniversaries of the great achievements of the Revolution and on every tenth day, the Republican Sunday. Like the Cult of Reason and the Supreme Being, these too were to prove ephemeral.

F.-A. Aulard, *Le culte de la Raison et le culte de l'Etre Suprême* (Paris, 1892) and *Christianity and the French Revolution*, trans. (New York, 1966); A. Dansette, *Religious History of Modern France*, vol. 1 (New York, 1961); A. Mathiez, *La Révolution et l'eglise* (Paris, 1910); J. McManners, *The French Revolution and the Church* (London, 1969).

J. A. Leith

Related entries: ATHEISM; CHAUMETTE; CIVIL CONSTITUTION OF THE CLERGY; CLOOTS; COMMITEE OF PUBLIC SAFETY; CULT OF THE SUPREME BEING; DAVID; DECHRISTIANIZATION; DESFIEUX; FABRE; HEBERTISTS; LEPELLETIER DE SAINT-FARGEAU; MARAT; PIUS VI; ROBESPIERRE, M.

CULT OF THE SUPREME BEING, a deistic and patriotic cult, inaugurated in Paris 8 June 1794. A familiar key term in the eighteenth-century French Enlightenment was *L' Etre Suprême*. It denoted a universal deity, who, quite different from the traditional Christian God, having created the universe, remained an impersonal being. Beyond this basic deistic premise, enlightened writers and their readers of the pre-Revolutionary and Revolutionary periods varied widely in their individual beliefs concerning other aspects of Christian doctrine, some verging on agnosticism or even atheism. Others retained not only a belief in a Supreme Being but also in the immortality of the soul and a happy afterlife for those who, according to enlightened morality, had deserved this. For some a belief in a Supreme Being was based on Newtonian science, with its implications that the universe operated automatically like clockwork, in accordance with natural law. Others, among whom the writer J.-J. Rousseau was the outstanding example, rejected this coldly mechanistic approach and conceived of the deity in pre-Romantic, emotional terms.

This deistic conception of a Supreme Being, in one form or another, thus was a familiar and acceptable idea to many of the generation who made the French Revolution, including enlightened members of the clergy. It was therefore to be expected that the Declaration of the Rights of Man and Citizen of 1789, drafted while the great majority of the clergy making up the First Estate still adhered to the Revolution, would be proclaimed "in the presence and under the auspices of the Supreme Being." When the Jacobin-controlled Convention accepted a much more radical constitution for the French Republic in June 1793, its Declaration of Rights was proclaimed "in the presence of the Supreme Being."

In the meantime, however, controversy over the confiscation of church property and the subsequent passage and implementation of the Civil Constitution of the Clergy, which led to papal rejection of these changes, which in turn led to the requirement for the clergy of an oath of loyalty to the Revolution, had resulted in a partial break between church and state.

This break with traditional Christianity, whose clergy had by now largely rejected the Revolution, stimulated the rise of what came to be a lay religion of nationalism and patriotism. Under the stimulus of a desperate war and a military crisis in 1793 and 1794, there developed a pattern of thought, action, and ceremony directed toward *la patrie* that included such obviously religious aspects as Revolutionary rituals, hymns, holy days, a new calendar with Sundays replaced by *décadis*, prophets, martyrs, and sacred objects.

The break with traditional Christianity became virtually complete, as many priests resigned, including J.-B.-J. Gobel, the constitutional archbishop of Paris, and radical supporters of the Revolution began an energetic program of dechristianization. In Paris during the fall of 1793, the city government, the Commune, had forbidden public ceremonies of the Christian church and decreed that "death was an eternal sleep." Plans were begun for substituting some kind of lay religion that would merge the dynamic new religion of national patriotism with enlightened conceptions of the deity.

The first of these projects was the Cult of Reason. The extreme radical wing of the dechristianization movement in the Paris Commune had seized the initiative, and on 10 November 1793 the Commune of Paris inaugurated the Cult of Reason at a festival in the former cathedral of Notre Dame, now converted to a Temple of Reason. Similar ceremonies followed elsewhere. Although several of the leaders were atheists, the movement itself was not atheistic, and the cult was dedicated not only to Reason but also to the Supreme Being, to Nature, Liberty, and *la patrie*.

M. Robespierre, soon to become the dominant figure in both the Jacobin club and in the National Convention, was firmly opposed to the actions of the extreme dechristianizers, for his deism was of the Rousseauist variety. In the spring of 1792 in an emotional speech at the Jacobin club, he had proclaimed, and maintained in spite of a hostile reception, his fervent belief in an eternal being, in a providence that personally watched over the Revolution. He further testified that in the first period of the Revolution, when he had been in the minority, he could not have held out without the consolation of such a belief. But he departed from his mentor Rousseau's harsh dictum in the *Contrat social* that nonbelievers should be banished, insisting that this truth be left in the writings of Rousseau.

On 21 November 1793, Robespierre launched his crusade against atheism in a speech at the Jacobin club, declaring it to be aristocratic, while belief in a Supreme Being was *toute populaire*. Then after the struggle with and the overthrow of the Hébertists, including the most radical leaders in the dechristianization movement, he laid the philosophical basis for a cult of the Supreme Being in a carefully prepared speech to the Convention on political morality, which is founded on love of *la patrie* and its laws.

In the meantime, plans were being made to inaugurate a series of festivals promoting national patriotism, to be held on each of the *décadis* in the Revolutionary calendar, one of which was to be devoted to the Supreme Being. A political crisis intervened, however, and it was not until after the overthrow of the Dantonists on 6 April 1794 that the next step was taken.

Robespierre on 7 May 1794 presented, in the name of the Committee of Public Safety, a report announcing the approaching Festival of the Supreme Being. This would provide a common denominator for the religious feelings of the majority of Frenchmen in a state religion that would help to consolidate the Revolution and the religious revolution that had begun with the break from Roman Catholicism, while avoiding the excesses of the dechristianization movement. His speech, "On the Relations between Religious and Moral Ideas with Republican Principles, and on the National Festivals," represented his most fundamental and personal thoughts on the subject of a belief in a Supreme Being and the immortality of the soul, which to him were the fundamental principles of the universal religion of nature. The report concluded with a decree, which was passed unanimously, proclaiming that the French people recognized the existence of the Supreme Being and the immortality of the soul. To promote Republican principles, national festivals on the key dates in the history of the Revolution would be celebrated, and on the *décadis* there would be celebrated national festivals dedicated to various subjects, the first of which would be the Supreme Being and Nature, this to take place 20 Prairial (8 June 1794).

This ceremony inaugurating the Cult of the Supreme Being, although Robespierre did not so name it, was carefully planned by the painter J.-L. David. It was the most carefully staged of all the Revolutionary ceremonies. A procession, drawing on the population of all the sections of Paris, was joined by the Convention, gathered at the Tuileries gardens. Robespierre delivered two short emotional speeches, linking the Supreme Being, from whom liberty and virtue had come, with the work of the Revolution and denounced in patriotic terms tyrants and despotism.

The procession then formed, complete with appropriate symbols. At the head of the Convention marched Robespierre as its current president. Arriving at the Champ de Mars, where a mound had been erected on which the marchers gathered, there was further singing, the taking of an oath by the men not to lay down their arms until crime and tyranny had been destroyed, and a final cry of "*Vive la République.*" Similar ceremonies were held in the provinces.

Thus was inaugurated what was to be a new religion for France, intimately tied up with the secular religion of national patriotism. It was also fatally linked to Robespierre who, although the original idea had not been his, had appeared as the pontiff of the new cult. Political differences, however, had surfaced during the ceremony. He himself testified to the insulting comments addressed to him during the procession. With his overthrow and execution in Thermidor, just fifty days later, the new cult was abandoned, together with the whole panoply of ceremonies decreed by the Convention. Under the Directory, seven different national festivals were decreed, but the Supreme Being was not included.

F.-A. Aulard, *Le culte de la Raison et le culte de l'Etre Suprême (1793-1794)* (Paris, 1904); A. Cobban, *Aspects of the French Revolution* (New York, 1968); D. L. Dowd, *Pageant-Master of the Republic: Jacques-Louis David and the French Revolution* (Lincoln, Neb., 1948); *Gazette nationale ou le Moniteur universel*, Nos. 259 and 262, 19 and 21 Prairial Year II; A. Mathiez, *Etudes sur Robespierre* (1758-1794) (Paris, 1958); J. McManners, *The French Revolution and the Church* (London, 1969); G. Rudé, *Robespierre, Portrait of a Revolutionary Democrat* (New York, 1976).

G. H. McNeil

Related entries: CALENDAR OF THE FRENCH REPUBLIC; CIVIL CONSTITUTION OF THE CLERGY; CULT OF REASON; DAVID; DECHRISTIANIZATION; GOBEL.

CUSTINE, ADAM-PHILIPPE, COMTE DE (1740-93), general. Son of an aristocratic family from Metz, Custine was a soldier almost from birth. As a small boy, he took part in his first military operation, a siege of Maestricht conducted by M. de Saxe. After completing his education, he joined the army and served throughout the Seven Years War. In 1761, he so distinguished himself that the duc de Choiseul promoted him to colonel and created a regiment for him. After the war, Custine attended Prussian maneuvers and came to advocate a Prussian-style military system for the French army. Then, in 1780, he went to America as colonel of the Saintonge Infantry Regiment. On his return, he was promoted to the rank of *maréchal de camp* (major general).

In 1789 Custine went to the Estates General as representative for the nobility of the Metz region. Although he did vote with the Right on certain issues, he attached his star to the Revolution. In October 1791, he became a lieutenant general. In April and May 1792, he led a body of troops that seized Porrentruy. In June he was given a large independent command within the *Armée du Rhin*. Once the duke of Brunswick had been turned back at Valmy, Custine took the offensive along the Rhine. He seized Speyer on 29 September, reaching Mainz on 21 October, and entered Frankfurt two days later. His success was important, although it was overrated at the time. For his efforts he was given command of all troops in the *Armée du Rhin* in November.

At this point, Custine was guilty of the same error that C. Dumouriez committed: he believed the Prussians could be easily separated from their coalition with Austria. Custine engaged in unauthorized and fruitless correspondence with Brunswick to try to open negotiations.

He was unable to hold Frankfurt for long, and the renewed allied offensive in March 1793 hurled his forces back. Unfortunately, he left 20,000 men isolated at Mainz, and, in general, his conduct of the retreat left much to be desired. However, his reputation was little diminished, and after Dumouriez defected to the enemy, Custine was appointed to command the all-important *Armée du nord* on 13 May 1793.

In most ways, Custine was a general admirably suited to the task before him. The *Nord* had been badly shaken by defeat and retreat; it needed its confidence restored. Custine did a first-rate job preparing the *Nord*. He culled useless men from units, fully armed and equipped his front-line battalions, and conducted rigorous training throughout the army. Custine was a strict disciplinarian who shot men for pillage and once executed two men chosen by lot to punish a unit that had dishonored itself. Yet in both the *Rhin* and the *Nord*, he was immensely popular. Custine's work of May, June, and July 1793 laid the foundation for the victories won in the fall.

But as able as he was in these respects, he was politically inept. His Prussian style of command struck the representatives on mission as unsuitable for Revolutionary France. He was contemptuous of civil authority, saying once, "When a decree of the Convention does not please me, I throw it in the fire" (Bertaud, p. 154). He quarreled with the representatives and disregarded directives from the Committee of Public Safety. He charged his fellow generals and the war ministry with incompetence.

Custine was already under suspicion when the fortress of Condé fell into enemy hands on 12 July 1793. His failure to save Condé brought his recall to Paris where he went, believing the government would not dare replace him. Yet on 22 July he was arrested. The fall of the abandoned French garrison at Mainz, followed by the loss of Valenciennes, sealed his fate. He was found guilty of criminal correspondence with the enemy, Brunswick, and of aiding the enemy to conquer French fortresses and magazines.

The historian J.-P. Bertaud (1979) has argued, "The trial that followed was not that of a traitorous general, but of the '*généralat,*'...opposed to the Revolution.... It was necessary that Custine die in order that the revolutionary people and their government demonstrate that the army was the armed fist of the Revolution." Custine went to the scaffold on 28 August 1793.

J. P. Bertaud, *La Révolution armée* (Paris, 1979); A. Chuquet, *Les guerres de la Révolution*, vols. 6–8 (Paris, 1892–96); R. W. Phipps, *The Armies of the First French Republic and the Rise of the Marshals of Napoleon the First*, vols. 1–2 (London, 1926, 1929); G. de Vernon, *Mémoire sur les opérations militaires des généraux-en-chef Custine et Houchard* (Paris, 1844).

J. A. Lynn

Related entries: BATTLE OF VALMY; BRUNSWICK; DUMOURIEZ.

D

DANCE. See *CARMAGNOLE*.

DANTON, GEORGES-JACQUES (1759-94), militant, deputy to the National Convention, member of the Committee of Public Safety. Danton was born on 26 October 1759 in Champagne in the town of Arcis-sur-Aube, where he later bought national property and which he visited repeatedly during the Revolution. His father died when Danton was two. In 1773 he entered the Oratorian school at Troyes and there fell in love with the classics. He is supposed to have traveled by foot to Reims, in 1775, ''to see how a king is made.'' By 1780 he was off to Paris to study law. Through brash self-assurance he became a lawyer's clerk. Because of his wretched handwriting, his master sent him to attend the courts, giving him the opportunity to hear the great lawyers of the day. Falling ill, Danton discovered the works of Rousseau, Beccaria, Montesquieu, Buffon, and Diderot, and he learned English and Italian. He still needed a degree and purchased a diploma at Reims; then he returned to Paris to practice. He had few cases initially. But then Danton fell in love with G. Charpentier, daughter of the proprietor of the Café Procope, near the Palais de Justice. They were married, and his father-in-law provided part of the sum with which he purchased the post of advocate to the royal councils (1787). Prior to the suppression of this post in 1791, he won a large number of cases.

He came to national attention as a Revolutionary through local Paris politics, but his ascent was gradual and it had its critics and its setbacks. The lawyer C. Lavaux later recalled seeing Danton at the Cordeliers convent, meeting hall for his district. It was 13 July 1789. Danton, in a frenzied voice, was urging his fellow citizens to take arms against 15,000 brigands mobilized at Montmartre and against an army of 30,000 about to pour into Paris and massacre its inhabitants. Although enrolled in the bourgeois guard, Danton did not participate in the siege of the Bastille the next day. In October, after becoming president of his district, he prepared its manifesto, which requested the other Paris districts to join in sending commissioners to the Commune and asking the marquis de Lafayette to go to Versailles to have the king reassign the Flanders Regiment. But Danton, now captain of the district's battalion of National Guards, did not go to Versailles himself. He also engaged in an extended struggle with J.-S. Bailly over the right his district claimed to impose binding instructions on its five representatives to the Assembly of the Paris Commune. He fought with Bailly also over J.-P. Marat, whom Bailly had sought to arrest. The resistance of the district to the Châtelet's agents led to an arrest decree being issued against Danton. The Cordeliers appealed to the National Assembly; it was brought also before the Assembly of the Commune. Ultimately the Châtelet abandoned its pursuit of Danton, and he emerged more popular than ever as his district's president.

He was also widely known in Paris. In January 1790 he was elected to the provisional Commune, where he displayed surprising moderation, as he did a year later when elected to the General Council of the department of Paris. He exercised little influence in each position. When the Cordeliers district lost its identity after the reorganization of Paris into forty-eight sections, he was elected by his section to the General Council of the Commune, but the other sections refused to ratify this choice, perhaps because of rumors that he was for sale.

About this time (August 1790) the Cordeliers club was born. A more democratic society than the Jacobins, it was composed of activists like Danton himself and had such early members as L.-C.-S. Desmoulins, A.-M. Legendre, P.-F. Fabre d'Eglantine, A.-F. Momoro, J.-P. Marat, along with P.-G. Chaumette, A.-N. Vincent, and J.-N. Billaud-Varenne.

In November, Danton addressed the National Assembly as a delegate from the Paris sections, who were angry over the harsh repression of the Nancy mutiny. He called for the dismissal of three royal ministers, J.-F. La Tour du Pin, J.-M. Champion de Cicé, and F.-E. G. comte de Saint-Priest. He was applauded by the Left, and the three subsequently resigned. But questions arose about his apparent friendliness to a fourth minister, A.-M. comte de Montmorin. Was Danton in Montmorin's pay?

In March 1791 Danton appeared at the Jacobins, asking that a new national legislature replace the stagnating Assembly. In April he clashed with the marquis de Lafayette in support of a mob intent on preventing the king from going to Saint-Cloud. On 21 June he criticized Lafayette severely, accusing him of complicity in the king's attempted flight. He opposed the Assembly's effort to re-establish Louis XVI on the throne and was a member of the Jacobin committee responsible for the petition calling for the king's replacement "by every constitutional means," implying a regency under the duc d' Orléans. He took no part in preparing the Cordeliers' more clearly republican petition, and he prudently left for the country the day of the Champ de Mars "massacre." When an arrest warrant was issued against him, he visited his recently purchased national properties at Arcis and then traveled with his father-in-law to England.

He returned to France to take part in the elections for the Legislative Assembly.

Not elected, he dropped from view, only to reemerge in December as candidate for the position of deputy *procureur* of the Paris Commune. He defeated J.-M. Collot d'Herbois for this post. He made a remarkable maiden speech (20 January 1792) in which he referred to nature as having endowed him with an athletic frame and the fierce countenance of liberty. He offered his resolve to fight against counterrevolution but wished also to win the esteem of those who dreaded the storms of liberty. He spoke, too, of his support of the constitutional monarchy.

On the question of the desirability of war, he stood with M. Robespierre in opposition. But he rallied to the Gironde when the possibility of his becoming a minister arose. Rebuffed, he became hostile to the Gironde and to the court.

Although Danton did not participate in the demonstration of 20 June against the crown, he apparently played a significant role in the insurrection of 10 August, as he claimed at his trial. He initiated the sectional movement demanding the king's deposition. It is true that he did visit his mother at Arcis shortly before the insurrection, but he was in Paris on 9 August to carry out the coup that replaced the regular Commune with its insurrectional successor, thereby disorganizing the defense of the Tuileries. It was he who ordered the killing of A.-J. Mandat by J.-A. Rossignol. The Girondins needed a man as minister who had authority with the people. They would not have turned to Danton if they had not considered him a leader of the insurrection.

During the weeks that followed, he was clearly the most important figure in France. This minister of the Revolution was technically only minister of justice, but as the first minister elected, by 222 votes out of 285—and also because of his arresting personality—he dominated his fellow ministers in the Executive Council: G. Monge, J. Servan, G.-F. Lebrun, E. Clavière, and J.-M. Roland. He appointed Fabre d'Eglantine general secretary for the Ministry of Justice, and Fabre handled much of its business, even using—and perhaps abusing— Danton's ministerial seal. On 19 August Danton dispatched a circular to the courts of France explaining the insurrection nine days earlier as the nation's successful response to a plot in the Tuileries and seeking to reassure the provinces of his own desire to work for the maintenance of law, public peace, and national unity. He asked the judges of France to show greater support for the Revolution than some of them had shown in the past.

Danton gave much attention to the matters facing other ministers, who met with him in his home. When the news reached Paris that Longwy had fallen, there was near panic, Roland and Servan urging the transfer of the government to Blois. Danton rejected this in no uncertain terms. He urged the Legislative Assembly to order each municipality to collect and equip all the men within its jurisdiction fit to carry arms and to supply them with all they needed to fly to the frontier. Special commissioners were created to go into the departments to supervise these levies, make necessary requisitions, and instill fear. He sounded the note of Terror because he believed those who supported the Republic were a very small minority. He instigated one decree declaring that relatives of *émigrés* were to be hostages and another calling for the arrest of nonjuring priests. On

28 August he obtained authority for domiciliary visits to search for weapons and arrest suspects. On 2 September, told that Verdun was about to fall, he hurried to the Assembly to make one of his greatest speeches, rousing France to the national defense: "We ask that whoever refuses to serve in person, or hand over his arms, be punished with death . . . the tocsin which is about to ring is not a signal of alarm; it sounds the charge against the enemies of the country. To defeat them, gentlemen, we must dare, and dare again, and dare forever, and so France will be saved" (Fribourg, p.173).

In calling for action did Danton have only France's external enemies in mind or was he thinking also of "the traitors among us"? Later that day, there began the massacres at the Paris prisons, more than 1,400 dying. What was Danton's responsibility for them? Several days later he told the future Louis-Philippe that he was responsible, because he wanted a river of blood between the Parisians who were going to fight in Champagne and the *émigrés*, as a guarantee of loyalty. But one cannot be certain if his statement rang true. Danton was then at fever pitch. He needed the support of the Commune, some of whom, including personal friends, favored this action. The massacres had been foreseen. Danton had been filling the prisons with persons he had publicly denounced as traitors, and shortly before the massacres began, he had inspected lists of prisoners and marked the names of those who should be set free. He may have agreed to the massacres without giving the order for them. He let them occur, making no effort to stop them and rejecting proposals that he intervene. He did intercede in certain cases, however—in behalf of A. Duport and C. de Lameth and in intercepting a warrant for the arrest of Roland. He probably could have done more but chose not to.

As minister, Danton kept directly in contact with France's generals, especially C. Dumouriez. He also sought to separate Prussia from Austria and dispatched F.-J. Westermann to the king of Prussia for negotiations that led, after Valmy, to the retreat from France of the Prussian army.

He was elected a deputy to the Convention from Paris, receiving the highest number of votes obtained by any Paris deputy. He was named to two of the Convention's most important committees, the Diplomatic Committee and the Committee on the Constitution. Not confident that the new Republic would survive, he struck a conservative note, asking the Convention to declare that all private property would be maintained forever. He sought the collaboration of the Girondins who distrusted him. In October they demanded an examination of his accounts as minister. Danton had spent heavily, and for much of his spending there were no records. He could not respond effectively. These attacks drove him toward the Left. He had disassociated himself from Marat earlier, but when J.-B. Louvet attacked Robespierre, Danton sprang to Robespierre's defense.

He also considered acting in behalf of the king, for whom his support was solicited by T. de Lameth. Danton promised support, adding that he would defend the king only to the extent that he did not jeopardize himself. Danton missed a large part of the trial while on mission in Belgium, returning in mid-

January only in time to speak brutally for the penalty of death and to vote against a reprieve. The king's friends had hoped for much more.

The mission to Belgium was a mission to Dumouriez. It concerned the question of Belgium's relationship with France. Was Belgium, now French occupied, to be annexed or to remain independent? It also concerned, more immediately, quarrels between Dumouriez and J.-N. Pache, France's war minister, over the obtaining of military supplies and over plundering in Belgium on the part of ministerial agents. Danton returned twice more: at the end of January on a mission marked by brutality and pillage and at the end of February, after his wife had died.

He returned to the Convention on 8 March 1793 to announce an enormous peril facing the French in Belgium and to ask the Convention to send commissioners into every section of Paris, to call on the citizenry to fly to the rescue of Belgium. There followed the abortive insurrection against the Girondins known as the March Days, during which Danton took the lead in the creation of the Revolutionary Tribunal, as well as in seeking a stronger executive authority, a kind of parliamentary cabinet. Danton may have been behind this abortive insurrection. The signal for it had come from the Cordeliers, and he later opposed P.-V. Vergniaud's demand for the punishment of its leaders.

He continued to support Dumouriez against mounting demands for his dismissal, and on 20 March he visited him again to discuss a cantankerous letter Dumouriez had written to Pache. Two weeks later, unable to lead his troops against Paris, Dumouriez deserted to the Austrians. Danton and the Girondins both had connections with the general and were endangered by them. Even before his treason, they accused one another of being his accomplices. Danton told the Convention that Roland had asked Dumouriez to help in crushing his enemies, especially Danton. M.-D. Lasource accused Danton of complicity with Dumouriez in an effort to restore the monarchy after destroying the Convention. Danton delivered a powerful riposte, attacking the Girondins. The Montagnards embraced Danton. A year later, however, the Robespierrists repeated Lasource's charge of complicity.

Within the week, he was elected to the newly created Committee of Public Safety. He made diplomacy his special province, seeking through negotiations both to win the support of the smaller, neutral powers and to divide the coalition against France. He needed, therefore, to demonstrate the moderation of France, and to this end he opposed Robespierre's demand for the sentence of death against cowards who should suggest any compromise with the Republic's enemies, and he asked for a decree announcing that France would not interfere in the affairs of its neighbors. Danton was turning from France's earlier policy of offering its support to all peoples desiring to resist the oppression of their tyrants. He may even have encouraged certain smaller states to believe that the release of Marie Antoinette might be obtained in return for their support of France.

He gave indirect support to the insurrectional movement against the Girondins by defending Paris against Girondin efforts to investigate the movement through the Convention's Commission of Twelve, whose suppression Danton achieved on 31 May, but he did not figure prominently in the purge of the Girondins two days later. While he desired their expulsion, he did not desire their deaths. Their defeat in turn weakened Danton himself by strengthening the advocates of a war to the death both at home and abroad.

Crisis followed. A federalist revolt began in support of the Girondins. Danton's foreign policy of negotiation had not improved France's military position. The Vendéan revolt continued, and on 10 July the Convention learned that Danton's Westermann had been defeated in the Vendée. F. Chabot informed the Jacobins that Danton had lost his energy, and the Jacobins complained about his absence. He had now taken a second wife, L. Gély. Marriage distracted and softened him. On 10 July someone called for the reconstruction of the Committee of Public Safety. From the original Dantonist Committee, only R. Lindet and B. Barère were retained. Robespierre joined the new committee on 24 July. Although Danton was elected president of the Convention on 25 July, he never again enjoyed his former prominence.

But he had his moments. He urged that the new Committee of Public Safety become the provisional government of France and that the Convention place 50 million *livres* at its disposal. The committee, suspecting a trap, opposed his suggestions. On 12 August he proposed a *levée en masse*, which was to be the enlistment of the thousands of delegates to Paris from the primary assemblies in the mobilization of France against the external foe. On 5 September he displayed his old energy as he endorsed the proposal for a Revolutionary army, asking that every citizen be provided with a musket, and he urged the division of the Revolutionary Tribunal into sections so as to accelerate its action.

On 25 September some of his friends challenged the policies of the Committee of Public Safety. Robespierre struck back, terrifying his critics. Danton was not present. He was ill or sick at heart. J.-R. Hébert had turned the Cordeliers against him. He was troubled by A.-P. Custine's condemnation and by the fate marked out for Marie Antoinette and the Girondins. He took to his bed and then left for Arcis for six weeks in the country.

He returned to Paris in late November, however, to speak against the dechristianization policy with which his Hébertist opponents had become associated. In this he stood with Robespierre. He also, cautiously, began to oppose the Terror, which, he argued, should strike only the real enemies of the Republic, not those who were merely lacking in Revolutionary vigor. In the name of moderation, he asked for the recall from the provinces of the Hébertist agents of the minister of war. He also sought the help of Desmoulins, who attacked the Hébertists through the pages of his *Vieux Cordelier*. Although in these attacks Danton and Desmoulins were uncritical of the Committee of Public Safety, it felt endangered for it had made the Terror its own policy. Criticism of it implied a Dantonist alternative. Robespierre feared the ultra-Revolutionaries but he feared the so-called Indulgents as well, and he supported each group in turn against the other. Danton's friends came singly under attack.

Danton fell into a kind of torpor, which further encouraged his enemies. His old friends, such as Collot d'Herbois and J.-L. David, turned against him. He appeared rarely at the Jacobins or at the Convention. Friends arranged a meeting with Robespierre, but it degenerated into a quarrel over whether innocents were perishing. Late in February 1794, L. Saint-Just told the Convention in his report against the factions, "Those who are moved with pity for prisoners are guilty against the Republic: guilty because they do not long for virtue; guilty because they do not desire the Terror" (Madelin, p.321). It was the Hébertists, however, who were arrested first, tried, and guillotined. Danton praised the Convention and the committee, both of which had never seemed to him so great, and he called for united action and concord. The hall rang with applause. But this triumph was followed by the sudden arrest, at night, of Danton, J.-F. Delacroix, Desmoulins, and P. Philippeaux and, on the following day, by the reading of the report that Saint-Just had prepared with notes provided by Robespierre. It asked the Convention to bring them before the Revolutionary Tribunal on the charges of being the accomplices of the duc d'Orléans, Dumouriez, and Fabre d'Eglantine, and of having dabbled in a conspiracy to restore the monarchy. Their indictment was voted without a single voice opposed. No one dared speak for fear of perishing himself.

Because such a trial could endanger the government, it was carefully directed. The judges were threatened with arrest should they show any weakness. Only seven jurors were found pure enough to serve. Principals from the Company of the Indies affair such as F. Chabot were made Danton's codefendants so as to suggest that all were knaves; foreigners like the E. and J. Frei brothers were added, to suggest a foreign plot. Even so, matters went poorly for the government. P.-J. Cambon, a government witness for the Indies affair, defended Danton against the charge of treasonable relations with Dumouriez. Danton spoke with his old energy and so loudly that he was heard far beyond the courtroom. He caused the courtroom audience to break into applause. The jurors appeared to be weakening. M.-J.-A. Herman, presiding, interrupted Danton's defense. J.-B.-A. Amar and J.-H. Voulland hurried off to Saint-Just to urge him to obtain a special decree that would permit the court to bring the trial to an early end. And they succeeded. He was executed 16 Germinal Year II.

Danton was not a rectilinear Revolutionary—hence the rumors that swirled about him during his lifetime and the intense controversies among historians since. G. Lefebvre has carefully reviewed the evidence assembled by A. Mathiez to show his venality. It is true that Danton's ordinary income, together with the compensation he received for his venal office, was insufficient to take care of both his generous living expenses and the purchases he made, usually in cash, of national properties and of a house at Arcis. The testimony of A.-F. Bertrand de Molleville, J.-P. Brissot, and Lafayette make it almost certain that he was in the pay of the foreign minister Montmorin, probably soon after the October Days. He probably also drew on the civil list, to judge from an offhand reference by H.-G. R. Mirabeau. He may have been involved in the distribution of royalist funds undertaken to save the life of the king. It is very difficult to show, however, how such payments influenced Danton's conduct.

Danton was a political realist, and he was also an adventurer. Not knowing where the Revolution was bound, he kept open various options. He had connections with the duc d'Orléans; with constitutional monarchists like the Lameth brothers and A. Duport; with Cordeliers old and new; even, briefly, with the Girondins. He was an improvisor, as his speeches reflect; sensitive to the crowd; able to inflame his hearers and become intoxicated by their applause—a man overflowing with life, whose basic personal goal was to enjoy life; capable of great spurts of energy and also of laziness and even failure of nerve. He was not a scrupulous man. He resigned himself easily to the shedding of blood. He was not a vengeful man, however. He was willing to forget the Girondins once he had defeated them. His opposition to the Terror toward the end of 1793 was inspired by concern for himself and his friends, in part, but also by an understanding of the harm that the Montagnards' murderous disunity would do to the Revolution. He was a vital force, almost too much for the government as it sought to break him, during his trial. "Not a great man, not a good man, and certainly no hero; but a man with great, good, and heroic moments" (J. M. Thompson).

F.-A. Aulard, *Etudes et lecons*, 9 vols. (Paris, 1893-1924); A. Fribourg, ed., *Discours de Danton* (Paris, 1910); N. Hampson, *Danton* (London, 1978); G. Lefebvre, *Etudes sur la Révolution française* (Paris, 1954); L. Madelin, *Danton* (London, 1921); J. Robinet, *Le procès des Dantonistes* (Paris, 1879); J. M. Thompson, *Leaders of the French Revolution* (New York, 1967).

S. Lytle

Related entries: CHATELET; CHAUMETTE; COMMISSION OF TWELVE; COMMITTEE OF PUBLIC SAFETY; COMPAGNIE DES INDES; CORDELIERS CLUB; DECHRISTIANIZATION; DESMOULINS; DUMOURIEZ; FABRE; FIRST COALITION; FLANDERS REGIMENT; FOUQUIER-TINVILLE; HEBERTISTS; INDULGENTS; LASOURCE; MOMORO; MUTINY OF NANCY; PACHE; REVOLUTIONARY TRIBUNAL; ROBESPIERRE, M.; SAINT-JUST; SECTIONS; SEPTEMBER 1792 MASSACRES; 10 AUGUST 1792; TERROR, THE; VARENNES; VENDEE; *VIEUX CORDELIER*; WESTERMANN.

DAUNOU, PIERRE (1761-1840), framer of the Constitution of the Year VIII (1799). See CONSTITUTION OF 1799.

DAUPHINE, province in southeastern France. For a brief time in 1788 the eyes of France focused on Dauphiné as it became one of the major centers of the pre-Revolution. The Dauphinois revolt proved to be an important catalyst for immediate change and a source of many of the Revolution's early ideas and slogans.

The government's financial crisis and the efforts of C.-A. de Calonne and E.-

C. de Loménie de Brienne to solve it form the background for the Revolution of 1788 in Dauphiné. The resistance of the parlements to their reforms finally led to the Edicts of May 1788, disbanding the parlements and establishing an entirely new judicial system. In Dauphiné, as in Béarn and Brittany, the edicts provoked a violent reaction, but the Dauphinois revolt provided the strongest hint of the revolution to come.

After much protest against the May Edicts, with specific discussion of the importance of the parlement to the economy of the city, Grenoble rose in revolt on 7 June 1788 to prevent the departure of the *parlementaires* to their places of exile. Troops attempting to gain control of the situation were bombarded with roof tiles, thereby giving the uprising its name, the *journée des tuiles*.

The uprising was short-lived, but its violence frightened the forces of order. The real significance of the revolt, however, was in the assemblies that followed it. The Assembly of Grenoble, which met on 14 June 1788, was the first of these. Led by J.-J. Mounier, the assembly called for the return of the parlement, the convocation of the ancient estates of Dauphiné (with vote by head and the doubling of the third estate) and for the convocation of the Estates General. Finally, the assembly demanded the convocation of a provincial assembly, which, after much resistance from the government, finally met at Vizille in July.

The three estates at Vizille ratified the resolutions of the Assembly of Grenoble, accepting double representation of the Third Estate and vote by head. They called for the restoration of the parlements, the convocation of the provincial estates, and the convocation of the Estates General. Additionally, the assembly repudiated Dauphiné's long-cherished privileges, advocating the union of the provinces.

The events that followed the turmoil of the summer of 1788—the replacement of E.-C. de Loménie de Brienne by J. Necker, the calling of the Estates General, and the reinstatement of the parlements—left much of France divided over issues such as vote by head and the doubling of the third estate in the Estates General. The three orders of Dauphiné remained united. The Assembly of Romans, the first legal assembly to be held in Dauphiné since the passing of the Edicts of May, met on 5 September 1788 to draw up a constitution for the forthcoming provincial estates. The constitution established an estates with twenty-four clergy, forty-eight nobles, and seventy-two members of the third estate. Deliberation was to be in common, with vote by head. The constitution built an entire system of provincial government, with an estates meeting regularly every year.

On 1 December the first provincial estates of Dauphiné to be held in 160 years was opened. It elected the province's deputies to the Estates General and produced a mandate requiring them to refuse to vote on anything until the principle of vote by head was accepted. In addition, they were to refuse any financial reforms until the writing of a constitution had begun. This mandate foreshadowed later actions taken by the Third Estate in the Estates General.

With the closing of the provincial estates, Dauphiné left the Revolutionary limelight until the outbreak of the Great Fear. Dauphiné was the only province in which the Great Fear caused a peasant revolt. Mustering initially on 28 July

1789 in response to rumors of an invasion, the peasants turned to burning and pillaging châteaux when the rumors proved to be unfounded. Along with the wine cellars, the seigneurial titles and *registres des gros fruits* were the peasants' major objectives. Miraculously, not one nobleman was killed. Calm was finally restored in most areas by 10 August, and Dauphiné was almost silent during the remainder of the Revolution.

Local popular tradition has awarded Dauphiné the title Cradle of the Revolution. If this distinction is deserved, it is because the Dauphinois pre-Revolution brought the first clear articulation of the ideas around which the Third Estate crystallized in the Estates General.

J. Barnave, *Esprit des édits enregistrés militairement au Parlement de Dauphiné le 10 mai 1788* (n.p., 1788); A. Champollion-Figeac, *Chroniques dauphinoises et documents relatifs au Dauphiné pendant le Révolution: 1ère période historique*, 2 vols. (Vienne, 1880–81); J. Egret, *Les derniers états de Dauphiné* (Grenoble, 1942) and *Le parlement de Dauphiné et les affaires publiques dans la deuxième moitié du XVIIIᵉ siècle*, 2 vols. (Paris, 1942); J.-J. Mounier, *Nouvelles observations sur les Etats-Généraux de France* (n.p., 1789).

T. A. DiPadova

Related entries: BARNAVE; CALONNE; GREAT FEAR; GRENOBLE; LOMENIE DE BRIENNE; MOUNIER.

DAVID, JACQUES-LOUIS (1748-1825), the outstanding French painter of the last years of the Old Regime, the Revolution, and the Napoleonic period and the leading exponent of the neoclassical style. David's style was an attempt to revive a purer form of classicism in reaction against the rococo style of the earlier eighteenth century. The neoclassical movement was partly a product of recent excavations at Pompeii, the idealization of Roman art by the German aesthetician J.-J. Winckelmann, and the engravings of Roman buildings by G. B. Piranesi; but it was also the result of a search for greater earnestness and severity in contrast to the frivolity of F. Boucher and J.-H. Fragonard. The new style, with its emphasis on sculptured forms, clear lines, classical settings, and theatrical poses, was ideally suited for portraying heroic events. Thus in succession it was used under the Old Regime to depict acts of civic virtue from antiquity, during the Revolution to portray patriotic deeds, and in the Napoleonic era to celebrate memorable events.

Like most of the other eminent artists of the Old Regime, David trained at the school of the Academy of Painting and Sculpture in Paris where, after five attempts, he won the grand prize in painting in 1775, which allowed him to continue his studies in Rome. His mentor, J.-M. Vien, had already guided him toward classical models, but his experience in Italy reinforced his devotion to Roman antiquity that his early works revealed. After his return from Italy in 1780, his paintings on themes drawn from ancient history seemed to fulfill the *philosophes*' demand for art which would inspire noble actions. *Belisaire*, done soon after his return, showing the Roman general, dismissed and blinded by a jealous emperor, begging at the base of a triumphal arch, was a condemnation of the outrageous treatment of a leader who had served his country well. This work won him associate membership in the Academy. In 1783 he displayed *Andromaque pleurant la mort d'Hector*, which he presented for full membership in the Academy. Then David did a series of heroic scenes in a bold neoclassical style that won wide acclaim. During a second visit to Rome, he completed the *Serment des Horaces*, portraying three Roman warriors swearing on their father's sword to do or die for their country. This depiction of patriotic zeal created a sensation at the Salon of 1785. The *Mort de Socrate*, a theatrical scene of the final moments of the philosopher who chose death rather than sacrifice truth, was much admired in 1787. Then, just as the Revolution broke out, David displayed his *Licteurs rapportant à Brutus les corps de ses fils*. Although commissioned by the government of Louis XVI, this painting of a Roman who had ordered his sons to be put to death for plotting against the Republic was reproduced or imitated repeatedly during the Revolution as a striking example of patriotism.

For artists, the Revolution presented both problems and opportunities. The traditional patronage of the court, the aristocracy, and the church was threatened and eventually destroyed, but the Revolution also seemed to offer artists an opportunity to serve a higher purpose by recording major events, portraying examples of patriotic zeal, or creating Revolutionary allegories. In 1790 the Jacobin club of Paris commissioned David to do a painting of the Tennis Court Oath in which the members of the Third Estate swore, in defiance of the royal government, not to disband until they had given France a constitution. When a plan to finance the work by selling subscriptions for small engravings failed, the Legislative Assembly agreed to pay the bill, but by that time the painter was engaged in other activities, and the work was never completed. He did, however, display a drawing of the scene at the Salon of 1791, which was frequently reproduced. It is now difficult to think of the Tennis Court Oath without visualizing the scene as David portrayed it: J.-S. Bailly administering the oath atop a table in the center, the deputies with their right arms upraised dramatically, the sun bursting in through the windows as the wind lifts the curtains.

David's major contribution to the Revolution, however, was his role as planner of festivals. The *philosophes* had asserted that, if properly used, festivals could serve to educate and uplift the common people. The Festival of Federation had further convinced the Revolutionaries of the value of festivals to influence the masses. In July 1791 David played a major role in designing the classical funeral carriage and other decorations for the triumphal translation of the remains of F.-M. Voltaire, who was seen as a precursor of the Revolution, to the Pantheon. It was the first completely secular celebration of the Revolution. Then during the struggle for power between the moderates and the radicals in the spring of 1792, David planned the festival in honor of the soldiers, including the Swiss of Châteauvieux, who had rebelled against their aristocratic officers at Nancy in August 1790. At first condemned as mutineers, they were now hailed as heroes.

Once again David combined neoclassical designs with new Revolutionary symbols. The central feature of the procession was a huge triumphal chariot bearing a statue of Liberty and adorned with patriotic low reliefs.

Following the overthrow of the monarchy, David was elected to the National Convention. He became the chief planner and designer of Revolutionary festivals and ceremonies, ''pageant-master of the Republic,'' as D. Dowd has called him. These Revolutionary festivals were much more than pageants; they were mass rallies designed to make the masses participants rather than spectators. The objective was to arouse support for the new republican institutions. David planned the funeral procession for L.-M. Lepelletier, who was assassinated in January 1793 for having voted to execute the deposed king. He also planned the funeral rites for J.-P. Marat, the fiery editor of *L'ami du peuple*, assassinated in July 1793 by C. Corday.

David also perpetuated the memory of these two republican martyrs in works of art. He did a sketch of Lepelletier lying on his deathbed, a sword hanging over the wound in his side. The Montagnard government was especially anxious to exploit the assassination of Marat, the Friend of the People, in order to dramatize the danger of counterrevolutionary plots and thus justify the purge of the Girondists in early June. David portrayed the dead journalist slumped lifeless in the bathtub where he had worked on his newspaper while soaking in a solution to relieve a skin ailment. At first the scene appears strikingly realistic, but a closer scrutiny reveals that it has been carefully devised to create a certain impression. Despite the fact that he has died violently, Marat appears with a benign expression on his face, still holding the note from his assassin in his left hand and clutching his pen in the other. The ink pot and papers on the stand have scarcely been disturbed. David has portrayed the bloodthirsty journalist like a dead Christ figure, a veritable Revolutionary *pietà*. Cheap reproductions were distributed widely.

Meanwhile he had planned the great Festival of Unity and Indivisibility on 10 August 1793 to mark the first anniversary of the overthrow of the monarchy and the proclamation of the new republican constitution. It was imperative to rally public opinion behind the new order, which was threatened by foreign invasion, internal revolt, and economic problems. This grandiose festival reveals clearly how such ceremonies united all the available means of mass persuasion; inspirational speeches, printed slogans, musical corps, colored banners, allegorical figures, large floats, triumphal arches, and civic altars all combined with a massive parade. In this festival there was a long procession composed of deputies of the Convention, officials from the departments, representatives of the primary assemblies, contingents of ordinary citizens, and groups of musicians. The cortege stopped at six stations, decorated with temporary statues and architectural structures, as it wound its way through the city.

In addition to his planning of festivals, David was active in many other ways at the peak of the Revolution. He served as a member of the Committee of Public Instruction and of the Committee of General Security, the important police committee of the Revolutionary Government, but his main contributions were as virtual arbiter of the arts. He led the movement to destroy the old Academy, which was eventually replaced by the Popular and Republican Art Association. He designed costumes and sets for various Revolutionary theatrical productions. On commission by the government, he drew political cartoons, which were reproduced for distribution throughout the country. Also on commission by the government, he designed national costumes intended to give Frenchmen a distinctive dress symbolizing their new status. Moreover, he did a painting of the teenage martyr F.-J. Bara, a drummer boy who had died in the Vendée crying out *"Vive la République"* in defiance of the counterrevolutionaries who had captured him. David showed him, stripped naked, clasping the tricolor to his breast as he expired. The government ordered reproductions to be displayed in all the classrooms of France.

David was one of the chief sponsors of the great contest in the spring of 1794 in which artists and architects were called on to design republican shrines, assembly halls, Revolutionary monuments, inspirational paintings, and ideal peasant dwellings. The Tuileries Palace was to be transformed into a National Palace surrounded by a public garden decorated with Revolutionary sculptures and low-reliefs. David's proposal for a giant figure of the people for the point of the Ile de la Cité where the statue of Henry IV had once stood was made part of a plan to erect republican monuments throughout the capital. Similar projects were proposed for other cities. If it had not been frustrated by the Thermidorian Reaction, this grandiose program would have put an ideological stamp on Paris and the departments.

David was so closely associated with M. Robespierre and the Terror that he barely escaped execution after 9 Thermidor. He was bitterly denounced in the Convention and imprisoned twice, but he survived by claiming that he had been too ill to support the move against Robespierre, that he had been deceived by him, and that henceforth he would follow principles rather than men. It was while imprisoned that he made the first sketch of his painting of the *Sabines*, which was not finished until 1799. After this narrow escape following Thermidor, he resolved to avoid involvement in politics, rejecting an invitation by Napoleon to join the Italian army to paint its campaigns, but gradually he was lured into the general's camp. After the great victory of Marengo by Napoleon in 1800 under the new consulate, David did his famous equestrian painting of Napoleon crossing the Alps. When Napoleon became emperor, he named David his chief court painter and another career opened for the artist.

A. Brookner, *Jacques-Louis David* (London, 1980); E.-J. Delecluze, *Louis David, son école et son temps* (Paris, 1855); D. L. Dowd, *Pageant-Master of the Republic: Jacques-Louis David and the French Revolution* (Lincoln, 1948); L. Hautecoeur, *Louis David* (Paris, 1954); J. A. Leith, *The Idea of Art as Propaganda in France, 1750-1799* (Toronto, 1965).

J. A. Leith

Related entries: CORDAY; FESTIVAL OF FEDERATION; MARAT; TENNIS COURT OATH; THERMIDORIAN REACTION.

DECADE (1793-1805), a period of ten days, the subdivision of the month in the new Revolutionary calendar, adopted in 1793, to take effect as of 22 September 1792 (1 Vendémiaire Year II). The *décade* consisted of ten uniform units: *primidi, duodi, tridi, quartidi, quintidi, sextidi, septidi, octidi, nonidi*, and *décadi*. The year included thirty-six and a half *décades*; the last five days were first referred to as excess *(épagomènes)* days and then, from the Year III, as *sansculottides*.

The choice of the *décade* was imposed not only for the purpose of rationalization (uniformity based on the metric system) but also as a firm ideological commitment to bring an end to the week, which "has served the pretentious designs of all sects" *(Instructions sur l'ère de la République)*. As P.-F. Fabre d'Eglantine had given the days a uniform name, it was decided to give each *quintidi* the name of the animal, fish, bird, or mammal that was most useful in that season and to each *décadi* that of a farming implement appropriate to the month. These names, however, were seldom used.

One of the major problems posed by the *décade* as a test of the restructuring of time is how much the *décadi* was observed. Imposed progressively, the *décadi* was rather well established in the Year II, at least in the cities; its usage subsequently became more lax and caused repeated confrontations between central and local authorities, between local authorities and those supposed to use it. It seems that except for some periodic revivals (as in the Year IV), the *décade* generally fell into disuse quickly. The history of the *décadi*, which largely remains to be done, is intimately related to the cult and festivals established to solemnize it.

Officially, use of the *décade* ended with that of the Republican calendar, by the *Senatus consultum* of 22 Fructidor Year XIII (9 September 1805).

A. Soboul, ed., *Concordance des calendriers grégorien et républicain* (Paris, 1963).

M. Vovelle

Related entries: CALENDAR OF THE FRENCH REPUBLIC; FABRE.

DECHRISTIANIZATION, a violent movement aimed at the destruction of established religion, which developed most fully between the winter of 1793-94 and the spring of 1794 (Brumaire-Prairial Year II). Historical tradition and even contemporary usage in France employ the term *déchristianisation*, which is difficult to translate into another language, in two senses. It is sometimes used to designate a condition that developed over a rather long period of time; for example, one speaks of the present dechristianization of French society. The term is also applied to a spontaneous, collective attempt to eradicate religion that arose directly out of the development of the French Revolution, and it is this meaning of the term that will be treated here.

Dechristianization should not be confused with Revolutionary anticlericalism, which was a heritage of the Enlightenment and found expression, during the early years of the Revolution, in the nationalization of clerical property and the subsequent Civil Constitution of the Clergy, or with the intensification of measures against refractory priests and *émigrés*, especially in 1792, although these did prepare the way for the flare-up of dechristianization. The latter occurred as a movement that affected France essentially between Brumaire and Germinal Year II. It was not entirely comparable to the wave of panic engendered by the Great Fear of 1789, which spread much more rapidly and was spontaneous. The wave of dechristianization, which spread through the country over a period of six months, was neither a panic nor truly spontaneous; on the other hand, it was not imposed from above, since the Revolutionary government disavowed it very early, in Frimaire Year II. It was, in fact, an organized, collective reaction with a highly politicized attitude.

Dechristianization had its origins in central France, in the Nièvre where the representative J. Fouché was active. The example rapidly spread and found an echo in Paris and nearby rural communities, doubtlessly through the intervention of P.-G. Chaumette. Then, due to the influence of popular societies or of the sectional movement and local Revolutionary leaders, communities renounced the practice of religion and closed their churches in order to transform them into temples of Reason, robbing them of their bells, silver, and sacred furnishings, which were then offered to the Republic in mocking processions and masquerades, while priests, and even constitutional bishops, renounced their positions and sometimes married. During this first phase, which took place between Brumaire and Frimaire Year II, the most spectacular episode, outside of those over which Fouché presided at Nevers, was the Festival of Liberty and Reason celebrated at Notre Dame of Paris on 20 Brumaire (10 November 1793) shortly after the defrocking of the constitutional bishop J.-B.-J. Gobel.

Initially the National Convention was taken by surprise and did not react unfavorably toward this movement, which took hold among Hébertist circles and *sans-culottes* who had been politicized by zealous propagandists. Very quickly, however, a reaction set in, from G.-J. Danton to M. Robespierre; there was a fear that this violent activity would alienate popular elements still attached to religion, and dechristianization came to be viewed as a Machiavellian stratagem for a counterrevolutionary plot. On 16 Frimaire, on the motion of Robespierre, the Convention forbade "all violent activities and measures against any religion." Dechristianization did not come to an end, however; although it was in retreat in Paris and in its original centers from Frimaire on, it spread throughout the provinces in the following months. In the southeast, for example, it achieved its culmination at Lyon in Frimaire, reached the Dauphinois Alps in Pluviôse, then in Ventôse the Rhône Valley and the Mediterranean Midi, where it was still active in Germinal. In this diffusion from the center of France toward the periphery, it did not really begin to subside until Floréal Year II (April–May 1794). Within the context of the dechristianizing campaign, it is difficult to evaluate the reassertion of control by Robespierre and the Montagnards, which, on 18 Floréal (7 May), led to the Convention's celebrated proclamation that "the French people recognize the Supreme Being and the immortality of the soul." This declaration was sanctioned and apotheosized at Paris and throughout the provinces by the celebration of the Festival of the Supreme Being on 20 Prairial Year II (8 June 1794). It is unclear whether this was the ultimate end or simply a pause in an enterprise that had been evolving during the preceding months.

The chronological outline suggests the geography of the movement. All, or nearly all, of France was affected by the spread of this movement in six months. However unevenly, it is a very revealing measure, like the cartography of Revolutionary toponymy (as place names were Revolutionized) and presents a map of striking contrasts that foreshadows the map of religious practice today: areas of intensive dechristianization in the Parisian Basin, and especially in the center of France, in a horseshoe from the Lyonnais to Aquitaine around the Massif Central, and finally in the Mediterranean Midi. In contrast, the Armoricain west, the north and northeast, and the southern slope of the Massif Central are refractory. A more precise geography shows large stubborn zones, often conservative mountain regions, such as the Alps, but these do not follow any mechanical kind of geographic determinism. Forced and voluntary dechristianization thus has set the map of dechristianization as it was at the end of the eighteenth century.

Within these spatial and temporal parameters, it is necessary to detail different aspects of dechristianization in practice. It is useful, and without doubt legitimate, to distinguish a destructive aspect from its innovations or hasty creations.

Under the first rubric, attacks against people were combined with attacks on property. Renunciations of the priesthood were one of the most striking aspects of the movement; sometimes spontaneous (about one in ten), more often forced, these affected a considerable number of priests, which can be estimated at around 20,000 for all of France, one-sixth of the total under the Old Regime and a much higher proportion among the constitutional clergy. This phenomenon varied considerably according to region, just as it took very diverse forms, from simple suspension from the priesthood to explicit renunciation. The marriage of priests extended their renunciation in about 5,000 cases; in this too, certain regions, such as the Lyonnais, were affected more than others.

The attack on places of worship led to the closing of churches or the suspension of worship. It can be estimated that by the end of the winter of 1793–94, these closings had taken place in a major part of France. Sometimes people destroyed the church bells, as in the Lozère and the department of Mont Blanc; almost everywhere the bells and silver from the holy vessels had to be handed over. In these cases, a destructive fervor coincided with a contribution to the Revolutionary war effort. This went even further, however, to the extent of iconoclasm: paintings, statues, confessionals, all the remnants of fanaticism and superstition were burned on pyres. It was to designate these activities that H.-B. Grégoire coined the term *vandalism* in his denunciation of them before the Convention.

This destruction, far from being gratuitous, was part of a collective plan; the *auto-da-fé* and the masquerade, which paraded the spoils from the churches in grotesque processions, were the most popular and spontaneous forms taken by the search for a substitute ritual. This found expression in the reopening of churches as temples of Reason, reserved for new civic festivals and, later, for the *culte décadaire*. These new festivities of the Year II, in addition to the celebration of Revolutionary anniversaries, gave meaning to forms of Revolutionary religiosity, which included the cult of the martyrs of liberty (the triad J.-P. Marat–L.-M. Lepelletier–M.-J.Chalier, to whom were added the child heroes F.-J. Bara and J.-A. Viala). These expressions, of which the festival is the best measure, were expanded by sending out teachers of morality, who were virtually civic apostles of this new type of missionary conquest on certain fronts, notably in the Midi.

Among the positive accomplishments of dechristianization should also be included the ambitious attempts to restructure time and space. This first took the form of the establishment of the Revolutionary calendar, beginning in the winter of 1793. The second consisted of extensive toponymic changes and the suppression of the names of saints and of everything reminiscent of the old religion and the substitution of names with a civic, moral, or mythological character.

The general outline presented here leaves open a certain number of problems and projects, on which current research is focusing. The intensive study of the ideology of dechristianization has barely begun to exploit the vast corpus of dechristianizing discourses and speeches by using the methods of historical linguistics. But it would also be appropriate to approach the problem by examining oral traditions that retain traces of this historical trauma. A beginning has also been made in dealing with sociological aspects of the movement. If the victims (the priests who gave up their vocation and who married) are now well known, the persecutors—two–thirds of whom were from the middle classes, with more popular elements prominent at local levels—are much more difficult to know and, hence, to analyze. An interesting but roundabout way of achieving a better understanding of this movement could be to study those who rejected dechristianization, not only the geography of refractory regions but also by analyzing hostile groups (such as women and peasants) and the means of expression used by these Christians without a church (such as female prophecy and messianic texts).

The last remaining unresolved problem is the interpretation of the movement. Today, except in certain milieux, no one believes that dechristianization was a strategic ruse or a hoax, manipulated by certain groups, like the Hébertists, to divert the masses from real problems and to keep up an artificial agitation. Used at the time and partially revived by A. Mathiez and, later, D. Guérin, this interpretation disregards the fundamental character and spirit of this phenomenon. As some historians, like M. Vovelle, have begun to do, it is useful to link the study of the violent dechristianization of the Year II with that of dechristianization during the course of the eighteenth century, which prepared the way for it. It also is useful to be concerned with the effects and repercussions on the nineteenth century of this turning point that set collective religious attitudes in a lasting form.

F.-A. Aulard, *Le Christianisme et la Révolution française* (Paris, 1925) and *Le culte de la Raison et le culte de l'Etre Suprême* (Paris, 1892); A. Mathiez, *Robespierre et le culte de l'Etre Suprême* (LePuy, 1910); B. Plongeron, *Conscience religieuse en Révolution* (Paris, 1969); A. Soboul, "Sentiments religieux et cultes populaires pendant la Révolution, Saintes patriotes et martyrs de la Liberté," *Ann. hist. de la Révo. française*, 29 (1957); M. Vovelle, *Religion et Révolution: la déchristianisation de l'an II* (Paris, 1976).

M. Vovelle

Related entries: CHAUMETTE; CIVIL CONSTITUTION OF THE CLERGY; CLOOTS; CULT OF THE SUPREME BEING; FOUCHE; GOBEL; GREAT FEAR.

DECLARATION OF PILLNITZ, a statement by the Holy Roman Emperor Leopold II and Frederick William II, King of Prussia, on 27 August 1791, threatening intervention against the French Revolution. Since the beginning of the Revolution, numerous projects had been considered in royalist circles for the European powers to issue a manifesto against it, an idea that would lead ultimately to the Brunswick Manifesto of 25 July 1792. During the first two years of the Revolution, however, the European monarchs—except Gustavus III of Sweden—showed little inclination to intervene.

The failed attempt of the French royal family to escape from Paris in June 1791 jarred the European courts out of their complacency and led to the first official statements concerning the possibility of intervention. Emperor Leopold II issued his Padua Circular on 6 July, proposing that the European courts cooperate in saving the French monarchy and royal family. Circumstances, meanwhile, cleared the way for possible Austrian action. On 25 July, Austria and Prussia signed an alliance, and on 4 August Austria concluded peace with Turkey. In Coblentz, the *émigrés* clamored for an immediate Austro-Prussian intervention in France, heralded by a threatening manifesto endorsing their own political objectives. The comte d'Artois and C.-A. de Calonne hastened to Vienna in August to press their views on the Austrian government.

Leopold II, however, soon overcame his first flush of indignation following the flight to Varennes. Marie Antoinette, feigning collaboration with the *constitutionnel* faction in Paris, wrote him on 30 July, urging that he recognize Louis XVI's intended acceptance of the new French constitution. Shortly after, she wrote to him secretly, telling him to disregard her earlier letter, which she had written only to dupe the *constitutionnels*. But Leopold deemed it best, both for his own sake and for the French royal family's, to recognize Louis XVI's acceptance of the constitution as voluntary. By August he no longer saw any immediate need to intervene, although some gesture of concern still seemed appropriate.

The emperor and the king of Prussia met at Pillnitz in Saxony in late August and were followed there by the importunate Artois and Calonne. The two monarchs discussed a range of concerns, chiefly having to do with Poland. Although French affairs received less attention, on 27 August the emperor and king issued their Declaration of Pillnitz. In this brief document they stated that having heard the representations of the comtes de Provence and d'Artois, they considered the present position of the French king "a matter of common concern to all the sovereigns of Europe" and invited the other powers to join them in employing the "most effective means" to strengthen the "foundations of a monarchical government" in France, "in which case" *(alors et dans ce cas)* Austria and Prussia would be prepared to act promptly, employing the necessary forces (Stewart, pp. 223-224). To this end they would hold their troops in readiness.

The declaration was purposefully vague, and Leopold was sure that the requirement that the other powers participate would protect him from the need for further action. Response to his Padua Circular had been lukewarm, and he was sure that Britain would refuse to cooperate. Although Frederick William II showed a certain romantic enthusiasm for action, Leopold considered the Pillnitz Declaration as no more than a gesture to encourage the royal family and its supporters in France, to make the French government aware of official concern abroad, and perhaps especially to placate the troublesome *émigrés* in Coblentz.

The Pillnitz Declaration was nonetheless the first international condemnation of the Revolution and as such had important repercussions. The *émigrés* capitalized on it by representing it as an actual ultimatum. In France it appeared as an imminent threat to the Revolution and thus provided justification for the growing belligerence of the Girondist and other prowar factions in late 1791 and early 1792, which subsequently led to the French declaration of war against Austria and Prussia in April 1792.

A. Sorel, "La fuite de Louis XVI et les essais d'intervention en 1791: Varennes et Pillnitz" *Rev. des Deux-Mondes* 3 (1886); J. H. Stewart, ed., *A Documentary Survey of the French Revolution* (New York, 1951).

H. A. Barton

Related entries: ARTOIS; BRUNSWICK MANIFESTO; CALONNE; *EMIGRES*; FREDERICK WILLIAM II; LEOPOLD II; PROVENCE; VARENNES.

DECLARATION OF THE RIGHTS OF MAN AND OF THE CITIZEN, the enactment that placed French constitutional law and social life on a new philosophical basis and became a symbol of the aspirations of Revolutionaries in France and throughout the world in the 1790s and ever since. The title of the declaration at once suggests the affiliation with a philosophy of natural law and social contract. The avowed purpose of the enactment was not to create but to recognize and describe rights. These were thought of as inherent in each human being and as carried over from the state of nature into the social state when man became citizen.

In article 2, the inherent rights are listed: "liberty, property, security, and resistance to oppression." Equality is not one of these rights but is the way in which nature distributes them: "Men are . . . equal in rights" (article 1). To preserve these rights is said to be the purpose of every society exercising political powers. The only right for which a general definition is given in the declaration is liberty: it is "being able to do everything which does not harm another" (article 4). Specifically, each person is free to hold to his own opinions, "even religious opinions" (article 10), and is free to speak, write, and print them (article 11). Property right entitles a person to keep his property until it is legally ascertained that public need requires confiscation and, in that case, until a just indemnity is paid (article 17). Security includes a right, asserted against government, not to be arrested or imprisoned unreasonably or treated unreasonably while in custody (articles 7, 8, 9); but security means more than this, for, in general, individuals' rights must be protected by a public force (article 12).

The phrase *resistance to oppression* was not intended to license every revolt in the future. The declaration, it is true, never directly defines oppression. It does, however, make clear the nature of the opposite: constitutional government. It states that governmental authority must emanate expressly from the nation (article 3), that each person's natural liberty can be limited only by the law (article 4), that the law can forbid only actions harmful to society (article 5), that the law, being "the expression of the general will," can be made only by the citizens or their representatives (article 6), and that a citizen summoned in accordance with the law must immediately obey (article 7). The law, therefore, is the link between man, free in nature, and the citizen, engaged in the reciprocities of social life. A higher law inherent in nature bounds the sphere of the everyday man-made law, which limits and protects, and thereby maintains, the constitution and the happiness of all.

In the declaration are condensed many years of political experience and thought. The actual text was adopted, in all essentials, in debates in the National Assembly during one week, 20–26 August 1789. Later changes were very small clarifications. A correction was voted in article 4 on 2 October 1789 when the document was prepared for transmittal to the king. Amendments were voted in articles 6, 12, 14, and 17 on 8 August 1791, when the declaration was prepared for incorporation in the revised constitution.

The declaration's immediate antecedents extended throughout the first half of 1789. In the spring, in electing deputies to the Estates General, the voters of the Paris nobility and various other constituencies included in their *cahiers de doléances* a demand for a specific declaration of the rights that belong to every man. The Third Estate of Paris, and a few other constituencies, drew up complete texts and put them in their *cahiers* to be proposed by their deputies. Indeed, in one of its aspects, the declaration that was actually adopted is the ultimate *cahier de doléances*. It states fundamental principles in virtue of which existing practices are condemned by the spokesmen for the social body. It says that "social distinctions" cannot be based on anything other than "common utility" and hence, by implication, not on antique origin or illustrious descent (article 1); and authority cannot come from any source other than the nation, and hence, by implication, not from divine right or the king's sole will (article 3). The declaration implies a list of objects of complaint, among them, cruel punishments (article 8), interference with non-Catholics' worship (article 10), prior restraint of publication (article 11), inequities and arbitrariness in the tax system, and secrecy of the government budget (articles 13, 14).

The declaration grew out of French experience in the 1770s and 1780s. It was also a sketch of a future ideal society. Once organized, the National Assembly set to work in early July to plan the writing of a constitution. On 11 July, the marquis de Lafayette read to the Assembly his draft of a bill of rights. He had sought, but did not follow, suggestions from T. Jefferson. More than twenty other members prepared draft declarations. All these proposals were referred to the *bureaux* of the Assembly. The *bureaux* were a parliamentary method of facilitating discussion, a committee of the whole divided into thirty subcommittees, each having forty members. They were to consider proposed declarations of rights during the last few days of July. None of the *bureaux*, however, recommended any draft declaration, except Bureau 6, which adopted a watered-down abbreviation of one by E.-J. Sieyès.

Whether to adopt any declaration at all was debated in the Assembly in regular session on 1, 3, and 4 August. Many members were opposed. A motion was made that there be a declaration of duties, too; it was supported by 433 members but rejected by 570. On 12 August the Assembly elected a committee of five, headed by H.-G. R. Mirabeau, to examine all the draft declarations and propose one for detailed consideration.

The proposal from the Committee of Five was debated for two days and, on 19 August, rejected. The Assembly proceeded to select one draft declaration to be considered in detail. By a majority vote, it decided to discuss the draft declaration prepared three weeks earlier by Bureau 6. Members who supported a strong and clear declaration of rights interpreted this vote as a defeat and vowed to obliterate the Bureau 6 draft with amendments. This they largely succeeded in doing, by substituting phrases and paragraphs drawn from various earlier draft declarations, as follows:

Date	Article	Principal author(s)
20 August	Preamble	Mirabeau, spokesman for the Committee of Five
	1, 2, 3	J.-J. Mounier, based on a draft by Lafayette
21 August	4, 5	A. de Lameth
	6	C.-M. Talleyrand
22 August	7	A. Duport, with additions by G.-J. Target and P.-V. Malouet
	8, 9	Duport, with amendments by Target
23 August	10	comte de Castellane, but with major amendments
24 August	11	duc de La Rochefoucauld d'Enville
	12, 13	Bureau 6, based on a draft by Sieyès
26 August	14, 15, 16	Bureau 6, based on a draft by Sieyès
	17	Duport

The declaration was shaped at certain points by its critics and opponents, who usually included about one-fifth of the Third Estate deputies, besides many noblemen and clergymen. They feared that natural law doctrine and ideas of equality and individual reason would intoxicate common people, especially the propertyless. They saw traditional religion as the foundation of social order and felt that dissent had to be discouraged and contained—hence, for instance, the amendments that made of article 10 a lame and grudging affirmation of religious freedom.

For a century, modern scholars have sought the origins of the ideas in the declaration. Various candidates have been proposed as originators: J.-J. Rousseau, the physiocrats, and J. Locke are the principal ones. Scholarly debates and studies of the ideas of Lafayette, Mounier, Duport, and Sieyès, however, point to the conclusion that there was not a sole intellectual source. The discourse in which the draftsmen thought and argued was that of the Enlightenment, whose own origins were neither sudden nor simple.

The later career of the declaration is one of the most extraordinary in the social history of ideas. It rapidly acquired the status of a catechism in France and of a revolutionary clarion in other European countries. It is incorporated by reference in the constitution of the Fifth Republic and so remains part of the law of the French state.

Ann. Hist. de la Revo. française 50 (1978), special no. on "Déclaration des droits de l'homme"; G. Lefebvre, *Quatre-vingt-neuf* (Paris, 1939), tr. R. R. Palmer as *The Coming of the French Revolution* (Princeton, 1947); S. Kent, "The Declaration of the Rights of Man and Citizen," *Great Expressions of Human Rights*, ed. R. M. MacIver (New York, 1950); J. Sandweg, *Rationales Naturrecht als revolutionäre Praxis. Untersuchungen zur "Erklärung der Menschen-und Bürgerrechte" von 1789* (Berlin, 1972).

P. Dawson

Related entries: CAHIERS DE DOLEANCES; JEFFERSON; LAFAYETTE; MIRABEAU; NATIONAL CONSTITUENT ASSEMBLY; SIEYES.

DECREES, VENTOSE. See VENTOSE DECREES.

DELESSART, CLAUDE-ANTOINE VALDEC. See LESSART.

DEPARTMENTS *(départements)*, largest units of local government established in France by the decrees of 14 and 22 December 1789 and 26 February 1790. The new administrative structure provided for by the Constitution of 1791 divided France into eighty-three departments, each with subordinate districts, and in each district, at the base of the pyramid, the mass of municipalities (communes). This system replaced the old provincial structure, with its potentially divisive loyalties, by a structure of units large enough to be administratively viable but small enough to presume some contact between the elected local officials and the citizens to whom they were responsible.

Although the departments were produced by legislative compromise, the legislators did try to reconcile traditional divisions, administrative convenience, and the contending ambitions of local vested interests, as well as to maintain some rough equity among the new units. The three fundamental criteria used to weigh one area against another were surface size, population, and taxable capacity, although complete departmental equality was impracticable; the range is suggested by the five legislators to whom the Hautes-Alpes was entitled, as against the Somme's sixteen and Paris's twenty-four. For the most part, the entrenched boundaries between the old provinces were respected; thus Brittany became five departments and Berry two. The most contentious matters were the number of departments to be formed in any one area, the number of districts within any one department, and the location of *chefs-lieux* at any level. It was widely believed that by becoming any kind of administrative headquarters, a community might gain in wealth as well as prestige, and the wish to satisfy as many interest groups as possible, plus ignorance of the demands and cost of the system, produced a proliferation of the districts, which linked department with communes. Even in 1790–91 some citizens saw this as extravagant, but local jealousies were strong, and reconstruction came only with Napoleon. The general departmental structure itself needed little change and has proved remarkably durable.

The 1790 intention was administrative decentralization, with the local executive chosen from below, not appointed from Paris. Communal officials (*maire, procureur, notables*) were elected by the active citizens, who also chose the secondary electors. These electors, sitting as a departmental assembly, chose the thirty-six members of the departmental council and its executive officer (*procureur-général-syndic*) and then, sitting by districts, the twelve members of the district administrations and the district *procureurs-syndics*. The members of the departmental council chose from among themselves eight directors, and a president to instruct the *procureur-général-syndic* in daily business, and the district officials similarly chose a directorate of four. Communal councils met monthly; other councils met annually to review the year's activities and to fill any vacancies. Communal office was for two years, with half the council retiring annually; districts and departments had the same system but four-year terms. The *procureur-général-syndic* and the *procureurs-syndics* had modest salaries; the directors received attendance money.

The departments were directly responsible to the king's ministry—generally to the minister of the interior but also to the minister of finance for tax collection and money matters, to the minister of justice for administrative support needed by the courts, and to the minister of war for matters concerning the army or the new *gendarmerie*. It was stressed that despite their electoral base, they were not representative bodies, their task being solely to enforce legislation forwarded by the ministry. Within the hierarchy, the law firmly subordinated districts to departments and communes to both the upper levels.

The Constituent Assembly had listed, among the duties of departmental officials, first and above all the supervision of everything related to tax collection.

They had also to deal with vagrancy and poor relief, supervise charitable and educational institutions and prisons, encourage agriculture and industry, look after public property (this covered church maintenance as well as road repairs), and deal with public health matters, the militia, and the National Guard. But the Constituent had not thought of everything. It had not foreseen the burden of implementing the Civil Constitution of the Clergy or the problem of *émigrés* and their property; it forgot population returns, reports on food supply, and the organization and control of the *gendarmerie*, and it forgot that troops on the move had to be fed and billeted. Beyond this mass of recurring responsibility was the huge amount of work needed to circulate and implement the unending stream of legislation from Paris, demanding both the establishment of new institutions and also the collection of all the information needed by the legislature before its decrees could be drafted or alternatively before they could be enforced. Local staffing had not envisaged Revolutionary reconstruction on so massive a scale, and in the communes, where much of the basic effort was needed, extra expenditure was discouraged by Paris.

The new system has been criticized for its financial weaknesses and its administrative clumsiness. The pay was low—the hard-worked and often underqualified communal officials were not paid at all—and general financial support was stingy. The national government had no immediate local representation; hence, allegedly, local deference to central policy was lacking. The system of government by committees implied a weak local executive. The combination of indirect election with the 1789 property franchise allegedly consolidated, if it did not create, a social gulf between departmental and communal officials, which estranged the department from the general public and encouraged administrative rebellion. And there were too many jobs for the number of people qualified to fill them. The structure was therefore doomed to internal collapse through bankruptcy and conflicts within its membership and to modification from outside because of the localist self-assertion of the departments, which, in combination with the officials' social orientation, brought them in 1793 into federalist confrontation with the Jacobin government.

Some of these criticisms may be exaggerated. Between 1790 and 1793, departments battled their way through frightening financial difficulties without actual collapse; secretaries paid the office bills, local lawyers supplied tables and bookcases for the judges, townspeople billeting soldiers and stabling their horses waited many months for payment. The underlying problem was not local government income, for which some provision had been made, but resistance to new and unexpectedly high tax burdens, which produced problems at all levels of government. Nor was executive authority wholly lacking. Committee government did not necessarily mean lack of a firm policy, which could be and was backed by troops. Criticism of ineffective local government early in the Revolution must take account not only of the enormous disruption of 1789 but also of the need in 1790–92 to rebuild the whole apparatus of government and get it working. Given the conditions, the degree to which by 1792 the new tax system was implemented and the amount of tax money collected seem creditable rather than otherwise.

Possibly the system was overly ambitious. It was said in 1790 that there was too much strain on available manpower, and a dozen departments also claimed that unless official pay was increased, only *les riches* would take office that involved compulsory residence in the *chef-lieu*. Certainly there was a great loss of talent in 1791–92 when thirty-eight departments lost one or more *procureurs-généraux-syndics* to the Legislative Assembly or the National Convention; in all forty-seven men thus moved on. (For various reasons, the Bas-Rhin had six *procureurs* within four years.) Fragmentary evidence suggests that many of those elected to important departmental office might be unlikely to remain, being young, presumably ambitious professional men; of the twenty-nine departmental *procureurs* reaching the Convention, twenty were lawyers and only eight were over forty-five. What kept the machine working may have been bureaucratic continuity at the office level. Office staff could be drawn from the old bureaucracy, plus recruits such as *feudistes* whose professional skills were useful in a transition period; and the departmental secretary, a crucial but nonpolitical figure, might well serve through the 1790s and beyond.

The relationship of the departments with central authority was more complex than is sometimes supposed. Subordination to Paris was an administrative tradition that the new executives accepted in 1790. But there was increasing tension, not only from departments putting their own interests first but also between a royalist ministry and patriotic departmental officials who felt that the intentions of the legislature were not being recognized. Especially after September 1791, this raised constitutional problems, since a questionable ministerial ruling might tempt departments into claiming a duty of independent judgment. Departments found too that they had to improvise to cover gaps in the decrees and that the legislature itself could make mistakes. When the self-reliance thus engendered finally became entangled with old local loyalties, local conservatism, and real political distrust, federalist protest is as understandable as the response it evoked in Paris.

A warning sign came in June 1792, when conservative departmental administrations protested at the invasion of the Tuileries. The king's execution in January 1793 was tacitly accepted, but in the following months there was much Girondin-encouraged uneasiness at Parisian pretensions, and in June the expulsion of the Girondin leaders produced widespread, if short-lived, administrative revolt. This had roots varying with the local political situation and did not necessarily reflect merely the social character of departmental officials (in the west, thoroughly bourgeois officials were defending the Republic against a conservative peasantry); its occasional persistence as open counterrevolution had highly specific causes. Nevertheless the Jacobin decree of 14 Frimaire Year II (4 December 1793) reflected an awareness that departmental independence might threaten the Republic's survival. Some departments had shown that they could use regional discontent as a weapon against the national government. The decree therefore robbed departments of all responsibility for executing Revolutionary policy, which went instead to municipalities and to district national agents. The democratic element here seems less significant than the introduction (at municipal level too) of Paris-based supervision.

After Thermidor, departmental quasi-autonomy was never recovered. Departments regained their range of responsibility (17 April 1795), but the 1795 Constitution, which abolished districts, also established national *commissaires* linking the departments with Paris. National control was limited by unevenly effective government, but the prefectorial system was already in embryo.

The failure of the 1790 decentralization is notorious. What deserves more emphasis is its 1790–92 achievement, when there was no precedent and little help for a wide range of essential tasks. Paris provided salaries for judges but nothing for their housing or books; Paris caused officials to be elected but supplied no maps of their jurisdictions; Paris created justices of the peace but did not inform them of their duties; Paris said that communal officials could easily grapple with the sixty-two pages of the new land tax decree. Frontier administrators had even to decide what made a man French, a necessary preliminary to determining whether he could be classed as an *émigré*. Not surprisingly, different departments sometimes solved their problems differently. What is remarkable is that after two years of struggle by desperately overworked officials, the new structures were in place and were, more or less, operative, the church excepted. Even the heavy and unpopular work on the tax rolls was well underway.

The breakdown of the 1790 system ran parallel to that of the central political system. Their common electoral base presupposed a consensus that disappeared. But early in the Revolution, the departmental officials had been the hinge between Revolutionary decision making in Paris and its execution in the provinces, and it was they who had to oversee the transition between the old France and the new. It is often said that the creative achievement of the Revolution was the work of the Constituent Assembly. But the Constituent merely issued the decrees. The departmental officials had to do their best to implement them.

L. Cahen and R. Guyot, *L'oeuvre législative de la Révolution* (Paris, 1913); A. Cobban, "Local Government during the French Revolution," *Eng. Hist. Rev.* 58 (1943); A. Forrest, *Society and Politics in Revolutionary Bordeaux* (Oxford, 1975); J. Godechot, *Les institutions de la France sous la Révolution et l'Empire* (Paris, 1951); A. Patrick, "Paper, Posters and People: Official Communication during the French Revolution, 1789–94," *Hist. Stud.* 70 (1978).

A. Patrick

Related entries: ACTIVE CITIZEN; CIVIL CONSTITUTION OF THE CLERGY; CONSTITUTION OF 1791; CONSTITUTION OF 1795; FEDERALISM; 9 THERMIDOR YEAR II.

DESFIEUX, FRANCOIS (1755-94), wine merchant, Revolutionary militant, alleged royalist agent. Desfieux was born in Bordeaux in 1755. He founded and presided in that city over the Club du café national in 1789 and a similar society at Toulouse. In Paris for the Fête de la fédération (1790), he became a Cordeliers and a Jacobin, remaining with the Jacobins at the time of the Feuillant secession in July 1791 and serving them as treasurer, secretary, vice-president, and long-time chairman of their Committee of Correspondence. He served the new government as a juror on the Tribunal of 17 August (1792), as president of his Paris section (L.-M. Lepelletier) in 1793, and as agent for the foreign minister P.-M. Lebrun-Tondu and the war minister J.-B.-N. Bouchotte. He was an active denouncer of other Revolutionaries: the Feuillants (he testified at J.-S. Bailly's trial); the *enragés* (when their continuing radicalism became an embarrassment to the Committee of Public Safety); and above all the Girondins, some of whom, such as A. Gensonné, had been his political rivals in Bordeaux. On the eve of 10 August he accused J.-P. Brissot and M. Isnard of seeking the indictment of M. Robespierre through the Club Réunion. One of the first to demand a Revolutionary Tribunal, he called the Jacobins to action against the Girondins during the March Days (1793), urging this in the name of Robespierre. Desfieux repeatedly demanded their trial and testified against them, stating that J.-M. Roland had planted in the *armoire de fer* a document incriminating him as a royalist agent.

Desfieux was repeatedly accused of fraud and bankruptcy as a businessman at Bordeaux, of mishandling funds as the Jacobins' treasurer, of stealing documents from the Jacobins, of accepting the money of "intriguers" (which he claimed was to his credit), of defending the September 1792 Massacres, of protecting the gambling house Sainte-Amaranthe for a share of its proceeds, and of being a royalist agent, as was contended with precision by the Girondin J.-A. Dulaure (1793) through his newspaper, *Le thermomètre du jour*. When Desfieux testified against the Girondins in October 1793, he was already in trouble, having been arrested briefly (and then released through the intervention of J.-M. Collot d'Herbois). Robespierre's "Notes against the Dantonists" accused Desfieux of secretly aiding the Girondins. They accused him also of having provoked the March Days in behalf of G.-J. Danton, so as to give C. Dumouriez an excuse for marching on Paris and restoring the monarchy. The real reason appears to have been, instead, his close personal connection with the Belgian P.-J. Proli who, in late September (1793) had organized a central committee of the popular societies of Paris to circumvent new legislation intended to stifle the recent militancy of the Paris sections. It was because they were dangerous to the government as Revolutionary militants who, moreover, had foreign connections, that he and Proli were arrested in October and then brought to trial with J.-R. Hébert in the second of the trials of Germinal (1793), accused of seeking to excite rebellion against the National Convention and the established authorities, and guillotined.

Desfieux. . .à ses concitoyens (Paris, n.d.); J. A. Dulaure, *Supplément aux crimes des anciens comités de gouvernement* (Paris, Year III); A. Tuetey, *Répertoire générale des sources manuscrites*, vol. 2 (Paris, 1914).

                                                                                    S. Lytle

Related entries: ARMOIRE DE FER, GIRONDINS; HEBERTISTS.

DESMOULINS, LUCIE-CAMILLE-SIMPLICE (1760-94), politician, publicist. Born at Guise on 2 March 1760, C. Desmoulins was the eldest child in a large middle-class family. His father, an official at the local *bailliage* court, directed his son toward a legal career. The elder Desmoulins contacted his well-connected cousin, J.-L. Viefville des Essars, a subdelegate to the intendant at Soissons, who procured a scholarship for Camille to the very prestigious collège Louis-le-Grand in Paris. There Camille won recognition for his abilities. He also met and fraternized with a fellow student, M. Robespierre. In 1785 Desmoulins graduated, qualified to practice law.

Education had given Camille not only credentials for a future career but also an appreciation of republican principles, which he found in his studies of the classics. He thus developed a hostility to monarchy; not surprisingly he also idolized the *philosophes*, especially the abbé de Mably and F.-M. Voltaire. Corollary to Desmoulins' beliefs was an antipathy to organized Christianity despite an admiration for Christ.

Desmoulins combined with these dangerous viewpoints a particularly strong joie de vivre, which he maintained through life. Possessed of a lively wit, he enjoyed people and rushed hurriedly into friendships. Very convivial, he relished material comforts although not always able to afford them. His eagerness, even impulsiveness, was contagious, and people generally liked him. Yet his impetuousness sometimes produced abrupt changes of mood and shifts in loyalties. This apparent instability, as well as the ill fit of his ingenuous personality with the somewhat starchy society of France, led many not to take him seriously.

In 1785, the effervescent Camille, secretly nursing some very heady beliefs, launched his law practice, although it quickly came to grief because of a pronounced stutter. Intensifying his failure was a thwarted love of Lucile Duplessis, whose parents would not allow her to marry someone so obviously without prospects. The political events from 1787 to 1789 promised new careers, revived hopes of gaining Lucile, and promoted changes consistent with his ideology. Consequently, Desmoulins entered the fray on the side of reform.

Desmoulins' initial effort was to contribute to the hail of pamphlets suggesting a blueprint for the new France. His brochure, *La philosophie au peuple français*, now lost, apparently received some attention. Desmoulins also unsuccessfully sought to represent his home town in the Estates General. What really vaulted Desmoulins into the limelight was his role in the taking of the Bastille. Rising bread prices and troop concentrations around Paris in July 1789 convinced many in the city that a plot existed to ruin them. When the dismissal of J. Necker, a very popular minister, became public on 12 July, significant portions of the population concluded that matters were coming to a head. The Palais Royal, a center for political agitation, filled with anxious people. Several orators, including Desmoulins, harangued the crowd. He may have shared his audience's belief in a conspiracy, but he was also connected to those who thought an insurrection could force acceptance of the proposals of the representatives at Versailles. For once not stuttering, he encouraged the Parisians to arm themselves for protection. Excited by Desmoulins, the crowd swirled out from the Palais Royal, swelled, and by 14 July gathered enough arms to overturn royal power in the city. Although the rioters acted largely in self-defense, contemporaries believed the victory marked a revolution in human affairs. Fortune smiled on Desmoulins, for simultaneously another of his pamphlets appeared. Although composed in June, *La France libre* espoused doctrines that suited the situation perfectly, for advocated in it was a republicanism that could justify popular political participation. Desmoulins followed this booklet with another, *Discours de la lanterne aux Parisiens*, which also defended Revolutionary action by explaining the political conditions under which violence was acceptable. These pamphlets, along with Desmoulins' successful speech, made the formerly obscure man a hero.

Desmoulins first gravitated toward the comte de Mirabeau's circle but soon located his political allies in the Cordeliers district and club, dominated by G.-J. Danton (1759–94). The Cordeliers shared his approval of popular participation and Danton, like Desmoulins, was warm and gregarious. To continue playing a role in the Revolution, Desmoulins decided to produce a newspaper, which he entitled *Les Révolutions de France et de Brabant*. This journal, first published on 28 November 1789 and continued on a somewhat regular weekly basis through eighty-six issues until late July 1791, actually continued his pamphlets. The journalist minimally reported news events but lavished space on political commentaries that proved very important. Desmoulins' writing, reflecting his personal buoyancy, possessed a vibrancy that when joined to criticism was as lacing as more serious analyses. His caustic attacks on opponents of the Revolution provoked numerous legal and political rejoinders. Only once, however, did Desmoulins suffer a reverse, and that was to pay damages so he could maintain his assaults unabated. He also proffered a positive vision of the Revolution, calling repeatedly for popular sovereignty and direct democracy. The *Révolutions de France et de Brabant* attracted approximately 3,000 subscribers, a healthy figure for the time, but its impact may best be measured by the fear it engendered among those it attacked. Their lawsuits and political efforts show Desmoulins' significance. This accomplishment, as well as his specific targets and ideology, made him important to the Cordeliers and linked him firmly to their aims. His fame also helped him achieve personal aspirations, since in December 1790 the Duplessis family finally allowed his marriage to their daughter. One small blemish marred Desmoulins' world. Fatigue, problems with printers, and the appeal of married life persuaded him to give up his paper in 1790, but after only three weeks, pressured by his political colleagues and desiring their approval, he resumed his popular publication with great success.

In the summer of 1791 Desmoulins sustained his first significant setback after two years of spectacular achievements. After Louis XVI's abortive escape attempt in June, the National Assembly reinstated the king, since, having completed a constitution requiring a monarch, they had little choice but to place him back on the throne. The Cordeliers, Desmoulins among them, violently objected and mounted a campaign culminating in a demonstration at the Champ de Mars on 17 July. The government's decision to disperse the rally ended in a slaughter, and many Cordeliers leaders feared that repression would center on them. Desmoulins then went into hiding, giving up his journal.

Although the repression never materialized and an amnesty was proclaimed in September 1791, Desmoulins did not return to writing. Attracted to domestic life with his young bride and physically exhausted, as he had been the previous year, he resumed his law practice. No more successful than before, he reentered the political wars in 1792 when J.-P. Brissot accused him of defending a politically questionable client. After penning a scurrilous attack on Brissot, Camille then joined again with Danton who, allied with the Mountain, opposed Brissot and the monarch. Tarnishing Desmoulins' comeback was an unfortunate effort at journalism. With his friend L.-M.-S. Fréron, he began a periodical, *Tribune des patriotes*, but it lacked flair and lasted through only four issues. But Desmoulins did play an important role in organizing the 10 August insurrection, and when Danton gained a portfolio in the new government, he appointed Desmoulins as one of his secretaries. When the government was dissolved in favor of the National Convention in September, Desmoulins was not out of work because he had been elected a representative.

This revival did not signify a return to real importance for Desmoulins, however. He wrote a condemnation of the Brissotins and voted for the death of the king, but stuttering limited his role in the Convention, where he rarely appeared. Leading members of the Convention viewed him as too unstable to be sent out on mission. He tried to reestablish his first journal, but his enthusiasm flagged, and he dropped it after two months.

The final episode in Desmoulins' life opened at the end of 1793 with his publication of the *Vieux Cordelier*. Under attack by the very radical Hébertists for poor attendance at the Convention and for socializing with the wealthy, Desmoulins published the journal as his defense. Perhaps the Terror also offended him because after blasting his assailants, he printed subtle but telling indictments of the Terror and called for clemency. Many historians have suggested that Desmoulins acted to support Danton and his associates who were at the same time attacking the Hébertists and trying to limit the Terror. Old school ties restrained Robespierre, and Desmoulins' amiability restrained others, but eventually Camille found himself linked to the Dantonists. When the Committee of Public Safety decided to eliminate those political opponents, Desmoulins was included. He was executed on 13 April 1794.

A. Chuquet, "La jeunesse de Camille Desmoulins," *Ann. révo.* 1 (1908); J. Claretie, *Camille Desmoulins and His Wife* (London, 1876); E. Fleury, *Etudes révolutionnaires, Camille Desmoulins et Roch Marcandier: La presse révolutionnaire* (Paris, 1851); J. Janssens, *Camille Desmoulins, le premier républicain de France* (Paris, 1973)

J. Censer

Related entries: BASTILLE, THE; BRISSOT; CHAMP DE MARS "MASSACRE"; CORDELIERS CLUB; DANTON; HEBERTISTS; MABLY; MIRABEAU; NECKER; *REVOLUTIONS DE FRANCE ET DE BRABANT*; 10 AUGUST 1792; VARENNES; *VIEUX CORDELIER*; VOLTAIRE.

DESSALINES, JEAN-JACQUES (1758-1806), black emperor of Haiti. See SAINT-DOMINGUE; TOUSSAINT L'OUVERTURE.

DESTUTT DE TRACY, ANTOINE-LOUIS-CLAUDE. See TRACY-DES-TUTT.

DIDEROT, DENIS (1713-84), author, *philosophe*, encyclopedist. Son of a cutler in Langres, Diderot early rebelled against an ecclesiastical career. After studies at the University of Paris and an apprenticeship in law, he entered more than a decade of obscurity, bohemianism, and self-education. In 1746 he was commissioned, together with the mathematician J. Le Rond d'Alembert, to direct the translation of E. Chambers' *Cyclopaedia*, and shortly the two became editors of an expanded project, which would include new articles—the genesis of the great *Encyclopédie*.

In the meantime, Diderot published anonymously the *Pensées philosophiques* (1746), which promptly was condemned by the Paris Parlement. Deistic in tone, the work attacked religious dogma and superstition while defending both the rightful place of human passions and the indispensable role of critical rationality. In 1748 a pornographic, satirical novel, *Les bijoux indiscrets*, and a treatise on mathematics were published. The *Lettre sur les aveugles* appeared in 1749, with highly original speculations on the psychology of the blind. Questions on the possible relativity of morality and metaphysics, in the absence of sight, led to an implied rejection of Christian absolutism and a suggestion of a materialistic, evolutionary view of the universe. It was primarily because of this book that Diderot was imprisoned in Vincennes for several months in mid-1749.

Back in Paris he resumed work on the *Encyclopédie, ou Dictionnaire raisonné des sciences, des arts et des métiers*, which eventually, in its original edition, would fill thirty-five enormous volumes of text and plates. Volume 1 appeared in 1751; subsequent volumes, supervised mainly by Diderot and including many key articles from his own pen, appeared yearly through 1757. Censorship problems caused a break until late 1765, when the remaining ten original volumes of text appeared, prepared under Diderot's sole editorship. The *Encyclopédie* had become an imposing compendium of knowledge, often technical or technological and sometimes subversive of the established order.

Meanwhile, in 1753, Diderot's anonymous *Pensées sur l'interprétation de la nature* attacked the oversimplifications arising from rationalism, stressed empiricism, and hinted again at a theory of cosmological and biological evolution. Two presumably realistic bourgeois dramas of everyday life followed—*Le fils naturel* (1757) and *Le père de la famille* (1758). Both reflected the new public mood emphasizing virtue and self-conscious moralism. In 1757-58 came the break from his closest friend, J.-J. Rousseau, and in the same period he wrote the first of two friendly criticisms of C.-A. Helvétius, whom Diderot saw as too much a psychological leveler and egalitarian.

Since 1756 Diderot had been submitting articles for M. Grimm's *Correspondance littéraire, philosophique et critique*, a newsletter addressed to private subscribers outside France. From 1759 through 1781, Diderot's most notable contributions were reports on the biennial Paris salons or art exhibitions. In these reports, Diderot showed himself especially fond of J.-B. Greuze's moralistic paintings, was appalled by the frivolity and licentiousness of F. Boucher, and was charmed by the color and veracity of J.-B.-S. Chardin's portrayal of everyday objects and bourgeois life.

Aside from further contributions to the *Encyclopédie*, most of the substantial works Diderot wrote after 1760 were not published during his lifetime; he wrote mainly for his own pleasure and, very deliberately, for posterity. Today these works include some of the most admired of all his productions: *La Religieuse, Jacques le fataliste, Supplément au Voyage de Bougainville* (all published in 1796), *Le neveu de Rameau* (1821), and *Le rêve de d'Alembert* (1830). In 1760 he began *La religieuse (The Nun)*, the tale of a girl forced into convent life and never reconciled to it. Diderot reveals himself not only as an anticlerical but as a subtle psychologist. *La religieuse* is also an experiment in novelistic form, with a *Préface-Annexe* of presumably factual documents and explanations, which are also partly fictionalized. *Le neveu de Rameau* is a brilliant, enigmatic, satirical dialogue between "Diderot" and the erratic, exuberant, cynical, outrageous nephew of the famous composer J.-P. Rameau. Actually the younger Rameau (the "Lui" of the dialogue) may well represent in part another side of the idealistic, intellectual Diderot officially appearing as the "Moi."

In 1765 Diderot received a substantial income for life when Catherine II of Russia bought his library but permitted him to keep it as its salaried curator. In 1769 he wrote *Le rêve de d'Alembert*, a group of three conversations centering on d'Alembert talking in his sleep. The dialogues touch on such matters as materialistic determinism and flux in nature. Diderot himself appears in the first dialogue, but equally important spokesmen for his ideas are the dreaming d'Alembert and the celebrated Dr. Bordeu. The latter concludes with permissive views on sexual morality that would have scandalized his age.

Most readers best remember Diderot's *Supplément au Voyage de Bougainville* (1772), for similar reasons. Here Diderot praises the unspoiled noble savages of Tahiti in order to criticize many of the unnatural restraints of European society. His last novel was *Jacques le fataliste et son maître*, a stunningly experimental novel with roots in earlier realistic or picaresque tales. Accidents and digressions continually interrupt the story that Jacques is telling his master about his love affairs. In the meantime, the narrator establishes himself at the very center of the action, creating, interrupting, and manipulating the narrative, chatting with the reader, and suggesting alternative developments. As to the issue of fatalism, most modern critics see Diderot as ridiculing its more simple-minded manifestations but retaining both his own more complex materialistic determinism and his belief in human moral potentiality and dignity.

Diderot responded to Catherine II's invitation to Russia in 1773. While there for five months, he talked to her about the need to examine and reform outmoded laws and the need for reason and justice and freedom; he discussed openly the vices of despotism and the desirability of establishing a substantial middle class. Catherine showed interest in his ideas but little inclination or opportunity to put them into effect. In the mid-1770s he collaborated on the third edition of the abbé Raynal's *Histoire des deux Indes*, emphasizing antislavery, anticolonialist views. Diderot's last large work was his *Essai sur les règnes de Claude et de Néron* (1782), a tribute to the philosopher Seneca and an apologia for Diderot's own career.

Diderot's connection with the Revolution is a bit problematical. His political theory, except for two important *Encyclopédie* articles ("Autorité politique" and "Droit naturel"), was not widely known during either his lifetime or the Revolution, and it can claim no striking originality. Although in his later years it veered from enlightened absolutism toward greater liberalism and sometimes even democracy, its fundamentals remained belief in social virtue, justice, private property, and the political necessity of education. His empiricism and practicality put him in tune with a utilitarianism advocating constitutional, bourgeois monarchy. Hints of possible recourse to revolution exist in his later writings, but generally he was a reformist and a gradualist, spurning disorder and violence. Yet Diderot's broader influence on the Revolution is indubitable as an unusually wide-ranging and articulate representative of the Enlightenment. Perhaps no other thinker of the age probed deeper than he into the assumptions underneath established principles and ways of thought.

D. Diderot, *Oeuvres complètes*, ed. R. Lewinter, 15 vols. (Paris, 1969-73), *Oeuvres politiques*, ed. P. Vernière (Paris, 1963); J. Proust, *Diderot et l'Encyclopédie*, rev. ed. (Paris, 1967); A. Strugnell, *Diderot's Politics: A Study of the Evolution of Diderot's Political Thought after the Encyclopédie* (The Hague, 1973); A. M. Wilson, *Diderot* (New York, 1972).

H. S. Vyverberg

Related entries: ENCYCLOPEDIE; ROUSSEAU.

DIETRICH, PHILIPPE-FREDERIC, BARON DE (1748–93), mayor of Strasbourg. Dietrich was the great-grandson of D. Dietrich (1620–94), president of the Strasbourg municipal government who signed the act of capitulation in 1681. His father, Jean (1748–95), was the founder of the ironworks in Niederbronn, Alsace, who received a title of nobility from Louis XV. Philippe-Frédéric inherited most of his parents' landed Alsatian estates and the ironworks. He traveled widely in Europe and published extensively on minerology. His principal work was *Description des gîtes de mineral et des bouches à feu de la France* (3 vols., Paris, 1786–1800). His publications earned him a reputation in the scientific and academic world.

Dietrich supported the Revolution of 1789 and was elected mayor of Strasbourg in February 1790. It was in his home that C.-J. Rouget de Lisle (1760-1836) first sang, on 26 April 1792, his "*Chant de guerre pour l'armée du Rhin*," later known as the "*Marseillaise*."

In August the Jacobins effected Dietrich's removal because of his demand for punishment of the instigators of the *journées* of 20 June and 10 August. Dietrich fled to Basel but returned in November 1792. He was arrested but acquitted by a tribunal in Doubs. The Paris Revolutionary Tribunal condemned him to death on 28 December, and he was executed the following day.

A. Mathiez, ''Un complice de Lafayette. Frédéric Dietrich,'' *Ann. révo.* 12 (1920); G. G. Ramon, *Frédéric de Dietrich: Premier maire de Strasbourg sous la Révolution française* (Nancy, 1919).

G. D. Homan

Related entries: MARSEILLAISE, LA; ROUGET DE LISLE; REVOLUTIONARY TRIBUNAL.

DILLON, ARTHUR, COMTE DE (1750-94), general. Born at Braywich, Ireland, Dillon was named colonel of the family regiment at the age of seventeen. When France went to war with England in 1778, the Dillon Regiment was sent to North America. Colonel Dillon was cited for bravery at the siege of Savannah and promoted to general of brigade in 1780. He also took part in the capture of Tobago, Saint-Eustache, and Saint-Christophe. He served as governor first of Saint-Christophe and then of Tobago in the 1780s. Elected to the Estates General in 1789 by the Second Estate, he defended the interests of the French colonies during the early years of the Revolution.

When war was declared in April 1792, the now Lieutenant General Dillon commanded the Army of the North. He served with distinction under General C. Dumouriez in 1793. As the result of a letter General Dillon wrote to the prince of Hesse-Cassel concerning the latter's withdrawal into Germany, Dillon was denounced as being in correspondence with the enemy. At the height of the Terror, he was arrested and taken before the Revolutionary Tribunal, where he was tried and condemned to death. His execution took place in Paris in 1794. General Dillon is a classic example of a royalist officer who remained in the service of his country, only to meet a tragic death at the hands of his countrymen.

R. F. Hayes, *Irish Swordsmen of France* (Dublin, 1934); A. H. de Jomini, *Histoire des guerres de la Révolution*, vol. 15 (Paris, 1820–24); G. Six, *Les Généraux de la Révolution et de l'Empire* (Paris, 1947).

J. G. Gallaher

Related entries: DUMOURIEZ; REVOLUTIONARY TRIBUNAL; TERROR, THE.

DILLON, THEOBALD, COMTE DE (1746-92), general. Born in Dublin, Ireland, Théobald Dillon entered the French army at the age of fifteen. He served in the Dillon Regiment with the rank of lieutenant until 1778, at which time he was promoted to captain and sailed with the regiment for America. He fell seriously ill after taking part in the siege of Savannah and returned to France. Promoted to colonel in 1780, he was named second in command of the family regiment and seven years later assumed command.

When the French Revolution began in 1789, Colonel Dillon believed it his obligation to remain in France and to continue his service to the king, even though other members of his family, except comte Arthur Dillon, emigrated to Coblentz. Named major general in 1791, he commanded the fortified city of Lille when war broke out in 1792. On 28 April General Dillon was ordered to feign an attack on the town of Tournay to divert Austrian attention from the real French offensive to capture Mons. As Dillon approached Tournay, he came upon a strong enemy force that was also advancing. The French general signaled a withdrawal, and the Austrians advanced. The French troops were soon in a disorderly rout, shouting treason. When General Dillon attempted to rally his troops before Lille, he was shot in the head, killed by one of his own men. His body was burned in the main square of Lille. Only with great difficulty did his wife and newly born child escape the same fate.

R. F. Hayes, *Irish Swordsmen of France* (Dublin, 1934); A. H. de Jomini, *Histoire des guerres de la Révolution*, vol. 15 (Paris, 1820-24); G. Six, *Les Généraux de la Révolution et de l'Empire* (Paris, 1947).

J. G. Gallaher

Related entry: DILLON, A.

DIRECTORY, the five-member executive that governed France between 1795 and 1799 and gave its name to this period of the French Revolution. Established according to the Thermidorian Constitution of 1795, the first Directory took office in Brumaire Year IV. The first five Directors—P. Barras, L.-M. La Revellière-lépeaux, J.-F. Reubell, L. Carnot, and C.-L.-F. Letourneur—inherited a desperate financial situation. The treasury was empty, the Revolutionary paper currency *(assignats)* almost valueless, taxes unpaid, and public institutions starved of funds. In the exceptionally cold winter of 1795, food supplies were exiguous, and famine and starvation threatened many parts of France.

The regime, however, rejected the Jacobin solution to such an emergency: political centralization and economic controls. Like their predecessors the Thermidorians, the Directorials espoused a liberal economic policy, just as they presided over a liberal, parliamentary political system. The Directory, however, failed to live up to its liberal principles. Time after time, the regime resorted to illiberal means to preserve and prolong its existence, for the period was punctuated by a series of coups d'état: Fructidor Year V, Floréal Year VI, Prairial Year VII, and finally Brumaire Year VIII. The Constitution of the Year III was made to work only by the introduction of exceptional measures, which violated it.

In addition to its inheritance of financial collapse and economic hardship, the Directory could not fully escape the legacy of political schism and the memories of the bitter and bloody conflicts of the previous years. The Directory set out to promote a brand of moderate, liberal republicanism, avoiding the excesses of the Jacobin Terror and of royalist restoration. In this way, it would protect the social gains of the bourgeoisie and especially the purchasers of the *biens na-*

tionaux against both a clerical, monarchical reaction and a social revolution from below.

The Directory never succeeded in erasing the divisions of the recent past and in cultivating a strong center party on which its support might rest. At first, the Directory was forced to adopt a *politique de bascule*, teetering first to the Left and then to the Right, as a new crisis forced it to seek new bases of support. In Floréal Year IV the discovery of the Babeuf conspiracy provoked a reorientation of government policy toward the Right. In the following year, royalist electoral victories drove the Directory to seek support on the Left.

The royalist electoral victories of the Year V brought about the first Directorial coup in Fructidor of that year when fifty-three deputies were deported as accomplices of an alleged conspiracy, and electoral results were annulled in forty-nine departments. The Constitution of the Year III had severely restricted the Directory's freedom to maneuver. The executive, confronted by a hostile legislature, could not legally dissolve it. The troops of General P.-F.-C. Augereau instead arrested leading royalists, an ominous sign of the Directory's readiness to violate the constitution and of the role of the army in domestic politics. F. Barthélemy, who had replaced Letourneur as director, was deported, and Carnot fled. They were replaced as directors by P.-A. Merlin de Douai and N.-L. François de Neufchâteau.

In the elections of the Year VI, the situation was repeated but in reverse. This time the Jacobins made important gains, and 163 ex-*conventionnels*, including 71 regicides, were elected. The Directory was once again unsure of an overall majority in the legislature and refused to tolerate what some historians have described as a nascent party of constitutional opposition. The coup of Floréal Year VI, unlike that of Fructidor Year V, did not require armed intervention, but 127 deputies were deprived of their seats, and many officials in minor posts were purged or *floréalisés*. Once again, the Directory had overruled the expressed wishes of the electorate by violating its own liberal constitution. These repeated electoral annulments had the effect of discrediting the entire democratic process and of reducing still further the limited number of Directorial sympathizers. It was clear that the Directory was failing to strengthen the middle ground between royalists and neo-Jacobins. The Directory failed to create the consensus of moderate republican opinion that would make the regime secure.

In Floréal Year VII, the Directory was drastically weakened by the departure of Reubell, its strongest pillar of support, who was replaced by the abbé Sieyès, a man committed to the revision of the Thermidorian constitution. The Directory now came under intense criticism from the Council of Five Hundred for its financial and military administration, and the victories of the allied coalition seemed to presage a repetition of the emergency of 1793. The Directory was forced to submit to the replacement of J.-B. Treilhard (elected director in Floréal Year VI in place of François de Neufchâteau) by L.-J. Gohier. Soon afterward P.-A. Merlin de Douai and La Revellière-lépeaux were replaced by P.-R. Ducos and General J.-F. Moulin. Although these events are known as the coup of

Prairial Year VII, the coup differed from its predecessors in that this time it was the legislature that purged the Directory and not vice versa.

The Directory survived the revival of Jacobin enthusiasm that followed military defeats, but the introduction of a forced loan and a new law of hostages frightened the propertied *notables*. A royalist rising in the southwest was crushed (1799), but the future now lay with Sieyès and all those sympathetic to a revision of the unworkable constitution of 1795. By Brumaire, this group included disaffected generals, like J.-E. Championnet, who had fallen afoul of the civilian administration, as well as N. Bonaparte and his brother Lucien.

The Directory's failure to achieve a lasting consensus is apparent in the history of Directorial elections. The Directory's only consistent support came from the southwest, the margins of the Massif Central, and the borders of the royalist west, although it did make important gains in eastern France in the Year VI, and the isolated department of the Haute-Vienne consistently voted Jacobin. A more vivid indicator of Directorial weakness is the abstention rate in these elections, which approached 90 percent in the Year VII in the Meurthe, the Sarthe, and parts of Alsace. The high level of desertion and draft dodging are further testimony to the abstention of the masses.

It could be argued that the regime's failure was inherent in its very origins. The Two-thirds Law, which attempted to perpetuate the *conventionnels* in office, has been seen as a kind of coup d'état carried out before the new regime had even been installed. On the other hand, the Directory did make a clear and sincere attempt to maintain the rule of law against militant Jacobinism and White Terrorist vengeance. This attempt, however, ran into difficulties very early. The minister of justice in the Year IV, Merlin de Douai, could not find administrators vigorous enough to maintain impartial justice against the most violent forms of rural disaffection. Due process of law was sabotaged at the local level by the prevarication of judges, the obstinate silence of key witnesses, and the connivance of local officials. Many local officials dared not implement government orders to pull down crucifixes or levy forced loans in their local communities. In the circumstances, it was remarkable that the Directory did endure for almost four years, longer than any previous Revolutionary regime.

The Directory must be credited with some important fiscal and administrative reforms, which laid the basis for the constructive work of the Consulate. The fiscal structure was rationalized and was based on four main taxes, *les quatre vieilles*, which remained the basis of the French tax system for a century. These were the land tax, a tax on movable property, the *patente*, and the tax on doors and windows. Even these sources of income, however, were insufficient for the immediate needs of the Directory, which resorted to short-term expedients like the forced loan and other forms of indirect taxation.

The Directory brought to an end the financial chaos and rampant inflation associated with the *assignats*. In the Year IV the introduction of a new paper currency, the *mandats territoriaux*, guaranteed by unsold *biens nationaux*, brought no lasting improvement. The Directory therefore returned to metallic currency.

Although specie was scarce, public officials received their salaries in grain, and a deflationary spiral set in; nevertheless the foundation was laid for economic reconstruction.

In the Year VI, Finance Minister D.-V. Ramel-Nogaret took desperate remedies to balance the budget, when the government euphemistically consolidated two-thirds of its debts. This measure destroyed the government's credit and probably ruined thousands of hard-pressed *rentiers*, but it made balanced budgets possible in the future. This and other attempts at reconstruction were achievements for which the Bonapartists, usually so eager to denigrate the Directory, had reason to be grateful.

The Directory remained a Revolutionary regime in that it was a staunch enemy of royalist counterrevolution and continued the Republic's anticlerical policies. After the coup of Fructidor Year V, the clergy were asked to take an oath swearing their hatred of the monarchy. The pope condemned this new imposition, and about 10,000 priests were sentenced to deportation for refusing it. Many of this number were never actually arrested and many of them were from conquered Belgium, where French secularizing legislation was introduced in 1796. The Directory's intransigence in religious matters did little to heal the schism created in 1790-91 by the Civil Constitution of the Clergy and the subsequent oath. The constitutional church never put down strong roots, and the cult of theophilanthropy, which enjoyed official patronage, attracted only a small intellectual elite. The Directory's contribution to secondary education in the Ecoles centrales was more successful in promoting the secular ideals of the Enlightenment within a Republican framework. Religious peace, however, was not achieved until the negotiation of the Concordat between Bonaparte and the papacy.

The Directory continued the Revolutionary drive to extend the benefits of French democratic egalitarianism to the oppressed peoples of *ancien régime* Europe. Yet its treatment of other nationalities was often extremely cynical. Financial difficulties forced France to support its armies out of resources plundered from liberated territories. An indemnity was imposed on the Dutch and their fleet put at France's disposal. Huge sums were extracted from Italy in the form of war indemnities and art treasures. The Directory was thus relieved of one financial burden; the conquered territories were condemned to meet the expenses of their own liberation.

Relations between the government in Paris and its generals in the field were strained. Bonaparte's personal prestige was high after the successful Italian campaign of 1796-97, and his personal policies prevailed in the negotiations with Austria at Leoben and Campoformio in 1797. The creation of satellite republics in northern Italy could not be a permanent peace-keeping solution, and in delivering Venice to the Hapsburgs, Bonaparte showed a cynical disregard for the Revolutionary aim of freeing oppressed nations from monarchical tyranny. The attempt to divert Bonaparte's ambitions toward the eastern Mediterranean theater backfired when the French fleet was destroyed at the Battle of the Nile in 1798. Bonaparte in any case returned to France in Vendémiaire Year VIII.

By this time, the revisionists could also count on the support of other generals who resented attempts by the regime's civil *commissaires* to regulate the plunder of Italy.

By Brumaire Year VIII, the bourgeoisie, whose interests the Directory had served, saw their safety in a change of regime. The Constitution of the Year III had entrusted power to a limited elite of property owners, whose rights the Directory had defended. The constitution had installed a two-tier electoral system, which effectively left the final choice of deputies to a plutocracy of about 30,000 men. The Directory presided over a bourgeois constitution in the sense that the right to education, to work, and to public assistance were no longer recognized as responsibilities of the state. The regime denationalized the war industries, farming out contracts to private entrepreneurs and sometimes to the personal acolytes of the directors themselves. The regime dismantled the economic controls of the Year II, prematurely minimizing the requirements of war. Having silenced the demands of the popular movement in the Year III, the Republic could afford to return to the principles of economic liberalism and their consequences: accelerating inflation and astronomically high food prices. At the same time, the continuing sale of *biens nationaux* favored the operations of property speculators. In many ways, the bourgeois Republic of 1795-99 is best seen as the direct descendant of the liberalism of the early Revolutionary years.

The Directory was an important transitional stage in the history of the French bourgeoisie, which had overthrown the remnants of feudal society and now faced the task of reconstructing French social and political institutions. The Revolutionary bourgeoisie was essentially a professional and administrative bourgeoisie, which welcomed new opportunities for investment in landed property. The sale of the *biens nationaux*, which continued under the Directory, provided an excellent opening for profitable investment at prices made ludicrously cheap by inflation. Administrative officials and the commercial classes were important beneficiaries from these sales.

Government contractors, too, were favored by the regime's insistence on offering the task of supplying its troops to private entrepreneurs. Individuals like G.-J. Ouvrard were able to amass considerable private fortunes from the business of feeding the French navy. Undertaking government contracts, however, was sometimes a risky business since the government could not be relied on to pay the *fournisseur* on time. The spectacular rise of men like Ouvrard has given an unfair impression of Directorial society as one dominated by a brash and exceptionally vulgar coterie of *nouveaux-riches*. Outside Parisian high society, the reality was typified by a modest and sober bourgeois, with a stable family, and a desire to protect newly acquired property.

Such a *notable* eventually found that Bonaparte provided a safer guarantee than the Directory. The Directory had shown scant respect for political freedoms, and by Brumaire its popularity was at low ebb. It would be unwise to conclude, however, that a Bonapartist dictatorship was the inevitable outcome or even the one most widely desired. Bonaparte had the support of disgruntled military leaders and of constitutional revisionists, but France had survived the military crisis of the Year VII without the aid of Bonaparte, who was stranded in Egypt. The plebiscite of the Year VIII did not suggest a groundswell of support for Bonaparte since Lucien, as minister of the interior, was responsible for the deliberate falsification of the voting results. The secret of Bonaparte's success was popular apathy and yet further cynical treatment of the wishes of the electorate. Strictly speaking, the plebiscite of the Year VIII obtained fewer votes than did the Jacobin Constitution of 1793. Once in power, Bonaparte stigmatized the Directory for its corruption, incompetence, and parliamentary instability. He nevertheless inherited the Directory's positive achievements of fiscal and administrative reform.

C. Church, "In Search of the Directory," in J. F. Bosher, ed., *French Government and Society, 1500-1850: Essays in Memory of A. Cobban* (London, 1973); A. Goodwin, "The French Executive Directory: A Re-evaluation," *History* 22 (1937); G. Lefebvre, *La France sous le Directoire (1795-1799)*, ed. J.-R. Suratteau (Paris, 1977); M. Lyons, *France under the Directory* (Cambridge, 1975); A. Soboul, *Le Directoire et le Consulat* (Paris, 1967); M. J. Sydenham, *The First French Republic, 1792-1804* (London, 1974); D. Woronoff, *La République Bourgeoise, 1794-99* (Paris, 1972).

M. Lyons

Related entries: ASSIGNATS; BABEUF; *BIENS NATIONAUX*; CISALPINE REPUBLIC; CISPADANE REPUBLIC; CONSPIRACY OF EQUALS; CONSTITUTION OF 1795; COUP OF 18 BRUMAIRE; COUP OF 18 FRUCTIDOR YEAR V; COUP OF 30 PRAIRIAL YEAR VII; COUP OF 22 FLOREAL YEAR VI; *MANDATS TERRITORIAUX*; PRELIMINARIES OF LEOBEN; SIEYES; THEOPHILANTHROPY.

DOCTRINE OF NATURAL FRONTIERS, political position holding that nature had established the Alps, the Rhine, the Pyrenees, and the ocean as France's territorial limits and that the French should seek to attain them. Erroneously attributed to the pre-Revolutionary Bourbon monarchy, the doctrine was in fact first proclaimed by certain French and foreign Revolutionaries. For a time in the 1790s, the attainment of the natural frontiers became a foreign policy objective.

The idea that nature had designed the frontiers of France seems first to have been suggested just before the Revolution by Anacharsis Cloots, a Prussian-born baron resident in France. In a work published in 1785, he urged the French government to extend its frontiers to the Rhine and the Alps. Another early advocate of the doctrine, M. de Cubières, a French poet and minor office holder, predicted in 1791 that the Sardinian Duchy of Savoy would eventually join France not only because of economic and cultural considerations but also because of the promptings of nature. Savoy, he suggested, was separated from Sardinia and joined instead to France by the "eternal Alps." Before 1792, however, with France at peace and entertaining no idea of territorial expansion, talk about natural frontiers was academic.

They were first seriously discussed in late 1792 and early 1793. At this time expansion of the Republic began to appear as a solution to problems of military supply, finance, and security that had arisen in the war against Austria and its allies. At the outset of the war, the French had hoped to persuade the peoples of occupied enemy territories along the eastern border to form independent sister states which, modeled on Revolutionary France and allied with it, would help secure it against enemies. Only Savoy and Nice responded favorably to the new ideology; when they voted for union with France, the National Convention annexed them. In Belgium and the occupied part of the Rhineland, however, the people not only refused to adopt French-style governments on whose co-operation France could count but failed to assist the French, whose armies were experiencing shortages of supplies and of funds needed to purchase them. To solve the critical problems resulting from this situation and to provide security for France, the Convention, after first trying to institute Revolutionary governments by force in the occupied areas, decided instead to annex them. The decision to embark on expansion, taken toward the end of January 1793, necessarily raised the question of what limits the Republic should have. For many Revolutionaries, the answer was the natural frontiers.

As early as November 1792, some Revolutionaries, already sensing that conditions might prompt an expansionist program, had suggested that the Republic should attain the natural frontiers. The German revolutionary J. G. A. Forster, engaged in trying to persuade the population in the occupied part of the Rhineland to join France, termed the Rhine the "natural frontier of a great republic." J.-P. Brissot spoke of expansion to the Rhine and Alps, and at the Paris Jacobin club, E.-B. Courtois and P.-A. Dartigoeyte observed pointedly that nature had divided mankind into separate nations by barriers of sea and mountain. Proposing to the Convention the annexation of Savoy, the abbé Grégoire stated that failure to join Savoy to France would thwart nature's order. He added that if the perils posed for France in the current struggle made annexation of more than Savoy advisable, the limit of expansion would be found in the frontiers traced for France by nature's hand. More emphatic endorsements than these of the natural frontiers doctrine came after the decision to annex the occupied territories. On 31 January 1793, G.-J. Danton, after informing the Convention that nature had imposed the limits of the Republic at the Rhine, the ocean, and the Alps, added that France would attain these limits despite foreign opposition. Two weeks later L. Carnot, reporting for the Diplomatic Committee on the matter of expansion, reiterated that the natural frontiers were the Rhine, the Alps, and the Pyrenees. His report sanctioned the annexation of any territory—whether belonging to a declared enemy or a neutral sovereign—between the existing frontier and the line of the Rhine and the Alps, if national interest required it.

The appeal of the natural frontiers stemmed from the eighteenth-century infatuation with nature as general arbiter of all things. The Revolutionaries, however, had practical reasons for adopting the so-called choice of nature as the Republic's limits. The acquisition of the territory between the prewar frontiers and those of nature would give the Republic the military and economic security that it needed. The natural frontier was a strategic frontier; with the Rhine and the Alps attained, the Republic would possess solid and defensible barriers. Moreover, the human and material resources of Belgium and the Rhenish zone, including the wealth confiscated from the church and from counterrevolutionaries, would help France wage a successful war.

In early 1793, the French, against the will of a majority of the population, annexed a large part of Belgium, Liège, and the left bank of the Rhine but then lost most of it to the enemy. When, after the summer of 1794, the French regained the military initiative and seized all territory as far as the Rhine, they again faced the question of the Republic's limits. With the decision to retain Savoy and Nice, the Republic kept its frontier on the Alps. Opinion was divided, however, over retaining the Rhine frontier. Most Republicans, notably J.-F. Reubell, *conventionnel* and later one of the five directors, were partisans of the Rhine frontier on strategic, financial, and economic grounds. Between 1795 and 1797, Reubell's opinion gradually prevailed. The Convention reannexed Belgium and Liège in October 1795 but left unsettled the question of the Rhenish left bank until a continental peace agreement was reached. Under the Directory, the question was resolved when the Austrians, defeated by N. Bonaparte in Italy, agreed in the Treaty of Campoformio (October 1797) to cede Belgium to France and recognize its rule on almost the entire left bank of the Rhine. The Republic had virtually attained the natural frontiers.

The framers of France's foreign policy did not long adhere to the doctrine of the natural frontiers. Even the Directory, before it collapsed in 1799, was considering acquisitions beyond the Alps. It had annexed the Ionian Islands in 1797 but lost them the next year to the forces of the Second Coalition. Early in 1799, the Directory took the first steps toward joining Piedmont to the Republic, but French military reverses prevented annexation at this time. Bonaparte was not the man to be bound by the rulings of nature, and he had not long been master of France before he began annexing territory beyond the natural frontiers.

J. Godechot, *La grande nation; l'expansion révolutionnaire de la France dans le monde de 1789 à 1799*, 2 vols. (Paris, 1956); R. Guyot, *Le Directoire et la paix de l'Europe, 1795-1799* (Paris, 1911); J. P. McLaughlin, "Ideology and Conquest: The Question of Proselytism and Expansion in the French Revolution, 1789-1793," *Hist. Papers, Can.* (1976).

J. P. McLaughlin

Related entries: BELGIUM; CLOOTS; DANTON; FIRST COALITION; FORSTER; REUBELL; SECOND COALITION; TREATY OF CAMPOFORMIO.

DOLIVIER, PIERRE (1746-?), abbé and advocate of extensive social reform. Curé of Mauchamps in the *bailliage* of Etampes, Dolivier lived in a community of small wine growers and day laborers, dominated by two large farmers who controlled most of the cultivated land. At the behest of his parishioners who demanded cheap bread, Dolivier served as their spokesman. In 1788 in *La lettre* *d'un curé du bailliage d'Etampes* and then the following year in *La voix d'un citoyen sur la manière de former les Etats généraux*, he demanded fixing the price of bread. In *Le voeu national* of 1790 he, as so many others, criticized the work of the Constituent Assembly. Denouncing suffrage based on property ownership, he appealed for social equality in the future, writing, "I wish that in its social policy the state establish a just equality of means so that each member can attain the full enjoyment of every right that is due him."

These social demands became more precise in the course of the conflicts during the spring of 1792. When the mayor of Etampes, J.-H. Simonneau, was killed by rioters, Dolivier took up their defense in a *Pétition*, arguing that it was the rising price of wheat, hunger, and "the rigid and repulsive inflexibility" of the mayor that led to his murder. Was it just, he asked, that only the rich man enjoy the right to property, and should not he be limited by controls? From this claim, so common among the *sans-culottes*, Dolivier went on to call into question landed property in a memorandum that M. Robespierre would not publish in his *Défenseur de la Constitution*. He wrote: "The nation alone is the true proprietor of its soil. Then, admitting that the nation can and should determine the types of private property and rules for its transfer, can it do so in a way that it will be deprived of its sovereign right to the products of the land and can it accord rights to proprietors that leave no rights, not even those of an inalienable nature, to those who are not proprietors?"

During the last months of 1792, which were marked by a substantial increase in the price of provisions and grain disturbances, Dolivier again took up his pen. In his *Essai sur la justice primitive*, which he did not publish until 1793, he distinguished between natural and civil property. The first did not extend beyond the person of each individual; the second was born of a common and unrestricted right, which had become a particular and exclusive right. Because of the failure to keep this last type of property right within its just limits, it had become "an inexhaustible source of perverseness and unhappiness for the people." No one should possess land in his own right; everyone should have it at his disposal. Did this mean the abolition of private property and the right of every individual to the product of his labor? At the time, Dolivier demanded only the division of cultivation, and not of property, in such a way that no farm would exceed "the tillage of a single plough," the ideal of the small farmer, as of a number of *sans-culottes*.

F.-N. Babeuf was aware of Dolivier's writings. His *Essai sur la justice primitive* was found among the papers of Babeuf, who had also noted Dolivier's name as an eventual member of the National Assembly that he planned to convene after the seizure of power by "the Equals."

M. Dommanget, *Les curés rouges* (Paris, 1976); J. Droz, ed., *Histoire générale du socialisme*, vol. 1 (Paris, 1972); J. Jaurès, *Histoire socialiste de la Révolution française*, vol. 2 (Paris, 1970).

J.-P. Bertaud

Related entries: BABEUF; CONSPIRACY OF EQUALS.

DON GRATUIT, fiscal contribution to the crown, ostensibly voluntary in character, voted by the assembly of the clergy. Ecclesiastical property was exempt from taxation under the *ancien régime* on the grounds that ecclesiastical revenues were earmarked for sacred purposes, specifically the support of the clergy, the maintenance of divine worship, and the relief of the poor.

The First Estate granted the *don gratuit* for the first time in 1561, by the contract of Poissy, in order to avert the threat of alienation of church lands. Negotiation of subsequent contracts accounted for the institutionalization of the assembly of the clergy (the so-called foreign clergy of provinces annexed after 1561 made other arrangements), which met on a regular basis every five years and in extraordinary session, usually in time of war, when the crown found itself in financial straits. Critics charged that the *dons gratuits*—which averaged 3,608,000 *livres* per year, approximately 3 to 5 percent of the annual revenue of the church, during the eighteenth century—represented an inadequate contribution given the extent of ecclesiastical property. Repeated borrowing to raise these sums resulted in the accumulation of a substantial clerical debt, payment of which became an issue for the National Assembly. On the eve of the Revolution, the clergy opposed efforts to subject its property to a uniform land tax, just as it had resisted the *dixième* of 1710, the *cinquantième* of 1725, and the *vingtième* of 1749, by identifying its fiscal privileges with the cause of religion itself and with the constitutional order of the *ancien régime*.

P. Gagnol, *Les décimes et dons gratuits* (Paris, 1911); G. Lepointe, *L'organisation et la politique financière du clergé de France sous le règne de Louis XV* (Paris, 1923); N. Ravitch, ''The Taxing of the Clergy in Eighteenth-Century France,'' *Ch. Hist.* 33 (1964).

J. Merrick

Related entries: CIVIL CONSTITUTION OF THE CLERGY; TITHE; *VINGTIEME*.

DROIT D'AINESSE. See PRIMOGENITURE.

DROUET, JEAN-BAPTISTE (1763-1824), local official who helped apprehend Louis XVI during the flight to Varennes. Drouet was born in 1763 at Sainte-Menehould, where he later became the town's postmaster. On 21 June 1791 he recognized the fleeing Louis XVI and took a shortcut to nearby Varennes where he arrived before the king and his escort. Drouet alerted the authorities and took part in the arrest of the sovereign and his family. This act made his fortune. A committed patriot, he became a deputy to the Convention, where he played an active role in its debates and discussions. This impulsive and simple man, still largely a peasant, took his place in the corridors of power. He joined the Jacobins, became a member of the Committee of General Security, and voted for the death of the king. On 2 June 1793 he played an important part in the expulsion of the Girondin deputies from the Convention. Later he endorsed price regulations and the maximum.

As a commissioner to the Army of the North, he was present at Maubeuge during its siege, and was taken prisoner by the Austrians in the course of a daring sortie. Along with other prisoners he was released in 1795 in exchange for Madame Royale. He returned to the Convention, as earnest and energetic as ever.

In Germinal Year IV (March-April 1796), he was suspected of circulating violently antigovernment pamphlets. He was in touch with F.-N. Babeuf and other members of his conspiracy, and after discussions with them, he joined this insurrectionary movement and participated, as a Jacobin, in meetings with the Babouvistes. Following a general assembly of the secret directory at his home on 19 Floréal (8 May), he and other conspirators were arrested two days later and incarcerated in the Abbaye prison.

The legislature discussed his case at several sessions and finally decided to bring an indictment against him. It was due to his position as a deputy that the members of Babeuf's Conspiracy of Equals were later tried by the High Court of Justice at Vendôme. On 1 Fructidor (18 August), however, he escaped from prison—undoubtedly with the complicity of P. Barras—and took refuge in Switzerland. He was judged in absentia at Vendôme and acquitted. In fact, he had not participated in the plot but had only engaged in transactions between the Montagnards and Babouvistes. He was an influential and very popular personality whom Babeuf ardently desired to have in his movement. After traveling around, he was allowed to return to France after 18 Fructidor (4 September 1797).

In the Year VII (1798-1799) Drouet organized the Society of the Manège, which regrouped the "last" of the Jacobins. Then J. Fouché appointed him commissioner of the Directory to the department of the Marne. Later N. Bonaparte named him subprefect of Sainte-Menehould, and he remained at this post for fourteen years. Proscribed under the Restoration, he lived in hiding and died, under a false name, at Mâcon in 1824.

G. Benoit-Guyod, *Qu'est devenu Drouet, l'homme de Varennes?* (Paris, 1946); H. Manevy and R. Vailland, *Un homme du peuple sous la Révolution* (Paris, 1947).

R. Legrand

Related entries: BABEUF; COMMITTEE OF GENERAL SECURITY; CONSPIRACY OF EQUALS; COUP OF 18 FRUCTIDOR YEAR V; VARENNES.

DUBOIS-CRANCE, EDMOND-LOUIS-ALEXIS (1747-1809), military man and legislator, chiefly responsible for the decree of the Amalgam in 1793. Born at Charleville on 17 October 1747, Dubois-Crancé was the son of an intendant. At the age of fifteen he enlisted in the musketeers of the king. Ten years later he left the service to retire to his chateau of Balham. Elected a deputy to the Estates General by the Third Estate of the *bailliage* of Vitry-le-François, he was one of the proponents of the Tennis Court Oath. In the Constituent Assembly, he specialized in military questions and was one of the first to call for the conscription of all able-bodied young Frenchmen. He participated in the formulation of laws that created uniformity of pay (by branch), of recruitment, and of promotion for cadres. He also played a prominent role in the work of the

Committees of Finance and Subsistence. Beginning in June 1791 illness forced his absence from the Assembly. He returned only in September, and the political dissensions that he witnessed there inspired him to write a satirical book, *True Portrait of Our Legislators*.

During the Legislative Assembly, Dubois-Crancé once again served in the army. Attached to the staff of the Army of the Midi, he became adjutant general with the rank of colonel. Four departments elected him to the Convention; he chose to sit for the Ardennes. In the Convention he voted for the king's death. He was sent to A.-P. Montesquiou-Fézénsac's army and sat on the Committee of General Defense from January to April 1793. There he presented a general plan for the coming campaign in January and defended the principle of the Amalgam; due to his intervention, the National Convention adopted his project for a single uniform, a single pay scale, identical discipline, and uniform rules for promotion for the personnel of the former royal army and of the battalions of volunteers. The formation of demi-brigades that would establish genuine unity in the army was, however, suspended; this would not be realized until the end of 1793 and during 1794.

Sent as a representative on mission, he directed the siege of Lyon but was accused of being lax. Recalled on 6 October 1793, he was denounced by G.-A. Couthon and his arrest was ordered. On 19 October the order was retracted. As an ally of the Thermidorians, he sat in the Council of Five Hundred from 1795 to 1797. He served as inspector general of the Army of the Rhine from 1797 to 1799. He became minister of war on 14 September 1799; and, powerless, he witnessed the coup d'état of 18 Brumaire. On 27 April 1801 he retired as a general of division and returned to Balham, where he later became the mayor. He died at Rethel in 1809.

T. Jung, *L'armée et la Révolution, Dubois-Crancé*, 2 vols. (Paris, 1884).

J.-P. Bertaud

Related entries: AMALGAM; COUTHON; TENNIS COURT OATH; THERMIDORIAN REACTION.

DUCOS, PIERRE-ROGER, COMTE (1747-1816), director and provisional consul. Born 23 July 1747 at Montfort, Ducos studied law at Toulouse and practiced at Dax (Landes), becoming president of the criminal tribunal of the department. He helped draft the *cahier* of the Third Estate of his region and then served as procurator of the commune of Dax and as justice of the peace. Elected by the Landes to the Convention, he joined the Plain after voting for the king's death. His most important work in the Convention was as a member of the Committee of Public Relief. After the days of 31 May and 2 June 1793, he declared himself against the Girondins. He favored separation of church and state. On 22 November 1793 he served as secretary of the Convention and in January 1794 as president of the Jacobin club.

Carried over into the Council of Ancients as a *conventionnel*, he was elected to that body by seven departments in 1796. At times he served as secretary and as president, the most important of the latter occasions being 18 Fructidor. When his reelection was annulled in 1798 on grounds of Jacobinism, he had to leave the Ancients on 30 Floréal Year VI and once again became president of the criminal tribunal of Landes.

After the coup of 30 Prairial Year VII, P. Barras, expecting Ducos to be his pawn, succeeded in having him chosen a director. In part because he thought Barras' policy would lead to a Bourbon restoration, however, Ducos soon became such a follower of E.-J. Sieyès that he was considered Sieyès' shadow. Ducos was one of the three directors who forced J.-P. Bernadotte to resign as minister of war after Bernadotte had refused a Jacobin request to arrest him and his two protectors and head a new government. Ducos was also one of the directors whose resignation made it impossible for the Directory to function and facilitated the coup d'état of Brumaire. His reward was an appointment as a provisional consul. There were reports that Sieyès and Ducos had split a considerable sum (700,000 to 800,000 francs), which the Directory had reserved for its existing members. To Sieyès' surprise, Ducos said that N. Bonaparte should be the first presiding consul.

In his capacity as provisional consul, Ducos cooperated with Sieyès, J.-J. Cambacérès, and C.-F. Lebrun in choosing a majority of the initial members of the conservative Senate. He became its first vice-president. In 1804 he received the senatorship of Amboise, with its accompanying income. In the same year he was named a grand officer of the Legion of Honor and of the Order of La Réunion, and in 1808 he was named a count of the empire.

As a senator, he voted for the deposition of Napoleon in 1814. Despite that fact, he became a peer of France during the Hundred Days. Exiled in 1816 as a relapsed regicide, he was not permitted to remain in Baden or Wurttemberg. En route to Austria, he died at Ulm on 16 March 1816 as a result of his carriage horses' having bolted.

J. B. Morton, *Brumaire, the Rise of Bonaparte: A Study of French History from the Death of Robespierre to the Establishment of the Consulate* (London, [1948]).

R. B. Holtman

Related entries: CAMBACERES; COUNCIL OF ANCIENTS; COUP OF 18 BRUMAIRE; COUP OF 18 FRUCTIDOR YEAR V; COUP OF 30 PRAIRIAL YEAR VII; GIRONDINS; LEBRUN; SIEYES.

DUMONT, PIERRE-ETIENNE-LOUIS (1759-1829), political commentator. Born on 8 July 1759 at Geneva where his family had been reputable citizens since the Reformation, E. Dumont became a popular minister there. The victory of the aristocratic faction over the liberal movement, to which Dumont belonged, caused him to leave Geneva in 1783 and go to Saint Petersburg, where he served as pastor of a Protestant church for eighteen months. He made the acquaintance of several prominent English statesmen when he went to London in 1785 to serve as tutor for the marquis of Landsdowne's sons. Contemporaries depicted

Dumont as a witty, erudite man of high, rigid principles, who, though an excellent writer, disliked public acclaim.

Dumont's career took a decisive turn when he visited Paris in 1788 and met the comte de Mirabeau. It was the beginning of a close relationship between two men who were almost total opposites in character and behavior. Although critical of Mirabeau's extravagant life-style, unstable temperament, and thirst for popularity, Dumont said no other Revolutionary figure had such a keen understanding of political events and issues. In the spring of 1789, Mirabeau persuaded him to join his *atelier*, or workshop, which consisted of three other former Genevans. They formed a brilliant speech-writing and editorial staff for Mirabeau, with Dumont and J.-A. Duroverai specializing in political affairs, while E.-S. Reybaz and E. Clavière handled economic issues.

As part of Mirabeau's *atelier*, Dumont was a minor participant in and an astute observer of the early phases of the Revolution. He and Duroverai tried unsuccessfully to arrange an alliance between Mirabeau and J. Necker. According to Dumont, he wrote the speech of 8 July 1789 in which Mirabeau attacked the summoning of troops to Versailles and the subsequent petition of the National Assembly requesting the king to remove them. The workshop also drew up a draft for the Declaration of the Rights of Man, which the deputies rejected. Dumont believed that Mirabeau may well have been part of a conspiracy during the October Days to make the duc d'Orléans lieutenant general of France. He noted that the Assembly's decree of 7 November 1789, which forbade deputies to serve in the ministry, dealt a severe blow to Mirabeau's ambitions and to the hopes of his entourage. In addition, Dumont and C. Duroverai took over the editorship of Mirabeau's journal, *Le courrier de Provence*, in June 1789. Although the journal was quite successful at first, Dumont withdrew from it early in 1790 due to mismanagement and dishonest practices by its publisher, L.-L.-E. Le Jay, and his wife, a former mistress of Mirabeau.

In March 1790, Dumont decided to return to England for the following reasons: his unhappiness over the journal, his growing disillusionment with the course of the Revolution and with Mirabeau, his role as a subaltern writer, the linkage of his name with Mirabeau's in several political pamphlets, and the increased alienation of many of his French and English friends because of his political activities.

Dumont came back to Paris for brief visits in 1791 and 1792. He was persuaded that the power of the radical Left had increased after Mirabeau's death and that the flight to Varennes had given rise to republicanism in France. During his final stay in Paris, he tried unsuccessfully to effect an alliance between the Feuillants and the Girondins. He blamed the problems of the monarchy primarily on the weakness of Louis XVI.

In 1792, Dumont's letters to his close friend, Sir S. Romilly, were published under a pseudonym. Dumont's most important work on the French Revolution, the *Recollections of Mirabeau*, was published posthumously in 1832. Although the book is essentially a series of sketches that the author intended to use as a basis for a broader account of the Revolution, historians have found it to be a valuable primary source on the period of the National Constituent and Legislative assemblies.

Dumont's major claim to scholarly fame is eight volumes of J. Bentham's works, which he edited during his residence in England from 1792 until 1814. With the restoration of Genevan independence, Dumont returned to his birthplace, where he became head of the Supreme Council and was active in judicial and penal reforms until his death on 29 September 1829.

E. Dumont, *Recollections of Mirabeau and of the Two First Legislative Assemblies of France*, 2d ed. (London, 1832) and *Souvenirs sur Mirabeau et sur les deux premières Assemblées legislatives*, nouv. ed. (Paris, 1951); H. R. Greenvelt [E. Dumont], *Letters, Comprising an Account of the Late Revolution in France...in the Years 1789 and 1790* (London, 1792).

D. M. Epstein

Related entries: CLAVIERE; MIRABEAU; NECKER; OCTOBER DAYS; ORLEANS; VARENNES.

DUMOURIEZ, CHARLES-FRANCOIS DU PERIER (1739-1823), general, foreign minister, minister of war. Born of an aristocratic family, Dumouriez was raised in a military environment. His father was a *commissaire des guerres* and one-time soldier in the Picardie Regiment. The young Dumouriez saw his first military action in 1757, when he accompanied his father to Germany, and he gained a commission as cornet in a cavalry regiment the next year.

At bottom, Dumouriez was an adventurer, and after leaving active service in 1762, he embarked on a series of wanderings and unusual missions. Voyages to Corsica, where he attempted to play an active role in that island's struggles with Genoa, were followed by travels to Portugal and Spain. Much of this was undertaken with the sanction of the duc de Choiseul, then minister of Louis XV. Recalled to France, Dumouriez was sent with French forces to pacify Corsica. On his return, Dumouriez, now a colonel, was dispatched as a French agent to assist the Poles who were leagued together in a confederation to resist Russian dominance of Polish affairs. Returning to France in 1772, he went on mission to Hamburg. He next spent some time imprisoned in the Bastille, owing to his involvement in a plot against the duc d'Aiguillon. However, Dumouriez soon returned to the service of the army and the king. Among his duties was an evaluation of the new Prussian-inspired tactics advocated by the baron de Pirch. Dumouriez' tactical knowledge was further enhanced by his long friendship with J.-A. Guibert, perhaps the most important French tactical writer of the eighteenth century. In 1778 he was appointed commandant of the Cherbourg garrison, a post he held until 1790. There he climbed the ladder of promotion as high as *maréchal de camp* (major general).

The Revolution presented Dumouriez with many opportunities. Indeed, A. Sorel wrote of Dumouriez, "The French Revolution was not, in his eyes, a regeneration of humanity, it was a career" (p. 405). In July 1789, he was named head of the National Guard in Cherbourg, where he used his double authority to keep order with a strong hand. A military reorganization eliminated his command in 1790, and he went to Paris. There, he received an important mission from the marquis de Lafayette, who sent him to assist and advise rebels in the Austrian Netherlands. His brief experience here focused his attention on that territory for years to come. After seven months as a general of the new twelfth military administrative division, Dumouriez returned to Paris, ingratiating himself with the Girondists. His claim to diplomatic expertise gained him the foreign minister portfolio on 15 March 1792. Virtually minister of war as well, Dumouriez attempted unsuccessfully to isolate the Austrian Hapsburgs from Prussia.

When war came in April, it was Dumouriez' plan to fight it in the Austrian Netherlands. He believed the population would rise to welcome the French army, but his expectations of quick success were unjustified. In April and May, French troops were sent reeling from their attempted offensive. Dumouriez played the part of the loyal royalist. Controversy and intrigue brought a shift of ministries, however, and Dumouriez, alienating J.-P. Brissot and the Girondists, was forced from the government on 15 June. Now a lieutenant general, Dumouriez won an appointment to the *Armée du Nord* where he took over the camp at Maude. He devoted his considerable talents to preparing the troops there. Lafayette's attempted coup and subsequent flight left the *Armée du Nord* without its commander. On 16 August 1792, Dumouriez was appointed its chief. He was soon ordered to lead part of his army south to deal with the duke of Brunswick's invasion. In the wooded hills and defiles of the Argonne, Dumouriez skillfully delayed the Prussian advance, but the invaders turned the French line, and Dumouriez was forced to retire toward Sainte-Menehould and Valmy, where he joined with General F.-C. Kellermann's *Armée du centre*. On 20 September these two French armies stood at Valmy. Dumouriez' weary troops were stationed in support of Kellermann's army that day of victory.

When the Prussians began their retreat, Dumouriez ordered his army north while he went to Paris, where he pleaded for his long-desired attack on the Austrian Netherlands. His fixation was based partially on a hope that the liberated people would choose him as their leader and that he could carve out a state for himself. After winning government approval, Dumouriez went to Valenciennes to lead the main body of his army. His final offensive plan was blunt, calling for a direct advance on Mons. The advance began on 3 November, and three days later he met the enemy at Jemappes, near Mons. The hard-fought Battle of Jemappes not only won Mons but set in motion an Austrian retreat that left the southern Netherlands in French hands before the end of 1792.

In pursuit of personal ambition, Dumouriez appealed to whatever factions in the new territory might give him their support, but he received neither the welcome nor the aid he expected. The diplomatic consequences of the French conquest, meanwhile, embroiled France with England and the Dutch Netherlands. Believing a wider war inevitable, the government ordered Dumouriez to invade the United Provinces. However, on 1 March 1793 the Austrians counterattacked into their old provinces, pushing back the French. Dumouriez abandoned the Dutch venture and rushed to meet the Austrian advance. The forces collided at Neerwinden on 18 March, where the French suffered a crippling defeat. After this battle, Dumouriez began to negotiate with the enemy. He concluded a treasonous armistice with the Austrians, who agreed not to attack the retreating French. In exchange, Dumouriez was to march his army on Paris to reestablish the monarchy. Dumouriez envisioned himself as regent to the young Louis XVII. The National Convention grew suspicious and sent the minister of war to investigate and, if necessary, to arrest Dumouriez; but the latter struck first and arrested the minister and his aides. Nonetheless, Dumouriez was unable to gain his soldiers' allegiance to his new plans, and on 5 April he crossed over to the Austrians.

His treason undermined French confidence in their generals. In the Army of the North, Generals A.-P. Custine and J.-N. Houchard ultimately fell victims to the suspicion created by Dumouriez' defection. Furthermore, he condemned French forces to weak and uncertain command throughout 1793 since no general believed himself secure.

After his flight, Dumouriez traveled without receiving a welcome anywhere. He later employed his military knowledge against N. Bonaparte. In 1800 he gave the Russians a project for invading the French coast. Later Admiral Nelson recommended Dumouriez to the English government, and three years later he became a salaried adviser to the cabinet. England became his home. With the Restoration of the Bourbons, he hoped to be rewarded by Louis XVIII, but Louis withheld the honors that the proud Dumouriez felt due him. Dumouriez lived out his days as an exile in England.

Dumouriez deserves both praise and condemnation. In defense of his strange opportunistic career, L.-A. Thiers wrote, "If he abandoned us, he had also saved us" (p. 42).

A. Chuquet, *Dumouriez* (Paris, 1914); C.-F. Dumouriez, *La vie et les mémoires*, 4 vols. (Paris, 1822-23); R. W. Phipps, *The Armies of the First French Republic and the Rise of the Marshals of Napoleon the First*, vol. 1 (London, 1926); A. Sorel, *L'Europe et la Révolution française*, vol. 2 (Paris, 1908); L.-A. Thiers, *Histoire de la Révolution française*, vol. 4 (Paris, 1857).

J. A. Lynn

Related entries: BATTLE OF JEMAPPES; BATTLE OF NEERWINDEN; BATTLE OF VALMY; GIRONDINS; GUIBERT.

DU PONT DE NEMOURS, PIERRE-SAMUEL (1739-1817), physiocrat, author and editor, deputy to the Constituante and Council of Ancients. Du Pont was born in Paris 14 December 1739, the son of a watchmaker. His search for employment began through his study of schemes being suggested for the regeneration of France after the Seven Years War. Earlier attempts at drama and poetry were tossed aside as he turned his attention to issues of population, taxation, agriculture, and others concerning the status of the French economy. His inchoate ideas were gradually brought into focus through his efforts to get them on paper, his correspondence with others who might share his interests, and his fortunate assignment from C.-B. Meliand, intendant of Soissons, to study various aspects of the economy of the region. These activities brought conviction of the primary significance of land in any economic and social order, which was displayed in a pamphlet Du Pont published in 1763 in response to a proposal for tax reform. He argued that the reform proposal grossly overestimated the number of taxpayers since all taxes ultimately were borne by proprietors of land.

Such ideas were in accord with those being propagated by F. Quesnay, personal physician to Madame de Pompadour but later to be celebrated as leader of a group of thinkers called physiocrats. Probably through the hands of the marquis de Mirabeau, who had been converted to Quesnay's ideas, a copy of Du Pont's pamphlet came to the doctor's attention. The young author was summoned to Versailles and became almost at once another ardent disciple.

Du Pont now seized on every opportunity to publish in support of what he came to regard as the true doctrine and best hope for the regeneration of France. His efforts won him the friendship of A.-R.-J. Turgot and appointment as editor of two journals, especially the *Ephémérides du citoyen*, an influential organ of physiocratic teachings. These fortunate developments allowed him to work with Turgot, the intendant of Limoges, and to marry M. Le Dée (d. 1784), by whom he had two sons, Victor and Eleuthère-Irénée. The younger son subsequently (1802) established powder mills in America along the Brandywine, the embryo of one of the world's industrial marvels, the E. I. du Pont de Nemours Co.

Du Pont's work in spreading physiocratic ideas, including his editing of some of Quesnay's writings under the title *Physiocratie*, served to make his reputation abroad. He corresponded with crowned heads and from some (in Sweden, Baden, and Poland) received both assignments and honors. He was in Poland serving as secretary for a commission on education when Turgot summoned him to a government post after the former intendant had been named controller general of finances under the new king, Louis XVI. During Turgot's twenty months in office, Du Pont labored diligently as a private secretary. He drafted many reports, notably one that was revived later under C.-A. de Calonne. The *Mémoire sur les municipalités* advocated a hierarchy of representative assemblies, with representation based on property ownership and income, not on social class. The work for Turgot was crucial in Du Pont's career. It taught him much about the intricacies of government and the problems of the practical administrator and reformer; it placed him among the most ardent disciples of Turgot and inspired him later to write an important biography and to publish a valuable edition of Turgot's writings; it also set the pattern for much of Du Pont's later activities. He was to attain a reputation as a remarkably diligent workman and prolific writer of reports in relatively minor posts.

Turgot's dismissal in 1776 removed Du Pont from any official post, although he was retained on salary (seldom paid) subject to recall. J. Necker did recall him in 1778, and, from that time, he engaged in a wide variety of duties, mostly involving the collection of information and the writing of reports. His principal mentor became C.-G. Vergennes, minister of foreign affairs, especially after Turgot's death in 1781. However minor his posts, his varied duties considerably broadened his knowledge and brought him many new contacts and friends, including C.-M. Talleyrand and T. Jefferson. He did much of the tedious work behind Calonne's reform program of 1786 and served as one of the secretaries for the Assembly of Notables. Calonne's failure cast Du Pont even further to the side and cost him some of his positions and income. He persevered, however, and Vergennes, in 1783, obtained for him a *lettre de noblesse* in recognition of his services.

His reputation helped him win election to the Estates General in 1789 as deputy of the Third Estate from Nemours (where Du Pont owned landed property). It was at that time that he added to his name the phrase *de Nemours* to distinguish himself from three other Du Ponts in the Estates General. Du Pont was remarkable for his activity within the Assembly. He served on numerous committees, drafted many reports, spoke frequently, and served as president of the Assembly in August 1790. His greatest efforts were in the area of finance and taxes, where he strove in vain to bring about orderly management. Although he was later to claim that physiocratic theories had influence on the reforms of the Constituent Assembly, in his own efforts, especially in matters of government finance and taxes, Du Pont displayed a willingness to adapt theory to circumstance. In political matters, his endeavors to retain a powerful monarchy were more in accord with physiocratic ideas.

The self-denying ordinance, of which he disapproved, barred Du Pont from service in the Legislative Assembly. Before the close of the Constituent, he had determined to open a printing establishment. His friend A. Lavoisier, the famous chemist who had introduced Du Pont's younger son, Eleuthère-Irénée, to advanced techniques in powder manufacture at the Essone works, came forward with a loan backed by a mortgage on Du Pont's landed property (Bois-des-Fossés) near Chevannes. This support enabled Du Pont to purchase a printshop and to carry on a profitable business, which included the printing of *assignats* against which he had earlier mounted a fruitless attack. Additionally, Du Pont published a weekly journal, the *Correspondance patriotique entre les citoyens qui ont été membres de l'assemblée nationale constituante*, which, until June 1792 when Du Pont relinquished the editorship, championed moderation and denounced moves to curtail the royal prerogative. Du Pont's stolid defense of the monarchy involved sword as well as pen, for on 10 August he led a small armed detachment that sought to protect the king. His ideas and activities had brought occasional attacks from more radical elements; after 10 August Du Pont yielded to the pleas of his family and associates that he go into hiding, while his son, no longer at Essone, continued to supervise the operation of the printshop. After temporary sojourns in and near Paris, he eventually retreated to Bois-des-Fossés, where for the next twenty-one months, aside from trips to obtain documentary proof that he had not emigrated, he busied himself in supervising his estate, carrying on scientific investigations of various natural phenomena, and writing on a variety of subjects.

During the purges of June-July 1794, Du Pont was seized at his rural retreat and hurried off to La Force prison. The fall of M. Robespierre (on 27 July), five days after Du Pont's arrest, probably saved his life but did not bring his immediate release from prison. His five or six weeks behind bars were alleviated by the considerable freedom allowed him to write and to have various material comforts provided by his family. In early September, he returned to Bois-des-Fossés. Two important developments now occurred: his decision to remarry and his successful effort to gain election to the upper house of the new legislative body decreed by the Constitution of 1795. Both these objectives were attained by early fall 1795. On 26 September, Madame F. (Robin) Poivre became the second Madame Du Pont de Nemours. A month later Du Pont took up his duties as deputy to the Council of Ancients from the department of the Loiret.

By this time Du Pont had accepted the Republic, so long as it could be kept to a moderate course under responsible leadership. He was frequently opposed to the majority of the Directory and to the Council of Five Hundred and never hesitated to criticize proposals and actions he regarded as arbitrary or ill conceived. He opposed inequitable taxation of proprietors and unreasonable treatment of the *émigrés*. It is not surprising, though unjust, that Du Pont was to be denounced by some as a secret royalist. His forthright expression and abundant activity retained for him the respect of the majority in the Council of Ancients, which chose him as one of its four secretaries in July 1796 and as presiding officer a year later. Outside the council, he was busy in his editing and publishing chores, writing papers, preparing a new edition of his *Philosophy of the Universe* (which he considered his major work), participating in meetings of the National Institute (to which he was elected soon after its establishment), and in furthering the new cult of theophilanthropy. All ended when Du Pont was arrested following the coup d'état of 18 Fructidor Year V (4 September 1797).

While not supportive of many of the views of the Directorial majority, which proclaimed the purging of subversive royalists through these arrests and proscriptions, Du Pont could not be held as a danger to the Republic. Details of his release are lacking, but within twenty-four hours Du Pont was freed, along with Irénée, who had also been arrested. Unfortunately, during their enforced absence, their printshop had been invaded and severely damaged by a mob. These misfortunes convinced Du Pont that France no longer offered a suitable arena for his activities, and he now considered going to America, where his son Victor had been stationed with the French consular services and where he had friends. His ultimate scheme was to establish somewhere in the United States a large agricultural colony that might be operated on physiocratic principles. Until that goal could be reached, he was willing to seize on other expedients in order to get a start. Such an expedient, it seemed to him, would be to establish in America a commercial brokerage house to facilitate, and to engage in, trade between France and the United States.

It required two years for him to develop the enterprise and to induce others to invest in it. Eventually, Du Pont de Nemours Père, fils et Cie. was established, and the entire family left for the New World in September 1799.

The company's prospects were dim, as Victor had foreseen. The land scheme had to be indefinitely postponed because of the speculation rage in America, and trading relations were slow to recover from the recent period of bad feelings between France and the United States. More capital was required, and Victor and Irénée returned to Europe early in 1801 in search of it. Irénée carried with him the separate scheme to establish powder mills in America that would employ the techniques he had learned a decade earlier at Essone. Finally, with success still a chimera despite Du Pont's optimism, three enterprises were established. The parent company would return to France with Du Pont in charge, Victor would have his own brokerage firm in New York, and Irénée his powder works, under construction along the Brandywine in Delaware. Only the last succeeded, despite serious problems, owing largely to the determination and hard work of its founder. Victor finally (in 1805) declared bankruptcy, and Du Pont liquidated (in 1811) his firm by saddling Irénée's with its obligations. Despite these problems, the family's relationship survived.

Back in Napoleonic France, Du Pont sought useful public service. Returning to France, he carried with him, at President Jefferson's behest, some papers bearing on negotiations over Louisiana, but his part in the famous purchase was minor. The failure of the first consul and later emperor to call on his talents made it easy for Du Pont to revert to his initial low opinion of Napoleon, though he was careful not to express it in public. He thought frequently of returning to America, but his involvement in numerous activities and Madame Du Pont's reluctance to leave again kept him in France. Though deeply distressed by the absence of any call to government office, Du Pont could never be idle. His most significant accomplishment during these years was the editing in nine volumes of Turgot's works. He spent over eight years in work with the Paris Chamber of Commerce; he served as a director and became involved for a year in the complicated finances of the Banque Territoriale; later, in 1810, he assumed the administration of a system of household relief in Paris. These, and other matters of even less significance, did not keep him from writing. He corresponded prodigiously, produced many reports relevant to his various responsibilities, and published a number of essays and reviews on diverse subjects. In April 1814 Talleyrand recalled him to public service as Napoleon's domination collapsed.

The post awarded him, secretary general of the provisional government, was hardly important. It lasted sixteen days and involved only the keeping of records and the certifying of decrees. It did, however, place Du Pont's name prominently on the printed *Acte d'abdication* of Napoleon. The restored Bourbon government found no further employment for him, though it did nominate him to the Legion of Honor and restored his former positions in the Council of State and Bureau of Commerce. Still without the useful employment he sought, he began to contemplate seriously moving to the United States.

Calm contemplation was ended by Napoleon's return from Elba. Believing himself in mortal danger because of his service with the provisional government and acceptance of honors from the restored Bourbons, Du Pont left Paris hastily on 15 March 1815 and obtained a falsified passport enabling him to depart for the United States two weeks later. He did not return to France, despite his wife's urging. His distress over their separation, his failing health, and disillusionment with the course of events in France after Napoleon's second abdication, were more than balanced by the care and solicitude of his sons and their families, and his own nature overcame any thoughts of idle brooding. He spent hours writing letters, preparing papers on many subjects, and translating *Orlando Furioso*. His greatest disappointment was his failure to see Jefferson personally in a visit to Monticello, owing to a confusion in arrangements.

Du Pont died on 7 August 1817 from unknown physical complications caused after he was thoroughly soaked and exhausted from participation in a bucket brigade that extinguished a fire in a charcoal house before it could spread to nearby powdermills.

Bouloiseau, M. *Bourgeoisie et Revolution: les Du Pont de Nemours (1788-1799)* (Paris, 1972); B. G. Du Pont, *Du Pont de Nemours*, 2 vols. (Newark, Dela., 1933); E. I. Du Pont, *Life of Eleuthère Irénée du Pont from Contemporary Correspondence*, ed. and tr. B. G. Du Pont, 12 vols. (Newark, Dela., 1923-27); P. Jolly, *Du Pont de Nemours, Soldat de la Liberté* (Paris, 1956; tr., with some additions, as *Du Pont de Nemours, Apostle of Liberty and the Promised Land*, by E. Du Pont Elrick, Wilmington, Dela., 1977); A. Saricks, *Pierre Samuel Du Pont de Nemours* (Lawrence, Kans., 1965).

A. Saricks

Related entries: ASSEMBLY OF NOTABLES; *ASSIGNATS*; CALONNE; SELF-DENYING ORDINANCE; THEOPHILANTHROPY.

DU PORT, ADRIEN-JEAN-FRANCOIS (1759-98), lawyer, magistrate, deputy to National Assembly. Prominent noble of the robe, magistrate in the Parlement of Paris, Du Port (born in Paris on 5 February 1759) early placed himself in the ranks of reformers, though he remained always a supporter of monarchy. A foe of ministerial despotism, he championed various movements for change before 1789. In 1787 he proposed to the Parlement of Paris that it institute an inquiry into C.-A. de Calonne's malfeasance, an action that led to Calonne's fleeing to England. In November 1787, Du Port supported the edict that gave civil status to Protestants and in January 1788 he denounced *lettres de cachet*. His reputation as an ardent reformer rests, however, on his activity during 1788-89 when preparations for the convocation of the Estates General held the center of attention. Together with C. and A. de Lameth, he played a leading role in advocating changes in the organization of that ancient institution and in suggesting plans for the regeneration of France. The group of rather prominent individuals advocating such change has come to be known as the patriot party (or *les patriotes*), and Du Port's splendid house on the rue du Grand-Chantier was often their central meeting place. Certainly, the celebrated, if rather mysterious, Committee of Thirty regularly met there to plan campaigns of public enlightenment.

Du Port was eager to participate in the reforms that could come from the meeting of the Estates General, if that body could be properly constituted. He was chosen as a deputy of the nobility from Paris and in late June 1789 was one of the forty-six nobles who defected to the Third Estate. The break in the ranks of the first two estates soon brought the transformation of the Estates General to the National Assembly and opened the door to significant change.

Du Port was disturbed by the disorders of the summer of 1789, disorders he feared might undercut the potential for substantial reform. He called for the establishment of a provisional tribunal to deal with cases of treason *(lèse-nation* in the parlance of the time). Principally, however, he became one of the most active of speakers and publicists for reform. He favored a forthright declaration of rights and opposed the creation of an upper house in the legislature in the early constitutional debates in August and September 1789. In matters touching law courts and justice, he had a significant role. Many of his remarks and reports delivered before the Constituent Assembly were printed, although they do not convey an adequate impression of how frequently he spoke. He had much to say on the use of juries in criminal and civil cases, on the reorganization of the court system, on reasons for eliminating the death penalty. He vigorously opposed M. Robespierre on the self-denying ordinance in May 1791; he professed to fear civil war and disruption if those who had brought about the changes did not oversee their execution.

Du Port served as president of the Constituent Assembly from 13 to 27 February 1791 and was chosen as one of the three commissioners to receive the declaration of the king after the abortive flight to Varennes. By that time, especially after H.-G. R. Mirabeau's death in April 1791, Du Port had forged an influential coalition with A.-P.-J. Barnave and A. Lameth (often called the Triumvirate, though dubiously so, since Alexandre's brother, Charles, was also intimately involved) seeking the consolidation of moderate measures. He became one of the pillars of the Feuillant Club, which was devoted to the end of preserving a constitutional monarchy. The danger of resort to more radical measures, including the threat of a Republic, became intense in the summer of 1791 after the unsuccessful flight of the royal family. Du Port and his associates strove mightily to strengthen the monarchical constitution and the other reforms that had been accomplished. For them the Revolution had gone far enough and should now be brought to a halt.

Barred from service in the Legislative Assembly by the self-denying ordinance but not from other public office, Du Port was elected president of the criminal court of Paris after the adjournment of the Constituent. While this position was an appropriate one for a person of his legal training and experience, he could not enjoy it unreservedly because of distress over the drift of events, especially after the declaration of war in April 1792. His moderate voice was lost in the growing clamor. The situation in France was becoming increasingly impossible for him, and the events of 10 August 1792 and their aftermath were disastrous to his cause. He fled from Paris but was arrested near Nemours and imprisoned as a suspected traitor. He was, however, set free by the law court at Melun under circumstances that remain far from clear; it seems likely that his release owes something to the intervention of G.-J. Danton.

Du Port emigrated and stayed in England until after Robespierre's fall on 9 Thermidor. He welcomed the return to mid-course government under the Constitution of 1795. The coup of 18 Fructidor Year V (4 September 1797) drove him again into exile. He took up residence in Appenzell (Switzerland), where he remained until his death on 15 August 1798.

A. Du Port, *Discourse...sur le religibilité des membres du Corps législatif* (*17 mai 1791*) (Paris, 1791) and other pamphlets by Du Port in the Frank E. Melvin Collection, University of Kansas Libraries; G. Michon, *Essai sur l'histoire du parti Feuillant: Adrien Du Port* (Paris, 1924).

A. Saricks

Related entries: CALONNE; COMMITTEE OF THIRTY; JUSTICE; SELF-DENYING ORDINANCE; 10 AUGUST 1792; TRIUMVIRATE.

DUPORTAIL, LOUIS-LEBEGUE (1743-1802), minister of war. Raised in a small town near Orléans, Duportail decided early on a military career and was admitted to the Royal Corps of Engineers as a lieutenant colonel in 1776. The following year he went to America to participate in the War for Independence. He was motivated more by an aristocratic sense of honor than by any political ideology and made this clear in repeated attempts to have Congress promote him to a higher rank. He became a close personal adviser to General G. Washington, who had great respect for his abilities as a strategist. In 1779 Congress established a Corps of Engineers, and Duportail, promoted to brigadier general, was appointed its first chief. During the war he also got along very well with the marquis de Lafayette, an association that bore fruit a decade later when Lafayette succeeded in having Duportail appointed minister of war on 16 November 1790.

Duportail found the ministry virtually unchanged since the Old Regime and the army in a chaotic state. Three major problems immediately engaged his attention: many of the officials in the ministry were holdovers from the Old Regime and needed to be replaced, the emigration of noble officers and the desertion of enlisted men had created an acute shortage of soldiers, and a clear and workable relationship between the army and the newly created National Guard had to be developed.

Duportail's greatest asset in confronting these problems was his excellent relationship with the leaders of the Constituent Assembly, particularly A. Du Port, A.-P.-J. Barnave, and C. and A. de Lameth. For example, at the very time when these men were dominating the Parisian Jacobin club and developing a national network of Jacobin affiliates, Duportail supported a controversial bill allowing soldiers to join these patriotic societies. As a result, he incurred the wrath of the conservative *monarchiens*, who criticized him for not working more on the king's behalf. But in contrast to his predecessor, J.-F. La Tour du Pin, Duportail recognized that the Revolution had at least partially transferred control of the military from the king to the Assembly. His commitment to the principles of 1789 was also evident in a different way during the political crisis following the king's flight to Varennes. Siding clearly with the antidemocratic movement led by the Feuillants, Duportail believed that Revolutionary republicans were no less subversive than counterrevolutionary aristocrats and warned that he would use the army to protect the nation from both. No other minister was more loyal to the Constitution of 1791.

Duportail's power eroded swiftly during the first weeks of the Legislative Assembly, when the Brissotins were determined to make him their first ministerial victim. Through repeated attacks, they charged Duportail with failing to replace aristocratic officials, ignoring the National Guard, and persecuting soldiers who dissented from Feuillant policies. Duportail responded that administrative reorganization was a tedious process and that the Assembly would have to be patient. There was much truth in this rejoinder, but the Brissotins were shrewd in attacking Duportail mostly for his administrative blunders. In fact, Duportail was a much better military strategist and theorist than bureaucratic reformer and he achieved little control over the ministry. On 2 December 1791, the king accepted his resignation.

After the insurrection of 10 August 1792, the Legislative Assembly issued a warrant for Duportail's arrest. He fled to the United States, where he bought a farm and taught himself agriculture. He died while returning to France in 1802 to help Napoleon.

A. P., vols. 25-35 (1879-1913); E. S. Kite, *Brigadier-General Louis Lebègue Duportail, Commandant of Engineers in the Continental Army, 1777-1783* (Baltimore, 1933); *Le Moniteur universel. Réimpression de l'ancien Moniteur; seule histoire authentique et inaltérée de la Révolution française, depuis la réunion des Etats-généraux jusqu' au Consulat (mai 1789-novembre 1799)*, vols. 7-10 (Paris, 1858-63).

G. Kates

Related entries: EMIGRES; FEUILLANTS; *MONARCHIENS;* TRIUMVIRATE.

DUQUESNOY, ADRIEN-CYPRIEN (1759-1808), constitutional monarchist, royalist. A provincial attorney, Duquesnoy was elected to the Estates General of 1789 from Bar-le-Duc. Generally a moderate and conciliatory man, he took strong stands when necessary. He took the Tennis Court Oath and approved the resistance of the Third Estate to the king's speech at the *Séance royale* of 23 June. He was also a member of the Constituent Assembly, where he often worked closely with H.-G. R. Mirabeau. Duquesnoy was a firm advocate of the division of France into departments, believing that provincialism was harmful to the interests of the state. He was also a dedicated supporter of a unicameral legislature. He supported J. Necker's fiscal reforms, the Civil Constitution of the Clergy, and Mirabeau's motion that the king, with certain prerogatives retained by the Assembly, should have the right to declare war and make peace. Among the matters he opposed were certain imperfections he detected in the Declaration of the Rights of Man, the limiting of suffrage to property owners, and distinctions between active and passive citizens.

It is believed that before his term with the Constituent Assembly ended, he had developed royalist sympathies, and he was one of the publishers of a royalist political periodical, *L'ami des patriotes*, which disappeared after 10 August 1792. He was serving as mayor of Nancy when his name was discovered among the incriminating papers found in the famous *armoire de fer* of the Tuileries. He was arrested early in 1794, but through a merciful gendarme his papers were destroyed, and he was put in La Force prison with common criminals instead of being jailed with the political prisoners. The arrival of the Thermidorian Reaction following M. Robespierre's overthrow spared Duquesnoy; he was acquitted by a reconstituted Revolutionary Tribunal. He remained out of public affairs until the appearance of Napoleon, under whom he achieved modest success.

Duquesnoy's two-volume *Journal* on the Constituent Assembly is regarded by historians as a good source on the deliberations of that body and on the internal struggles between the moderates and those with more ambitious Revolutionary designs against the government.

C. Beaulieu, ''Duquesnoy,'' *Biographie Universelle* (Michaud), vol. 12 (Graz, 1967); R. de Crèvecoeur, ed., *Journal d'Adrien Duquesnoy sur l'Assemblée Constituante, 3 Mai 1789–3 Avril 1790*, 2 vols. (Paris, 1894); P. Faure, ''Duquesnoy,'' *Dictionnaire de Biographie française*, vol. 12 (Paris, 1970).

R. L. Carol

Related entries: ACTIVE CITIZEN; *ARMOIRE DE FER*; CIVIL CONSTITUTION OF THE CLERGY; NECKER; PASSIVE CITIZEN; PRISONS; TENNIS COURT OATH.

E

EDEN TREATY OF 1786, commercial treaty between France and the United Kingdom. The Treaty of 1783 ending war between France and the United Kingdom promised that both sides would attempt to agree on new trade arrangements. Throughout the eighteenth century, legal trade between the two nations had been at a reduced level due to restrictions and high tariffs. Smuggling, however, proceeded at a very high rate. Some statesmen in the London government were impressed with A. Smith's arguments for free trade, while others saw British advantage in an opening of France to British exports. At Versailles, interest in freeing trade was even greater. Foreign Minister C.-G. Vergennes and his deputy J.-M.-G. Rayneval wished to foster a rapprochement between France and England and, more specifically, to help augment public finance by increasing customs revenues, promoting French exports, especially wine, and encouraging competition, which "insures the perfection and success of our manufactures" (Rayneval).

Negotiations began in earnest in April 1786 when W. Pitt's special envoy, W. Eden, arrived at Versailles. The diplomats signed the treaty in September 1786. It was ratified a few months later and went into effect in July and August 1787. The French achieved a 69 percent reduction in British tariffs on their wine but failed to gain admission for their silks. On other major trading items, both sides cut tariffs on hardware and metal to 10 percent ad valorum, on cottons and woolens, porcelain, pottery, and glass to 12 percent. Other provisions eased regulations on merchants and shipping.

The best French and British estimates of legal trade between the countries in this period differ considerably, but they do agree that it increased sharply, more than doubling from the mid-1780s to the early 1790s. No one can say with precision how much of this came as a result of a shift from smuggling to legal trade, but certainly a large part did, benefiting government revenues and consumers in each country. The unreliable statistics do not permit us to say which country increased its legal exports to the other more, but figures from both sides show Britain with a favorable balance of about two to one in the late 1780s. At the time and since, many Frenchmen claimed that the treaty allowed a flood of British goods to harm French industry and its workers. Research by L. Cahen finally challenged these views, 150 years later, but the question still needs a thorough investigation.

One aspect of the hesitant liberal reform policy of Louis XVI's government, the 1786 treaty was not in force long enough to have a major economic impact, but misperceptions and exaggerations of its negative effect in France did generate opposition to the regime. Vergennes' hopes to appease British resentment over losses in the American war died with him, in February 1787, and with the heightened tension between the two countries arising from the Dutch Revolution of 1787.

L. Cahen, "Une nouvelle interprétation du traité franco-anglais en 1786-87," *Rev. hist.* 185 (1939); J. Ehrman, *The British Government and Commercial Negotiations with Europe: 1783-1793* (Cambridge, 1962).

J. M. Laux

Related entries: LOUIS XVI; PITT.

EDICT OF TOLERATION (November 1787). See RABAUT SAINT-ETIENNE.

EDUCATION. In 1789 France did not have a comprehensive system of instruction with schools established or controlled by the royal government. Religious communities handled much of the task of providing basic education to boys and girls. At the secondary level, only boys received public education, mostly in the classics, in *collèges* operated by special boards, municipalities, and, especially, teaching orders. At each level many children, but mainly the wealthy and well-born, had private tutors. At the highest level, over twenty universities had faculties of arts, theology, law, and medicine. There were also the Collège de France, providing high-level lectures, and specialized royal creations, such as a school of mining and the military school.

Many Frenchmen in the previous several decades maintained that instruction was not sufficiently practical, patriotic, and secular. Yet even more persons seem to have been content with the old institutions and methods. As late as 1789, education was not a major concern of those who drew up the *cahiers,* although some did call for a national system.

During the early years of the Revolution, the old institutions continued, although manifestations of Revolutionary patriotism changed the atmosphere in many schools. The Constituent Assembly devoted little attention to education, but its Constitution of 1791 did create the Committee of Public Instruction. In that committee's name C.-M. Talleyrand, in September 1791, presented a report stressing the importance of education and calling for a system to make it available, in various forms, to all French people. The Constituent did not act on the report, but nevertheless a belief was pervasive that the creation of the new system was imminent.

Other factors contributed to that belief. First, the Revolution led to renewed criticisms that instruction was impractical and nonpatriotic. Second, the Constituent took actions that did much to cripple the existing institutions. It reduced the revenues of many schools at all levels by suppressing the tithe, the *octrois*, and feudal dues. It also prescribed a civic oath first for ecclesiastics and then for the relatively few laymen who taught, causing many teachers to leave their posts. The damage done by these actions often has been overstated. Few schools lost all or even a major part of their revenues. In some *collèges*, a majority, or even all, of the teachers were jurors. Yet at least half the teachers in *collèges* and universities did not conform, and the percentage was even higher for ecclesiastics in primary schools.

By the time the Legislative Assembly convened, some schools at all levels had closed, and discontent with the old ways was growing. The Committee of Public Instruction, with the marquis de Condorcet the primary author, prepared a new plan for a comprehensive educational system. Public instruction would be provided in primary schools, secondary schools, institutes, *lycées*, and a National Society of Sciences and Arts. Word of the plan created great hopes but also some fears. Letters poured into Paris from local authorities pleading for one of the institutes to offset the loss to cities of bishoprics, law courts, or other administrative units during the Revolution. Unfortunately, Condorcet's plan was presented to the Legislative on the day that France declared war on Austria. The legislators devoted little attention to the plan and did not adopt it.

On the practical side, the Legislative did nothing to check the deterioration of existing institutions except to vote what must have been a highly inadequate sum to aid teachers whose *collèges* and universities had lost revenues because of Revolutionary legislation. More important, in August 1792 it continued the work of destruction by dissolving teaching orders. Some former religious orders continued to teach as laymen, at least at the secondary level, but schools nevertheless had received another blow.

When the National Convention began to sit, education at all levels was in a greatly reduced and disorganized state, although instruction was far from non-existent. Teachers were scarce, although some remained and others had been replaced. In even shorter supply were funds and students. The government had made up for little of the lost revenue. Students had left the schools in droves for reasons such as that ecclesiastics no longer taught, the quality of instruction had dropped, fighting for the Revolutionary *patrie* was appealing, or the times were not right for sitting in the classroom.

The period of the Terror saw the continuation of hopes for a system of national education and the consideration of several plans to effect it. Two of those plans, debated by the Convention in 1793, are illustrative of the controversy over education. The Committee of Public Instruction in June presented a new comprehensive plan, which the Montagnards attacked for being insufficiently radical.

The Convention preferred, and adopted in August, a plan drawn up by L.-M. Lepelletier (martyred the previous January) and supported by M. Robespierre that called for all children to be given practical and patriotic instruction at the primary level under Spartan conditions in state boarding schools. The Lepelletier plan was, however, never carried through. The upshot was that the Convention saw many educational plans, but pressing events, factional struggles, and, perhaps, too great a passion for perfection prevented it from putting any into operation.

During the Terror, the Convention's practical actions concerning education amounted to little. In March 1793 it confiscated all endowments of educational institutions, although the buildings of *collèges* were spared. Teachers' salaries were to be a national charge. The following September it closed the military schools and the universities as being elitist institutions. And in December it decreed that all could teach who had a certificate of good morals and *civisme*— to avoid fostering a hierarchical corps of teachers.

The Convention's actions caused confusion and dismay. Many primary schools and *collèges* closed, especially in areas wracked by civil insurrection. But some remained open, giving mostly a narrowly practical and patriotic education. (Teaching of the Constitution and the republican laws was a must.) Some teachers undoubtedly were good, but many were no more than unqualified superrevolutionaries. For the schools remaining open, finances were a problem. Some local authorities paid teachers' salaries at the level prescribed in March 1793, but others expected the money to come from Paris. As a result, many teachers went unpaid.

After Robespierre's death in July 1794, the Convention slowly began to construct the long-awaited system of national education. First it turned to the primary schools. In November 1794 a decree established one such school for every thousand inhabitants, with separate divisions for girls and boys. The Convention would choose the textbooks, the people would select the teachers, and special juries appointed by district officials would administer the schools. Instruction would be in French and would stress practical matters (such as the three R's, land measurement, and elementary science) and patriotism but not religion. The decree, however, also permitted private citizens to open independent schools, under the supervision of public authorities, with the obligation to teach the Rights of Man and the constitution but also with the freedom to give religious training. In February 1795 the Convention established what amounted to super secondary schools called *écoles centrales*, one for every 300,000 inhabitants. Authorities in Paris would select their textbooks and would appoint a national jury to select and supervise the teachers. The teachers themselves would run the schools.

In October 1795 the Convention approved a report drawn up by P. Daunou that incorporated the previous laws on primary schools and the *écoles centrales*. For the latter, it said that organization was to be by courses, with one professor for each in drawing, natural history, classical languages, modern languages, mathematics, experimental physics and chemistry, literature, history, and legislation (no law schools existed then).

Creating the schools was a different matter. For primary ones, the most serious problem was in finding suitable textbooks and teachers. Religiously oriented independent schools multiplied and thrived; probably fewer than half the local jurisdictions of France actually had public primary schools after 1795. Above them, between ninety and one hundred *écoles centrales* slowly emerged. They attracted sufficient students, at least partly because of a law of 1797 that required attendance at one for obtaining governmental posts. Nevertheless, these *écoles* have been deemed unsuccessful then and subsequently because they lacked boarding facilities, their teachers were unqualified, they had no admission tests or standards, certain of their courses (such as history and legislation) were vaguely defined, and, especially, all the discrete courses lacked correlation and coordination. Students, in essence, selected their own courses, and they preferred drawing and mathematics. The *écoles* were abolished by N. Bonaparte in 1802.

Individuals in the assemblies of the Directory knew of the weaknesses in the Daunou Law, debated them much, but did little. A decree of 1798 tried to reduce the number and influence of independent (religious) primary schools by increasing supervision of them, but the law had little effect.

Revolutionary authorities had greater success in constructing special schools (at least partly to replace the universities), although two such schools clearly failed. The Ecole de Mars, intended to provide military training based on merit, was too rigorous and Spartan; it lasted only from July to October 1794. The Ecole normale, to train teachers, gave instruction that was too specialized and high powered; it lasted only from January to May 1795. But successful and lasting institutions began as well, including three medical schools (December 1794) and the Ecole polytechnique (1795). The Collège de France was the only instructional institution to exist throughout the Revolution.

The record of Revolutionary authorities in providing education for all young men and women clearly was not a good one, but it may not have been as bad as usually thought. The difficulties in studying that record are great. We need to know better the number and quality of schools existing as of 1789, and we need more synthetic works concerning what Old Regime institutions existed until their formal abolition and how completely the actions of the assemblies were carried out. What we have now are some good regional or single-institution studies or general works that concentrate on plans never put into operation and on the laws themselves.

E. Allain, *L'Oeuvre scolaire de la Révolution, 1789–1802* (Paris, 1891); C. Bailey, "The Tortuous Liquidation of Old Regime *Collèges*, 1789-1795," *Pro. of the WSFH* (1978); H. C. Barnard, *Education and the French Revolution* (Cambridge, 1969); C. Hippeau, *L'instruction publique en France pendant la Révolution*, 2 vols. (Paris, 1881, 1883); R. R. Palmer, "The Central Schools of the First French Republic: A Statistical Survey," *Hist. Reflec.* 7 (1980); F. Ponteil, *Histoire de l'enseignement en France, 1789–1964* (Paris, 1966).

C. Bailey

Related entries: CERTIFICATES OF CIVICISM; CONDORCET; LEPELLETIER DE SAINT-FARGEAU; 9 THERMIDOR YEAR II; *OCTROI*; TERROR, THE.

EGALITE, PHILIPPE. See ORLEANS.

EGYPTIAN EXPEDITION (1798–1801), military expedition led by General N. Bonaparte to the Near East. The Egyptian expedition was undertaken as part of the war against England. France did not have naval strength to invade the British Isles, but the ships and men were available for a Mediterranean venture. Egypt could become a staging area for future operations against India, England's major overseas holding since the loss of the American colonies. Furthermore, the other principal European powers, Prussia, Austria, and Russia, having recently divided Poland between themselves (1795), would not consider their interests threatened by a French presence in Egypt and therefore would not object to it. Finally, the island of Malta could be taken on the way to Egypt and used by the French as a key naval base in the center of the Mediterranean.

For these reasons General N. Bonaparte, the supreme commander of the expedition, sailed from Toulon on 19 May 1798. The expedition consisted of thirteen ships of the line, six frigates, and a sufficient number of troop and cargo vessels to transport 35,000 officers and men and 167 savants. The expedition had been gathered in five ports in southern France and Italy (Marseille, Genoa, Civita Vecchia, Corsica, and Toulon) and converged on Malta. On 11–12 June the French captured the strategically located island and, after reorganizing its government, sailed on to the east.

The French arrived off Alexandria on 30 June and immediately landed 4,300 men on the beach eight miles to the west. The city was assaulted and captured with only light fighting. Napoleon then led his army to the west leg of the Nile and south towards Cairo. At Shubra Khit, a Mameluke army made a weak attempt to stop the French, but after a brief skirmish it fled to the south. On the west bank of the Nile, some ten miles south of the great pyramids of Giza, the entire Mameluke army waited for the French. The battle, which took place on 21 July, was entirely one-sided. The 6,000 Mameluke cavalry, under the leadership of Murad Bey, was totally ineffective against the four French divisions formed in squares. Unable to break the squares and suffering heavy losses from the French artillery and musket fire, the Mamelukes retired to the south, leaving behind their irregular infantry, perhaps 15,000 men, who suffered very heavy losses in the rout that concluded the battle. Cairo surrendered the next day, and Bonaparte was in control of the lower Nile. He ordered General L. Desaix to pursue the Mamelukes up the Nile. For the next nine months, Desaix' little army followed the Mamelukes south until it reached Aswan and the first cataract on the Nile. Middle and Upper Egypt were declared to be under French control, but in fact only those towns along the river that the French held in strength were effectively controlled.

In Cairo Bonaparte set about reorganizing the conquered land. Taxes were collected to support the new government, a mint was established to coin money, a postal service was set up, patterned after the French service, a new hospital for the poor was built, a health department was created, and the first printing presses in Egypt, which the French had brought with them, were put into operation. The Egyptian Institute was founded on 22 August for the purposes of research, study, the publication of facts about the country, and to introduce the ideas of the Enlightenment. It was the men of the institute who found the Rosetta Stone, surveyed the isthmus of Suez with the construction of a canal in mind, and were the first Europeans to visit and report on the wonders of ancient Egypt. They laid the foundation for modern Egyptology.

The French expedition suffered a major setback on 1–2 August 1798 when Admiral H. Nelson attacked and destroyed the entire French fleet, anchored at Aboukir Bay. This confirmed English control of the Mediterranean and cut the Army of Egypt off from all but the most scant communications with France. Then the formation of the Second Coalition brought Austria and Russia back into the war on the side of England. The combination of English gold and the French invasion of Egypt led the Ottoman Empire, which claimed sovereignty over Egypt, to declare war on France. In the spring of 1799, with affairs in good order in Egypt, Bonaparte undertook an expedition into Syria. The purpose of this action was threefold: to secure the conquest of Egypt by defeating the Turkish army, which was preparing to invade Egypt by way of Syria; to force the Porte of Syria to declare for France, thus securing the French right flank; and to deprive the English blockading squadron of the supplies it was obtaining from Syrian ports.

Bonaparte left Cairo on 10 February 1799 with 10,000 men. After a long, hot march through the desert and along the coast, he reached Acre on 20 March. The city was besieged for two months, during which time Napoleon defeated the Turkish army at Mount Tabor (16 April). Acre held out with the aid of the English until Bonaparte decided to withdraw to Egypt. The lack of siege guns, illness in the French army, the plague, which was rampant within Acre, and news of allied victories in Europe all seemed to have been considerations in his decision to return to Egypt. Almost half the men who took part in the Syrian expedition did not return.

Shortly after his return to Cairo, Bonaparte received news that a Turkish army, some 15,000 men strong, had landed at Aboukir. He rushed to the coast where he was able to muster a force of 10,000 men. On 25 July he attacked the Turks in their defensive position and drove them into the sea, with the exception of several thousand who took refuge in the fort at the end of the peninsula. Fort Aboukir held out until 2 August, when it surrendered. The military situation was secure, at least temporarily. On 23 August, Bonaparte turned over command of the expedition to General J.-B. Kléber and returned to France. Kléber had been an outspoken advocate of a complete French evacuation of Egypt even before Bonaparte's departure. Once in command of the French army, he opened negotiations with the Turks and the English to achieve this end. On 28 January 1800, the Convention of El-Arish was signed by all three parties, and it remained only for its terms, the French evacuation of Egypt, to be carried out. Kléber was assassinated on 14 June, and command of the French forces was assumed by General J.-F. Menou, the senior officer. Menou presided over the disaster that overtook the expedition.

In the spring of 1801, an English army landed at Aboukir and defeated Menou. This force was then joined by a Turkish army, and together they besieged General A.-D. Belliard in Cairo and Menou in Alexandria. Cairo capitulated in July and Belliard's army of 12,000 was evacuated by the English to France, where they arrived in October 1801. Menou held out at Alexandria with 7,000 men until September, when the last of the French troops were transported to France aboard English ships.

L. Berthier, *Campagne d'Egypte* (Paris, 1827); J. C. Herold, *Bonaparte in Egypt* (New York, 1962); C. de la Jonquière, *L'Expedition d'Egypt, 1798–1801*, 5 vols. (Paris, 1899–1907); J. Thiry, *Bonaparte en Egypte* (Paris, 1973).

J. G. Gallaher

Related entries: BATTLE OF ABOUKIR; KLEBER; MENOU; SECOND COALITION.

18 BRUMAIRE, COUP OF. See COUP OF 18 BRUMAIRE.

ELISABETH DE FRANCE, PHILIPPINE-MARIE-HELENE, MADAME (1764-94), youngest sibling of Louis XVI. Madame Elisabeth was the daughter of Louis, dauphin of France, and his second wife, Marie-Joséphine de Saxe. A conventional aristocratic upbringing left her serious, pious, and charitable. Various projects for her marriage came to nothing. After 1781 she maintained her own household at Montreuil and rarely appeared at court since her fondness for her brother, Louis XVI, did not extend to Marie Antoinette.

As early as 1787 she was suspicious of the intentions of the notables and also of her brother's political sense, although she remained loyal to him. She was profoundly hostile to the National Assembly and favored firm action against the deputies. Taken to Paris after the march to Versailles (October 1789), she grew to believe that only civil war could save the monarchy. Both before and after the flight to Varennes, in which she took part (21 June 1791), she urged her brother to escape abroad. After the attack on the Tuileries (10 August 1792), she was held in the Temple Prison with the royal family. On 9 May 1794 the Revolutionary Tribunal of Paris interrogated her. The following day, she was condemned to death for counterrevolutionary plotting with royalists and *émigrés* and guillotined.

P.-J.-B. Buchez and P. C. Roux, eds., *Histoire parlementaire de la Révolution française*, vol. 34 (Paris, 1837); F. Feuillet de Conches, *Correspondance de Madame Elisabeth de France* (Paris, 1868).

L. J. Abray

Related entries: OCTOBER DAYS; REVOLUTIONARY TRIBUNAL; 10 AUGUST 1792; VARENNES.

ELLIOT, HUGH (1752-1830), English *agent provocateur*. See NOOTKA SOUND CONTROVERSY.

EMERY, JACQUES-ANDRE, ABBE (1732-1811), theologian. A member of the Sulpician Order, Emery was born in 1732 in Gex. As a royalist and the superior of a seminary, he took the lead in recommending the decree of August 1792, which prescribed that all priests holding public office must take an oath of loyalty to liberty and equality. Noncompliance to this decree by any priest would mean the loss of pension and even deportation. Emery was imprisoned during the Terror but was saved from execution by M. Robespierre's overthrow on 9 Thermidor.

On 30 May 1795, after the reopening of churches to the so-called refractory clergy, the Directory demanded that they participate in the *décadi* ceremonies and take an oath of loyalty to the constitutional laws. Provincial clerics rejected this. Emery, as head of the Paris archepiscopal council, pleaded for its acceptance because he believed that a policy of reconciliation with the Republic would be in the best interests of the Catholic church. When Napoleon became first consul, Emery persuaded him to declare that *émigrés* and deportees would be able to return to France provided they swore an oath of loyalty to the Republic. Emery remained politically and religiously active during Napoleon's administration.

M. Lyons, *France under the Directory* (London, 1975); J. McManners, *The French Revolution and the Church* (London, 1969); W. M. Sloane, *The French Revolution and Religious Reforms* (New York, 1901).

N. Chaudhuri

Related entry: CIVIL CONSTITUTION OF THE CLERGY

EMIGRES, French nobles, clergy, and members of the third estate who chose or were forced to live in exile between 1789 and 1814. The fall of the Bastille on 14 July 1789 triggered the flight from France of the comte d'Artois, the prince de Conti, the baron de Breteuil, the duc de Broglie, the prince de Bourbon-Condé, the duchesse de Polignac, and others who constituted the first wave of over 150,000 French citizens who for one reason or another became *émigrés* during the French Revolutionary era. The comte de Provence made good his escape from France in June 1791; he and his brother, Artois, established headquarters at Coblentz, where the army of the princes gradually was created. It was disbanded soon after the Austrian and Prussian armies (the little army was attached to the Prussian forces) retreated after the Battle of Valmy in September 1792. Organized at about the same time, the army of the prince of Condé continued as a symbol of *émigré* military resistance to republican France, supported by Austria, England, and Russia until it too disappeared in 1801.

When Louis XVI was executed in January 1793, Provence recognized the eight-year-old son of the deposed king as Louis XVII and declared himself regent. After the child died in the Temple in June 1795, Provence proclaimed himself king as Louis XVIII and preserved the trappings of kingship as best he could with subsidies from European monarchs hostile to the Revolution. Provence and Artois kept the idea of French royalty alive with threats, proclamations, declarations, intrigues, and pressure for recognition.

Provence was the titular head of the exiles, but Artois was the most determined and uncompromising of the princes who played a leading role in orchestrating *émigré* diplomacy, encouraging conspiracies, and launching military projects that had as their objective the overthrow of the Revolutionary regime and the restoration of *ancien régime* institutions. The English, hoping to establish a second front in western France against the republican armies, sponsored two invasion projects in 1795. The first failed miserably at Quiberon; nothing came of the second when the ships transporting Artois and his entourage returned to England without making contact with the insurgents ashore. F.-A. Charette de la Contrie, G. Cadoudal, the comte de Frotté, and N. Stofflet were among those royalist agents sponsored by the princes who led rebel forces in western France. Ultimately they were captured and executed; and royalist leaders H. de la Roche-jaquelin and J. Cathelineau died from wounds received in battle with republican troops.

Indeed, *émigré* attempts to overthrow the Revolutionary regime in Paris provided that government with precisely the justification it needed for extreme measures against those who opposed the Revolution. French peasants and members of the middle class supported the Revolution more enthusiastically when it appeared that their gains were threatened by *émigré* princes, nobles, and clergy who sought foreign aid for the restoration of their special privileges. On 28 June 1791, the National Assembly forbid French citizens to leave the country without a passport. In October, the princes were ordered by Louis XVI to return to France or be stripped of their rights. And on 12 February 1792, the Legislative Assembly declared as traitors those who corresponded with the prince de Condé and other exiles and ordered the arrest of citizens fleeing from France. Machinery was created for the sequestration of *émigré* property, and in April those listed as *émigrés* who had left France after 1 July 1789 and had not returned by 1 May 1792 were banished forever. The death penalty was decreed for the princes of the blood and others conspiring against the constitutional monarchy.

On 27 May 1792 the Legislative Assembly approved legislation that required clergymen who refused to take the oath to the Civil Constitution of the Clergy to leave France within fifteen days or be forcibly expelled. Some 30,000 clergymen were subject to deportation by terms of this legislation, and thousands left France. In October, the National Convention banished the *émigrés* from France forever and decreed the death penalty for those who returned to their homeland. The Constitution of 1795 also provided for perpetual banishment of the *émigrés* and the nonjuring clergy; despite this, by 1797 the number returning had reached tidal proportions. The punitive legislation still was on the books, but it was rarely enforced. Napoleon's new constitution for the Consulate forbade their return, but on 20 October 1800, a partial amnesty opened the door for the legal repatriation of some 52,000 *émigrés*. Finally, on 26 April 1802, a general amnesty signed by Napoleon permitted all but about 1,000 of the most notorious exiles to return to France. When Provence became king in 1814, all save a handful returned to their homeland. The Indemnity Law of 1825 provided 1 billion francs to compensate those whose property had been confiscated during the Revolution, whether they were Jacobins, Girondin, nobles, peasants, or *sans-culottes*.

The first wave of *émigrés* was made up of nobles whose determination, along with their contacts with European ruling classes, gave the emigration a royalist character, long after the period when the nobles constituted a majority of the exiles. Most aristocrats were deliberate expatriates, but the nonjuring clergy were at first ostracized by the Revolutionaries and then ordered to leave France, although most returned when the Concordat of 1801 was approved. Over 6,000 noble army officers went abroad.

Some members of the Third Estate, who eventually constituted over 50 percent of the *émigrés*, compromised themselves by violating decrees of the Revolutionary government and participating in local revolts. Others left France to show their distaste for the religious changes. Fear, hatred, panic, and desire for adventure were among the motives of artisans and peasants who left their native soil and were listed as *émigrés*. From the fall of the Bastille until the execution of M. Robespierre, the departures were continuous, but the reflux began in the summer of 1794, and tens of thousands returned under the Directory.

Of the more than 150,000 *émigrés*, of whom probably not over 60,000 were outside France at any one time, some 97,000 are identifiable by social class. The nobles made up 17 percent of the *émigrés* (about 5 percent of all the nobles in France went into exile), and some 25 percent were members of the clergy, which meant that about 17 percent of all the Catholic clergymen in France went abroad. Fifty-one percent of the *émigrés* were members of the third estate, but they constituted less than 2 percent of that order as it existed in 1789.

All elements of French society were represented. On the national, departmental, and communal lists of *émigrés* were included, among others, 47 actors, 1,741 lawyers and magistrates, 150 ship captains, 47 bankers, 296 students, 248 school teachers, 85 stone masons, 4 chimney sweeps, 935 weavers, and 6 prostitutes. The Bas-Rhin, the Pyrénées-Orientales, the Var, the Bouches-du-Rhône departments, along with departments washed by the English Channel, furnished a disproportionate share of the exiles because of their proximity to foreign soil.

The *émigrés* were found almost everywhere. They made their way to the United States where they congregated mainly in such port cities as Boston, Philadelphia, New York, and New Orleans in order to be in closer contact with the homeland. It is estimated that 25,000 of the exiles, of whom 10,000 were priests, lived in England at one time or another during the Revolutionary era. Some 20,000 settled around Coblentz; thousands found homes in the capitals of dozens of the small German states. In Berlin, St. Petersburg, Geneva, Rome, Madrid, Lisbon, Hamburg, Turin, and other cities, colonies of *émigrés* awaited the day they could return to France. Spain gave asylum to some 4,000 of the exiles, and 6,000 settled in the Italian states. Some 2,000 (mostly clergymen) found their way to the Papal States where they were openly contemptuous of the rituals and ceremonies of the Italian Catholic church. Indeed, the *émigrés* were foreigners, generally looked on with distrust by their hosts and given little respect or consideration. The life-style of the French princes and many members of the court nobility offended people wherever they settled. Secular and regular clergy who found refuge in Spain were segregated in the convents of the fifty-eight Spanish dioceses and isolated from the general population to guard against the Gallican (or even Jacobin) tendencies of some of the expelled nonjuring French clergy.

Cut off from their properties and income in France, the *émigrés* soon were in want, and tens of thousands eventually found employment. Skilled craftsmen were in demand, but for nobles and clergymen, adjustment to the new conditions was very difficult. The comtesse de Tesse bought a property near Fribourg, but few members of the nobility had the resources to purchase land. The comte de Mounier established a school of political science at Weimar, and wives of *émigré* noblemen made and sold straw hats in London. The participation of the *émigrés* in industrial and commercial enterprises was limited since they possessed neither the funds nor technical knowledge for it. However, M. Brumel became a manufacturer of pulleys and drive wheels in England and invented a completely mechanized system of producing ships' blocks. He was the designer of the first tunneling shield (under the Thames River), an achievement for which he was knighted in 1841.

Many noble army officers found employment in the army of the prince of Condé, which continued to play a role, sometimes in almost phantom form, until 1801. French officers were so numerous in the British, Prussian, and Austrian armies that French units were organized. French *émigré* officers also served in the armed forces of Russia, Spain, Holland, Portugal, Sweden, and Turkey. Noble and clerical *émigrés*, as well as members of the middle class, found employment in organizing schools and establishing chapels, as well as teaching French, music, art, and a host of other disciplines. Provence and Artois and other princes of the blood were granted substantial subsidies by the English government, which they used to support themselves and their entourages. *Émigré* writers, artists, musicians, and actors associated themselves with the artistic life of the country in which they lived and frequently found the kings and heads of noble families to be patrons.

As the years passed, the ideological struggle occupied an increasing number of the exiles as they tried to rationalize the past and look to the future. Uncompromising defenders of the Old Regime, like the comte d'Artois, locked horns with other royalists who gradually realized that the institutions of pre-Revolutionary France were gone forever. F. Montlosier, for example, maintained that the monarchy could not be restored unless a substantial portion of the Revolutionary legacy was preserved. By 1814 Provence had adjusted to the realities sufficiently to grant the charter of 1814 and accept the constitutional monarchy that paved the way for a happy ending to the emigration.

It was not, however, so much the efforts of the exiles but the decision of the victorious allies and a handful of imperial politicians that restored the Bourbons in the name of legitimacy (and expediency). Three *émigré* princes of the blood (Louis XVIII, Charles X, and Louis-Philippe) served as kings of France between 1814 and 1848, and the return of thousands of nobles and members of the clergy to positions of power and influence in French institutional life during this period must be considered one of the most surprising and unexpected developments of the first half of the nineteenth century.

D. de Castries, *Les hommes de l'émigration, 1789–1814* (Paris, 1979); E. Daudet, *Histoire de l'émigration pendant la Révolution française*, 2d ed., 3 vols. (Paris, 1904-7); G. de Diesbach, *Histoire de l'émigration, 1789–1814* (Paris, 1975); H. Forneron, *Histoire générale des émigrés pendant la Révolution française* (Paris, 1905); D. Greer, *The Incidence of the Emigration during the Revolution* (Cambridge, Mass., 1951); J. Vidalenc, *Les émigrés français* (Caen, 1963); M. Weiner, *The French Exiles, 1789–1815* (London, 1960).

V. W. Beach

Related entries: ARTOIS; BASTILLE, THE; BATTLE OF VALMY; CALONNE; CHARETTE DE LA CONTRIE; CIVIL CONSTITUTION OF THE CLERGY; COBLENTZ; CONDE; DECLARATION OF PILLNITZ; LA ROCHE-JAQUELIN; PROVENCE.

ENCYCLOPEDIE (1751-72), great compendium, consisting of seventeen volumes of text and eleven of plates, presenting the accumulated knowledge and ideas of the age of the Enlightenment. Although the *Encyclopédie* has come to be regarded as one of the most characteristic works of the Enlightenment and one of the best-known encyclopedias in the history of humanity, its beginnings were unassuming. Early in 1745 two obscure writers, the German G. Sellius and the Englishman J. Mills, signed a contract with the French printer and bookseller A.-F. Le Breton to translate E. Chambers' *Cyclopaedia* into French with some expansions and corrections. By the end of the year, Le Breton had quarreled with the two men, the partnership had ended, and Le Breton had begun the enterprise again with three new partners—the Parisian booksellers A.-C. Briasson, M.-A. David, and L. Durand. In June 1746 they chose an editor, abbé J.-P. de Gua de Malves, but he proved incapable of handling such a project and resigned in August 1747.

Finally in October 1747, the publishers selected D. Diderot and J. Le Rond d'Alembert as coeditors. It is not certain whether they or Gua de Malves first thought of transforming the venture from a revised translation of Chambers' *Cyclopaedia* to an independent reference work. Clearly Diderot and d'Alembert were responsible for making the *Encyclopédie* a polemical work designed to improve Frenchmen, as well as to inform them. Except for P. Bayle's *Dictionnaire historique et critique*, no earlier encyclopedia had sought and aroused such controversy.

Between 1751 and 1757, Diderot and d'Alembert completed seven letterpress folio volumes. In order to do so, they wrote many articles themselves and encouraged contributions from scores of collaborators. Since the *Encyclopédie* contained politically and religiously unorthodox remarks, it angered many powerful Frenchmen. The government censored the work and in 1752 halted publication for a few months. Then between 1757 and 1759, the *Encyclopédie* became enmeshed in controversy. D'Alembert's article "Genève" caused an international incident by maintaining, among other things, that the theology of several Genevan pastors was more like deism than Calvinism and that this was, in addition, a sign of the city's enlightenment. After much wavering, d'Alembert chose to resign as editor rather than endure abuse and possible persecution. The publication of C.-A. Helvétius's irreligious book *De l'esprit* (1758) confirmed conservatives in their belief that there existed in France a conspiracy against Catholicism. In March 1759 the royal administration officially forbade further publication of the letterpress volumes of the *Encyclopédie*.

In spite of the ban, the *Encyclopédie* was officially permitted to publish volumes of plates and unofficially permitted to continue the publication of volumes of articles. With the help of the tireless L. de Jaucourt and other contributors, Diderot labored on as sole editor. He became infuriated in 1764 when he learned that the apprehensive publisher, Le Breton, was secretly censoring the work. Finally in 1772, to Diderot's relief, the work was completed. Moreover, despite its scandalous reputation, only a handful of encyclopedists, including Diderot and some liberal Catholic clergymen, actually suffered serious persecution from church and state.

The *Encyclopédie* consists of seventeen folio volumes of articles (71,818 entries) and eleven volumes of plates (some 2,900 engravings). This makes it larger than any alphabetical encyclopedia preceding it except for J. Heinrich Zedler's sixty-four folio volume *Universal Lexicon*. A monumental work of scholarship, the *Encyclopédie* deserves recognition as an outstanding reference book. It includes articles by such well known *philosophes* as J.-J. Rousseau, F.-M. Voltaire, the baron de Montesquieu, and baron d'Holbach. More important, it was the first encyclopedia to recruit many experts, who submitted articles in their respective disciplines, and to institute the practice of crediting articles to particular contributors. Among the 139 or so identified collaborators to the letterpress volumes are the sculptor E.-M. Falconet, the architect J.-F. Blondel, the grammarians N. Beauzée and C. Chesneau du Marsais, the engraver and designer J.-M. Papillon, the natural scientists L. Daubenton and N. Desmarest, and the surgeon A. Louis, to name but a few. Some of these men, and many others, contributed to the volumes of plates. Certainly the work contains contradictions and superficialities, but in many fields of learning, the coverage was up to date and thorough. In some, the *Encyclopédie* pioneered. For example, no other work of the century rivaled its comprehensive treatment of trades and industries, and in the emerging discipline of economics, the *Encyclopédie* includes contributions by the engineer J.-R. Perronet elucidating the principle of division of labor and by F. Quesnay foreshadowing his doctrine of physiocracy.

In religious matters, the *Encyclopédie* merits its reputation as a *machine de guerre* against Christianity. Articles by individual encyclopedists favor Catholicism, Protestantism, deism, skepticism, or atheism; thus no uniform attitude toward religion exists in the *Encyclopédie*. Still, unorthodoxy predominates. There are not only articles advocating religious toleration and attacking religious superstition but also contributions calling for the separation of church and state, mocking clergymen, casting doubt on the truths of the Bible, discrediting Catholic dogmas and rituals, and even some supporting determinism, materialism, and atheism.

All of this does not mean that the *Encyclopédie* was an inflammatory work. The political articles show that no one form of government was considered superior to all others. The republic of Geneva is eulogized, but a republic is deemed suitable only for a small territory. Some articles support limited monarchy; others praise absolute monarchy so long as it serves the general welfare. The contributors grant subjects the right to resist despots; on the other hand, a king like Henri IV is regarded as a hero for obeying the laws, tolerating criticism, and helping the poor.

The *Encyclopédie* does not seek a social revolution. It repeatedly attacks the behavior of courtiers and *les grands*; but the poet J.-F. de Saint-Lambert points out in his article, "Luxe," that rank is essential to public order. Other contributors declare that men are born equal; nevertheless, privileges for the nobility are sometimes justified.

The encyclopedists favor commerce and regard merchants as valuable citizens who deserve respect and a share of political power. But the *Encyclopédie* does not idealize the middle class. Some bourgeois are criticized for buying useless government offices and evading taxes. In "Tragique bourgeois," L. de Jaucourt affirms that merchants are inappropriate protagonists in a tragedy. The *Encyclopédie* often denounces tax farmers and other financiers, for they are considered rapacious and parasitical.

The *Encyclopédie* desires to improve the lot of the common people. It hopes to raise the status of artisans, generally opposes slavery, and tries to render conscription and the *corvée* less onerous on peasants. Yet the encyclopedists do not call for political democracy in France. Many articles in the *Encyclopédie* note the masses' ignorance and credulity.

When discussing specific eighteenth-century French officials and politics, the *Encyclopédie* is usually cautious. It indirectly reproaches O. Joly de Fleury, the attorney general of France who harassed Diderot, but its dedication is to comte M.-P. d'Argenson, the secretary of state for war and the former director of publications. The article "Librairie" praises C. Lamoignon de Malesherbes, the director of publications from 1750 to 1763. Also, in many places the work lauds Louis XV. The *Encyclopédie* criticizes the government's numerous failings yet calls on it to provide better education, discourage military desertion, combat beggary, and make taxes more equitable. The encyclopedists do not want to do away with the French monarchy; they want to improve it.

It still remains true that no other eighteenth-century encyclopedia so assailed Christianity and proposed so many religious, economic, and political reforms. Its message spread far and wide. More than 4,000 sets of the first edition were produced, although it cost so much that only the very rich could afford to buy it. Five other editions were published during the Old Regime (the Geneva folio, Lucca folio, Leghorn folio, Geneva-Neuchâtel quarto, and the Lausanne-Bern octavo). Over 20,000 more copies were distributed throughout Europe, and the price of a set then came within reach of the French middle class. The *Encyclopédie* became a best-seller. Even in its later expurgated versions, it helped undermine the church and the monarchy and thus unintentionally prepared the way for the French Revolution.

Those encyclopedists who lived until the Revolution had difficulty adjusting to it. They were divided in their political allegiances. Some remained monarchists; others turned republican. Few, however, upheld the Reign of Terror.

A comparison of the ideas of the *Encyclopédie* with the policies of the Revolution reveals some similarities. For example, both favor religious toleration and the abolition of torture, and both are imbued with a fervor for humanity and a hatred of tyrants. But the *Encyclopédie* does not call for the destruction of the parlements, wars of liberation, or popular sovereignty. The work seeks an intellectual rather than a political or social revolution.

R. Darnton, *The Business of Enlightenment: A Publishing History of the "Encyclopédie," 1775–1800* (Cambridge, Mass., 1979); F. A. Kafker, ed., *Notable Encyclopedias of the Seventeenth and Eighteenth Centuries: Nine Predecessors of the "Encyclopédie"* (forthcoming); J. Lough, *The Contributors to the "Encyclopédie"* (London, 1973), *The "Encyclopédie"* (London, 1971), *The "Encyclopédie" in Eighteenth-Century England and Other Studies* (Newcastle upon Tyne, 1970), and *Essays on the "Encyclopédie" of Diderot and d'Alembert* (London, 1968); J. Proust, *Diderot et l'Encyclopédie*, 2d ed. (Paris, 1967) and *L'Encyclopédie* (Paris, 1965); A. M. Wilson, *Diderot* (New York, 1972).

F. A. Kafker

Related entries: CAHIERS DE DOLEANCES; CORVEE; DIDEROT; ENLIGHTENMENT, THE; MALESHERBES; ROUSSEAU; VOLTAIRE.

ENLIGHTENMENT, THE, a movement of thought that rejected the principle of authority as the guarantor of truth and instead subjected the realms of religion, politics, morality, and social life to the scrutiny of critical reason. The Enlightenment had its roots in the scientific revolution of the seventeenth century and was an international movement with branches spreading from the Italian peninsula to the American colonies. It came to fruition, however, in the eighteenth century and was centered in France where it was led by the *philosophes*, a group of writers, journalists, scientists, and reformers. The most prominent figures were C.-L. Montesquieu, F.-M. Voltaire, J.-J. Rousseau, and D. Diderot. The typical literary genres of the Enlightenment included the *conte philosophique* or philosophical tale (for example, Voltaire's *Candide*, 1759), novelistic accounts of imaginary voyages (Montesquieu's *Persian Letters*, 1721), essays on society and politics (Rousseau's *Discourse on the Origins of Inequality*, 1750), and moralizing novels (Rousseau's *Emile, or Education*, 1762). The common purpose of the *philosophes* was embodied and epitomized in the grand collaborative enterprise of the Enlightenment, Diderot's *Encyclopédie* (1751–72), a multivolume work designed to summarize and popularize the most recent and best work in philosophy, science, and technology, not merely to inform the public but to change the general way of thinking.

The Enlightenment was never a unified body of doctrine with an institutional base like that of a church, academy, or university. Instead, it depended on the circulation of books and the exchange of correspondence, on friendships, and on the sort of intellectual intercourse that a cosmopolitan urban life makes possible. Moreover, since it extended over more than one generation, its unity is something more obvious in retrospect than it was to its creators, men who often quarreled bitterly among themselves and to the point of personal betrayal. Nevertheless, on the important issues of political rights and duties, there existed by the eve of the French Revolution a congeries of principles and values that most people who thought of themselves as unprejudiced, well informed, and progressive—that is, as enlightened—had assented to, if only because they took them to be self-evident truths.

Drawn principally from the liberal, individualistic political tradition founded by J. Locke, enlightened political and social ideas centered on freedom, first and fundamentally on the freedom of the individual to own, increase, and enjoy the fruits of his labor, free from the depredations of the state and of the unproductive, parasitical social orders of the clergy and aristocracy. The freedom of the individual depended on the rule of law to protect all citizens or subjects from the arbitrary and thus despotic exercise of force. Freedom was also demanded for the expression of ideas, even when they were incompatible with the dogmas of established religion.

This libertarian consensus did not constitute a formal, coherent political theory or program. It was a set of values and beliefs that disposed men to make specific political demands and to take action when the opportunity presented itself. The same can be said for two equally important aspects of what can be called the *philosophes'* creation of a new political mentality: their belief in the possibility of rational social reform and their elevation of productive labor to the status of every man's prime social duty.

Almost without exception, the *philosophes* contended that critical reason, modeled on the procedures of natural science, could be applied to defective social institutions in order to diminish, if not eradicate, the suffering that humanity had imposed on itself through ignorance, sloth, and a lack of intellectual courage. Although there were *philosophes* who thought that regression was possible and progress not inevitable, it was widely held that since man and not God was responsible for social evil, man himself could markedly diminish unnecessary suffering with reason and energy.

The Enlightenment's faith and hope in progress was allied, both conceptually and emotionally, to its reevaluation of labor. The *philosophes* did not entirely succeed in destroying the older ethic that held work in contempt and valued aristocratic leisure and priestly prayer, but they did create a rival ethic. By the time the Estates General was called, a *philosophe* and pamphleteer like E.-J. Sieyès could demand that idle aristocrats and do-nothing priests be excluded from the nation on the grounds that they did no useful work.

The relationship of these ideas, values, and attitudes to the French Revolution has been debated since the Revolution. The controversy is intricate and probably interminable. Two principal questions pose themselves. First, were the *philosophes* responsible for the coming of the Revolution? Second, did the Enlightenment provide the program that the Revolution's leaders consciously labored to realize? The first question is no longer raised seriously. Although some participants as well as contemporary conservative polemicists like E. Burke blamed the *philosophes* for the Revolution, it is clear that neither the *philosophes* nor their ideas played a role in the outbreak of a revolution caused by the French crown's bankruptcy and its stumbling mismanagement of the political and economic crises of 1789.

The problem of the Enlightenment as a blueprint for Revolutionaries is considerably more difficult, if only because the Revolution's institutions and dominant political ideals changed so rapidly and drastically. Nevertheless, until recently the consensus was that the deputies who abolished feudalism on 4 August 1789, drafted the Declaration of the Rights of Man and the Citizen, and framed the first constitution were deliberately attempting to put the ideas of the Enlightenment into practice. In fact, from this point of view the Declaration of the Rights of Man must be seen not as a document influenced by the Enlightenment but as one of the movement's principal texts.

Attacks on the interpretation linking Enlightenment ideas and Revolutionary practice come from several quarters, but the arguments reduce themselves to the following. The *philosophes*, it is said, were essentially moderate men who often expressed a fear of social disorder and who certainly would have abhorred revolutionary change had they lived to witness it. They produced, moreover, very little in the way of formal political theory. Even the Enlightenment's most notable work of theory, Rousseau's democratic *Social Contract*, was not intended by its author to apply to a nation as large as France. In addition, it was not widely read, being far less known than Montesquieu's *Spirit of the Laws*, a work that supported not democracy but monarchy balanced by aristocracy. Finally, it has been argued that the general, abstract kinds of principles laid down in the Declaration of the Rights of Man, from which specific governmental reforms and institutions were to be deduced, actually constituted a break with the *philosophes* because the Enlightenment had after 1750 become increasingly empirical and wary of abstract, rationalistic principles.

None of these contentions is wrong, but all are somewhat irrelevant to the problem of the influence of ideas and values on the Revolution's course. The *philosophes*' prudent moderation, their political timidity, and impotence does not make their ideas any the less corrosive or, indeed, revolutionary in the hands of men determined to use them against a government no longer able to rule.

Indeed, the intentions of a writer matter little when it is a question of determining whether his ideas played a part in actual political change, in revolution. This is especially true in the case of Rousseau's vision of a virtuous, democratic republic. Intended though it was for a small polity about the size of a city–state, the argument advanced in the *Social Contract*, after 1792, inflamed the imagination of political activists who had overthrown Europe's largest monarchy and were building a republic amid its ruins. Before the failure of the constitutional monarchy, Rousseau's democratic theory was generally taken as a purely theoretical exercise. Afterward it became a political force. The relationship between books and events is a constantly shifting process. Had the Revolution ended after the establishment of a constitutional monarchy, Montesquieu would have become such a moderate revolution's honored theoretician and known to historians as the most influential of the *philosophes*. It did not end, and the first generation of radical democrats took sustenance from the *Social Contract*, a book that no one thought was applicable to France before 1789.

The Enlightenment's failure to produce a significant body of formal political theory has also been adduced to belittle its influence on the Revolution. Formal political theory is, however, not the only kind of thought that exercises an influence on political events. Values, structures of feeling, the search for exemplars, and religious belief can be equally important. And these are to be sought not in narrowly defined political works but in novels, plays, poetry, opera, and the visual arts, all of which often profoundly modify sentiments and, ultimately, behavior. Indeed, during the Enlightenment when the nature of the Bourbon state provided virtually no scope for political action and revolution was unthinkable, political aspiration and thought were expressed in many ways. For example, the Enlightenment's admiration for the austere civic virtues of the ancient Greeks and Romans was embodied in works as different as Voltaire's tragedies, Rousseau's *Discourse on the Origins of Inequality*, and, late in the century, J.-L. David's painting, *The Oath of the Horatii*. Before the crises of 1788 and 1789, the celebration of antique republican heroism was at most an oblique criticism of the monarchy's political values. After the onset of the Revolution, what had often been a politically sterile, inauthentic moral-aesthetic affectation provided Revolutionaries with a republican iconography, language, and symbolism. That at the least facilitated and fueled the growth of republican values.

Finally, there is the argument that the Revolution's founding document, the Declaration of the Rights of Man, as well as the reforms implemented in its name, actually broke with the new, empirically minded Enlightenment. This contention depends on a kind of historian's fiat that defines and then freezes the Enlightenment into a monolith. This procedure, however convenient for an understanding of the development of the Enlightenment, obscures the influence of ideas on the men who carried on the work of the *philosophes* into the Revolutionary period. It requires that men like the marquis de Condorcet, Sieyès, and A. Lavoisier be excommunicated from the Enlightenment because they continued to hold and act on ideas that the Enlightenment is alleged to have abandoned. In fact, the first wave of Revolutionaries were in the process of redefining and giving substance to the Enlightenment's often general, moderate, or vague political yearnings in a revolutionary situation. In so doing they necessarily modified greatly a living and mutable body of thought that, under the circumstances, itself became a revolutionary force. Moreover, in the Revolution's crucible, these radicalized Enlightenment ideas were used to justify massive administrative and political change, new forms of government, democracy, and even Terror in a way that no one, and above all their progenitors, could have foreseen. The Revolutionaries also introduced new ideas or sentiments that were incompatible with much of what they had inherited. The emergence, for example, of armed nationalism and ideological warfare both as idea and practice marks a real departure from the internationalism, cosmopolitanism, and antimilitarism of many of the *philosophes*.

It is probably impossible to say at what point during this reciprocal interplay of Enlightenment ideas and unprecedented political events so transformed the body of Enlightenment ideas that a new movement of thought began. But the fact that ultimately the Enlightenment underwent such a metamorphosis does not in the least mean that it had no influence on the Revolutionary events that brought it to an end.

E. Cassirer, *The Philosophy of the Enlightenment* (New York, 1951); W. F. Church, ed., *The Influence of the Enlightenment on the French Revolution*, 2d ed. (Boston, 1974); A. Cobban, *In Search of Humanity* (New York, 1960); R. Darnton, *The Business of Enlightenment* (Cambridge, Mass., 1979); P. Gay, *The Enlightenment*, vols. 1–2 (New York, 1966, 1969); N. Hampson, *The Enlightenment* (London, 1968); D. Mornet, *Les origines intellectuelles de la Révolution française* (Paris, 1933).

R. Bienvenu

Related entries: BURKE; CONDORCET; DAVID; DECLARATION OF THE RIGHTS OF MAN AND OF THE CITIZEN; *ENCYCLOPEDIE*; *ESPRIT DES LOIS, L'*; LAVOISIER; MONTESQUIEU; ROUSSEAU; SIEYES; SOCIAL CONTRACT; TERROR, THE; THEORY OF REVOLUTIONARY GOVERNMENT; VOLTAIRE.

ENRAGES, a group of leaders of the Paris sections and popular societies during 1792 and 1793 who agitated the National Convention to adopt economic and social policies that would serve the interests of the poor and for the intensification of the Terror against counterrevolutionaries, food hoarders, currency speculators, and the corrupt rich in general. The description *enragés* is a historical invention. During the Revolution, *enragé* meant no more than "wild extremist," whether of the Right or of the Left. *Les enragés* first appear as a distinct and coherent ultra-Jacobin party of the Left in J. Michelet's *History of the Revolution*, published in 1853.

The boundaries of this party are vague. Some historians have extended them to include J.-R. Hébert and his followers in 1794 and G. Babeuf and the Equals of 1796. Others would add provincial agitators like T. de Montigny of Orléans. In an influential 1930 study, J. M. Zacker, however, defined the *enragés* as the four chief Parisian activists: J. Roux (1752–94), J.-T.-V. Leclerc (1771–?), J.-F.Varlet (1764–?), and C. Lacombe (1765–?). R. B. Rose in a more recent study adds A.-P. Léon (1768–?) to this list.

The most influential figure among this group was J. Roux, a priest and, from 1791, *vicaire* of the church of Saint-Nicolas des Champs, in the densely populated and working-class Gravilliers section in central Paris. Roux's preaching early took on a political and social tone, and by March 1792 he had joined the Cordeliers club. He also built a strong following of *Jacquesroutins* in the Gravilliers section assembly and in December 1792 was elected by the section to the General Council of the Paris Commune. Roux's influence was wider than his section, however. One of his most popular sermons, the *Discours sur les moyens de sauver la France et la Liberté*, first delivered at Saint-Nicolas in May 1792, was subsequently repeated before the general assemblies of ten of the forty-eight Paris sections and in the parish churches of Saint-Eustache, Sainte-Marguérite, Saint-Antoine, and the cathedral of Notre Dame itself. In this manifesto, subsequently printed, Roux first sounded many of the notes of what subsequently became the *enragé* program: a strict Revolutionary vigilance against religious fanaticism and traitorous public functionaries, a purge of aristocrats from public office, and a thunderous denunciation of *accapareurs* and *agioteurs* (food and currency speculators), for whom Roux demanded the death penalty. He also pressed for state control of the grain trade and the creation of a network of public granaries to ensure cheap and plentiful food.

Many of the same themes were echoed, in late 1792, by Varlet. Varlet, a compulsive agitator since the earliest days of the Revolution, had come to prominence during the agitation surrounding the overthrow of the monarchy on 10 August 1792. A street orator, Varlet became, with his mobile tribune, one of the landmarks of the Terrasse des Feuillants in the Tuileries Gardens. A member of both the Jacobins and the Cordeliers, he had a solid following in the Roi-de-Sicile (later Droits de l'Homme) section. At the time of the 10 August uprising, he presented and published a massively supported petition, *Voeux formés par des français libres*, which linked the demand for severe laws against food hoarding with a purge of all aristocrats from military command and with more generally canvassed demands for a republic and elections by universal suffrage. Shortly afterward, Varlet published a program for the National Convention elections that urged the adoption of the essentials of direct democracy: direct voting, recall, legislation by referendum, and action to redress the great inequality of fortunes.

Of the other *enragés*, Léon had first made a name for herself in February 1792 as a feminist militant by a proposal to drill and arm a legion of 300 women Revolutionaries. It was not until 10 May 1793 that she reappeared in the public eye, with the announced founding of an equally militant Club des citoyennes républicaines révolutionnaires. Lacombe, who collaborated with Léon in this foundation, was a provincial actress who had made her debut on the political stage in Paris as the orator of a Jacobin address to the Legislative Assembly in July 1792. Leclerc arrived in Paris as a delegate of the Lyon Jacobins at the beginning of May 1793 to lobby for all-out Terror against counterrevolutionaries and moderates.

There is no evidence of any political collaboration between any of the *enragé* leaders before the summer of 1793. During May 1793, however, elements of a common *enragé* platform began to emerge, as the struggle between the Girondin-dominated Convention and the extremists of the clubs, the sections, and the Commune approached its crisis. From the middle of May, Varlet, with the support of the Républicaines révolutionnaires, was busily canvassing support from the sections and the popular societies for the displacement of the existing government, the arrest of the leading Girondins, a roundup of suspects, a purge of the army and the administration, the expansion of a paramilitary Revolutionary army, and the extermination of speculators and monopolists. It was this program that provided a major inspiration for the uprising of 31 May 1793 and the defeat of the Girondins.

These *enragés* each played a prominent part in the uprising, and Varlet in particular exercised a strong influence on the Central Revolutionary Committee, which for a time exercised effective control over Paris. However, the *enragés* rapidly found themselves displaced by an alliance formed by the Montagnard leaders in the Convention, the Jacobin club, the Paris departmental administration, and the Paris Commune, all of whom closed ranks to resist the more extreme policies of the insurgents. In consequence, as the new Montagnard government consolidated its authority during the summer of 1793, the *enragés* moved into opposition, continuing, with the support of the Cordeliers club and the Paris sections, to urge the completion of what they saw as the unfinished revolution of 31 May. This confrontation was strikingly illustrated on 25 June when the Convention's celebrations of the promulgation of France's new democratic constitution (suspended until the peace) were interrupted by a delegation led by Roux, which demanded a more effective purge of the Convention and immediate action against the growing food shortage and high prices in Paris. Another aspect of the same agitation was a demand by the forty-eight Paris sections for a general maximum, or price control legislation. On 28 June 1793 M. Robespierre personally denounced Roux at the Jacobin club, to give the signal for a counteroffensive.

As a result, Roux and Leclerc were expelled from the Cordeliers club and Varlet was suspended, the Commune censured Roux, and J.-P. Marat attacked him in the *Ami du peuple*. Ironically, Marat's assassination on 14 July made possible a renewal of *enragé* activism. Both Roux and Leclerc immediately began to publish continuations of Marat's journal entitled, respectively, the *Publiciste du peuple français* and *L'ami du peuple*. By mid-August both journals were attacking the growing menace of Jacobin dictatorship and denouncing the unpurged Convention as the instrument of speculators, monopolists, and the rich generally. Some of the language Roux and Leclerc used resembles a modern-sounding class interpretation of the Revolution as an explicit triumph of the bourgeoisie over both the aristocracy and the people. Meanwhile they continued to emphasize the economically radical and terrorist aspects of the *enragé* program, against a background of growing food crisis in Paris and civil war outside. At the beginning of September, Leclerc's journal heralded a new challenge to Montagnard authority, which was supported by the Républicaines révolutionnaires: a demand for the immediate introduction of the constitution, with elections to replace the Convention.

The *enragés'* days were already numbered, however. In the *journées* of 4–5 September, the leaders of the Commune, P.-G. Chaumette and Hébert, skillfully stole the *enragés'* thunder, adopting the essentials of their program—the general maximum, the Revolutionary army, and the guillotine for food hoarders—so capturing the mass support of the sections and the popular societies. Thus, there was no effective resistance when the Commune and the Jacobin club moved to finish the *enragés*. Roux was arrested on 5 September 1793 and ultimately committed suicide in jail rather than face trial. In mid-September a threat of imprisonment was sufficient to persuade Leclerc to discontinue the *Ami du peuple*, and the Club des citoyennes républicaines révolutionnaires was closed by decree at the end of October. Varlet, though he had remained aloof from Roux and Leclerc's campaign since June, was arrested in mid-September for his part in a separate agitation by the militants of the Paris sections against the encroachment of the Convention and the Commune on their independence and freedom of action.

The repression of September 1793 marked the end of any semblance of coherent *enragé* program or party. The surviving *enragés* continued, individually, to play a minor role in Revolutionary politics. Leclerc and Léon (who married each other in November) and Lacombe were all arrested for alleged association with the Hébertist conspiracy of Ventôse Year II (March 1794). Varlet kept clear of this entanglement but was arrested soon after the overthrow of Robespierre for attempting to revive an independent *sans-culotte* opposition to the Thermidorian Convention. On their release from prison, the *enragés* returned to a political obscurity from which Varlet alone emerged, briefly and insignificantly, in 1830–31, as a Bonapartist pamphleteer at Nantes.

While the *enragés* failed to seize or hold on to power, their contribution to the history of the Revolution was not without significance. Together they formed an important element in the complex of forces that drove the Convention to abandon economic and political liberalism for a kind of collectivist totalitarianism. Most of the measures advocated by the *enragés* were in fact adopted by the Convention during 1793.

Attempts have been made to attribute a wider significance to the group. In 1845 K. Marx and F. Engels described Roux and Leclerc as precursors of the Communist tradition, passed down through G. Babeuf and F. M. Buonarroti to the nineteenth century, and the *enragés* have attracted some attention from historians of socialism. While they had no coherent socialist ideology, many of

their writings and utterances did reflect the inspiration of a Rousseauist egalitarianism, based on the premise of a primitive right to substance, prior to and
superior to the right of property. This provided the theoretical justification for
their practical proposals for state intervention in the economic process but was
never used to justify pure communism, as was the case with Babeuf. The *enragés'*
socialism was a pragmatic response to the pressures of the time rather than the
product of philosophical reflection.

M. Cerati, *Le club des citoyennes républicaines révolutionnaires* (Paris, 1966); W.
Markov, *Die Freiheiten des Priesters Roux* (Berlin, 1967); R. B. Rose, *The Enragés*:
Socialists of the French Revolution? (Sydney, 1968).

R. B. Rose

Related entries: BABEUF; BUONARROTI; CENTRAL REVOLUTIONARY
COMMITTEE; CHAUMETTE; CORDELIERS CLUB; HEBERT; LACOMBE;
LECLERC; LEON; ROUX; 10 AUGUST 1792; VARLET.

EQUALS, CONSPIRACY OF. See CONSPIRACY OF EQUALS.

ESPRIT DES LOIS, L' (1748), C.-L. de Secondat, baron de la Brède et de
Montesquieu's classic work of political theory. One of the most intensively
studied and debated books of the eighteenth century, *L'esprit des lois* contributed
more than virtually any other contemporary work to the political discourse of
the late eighteenth century generally and the French Revolution in particular. A
subtle and complex treatise, *L'esprit des lois* exerted a perceptible influence on
Revolutionary figures as different as M. Robespierre and J. de Maistre. If few
among its many readers extracted from the work the same message, almost all
remained in some respect students of the same master.

L'esprit des lois was the product of a lifetime of social observation and
analysis, remarkable erudition, and constant travel. By the time Montesquieu
began to compose the work, he had already established himself as a major literary
figure, particularly on the basis of his notorious *Lettres persanes* (1721). In
publishing *L'esprit des lois* Montesquieu placed himself again in the thick of
controversy by strongly advocating the *thèse nobiliaire*. But his work was far
more than a polemic on behalf of the French nobility; it provided nothing less
than one possible foundation for an entire science of society, treating within its
broad scope a multitude of fundamental political, economic, and social subjects.

The significance of *L'esprit des lois* for the French Revolution may be said
to lie in two principal areas.

It lies first in Montesquieu's demonstration of the integral connections between
political structures and a broad range of social phenomena, including class structure, religion, and commercial activities. Montesquieu put forward a typology
of political societies—democratic and aristocratic republics, monarchies, and
despotisms—in the conviction that the inner dynamics of real societies can best
be understood by working out models of social interaction and examining real
societies in the light of these models. Applied one way, Montesquieu's social

science lent support to the notion that the central institution of society was the state and that therefore the key to social regeneration was redesign of the government and its laws. Revolutionaries paid particular attention to Montesquieu's account of the republican form of government, taking to heart his idea that the guiding principle of republics was virtue. Counterrevolutionaries came to apply the lessons of *L'esprit des lois* altogether differently. They used the close connection established by Montesquieu between the state and society as the basis for their argument that just because the two were integral parts of one whole, swift change in the state would make it incompatible with the society it was supposed to govern. No change, they contended, could be legitimate if it interrupted the internal harmony of a society, a political principle that the Revolutionaries had violated in their brutal use of political levers to effect social change. The proof of the Revolutionaries' folly seemed to lie in that fact that none of the Revolutionary constitutions, from that of 1791 to those of N. Bonaparte, had resulted in social or political equilibrium.

The second major contribution of *L'esprit des lois* to French Revolutionary thought consisted of Montesquieu's notion of despotism. By the time Montesquieu wrote *L'esprit des lois*, the term *despotism* had already begun to reenter Western political discourse, to be used frequently in the controversies regarding the reign of Louis XIV. In linking despotism to a social system, Montesquieu broadened the term's meaning by demonstrating that under despotism, men were not merely subjects governed by arbitrary decree but veritable slaves. Of equal significance was Montesquieu's account of despotism as a corruption of monarchy. The clear implication of *L'esprit des lois* was that all members of a monarchical society like France lived under the constant threat of being enslaved within the kind of political society Montesquieu presented as "corrupt by its very nature." Montesquieu's notion of despotism proved enduring. In 1778 A.-H. Anquetil-Duperron could write that Montesquieu had definitively established the meaning of despotism and that since *L'esprit des lois* had appeared thirty years earlier, no one writing on this subject had done anything but copy him. The political impact was profound. In confirming old suspicions and raising new fears about the monarchy, *L'esprit des lois* helped not only to reinvigorate the resistance of the parlements to royal command but also to lay the ideological foundation for the broad, if loose, consensus of disaffection that made possible the Revolutionary crisis of 1787–89.

The measures Montesquieu recommended to prevent despotism proved to have a less universal following. In tying the defense of liberty to the defense of privilege, the strength of traditional corporate bodies, and the separation of powers, Montesquieu opened himself to attack from many who admired other aspects of his argument; these included F.-M. Voltaire, who, if he feared despotism, had little confidence in the wisdom of the parlements, and many Revolutionaries, like the marquis de Condorcet, who demanded equal rights for all and opposed in principle the separation of powers. Yet in championing the corporate structure of the Old Regime, Montesquieu was also not without enduring influence. To those who saw the salvation of society in the preservation of intermediary bodies between the individual and the state—and this group included not only counterrevolutionaries like L. de Bonald and J. de Maistre but also eventually such liberals as A. de Tocqueville—*L'esprit des lois* remained in this regard a guiding light from the age of *lumières*.

L. Althusser, *Montesquieu—La politique et l'histoire* (Paris, 1959); E. Carcassone, *Montesquieu et le problème de la constitution française* (Paris, 1927); R. Shackleton, *Montesquieu—A Critical Biography* (London, 1961).

T. E. Kaiser

Related entries: ENLIGHTENMENT; MONTESQUIEU; VOLTAIRE.

ESTATES GENERAL, the representative body of the Old Regime whose meeting in May 1789 was essential to the development of the French Revolution. This assembly, composed of representatives of the three orders (clergy, nobility, and Third Estate) and selected by cities, *bailliages*, and *sénéchaussées*, was called by the king in extraordinary circumstances. The first Estates General since 1614, this assembly was summoned to meet at Versailles on 27 April, although the date was later changed to 5 May, in order to propose solutions to financial problems, to reduce the treasury's deficit, and to relieve the public debt, problems that the two Assemblies of Notables in February 1787 and November 1788 had failed to resolve. The spirit of the Enlightenment had profoundly influenced liberal nobles such as F.-A. La Rochefoucauld-Liancourt, the marquis de Lafayette, the marquis de Condorcet, and the comte de Mirabeau, priests like the abbé Sieyès, and the majority of the bourgeoisie who formed the dominant element in the Third Estate. A patriot party developed around the Committee of Thirty and undertook active propaganda against royal absolutism, ministerial power, and pecuniary privileges. On 24 December 1788, this group had, despite the very strong opposition of the aristocracy, achieved the doubling of the number of deputies of the Third. The Estates General, elected between February and April 1789 in two or three stages, as provided for by the royal regulations of 24 January, included 1,139 members, of whom 291 represented the clergy, 270 the nobility, and 578 the Third Estate, a homogeneous group over half of whom were members of the legal profession, barristers and prosecutors. The Third also included merchants, financiers, entrepreneurs, professionals, and men of independent means. It is noteworthy that Sieyès and Mirabeau abandoned their order and were elected by the Third Estate. Each deputy was also responsible for presenting to the king a list summarizing the grievances and remonstrances of his electors. As the spokesmen for bourgeois claims, they demanded the abolition of privileges, equality of taxation, and a constitution, but they neglected a large number of popular desires expressed on the level of rural parishes and corporations of arts and crafts. It would be difficult to exaggerate the importance of the lists from villages, where every Frenchman at least twenty-five years old and inscribed on the tax rolls—and even women who were heads of families—had the right to be heard. The suffrage was, then, in principle very liberal;

nevertheless, economic circumstances and illiteracy worked in favor of the notables. No peasant, no craftsman, no small tradesman figured among the deputies to the Estates General.

The opening session was preceded, on 4 May, by a slow, very formal, anachronistic procession. In the presence of the king and the court, the members of the three orders heard Mass in the church of Saint-Louis at Versailles. Then, on 5 May, they "submitted" to speeches by the keeper of the seals, C.-L.-F. Barentin, and J. Necker, which contained neither program nor promises. The disappointment of the Third Estate was intense and was manifested from the beginning by the verification of credentials, which was done by separate orders and not in common. Furthermore, the king did not permit voting by head during the deliberations of the Estates. Discussions went on for a month, thereby allowing the deputies of the Third to affirm their positions, while popular agitation at Versailles and Paris increased. Then on 12 June by a roll call, they undertook by themselves the verification of credentials of all the deputies. Some parish priests came to join them. This was a beginning, and on 17 June, on the proposal of Sieyès, those present constituted themselves as the National Assembly and affirmed their right to approve or reject the levying of existing taxes. On 19 June, the clergy decided to join the Third, while the intransigent nobility appealed to the king, who ordered the convocation of a plenary session for 23 June to annul the decrees passed illegally by the Third and the closing of the Salle des Menus Plaisirs where it met. Taking refuge in a nearby tennis court on 20 June, 578 deputies, including five clergy, took the oath to "never separate . . . until the Constitution is established and consolidated on solid foundations." The nearly unanimous vote expressed the collective will of the Third to resist royal power. This firmness swept along the majority of the clergy and some nobles. The joint session on 23 June, a veritable *lit de justice*, was unable to break such spirit.

In the king's name, Barentin declared the decisions of the Third and the obligations imposed on certain deputies null. He also granted some concessions regarding the vote by head and common deliberations of the Estates, which could henceforth consent to taxes and loans and distribute public receipts among the ministries. He promised to sanction fiscal equality, guarantee personal liberties and freedom of the press, and consider proposals for the reform of indirect taxes, including the salt tax (*gabelle*), which he knew was very unpopular. "If you abandon me in such a fine enterprise, alone I shall provide for the welfare of my people . . . alone I shall consider myself their true representative," added Louis XVI, who, in front of the Third, upheld the power of the aristocracy, with the intention of maintaining traditional structures. Still, if this minimum program had been agreed to only a little while before, he would have been able to satisfy most public opinion. At this point it seemed like both charity and a challenge. Ordered to return to their respective chambers, the deputies of the Third refused, and J.-S. Bailly declared that the assembled Nation could not receive orders, while Mirabeau may have made the declaration, which, although unverifiable, has become famous: "We shall leave only at the point of bayonets."

The king rejected the use of force and the dismissal of Necker who had opposed the meeting of the royal session on 23 June. Beyond that, on 27 June he invited the privileged to join the other deputies. Thus, the National Assembly became legal without having recourse to violence. On 7 July it appointed some of its members to a Committee on the Constitution and on 9 July took the name National Constituent Assembly. The bourgeoisie quickly exploited its victory by electing a secretariat and creating an official journal of its sessions. The first motions made anticipated a total remodeling of the existing political regime, which was henceforth described as *ancien*. But questions remained: Was the king's attitude sincere? Would the nobility acquiesce? The concentration of troops around Paris showed that a *coup de force* was imminent. A popular response was predictable. Chances of maintaining a peaceful revolution were growing slimmer; they disappeared on 14 July.

J.-P. Bertaud, *Les origines de la Révolution française* (Paris, 1971); J. Godechot, *La prise de la Bastille* (Paris, 1965); G. Lefebvre, *The Coming of the French Revolution* (Princeton, N.J., 1947); R. R. Palmer, *The Age of Democratic Revolution*, vol. 1 (Princeton, N.J., 1959); *Recueil de documents relatifs aux séances des Etats généraux (mai-juin 1789)*, 3 vols. (Paris, 1953–74); M. Vovelle, *La chute de la monarchie, 1787–1792* (Paris, 1972).

M. Bouloiseau

Related entries: ASSEMBLY OF NOTABLES; *BAILLIAGE*; BAILLY; BARENTIN; COMMITTEE OF THIRTY; NECKER; TENNIS COURT OATH.

EVECHE.   See CENTRAL REVOLUTIONARY COMMITTEE.

F

FABRE, PHILLIPE-FRANCOIS (FABRE D'EGLANTINE)(1750-1794), poet and *conventionnel*. Fabre adopted the name *d'Eglantine* after supposedly winning a prize, a wreath of eglantine, in a literary contest in the floral games in Toulouse in 1771. He viewed the Revolution as a play and himself as a major actor both in and behind the scenes. As a comic satirist of society and politics, he produced eleven plays, all in verse, between September 1787 and March 1792. His most noted and finest was *Le Philinte de Molière* (1790), which incorporated his devotion to F. Molière, Rousseauism, and revolutionism.

With the opening of the Cordeliers club in the spring of 1790, Fabre d'Eglantine emerged as a leading spokesman and as its president. But the apex of his career was attained during the Revolutionary events of 1792–93. On 10 August 1792 he was one of the few Revolutionary leaders who actually participated in the attack on the Tuileries. He was selected by G.-J. Danton as one of his secretaries and became a member of his inner circle. Fabre's influence increased when he was elected as a Paris deputy to the National Convention.

He supported dechristianization by applying his poetic talents to the nomenclature of the Revolutionary calendar. As indicated in his report to the Convention on 24 October 1793, poetic or agrarian names were given to months, such as Vendémiaire, Brumaire, and Frimaire. Sundays were eliminated since each month was to be divided into three equal parts, or *décades*.

His implication in the foreign plot conspiracy and the affair of the Compagnie des Indes led to the destruction of the Mountain and intensified factionalism within the Convention. In October 1793 the alleged foreign plot was exposed by Fabre when he met with M. Robespierre, L.-A. de Saint-Just, and the Committee of General Security, where he proceeded to denounce such men as P. Proli, F. Desfieux, and P.-U. Dubuisson as foreign conspirators trying to destroy the Republic. Actually, the accusations were false and politically motivated to obtain public support. Subsequently, fearing attack as an ally of Danton, he denounced the Hébertists as partisans of violent and extreme measures. Fabre d'Eglantine's success was short-lived; soon he was charged with fraud in his connection with the Compagnie des Indes by F. Chabot. The opportunity of making profits by falsifying a decree that led to the compulsory liquidation of the *Compagnie* proved fatal to Fabre d'Eglantine.

Arrested on 13 January 1794, he was expelled from the Jacobins and denounced by Robespierre. Although the falsified decree was not produced at his trial, he was indicted as a Dantonist. He perished with Danton and C. Desmoulins on 3 April 1794, ending a checkered career at the early age of thirty-nine.

L. Jacob, *Fabre d'Eglantine chef des "Fripons"* (Paris, 1946); A. Mathiez, "Fabre d'Eglantine et la falsification du décret de liquidation de la Compagnie des Indes," *Ann. révo.* 6 (1913); C. Vellay, ed., *Oeuvres politiques de Fabre d'Eglantine* (Paris, 1914).

C. A. Gliozzo

Related entries: CALENDAR OF THE FRENCH REPUBLIC; COMMITTEE OF GENERAL SECURITY; COMPAGNIE DES INDES; CORDELIERS CLUB; *DECADE*; DECHRISTIANIZATION; DESFIEUX.

FARMERS GENERAL, financiers responsible for certain kinds of tax collection under the Old Regime. Founded in the 1660s by J.-B. Colbert, the General Farm was a complex bureaucracy established for collecting a conglomeration of royal taxes. Most notably left to another body was the land tax (*taille*). But by the eighteenth century, among the imposts received were the salt (*gabelle*) and tobacco taxes, internal customs duties, tariffs, excises, town duties, registry taxes, and sales taxes. Different jurisdictions and rules governed each assessment, so the General Farm possessed many layers of officialdom. Each province, however, had an office to coordinate many of these responsibilities. Numbered among functionaries necessary to this system were both highly sophisticated business persons and illiterate guards. All told, the Farm employed about 30,000.

Not only did the General Farm collect taxes; it dispensed payments. Very rarely did specie travel to the royal treasury in Paris to be redistributed. Customarily officials at all levels of the Farm, with an order from the government, paid diverse obligations of the administration. Such procedures enabled the government to purchase goods and services more readily.

But the main function of the General Farm, other than collecting taxes, was providing a strong fiscal mooring for the royal government. The Bourbons tried not to administer this bureaucracy themselves. Rather, Colbert had merged these various taxes to form an attractive investment for tax farmers. In essence, tax farmers advanced the government a specified sum for the privilege of collecting a particular tax. Colbert hoped then to use the reorganized and more efficient General Farm as a lure to provide an assured level of royal income.

The informal group that financiers initially formed to bid on the General Farm had by the eighteenth century become recognized and regulated by the monarchy as the Company of Farmers General. The number of these men varied from forty to sixty according to law, and although officially a single individual held each position, in practice others often owned parts of each share. For example, in 1780 the king possessed approximately 20 percent of the company through ownership of portions of many different holdings. Each named shareholder was expected to shoulder responsibility for managing the farmers general. All sat on some four to five boards, known as assemblies, which, divided by function, ran the organization. Nonetheless, because of the preeminence of certain assemblies and the role of the correspondent of each board, a handful actually directed the corporation.

The farmers general paid enormous sums to the treasury but made very handsome profits. Throughout most of the eighteenth century, the government leased out the General Farm for a six-year period. From 80 million *livres* in 1726, the annual revenue rose to 152 million *livres* in 1774. Moreover, the king's comptrollers borrowed, from anticipated revenues, immense sums, amounting to over 700 million *livres* in the 1780s alone. When the Old Regime collapsed in 1789, the monarchy owed the farmers general almost 70 million *livres* in long-term debt. But these payments and loans indicate the prosperity, not the destitution, of these tax farmers. No one knows their profits precisely, but estimates exist for 1774. Profits amounted to 156,000 *livres* per partner. Each earned in addition 161,000 *livres* in salary and in guaranteed interest on the capital advanced to the company (1,568,000 *livres*). This total income of 317,000 *livres* was very substantial. Moreover, one might consider all these earnings simply as a return on the money deposited in the capital fund since most investors did not actually work much, if at all, at the company. Such a return represented a 20 percent yield, four times the normal rate.

These tremendous financial gains, when coupled to traditional popular hostility to tax collectors, ensured that many Frenchmen would find these tax farmers odious. All Louis XVI's ministers objected to the earnings and power of this syndicate, and J. Necker actually took steps to break up the corporation. The desperate need for money, however, limited the measures that Old Regime ministers could adopt, but the farmers general did not fare well with the Revolutionaries. As early as August 1789, the National Assembly began dismantling the company. Inexorably, the legislature ended each of the taxes collected by the Farm, canceling the last on 20 March 1791. The Assembly also annulled the contract with the farmers general on the same day. Only a final accounting and liquidation remained, but the complexity of this operation made that slow and difficult work. This process was not finished when the Terror began. Then seen as bloodsuckers, some twenty-eight farmers general were arrested on 6 May 1794, subjected to Revolutionary justice, and executed on 8 May.

M. Marion, *Dictionnaire des institutions de la France* (Paris, 1976); G. T. Matthews, *The Royal General Farms in Eighteenth Century France* (New York, 1958).

J. Censer

Related entries: NECKER; *TAILLE*.

FAUCHET, CLAUDE (1744–93), deputy to the Legislative Assembly and the National Convention; founder of the *Bouche de Fer*. See *BOUCHE DE FER*; CERCLE SOCIAL.

FAVRAS, THOMAS DE MAHY, MARQUIS DE (1744–90), former officer of the Guards of the comte de Provence, counterrevolutionary conspirator arrested 24 December 1789 and hanged 19 February 1790, whose silence at his trial probably spared Provence great embarrassment. Born at Orléans into a family of lesser nobility of obscure origin, Thomas de Mahy adopted the *Favras* from a landed property and began to use *marquis* in the early 1770s. Favras entered Provence's service in 1771. He was an army veteran, poorly educated but ambitious, something of an autodidact, and apparently bold, generous, and rather naive. When he left Provence's service in the mid-1770s, he retained the latter's patronage and developed an interest in public affairs. In 1789 he published several pamphlets, for example on the amortization of the state's debts under the auspices of the Estates General and on the virtues of a *don patriotique* by the clergy.

After 14 July Favras tried to organize a force of former bodyguards and retired officers to defend the royal family. Out of these beginnings he developed a plan to remove the king from Paris until the city could be subdued by loyal troops. Characteristically, he was indiscreet and as a result was reported to the marquis de Lafayette, who placed him under surveillance. During the crisis of 5-6 October, Favras tried to take charge of the situation at Versailles but failed to persuade the minister of war to legitimize and reinforce the loyal contingent he claimed to have in hand. Favras then accompanied the royal family to Paris and continued his recruiting efforts, probably with encouragement of some sort from Provence.

After the October Days, an attempt to rescue the king and discipline Paris was widely anticipated. Without doubt Favras was preparing such a coup. More circumspectly, Provence, who in most of the historical literature is assumed to have been directing Favras, was attempting to raise money for some purpose, and when he permitted Favras to act as an intermediary in contacts with bankers, Lafayette's informers reported on these activities. On 24 December 1789, Favras and his wife were arrested and a document verifying Provence's relationship to the fund raising came into Lafayette's possession. On 25 December, there circulated in Paris a pseudonymous printed explanation that Favras had planned to raise 30,000 men, assassinate Lafayette and the mayor, and starve Paris into submission, and that the comte de Provence was the instigator. Provence immediately appeared before a specially convened meeting at the Hôtel de Ville and denied the charges, maintaining that his whole allegiance was to liberty and to the Revolution as led by his brother, and that only for personal needs had he authorized Favras to negotiate a loan. Provence was not challenged further, and such written commitments as he may have provided for the prospective lenders were never produced, whether because Lafayette had returned them to him or because they were otherwise disposed of.

Favras was tried at the criminal court of Paris. Although he wrote a lengthy testament and other statements, he went to his death without naming any accomplices. The disappearance of some of his papers encouraged speculation about a promised last-minute reprieve that never came and the possibility of a late attempt on his part to reveal the whole story—an attempt that was frustrated or from which he was dissuaded. Madame Favras, who had been set free, was given a pension by Louis XVI and Marie Antoinette. The Favras execution was the first case of a noble's being subjected to a commoner's penalty. The trial attracted much attention and contributed to an atmosphere charged with suspicion. Prompted by Lafayette and J. Necker, Louis XVI on 4 February 1790, while the trial was still in progress, went before the National Assembly and declared his loyalty to constitutional government. For the moment Lafayette's leadership was strengthened. His rival, H.-G. R. Mirabeau, who had coached Provence for his crucial self-justification at the Hôtel de Ville, had been formulating his own version of a royal rescue, a draft of which he had sent to Provence in mid-October. Historians have disagreed about the relative contributions of these prominent figures to the Favras affair, which was a surface symptom of many undercurrents between the October Days and the royal family's flight to Varennes.

E. Cleray, *L'Affaire Favras (1789–1790)* (Paris, 1933); M. Lecoq, *La conspiration du Mis de Favras* (Paris, 1955); Roman d'Amat, "Favras, Thomas de Mahy, marquis de," *Dictionnaire de biographie française, sous la direction de Roman d'Amat*, vol. 9 (Paris, 1961).

P. H. Beik

Related entries: LAFAYETTE; PROVENCE.

FAYETTISTES, followers of the marquis de Lafayette in the formation of the Society of 1789. See SOCIETY OF 1789.

FEDERALISM (1793), propagandistic label for provincial dissatisfaction with the coup d'état of 31 May–2 June 1793 that led to revolts against the central government by more than 60 departments. Independent action by departmental governments led to the political, and later historical, myth that their opposition was based on a desire to alter the structure of national government. In fact, of all the principal actors in the revolt only F.-N.-L. Buzot had any federalist ideas, although several Jacobins had also spoken on occasion of decentralization. Departmental authorities universally declared themselves to be protectors of the National Convention, France's legitimate authority, against the illegal activities of the Paris mob, the Commune, and a few demagogues. While local authorities inevitably represented the wealthier merchant and guild groups who dominated provincial cities, federalism remained a political movement supported by popular societies and primary assemblies.

Federalist revolts occurred simultaneously with royalist rebellions in the Vendée and elsewhere but differed in motivation. Most federalists energetically combated counterrevolution, sometimes in cooperative efforts with the new Jacobin authorities. However, federalism inadvertently contributed to the counterrevolution by distracting the central government from military action against counterrevolutionaries. Additionally, royalists sometimes offered their support to federalists in the hope of weakening the Republic. Federalism failed, despite its overwhelming local strength, because it was both unwilling and unable to struggle against Paris. Departmental armies sent against Paris were generally small and ineffective, but even more important, federalists were willing to be convinced by the Jacobins that democracy was secure—hence, the rapid passage and ratification of the 1793 Constitution. Recognizing their republican loyalties, Jacobin representatives usually treated the federalists leniently when the revolt collapsed.

The most serious military encounter occurred at Lyon. Following months of tension here, moderates expelled Jacobin groups from the local government and resolved to raise a 10,000-man army to march on Paris. The Convention declared Lyon a rebel city in mid-July and ordered the population to leave within three days or face expropriation. The Lyonnais responded by arresting M.-J. Chalier, a former mayor and leader of the Jacobins. Federalist recruiting was nevertheless slow, and the departmental guard, commanded by a former member of the Royal Guards, comte de Précy, failed to stop a Parisian force under General F.-C. Kellermann, which laid siege to Lyon 8 August. After prolonged heavy bombardment, the city capitulated on 9 October. Victorious Jacobins demolished a few houses of federalist leaders and exacted heavy reprisals; some 2,000 deaths have been documented. Lyon's federalism was republican; its leaders remained loyal to the Republic and approved the 1793 Constitution. Nevertheless, royalist sentiments were common in the resisting army and were probably responsible for the stubbornness of the military effort.

Anti-Parisian sentiment predominated in Marseille after the Jacobins ousted the popular, radical, but unaffiliated mayor J.-R.-P. Mouraille, alarming moderate elements that rehabilitated him and closed the Maratist popular society. On 12 June, the city declared itself in a legal state of resistance and a week later resolved to ignore all decrees from the Convention and to raise an army to march on Paris. Simultaneously, the representatives on mission were arrested, and efforts were made to coordinate action with other southern centers, such as Toulon and Montpellier, Lyon being too distant for effective joint action. Marseille's departmental army captured Avignon; but the Parisian general, J.-F. Carteaux, recaptured it and laid siege to Marseille. An English frigate under Admiral S. Hood entered the harbor to offer help, provided that the Marseillais swore allegiance to Louis XVII. The local government refused, and fighting between royalists and republicans broke out in the streets, ending only when Carteaux took the city on 25 August. Some federalists and royalists escaped to Toulon, where the revolt continued until December under the protection of the English and Spanish fleets. Toulon accepted the English conditions.

The Jura also created an armed guard to march on Paris, together with surrounding departments such as the Doubs, but little actual fighting occurred. Jacobin representatives on mission, J. Bassal and A. Garnier de l'Aube, encouraged Jacobin groups without much interference from local authorities. Federalists were dismissed from office in late July and the 1793 Constitution approved.

The Gironde actively supported its expelled deputies. On 7 June, the department proclaimed itself in revolt and formed a Committee of Public Safety, which arrested the Convention-appointed representatives on mission. A small departmental force of 1,000 men was formed from the National Guard, and decrees passed by the Convention were ignored. But passage of the 1793 Constitution removed much of the energy of the revolt in Bordeaux. On 1 August the departmental force was dissolved. Nevertheless, a *société de la jeunesse bordelaise* protected the municipal authorities from Jacobin arrest, and newly arrived representatives on mission, C. Ysabeau and M.-A. Baudot, had to flee in mid-August. The city submitted to Parisian authority only in mid-September, and, finally, in mid-October a Parisian army of 5,000 men arrived, led by representatives of the Convention. A number of federalists were arrested, but not executed.

Brittany and Normandy similarly resisted Parisian authority systematically but not very effectively. A Central Assembly of Resistance to Oppression was formed in Caen with representatives from the Norman and Breton regions and formed a departmental guard commanded by General F. Wimpffen, commander in chief of the Army of the Côtes-de-Cherbourg. The arrival of Girondist deputies encouraged the federalists. By late June, Breton and Norman troops moved to Evreux, securing the area for the federalists. Marching toward Paris, they encountered Parisian troops at Brécourt, near Vernon. The 2,000 federalist troops under Count J. de Puisaye broke and fled after a brief skirmish. No serious effort was made to rally the troops, and the rebellion collapsed. Normandy calmly awaited R. Lindet, Jacobin representative on mission, who arrived on 3 August; he treated the rebels leniently. The Central Assembly retreated to Rennes along with Breton troops and disbanded. Lindet was soon joined by J.-B. Carrier who arrived in early September, and he reorganized the local authorities.

L. Dubreuil, "Evreux au temps du fédéralisme," *Révo. française* 88 (1925); A. Forrest, "The Revolution in Bordeaux: The Significance of the Federalist Movement of 1793," *Bord. et les îles brit.* (York, 1973–75); A. Goodwin, "The Federalist Movement in Caen," *Bull. of the J. Rylands Lib.* 42 (1960); J. Grall, "Le fédéralisme (Eure et Calvados)," *Bull. de la Soc. des Antiq. de Norm.* 55 (1961); P. Nicolle, "Le mouvement fédéraliste," *Ann. hist. de la Révo. française* 13–15 (1936–38); D. Stone, "La révolte fédéraliste à Rennes," *Ann. hist. de la Révo. française* 43 (1971); M. J. Sydenham, "The Republican Revolt of 1793," *Fr. Hist. Stud.* 12 (1981); H. Wallon, *La Révolution du 31 mai et le fédéralisme en 1793* (Paris, 1866).

D. Stone

Related entries: BUZOT; CAEN; CARRIER; CONSTITUTION OF 1793; JACOBINS; KELLERMANN; LINDET, R.; LYON; MARSEILLE; NATIONAL CONVENTION; PUISAYE; REPRESENTATIVES ON MISSION; TOULON VENDEE; WIMPFFEN; YSABEAU.

FEDERATION, a movement of the early Revolution that sought to express the new national unity in public festivals that reached their climax in the celebration in Paris on 14 July 1790. From the eighteenth century, the theme of federation attracted the attention of the *philosophes*; the *Encyclopédie* devoted twenty-three articles to it, along with numerous references. A new desire developed for a ceremony that was both moral and civic and, at the same time, removed from the cult of monarchy and the mysteries of the Catholic religion.

In the spring of 1789, in the face of the aristocratic plot, the extent of which was exaggerated by popular panic, the solidarity of men devoted to the regeneration of the kingdom found new bonds. When the old state broke down, new municipal governments and bourgeois guards, moved by a sense of belonging to the same community, tried to form federations by uniting in fraternal gatherings. These federations (the first of which took place in the town of Etoile near Valence on 29 November 1789) spread spontaneously from village to village, from city to city, even from province to province. In January 1790, 150 delegates from eighty towns, representing 150,000 united guardsmen, federated at Pontivy, where the National Guards of Brittany declared that, irrespective of the region each came from, they were all citizens of the same nation. Federations multiplied: at Dôle in February, at Lyon on 30 May, and at Strasbourg on 13 June, when patriots from Alsace, Lorraine, and Franche-Comté together planted on the Kehl bridge a tricolor flag bearing the inscription, "Here begins the country of Liberty." In growing, the movement changed its character; ideology supplanted the concern for security; instead of a means, federation became an end: the affirmation that a nation was born.

These gatherings, expressing a political ideal, led to the creation of unprecedented festivals; they served to translate, with solemnity and dignity, the new consciousness of the nation—"an amorphous mass of disunited people" in the words of H.-G. R. Mirabeau—of its independent existence, and of its true sovereignty. For example, at Lille on 1 May 1790, the National Guard, at the suggestion of participants from Gravelines and Dunkirk, addressed a proposal for federation to Valenciennes, Avesnes, Douai, Boulogne, Montreuil, and other towns. The preparations included symbolic decorations: the Lillois inscribed "the nation, the law, the king" on one side of their flag and "Liberty, Equality, or Death" on the other, while the inhabitants of Douai had recourse to Latin. On the Champ de Mars (in Paris) there were four colossal statues representing Justice, Prudence, Strength, and Tolerance, while a bas-relief depicted the oath of the Horatii; near the central altar rose a statue of liberty; perfume pans and a hundred incense burners carried by young children created a mystical atmosphere.

This movement, which generated a new fervor, necessarily had repercussions in Paris, but neither the king, who distrusted Revolutionary spontaneity, nor the Assembly, which feared uncontrolled activity that might allow counterrevolutionaries to display their strength, desired to sanction such provincial federations by a national ceremony on the Champ de Mars, as had been proposed by J.-S. Bailly, in the name of the Commune of Paris, on 5 June. Ultimately, at the suggestion of C.-M. Talleyrand, it was decided that only the National Guard would send delegates. The date chosen was both an anniversary and a symbol: 14 July 1790.

This commemorative festival was intended to express the joy and unanimity of the entire people. As in all other utopias, it should take place in an urban environment and avoid any discord; it was to bring together in a fraternal pact representatives from the eighty-three departments. S.-N.-H. Linguet, J.-F.

Blondel, and others long debated the choice of the site and the setting. Eventually, the Champ de Mars was selected since it fulfilled the necessary requirements that would, according to J.-J. Rousseau, allow the people to be both spectators and actors, while encouraging an atmosphere of full communication.

The transformation of the Field of Mars into the Field of Federation took the form of genuine festival, a joyful carnival, a lesson in civicism. One contemporary described it as a bustle of shoveling, digging, and hauling, with men and women working together in the joy of collaborating in the construction of a new world. It represented the struggle for liberty, the arch of triumph conjured up the image of combat, and the place arrangement symbolized the allegiance of the monarch to the people and the law. In the center an altar gave the appearance of dedication to new divinities—the fatherland and the constitution—and the setting was not dominated by a dais, since access to the Supreme Being was available to all. There had been plans to construct a lasting monument to leave to posterity a testimony of this event and to illustrate the triad of the nation, the law, and the king. Instead, the architects decided to have temporary structures and to trust in the formative influence of public space to inspire enthusiasm and the desire of emulation. The 14,000 armed *fédérés*, representing the National Guard, came to meet, by groups, at the Champ de Mars.

In the course of a long ceremony, the bishop of Autun, Talleyrand, celebrated Mass. The marquis de Lafayette, in the name of all the National Guardsmen, took an oath "to be forever faithful to the Nation, the Law, and the King, to support the Constitution, decreed by the National Assembly and accepted by the king, and remain united with all Frenchmen by the indissoluble bonds of Fraternity." The king swore to respect the constitution and was acclaimed by the crowd. A ball at the site of the Bastille prolonged the festivities in a rustic and symbolic atmosphere; amid *farandoles* the chant of the *ça ira* broke out, and its egalitarian resonance continually excited the crowds. The celebration of the federation at the time consecrated patriotic sentiment and attested the strength of loyalty to the monarchy.

This ceremony was supposed to inaugurate a cycle of annual celebrations. In fact, in the provinces it was repeated on 14 July 1791, but with a more martial emphasis. At Abbeville soldiers swore to "die rather than suffer invasion," and at Lille there were cries of "Long live the Nation, long live the Law" to the sound of military music. Since the flight of the king to Varennes, the atmosphere had changed. On 17 July in Paris, the Champ de Mars became the scene of a deadly confrontation.

In 1792, the sections of Paris along with provincial municipalities decided to overturn the king's veto by assembling a camp of 20,000 *fédérés* (local National Guardsmen called to federal service) around Paris. Following the disastrous military campaign and the events of 20 June 1792, the *fédérés* converged on Paris, bringing with them a more hostile attitude toward executive authority than that of the Parisians. To the strains of the *"Marseillaise,"* the fatherland was proclaimed to be "in danger." By 1793 federalism replaced federation as a major issue, as the federalist revolts threatened to split the Revolution into two camps. This situation was the complete opposite of the spirit of federation, as exemplified by 14 July 1790.

P. Arches, "Le premier projet de fédération nationale," *Ann. hist. de la Révo. française* 28 (1956), and "Une fédération locale. La confédération des Pyrénées (1789-1790). Travaux d'approche." *Bull. d'hist. econ. et soc. de la Révo.* (1971); J. Ehrard and P. Viallaneix, eds., *Les fêtes de la Révolution* (Paris, 1977); M. Ozouf, "Le Cortège et la ville: les itinéraires parisiens des fêtes révolutionnaires," *Ann.: Econ., soc., civ.* 26 (1971), and "Symboles et fonctions des âges dans les fêtes de l'époque révolutionnaire," *Ann. hist. de la Révo. française* 42 (1970); M. Sepet, *La chute de l'ancienne France: la Fédération* (Paris, 1896); P. Thore, "Fédérations et projets de fédérations dans la région toulousaine," *Ann. hist. de la Révo. française* 21 (1949); R. Toujas, "La genèse de l'idée de fédération nationale," *Ann. hist. de la Révo. française* 27 (1955).

L. Trenard

Related entries: FEDERALISM; FESTIVAL OF FEDERATION.

FEMINISM. See GOUGES.

FERSEN, HANS AXEL VON, COUNT (1755-1810), Swedish officer and diplomat. Born in Stockholm, the son of a prominent political leader, Fersen belonged to the high nobility and received a cosmopolitan upbringing. Following a grand tour on the Continent, during which he met the French royal family at Versailles, and service at the court of Gustavus III in Stockholm, he returned in 1779 to France, where he quickly gained the favor of Marie Antoinette. Between 1780 and 1783 he served as an aide to General J.-B.-D. Rochambeau with the French expeditionary force in America during the War of Independence. Returning to France, he became proprietary colonel of the Royal-Suédois Regiment and divided his time between French and Swedish service. That he and Marie Antoinette became deeply attached to each other is beyond question, although the exact nature of their relationship remains unclear, despite much controversy.

After participating in Gustavus III's Russian war in 1788, Fersen was in France at the beginning of the Revolution and was soon made Gustavus' secret agent for French affairs, without the knowledge of the Swedish ambassador, baron de Staël, who was suspected of Revolutionary sympathies. In 1791, Fersen arranged for the escape of the French royal family from the Tuileries on 20 June, and he drove them on the first lap of their perilous journey. When the flight attempt failed at Varennes, Fersen was forced to take refuge in Brussels, where he remained at the center of attempts to organize counterrevolutionary action, on behalf of both Gustavus III and of the captive French royal family. His voluminous correspondence from this period provides an invaluable source regarding the French and European counterrevolution.

The assassination of Gustavus III in March 1792 ended any immediate prospect of Sweden's involvement in a war against the Revolution, thereby undermining Fersen's diplomatic position. Following the outbreak of the War of the First

Coalition (1792–97), he nonetheless commissioned the drafting of the Brunswick Manifesto of 25 July 1792, in which the allies threatened vengeance if the French sought to resist their invasion or to harm the royal family. After Marie Antoinette's execution in October 1793, Fersen remained largely inactive in Germany until 1797, when he served as Swedish ambassador to the Congress of Rastadt, where he had a stormy confrontation with General N. Bonaparte.

In 1799, Fersen returned to Sweden, where he served in various official positions. During the War of the Third Coalition (1805–7), he accompanied Gustavus IV Adolphus as a diplomatic adviser on his German campaign in 1805–6 and sought to moderate the king's dangerous rashness. Staunch legitimist that he was, he played no part in the Swedish revolution that overthrew Gustavus IV Adolphus in 1809, although he served in the provisional government that followed. By 1810, however, he became the focus of unfounded popular suspicions of having poisoned the new crown prince, Karl August of Augustenburg; and this led to his assassination by a Stockholm mob on 20 June 1810.

H. A. Barton, *Count Hans Axel von Fersen* (Boston, 1975); R. M. Klinckowström, ed., *Le comte de Fersen et la cour de France*, 2 vols. (Paris, 1878); Alma Söderhjelm, *Fersen et Marie Antoinette* (Paris, 1930).

H. A. Barton

Related entries: BRUNSWICK MANIFESTO; COUNTERREVOLUTION; FIRST COALITION; GUSTAVUS III; MARIE ANTOINETTE; VARENNES.

FESTIVAL OF FEDERATION (*Fête de la Fédération*) (14 July 1790), celebration organized to commemorate the fall of the Bastille and to express French unity under the Revolution. Held on 14 July 1790, the first anniversary of the taking of the Bastille, the festival was for many people a joyous affair that seemed to sum up what had been achieved by the Revolution and to symbolize the inauguration of a new era for Frenchmen. The idea of an annual celebration of the capture of the Bastille had been proposed by C. Villette within a few days of the event, but by the time the National Assembly began to draw up plans early in the following June (1790), developments had taken place that gave the celebration a new dimension and significance.

The past year had seen local rallies occur throughout France in which the new National Guards and regular troops from neighboring villages and towns swore to defend the Revolution. The main ritual was the consecration of flags, but there had also been parades, dances, bonfires, banquets, and emotional embraces. Women, youths, and children played a conspicuous role. The word *fédération*, popularized by the American Revolution, was gradually applied to these ceremonies. Local rallies had led to district and regional ones. Inspired by these examples, the planners proposed a national federation in which delegates from all eighty-three new departments would swear allegiance to the emerging constitution. It would be a dramatic display of unity.

The planners were aware of previous festivals such as Olympic games, Roman spectacles, church processions, and royal celebrations of births, marriages, coronations, and victories, but they hoped to create a new kind of festival to represent the unprecedented nature of the Revolution. There would be no animal combats, gladiatorial contests, or processions of chained captives such as had marred Roman festivals. Above all, the festival would be staged on a scale surpassing even the largest ceremonies of the past.

Such a grandiose festival would require a special setting. Since no auditorium could accommodate the hundreds of thousands of citizens who would participate, a vast outdoor space was required. Eventually the Champ de Mars was selected because it was near the city, offered a large empty space, and also evoked memories of the field on which the fathers of the nation had once assembled. The planners drew on the proposals of various architects to transform this space into a vast amphitheater. This circus would not only accommodate the masses but would array them in an impressive fashion. "*Le plus beau de tous les spectacles d'une grande fête, c'est le peuple même qui la contemple*," asserted an anonymous pamphleteer.

Various architectural structures, mostly based on classical models, were erected to create an imposing setting for the ceremonies. A temporary bridge was erected across the Seine leading to a triumphal arch decorated with low reliefs celebrating not bloody military victories but rather the conquest of liberty, the constitution, and the Rights of Man. A throne for the citizen-king, as some now called Louis XVI, was set up on a dais at the far end of the circus. His new status was expressed by the fact that an identical seat for the president of the National Assembly was placed to the right of the king on exactly the same level. These two seats were flanked on either side by places for the deputies of the National Assembly and the municipal officials of Paris so that the king and the representatives of the people formed one body. At the center of the circus, a civic altar was erected embellished with reliefs celebrating the constitution and the benefits of the Revolution. The equal faces of the altar faced all of France and the four corners of the world. Broad steps on all sides signified that the altar was accessible to everyone. There was no canopy over this altar so that there would be no barrier between the Supreme Being and his minister. Places for the contingents of the regular army and the National Guards from throughout France, all with their standards, encircled the field. Space for the public was created on the surrounding slopes.

All classes participated in the construction of this impressive setting. Contemporary observers and later historians have recounted how preparation for the festival became a sort of communal festival itself. Families and corporations marched out to the Champ de Mars accompanied by fifes, drums, and flags. General Lafayette worked a few hours himself. At times the workers sang a new refrain that appeared at the time, "*Ça ira*" ("It'll all work out"), expressing the optimism of the day. Contemporary engravings show common folk and fashionable women working hectically to get the site ready in time. The authorities were anxious to curb and direct this popular fermentation.

It rained the day of the festival, but the ceremony proceeded as planned. A long cortege of National Guards from all over France, units of the regular army, municipal officials, and deputies of the National Assembly marched through Paris, across the pontoon bridge, and under the arch into the Champ de Mars where possibly 350,000 were congregated. The banners of each contingent were blessed in turn at the altar. Following this, C.-M. Talleyrand, leader of the new constitutional church, celebrated mass. Then the marquis de Lafayette led the people in an oath "to be faithful forever to the nation, the law, and the king." Finally, to underline the fact that he too was now subject to the law, Louis XVI himself swore to uphold the constitution. The festivities included dances, fireworks, civic banquets, and special theatrical presentations, which continued for days after the main event. The planners were anxious to embrace the whole country; orders went out for simultaneous celebrations in all the communes of France.

What was omitted from the festival was as significant as what was included. It is important to note that in a celebration planned for the anniversary of the fall of the Bastille, there was no reenactment of that event. One writer had proposed an attack on a model of the Bastille erected in the middle of the Champ de Mars. Another had proposed that the cortege should carry through the streets a model of the old prison to be placed on the altar. The king would then smash the model with a hammer as he took the oath to uphold the constitution. The planners rejected these proposals because they wished to minimize reminders of past conflicts in order to achieve unanimity.

Successive regimes at later stages of the Revolution would also attempt to use festivals as a means of creating unanimity and stabilizing the Revolution. The festival, at first spontaneous in its origins, became an instrument for attempted social control. But subsequent major festivals—the Festival of Unity and Indivisibility in August 1793, celebrating the new republican constitution; the Festival of the Supreme Being in June 1794, striving to consolidate the Robespierrist Republic of Virtue; and the whole cycle of festivals after 1795, intended to rally citizens around the Directory—all failed to unite Frenchmen around the various institutions and ideologies that appeared through the turbulent decade.

J. Ehrard and P. Vialleneix, eds., *Les fêtes de la Révolution: Colloque de Clermont-Ferrand* (Paris, 1977); M. Ozouf, *La fête révolutionnaire* (Paris, 1976); J. Tiersot, *Les fêtes et les chants de la Révolution* (Paris, 1908).

J. A. Leith

Related entries: "*CA IRA*"; CULT OF THE SUPREME BEING; DEPARTMENTS; FEDERATION.

FEUDALISM (*féodalité*), a term used to describe a complex of economic, social, and legal relationships of the Old Regime. Few terms have caused so much difficulty for the historian of France. Most medievalists feel that feudalism was moribund by the end of the twelfth century; for eighteenth-century legists, feudal law and the entire *complexum feudale* was the source of countless legal treatises and an increasing number of remunerative lawsuits; and many twentieth-century historians believe that *féodalité* is what the French Revolution was all about. Feudalism as a form of land tenure in return for military service, of course, died with the end of knight service, although the legal pretense was maintained as late as 1697 when Louis XIV promulgated, albeit for the last time, the obligation of knight service in the *ban* and *arrière ban* for three months within the frontiers of the kingdom and for forty days outside of them. But by the eighteenth century, the military contract was gone in law as well as in fact, and the feudal complex was largely assimilated into private property, though without losing the original terminology and including much of the personal dependence that the terms themselves conveyed. The landed properties of the seigneurs were described as fiefs, and the tenants (quitrenters) were called vassals or *justiciables* in the legal registers or rent rolls (*terriers*). In a few remote areas of the kingdom—in the Pyrenees and Auvergne, for example—a fief holder might still insist on paying faith and homage with the traditional pair of gloves to his overlord, but most of these obligations had been commuted to a token money payment made to the royal Bureau des Finances. In general, feudalism had atrophied at the upper level of society except as a badge of prestige.

The substance of feudalism in the eighteenth century was at the level of landlord and peasant or, more precisely, between *seigneur* and *censitaire*. The legal situation is perhaps best understood by recalling the long process of alienation of the lord's domain since the thirteenth century. Bit by bit, the landed nobility had yielded portions of its land to small holders on condition that they pay a perpetual quitrent or *cens* and perform other obligations to the seigneur. These *censitaires* had many of the attributes of modern property owners. They could buy, sell, exchange, divide, bequeath, and inherit the parcels they worked so long as they paid their annual *cens* and performed their obligations to the seigneur. Hence by the eve of the Revolution, feudalism became closely identified with a package of seigneurial rights or claims on a mass of semi-independent small owners. It has almost nothing to do with serfdom, which had virtually disappeared in eighteenth-century France.

What were the seigneurial rights, and how prevalent were they in French society? How much of a burden were they for the *censitaires*, both materially and psychologically? Much historical controversy turns on this question. For those who regard the French Revolution as fundamentally antiaristocratic, the attack on seigneurial rights represents an important part of that interpretation. For Marxist historians in particular, the feudal complex is an important link to their general view that the French Revolution marks the replacement of a feudal aristocracy by a rising bourgeoisie. An increasing number of social historians, such as the late A. Cobban in England and F. Furet in France, have questioned the importance of seigneurialism as a cause of the Revolution, claiming that it was a dying institution, that it was deeply imbedded in other property relations, and that the rhetoric of *féodalité* was far more significant than the actual burden of the system.

Consider first the variety of seigneurial rights. The economic claims might be classified into five major groupings: (1) annual, perpetual quitrents either in coin or in produce known as *cens*, *champarts*, *agrières*, and *terrages*; (2) mutation fees (*lods et ventes*, *rachats*) paid to the seigneur when a tenure changed hands by sale or inheritance; (3) seigneurial monopolies (*banalités*), the obligation to use only the seigneur's mill, oven, or wine press; (4) free labor services (*corvées*) usually limited to no more than three day's labor per annum for the seigneur; and (5) pasturage rights (*parcours*, *triage*), which often conflicted with village claims to communal pasturage. To these should be added occasional market tolls, as well as fishing and hunting rights. The seigneurs also had certain honorific rights, which they often prized more highly than their monetary claims. These included special privileges in the parish church, an honored place in village processions and fêtes, as well as the exclusive right to raise pigeons (the dove-cot was the rural mark of the seigneury). Finally, the seigneur had rights of justice—that is, he or his agent was the judge of a local court of the first instance, which, although rarely remunerative, was of strategic importance to the managing of a seigneury. In fact, recent research (Y. Castan and O. Hufton) is beginning to show that seigneurial justice was far from moribund in the policing of the French countryside. A final judgment on the impact of *féodalité* may have to await the conclusions of this research, though the *cahiers* as a whole condemned seigneurial justice as inefficient, negligent, and biased in favor of the seigneur's economic interests. One of the first acts of the National Assembly was to abolish seigneurial justice.

How burdensome materially were the seigneurial rights for the average small landholder? Considering the extremes of regional variation in France and the difficulty of calculating peasant income, the question may never be answered precisely. Given the inflation over five centuries, a *cens* in coin fixed since the thirteenth or even fifteenth century was a negligible sum by the eighteenth century. On the other hand, a seigneurial rent paid in produce had kept up with inflation, and in many regions of France, these produce rents claimed as much as a tenth of the gross harvest. When we remember that peasant plots probably averaged about five acres, this was a substantial portion, especially when added to the cost of seed, royal taxes, and the church tithe. Mutation fees were no less variable, but in Brittany, for example, they represented one-eighth of the price of sale. One-thirteenth, however, was more normal for the *lods et ventes*. The seigneurial utilities—mill, oven, press—were usually leased to the larger tenants, who collected a share of the produce, and peasant complaints focused on these renters and millers rather than on the monopoly as such. The free labor services (*corvées*) were limited to only a few days per year and were beginning to be commuted into money rents. Labor services—cartage, for example—were at-tached to regular farm leases. Seigneurial pasturage rights were another matter, especially in the east of France, where seigneurial claims often conflicted with those of the village communities. In these cases seigneur and village fought over the principal farm capital, the livestock, in the royal courts, and one has the distinct impression that conflicts of this kind were increasing in the late eighteenth century. Similar legal contests were waged over the rights to woodland.

What appears to have irritated the small holders in the last decades of the century was the increasing use of specialists in the feudal law by the seigneur. Although this *feudiste* was not unknown in the early years of the century, there is no doubt that the techniques of measuring, recording, and collecting seigneurial obligations improved greatly in the last years of the Old Regime. The seigneurial rent rolls (*terriers*) were much better kept and served to legitimize the claims of the seigneur and increase the efficiency of collection. The *feudiste* became a regular member of the seigneurial staff along with the judge, the attorney, and the steward. This tightening of the administration of the seigneury has often been regarded as part of a seigneurial reaction, a conscious and novel effort to make the seigneurial rights pay. It might be better regarded as part of a more general and impersonal improvement in the techniques of private estate management, which had parallels in the public administration as well.

M. Bloch was one of the first historians to apply the term *seigneurial reaction* to a broader process of domain building since the late fifteenth century. Bloch demonstrated how seigneurial rights could be used, along with more modern lease-holding techniques, to place the *censitaire* in debt to the seigneur, often leading to foreclosures and a reuniting of the peasant parcels to the domain, land still held directly by the seigneur. For example, *cens* arrears were permitted to accumulate for twenty-nine years, the legal limit after which they became extinct due to nonobservance. Demanded by the seigneur after twenty-eight years in one lump sum, these accumulated arrears were often too much for small holders to pay. As a result, peasants often had to give up their plot of land in what amounted to a foreclosure. Of course, the process of loans and foreclosures was not new in the countryside, but the use of *cens* arrears was one of the avenues open to a domain-building seigneur. The *retrait féodal* was another means. This right permitted a seigneur to intervene in any sale of land among his *censitaires* and buy the parcel himself at the same price. The exercise of this right was deeply resented by the peasantry.

During the Revolution, many village communities complained about these practices, which, like the seigneur's incursions into common meadow or wood, were often labeled manifestations of the *puissance féodale*. But it is not at all certain that these techniques were new or part of a consciously planned seigneurial reaction in the last years before the Revolution. It seems likely, however, that many villagers, no doubt encouraged by a surfeit of country lawyers, began to question the legitimacy of many seigneurial rights, not only as unjustified burdens on their livelihood but also as an affront to their dignity. The inconveniences of feudal rights had been increasingly discussed by historians, legists, publicists, and enlightened reformers for a half-century. But the peasants' new awareness of these inconveniences deserves closer attention and may be related to the recent efforts of the royal administration to elicit local participation in public affairs. For example, at what point did the villagers in Burgundy, a province of very cohesive village communities, become uncomfortable, even hostile, when they were labeled vassals in the new *terriers*, at a time when the royal government began employing the term *citizen* in official documents? Dignity counted for something in the resentment against seigneurial rights, more perhaps than the material deprivation, which, after all, had existed for centuries.

What was the stake of the larger landlords in the seigneurial or feudal system? Owning a seigneury with its various rights was a mark of prestige as important to the socially mobile merchant or *officier* as it was to a marquis or duke with four quarterings of noble pedigree. There is some evidence that the seigneurs of eighteenth-century France—and most of them were noble or would-be noble landlords—insisted on their seigneurial rights (honorific as well as fiscal) at a time when they were increasingly debated in public life and contested by the villagers themselves. In 1780 the marquise de Choiseul said that her *vassals* in Lorraine would find her charitable and reasonable, *except* when they challenged her rights. Dignity played a role at both ends of the social spectrum.

This is not to say that the seigneurial rights did not have material as well as psychological importance to those who exercised them. In a period of increasing grain prices after 1750, produce rents made up a substantial portion of the landed revenues of the seigneurs. As with the burden of the dues on the peasants, regional variation was extremely wide. Less than 10 percent around Toulouse, Bordeaux, and Le Mans, seigneurial dues represented as much as 33 percent of total landed incomes in Brittany, Burgundy, and Auvergne. It also appears that the revenues from the seigneurial rights represented a higher proportion of total landed income on large estates. However, the abolition of seigneurial dues and seigneurial justice, though a heavy blow to many families, did not destroy the landed nobility or notability as a social group. On the whole, their domainal properties were large enough to sustain them, even after the sale of *émigré* lands in the course of the Revolutionary decade.

What was the effect of the feudal system on French agricultural growth? First, considering the extent of absenteeism and urbanization among the larger land-lords, a major portion of the surplus landed income was spent on luxury goods in the capital or on dowries and not reinvested in farm improvements. Seigneurial income was a substantial portion of that surplus, and the abolition of seigneurial dues did redistribute some of that income to the smaller landowners. However, it seems doubtful that the small owners were able to reinvest much of that added income either. Much of the produce rents was simply consumed. Having more to eat was certainly a kind of progress for the peasant family, but it does not represent economic growth. True, morale counts for something among small peasant farmers, and the legal transformation of the *censitaire* into a *propriétaire* was an important advance in status and security for the country people. Never-theless, efforts to link the abolition of feudalism with capitalist agriculture by Marxist historians like A. Soboul, who postulate a higher reinvestment rate on the part of the small and middling peasant farmers after the Revolution, have not yet been supported by the evidence. There seems, for example, to have been very little increase in farm yields before 1840.

On the other hand, there is little doubt that seigneurial dues, especially as they became more carefully recorded in the *terriers* of the late eighteenth century, were an obstacle to changing crop courses. Calculating the percentage of the harvest was a meticulous and difficult task; changing crops necessitated not only a new calculation and a new rent roll but also finding equivalences. For example, what was the equivalent in grain of a *terrage* of one-tenth of the wine harvest? Moreover, mutation fees and the threat of the *retrait* surely lessened a desire to sell or exchange parcels in the interest of consolidation of the soil. As for market tolls and river rights, there can be no doubt that they hindered marketing. Similarly, hunting rights and the right to keep pigeons often damaged the peasants' crops.

Seigneurial claims of pasturage are a more complicated problem. Many seigneurs argued that by expanding the right of *triage*, they were consolidating the larger blocks of meadow for more rational livestock raising, at the expense of inefficient communal herds and flocks. In these cases, especially prominent in mountain areas and in Lorraine, the French seigneurs came closest to enclosure in the English sense. As a social question, however, the seigneurial claims to expanded pasturage were a source of countless law cases, with the village communities trying to protect their common pasturage, especially for the poor. In cases like this, the seigneurial system became so enmeshed with capitalist agriculture that it is difficult to sort out its specific economic consequences.

Combined with the other administrative techniques, seigneurial claims were not invariably anticapitalist or even anti-economic growth. In any case, there were so many structural and attitudinal obstacles to agricultural growth that it seems unwarranted to make seigneurialism a crucial obstacle to capitalist development. However, in a society where the distribution of agricultural wealth and income was becoming less and less equitable, where agricultural growth was very slow, and where there was increasing public concern about mendicity, public health, illiteracy, and national resources generally, the seigneurial system was more readily singled out by reformers as irrational, lacking utility, socially disruptive, and even oppressive. This is not to say that the attack on feudalism was only ideological or rhetorically inspired, although changing perceptions of *féodalité* must not be ignored. But more perhaps than either an economic burden on the peasant, which it surely was, or an irrational relic of the past, which the enlightened reformers said it was, the feudal *complexum* was, above all, a residue of local judicial power in the hands of private parties that the French bureaucratic state found cumbersome and ultimately expendable. Had there been no Revolution, it is reasonable to assume that the seigneurial system would have gone the way of so many other institutions of medieval and even Renaissance France: tolerated in name but sapped of substance. There is no small irony in the fact that the Revolutionary government destroyed the nomenclature of feudalism without rooting out all of its economic and psychological content. Perhaps no revolution, before the twentieth century at least, could do that.

It was fundamental for the new regime that private property be clearly defined as allodial, freehold tenure, liberated from the quasi-political overtones and personal dependencies that characterized the *censitaire-seigneur* relationship. Pruned of its feudal encumbrances—many reformers said vestiges—the land could serve as a basis for full (active) citizenship and the creation of an electorate of independent property owners. The large majority of the deputies in the National Assembly had no desire to weaken property rights, which were declared sacred in the Declaration of the Rights of Man and the Citizen; however, such a legalistic transformation of the status of the land could not be easily understood by the average French peasant. More than in the *cahiers*, the peasants made their feelings abundantly clear in the summer of 1789 when they directed their attacks against the rent rolls kept in the château towers. The famous decrees of 4 August responded to this rural revolution by declaring the feudal system abolished forever. The suppression of seigneurial justice presented no special problems since the entire judicial structure of France was being overhauled anyway. This was an important and permanent change, for it removed the basis for any special police or judicial power in the hands of the local seigneur. However, the Feudal Committee, composed overwhelmingly of legal-minded deputies and led by P.-A. Merlin de Douai, was reluctant to abolish seigneurial dues, which, after all, represented a capital investment and therefore private property. After six months of discussion—during which many peasants throughout France stopped paying their seigneurial dues altogether—the Feudal Committee made a legal distinction separating those rights that bore on the person of the vassal from those that issued, presumably, from an original contract (*une primitive concession de fonds*). The former were abolished, but the latter category, which embraced the vast majority of dues (*cens, champarts, terrages,* even the *banalités, triages, corvées,* and mutation fees), was retained, even legitimized by the new law of March 1790. True, the vassals were now authorized to purchase exemption by paying twenty to twenty-five times the annual charge. The dues were made *rachetables,* as reformers such as P.-F. Boncerf had proposed as early as 1776. But very few peasants could accumulate this much capital to free their land from seigneurial charges. Passive resistance, however, continued in many parts of the countryside, and the dues were very irregularly paid, especially after the summer of 1792 and the establishment of the First Republic. On 17 July 1793, the Convention apparently brought the law into line with peasant practice. "All dues formerly seigneurial, feudal rights whether fixed or casual . . . are suppressed without indemnity," read article 1 of this law. Title deeds were to be burned publicly, and those who refused to comply with the new law were threatened with prison sentences.

Yet even this dramatic act at the beginning of the Terror did not end all the economic burdens of seigneurialism. Nothing prevented a landlord from raising his rents to compensate for the loss of seigneurial dues, so that tenants and sharecroppers did not necessarily benefit from abolition. The freedom of contract in new leases or agreements between tenant and landlord were explicitly guaranteed by another decree in November 1793. The economic benefits of abolition, therefore, were reserved largely to those farmers (*censitaires*) who were not tenants and who had owned land before 1789. In France this represented an important proportion of the rural population, perhaps 5 million proprietors, small and middling, in a population of 30 million in 1800.

In psychological terms, *féodalité* held on into the next century, partly in the form of a latent apprehension that the old dues would reappear along with the hated church tithes but also as a real anxiety about a return to personal dependence and harassment by an increasingly vague feudal power. This phrase was employed in many village communities during the Revolution of 1848 and even into the late nineteenth century.

Over the centuries, then, feudalism had changed from a military contract to a system of land tenure with a component of local justice. Having served as the mainstay of the medieval political order and as a method of military defense, *féodalité* gradually came to mean simply seigneurial rights. A. de Tocqueville was one of the first authors to realize that the forms and apparatus of feudal law seemed more oppressive as its utility atrophied. By the eighteenth century, feudalism had become an adjunct to land tenure and was increasingly associated with noble privilege. The Revolution, of course, did not abolish tenant farming, and given the continued economic and political power of the landlords, many of the old dues were simply transformed into regular rents based on a modern lease contract. But feudalism as a legal system of personal dependence, backed by seigneurial justice, was ended by the Revolution. More important than its economic effects—abolition of seigneurial dues did not launch an agricultural revolution in France or end economic dependence of tenants on landlords—were the psychological consequences of freeing the land from seigneurial dependence. Personal dignity demanded that the language of feudalism be eradicated from all public use. Equally important, *féodalité* remained a symbol of rural oppression, a cry of alarm like *aristocrate*. Although devoid of specific institutional content, the return of feudalism could still evoke an emotional response in the French countryside as late as 1900. J. le Roy's well-known novel, *Jacquou le Croquant*, with its theme of feudal oppression, was written in 1890. Even the French Communist party found the spectre of feudalism still useful in its rural electoral campaigns in the mid-twentieth century.

F.-A. Aulard, *La Révolution française et le régime féodal* (Paris, 1919); M. Bloch, *Les caractères originaux de l'histoire rurale française* (Paris, 1931); A. Cobban, *The Social Interpretation of the French Revolution* (Cambridge, 1964); J. Q. C. Mackrell, *The Attack on Feudalism in Eighteenth-Century France* (London and Toronto, 1973); A. Soboul, "La Révolution française et la 'féodalité.' Notes sur le prélèvement féodal," *Rev. hist.* 240 (1968); P. Sagnac and P. Caron, eds., *Les comités des droits féodaux et de législation et l'abolition du régime seigneurial, 1789-93* (Paris, 1907).

R. Forster

Related entries: *BANALITE*; *CENS*; *CHAMPART*; COBBAN; *CORVEE*; 4 AUGUST 1789; PEASANTRY.

FEUILLANTS (1791-92), political club known officially as the Société des amis de la constitution séante aux Feuillants. Although the club itself was not established until the summer of 1791, it is now more generally associated with the followers of A. Du Port, A. Barnave, and A. de Lameth, or the Triumvirate, as they were called. Du Port and Barnave were both attorneys from wealthy backgrounds. Lameth was from an old noble family and had been a colonel in the army. They became friends and political allies during the summer of 1789 and remained virtually inseparable until the autumn of 1791. These young and talented politicians rapidly rose to prominence among the so-called patriots, particularly at the Jacobin club, where Barnave demonstrated his extraordinary oratorical abilities. In the winter of 1789–90, an intense rivalry developed between the Triumvirs and the marquis de Lafayette. At this stage, their differences were more personal than ideological, and historians have had difficulty deciding on what issues they disagreed. Nevertheless, tempers flared to such a degree that Lafayette and his supporters left the Jacobins during the first months of 1790 to begin their own club, the Society of 1789. A pamphlet war ensued, in which the Fayettists accused the Triumvirate of risking anarchy for their own personal ambition. But victory belonged to the three young deputies. While the Society of 1789 became little more than an aristocratic academy, the Triumvirate tightened its grip on the Jacobins.

The Triumvirs were revolutionaries in the sense of their deep commitment to the principles of 1789. They worked hard to create legislation in accordance with the new notions of national sovereignty and equal rights under the law. But while every Frenchman was recognized as a citizen of the nation and thereby entitled to certain rights, the Triumvirs believed that participation in political affairs ought to be restricted to property owners of the comfortable classes. In fact, the Triumvirs shared a genuine fear of those without property. In his speeches, Barnave claimed that the primary function of government was to protect the property owner from the poor. Lameth echoed these sentiments in his memoirs, suggesting that without strong government, the poor would naturally strike against property owners. By 1791 the Triumvirs believed that their Revolutionary days were almost behind them. With the codification and ratification of the constitution, the Revolution would be complete.

Such might have been the case had it not been for a burgeoning democratic movement, which was winning converts daily in various Parisian clubs, such as the Cercle Social and the Cordeliers. Led by M. Robespierre, J. Pétion, and H.-B. Grégoire in the Constituent Assembly, the democratic leaders attacked the Triumvirate for excluding millions of citizens from the political process. Already in March, Madame Roland astutely noted that Barnave "wants liberty but hates equality." While the democrats were ignored by the Assembly, they developed considerable influence in the Jacobin club. By June a large segment of Parisian public opinion had come to distrust the Constituent Assembly. The king's flight to Varennes transformed the democratic struggle into a united republican movement. The Triumvirs responded by initiating an immediate rapprochement with the Fayettists. On 22 June Barnave told the Constituent Assembly that whatever differences may have existed prior to the crisis, he and Lafayette were now completely united.

Although the Fayettists and the Triumvirs had shared concern over the radicals in April and May, their rapprochement in June marks the real beginning of the Feuillants. From now on they would be the party of order. The achievements of the Constituent Assembly were to be preserved, but the Revolution was to go no further. The king was to be completely forgiven and restored to his office with the qualification only that he accept the constitution. Most important, the Feuillants were to use all of their resources to oppose the democratic movement. Thus the origin of the Feuillants lay in opposition to the Parisian democratic movement, and the Feuillants were even willing to sacrifice liberty and equality for the restoration of law and order. As Barnave said, "For the masses of men, tranquillity is more necessary than liberty" (Michon, p. 327).

The beginning of the Feuillant Club came less than a month after the king's attempted flight, in reaction to developments at the Jacobin club. The Jacobins had increasingly become paralyzed between the Constituent Assembly and the popular clubs, and they were unable to have much influence over the course of events after the king's ill-fated departure. On 15 July, a huge deputation of radicals from the Cercle Social and the Cordeliers interrupted the evening session, demanding Jacobin support for a republican petition. It is not exactly clear what happened next, but one thing is certain: the more moderate members believed that the radicals had gained too much influence. The next day almost all of those Jacobins who were deputies in the Constituent Assembly had seceded and established their own Society of the Friends of the Constitution in the convent of the Feuillants.

The Feuillants immediately set about to eclipse the Jacobins and destroy the democratic movement. With a well-organized governmental propaganda machine at their disposal, they were able to win the allegiance of more than 400 affiliate societies. Attempts at reconciliation were rejected by the Triumvirs, who would have nothing more to do with radicals like Robespierre and J.-P. Brissot. More important, on 17 July martial law was declared in Paris, and Lafayette's troops broke up a republican demonstration at the Champ de Mars by killing several people. This "massacre" succeeded in defeating the democratic movement (at least until the summer of 1792). Some minor radical leaders were arrested, and others fled Paris, abandoning their clubs and presses.

By August the Feuillants were in a very strong position. The club wrote up statutes that were designed to keep out troublemakers. Dues were set at 16 *louis* per quarter, a sum only the wealthy could afford. Meetings were closed to the public, and the initiation of new members was carefully supervised. Deputies of the Constituent Assembly had to have the endorsement of six of their peers; nondeputies had to be supported by no fewer than thirty-six electors.

Club meetings were devoted to discussions about how to strengthen the proposed constitution so that the radicals could never again threaten the nation without breaking the law. The results of the deliberations were reflected in the Constituent Assembly, where the deputies dropped the infamous *marc d'argent*, thereby permitting all active citizens to vote. But this was only a sop to the democrats. In its place, they greatly stiffened the qualifications for public office, effectively restricting the pool of potential deputies to a relatively small number of wealthy men.

The Assembly also decreed that the constitution could not be changed for at least ten years, and only then with difficulty. In effect, the Feuillants were trying to stop the Revolution by ensuring that the leaders of the new regime would be drawn only from the propertied classes. Modern historians have generally criticized the Feuillants for these reactionary measures and have accused them of hyprocrisy in demanding that the radicals adhere to the constitution during the crisis of June–July 1791, while they themselves were quite willing to tamper with it afterward. G. Michon even claimed that the Triumvirate secretly wanted the Constituent Assembly to create a second chamber modeled after Britain's House of Lords, a view supported by A. de Lameth in his memoirs.

Although the Feuillants dominated political affairs during the summer of 1791, time was not on their side. Unlike the radicals, their basis of support was not popular; it rested on their control of the Constituent Assembly. When that body completed its work at the end of September, the Feuillant leaders left national office. A decree passed in the spring had excluded Constituent deputies from reelection. While 345 new Legislative Assembly deputies joined the Feuillants, their number included no leaders as gifted as the Triumvirate. Moreover, the 136 deputies who joined the Jacobins included some extraordinary politicians, particularly those from the Gironde. Through repeated Girondin attacks, the Feuillants were put on the defensive, and their position was weakened.

For that reason the Triumvirs had misgivings about the Feuillant Club and later believed its establishment to be a mistake. As Barnave put it, "A conservative club, or a club on the defensive, is a thing against nature" (Michon, p. 283). In other words, a club was most effective when it could harness public opinion and lobby for various legislative concerns. But the Feuillants were generally not interested in developing a popular constituency. By restricting membership to an elite core and holding sessions behind closed doors, the Feuillants left themselves wide open to vindictive rumors. Radical journalists charged that a counterrevolutionary conspiracy was being developed at the club. In 1790 the Triumvirs had attacked the Society of 1789 for degenerating into an aristocratic club after seceding from the Jacobins. Now the Jacobins were doing the same thing to the Feuillants.

During the fall of 1791, the Feuillants were further plagued by internal problems. First, the Triumvirs and the Fayettists renewed their rivalry. The Triumvirs moved closer to the court, whose hatred for Lafayette was well known. Lafayette began to negotiate with the Brissotins over a war policy. The Triumvirs were convinced that war would lead to anarchy and supply the radicals with excuses to topple the constitution. Second, when the Feuillants were finally pressured into opening their sessions to the public in December, radicals wrecked the meetings with constant interruptions from the gallery. Finally, between December 1791 and March 1792, the Feuillants had to move their club three times before finding a new home at the Cloître Saint-Honoré.

In fact, the group that met at the Cloître Saint-Honoré during the spring of 1792 was but a skeleton of what the Feuillants had been the previous summer. Barnave had retired to Grenoble, and Lameth was serving in the army. Only Du Port remained in Paris, and he rarely went to the club. Weak and disunited, the Feuillants were finally suppressed after the insurrection of 10 August 1792.

If the Feuillants made one major error, it was their almost blind support for the king after June 1791. Before the Varennes episode, they had maintained a healthy distance from the court. But fearing a democratic crusade more than an aristocratic reaction, the Feuillants placed all of their hopes on the good intentions of the king. In July 1791 Barnave had begun a secret correspondence with the queen. She duped the Feuillants into believing that the court was following their advice when it was actually embarking on its own independent course. The Feuillants were not counterrevolutionaries, but they allowed themselves to be used by those who had little sympathy for the principles of 1789.

F.-A. Aulard, ed., *La Société des Jacobins*, 6 vols. (Paris, 1889–97); E. Bradby, *The Life of Barnave*, 2 vols. (Oxford, 1915); A. de Lameth, *Histoire de l'Assembleé Constituante*, 2 vols. (Paris, 1828–29); C. McClelland, "The Lameths and Lafayette: The Politics of Moderation in the French Revolution" (Ph.D. dissertation, University of California, Berkeley, 1942); G. Michon, *Essai sur le parti Feuillant, Adrien Duport* (Paris, 1924).

G. Kates

Related entries: BARNAVE; CERCLE SOCIAL; CHAMP DE MARS "MASSACRE"; CORDELIERS CLUB; DU PORT; LAFAYETTE; LAMETH, A.; *MARC D'ARGENT*; ROLAND DE LA PLATIERE, M.-J.; SELF-DENYING ORDINANCE; SOCIETY OF 1789; 10 AUGUST 1792.

FEUILLE VILLAGEOISE, LA, newspaper (30 September 1790–2 August 1795). *La feuille villageoise* was one of the most original and successful of the Revolutionary papers. Its originality lies in the fact that it was written for villagers. Although it was not the first or the only Revolutionary paper for rural readers, it was the most widely read, the most concerned with politics, and had the longest existence of any other paper of its kind. It was the first successful paper for the peasants in French history. Appearing on 30 September 1790, it survived until 2 August 1795. Five years of continuous publication attests to its popularity. Claiming nearly 15,000 subscribers in its first year and nearly 11,000 subscribers and 200,000 or 300,000 readers in its second year, it was one of the most widely read papers during the Revolution.

La feuille villageoise was founded by J. Cérutti (1738–92). His collaborators were P. Grouvelle (1757–1806) and J.-P. Rabaut de Saint-Etienne (1743–93), who left before the end of the first year. When Cérutti died on 3 February 1792, Grouvelle picked P. Ginguené (1748–1816) as his coeditor. When Grouvelle was named ambassador to Denmark in July 1793, Ginguené became sole editor. The editors were all urban literati. There was no peasant among them.

La feuille villageoise was created because the editors realized that the Revolution could not succeed without peasant support. It had a dual purpose: to be a newspaper as well as to provide an education. Its aim was to educate the villagers in the laws, events, and discoveries that interested them. It promised to teach history and geography. It also disseminated information about agronomy and rural handicrafts. Although it was not part of the original program, religion, politics, the war, and letters to the editor took up more and more space.

The editors were aware that the rustics' lack of money, time, and education were obstacles to their paper's success. They kept the price low. *La feuille villageoise* was one of the cheapest papers, a major reason for its success. The editors tried to reach the peasants through the intermediary of a rural elite. They appealed to the rich landowners and farmers, curés, doctors, and other *campagnards* to procure an annual subscription. It was mailed to the local post office. Appearing in Paris on Thursday, it was to arrive by Sunday so the rural elite could read it publicly and comment on it to groups of peasants after Mass. In the absence of subscription lists, an analysis of letters indicates its success. The largest number of letters came from the clergy, which supports A. Mathiez's contention that it was the organ of the constitutional clergy. Next came the administrators, with the liberal professions and businessmen trailing behind. The Jacobins also helped. While there were a few letters from cultivators, none were from real peasants. This does not invalidate the conclusion that the editors were successful since they intended to reach the villagers indirectly. The paper had it greatest circulation in the Paris basin, Normandy, the center, and the Rhône valley; it was weak in the north and northeast, the southeast, the Massif Central, the Aquitaine basin, and the west.

The editors, moderates all, proclaimed themselves independent of the government, political factions, and the Jacobins. Disliked by the Right and Left, the paper's admirers were moderates and Girondins. It was critical of the Mountain, the Paris Commune, and the *sans-culottes*. If it survived the Terror, it was because it avoided attacking the Mountain, was silent about the purge of the Girondins, and supported the Revolutionary government.

One aim of the editors was to provide a civic education. Although the peasants suffered most under the Old Regime, they benefited most from the Revolution. If the editors wanted to transform the peasants into citizens, they sacrificed rural political participation to the need for an efficient administration. Opposed to democracy and a republic, after 10 August 1792, they became enthusiastic republicans but dubious democrats.

The paper played an important role in combating religious fanaticism and superstition. In the Year II it propagated a natural religion and a secular morality. Its anti-Christian propaganda was much appreciated by the Revolutionaries. The editors tried to get the peasants to pay their taxes by arguing that taxes were necessary for public services and prosperity and that liberty was cheaper than tyranny. They defended the *assignats*. Although they defended free circulation of grain, they became staunch defenders of the Law of the Maximum. Violations of this law shattered their rural idyll. But they were pleased that the Revolution had enriched the peasants, transformed them into landowners, and made them independent. Fearing the effects of luxury, they told the peasants to stay on the farm and preserve their simple mores, which inhibited peasant mobility while retarding urbanization and industrialization.

The editors were *citadins* with little concrete knowledge of agrarian realities. Lacking a coherent agrarian program, they defended the assemblies' work or deferred to experts. They were indifferent to demands for the complete suppression of the feudal dues. They usually defended the landowners against their farmers and *métayers*. They viewed the sale of national land strictly as a financial operation. They looked on the transfer of *émigré* land as a means to multiply small proprietors. They extolled their social ideal of the owner-occupier. They advocated freedom of cultivation, private property, enclosure, suppression of collective rights, division of the commons, diversification of crops, voluntary consolidation of holdings, and a market economy. There was a contradiction between their advocacy of small subsistence farms and their desire for the development of commercial agriculture to feed the cities.

M. Edelstein, *La feuille villageoise: Communication et modernisation dans les régions rurales pendant la Révolution* (Paris, 1977).

M. Edelstein

Related entries: LAW OF THE MAXIMUM; PEASANTRY.

FIRST COALITION (1793-97), alliance of European nations that fought against France in the first series of Revolutionary wars. The formation of the First Coalition was primarily the work of England in the months following its entry into the war against France (1 February 1793). The fighting had begun the previous spring when France declared war first on Austria and then on Prussia. This was followed by numerous lesser states entering the conflict against France. However, it was England that united the belligerents with formal agreements beginning with Russia on 25 March, followed by Sardinia, Spain, the Kingdom of the Two Sicilies, Prussia, Austria, Portugal, Baden, and the two Hesses. Hanover, which belonged to George III, was also part of the coalition. The coalition was held together loosely by the common enemy, France, for a common agreement or treaty was never signed. Furthermore, the war aims of the coalition were almost as numerous as the members. The two principal goals were to save

European civilization, as it was understood by the aristocracy, by destroying the French Revolution, and the restoration of the law of nations, which would require France to return conquered territories. These two rather general aims were superseded by more particular aims of the various members of the coalition. England coveted French colonial possessions; Prussia desired territory on the Rhine; Austria territory in Italy; and Russia, Prussia, and Austria a further partition of Poland.

The principal source of weakness within the coalition was the desire on the part of major continental powers to complete the partition of Poland. The full weight of the allied armies was never directed against France. The bulk of the Prussian and Russian armies and major portions of the Austrian army remained in eastern Europe in order to deal with Poland and to watch one another. Thus, although France was weak in 1793 and 1794, the armies of the First Coalition, with divided interests and a lack of unity of command, were unable to achieve victory. France was also divided in these years. Following the establishment of the Republic in September 1792 and the execution of Louis XVI (January 1793), the royalists, the nonjuring clergy, the moderate republicans, and other anti-Jacobin factions raised the standard of rebellion against the government in Paris. Thus, in addition to fighting the allies on all frontiers, the government of the Convention was also fighting Frenchmen in the west and the south of France.

Through the spring and summer of 1793, allied armies won victories on all fronts. They advanced into France from the north, the east, and the south. But their lack of coordination, cooperation, and will, coupled with the enormous determination of the French government and the sacrifices of the French people, turned the tide in favor of the French by the summer of 1794. The Battle of Fleurus, on 26 June 1794, marked the turning point. The French army took new heart from this victory, and the allied armies began to withdraw. The French reoccupied the Netherlands and the left bank of the Rhine. At the same time the rebellion in the south was brought under control. Marseille, Lyon, and Toulon submitted to the authority of Paris. By 1795 France was militarily stronger than it had been at any other time since the war had begun.

At the same time the First Coalition began to fall apart. The principal defection was on the part of Prussia. In order to concentrate its strength on the east to ensure an adequate share of Poland, Prussia opened negotiations with France before the end of 1794. Prussian military might in the east made it impossible for either Austria or Russia, which had never contributed substantially to the coalition, to concentrate meaningful armies in the west. The Pitt government in England, disgusted by the fact that its allies were using the large sums of money it had contributed to support armies against France to subdue the Poles, refused any further aid. The First Coalition collapsed under its own ineffectiveness and its greed for Polish lands. The end of the coalition was brought about militarily by General N. Bonaparte's successful Italian campaign in 1796–97. After Austria signed the treaty of Campoformio (1797), only England remained at war with France.

A. H. de Jomini, *Histoire des guerres de la Révolution*, vol. 15 (Paris, 1820-24); R. W. Phipps, *The Armies of the First French Republic and the Rise of the Marshals of Napoleon I*, 5 vols. (Oxford, 1926-39).

J. G. Gallaher

Related entries: BATTLE OF FLEURUS; BATTLE OF VALMY; FREDERICK WILLIAM II; PITT; POLAND; TREATY OF CAMPOFORMIO.

FIVE HUNDRED, COUNCIL OF. See COUNCIL OF FIVE HUNDRED.

FLANDERS REGIMENT, line regiment at Versailles during the October Days 1789. The Flanders Regiment was stationed at Douai when the deputies to the Estates General arrived at Versailles. The marquis de Lusignan, colonel of the regiment, was a deputy of the Second Estate, and the regiment generally maintained good discipline through the summer of 1789. An inspection report of 3 September 1789 contained nothing but praise for the soldiers and the regiment was recommended by the minister of war to the king for its discipline and reputation.

For a time Louis XVI considered leaving Versailles and putting distance between the royal family and the Revolutionaries; and when he decided to stay he authorized the commandant of the National Guard of Versailles to bring in reinforcements from the regular army to maintain law and order. The Flanders regiment was selected.

The regiment contained about 1,100 soldiers when it arrived in Versailles, nearly half of them from the Ile de France and neighboring provinces. Although there had been some desertion, the spirit of the regiment was still considered excellent. Upon arrival it took the new civic oath and surrendered its two cannon to the municipal authorities, but this did not allay the popular suspicion that the Flanders Regiment was involved in a conspiracy to help the king escape to Metz. On 1 October, when officers of the royal bodyguard gave a dinner for officers of the Flanders Regiment, some of the latter allegedly trampled on the tricolor cockade, which intensified feelings in Paris. Meanwhile the rank and file had begun to associate closely with local citizens, and when the crowd of Parisians marched to Versailles on 5 October to present their demands to the King, the Flanders Regiment, which was in formation, obviously sympathized with the populace. The men, not the officers, placed themselves at the disposal of the marquis de Lafayette, who was following the crowd with a contingent of the Paris National Guard.

The Flanders Regiment did not participate in the struggle between the mob and the royal bodyguard the next day, although many soldiers left their quarters to fraternize with the National Guard. About 300 of them helped to escort the king from Versailles to Paris, and over one hundred deserted, many of them later joining the paid companies of the Paris National Guard.

In 1791, the Flanders Regiment lost its illustrious name and became simply the 19th Regiment. Later, the first battalion was not amalgamated and the second became part of the 38th demi-brigade.

P. Daniel, *Abrégé de l'histoire de la milice françoise*, 2 vols. (Paris, 1783); J. Godechot, *The Taking of the Bastille: July 14, 1789* (New York, 1970); L. Gottschalk and M. Maddox, *Lafayette in the French Revolution, Through the October Days* (Chicago, 1969); G. Lefebvre, *The French Revolution*, vol. 1: *From its Origins to 1793* (London, 1962); S. F. Scott, *The Response of the Royal Army to the French Revolution: The Role and Development of the Line Army, 1787-93* (Oxford, 1978).

J. Luvaas

Related entry: OCTOBER DAYS.

FLESSELLES, JACQUES DE (1721–89), royal magistrate. After a long career as intendant (Moulins, 1762–65, Rennes, 1765–67, and Lyon, 1767–84), Flesselles served as an adviser to the administration of Parisian food supplies before accepting the post of *prévôt des marchands* (the royally appointed head of the municipal council of Paris) on 21 April 1789. He took part in the final preparations for the Estates General. On 25 June he seated twelve electors on his council, having refused a similar request on 27 May. Summoned to the Hôtel de Ville by the people on 13 July, he joined with a permanent committee of electors sworn to the defense of Paris against royal armies. He tried in vain to limit the distribution of arms to a select guard and incurred the wrath of the people for misleading them in their search for weapons on 14 July. Delegates from the sections charged him with treason. During the popular siege of the Bastille, Flesselles tried to negotiate a cease-fire with marquis de Launey but hesitated to order surrender or siege in the city's name. In the tumult at the Hôtel de Ville following the fall of the Bastille, a group from the Palais-Royal section pressed Flesselles to answer for his conduct. He was shot with a pistol as he set out on foot from the Hôtel de Ville. His head was paraded on a pike with that of Launey.

Dictionnaire de biographie française, ed. Roman d'Amat, vol. 79 (1976); H. Fréville, *Intendance de Bretagne* (Rennes, 1953); J. Michelet, *Histoire de la Révolution française*, critical edition by G. Walter (Paris, 1952).

T. M. Adams

Related entries: BASTILLE; LAUNEY.

FLEURUS, BATTLE OF. See BATTLE OF FLEURUS.

FLOREAL, COUP OF 22. See COUP OF 22 FLOREAL.

FLORIDABLANCA, DON JOSE MONINO Y REDONDO, CONDE DE (1728–1808), Spanish statesman. Floridablanca was born at Murcia in 1728, the son of a retired army officer. He received a good education, which he completed at the University of Salamanca, where he studied law. He entered the legal profession, earned a substantial reputation, and in 1766 entered the service of

King Charles III. The king was a reformer, an enlightened despot who sought to strengthen the royal government, reduce the power of corporate groups, such as the church and aristocracy, and improve the lot of the common people. Floridablanca was in complete accord with these ideas and was well versed in the writings of the French *philosophes* and physiocrats.

His first mission was to prepare the decree expelling the Jesuits from Spain in 1767. Five years later, he became ambassador to the Vatican, where he worked to secure Pope Clement XIV's suppression of the entire Jesuit order in 1773. For his success, he was ennobled by Charles and in 1776 became that monarch's first minister and secretary for foreign affairs. He subsequently worked closely with Charles on a wide range of internal reforms designed to stimulate economic activity and promote learning, science, and the fine arts, and Spain did experience a revival of commerce, industry, and learning during the last decades of the eighteenth century.

In foreign affairs, Floridablanca ended long-standing disputes with Portugal over rival claims in South America and put relations with Lisbon on a friendly basis. He also became involved in the American Revolution, although he was not anxious to assist the rebels in gaining their freedom from Britain because he feared the American example might stir up similar demands in Spain's colonies. He tried simply to keep the war going in order to prevent Britain from interfering with Spanish imperial interests. French pressure finally forced him to lead Spain into the conflict. Floridablanca demanded Gibraltar, Minorca, and Florida as compensation for Spanish participation. Unable to take Gibraltar, the Spanish had to satisfy themselves with Minorca and Florida and to accept American independence.

The advent of the French Revolution caused a major change in Spanish policy. Floridablanca believed strongly in enlightenment and enlightened despotism and disapproved of the changes taking place in France. He feared the spread of Revolutionary ideas to Spain and was concerned that a weakened monarchy would reduce the value of the Family Compact. In 1790, Spain, in fact, had to bow to British threats in the Nootka Sound dispute because the French National Assembly refused to permit Louis XVI to support Spain.

In 1791 Floridablanca sought to seal Spain from the contamination of French ideas; he forbade the importation of French books and newspapers. To preserve Louis XVI's throne, he also supported all efforts of the Austrian emperor to intimidate the Revolutionaries by threats of armed intervention.

Charles IV had ascended the Spanish throne in 1788; he was a reactionary who was easily influenced by court favorites. One of them, M. Godoy, persuaded the monarch to remove Floridablanca from office in 1792. Briefly imprisoned, Floridablanca was soon released and allowed to retire from public life. He remained in seclusion until 1808, when he was asked to become president of the central junta, which was leading the resistance to J. and N. Bonaparte. The junta, in the face of the advancing French armies, left Madrid for Seville, where Floridablanca died shortly after.

M. G. Alcázar, *El Conde de Floridablanca* (Madrid, 1920); R. Herr, *The Eighteenth Century Revolution in Spain* (Princeton, 1958); F. Rousseau, *Règne de Charles III d'Espagne (1759–1788)*, 2 vols. (Paris, 1907).

S. T. Ross

Related entries: DECLARATION OF PILLNITZ; NOOTKA SOUND CONTROVERSY.

FORSTER, JOHANN GEORG ADAM (1754-94), German revolutionary. Georg Forster was born in the Polish village of Nassenhuben, near Gdansk on 26 November 1754. His father, J. R. Forster, descended from British immigrants, was a clergyman who left his ministry to become an amateur scientist of some note. After living briefly in Russia among German colonists at Sartov on the Volga, the family settled in England in 1766. The father and son accompanied Captain J. Cook on his second voyage around the world (1772–75). Their subsequent travel account—*A Voyage Round the World* (London, 1777) and *Johann Reinhold Forsters und Georg Forsters Reise um die Welt* (Berlin, 1779)—established young Forster's reputation in the German Enlightenment and widely influenced this literary genre.

Forster later held a professorship of natural sciences at the Collegium Carolinum in Kassel from 1778 to 1784 and between 1784 and 1787 at the Polish University of Vilna (Lithuania). In 1788, with his wife, Therese, he moved to Mainz where he assumed the post of university librarian, a position that allowed him ample time for his literary work.

In 1789 Forster hailed the French Revolution as a nonviolent and enlightened approach to necessary change, although he did not commit himself as enthusiastically as many other German intellectuals. In 1790 he accompanied young A. von Humboldt, as his mentor, on a trip to England and subsequently published *Ansichten vom Niederrhein, von Brabant, Flandern, Holland, England und Frankreich*, his most important literary accomplishment. This work, published in Paris in the Year III, condemned despotism and insisted on freedom for citizens, although still within the terms of the humanitarian Enlightenment. It was only in 1791 while reviewing and refuting E. Burke's well-known pamphlet that he became a fervent partisan of the Revolution; he then told his father-in-law, "*Ja, es gibt Fehler und Gebrechen auf beiden Seiten. Aber wer Vernunft und Gefühl hat und nicht wählen kann, den bedaure ich*" ("Yes, there are defects and failures on both sides. But I pity whoever has reason and feeling and cannot choose").

After the war began in 1792, as the French approached Mainz, the elector-archbishop fled abroad. A.-P. Custine's army occupied the city on 21 October without resistance, and local republicans with the assistance of German refugees established a Jacobin club two days later. Although Forster initially was reticent toward the *clubbistes*, he joined their ranks on 5 November and rapidly emerged as their most prominent figure, serving as club chairman in January and March 1793. On 13 January he planted the liberty tree of Mainz. He became thoroughly absorbed by political duties, and, as vice-president of the new administration, he campaigned in the elections for the German Rhenish National Convention, which convened on 17 March with Forster as vice-president. As one of the fathers of the Republic of Mainz, Forster carried the motion for its reunion with the greater French Republic on 21 March and subsequently led the deputation to Paris that requested approval for the incorporation of Mainz from the National Convention, which agreed. Shortly after, Mainz was besieged and capitulated, and citizen Forster was forced to remain in Paris. Denounced as a traitor to the nation by most of his former admirers in Germany, including F. Schiller, and abandoned by his wife, he devoted himself to writing and performing diplomatic missions for the French government. Already seriously ill and increasingly distrusted by French Revolutionaries as the foreign war wore on, Forster suffered a lonely death in Paris at the age of thirty-nine, on 10 January 1794.

For a long time, rising German nationalism retained the image of an isolated Forster as a "bad German." In fact, this very talented and diversified intellectual was an idealistic cosmopolitan of the Enlightenment, a soft-hearted deist and sentimental bourgeois philosopher whose liberal and democratic intentions were free of personal ambition. He was impressed by his experiences in Britain and, as an inhabitant of the Franco-German borderlands, he fully accepted the French Revolution only as the result of a long and complex process. At first he preferred the constitutionalists like H.-G.R. Mirabeau; in 1792–93 he sympathized with the Girondins, who represented for him the Revolution in power; and his changing position during the Terror is still a matter of debate. In the end, he recognized the sheer necessity of a strong Jacobin Revolutionary government, with its inevitable hardships, in order to defend the Republic against its mortal enemies. He respected M. Robespierre but remained closer to the Dantonists and was disturbed by so much violence and bloodshed. Yet he never lost his faith in the ultimate victory of the Revolution, even if it did not fulfill all of his dreams. In his "last letter to Therese" on 4 January 1794 he wrote, *"Wir haben überall ganz löwenmassig gesiegt."* ("On the whole we have conquered like lions.")

H. Fiedler, ed., *Georg Forsters Bibliographie, 1767 bis 1970* (Berlin, 1971); *Georg Forster, Werke* (Berlin, 1958–); K. Kersten, *Ein europäischer Revolutionär: Georg Forster, 1754–1794* (Berlin, 1921); G. Steiner, ed., *Georg Forster: Werke*, 4 vols. (Leipzig, 1971), and G. Steiner, *Georg Forster* (Stuttgart, 1977); L. Uhlig, *Georg Forster: Einheit und Mannigfaltigkeit in seiner geistigen Welt* (Tübingen, 1965).

W. Markov

Related entries: BURKE; CUSTINE; ENLIGHTENMENT; GIRONDINS.

FOUCHE, JOSEPH (1763-1820), duke of Otranto, terrorist and minister of police. Born in Nantes, Fouché was educated by the Oratorians, although he never took full holy orders. He taught physics and mathematics in several of their schools, including that in Paris. At Arras, in the literary circle known as the Rosati, he met M. Robespierre and was exposed to the rising demands for social change.

After the outbreak of the Revolution, Fouché became active in the club at Nantes known as the Friends of the Constitution, and in August 1792 he was elected as a deputy from the Loire-Inférieure to the National Convention. He married the daughter of a well-to-do merchant of Nantes and, following his election, submitted a strong memorial to the Convention opposing the abolition of the slave trade. Nevertheless, his increasingly radical views placed him among the regicides voting in January 1793 for the execution of Louis XVI. He soon won notoriety as a representative on mission from the Convention, working ruthlessly to repress the Vendée revolts and later the rebellion at Lyon, where 1,667 death sentences were imposed. In the Nièvre he sought to help the peasants by urging the redistribution of wealth from the rich to the poor. His antireligious views, which had become extreme, led him to ransack churches and send the spoils to the treasury. At Nevers he proposed that priests should marry and ordered signs at the entrances of all cemeteries proclaiming death to be an eternal slumber. Fouché published a number of pamphlets in 1793, the chief being *Réflexions sur le jugement de Louis Capet, Réflexions sur l'éducation publique,* and *Rapport et projet de loi relatif aux collèges.*

In the Convention, Fouché, although an avowed terrorist, opposed the increasingly autocratic Robespierre who advocated the new Cult of the Supreme Being, while Fouché's views embraced atheism. Early in July 1794, Robespierre had him dismissed from the powerful Paris Jacobin club. Along with J.-L. Tallien, Fouché now took the lead in effecting the overthrow and execution of Robespierre on 9 and 10 Thermidor (27–28 July). Continued disagreements over policy in the Convention led Tallien and F.-A. Boissy d'Anglas to attack and imprison him. He was released at the time of the proclamation of the new constitution in September 1795.

A member of neither assembly under the new Directory, Fouché in 1797 won a lucrative post as supplier of military materials to the government. Evidence suggests that he entered into secret negotiations with the reviving royalists, of whom there were many, but in the end he turned to the other extreme, the Jacobins, and to P. Barras, the most powerful of the directors. He helped Barras during the coup of Fructidor (September 1797) and, after its success, was quickly appointed minister to the Cisalpine Republic at Milan in order to secure the ratification there of the newly French-imposed constitution. This he did, but he was soon removed for being too high-handed. By early 1799 he was back in Paris and then served very briefly as minister to the Hague.

During the tense summer of 1799, E.-J. Sieyès, by now the leading figure in the Directory, appointed Fouché minister of police (20 July). In this capacity he proved himself active, subtle, and unscrupulous. Many suspected counter-revolutionary newspapers were banned and sixty-eight journalists deported for holding disloyal views. On 13 August Fouché closed the Paris Jacobin club, a center for radical criticism of the regime. Royalists and Jacobins were ruthlessly prosecuted whenever he unearthed their criticisms. In a report of 4 October, he informed the directors that the majority of Frenchmen favored the Republic, a conclusion readily accepted by the historian F.-A. Aulard.

Fouché was among those, including P. Barras and C.-M. Talleyrand, who, in 1799, were seeking a general to take over the tottering Directory. On N. Bonaparte's return from Egypt in mid-October, Fouché quickly and secretly joined forces with him, supplying much information from the police records and working more closely with Sieyès than with Barras, whom he considered a spent force. His principal and valuable role during the actual two days of the Brumaire coup (9-10 November) was to remain in Paris away from the drama being enacted at Saint Cloud and to be ready for any dangerous eventuality arising from the conspiracy. He overstates his role in his dubious memoirs, as does his principal biographer, L. Madelin. After the successful coup, Bonaparte understandably retained him as minister of police during the first three years of the Consulate (1799-1802). When he did temporarily leave office, he took with him a large portion of the secret funds he had accumulated.

Fouché ably employed the ruthless skills he had developed during the Revolution in his intermittent service of Napoleon. When the Ministry of Police became part of the Ministry of Justice in 1802, Fouché was made a senator. He was reappointed to his old post in 1804 and served later as minister of the interior. In 1809 he became duke of Otranto. With much reason, however, Napoleon grew increasingly suspicious of Fouché, who had drawn close to Talleyrand. When the emperor was engaged in the Austrian campaign of 1809 and the British threatened Antwerp, Fouché on his own initiative mobilized 60,000 National Guards, proclaiming that the presence of Napoleon was unnecessary to repulse the enemy. He also gave a military command to J.-B. Bernadotte, whom Napoleon distrusted, and secretly started unavailing peace overtures to Britain. In the light of all this, Fouché was dismissed in June 1810, subsequently holding the two undistinguished posts of governor of Rome (1810) and of the Illyrian Provinces (1813).

Napoleon never fully trusted Fouché and is reported to have said at Saint-Helena that he should have had him shot. Fouché was similarly unsuccessful in obtaining the permanent favor of the restored Bourbons in 1814 and 1815, although he did serve a brief term as ambassador to Dresden. He retired to Prague and then to Trieste, where he died on 25 December 1820.

Fouché was a ruthlessly efficient bureaucrat, the pioneer of the police type familiar in the modern world. What distinguishes him is his endless capacity to intrigue on behalf of—or against—royalists, Jacobins, or even Bonapartists as the occasion demanded. With his unexpressive, dead-white countenance and his eerie, lackluster eyes, he had few friends. He carried into the Napoleonic empire what he had learned in the Revolutionary decade, mingling this with newer policies inescapable in a modern age of warfare and conquest.

J. Fouché, *Mémoires*, ed. L. Madelin (Paris, 1945) (not actually written by Fouché but compiled in 1824 from his notes and papers); L. Madelin, *Fouché*, 2 vols. (Paris,

1901, latest reprint, 1955); H. A. Wallon, *Les Représentants du peuple en mission et la justice révolutionnaire dans les départements en l'an II (1793-1794)*, 5 vols. (Paris, 1889–90); S. Zweig, *Joseph Fouché: The Portrait of a Politician* (New York, 1930).

E. J. Knapton

Related entries: CISALPINE REPUBLIC; COUP OF 18 BRUMAIRE; COUP OF 18 FRUCTIDOR YEAR V; CULT OF THE SUPREME BEING; FEDERALISM; 9 THEMIDOR YEAR II; VENDEE.

FOUQUIER-TINVILLE, ANTOINE-QUENTIN (1746-95), public prosecutor. In 1793, as a means of avoiding the type of massacres that had occurred when mobs took the law into their own hands, the National Convention created the Revolutionary Tribunal and named Fouquier-Tinville public prosecutor. Born near Saint-Quentin, he had spent years in a marginal existence as a lawyer in Paris, but the history of Fouquier-Tinville from 1793 became essentially the history of the Revolutionary Tribunal of the Terror.

The tribunal's early trials, usually of *émigrés* who had returned to France, an illegal act punishable by death, were apparently conducted fairly in terms of presentation of evidence, interrogation, and defense procedures. However, when the Revolutionists, frantic over the desertion of C. Dumouriez, forced the executions of military figures with proven close ties with the general, the awesome machinery of Revolutionary justice had begun to operate. Those who paid with their heads ranged from C. Corday, J.-P. Marat's assassin, to the pitiful servant C. Clère who, in a drunken stupor, had babbled nonsense that was construed as counterrevolutionary.

The demand for a trial of Marie Antoinette showed the acceleration of Revolutionary fervor and its impact on the tribunal. Fouquier indicated that if he received sufficient evidence, he would do what was expected of him. The conduct of the trial illustrated the deterioration of court proceedings. Even so, at the trial of twenty-one Girondins in October 1793, the forms were observed by Fouquier. The prolonged proceedings irritated extremists like J.-R. Hébert, who complained in the Convention against the slowness of the tribunal, declaring that the nation had already judged those accused. Fouquier's apparent reluctance to abandon legal procedures prompted the Convention to decree that in any case, if the jury believed itself well enough informed of the facts after three days of trial, it could terminate proceedings. In the Girondins' case, some of the jury stated they had not had enough time to form an opinion. Fouquier called a recess, addressed the jury privately, and evidently communicated the Convention's intent. When the court reconvened, the jury announced it had heard enough evidence and the trial ended without further testimony being given. Despite the multiplicity of charges, the number of defendants, and degrees of complicity or guilt, the jury, after three hours of deliberation, found the Girondins collectively guilty.

The shortcut to the guillotine had begun, and following the Girondins to the scaffold were such figures as Madame Roland, P. Egalité, A. Chenier, and Madame du Barry. The charges of depravity and licentiousness against the mistress of the beheaded king's grandfather indicated a puritanism of the Revolutionary regime, illustrated further by the prosecution of prostitutes who, as alleged tools of despotism, were accused of having enslaved citizens in debauchery and aided conspiracies against the state by corrupting society, sufficient enough charges to invoke the death penalty.

Clerics were prosecuted by Fouquier with equal vigor. Those who had refused to swear the constitutional oath (nonjuring clergy) were automatically accused of being counterrevolutionaries. Even clergy who had sworn the oath (juring) did not find their jeopardy removed; they were accused of dissembling or of such things as nonparticipation in Revolutionary activities. Citizens who aided nonjuring clergy, or who resisted or maligned the constitutional clergy, were similarly prosecuted. By the end of 1793, Revolutionary justice began to reach into the ranks of former constitutionalists and Feuillants, such as A. Barnave and J.-S. Bailly, guillotining most of them.

In 1794 Fouquier was given a double task: to eliminate the extremists (*enragés, ultras*) led by Hébert and the moderates (*indulgents, modérés*) whose leader was G.-J. Danton. Hébert and his associates were tried and executed. The trial of Danton and his group (among them L.-C.-S. Desmoulins, Fouquier's distant relative and early benefactor) showed the further erosion of the judicial process. Sixteen Dantonists were tried simultaneously with a group that included P.-F. Fabre d'Eglantine, charged with speculation and manipulation of the stock of the India Company. When Danton's outbursts aroused public sympathy, Fouquier foresaw difficulty; bound, as always, by the rules, he passed the problem to the Convention where L. Saint-Just manipulated a vote allowing the tribunal to suppress testimony if it troubled the proceedings. Armed with the decree, Fouquier did just that, and Danton and the other accused were guillotined.

The Law of 22 Prairial emerged from the Convention and proved to be a most effective weapon of the Terror. It provided among other items that no authorization of the assembly was necessary to bring its own members before the Revolutionary Tribunal. Treason was defined in such broad terms that anyone could be charged with that crime. The law also stated that the tribunal had no obligation to hear witnesses or allow attorneys for the defense and that the accused need not be present at the trial. Death was the only penalty provided. Mass trials now included both figures of importance and ordinary criminals, considered as worthless rabble by the Terror, who had been crowding the Paris prisons.

With the events of Thermidor came the trial of M. Robespierre, Saint-Just, and their coterie; those who had praised and supported them now called for their heads. Fouquier, going through whatever formalities remained, produced what he knew was wanted, and the architects of the Terror followed the multitude of their victims to the guillotine. However, along with the leaders, one of their chief instruments, the public prosecutor himself, would have to pay for his share in their excesses.

At first, the Convention hesitated in ordering his trial since many of its members had given him the legal tools to achieve their purposes, but finally his arrest was ordered. Addressing the Convention, Fouquier used his oft-repeated argument that he had merely been obeying the law and acting as a public official, but his defense was rejected and he was returned to prison.

The charges against Fouquier were directed at three areas: first, his crimes, such as pushing the Tribunal into hasty judgments and having it condemn innocent people, were listed; his association with the men of the Terror was the second area; and his social character (violence, vindictiveness) was the third. In April 1795 the final phase of the trial began before a renewed Revolutionary Tribunal. After having granted to Fouquier processes and rights denied the accused in his court, the case was turned over to the jury, which, on 5 May, found him guilty and sentenced him to death.

The result was not unexpected since it was mainly a trial of the tribunal of the Terror, just as the trial of the king had been more the trial of the institution of the monarchy than of the king as a person. Fouquier's last letter, on the night of his execution, showed him unrepentant, repeating that he had acted under orders. At his execution on 6 May 1795, the crowd cheered when the executioner raised the bloody head of Fouquier-Tinville at each corner of the scaffold.

C. Bertin, *Les grands procès de l'histoire de France*, tome II (Paris, 1966); J. Castelnau, *Fouquier-Tinville* (Paris, 1957); A. Dunoyer, *The Public Prosecutor of the Terror* (London, 1914); P. Labracherie, *Fouquier-Tinville, Accusateur Public* (Paris, 1961); J. Whitham, *Men and Women of the French Revolution* (New York, repr. 1968).

R. L. Carol

Related entries: COMMITTEE OF PUBLIC SAFETY; DUMOURIEZ; *ENRAGES*; GIRONDINS; HEBERT; INDULGENTS; LAW OF 22 PRAIRIAL; MARIE ANTOINETTE; REVOLUTIONARY TRIBUNAL.

4 AUGUST 1789, session of the National Assembly that abolished feudalism. *Feudalism* was the term used in eighteenth-century France to describe the traditional dues and services a peasant owed his manorial lord. Reformers sometimes applied the term more generally to the entire system of privilege characteristic of the Old Regime. On the night of 4 August, the National Assembly decreed an end to feudalism in both these senses, an event ever since regarded as one of the most glorious moments of the Revolution.

The decree was a direct consequence of the peasant insurrections against tithes, taxes, and seigneurial dues that spread through much of France in the spring and summer of 1789. There was little sympathy at Versailles for the peasants' actions since the landowning middle class had almost as much to lose from the disturbances as did the privileged orders. But the radical minority in the National Assembly known as the patriot party feared that repression by the Assembly might undermine popular support for the Revolution and increase the power of the king and his army. The patriots preferred a legislative remedy for the peasant grievances, a course that might calm discontent and rescue at least some threatened property rights.

In the days preceding 4 August, the Assembly was engaged in debate over the principles of the new constitution. The patriots sought to abolish all distinctions between privileged and unprivileged, but they lacked majority support. However, the crisis created by the peasant revolts now presented the opportunity for a clever parliamentary maneuver. A committee of about 100 deputies (probably the Breton Club) resolved to destroy all the privileges of classes, provinces, towns, and corporations. This was to be accomplished through an appeal by members of the liberal aristocracy to the patriotism and humanity of their colleagues, but it would likely have failed except for the climate of fear created at Versailles by exaggerated reports of looting and bloodshed in the provinces.

The evening session of the Assembly on 4 August began with the reading of a proposed decree to guarantee "the sacred rights of property and personal security" by ordering the enforcement of all existing laws. The vicomte de Noailles rose to speak. He invited the Assembly instead to examine the just grievances of the peasants and to respond by relieving them of the burden of feudal dues. Then the duc d'Aiguillon broadened the debate with an attack on the tax exemptions and other privileges enjoyed by corporations, towns, and some individuals. Speaker after speaker came forward and denounced the horrors, vexations, and inequities of feudalism. Each either offered to sacrifice his own privileges or proposed reforms that applied to others. Both opponents and partisans of the reforms later commented on the enthusiasm and spirit of selflessness that had gripped the Assembly that night. They used words like *drunkenness* and *delirium* to describe the mood. Unfortunately, the only surviving minutes of the historic session were edited to give an impression of unanimity. Other sources indicate some feeble resistance to the rush of events, with dissenting voices, by these accounts, shouted down. In any case, the confusion of the proceedings in a noisy and excited hall made it impossible to keep a detailed or accurate record. When the session finally broke up at 2 A.M., the exhausted secretaries could only list the results. These included the suppression of court pensions, venal offices, tithes in kind, and all municipal, provincial, and corporate immunities, tax exemptions, and privileges; provision for the abolition or redemption of seigneurial dues and rights; a reform of the guild system; and equality of taxation. Louis XVI was proclaimed Restorer of French Liberty.

In the following days (6–11 August), the Assembly turned to an article-by-article discussion of a decree to put its decisions into effect. Counterattacks by the privileged were rarely successful. The clergy, foolhardy enough to challenge the abolition of tithes in kind, was stripped of all its tithes. Most conservatives were reluctant to risk unpopularity by opposing the decree and counted on the king to refuse his acceptance. The Assembly presented the final decree to Louis XVI on 13 August and celebrated it with a Te Deum. The decree began: "The feudal regime is entirely abolished. . .''; but this was an exaggeration. Because of the deputies' afterthoughts, certain measures voted on 4 August, most notably the reform of the guilds, had simply disappeared from the legislation. The effect of other measures, principally those relating to seigneurial dues, had been diluted. And yet the king, as anticipated, withheld his approval. On the grounds that the decree was a constitutional measure and therefore not subject to royal veto, on 19 September the Assembly invited the king to promulgate it without delay. Louis XVI would consent only to publish it. The October Days forced him to change his mind and to promulgate the decree by letters patent on 3 November 1789.

The most important articles in the decree of 5–11 August dealt with seigneurial dues and rights. These introduced a distinction between feudal dues and rights, reputedly derived from the personal servitude of a vassal, and those dues that fell on land and might therefore be considered a legitimate form of property. The former were abolished without compensation, but the peasantry had to redeem the latter in cash. The conservatism of the Committee on Feudal Rights, entrusted with interpreting the legislation, was soon apparent. The decree of 15 March 1790 limited abolition to a relatively restricted list of dues, while the decrees of 3 and 9 May 1790 made the procedure for redemption of the remainder complicated and, at twenty to twenty-five times the annual value of the dues, far too expensive for most peasants. The peasantry eventually freed itself only by continued protest and stubborn refusal to pay anything. The Legislative Assembly suppressed all dues that could not be justified by an original title-deed on 25 August 1792, and the National Convention finally abolished all dues without exception on 17 July 1793. Even so, it has been argued that many dues were simply incorporated into higher rents and therefore survived, at least for tenants, in another form. But whatever the shortcomings of the decree of 5–11 August, it altered forever social and economic relations in the countryside. As for its broader impact, the decree was the first step in a series of Revolutionary legislation that transformed a country of subjects divided by privilege into a united nation of citizens equal before and under the law. It marks the end of the Old Regime and the birth of modern France.

J.-P. Hirsch, *La nuit du 4 août* (Paris, 1978); P. Kessel, *La nuit du 4 août 1789* (Paris, 1969); A. Mathiez, ''Les corporations ont-elles été supprimées en principe dans la nuit du 4 août 1789?'' *Ann. hist. de la Révo. française* 8 (1931).

M. D. Sibalis

Related entries: AIGUILLON; FEUDALISM; GREAT FEAR; OCTOBER DAYS; PATRIOT PARTY.

14 FRIMAIRE, LAW OF. See LAW OF 14 FRIMAIRE.

FOX, CHARLES JAMES (1749-1806), British statesman, leader of Whig opposition 1784-97. The most persistent objective in Fox's long tenure as leader of the opposition was to maintain the unity of the Whig party in order to replace W. Pitt with himself as prime minister. Within this context, the French Revolution was Fox's undoing. The Whig conservatives under E. Burke and W. Windham viewed the Revolution as a threat to everything they held sacred: church, state, property, civilization; in contrast, the Whig liberals under C. Grey and R. B. Sheridan saw the Revolution as an opportunity for Frenchmen to gain the same liberties enjoyed by Englishmen. Although closer philosophically to the latter, Fox urged moderation and prudence throughout 1789–91 in order to save the party. He tried to temper Burke's fanaticism and Grey's radicalism by minimizing the objectives and effects of the Revolution. For him, the upheaval in France was analogous to the English and American revolutions—struggles for freedom and constitutional governments—which all Whigs, old and new, could proudly defend. His understanding of French politics was as faulty as Burke's, but, unlike Burke, he failed to grasp the magnitude of the Revolution. For him, the marquis de Lafayette and the vicomte de Noailles were essentially English Whigs, and the Jacobins were no different from the Feuillants.

From the flight of Louis XVI to Varennes to the September 1792 Massacres, Fox's friends gradually drifted away, seeing more virtue in Burke's *Reflections* than in Fox's defense of the Revolution. In desperation, Fox pleaded with members of the center, notably Lords Portland and Fitzwilliam, to put aside differences within the party and not to give general support to Pitt's government. By the beginning of 1794, however, the split was final, and with it ended Fox's dream of a Whig ministry.

Fox's position on the Revolutionary wars was even more incomprehensible to the center and right Whigs. For them, the wars were patriotic struggles to save England from the "cannibal republic," which threatened to destroy the very foundations of British society and government. Only a crusade to crush the Revolution, extirpate Jacobinism, and restore the monarchy could save Britain. Fox, in contrast, rejected national security as an issue, often repeated Cicero's maxim that "the most unjust peace is better than the most just war," and urged the government to negotiate a treaty without indemnities to end "Pitt's war." Fox was at his best in defending British liberties against Pitt's repressive acts, in circumscribing the limits of the war, and in moderating the hysteria in Britain in the winter of 1792, but he was at his worst in defending French aggrandizement, rationalizing the excesses of the Revolution, celebrating British defeats abroad, and using every political exigency as a means for achieving political power.

British Library, Fox MSS, Additional Manuscripts; J. W. Derry, *Charles James Fox* (London, 1972); Lord J. Russell, *Memorials and Correspondence of Charles James Fox*, 4 vols. (London, 1854).

H. V. Evans

Related entries: BURKE; LAFAYETTE; PITT.

FRANCIS II (1768–1835), archduke of Austria, king of Hungary, Holy Roman Emperor (1792-1804); became Francis I, emperor of Austria, 1804–35. Francis, born in 1768, was the son of Leopold II (1790-92). Shortly after Francis assumed the throne on 1 March 1792, war broke out with France on 20 April, a conflict that would last, with various interruptions, until 1815. Francis, however, was a man of peace who waged a defensive war and who had no desire to destroy the Revolution in France. Although Austria suffered many defeats at the hand of

France during the Revolution and the Napoleonic era, Francis displayed much steadfastness. On 11 August 1804 he took the title of Francis I and in 1806 agreed to the dissolution of the Holy Roman Empire. In order to gain time to recuperate, he accepted Metternich's idea to marry his daughter Marie Louise (1791–1847) to Napoleon.

In the post-Napoleonic years, Francis was one of the principal advocates of monarchical absolutism, opposing and suppressing liberal and nationalist movements in Europe. At home, he used the power of his centralist state to suppress political dissidents. Although suspicious of new ideas, he introduced a new Code of Criminal Law and a Civil Code. Cultural life flourished in spite of censorship during his reign. Francis was very popular with his subjects, who referred to him as "good Emperor Francis." He was married four times and had thirteen children.

Viktor Bibl, *Kaiser Franz der letzte römisch-deutsche Kaiser* (Leipzig, Vienna, 1938); Paul Bernard, *Jesuits and Jacobins. Enlightenment and Enlightened Despotism in Austria* (Urbana, 1971).

G. D. Homan

Related entry: FIRST COALITION.

FRANC-MACONNERIE. See FREEMASONRY.

FRANCOIS DE NEUFCHATEAU, NICOLAS-LOUIS (1750-1828), deputy to the Legislative Assembly, minister of the interior, director. Born at Saffrais (Lorraine), the son of a schoolteacher, the future politician was educated at the Jesuit collège at Neufchâteau. He was a child literary prodigy, becoming an associate member of the academies of Dijon, Lyon, Marseille, and Nancy at the age of fifteen. After leaving for Paris in about 1768, he returned briefly to Toul in 1770 as professor of poetry at the episcopal collège of Sainte-Claude, from which he was rapidly ejected for introducing the works of the *philosophes*. He took up law and obtained a doctorate at Reims University. Returning to Paris in 1773, he did some desultory legal work but was principally a man of letters. He purchased the office of lieutenant général of the *bailliage* of Mirecourt-en-Lorraine in 1776. In 1783, he became *procureur-général* of the Conseil supérieur at Le Cap Français in Saint-Domingue. When this office was abolished in 1787, he withdrew with a pension to an estate in Lorraine where he developed the interest in agriculture that was to remain with him for the rest of his life.

Before the Revolution, François was an archetypal man of the Enlightenment. He established many close contacts in literary and philosophical circles. From the age of fifteen, he pursued an active correspondence with F.-M. Voltaire who thought well of his talent, as did J. Grimm. He was linked with J. Le Rond d'Alembert and S.-N.-H. Linguet, contributed to the *Almanach des Muses*, wrote pieces against E. Fréron, and stayed at the home of J.-B.-M. Dupaty. He had great facility as a versifier and remained a prolific minor poet throughout his life. He imbibed many of the humanitarian and antiecclesiastical attitudes of the *philosophes*, and his correspondence reveals a wide-ranging and inquiring mind. His later writings on agriculture place him among the important eighteenth-century agronomists. His pre-Revolutionary political attitudes were those of an enlightened reformer.

In 1789, François drafted the Third Estate's *cahier* for the *bailliage* of Toul but refused election as a deputy on financial grounds although agreeing to be a *suppléant*. He became justice of the peace at Vicherey and was elected to the directory of the department of the Vosges in June 1790. Elected for the Vosges to the Legislative Assembly, he attracted attention above all for his anticlericalism. In particular, he proposed the text voted on 29 November 1791 (but subsequently vetoed) that rendered nonjuring priests automatically responsible for troubles breaking out in their communes. He also published an amount of anti-Christian verse, some of it being used in Parisian Festivals of Reason during later 1793. It was on François' proposition that the Assembly swore, on 28 August 1792, not to leave Paris until replaced by the Convention, and it was François, as last president of the Legislative, who made the valedictory speech to the incoming assembly.

Alleging health reasons, François refused election to the Convention and also the post of minister of justice offered to him in October 1792. He returned to be justice of the peace at Vicherey and spent 1793 publishing memoranda on agriculture and food supply. However, it was his literary activities that brought him into trouble. The production of his *Paméla* at the Théâtre-Français in August 1793 brought to a head the conflict between the patriot actors around Talma and the reactionary Comédie-Française. The play scandalized the Jacobins by its seemingly pro-noble implications. François was arrested by the Committee of Public Safety on 2 September and remained incarcerated in the Luxembourg until 17 Thermidor (4 August 1794).

Although he was appointed a judge on the Tribunal de Cassation on 14 Nivôse Year III (3 January 1795), it was under the Directory that François became prominent. He began the period as *commissaire* of the Directory with the departmental administration of the Vosges. On 28 Messidor Year V (16 July 1797), he was appointed minister of the interior in the critical ministerial reshuffle that marked the definitive split between the members of the First Directory and preluded the coup of 18 Fructidor (4 September 1797). According to L.-M. La Revellière-lépeaux, he came in as the nominee of J.-F. Reubell (from neighboring Alsace). However, he was probably acceptable to La Revellière-lépeaux because of his antireligious attitudes, and he also seems to have been close to P. Barras. He lasted in the ministry until the coup of 18 Fructidor when he was elected to the Directory, at the top of the Councils' list. On the first rotation of membership, the lot fell to François, who stepped down on 1 Prairial Year VI (20 May 1798). He was immediately sent to negotiate with the Austrians at Seltz (25 May-7 July) over the enforced departure of ambassador J.-B. Bernadotte from Vienna. He returned as minister of the interior again on 29 Messidor Year VI (17 July 1798) and finally resigned on 4 Messidor Year VII (22 June 1799), after his attempts to manipulate the elections through the Directory's *commissaires* in the departments had been bitterly attacked by neo-Jacobin deputies.

François had little political stature: his action as a director was negligible; his handling of the Seltz negotiations was without talent; and his manipulation of the Year VII elections was too overt. As minister of the interior, however, he had profound and enduring effect on the development of modern government in France, especially during his second ministry. His reorganization of the ministry after the Revolutionary disarray was instrumental in the transition from the *ancien régime* administration to the Napoleonic. His enormous energy (two large volumes of ministerial circulars) was not merely devoted to general enquiries and regulations but also to the pursuit of practical results in a great diversity of matters. He surrounded himself with technical experts and founded the first government statistical service. His action was dominated by two preoccupations: the securing of the Republic and the development of the economy. In the first field, apart from his attempt to produce a stable nonpartisan majority in the elections of the Year VII, he was concerned primarily to promote republican education. He developed the primary school system, established competitions among the *écoles centrales*, published textbooks on reading and on the constitution, and attempted to reform the poor school (Collège d'Egalité) under the name of the Prytanée français. Under a wider definition of education, one should place his constant promotion of republican fêtes for which he wrote special hymns. As for the economy, his particular interest remained with agriculture. He sought to reverse the process of deforestation and issued propaganda to improve conditions. More generally, François attempted to catalog all the resources, produce, and manufactures of France in a standardized survey of the departments, which largely foundered after his departure. In this respect, he foreshadowed the basic information-gathering and processing techniques of later governments. His most concrete economic achievement was the first French exhibition of manufactured goods (5 Complémentaire Year VI–10 Vendémiaire Year VII, or 19 September–1 October 1798) held to stimulate production and trade.

Under the Consulate and the Empire, François became an unconditional supporter of Napoleon. Appointed one of the first twenty-nine senators, he was secretary of the Senate under the Consulate and its president from 1804 to 1806. He was elected to the Académie française in 1803 and became grand trésorier of the Légion d'Honneur in 1804. Nominated to the *sénatorerie* of Dijon in 1804, he transferred to that of Brussels in 1806 and was created count in 1808. Throughout these years, he continued to experiment with agriculture and to write improving textbooks for the farming public. However, in public life, he had become merely an endless speechmaker on state occasions, a turner of fine phrases in praise of the regime. Under the Restoration, he never found the royal favor that he craved.

A.N., AB[xix] 75-91; J. Lhomer, *François de Neufchâteau* (Paris, 1913); P. Marot, *Recherches sur la vie de François de Neufchâteau* (Nancy, 1966).

C. Lucas

Related entries: *BAILLIAGE*; BERNADOTTE; *CAHIERS DE DOLEANCES*; COUP OF 18 FRUCTIDOR YEAR V; EDUCATION; LA REVELLIERE-LEPEAUX.

FREDERICK WILLIAM II (1786-97), king of Prussia. Born in Berlin on 25 September 1744, he succeeded his uncle, Frederick II (the Great) as king of Prussia on 17 August 1786. This corruptible and irresolute Hohenzollern was influenced by cliques of favorites, including advisers, ministers, generals, and ministers. Interested in music, the arts, and Rosicrucian mysticism, he firmly rejected the Enlightenment by such acts as the Wöllner edict of 1788 and by reprimanding I. Kant.

In 1786–87 he contributed to the defeat of the Dutch patriots and the restoration of the conservative Orangist government. Although in 1791 he acquired Ansbach and Bayreuth by inheritance, his major territorial ambition consisted of grabbing more of Poland—Thurn, Danzig, Gdansk. Thus, he was ambivalent about using Revolutionary France against Austria or joining the latter in a crusade against the Revolutionaries. Gradually he allowed himself to be won over by the war party and committed Prussia to the Convention of Reichenbach on 27 July 1790, the Declaration of Pillnitz on 27 August 1791, and an alliance with Austria on 7 February 1792, followed by a military convention on 25 February. After joining Austria in the war, he continued to take the superiority of the Prussian army for granted until the débacle of the campaign of 1792, which resulted in the Prussian defeat at Valmy (20 September) and the disastrous retreat through Champagne that followed. Thereafter Frederick William remained on the defensive in the west in order to retain a free hand for the Second Partition of Poland with Russia (23 January 1793) and for the repression of Polish resistance, which lasted until 1794. The king later withdrew from the First Coalition and on 5 April 1795 concluded a separate peace, neutralizing northern Germany, with the French Republic at Basel. He compensated himself in the Third Partition of Poland (24-26 October 1795), whereby Prussia annexed territory including even Warsaw, the Polish capital.

W. M. von Bissing, *Friedrich Wilhelm II, König von Preussen* (Berlin, 1967); W. Real, *Von Potsdam nach Basel* (Basel, 1958); G. Stanhope, *A Mystic on the Prussian Throne* (London, 1912).

W. Markov

Related entries: BATTLE OF VALMY; CHARLES IV; FIRST COALITION; FRANCIS II; DECLARATION OF PILLNITZ; KOSCIUSZKO; POLAND; TREATY OF BASEL.

FREEMASONRY, an eighteenth-century movement in England and France that was simultaneously fraternal, intellectual, and religious, whose origins and impact on the French Revolution are still controversial. Whatever its origins—the secrets of the alchemists, the heritage of the Templars, the signs of the *compagnonnages* (trade guilds)—by the beginning of Louis XV's reign the characteristic elements of Freemasonry were in place: the three grades, the initiation ceremony, the legend of Hiram, the secret, and Anderson's Constitutions. Freemasonry, which quickly spread following the Jacobite diaspora, was first condemned in 1738 by a papal bull (not registered in France) and then again in 1751. The chevalier de Ramsay had furnished a vague and tolerant doctrine, readily acceptable to lodges of different tendencies. In 1743 L. de Bourbon-Condé, comte de Clermont, succeeded the duc d'Antin as grand master and established new statutes. At the end of Louis XV's reign, there were about 50 lodges in Paris, 169 in the provinces, and 11 in the colonies. With this flourishing, obedience became fragmented; the mastership of the comte de Clermont became difficult because of the independence of provincial lodges, the diversification of rites, and the success of the Scottish rite. In 1771 Louis-Philippe, duc de Chartres and future duc d'Orléans, was elected grand master, with A. de Montmorency-Luxembourg as administrator. In 1773 they founded the Grand Orient of France and reorganized the Masonic network, which enjoyed an astonishing prosperity: 629 lodges, of which 63 were in Paris, 442 in the provinces, 38 in the colonies, 69 military lodges, and 17 lodges abroad, altogether around 30,000 brothers. The Grand Orient maintained relative cohesion among the mass of Masons; although 46 masters in Paris refused to submit to the discipline of the Grand Orient and established the Grand National Lodge, this dissident element lost its influence after 1778.

According to the records of the Grand Orient and the National Lodge, Freemasons were recruited, at their apogee in 1773, among urban elites. It is difficult to determine the motivation of the initiates. One of the lodges, which was typical in combining virtue, patriotism, and humanity as criteria, was that of the "Nine Sisters," which welcomed B. Franklin, F.-M. Voltaire, and J.-B. Greuze and created a kind of open university where B. Constant, the marquis de Condorcet, and G.-J. Danton participated side by side. In the provinces rationalist brothers, thanks to para-Masonic institutions, so spread the new spirit that it has been alleged that the *Encyclopédie* was a Masonic accomplishment.

The lodge was not strictly a corporate body, or an academy, or a sect, or a party; rather it was all of these together. Among the various tendencies, the Scottish insistence on obedience prepared the way for a renewal of faith and was a forerunner of Romanticism. In the Masonic universe, the proselytes of the irrational came from different positions: Christians like J. de Maistre, nonbelievers searching for a truth outside the church, and men like M. de Pasqually, L.-C. de Saint-Martin, and J.-B. Willermoz who set Freemasonry on the path to esoterism and occultism. Some resorted to alchemy, magic, astrology, numerology, and neo-Pythagorism. Beyond doubt, the increasing Revolutionary crisis was marked by the rapid multiplication of occult sciences and esoteric religions.

To contemporaries, the Revolutionary events appeared so surprising that they searched for exceptional, even supernatural, causes. In 1789 when G. Balsamo, known as Cagliostro, was tried by the Inquisition in Rome, he blamed Free-

masonry. Abbé A. Barruel explained that the kingdom of Louis XVI was suffering divine punishment for its evil ways and for its philosophical insolence (in
Le patriote véridique ou discours sur les vraies causes de la Révolution actuelle).
In 1792 the abbé Lefranc published *Conjuration contre la religion Catholique
des souverains dont le projet conçu en France doit s'exécuter dans l' Univers
entier*, in which he repeated the thesis of an earlier brochure dating from 1782,
*Le secret de la Révolution révêlé à l'aide de la Franc-Maçonnerie et la con-
juration contre la religion catholique*. According to him, Illuminati, who met
at the convent of Wilhelmsbad in 1782, decided on the execution of Louis XVI
and the destruction of the monarchy. He based his claim on the warning of J.-P.
Luchet, the librarian of the Landgrave of Hesse-Cassel, who, in his *Essai sur
le secte des Illuminés* (1789), maintained that the fate of the West depended on
the Illuminati of Bavaria. In fact, this very divided group had been outlawed by
the Elector in 1784. After Luchet, however, K. F. Bahrdt, L. A. Hoffmann, J.
G. Zimmermann, J. Robinson, and J. A. Starck publicized the admissions of
Cagliostro, claimed that H.-G. R. Mirabeau belonged to the Illuminati, and
attributed responsibility for the Revolution to J. Bode because he had come to
Paris in 1787 for the congress of the *Philadelphes*. In 1796 in his *Mémoires
pour servir à l'histoire de la Révolution*, abbé Barruel spread the thesis of a
conspiracy concocted in the bosom of the Masonic lodges that brought together
the sophists of disbelief, rebellion, and anarchy; he confirmed that the French
Freemasons were the disciples and instruments of the German Freemasons.

It is true that the Illuminati influenced some Revolutionaries like N. de Bonneville, who in 1788 published *Les Jésuites chassés de la Franc-Maçonnerie* and,
together with the abbé Fauchet, in 1790, founded the Cercle social and began
publishing the *Bouche de fer*. Nevertheless, it cannot be claimed that Bode
worked out a conspiracy plot that was going to lead to the Revolution. This
romantic explanation was refuted in 1801 by J.-J. Mounier in *De l'influence
attribuée aux Philosophes, aux Francs-Maçons*. In spite of this, such a thesis
has survived, and opponents of the Revolution have used it. On the other hand,
the heirs of the Enlightenment have congratulated themselves on the role played
by Freemasonry in the political, social, and cultural transformations that took
place in the course of the Revolutionary crisis.

In *Révolution et la libre pensée* (1923) and *Sociétés de pensée et la Révolution
en Bretagne* (1925), A. Cochin exposed the conspicuous role of the lodges in
the coming of the Revolution, which was set in motion by ''the Machine'': the
literary circles, the agricultural societies, the academies, and the reading rooms.
Cochin does not charge that this was a plot but rather an unintentional preparation.
It is also worthy of note that the activities of the elite might well have been
directed by cafés and clubs that were also concerned with political and social
problems.

B. Fäy dealt with the development of Revolutionary mentality in two works,
L'esprit révolutionnaire en France et aux Etats-unis (1924) and *La Franc-Maçonnerie et la Révolution intellectuelle du XVIII siècle* (1935). Like Barruel, he

concluded that the role of the lodges was crucial for the Revolution, for the new ideas were powerful and influential, even if false and dangerous, and seduced the French elite, all the more since they came from England. While Barruel accused the Germans, Fäy accused the English and their mystique, which set off a Masonic crusade. Franklin had provided a credo to those who, escaping the domination of the church, propagated hope thanks to the example of the American Revolution. The upper nobility also committed suicide by its intellectual frivolity and naiveté. While it is true that the first patriot leaders were nobles who were initiates, that the *cahiers de doléances* owed much to the duc d'Orléans and his network, that 400 to 1,100 deputies to the Constituent Assembly endorsed the Enlightenment, and that Masonic connections were important at the time of the Battle of Valmy, Fäy's brilliant hypothesis appears nevertheless both excessive and insufficient.

In contrast, G. Martin attributes considerable responsibility to Freemasonry for the beginning and the spread of the Revolution but by way of congratulation. In *La Franc-Maçonnerie française et la préparation de la Révolution* (1926) and his manual, *Histoire de la Franc-Maçonnerie française* (1929), he rejected the conspiracy thesis: Freemasons did not plan the execution of Louis XVI, even though Dr. J.-I. Guillotin was a member of the Grand Orient. For this historian, himself a Freemason, the lodges deserve credit for elaborating a reform program expressed in the *cahiers de doléances*, for creating the Committee of Thirty, which was active in the electoral campaign of 1789, for contributing to the establishment of the Jacobin club, and for being responsible for the night of 4 August through the speech of the brother, G.-G. Leguen de Kerendal, and the compliance of the duc de Noailles. But was the political conduct of the Freemasons dictated by Masonic considerations? A. Mathiez recalled that on 29 July 1789, the Grand Orient decided to preserve absolute neutrality in the face of events; he estimated that the political influence of the Masonic lodges was nearly nonexistent.

On the other hand, R. Priouret, in *La Franc-Maçonnerie sous les lys* (1953), showed the role played by occult obedience in the counterrevolution; many Freemasons sought refuge in mystical meditation, emigrated, or were victims of the Terror. In his *Histoire de la Franc-Maçonnerie française* (1935), A. Lantoine minimized the importance of ideology in revolutions. This writer, a member of the Council of the Grand Lodge of France, accorded little significance to the Masonic movement in the development of the Revolution; at the most, some of their formulas—the revenge of the Templars—were incorporated into threats against the papacy and royalty.

Alongside these theses, it is evident from different monographs that probably the lodges played a role in the propagation of Revolutionary concepts and provided the opportunity to speak and discuss. Indisputably, however, the enlightened middle class and the liberal nobility could have had the same experience just as well in other societies.

The contribution of Masonic practices can be recognized in the organization of Revolutionary festivals, but the organizers of these festivals could have just as readily borrowed, more or less consciously, from the Catholic liturgy. It was a Freemason who erected the first altar of the Fatherland in 1789; the marquis de Lafayette was the central figure in the Fête de la Fédération of 1790; J. Fouché organized the Festival of Equality at Lyon in 1794; and J.-L. David, similarly a Freemason, was the great organizer of festivals during the Directory. The Masonic vocabulary can be recognized in Revolutionary iconography: the luminous delta bearing the eye of reason, the Mountain, the Tree of Liberty, and others. There were also practices borrowed from the Masonic tradition, which itself was derived from Christian tradition: the oath, the kiss of peace, the embrace, the fraternal use of *toi*. Likewise, the music of the lodges was repeated in Revolutionary ceremonies; the musicians, often initiates, borrowed from their repertoire and adapted Masonic hymns and songs. It is necessary, however, to be more precise about what their music actually owed to the fact that they were Masons.

What prevents the historian from treating Freemasonry as a political element in the Revolution is the diversity of behavior by Freemasons in the face of various Revolutionary waves. During the constitutional phase of the Revolution, the Masonic elite (known through research) accepted and even sometimes instigated reforms; these notables reacted according to their temperament, their background, their interests. From the spring of 1789, reservations were expressed; soon some Freemasons emigrated, and others joined the Feuillants or the Girondins; and a few, like J.-B.-A. Amar, became Montagnards. Many, as in Lyon, allied with the federalist revolts or even the *chouan* rebellion. The lodges stopped meeting in 1791 or 1792, some because their membership disappeared, others as the result of an explicit decision. The Terror was the negation of their ideal. On their part, some Montagnards considered Freemasonry an institution of the Old Regime, tainted by superstition and prejudice.

Masonic revival came slowly. M. Roettiers de Montaleau strained to keep alive the Masonic ideal during the Terror; he saved the archives of the Grand Orient from theft and destruction. Imprisoned, he was freed by M. Robespierre's fall. In 1796 he announced the resurrection of the Grand Orient and received the unusual title of grand venerable. Few lodges resumed activity during the first Directory; the Masons who attempted to reconstitute the order were sometimes considered Clichyens (royalists), sometimes moderates (as at Marseille), sometimes Jacobins (as at Toulouse)—striking evidence of their political pluralism. The coup d'état of 18 Fructidor constituted a new check. Only in 1799 did the Grand Lodge and the Grand Orient reunite. Under the Consulate the movement truly revived.

A. Bouton, *Les Francs-Maçons manceaux et la Révolution française, 1741-1815* (Le Mans, 1958); P. Chevallier, *Histoire de la Franc-Maçonnerie* (Paris, 1976); J. Droz, "La légende du complot illuministe," *Rev. Hist.* 226 (1961); B. Fäy, *La Franc-Maçonnerie et la Révolution intellectuelle du XVIIIe siècle* (Paris, 1935); "La Franc-Maçonnerie et la Révolution française," *Ann. hist. de la Révo. française*, 41 (1969); D. Ligou,

Histoire de Francs-Maçons en France (Toulouse, 1981); D. Ligou, ed., *Dictionnaire universel de la Franc-Maçonnerie* (Paris, 1974); P. Naudon, *Histoire générale de la Franc-Maçonnerie* (Paris, 1981); L. Trenard, "Lumières et Maçonnerie dans le seconde moitié du XVIIIe siècle," *Rev. des Et. Mais.* 5–6 (1980).

L. Trenard

Related entries: BOUCHE DE FER; CAHIERS DE DOLEANCES; CERCLE SOCIAL; CHOUANNERIE; COMMITTEE OF THIRTY; COUNTERREVO-LUTION; ILLUMINATI.

FRENCH GUARDS, elite regiment of royal household troops. Founded in 1564, during the religious wars in France, to protect the royal family in court and in the various châteaux where they lived, the French Guards were placed on a permanent footing during the reign of Henry III and grew steadily in size throughout the eighteenth century. By 1789 the regiment had become an exclusively ceremonial unit, some 3,600 strong and quartered in Paris, where many of the soldiers worked at various trades in off-duty hours.

This contact with the working classes quickly eroded the discipline of the French Guards after the Estates General assembled at Versailles. By late June 1789 individual soldiers began to refuse police duties. On 27 June five companies deserted and joined the crowd at the Palais Royal, and when the colonel arrested the ringleaders, T. Jefferson, the U.S. minister, observed that these Guards were arrested because of their support for the people, although other pretexts were given. On 6 July some soldiers of the Guards stationed at Versailles quarreled with German speaking hussars, and several days later others clashed with the Royal Allemand cavalry. By 13 July many had joined the Paris mobs in raising barricades in the streets. On 14 July five of six battalions of the regiment defected and one detachment of about 100 French Guards organized the final attack on the Bastille. The fall of this hated symbol of the *ancien régime* has been attributed to the confluence of two powerful currents, the great national uprising and the defection of the regular army. In this revolution of the soldiers, the French Guards played an influential role.

Soldiers who had participated in the capture of the Bastille were awarded the medal of the French Guards. When the Paris National Guard was organized a few days later, many of the French Guards entered the thirty paid companies that served as a permanent nucleus. Their new duties were much the same as the old—to guard the Tuileries after the royal family had returned to Paris.

The regiment was officially dissolved on 1 September 1789, but because of their early commitment to the Revolution, the French Guards were allowed to keep their flags, insignia, and regimental property. The musicians of the regiment were picked up by the district of the Filles-Saint-Thomas, and as the band of the National Guard continued to perform for ceremonial occasions.

Although some suspected that the former French Guards would sympathize with the counterrevolution, nearly all seemed to be loyal to the new regime. In January 1790, some 2,000 of them formally deposited their old regimental standards and swore loyalty to the Revolution and the Commune.

P. Daniel, *Abrégé de l'histoire de la milice françoise*. 2 vols. (Paris, 1783); J. Godechot, *The Taking of the Bastille: July 14th, 1789* (New York, 1970); L. Gottschalk and M. Maddox, *Lafayette in the French Revolution, Through the October Days* (Chicago, 1969); E. L. Higgins, ed., *The French Revolution as Told by Contemporaries* (Boston, 1938); G. Lefebvre, *The French Revolution*, vol. 1 (London, 1962); S. F. Scott, *The Response of the Royal Army to the French Revolution: The Role and Development of the Line Army, 1787-93* (Oxford, 1978).

J. Luvaas

Related entries: BASTILLE; COUNTERREVOLUTION; NATIONAL GUARD.

FRERON, LOUIS-MARIE-STANISLAS (1754-1802), journalist and *conventionnel*. Fréron was an unlikely Revolutionary. His father, whom he idolized, edited the clerical and reactionary periodical, *Année littéraire*. Stanislas Lescynski, ex-king of Poland and father-in-law of Louis XV, was present at his baptism on 17 August 1754. And Madame Adélaide, the aunt of Louis XVI, pampered him as a child.

From age sixteen to twenty-four he attended the collège of Louis-le-Grand, where his classmates included M. Robespierre and L.-C.-S. Desmoulins. But Fréron was a lackluster student, and the broadening effects of this experience were not readily apparent. The turning point in his life probably came in 1781 when he lost control of his dead father's journal to his maternal uncle, the abbé Royou. Thereafter he became a denizen of the Parisian intellectual underworld, adopting a libertine and parasitical life-style.

In 1789 Fréron was chosen an elector of the Bonne-Nouvelle district of Paris and then, after the assault on the Bastille in which he was involved, a representative of the Commune. Returning to journalism, he founded (23 May 1790) *L'orateur du peuple*, a radical sheet written in the style of J.-P. Marat's *Ami du peuple*. At the Club des Cordeliers where he was a mainstay, G.-J. Danton and Marat were among his political comrades-in-arms, but his warmest friends were Desmoulins and his wife, Lucile. The trio lived in the same apartment building and often spent holidays together at Bourg-la-Reine.

Following the Champ de Mars "massacre" (17 July 1791), Fréron went into hiding at Versailles; however, he soon returned to Paris and immersed himself again in politics. On 9–10 August 1792, he participated in the attack on the Tuileries Palace. Chosen a deputy of Paris to the National Convention on 14 September, he took his seat on the extreme Left with the Montagnards. He not only voted for the death of the king (January 1793) but demanded that the execution be carried out within twenty-four hours.

On 19 March 1793, he was appointed, with P. Barras, to be a representative on mission to the Hautes- and Basses-Alpes. During their eleven-month stay in Provence, the two men were ferocious terrorists. Indeed, Fréron's letters leave the impression that he delighted in seeing blood flow. When Toulon was recaptured in December 1793, he boasted of having had 800 people shot. The excesses he and Barras committed at Toulon and Marseille, together with the charges of debauchery leveled against them by local patriots, led to their recall on 23 January 1794.

On his return Fréron found himself in a precarious position. The Committee of Public Safety gave him a frigid reception, and Robespierre treated him with open contempt. During the purge of the Dantonists (March–April 1794), he cowered in the background, doing nothing to try to save C. and L. Desmoulins from execution. A desire to avenge Desmoulins may have prompted him to join the conspiracy of 9 Thermidor that overthrew Robespierre. But fear for his own life was probably the paramount factor.

During the Thermidorian period, Fréron was one of the most prominent of the turncoat terrorists. On 11 September 1794, he revived *L'orateur du peuple*, which became the voice of reaction. He was also the chief of the "gilded youth," a middle-class paramilitary force, always ready to assail Jacobins on the street. His name aroused such violent passions that he was not chosen as a deputy to the Council of Five Hundred or Council of Ancients in 1795, but Barras secured him an appointment as commissioner to Marseille. In his "second proconsulate" at Marseille, he had a romance with the teenage beauty, P. Bonaparte. Their plans to marry were blocked by Napoleon, however, and by his own recall to Paris in 1796. The last years of his life were unhappy. After numerous attempts to secure a governmental post, he was finally named to be a subprefect at Les Cayes in Santo Domingo. He contracted dysentery and died shortly after his arrival there (15 July 1802).

R. Arnaud, *Journaliste, sans-culotte et thermidorien. Le Fils de Fréron* (Paris, 1909); E. Poupé, *Lettres de Barras et de Fréron* (Draguignan, 1910).

M. Kennedy

Related entries: COMMITTEE OF PUBLIC SAFETY; CORDELIERS CLUB; DESMOULINS; *JEUNESSE DOREE*; 9 THERMIDOR YEAR II; ROBESPIERRE, M.; THERMIDORIAN REACTION.

FRERONISTES. See *MUSCADINS*.

FRIMAIRE, LAW OF 14. See LAW OF 14 FRIMAIRE.

FROMENT, FRANCOIS (1756-1825), chief instigator of the first popular counterrevolutionary movement, centered in the department of the Gard as the government of this new administrative unit was being organized. See BAGARRE DE NIMES.

FRONTIERS, DOCTRINE OF NATURAL. See DOCTRINE OF NATURAL FRONTIERS.

FROTTE, LOUIS DE (1755?-1800), royalist. See *CHOUANNERIE*.

FRUCTIDOR, COUP OF 18. See COUP OF 18 FRUCTIDOR.

G

GABELLE, widely despised salt tax of the Old Regime. The *gabelle* originally was a tax levied occasionally by French kings in the fourteenth century on a variety of commodities, but it was established permanently on salt during the later stages of the Hundred Years War. Of the many royal taxes of the Old Regime, it was probably the most generally hated and condemned, but the government felt unable to abolish or replace it because it was its second largest source of revenue (only slightly less than the *taille*). The revenue came from leasing to entrepreneurs for a specified period the exclusive right to sell salt in the kingdom at varying stipulated amounts above its actual cost. In order to assure the profitability of the agreement, the government required subjects to purchase certain minimum amounts of salt. The varying prices and minimums had been last established for the six districts into which the country was divided by an ordinance of 1680. Besides having responsibility for the purchase, distribution, and sale of salt, the tax farmers were empowered to search premises for illegal salt and to arrest and try alleged violators of the tax regulations. Complaints were frequent about the lack of availability of salt when needed, poor quality, and short measure, as well as abuses of the tax farmers' police powers.

The most obvious shortcoming of the *gabelle*, however, was its arbitrary and therefore seemingly unjust incidence. In the six districts, salt ranged in cost from 40 *sous* per *livre* in the largest (*pays de grande gabelle*) to less than a *sou* in the *pays exempts*. Exemptions and lower rates of tax were usually the result of special agreements made with the crown by certain areas added to the domain after the initial levy. Variations of this magnitude, however, especially in contiguous areas, led not only to resentment but also to large-scale smuggling, in spite of heavy penalties (salt smugglers were the largest single source of manpower for the galleys).

Besides the arbitrary and unfair geographical variations, there were also the customary Old Regime class, individual, and institutional exemptions from which clergy, nobility, certain categories of royal officials, and some towns and cities like Paris and Versailles all benefited. Denounced generally by the *cahiers* and public opinion, the *gabelle* was finally abolished by the National Assembly in 1790.

M. Marion, *Dictionnaire des institutions de la France aux XVIIe et XVIIIe siècles* (Paris, 1923).

R. W. Greenlaw

Related entry: TAILLE.

GARAT, DOMINIQUE-JOSEPH (1749-1833), writer and politician. A native of Basses-Pyrénées, Garat established himself in pre-Revolutionary Paris as an advocate, history professor, writer, and orator. When the Estates General was elected, he was chosen to represent the *bailliage* of Labour; his earliest conspicuous Revolutionary service was analyzing and reporting the proceedings of the National Constituent Assembly for the *Journal de Paris*. Irresolute and changeable, though of vaguely popular convictions, Garat was able to play a continual and varying role in the great events of the Revolution, largely by being a pliant tool of others. Even more than E.-J. Sieyès, Garat could claim that his most significant achievement during the Revolutionary-Napoleonic era was to have survived.

In September 1792 he replaced G.-J. Danton as minister of justice in the Girondist-dominated Provisional Executive Council. In this office, Garat had to notify Louis XVI of the judgment against him and to serve as official witness of the king's execution. In March 1793, Garat took over the Ministry of the Interior, which J.-M. Roland de la Platière had vacated; it was a post in which he proved inadequate, uninformed, and unable to curb corruption and insubordination and from which he resigned in August 1793.

In October 1793 he was arrested as a Girondist sympathizer, but his friendly relations with P. Barras and M. Robespierre saved him from harm. When Montagnard fortunes turned, Garat sided against Robespierre and, during the Thermidorian Reaction, following Robespierre's fall from power, he was named a member of the Convention's Executive Committee on Public Instruction. Under the Directory he was elected to the Council of Ancients (1799) and became that body's president. With the Brumaire coup d'état, Garat rallied to Napoleon; he was elected to the Senate (1800) and became a count of the Empire (1808) and a commander of the Légion d'honneur (1810). Garat, consistent in his fickleness, voted for dethroning Napoleon in 1814 but served as a member of the Chamber of Representatives during the Hundred Days (20 March 1815–22 June 1815), between Napoleon's return from Elba and the Battle of Waterloo. With Louis XVIII's return to Paris (July 1815), Garat retired quietly to his native Basses-Pyrénées.

Recognition of Garat's literary activity was seen in his election during the Directory to the Moral and Political Section of the Institute. After the second Restoration, he was excluded from the Institute, only to be elected to the Academy of Moral and Political Science following the 1830 Revolution. This final recognition of this politician for all parties occurred a year before his death on 9 December 1833.

D.-J. Garat, *Considerations sur la Révolution française* (Paris, 1792), and *Mémoires de Garat* (Paris, 1862).

C. A. Le Guin

Related entries: COUNCIL OF ANCIENTS; COUP OF 18 BRUMAIRE; DANTON; ROLAND DE LA PLATIERE, J.-M.; SIEYES; THERMIDORIAN REACTION.

GAXOTTE, PIERRE (1895-   ), historian, journalist, and man of letters, elected to the Académie française in 1953. The son of a republican notary, Gaxotte was born in Revigny (Meuse), and educated first at local schools in Lorraine, then at the Lycée Henri IV and the Ecole Normale Supérieure in Paris. He joined the Action française in the 1920s and served as C. Maurras' secretary for a time. He was editor in chief of the weekly magazine *Candide* from 1924 to 1940, as well as a contributor to other periodicals sympathetic to the Action française.

While practicing journalism, Gaxotte published three best-selling books about the eighteenth century: *La Révolution française* (1928), *Le siècle de Louis XV* (1933), and *Frédéric II* (1938). These surveys are popular histories. They contain no reference notes, rely primarily on secondary sources, and stress colorful detail and drama. They reveal Gaxotte's conservatism. He interprets the reigns of Louis XV and Frederick II favorably but loathes the French Revolution from beginning to end. He sees it as characterized by anarchy, domestic violence, foreign wars, inflation, bankruptcy, famine, and a communistic Terror. Among those he holds responsible for this disaster are the weak-willed and naive Louis XVI, the parlements, the *philosophes*, the members of various social, literary, and political clubs, and the leading Revolutionary politicians. A partisan and present-minded historian, Gaxotte finds occasion in his *Révolution française* to disparage twentieth-century Freemasons, liberals, communists, and leftists in general.

Gaxotte has remained a prolific writer. Among his publications are reminiscences of his childhood, *Mon village et moi* (1968), and editorials for *Le Figaro*. The 1975 edition of his *Révolution française*, revised with the collaboration of J. Tulard, has added extensive bibliographies.

A. Cobban, *Historians and the Causes of the French Revolution* (London, 1958); P. Farmer, *France Reviews Its Revolutionary Origins* ... (New York, 1944); S. Wilson, ''The 'Action Française' in French Intellectual Life,'' *Hist. J.* 12 (1969).

F. A. Kafker

Related entries: LEFEBVRE; MATHIEZ; SOBOUL.

GENERAL DEFENSE, COMMITTEE OF. See COMMITTEE OF GENERAL DEFENSE.

GENERAL SECURITY, COMMITTEE OF. See COMMITTEE OF GENERAL SECURITY.

GENERAL WILL, the political concept most closely associated with J.-J. Rousseau and employed during the Revolution to reconcile the liberty and equality of individuals with the welfare of society. This concept came to the fore during the period of the Enlightenment in the course of debates on political science, society, the individual, and the state. In the articles of the *Encyclopédie* on the legislator and natural law, D. Diderot considered the problem of the general will from a moral point of view; it seemed to him inadmissible that the individual be the sovereign judge of what is just and unjust, good and evil. The particular will of the individual was always suspect. The general will was the only judge. In order to judge, it was always necessary to refer to the general welfare and general will. Whoever found himself in disagreement with this general will denied his human quality; it was the general will that determined the nature and limits of all one's obligations.

In his article on "Political Economy" in the same encyclopedia and in the *Social Contract*, Rousseau declared that the social contract could not constrain individual wills. Every agreement of subjugation closely resembles a convention that reduces a people to slavery and demands of it blind submission; such an agreement is a pseudo-contract, juridically null and morally senseless. Rousseau broke with the philosophy of the contract that had prevailed until that time. For T. Hobbes and H. Grotius, a contract was a voluntary and reciprocal engagement between parties, and the contractual document in no way changed their nature. According to Rousseau, political authority should not impose itself on particular wills; the latter, joining together to promote a general will, should establish themselves as the political authority. Thus, the contract is the birth certificate of a people: "this act of association produces a moral and collective body" (*Social Contract*).

Every democratic enterprise depends on the rule of the general will to exist and to impose obedience legitimately. This should not be confused with the will of all, for if all men let their greedy and mean nature express itself, they would not agree on a common language and there would be, in Rousseau's terms, only "incomprehensible nonsense." In fact, the general will is not the will of the people in the sociological sense of the word; it is rather the will of the people as they emerged from the contract to serve as the basis of sovereignty—the people as citizens.

Direct democracy guarantees every person a total freedom, and it alone can guarantee an autonomy as perfect as if he lived outside society. With a democratic constitution, "each individual by uniting with all others, however, obeys only himself and remains as free as before" (in the state of nature). To put it another way, as long as subjects submit only to laws adopted by the body of citizens, "they obey no one, but only their own will," from which it follows that "one is free and obeys laws since they are only the registration of our wills" (*Social Contract*).

After this affirmation of ethical values, Rousseau develops an argumentation of a pragmatic nature. "The general will can alone direct the energies of the

State toward the purpose of its formation which is the common welfare." Democratic laws are "equitable because they are common to all, useful because they can have no other object than the general welfare"; they cannot be "unjust since no one is unjust toward himself." The general will is always right; it cannot err. This is not a question of the infallibility of the majority who can also err. But if correct, exact, and complete information is submitted to the people, the people will discover the correct solution. This is an optimistic postulate: man is born good; in a group he can be still better; he expresses himself by laws that are the expression of the general will. These laws are desired by all and applicable to all.

It is difficult to prove the influence of the *philosophes* on the opinions expressed in the *cahiers de doléances*. Still, the nobility and the bourgeoisie agreed on the substitution of the rule of law, as accepted by the representatives of the nation, for absolute power. Without question, the members of the Constituent Assembly looked to the formula of the *Social Contract* for the Declaration of the Rights of Man and Citizen: "Law is the expression of the general will." Article VI makes this more explicit: "All citizens have the right to participate personally or through their representatives in its formulation. It should be the same for all, for those whom it protects, for those whom it punishes." This same principle was repeated in the preamble to the constitution.

The Declaration of Rights recognized the right of all citizens to participate personally or by their representatives in the formation of law; subsequently the Constituent Assembly established an exclusively representative regime and instituted a system of voting based on property, with passive citizens and active citizens and two-stage elections. Thus, the regime established by the Constitution of 1791 did not create direct democracy and deviated from Rousseau's principles. J.-J. Mounier and E.-J. Sieyès felt that the majority of citizens were not sufficiently informed and did not have sufficient leisure to participate directly in making laws. The marquis de Condorcet protested against this in the name of every individual's right to maintain personal sovereignty.

The fall of the monarchy on 10 August 1792 led to the meeting of the National Convention to elaborate a new constitution. During the period of Girondin supremacy, Condorcet was in charge of this project. The task required conciliating obedience to the law, submission to the general will, and popular sovereignty while also taking into account circumstances and principles. The size of the Republic condemned it to being representative; the people thus would delegate but not abdicate their sovereignty. The people would be consulted by means of the referendum, and the Council of Ministers was to be the masterpiece of the Girondin plan. L. Saint-Just criticized these arrangements; according to him, the ministers would submit to pressures while stressing the general will.

In turn, Saint-Just presented to the Montagnard Convention his plan for a constitution, which reintroduced the principle of the general will as conceived by Rousseau. The basis for this lay in the election of the national representatives by the people as a body since representatives of factions did not express the general will, which is indivisible. During the summer of 1793, Saint-Just was obsessed by the risks that a federation would create. The basic principles of the Montagnards were incorporated into the constitution that was voted on 23 June 1793 and into the Declaration of the Rights of Man and Citizen that preceded it: "Law is the free and solemn expression of the general will; it is the same for all, for those whom it protects, for those whom it punishes; it can prescribe only what is just and useful for society." Article 26 condemned federalism: "No portion of the people can exercise the power of the whole people." Article 29 reaffirmed the sovereignty of each individual. This constitution was the result of circumstances, hasty and incomplete. Compared to Condorcet's plan and M. Robespierre's promises, this constitutional achievement marked a departure in democratic thought. The Montagnard constitution limited the application of national sovereignty and of direct suffrage. The deputies alone were elected individually and directly in primary assemblies; judges, civil servants, and administrators were selected in a two-step process, and the Executive Council was elected in three steps. This mechanism risked perverting the general will, and its partisan intent is evident. The use of the referendum, provided for by Condorcet, is very restricted in this document. This constitution was never implemented; in October 1793 the Committee of Public Safety declared that the government would be Revolutionary until the peace.

Robespierre insisted that it was the duty of every citizen to contribute to the success of the Revolution. In a manner of speaking, each individual should bring to the common mass that portion of public power and sovereignty that he possesses; otherwise, he is excluded from the social pact. The individual's freedom disappeared before the government's objective. Already, in 1791, in *The Spirit of the Revolution and Constitution of France*, Saint-Just had suggested that it was impossible to convince rogues and egotists of the benefits of the social contract. The resistance of some criminals should not be considered as part of the general will. Rousseau had also noted that the sovereign will could not be tyrannical since the general will should be just and reasonable. For Saint-Just, the objective content of the concept of liberty was essential; the spontaneous expression of the will of the people is acceptable only if it coincides with the common welfare, reason, and virtue. In his *Discourse on the Constitution of 1793*, Saint-Just refined his definition of the general will; it "is formed from the majority of particular, individual wills, acquired without any outside influence." He condemned purely speculative will and spiritual views, for which he substituted the interests of the social body.

Robespierre did not accept this conception in the same terms; he called into question the methods of expressing the general will and the relations between the executive and legislative branches. Robespierre wanted to forewarn the people of their own faults and of the corruption of deputies, but he did not want to interfere with their choice of representatives. The true majority was that which coincided with the general will, even if the latter was expressed through a parliamentary minority. This position justified direct popular action and even the duty of resisting oppression. For the Incorruptible, the Paris Commune and sections expressed the general will against the tyranny of the Girondin Convention.

In drawing up the Constitution of the Year III (1795), the Thermidorian Convention did not retain these concerns. It abolished the right of insurrection, however justified, demanded respect for the laws passed by representatives, and rejected the idea of sovereignty in the organization of public powers. Sieyès explained that the people had wished to arrogate to themselves the sovereignty that they had taken from the king, but the state was not an absolute. In the autumn of 1795 antiparliamentary sentiment spread.

During the Directory, insurrections were launched against the representative body in the name of direct democracy, but usually it was royalism that benefited. The regime that arose from the Convention dominated by the Plain no longer enjoyed the consensus that provided real legitimacy.

The outrage committed against the inviolability of representatives, the terrorist measures, and the dictatorship of the committees had destroyed confidence in the general will as expressed by elected representatives. In his turn, Napoleon claimed to personify the general will of the French nation.

L.-L. Cahen and R. Guyot, *L'oeuvre législative de la Révolution* (Paris, 1913); R. Derathé, *Rousseau et la science politique de son temps* (Paris, 1950); *Etudes sur le Contrat Social de J.-J. Rousseau: Actes des journées d'études tenues à Dijon en 1962* (Paris, 1964); J. Matrat, *Robespierre ou la tyrannie de la majorité* (Paris, 1971); A. Ollivier, *Saint-Just ou la force des choses* (Paris, 1954); J. L. Talmon, *Les Origines de la démocratie totalitaire* (Paris, 1966).

L. Trenard

Related entries: ACTIVE CITIZEN; CONDORCET; CONSTITUTION OF 1793; DECLARATION OF THE RIGHTS OF MAN AND OF THE CITIZEN; DIDEROT; *ENCYCLOPEDIE*; PASSIVE CITIZEN; ROUSSEAU; SAINT-JUST; *SOCIAL CONTRACT*.

GENET, EDMOND-CHARLES (1763-1834), diplomat. Born in Versailles of a cultured and courtly family traditionally employed in the Ministry of Foreign Affairs, Genêt entered his father's office in 1777. There he came into contact with the American Revolution and after education abroad served in Vienna and London before succeeding his father as head of translation in 1781. Later he went to Russia as secretary of the legation and was made chargé d'affaires after the emigration of the ambassador. The treatment he received from *émigrés* and Russian authorities made him an active republican. Expelled in July 1792 as a protest against 20 June, he was received as a martyr by the Girondins on his return. He was appointed minister to the United States on 19 November 1792, but his departure was delayed until January in case the royal family came with him. Fêted on his arrival at Charleston in April 1793 by local republicans, he became very involved in American politics. Although he had been sent to negotiate a trade alliance and to convince the Americans that France was a friendly power, not the source of subversion claimed by the English, he tried impetuously to enforce the terms of the alliance of 1778. He sought American arms and participation in ventures against Canada, Louisiana, and Florida and publicly attacked G. Washington.

The authorities in Paris censured him in the summer of 1793 for his actions. When he appealed over President Washington's head to the populace for support, many Americans finally turned against him. Washington demanded his recall and, as the Committee of Public Safety found his aggressive Girondin diplomacy unacceptable, they appointed commissioners to arrest him in America. The commissioners were delayed by contrary winds, but the press campaign against him in France revealed his isolation. Rather than return and face trial, he chose to settle in the United States, marrying the daughter of Governor Clinton of New York and spending his remaining years as a progressive farmer. He also remained an active correspondent with his sister, Madame Campan.

G. Balte, *Citizen Genêt, Diplomat and Inventor* (Philadelphia, 1946); W. L. Blackwell, "Citizen Genêt and the Revolution in Russia." *Fr. Hist. Stud.* 3 (1963); M. Bouloiseau, "Edmond-Charles Genêt à St. Petersbourg (1789–92)," *Bull. d'hist. econ. et soc. de la Révo. française* (1969).

C. Church

Related entries: COMMITTEE OF PUBLIC SAFETY; GIRONDINS.

GENSONNE, ARMAND (1758-93), Girondin political leader in the Legislative Assembly and National Convention. Born in Bordeaux on 10 August 1758, Gensonné had become a prominent young lawyer there by the beginning of the Revolution. He was active in the National Guard and in local politics, along with a number of men with whom he formed close political associations, including P.-V. Vergniaud, J.-B. Boyer-Fonfrède, and M.-E. Guadet. In 1791 he was appointed to the *tribunal de cassation* of Bordeaux and shortly afterward elected to the Legislative Assembly, where he allied with the Girondins. Like many of his colleagues, Gensonné endorsed a belligerent foreign policy; it was he who proposed the declaration of war on Austria that the Assembly passed by an overwhelming majority on 20 April 1792. He further advocated harsh treatment of the so-called Austrian Committee and former ministers suspected of encouraging Louis XVI's opposition to the Revolution. Following the Parisian *journée* of 20 June 1792, however, he began to moderate his attitude toward the monarch.

After the overthrow of the monarchy on 10 August 1792, Gensonné was elected deputy to the National Convention from the department of the Gironde. Like Vergniaud, he condemned the September 1792 Massacres and demanded an investigation. He was highly critical of the Paris Commune and an outspoken opponent of the Montagnard element in the Convention, which depended heavily on Parisian support. On the crucial issue of the king's fate, Gensonné staunchly supported a popular referendum but voted for the death penalty. He found himself a central figure in the bitter struggle between Girondins and Montagnards. In March 1793 he was elected president of the Convention. As the Montagnards intensified their attack on the Girondins, one of their most effective tactics was to implicate their opponents in the recent treason of General C. Dumouriez, and it was undeniable that Gensonné had maintained a close relationship and correspondence with the traitor. When Parisian crowds forced the purge of Girondin leaders from the Convention at the end of May and the beginning of June, Gensonné was among those taken into custody. He wrote a moving *Testament* to his constituents in Bordeaux, indicating his willingness to sacrifice his life for the sake of liberty and urging the Bordelais to continue this struggle. Along with a score of his colleagues, he was brought to trial before the Revolutionary Tribunal on 24 October; he was found guilty, sentenced to death, and executed on 31 October 1793.

R. Brouillard, "Désaccord entre Girondins: la motion de Gensonné du 27 octobre 1792," *Rev. hist. de Bord. et de la Gir.* 34 (1941) and "Dumouriez et les Girondins— correspondance inédite de Gensonné," *Rev. hist. de Bord. et de la Gir.* 36 (1943); A. Forrest, *Society and Politics in Revolutionary Bordeaux* (London, 1975); M. J. Sydenham, *The Girondins* (London, 1961).

S. F. Scott

Related entries: AUSTRIAN COMMITTEE; CENTRAL REVOLUTIONARY COMMITTEE; DUMOURIEZ; GIRONDINS; GUADET; MONTAGNARDS; SEPTEMBER 1792 MASSACRES; VERGNIAUD.

GEORGE III (1738-1820), king of Great Britain. When the Estates General convened in 1789, the people of Britain were still celebrating the miraculous recovery of George III from porphyria, an unknown disease associated with insanity in the eighteenth century. During the decade of the Revolution, his health improved, enabling him to engage actively in every aspect of Britain's political affairs.

Throughout his life, George III remained an uncompromising spokesman for the *ancien régime*, opposing parliamentary reform, Catholic emancipation, and the abolition of slavery. He saw the Revolution as a string of barbarous acts committed by "the most savage people," and considered all pro-revolutionary societies in Britain as "daring outrages." The excesses of the Revolution increased British francophobia and enabled the government to solidify its position by splitting the Whig opposition. Although he adhered to a policy of neutrality toward France prior to the outbreak of war, the Hanoverian king was philosophically incapable of neutrality. When war came, he viewed it as a crusade to overthrow Jacobinism and restore the Bourbons. He enthusiastically supported W. Pitt's repressive acts and vigorously opposed all attempts at a negotiated peace, including Amiens (1802). He viewed Napoleon as an impious, usurping Corsican tyrant. Failing health through repeated attacks of porphyria after 1800 left him debilitated, blind, and mentally disturbed. The Regency Bill (1811) finally removed him from power, but his popularity as king never waned.

A. Aspinall, ed., *The Later Correspondence of George III*, 5 vols. (Cambridge, 1962–70); S. Ayling, *George the Third* (London, 1972); J. Brooke, *King George III* (London, 1972).

H. V. Evans

Related entries: JACOBINISM; PITT.

GERLE, CHRISTOPHE-ANTOINE (1736-1805). See THEOT.

GERMINAL, UPRISING OF 12.   See UPRISING OF 12 GERMINAL.

GIRONDE, southwestern department and term used to describe elected deputies to the Legislative Assembly and the Convention (most notably P.-V. Vergniaud, A. Gensonné, and M.-E. Guadet) whose prominence as liberal republicans caused the name of this constituency to become associated with the leading politicians of this persuasion. The election of men conspicuously identified with civil liberties and laissez-faire economic policies reflected the commitment of this commercial wine-growing region to the Revolution's earlier, primarily antifeudal phase, and manifestations of Revolutionary ardor continued to mark the department's political life during the period of the Girondins' national ascendancy from the autumn of 1791 to the spring of 1793. Despite apprehensions among powerful business interests in Bordeaux, the *chef-lieu*, that the war against Austria and Prussia that their deputies championed would lead to an economically damaging conflict with England, 8,000 volunteers were forthcoming from the Gironde before the end of 1792; and after those fears were realized in 1793, local leaders at their own expense outfitted corsairs to defend the southwestern coast from English warships. Battalions from Bordeaux also participated in the Republic's initial expedition against the Vendée rising. The department's major elective bodies—influenced by the particularist tradition of the historic province of Guienne as well as by personal loyalties and liberal ideological convictions—supported the Girondin deputies of the Convention in their struggle against the Mountain and Paris.

   In the wake of the Girondins' fall, representatives of the commune of Bordeaux and of the General Council of the Gironde combined to form a Commission populaire de salut public (7 June 1793), which dispatched agents to other departments to encourage the federalist revolt and which sponsored a Force départmentale to resist the central government. Important localities such as La Réole, however, failed to back the insurgency; the departmental army proved ineffective; and the Commission populaire decreed its own dissolution on 1 August 1793. During the following month, forces loyal to the Committee of Public Safety easily subdued the area. The reprisals that ensued were less extensive than in places like Lyon where federalist resistance was more tenacious. J.-L. Tallien, one of the *conventionnels* charged with exacting retribution, was accused in Paris of undue leniency. But as the Terror intensified, more than 300 executions did take place (most dramatically of fugitive deputies Guadet, J.-B.

Salles, C.-J.-M. Barbaroux, and J.-B. Birotteau, who had fled to the southwest after the failure of the federalist revolt in Normandy and Brittany). Deputies on mission attempted to have the word *Gironde* suppressed as a place name and to rechristen the department Bec d'Ambès. During these same months (October 1793–July 1794) the business and professional elites, which had dominated the Gironde since 1790, were displaced, and administrative power was vested in a military commission directly responsible to Paris and staffed in its lesser echelons by lower-middle-class functionaries from the region. After Thermidor, however, men of the *haute bourgeoisie* again succeeded to most positions of prominence and authority in the department.

P. Bécamps, *Les suspects à Bordeaux et dans le département de la Gironde, 1789–1799* (Paris, 1954); R. M. Brace, *Bordeaux and the Gironde, 1789–1794* (Ithaca, 1947); A. Forrest, *Society and Politics in Revolutionary Bordeaux* (Oxford, 1975).

M. R. Cox

Related entries: FEDERALISM; GIRONDINS; LYON; MONTAGNARDS; REPRESENTATIVES ON MISSION; TALLIEN; VENDEE.

GIRONDINS, political faction during the Legislative Assembly and the early Convention (1791–93). After the start of the Legislative Assembly, a loosely knit group of left-wing deputies began to meet regularly for meals, entertainment, and in salons. Although this group never formally became a political party and did not even vote as a bloc in the Assembly, it became increasingly known as a distinct political faction, referred to by various names at the time (among them, Brissotins, Rolandins, Nationals), the term *Girondins* becoming universal only after the publication of A. Lamartine's famous history in 1847. The Girondins themselves were composed of two fairly distinct subgroups, each of which had roots going back to pre-Revolutionary days. The first was a group of gifted deputies from the Gironde, including P.-V. Vergniaud, M.-E. Guadet, A. Gensonné, J.-A. Grangeneuve, and J.-F. Ducos. These men were exceptional orators who had been active in Bordeaux political affairs. Their speeches to the Legislative Assembly made an immediate and strong impression. The other group was made up of intellectuals and journalists who had been active in the Paris municipal revolution. They included J.-P. Brissot, the marquis de Condorcet, J. Dusaulx, and C. Fauchet.

At the outset, the Legislative Assembly included more Feuillants than Girondins, but most deputies had not yet aligned with any faction. The Girondins needed a patriotic cause that could divide the Feuillants and gain the support of the independents. They found their cause in the call for a declaration of war against Austria. In speeches first to the Paris Jacobins and then to the Assembly, the Girondins argued that a war with Austria would rally the French around the Revolution, liberate oppressed peoples from despotism, and test the loyalty of Louis XVI. This was a shrewd and timely foreign policy, which quickly benefited the Girondins. Their first victory came on 1 December 1791, when the Feuillant minister of war, L.-L. Duportail, was forced to resign because of Girondin attacks. By March 1792, the Girondins had demonstrated that they could secure a majority of votes in the Assembly, and Brissot had become the nation's most powerful deputy.

In March, Louis XVI dismissed his Feuillant ministers and appointed a new cabinet, which included two of Brissot's friends, E. Clavière as minister of contributions and J.-M. Roland de la Platière as minister of the interior. Together with C. Dumouriez at the Ministry of Foreign Affairs and, later, J. Servan de Gerbey at the Ministry of War, the new cabinet had an unambiguously prowar posture. War against Austria was finally declared on 20 April 1792.

By this time, the pacifist Feuillants had degenerated into various splinter groups, but their place was taken by a very small group of radical Jacobins, led by M. Robespierre, who opposed the war because of its effect on the urban poor. The break that now occurred between Girondins and radical Jacobins was manifested in L.-C.-S. Desmoulins' vicious pamphlet, *Jean-Pierre [sic] Brissot demasqué*. But this schism became important only when the first battles went badly, and the French began to realize that the war might be long and require costly sacrifices.

The Girondins worried about the effect the first losses would have on public opinion. Roland secretly subsidized various pro-Girondin journals and employed the former novelist J.-B. Louvet to begin the *Sentinelle*, a propaganda sheet written for Paris *sans-culottes* and posted throughout the capital. More important, the Girondins blamed the military losses on the treasonous behavior of the king. Roland, Clavière, and Servan had never been on good terms with Louis XVI, and in May their relations with him deteriorated even further. The king consistently refused to endorse Girondin legislation. During the first week in June, Roland sent the monarch a letter (actually written by his wife) warning him of a new insurrection if his behavior did not become a good deal more patriotic. When Louis ignored the letter, Roland leaked it to the papers, and the king dismissed all the Girondin ministers and in their place appointed Feuillants.

An older generation of historians once claimed that the Girondins were responsible for the insurrection of 20 June 1792, which occurred only a week after their dismissal from the cabinet. But no hard evidence has ever linked Brissot and his friends to this *sans-culotte* uprising. A closer look at the sources reveals that for some time after their dismissal, the Girondins hoped that the king would come to his senses and reinstate Clavière, Roland, and Servan. This placed the Girondins in a very ambiguous position on the eve of the 10 August insurrection, a position that would haunt them later. On the one hand, they posited themselves as popular leaders who were trying to steer the Revolution in a more democratic direction. But on the other hand, they wavered from actually calling for a popular revolution against the monarchy, clinging to the hope that the king would recall them to the cabinet.

After the 10 August insurrection, Clavière, Roland, and Servan were appointed to the first republican cabinet. Their power was further strengthened by the elections to the Convention, in which the older Girondins were joined by new deputies such as C.-J.-M Barbaroux, L.-S. Mercier, F. Lanthenas, J.-A. Creuzé-Latouche, and T. Paine. But the new government was now opposed by a more potent force than the monarchy: the revolutionary Paris Commune, which embodied the growing political aspirations of the *sans-culottes*. In the Convention these forces were well represented by M. Robespierre, G.-J. Danton, and the Montagnards, who accused the Girondins of corruption, opportunism, military ineptitude, and reactionary economic policies. During the fall of 1792 several Girondins, including Brissot, were expelled from the Paris Jacobins, and the stage was set for a struggle over control of the Convention itself.

The trial of Louis XVI provided the Convention with its first major showdown between Girondins and Montagnards. The Montagnards were highly disciplined and united in their call for the king's conviction and for his immediate execution. In contrast, the Girondins were divided on the various issues of the trial and advocated no common policy. While some historians find a tendency among Brissot and his allies toward the more moderate position of national referendum on the king's sentence and for his expulsion from the nation instead of his death, several Girondins voted with the Montagnards on each of the trial's major issues, and the Girondins' leadership of the Convention was seriously diminished. A few Girondins, such as A.-G. Kersaint, withdrew from political life, and the day following the king's execution, Roland resigned as minister of the interior.

Although the trial marked the end of Girondin control of the Convention, the Montagnards could not yet secure a majority of deputies. The spring of 1793 was characterized by a stalemate in which neither side could pass strong legislation needed to address an escalating war, counterrevolution in the Vendée, and serious economic problems. In April the Central Revolutionary Committee of the Paris sections called for the expulsion of twenty-two Girondins. But the Convention did little until the crisis of 31 May–2 June, when 20,000 armed *sans-culottes* surrounded the Convention and virtually forced the reluctant deputies to order a Girondin purge. Twenty-nine Girondins were expelled from the Convention, and a general repression followed in which the Girondins were successfully eliminated as a political force.

There remains much controversy among historians regarding the extent to which the Girondins constituted a formal political entity with any united set of policies and behavior. To be sure, one of the main reasons for the demise of the Girondins between November 1792 and May 1793 was their staunch individualism in contrast to the more disciplined Jacobins. But despite their disunity, there were some general principles that the Girondins shared and made their network of friendships so politically potent. First, the Girondins stood for representative democracy. They believed in a democratic republic and of all French Revolutionary groups were the most receptive to American political ideas. Second, the Girondins believed in laissez-faire economic policies. Following A. Smith and the physiocrats, they pursued an economy in which the grain trade was left completely in private hands and in which prices were determined strictly by the market. This position made the gap between them and the *sans-culottes* unbridgeable. Third, the Girondins took a greater interest in the amelioration of the condition of blacks and women than other political groups; abolitionist clubs such as the Amis des Noirs and feminist groups such as the Cercle Social were dominated by Brissot and his friends. Finally, the Girondins were very interested in preserving the Civil Constitution of the Clergy even when it became clear that this religious compromise no longer served the national interest.

Actes du colloque Girondins et Montagnards (Sorbonne, 14 décembre 1975), A. Soboul, ed. (Paris, 1980); E. Bire, La legende des Girondins (Paris, 1881); A. Patrick, The Men of the First French Republic: Political Alignments in the National Convention of 1792 (Baltimore, 1972); A. Mathiez, Girondins et Montagnards (Paris, 1930); M. J. Sydenham, The Girondins (London, 1961).

G. Kates

Related entries: BRISSOT; CENTRAL REVOLUTIONARY COMMITTEE; CERCLE SOCIAL; CIVIL CONSTITUTION OF THE CLERGY; CLAVIERE; FEUILLANTS; GENSONNE; GUADET; PARIS COMMUNE; ROLAND DE LA PLATIERE, J.-M.; SANS-CULOTTES; SOCIETE DES AMIS DES NOIRS; VERGNIAUD.

GLACIERE. See AVIGNON; ROVERE.

GOBEL, JEAN-BAPTISTE-JOSEPH (1727-94), bishop. Son of a comital procureur fiscal and avocat in the conseil souverain of Alsace, Gobel was named bishop in partibus of Lydda and succeeded his uncle as coadjutor of Basel in 1771. Elected to the Estates General, he proposed the qualification concerning public order incorporated into the article on toleration in the Declaration of the Rights of Man and the Citizen. Despite some initial reservations, Gobel subscribed to the Civil Constitution of the Clergy before the National Assembly on 2 January 1791. He was elected constitutional bishop of Paris and consecrated by C.-M. Talleyrand in March. As bishop he published a number of pastoral instructions supporting the Civil Constitution and urging obedience to the laws adopted by the Revolutionary assemblies. He also frequented the Jacobins and sanctioned clerical marriage.

Under pressure from the leaders of the dechristianization movement, Gobel abdicated his office and donned the bonnet rouge before the Convention on 7 November 1793, explaining that no public and national worship should be practiced other than that of liberty and equality. Arrested, along with the Hébertists, for allegedly conspiring against the Republic, the former bishop was guillotined on 13 April 1794.

G. Gautherot, "Gobel, évêque métropolitain constitutionnel de Paris," Rev. des ques. hist. 83 (1909) and Gobel, évêque métropolitain constitutionnel de Paris (Paris, 1911).

J. W. Merrick

Related entries: CIVIL CONSTITUTION OF THE CLERGY; SYMBOLISM.

GODOY, MANUEL (1767-1851), Spanish minister of state. See CHARLES IV.

GOHIER, LOUIS-JÉROME (1746-1830), deputy, minister of justice, director. Born in Brittany, Gohier was an *avocat* in Rennes, before being elected deputy for the Ille-et-Vilaine to the Legislative Assembly. In February 1792, he spoke in favor of the sequestration of *émigré* property and in June 1792 made an anticlerical speech on the secularization of the *état-civil*. After 10 August 1792, he was entrusted with the examination of the king's civil list and royal correspondence, which demonstrated the duplicity of the court. On 20 March 1793, he replaced D.-J. Garat as minister of justice, a post he retained until 1795; this later earned him a reputation as a Jacobin. As minister, he supervised the arrest of the Orléans family and, after 2 June 1793, of the proscribed Girondin deputies. After 1795, he resumed a legal career in Paris, becoming president of the *tribunal civil, tribunal criminel,* and eventually of the *cour de cassation*. In the Year VI, he was elected deputy for Paris to the Council of Five Hundred by the dissident assembly at the Oratoire. His election was annulled in the anti-Jacobin coup d'état of Floréal Year VI.

On 30 Prairial Year VIII, he was elected a director, after previously unsuccessful attempts in the Years V and VI. He was president of the Directory at the time of N. Bonaparte's coup of 18 Brumaire. Gohier rejected suggestions that Bonaparte, who was under the statutory age of forty, could become a member of the Directory, and his devotion to constitutional legality made him the enemy of the *brumairiens*. In his memoirs, written during the Bourbon Restoration, Gohier attacks Bonaparte and E.-J. Sieyès as traitors to the Constitution of the Year III, justifies the Directory, and defends his own support for the ministers J.-B.-J. Bernadotte (war) and R. Lindet (finances).

At midnight on 17 Brumaire, J. Beauharnais invited the Gohiers to breakfast at 8 A.M. on the 18 Brumaire, but Gohier was suspicious enough to send his wife alone. He refused to resign as director, but his influence was effectively neutralized by the Bonapartists, who confined him to the Luxembourg palace, guarded by General J.-V. Moreau's troops, until 20 Brumaire. He retired from politics but in 1802 was appointed commercial secretary in Amsterdam. He retired definitively from public life in 1810, when France annexed Holland.

L. J. Gohier, *Mémoires des contemporains*, 2 vols. (Paris, 1824); M. J. Sydenham, *The First French Republic, 1792–1804* (London, 1974).

M. Lyons

Related entries: COUNCIL OF FIVE HUNDRED; COUP OF 18 BRUMAIRE; DIRECTORY; GARAT; SIEYES.

GONCHON (''L'ORATEUR DU PEUPLE'') (no known dates), popular militant of the faubourg Saint-Antoine. Born at Lyon (possibly in the city's silk-weaving suburb of La Croix-Rousse where there was a family of that name), Gonchon became a *dessinateur en soie*, one of the elite trades in the silk industry. At some unknown date, perhaps after his time in the army as a dragoon, he moved to the faubourg Saint-Antoine in Paris where he became a small entrepreneur, directing a silk embroidery workshop that produced novelties of his own design. He had an orthodox career as a minor militant during the early Revolution. Although not an official *vainqueur de la Bastille*, he was among those who delivered the French Guards from the Abbaye and marched with them against the Bastille. He went to Versailles on 5 October 1789, participated in the dispersal of an aristocratic assembly at the Capucins in 1790, signed the Champ de Mars petition in 1791, and received favorable mention in the radical newspaper, *Le père Duchesne*. However, it was in 1792 that he became prominent as the most frequent spokesman for the repeated deputations from the faubourg Saint-Antoine to the Legislative Assembly. Initially referred to as "L'Orateur des hommes du 14 juillet," he soon became known as "L'Orateur du faubourg Saint-Antoine" or as "L'Orateur du peuple," a title whose implicit claims were rivaled only by another radical, Anarchasis Cloots, "L'Orateur du genre humain."

Gonchon's main talents lay in his oratorical powers and his sense of dramatic self-production. With his outsize pike topped by a huge Phrygian bonnet, he became a symbol of the faubourg. His speeches at this time reflected fairly accurately the opinions of the faubourg, although he does not seem to have shaped these opinions. He reflected the faubourg in his defense of the 20 June demonstration, his denunciation of despotism, his identification of a new aristocracy of wealth, and, above all, in his consistent belief in the goodness, purity, and infallibility of the people, whose instincts and services to the Revolution he contrasted with those of constitution makers. He similarly reflected faubourg attitudes later in 1792 by his impatience with factional fighting in the Convention and his repeated calls for republican unity.

He went on several missions outside Paris after 10 August 1792: in August to explain the overthrow of the king to the departments threatened by the Prussians, in December on a patriotic propaganda mission in the Eure-et-Loire, from mid-January to mid-April 1793 as an official Apostle of Liberty with the army in Belgium, where he displayed moderate attitudes especially in religious matters. Indeed, Gonchon was fundamentally a moderate. The Girondists, who sensed this, made some attempts to attach him to themselves. However, although he certainly received a small sum from their agent, there is no evidence that he ever either understood the nature of the overtures or espoused their cause. He was an open enemy of C. Dumouriez, and his speeches against Convention factions were aimed at both Montagnards and Girondists. Nonetheless, his moderation and his long absence in Belgium put him out of touch with the faubourg. His antifaction speech to the Convention on 22 April 1793 contrasted with that of another official spokesman for the faubourg on 1 May who presented a list of radical demands close to the *Enragé* program. The evolution of his politics became fully visible when he was sent by the Ministry of the Interior to the southern departments on a mission of inquiry in May 1793. He was in Lyon at the end of May when the sectional revolt overthrew the Jacobin municipality. He wrote a series of ill-advised reports to the minister, sympathetic to the sections. These show that he was moved above all by what he saw as deliberately bloodshedding tactics by the Jacobins during the confrontation at Lyon. This suggests that the source of his growing moderation may have been a revulsion from the September Massacres, which he never mentioned in his speeches.

After his return to Paris, Gonchon was denounced increasingly as a Girondist. However, the government moved against him with considerable uncertainty, which doubtless stemmed from its fear of his presumed influence at a time when it was beginning to repress the popular movement. Arrested and released twice in September 1793 by the Committee of General Security, he was finally imprisoned in late October. He was released on 20 Thermidor Year II (7 August 1794) as a victim of M. Robespierre but rearrested a month later on denunciations about his federalist behavior at Lyon. He was finally set free on 29 Vendémiaire Year III (20 October 1794).

In the early period of the Thermidorian Reaction, he shared the anti-Jacobin attitudes of many popular militants. Between Brumaire and Pluviôse (November 1794 and February 1795), when the *jeunesse dorée* (militant reactionary youth) seemed capable of an antiterrorist alliance with popular elements, Gonchon acted as an organizer and spokesman for it. He led a crowd of youths in stoning the Jacobin club in mid-Brumaire, published a pamphlet calling for vengeance, organized a counter-festival on the anniversary of the king's death, denounced F.-N. Babeuf in Nivôse, and participated in the repression of sectional militants alongside a Girondist agent named Gadolle who had tried to manipulate him in late 1792. However, his attitudes changed when he was sent by the Committee of General Security to help restore order at Lyon (probably late Germinal, or mid-April), for he narrowly escaped assassination there by militant reactionaries. During the 13 Vendémiaire Year IV (5 October 1795) royalist insurrection in Paris, he was employed by the committees of government to arm the faubourg Saint-Antoine in support of the Convention.

Early in Year IV Gonchon acted as a governmental agent in attempts to tie the faubourg to the directorial regime. He distributed 15,000 *livres* out of the Ministry of General Police's secret funds. On 11 Floréal Year IV (30 April 1796), the Directory sent him to the Haute-Loire, Ardèche, and Gard to inquire into political disturbances. He remained there nearly a year, supporting local reactionaries against the neo-Jacobins in the electoral struggles of the Year V. In the Year VI (late 1797–1798) he seems to have been once again an agent of the Ministry of General Police in Paris. Clearly his life became increasingly difficult. In Nivôse Year VI (December 1798), he petitioned the Directory for a pension to enable him to start a new workshop to produce more novelties of his own invention. He subsequently dropped out of view.

A.N. F⁷ 4606, 7525; V. Fournel, *Le patriote Palloy; L'Orateur du peuple, Gonchon* (Paris, 1892).

C. Lucas

Related entries: BABEUF; CHAMP DE MARS "MASSACRE"; COMMITTEE OF GENERAL SECURITY; CLOOTS; DUMOURIEZ; FEDERALISM; GIRONDINS; *JEUNESSE DOREE*; PRISONS; SYMBOLISM; 10 AUGUST 1792; THERMIDORIAN REACTION.

GOSSEC, FRANCOIS-JOSEPH (1734-1829), Belgian composer, composition professor at Paris Conservatory (1795-1816). See MUSIC.

GOUGES, MARIE-OLYMPE DE (1748-93), pamphleteer and writer. Known as quixotic, garrulous, and seemingly unpredictable, Olympe de Gouges was born near Montauban simply as Marie Gouze, daughter of P. Gouze, a butcher, and O. Mouisset, a trinket peddler. Little is known of her youth except that she married L.-Y. Aubry, the proprietor of a restaurant, in 1765. Less than a year later, she bore a son, Pierre. When Aubry died, Gouges was left with an adequate income and a desire to relocate in Paris where she planned to become a flamboyant literary figure even though she had little formal education.

In 1784, Gouges experienced her first literary success when *Zamour et Myrza ou l'heureux naufrage* was accepted by the Comédie Française. To a certain degree, this was her only literary success. The playwright P.-A. Caron de Beaumarchais began to question the authorship of her works, and other writers wearied of her attempts to dominate their gatherings. In *Le philosophe corrigé*, she smugly dismissed her critics by declaring that they envied her talent. She turned then to political tracts. Regardless of the type of writing, Gouges' message remained substantially the same: an undercurrent of feminism, a challenge to detractors, and a desire to immortalize herself.

A political moderate, Gouges supported the institution of the monarchy, but she also pressed for relief for the poor and national workshops. Other causes included a women's journal, patriotic subscriptions, the creation of a second national theater for women, and a mission to bring the king's brothers back to France in order to silence rumors of international plots. This mixture of causes labeled her either as republican or royalist, depending on the accuser.

Gouges' most famous writing was *Les droits de la femme et de la citoyenne* (1791). The political pamphlet spelled out her firm commitment to feminism. Could men ever be just, she questioned, when they have created a tyranny against women? In an impassioned plea, which became both celebrated and apocryphal, Gouges wrote: "A woman has the right to mount the scaffold; she must also have the right to mount the tribune" (Gouges, Art. 10).

In December 1792, Gouges discovered a new cause to bring her notoriety. It was her "sublime duty as a republican" (Lacour, p. 57) to join C.-G. Malesherbes in his defense of the king. Her defense was clear: to recognize the distinctions between the man and the king. Her offer of counsel, however, was dismissed, and journals treated the event with amusement.

During the winter of 1793, her writings became invectives against M. Robespierre whom she called "the egotistical abomination" (Lacour, p. 62) of the Revolution. There were also two new causes she espoused: conciliation between the Girondins and Jacobins and a plebiscite to determine the government of France.

Les trois urnes ou le salut de la patrie, which set forward her plan of plebiscite, was the evidence Robespierre needed for her arrest. The pamphlet was clearly seditious under the Law of 29 March, and Gouges was arrested on 20 July 1793. Even in prison, Gouges did not realize the seriousness of the charges, and she continued to write tirades that branded her as a Girondin and aristocrat. Tried for her writings, she was found guilty and sentenced to death, but Gouges had one last plan. She pleaded that she was pregnant to postpone her execution. Physicians, however, declared that it was a ruse.

On 3 November 1793, Olympe de Gouges mounted the scaffold. The obituary that appeared in the *Feuille du salut public*, however, did not cite her crime solely as sedition. According to the journal, she was equally guilty of feminism, "for having forgotten the virtues which befit her sex."

A.N., W.293, dossier 210 (imprisonment and trial); M. Cerati, *Le Club des citoyennes républicaines révolutionnaires* (Paris, 1966); O. de Gouges, *Les Droits de la Femme* (n.p., n.d.); L. Lacour, *Les origines du féminisme contemporain: Trois femmes de la Révolution, Olympe de Gouges, Théroigne de Méricourt, Rose Lacombe* (Paris, 1900).

S. Conner

Related entries: BEAUMARCHAIS; MALESHERBES; ROBESPIERRE, M.

GREAT FEAR (c. 20 July-6 August 1789), currents of alarm and panic that swept the French countryside. The Great Fear arose in a situation of generalized fear and anxiety, which stemmed from a conjuncture of famine, unemployment, political turmoil, and revolution. It was at root a fear of brigands, armed hordes who were said to be roaming the countryside, looting, burning, pillaging, and massacring. Yet the explanation of the Great Fear is more complicated: it was the conviction that brigands and foreign troops were in the service of the aristocracy that gave the fear its particular character.

Misery was widespread in France in the spring and summer of 1789. The 1788 harvest had failed, and the subsistence picture became critical as the next year's harvest approached. Prices peaked in July 1789. There was serious unemployment in both agriculture and manufacturing. High prices, shortages, and purchases by provisioning agents for the cities provoked bread riots and the popular taxation of grain. Grain stores and shipments roused suspicions of famine plots—hoarding and speculation on the food of the poor. Tax farmers and customs inspectors were the objects of increasingly vituperative and violent attacks. Most especially, misery had swelled the numbers of wandering poor—beggars, itinerant workers, peddlers, deserters, and the destitute. Beggars were an accepted part of rural society, but unknown wanderers inspired the deepest apprehensions. As harvest time approached, farmers lived in perpetual dread of brigands who were known to cut crops or fire buildings when dissatisfied with the hospitality they had received. Periods of scarcity aggravated these fears.

The new element in 1789 was the expectation of reform. The calling of the Estates General for the spring of 1789 and the preparation of *cahiers* raised peasant hopes that the king would indeed redress their grievances. In many cases, the peasants took the expression of these grievances to be tantamount to their redress, refused to pay their taxes, tithes, or seigneurial dues, and demanded the restitution of usurped property or rights. In the antiseigneurial revolts that shook France in the spring and summer of 1789, the peasants often claimed to be acting on the authority of the king.

There had been urban riots and rural uprisings throughout the spring of 1789 in Provence, Dauphiné, Hainaut, Cambrésis, and Picardy, and in the Paris and Versailles region. Most of these revolts were a direct response to famine conditions and struck at public officials and the privileged orders. Rural uprisings multiplied after 14 July. Franche-Comté, Alsace, Hainaut, and the Mâconnais were shaken by extensive and violent armed revolts, which for the most part were distinctly antiseigneurial. Peasants refused payment of seigneurial dues or tithes, destroyed archives and even court records, attacked châteaux, abbeys, mills, and forges, invaded forests, and destroyed game. A chance explosion on 19 July at the Château de Quincey, where peasants claimed they had been invited to drink, launched the revolts in Franche-Comté and also served as chilling confirmation of an aristocratic plot. In Alsace peasants assaulted their Jewish creditors and forced cancellation of their debts. Revolts in the Mâconnais were among the most violent; whole towns joined in the march from château to château, burning archives and sacking homes. Destruction and revenge were the obvious and avowable goals in these revolts. The revolts contributed to the atmosphere of anxiety and unrest that was crucial to the Great Fear, but only the Franche-Comté and Mâconnais revolts were immediate causes of Fears. Moreover, the areas where rural revolts were most violent did not experience the Great Fear, which suggests that the fear germinated in areas only slowly mobilized by the Revolution.

Events in Paris provided a major impetus for the Great Fear. The foreign regiments stationed around Paris and J. Necker's dismissal on 11 July were seen as evidence of a plan to quash the Assembly and subdue the capital. The new Parisian municipality acted quickly in establishing a bourgeois militia to control the popular rising and prevent any aristocratic coup. Parisians in search of arms stormed the symbolically important Bastille. In mid-July rumors circulated in Paris, as they would in the countryside, that thousands of brigands were marching on the city, that the *émigrés* had engaged foreign troops, and that the scarcity was owing to an aristocratic plot to starve the people.

The aristocratic plot had its variant in the countryside. Peasants knew from long experience that seigneurs and clergy would fight to the end any restriction of their rights and privileges; it was only natural to believe that the aristocracy would try to ruin the king's efforts at reform. The emigration, which was just beginning, raised suspicions that princes and nobles were seeking foreign support against the Revolution. Regiments returning to their garrisons from Paris were more than once mistaken for foreign troops by the people, and exotic invasion forces were reported to have landed in various ports. The sort of syllogism that proved the aristocratic plot was a simple one: nobles had usurped the tithes; the tithes were meant to provide for beggars; therefore the beggars must be in the pay of the nobles. These connections linked the economic and political crises.

The countryside learned of events in Paris and in the Estates General through delegates' reports, correspondence, travelers, and peddlers. When news spread of Necker's dismissal and the events of 14 July, towns and villages immediately took defensive measures, established militia, seized arms, and posted guards. As royal administration in the provinces withered, local committees gradually supplanted the Old Regime government. Tensions heightened as it was widely reported that the cities, in efforts to tighten their security, had expelled their brigands, who along with escaped prisoners, galley slaves, and foreigners were proceeding to pillage the countryside.

There were several separate starting points for the fear. The fear that spread through Les Mauges and Poitou began in Nantes on 20 July, when it was reported that dragoons were coming to restore order in the city. While making defense preparations, the city sent out cavalry to search the countryside. Villagers in turn took alarm at seeing the Nantais troops, who they feared had come to seize their remaining grain stores. The Maine fear began on 20 or 21 July, probably as a result of a market disturbance. The Franche-Comté fear, developing directly from the revolt, began on the twenty-second and spread through the east and southeast. The Champagne fear began on 24 July when a herd of cows entering a woods was taken for brigands. In Beauvaisis, the fear began on 26 July near Estrées, where villagers took fright at a quarrel between poachers and guards, who they imagined were coming to cut their crops. The Valois fear, which sprang from similar harvest anxieties, crossed currents several times with the Beauvaisis fear. The fear that began in Ruffec on 27 July and had spread as far as Lourdes by 6 August developed from successively exaggerated accounts of beggars disguised as monks, who were in turn metamorphosed into brigands, thieves, and smugglers. Southeast of Paris, a current of fear that swept Hurepoix began when troops arrived at Limours on 28 July. Other currents swept northern Burgundy in late July.

The Great Fear is remarkable for the distances it covered and the speed with which it traveled. Though much of France experienced the fear, several areas were generally unaffected by it: most of Flanders, Hainaut, the Cambrésis, the Ardennes, the larger part of Normandy and the Normandy *bocage*, Brittany, Médoc, the Landes and the Basque country, Bas-Languedoc and Roussillon, Franche-Comté, Alsace, and the Mâconnais largely escaped the Fear. The fear traveled by what G. Lefebvre terms "warning" panics and "relay" panics. When the first sightings of brigands or troops were reported, towns would sound the tocsin, alerting the surrounding countryside, and the militia would be hastily formed and armed with any available weapon or implement. Warnings and calls for help were sent to neighboring villages, which were in turn thrown into panic as they prepared both to march to the assistance of the threatened village and to ensure their own security. Relay panics occurred as the warnings traveled from town to town. In some cases multiple warnings would arrive, seeming to menace a village from all directions. On other occasions, villagers responding to a call for help or even the messengers themselves would be taken for brigands, thereby amplifying and redirecting the original panic. The rumors were transmitted by letters from local or provincial authorities or notables, by postal employees or private *courriers*, by travelers, by persons fleeing in panic, and by servants or workers sent specifically to warn surrounding villages and call for help. Since the Great Fear was a series of concatenated local panics, its currents followed the local routes and pathways rather than the major thoroughfares.

One consequence of the Great Fear was a renewed suspicion of, and hostility toward, the aristocracy, and the seigneur in particular. When the apocalyptic warnings proved unfounded, peasants were inclined to blame the aristocracy for having tricked them. Since nobles were often the first to receive the reports of brigands and since they often played a prominent role in local defense arrangements, they were open to blame if the reports were untrue. Yet nobles or clergy who did not respond to the fear were guilty on all counts; not to fear the brigands when everyone else did was a sure sign of complicity, but in retrospect so was prescience. The Great Fear, which resulted in three murders, was not a particularly violent phenomenon. It was responsible for one major revolt, in Dauphiné, where scores of châteaux were damaged or burned by peasants who first assembled to fight the brigands. In most cases, the fear meant that peasants kept an even closer watch on the activities of nobles and clergy, inspected and looted their homes, harassed and threatened them, and demanded renunciations of fees and privileges. The Great Fear helped forge a sense of identity among the peasants, the Third Estate, and the Revolution and provided a precedent for the cooperation and mutual assistance between town and country that would be attempted in the August federations. Yet it was never an easy and rarely an enduring alliance. Frightened by rural unrest and rebellion, the Assembly on the night of 4 August renounced privileges and abolished the feudal regime; subsequent history may be seen as a long argument between peasants and bourgeois legislators over how far the abolition had to go.

The Great Fear is not an isolated incident in French history. There were similar panics in France in 1703 and 1848. Yet the broad conjuncture of economic and political circumstances gave the fear its poignancy and its virulence. G. Lefebvre's work remains the essential study of the fear. Study of popular risings and the psychology of panic and crowd action has proliferated since Lefebvre's time, however, and there is room for a new consideration of the fear in the light of this research. In establishing the Fear as a precise event, Lefebvre was responding to the animistic psychologism that characterized earlier discussions of it. One might now attempt to reexamine the fear in its relation to and as an expression of popular culture and mentalities.

H. Dinet, "La grande peur en Hurepoix," *Paris et Ile-de Fr.*, vols. 18–19 (1967–68), "Les peurs du Beauvaisis et du Valois," ibid., vols. 23–24 (1972–73) and "Recherches sur la grande peur dans la Bourgogne septentrionale: la peur de Bernon," *Ann. de Bourg.* 50 (1978); G. Lefebvre, "Foules révolutionnaires," *Etudes sur la Révolution française*

(Paris, 1954) [English translation, "Revolutionary Crowds," in J. Kaplow, ed., *New Perspectives on the French Revolution: Readings in Historical Sociology* (New York, 1965)] and *La Grande Peur de 1789*, rev. ed. (Paris, 1957) [English translation, *The Great Fear: Rural Panic in Revolutionary France* (New York, 1973)].

M. A. Quinn

Related entries: BASTILLE; FEUDALISM; 4 AUGUST 1789; LEFEBVRE; NECKER; TITHE.

GREGOIRE, HENRI-BAPTISTE (1750–1831), cleric and politician. Grégoire was born into an artisan family in a village in Lorraine and educated by the Jesuits. His intellectual gifts were identified early in his life, and he mingled with the enlightened circles that flourished in the later eighteenth century in Metz and Nancy. When he was only twenty-three, he won the prize of Nancy's academy with an *Eloge de la poésie*. After a few years of teaching, he was named curé in the village of Embermesnil, where he was to remain until the Revolution, except for travels in Switzerland and the German Rhineland, where the circulation of the ideas of the so-called Christian *Aufklärung* may have stimulated his own conviction that something similar was possible for France.

In 1788, he achieved prominence within Lorraine for winning the prize of the Metz academy for an essay on the question: "Are there means of rendering the Jews happier and more useful in France?" Grégoire insisted that the Jews should be emancipated and treated as citizens of France. He acknowledged that they had been corrupted by ghetto life and restriction to occupations like peddling and money lending but suggested they could be redeemed (and presumably converted to Christianity) through absorption into the French community. In Lorraine, Grégoire's advocacy of Jewish emancipation was an unpopular position.

By 1789, Grégoire had also emerged as a spokesman for the lower clergy of the province against what they considered the tyranny of the bishops. At the Nancy electoral assembly, he was chosen one of the two deputies from the First Estate to the Estates General.

At Versailles, Grégoire rapidly emerged as one of the leading advocates among the clergy for the creation of a single National Assembly. Although he was neither a good writer nor an effective speaker, his energy, dedication, and integrity characterized his political career, as they did all the other crusades of his long life. He was one of five priests to take the Tennis Court Oath and was president of the newly united National Assembly during the Bastille crisis. He continued to press, with little success, for Jewish emancipation, and he launched what would become a lifetime preoccupation: the emancipation and enfranchisement of the blacks of the Caribbean colonies.

Like many other French clerics, he warmly favored the reform of the church. As a Gallican Catholic of mildly Jansenist leanings, Grégoire was quite willing to see the Revolutionary government take the initiative. While he had some private reservations about the Civil Constitution of the Clergy, he accepted it. When he took the oath to support it, he said, "We are Christians and patriots."

Elected by two departments as their bishop under the new Civil Constitution, he chose the Loir-et-Cher. The experience was not a happy one, but Grégoire persisted to the end of his life in believing that a morally purified and politically enlightened state Catholicism was essential if Christianity were to triumph.

With the fall of the monarchy after August 1792, Grégoire was elected to the National Convention and returned to Paris. He was appointed to the Colonial Committee, despite the vehement objection and opposition of the West Indian planters, and continued his efforts on behalf of the blacks. A strong advocate of the annexation of Savoy, he was absent on mission at Chambéry when the trial of the king took place. While essentially sympathetic to the policies of M. Robespierre and the Mountain, Grégoire succeeded in remaining aloof from party squabbles. He continued to defend the constitutional church to the best of his ability, condemning both the dechristianizers and the clergy who apostasized in the face of persecution. He even continued to wear his clerical garb in the Assembly.

Elected to the Committee of Public Instruction, Grégoire made some major contributions to the notion of the formation of a national culture. He worked for the creation of basic texts for the schools, for the organization of public libraries and botanical gardens, and for the supplanting of dialects by the universal use of French. His inquiry on the use of patois is a mine of information on popular culture. In his efforts to preserve works of art as part of the national heritage, he coined the word *vandalism* to characterize their destruction.

When the Convention ended its deliberations in 1795, Grégoire was elected to the Council of Five Hundred. He continued, with scant success, to defend the surviving remnant of the constitutional church, and he organized the Société des amis des noirs to press the cause of the blacks. He began an international correspondence with other abolitionists throughout Europe. His proposals paralleled those of his English counterparts in that he advocated an expanded colonial empire as a means of undermining the slave trade and advancing France's economic interests simultaneously.

Rejected three times as a candidate for the Napoleonic Senate because of his religious views and his republicanism, Grégoire was finally elected in 1801. He was a member of the outspoken but important minority who opposed many of Napoleon's policies, including the signing of the Concordat with the papacy, which meant the definitive end of the constitutional church. Instead, Grégoire gave his support to the remnant that refused to accept reunion with Rome.

Excluded from political office with the Bourbon restoration, Grégoire retired to Auteuil, where he spent most of his final years in scholarship and writing. He wrote on black literature, on the condition of women, and he wrote his memoirs. He devoted his time above all to church history, seeking to demonstrate that the Gallican and not the ultramontane represented the genuine French religious tradition. His major work was a *Histoire des sectes*, published in two volumes in 1810 and suppressed for its criticisms of Napoleon, expanded in its posthumous third edition to six volumes. It is confusing and poorly organized but is invaluable as a source of information on popular religious movements in the eighteenth century.

Grégoire died at age eighty-one in 1831, embittered and frustrated at the failure of so many of his plans to come to fruition, but as dedicated as ever to revolutionary republicanism, the moral reformation of the world, and the regeneration of Christianity.

P. Catrice, "L'abbé Henri Grégoire (1750-1831), 'ami des tous les hommes,' et la régénération des juifs," *Mél. de sci. relig.* 36 (1979); M. de Certeau, D. Julia, and J. Revel, *Une politique de la langue: la Révolution française et les patois: l'enquête de Grégoire* (Paris, 1975); A. Gazier, *Etudes sur l'histoire religieuse de la Révolution française d'après des documents originaux et inédits* (Paris, 1887); H.-B. Grégoire, *Mémoires*, ed. H. Carnot, 2 vols. (Paris, 1838); R. Necheles, *The Abbé Grégoire, 1787– 1831: The Odyssey of an Egalitarian* (Westport, Conn., 1971).

C. *Garrett*

Related entries: BASTILLE, CIVIL CONSTITUTION OF THE CLERGY; DE-CHRISTIANIZATION; EDUCATION; MONTAGNARDS; TENNIS COURT OATH.

GRENOBLE, city in southeastern France, capital of Dauphiné and the Isère. The cradle of the Revolution, as its inhabitants boasted, Grenoble played an extremely important role in the first years of the Revolution. Revolutionary agitation began in this provincial capital of 20,000 in May 1788 when the local parlement refused to register the Edicts of May. When the monarchy attempted to exile the rebellious magistrates, a riot, the first of the Revolution, broke out, which is known as the Day of the Tiles because the populace hurled roof tiles at the royal troops. Frightened by this manifestation of popular violence, the magistrates quietly withdrew from the city, but the initiative had now passed to the city's bourgeoisie. On 14 June 1788, the three orders of Grenoble met and resolved to convene the estates of Dauphiné.

A week later, on 21 June, representatives of the province met at the château of industrialist C. Périer at Vizille, just outside Grenoble. Here for the first time, the Third Estate was doubled and votes were counted by head. Here two Grenoblois who would play important roles in the National Assembly, J.-J. Mounier and A.-P.-J.-M. Barnave, first emerged as leaders of the Third Estate. That fall, the government convoked another meeting of the estates of Dauphiné at Romans, where the deputies to represent Grenoble and the province at the Estates General were selected.

Thanks to the foresight of the municipal government, the summer of 1789 passed without violence in Grenoble. The fall did witness a quiet but desperate struggle between the local adherents of Mounier and Barnave. But in February 1790, the municipal elections revealed that the partisans of Barnave and a limited constitutional monarchy had triumphed over Mounier's more conservative adherents. A solidly bourgeois municipality, in which members of the liberal professions and wealthy merchants predominated with solidly patriotic, pro-Revolutionary sentiments, was elected.

For the next few years, Grenoble knew little unrest. The Revolution met the local bourgeoisie's expectations, and the Civil Constitution of the Clergy occasioned no dissension, for Grenoble's priests rallied to the constitutional church. High prices did cause misery among the poor and a small *sans-culottes* movement, with the artisan J.Chanrion at its head, did take shape. But the conciliatory stance of the municipal government and timely purchases of grain averted popular unrest. In August 1792, the Grenoblois cheered the advent of the Republic and professed their loyalty to the Convention.

This loyalty proved durable. In June 1793 there were signs of federalist agitation within the department of the Isère, but the city of Grenoble remained faithful to the Convention, and the federalists were quashed. For its loyalty, Grenoble seems to have been rewarded, for the city was never seriously troubled either by the Robespierrist government or its envoys. Government agents, of whom P. Chépy was the most important, frequently decried the Grenoblois' moderation, but aside from the installation of a new municipal government with strong *sans-culotte* elements and half-hearted attempts at dechristianization, the Robespierrist dictatorship left the Grenoblois to their own devices. Only two people, both refractory priests from another region, were guillotined in the city. The Terror in Grenoble was, in the words of a native son, Stendhal, "very reasonable."

More important to the city was the war. Grenoble was the headquarters of the Army of the Alps, and the presence of troops, particularly during the siege of Lyon, drove up grain prices and disrupted commerce. Nevertheless, the city tried to meet the challenge of provisioning and equipping an army. It is indicative of the political climate in Grenoble that the major factory for the production of firearms was launched jointly by the city's wealthiest merchant, C. Périer, and its most radical *sans-culotte*, J. Chanrion.

The history of Grenoble between the fall of Robespierre and the rise of Napoleon is not well known, but it seems that the Grenoblois reacted to the end of the Terror with their accustomed moderation. Unlike nearby Lyon, Grenoble was not the scene of violent counterterrorist activity, and the abandonment of the ill-enforced maximum and a purge of *sans-culotte* elements within the municipal government were the most important events precipitated by the change in regime. Once again, members of the liberal professions and wealthy merchants dominated the city government and continued to do so, despite a slight Jacobin resurgence after the coup of 18 Fructidor Year V. Only scattered resistance greeted the news of Napoleon's coup. Grenoble's bourgeoisie seems to have been happy that a stable government was at last established in Paris.

V. Chomel, ed., *Histoire de Grenoble* (Toulouse, 1976); A. A. Prudhomme, *Histoire de Grenoble* (1888).

K. Norberg

Related entries: BARNAVE; CIVIL CONSTITUTION OF THE CLERGY; DAUPHINE; DECHRISTIANIZATION; FEDERALISM; MOUNIER.

GRENVILLE, WILLIAM WYNDHAM, BARON (1759–1834), British foreign minister, 1791–1801. A member of the powerful Whig family fathered by G. Grenville, W. Grenville exerted more influence on British foreign affairs during the French Revolution than anyone else except George III and W. Pitt. After graduating from Eton and Oxford, where he distinguished himself in Greek and Latin verse, he studied law at Lincoln's Inn. In 1782 he was elected to Parliament for Buckinghamshire, the family's patronized seat, and when Pitt, his first cousin, became prime minister the following year, he was appointed privy councillor and made paymaster general, a lucrative position. After serving briefly as one of Britain's youngest Speakers of the House of Commons, he became Pitt's secretary of state for the Home Department in 1789 and foreign secretary in 1791. Between appointments he was raised to the peerage as Lord Grenville and served as Pitt's chief spokesman in the House of Lords.

During the early years of the Revolution, Grenville, like Pitt, attributed Britain's commercial prosperity to international peace and consequently urged a policy of strict neutrality toward France. As late as 7 November 1792, he was optimistic about keeping free of "all the continental evils," but after the sudden fall of the Austrian Netherlands a week later, he lamented that this "has brought the business [war] to a much nearer issue here than any reasonable man could believe a month ago" (Grenville, *Memoirs*, vol. 2, pp. 221-28). The Scheldt and propaganda decrees of late 1792 added to his fears of an inevitable war.

Following the outbreak of war in February 1793, Grenville pursued a fairly moderate policy toward France, decrying the extremities of the Burkites and questioning the wisdom of Pitt's Toulon declaration (1793) of restoring the Bourbons, but by 1795 he had become the leading counterrevolutionist in the cabinet. When the less hawkish Pitt initiated peace feelers in 1795, he tendered his resignation privately but withdrew it when Prussia made peace with France. Thereafter he consistently supported every program to aid the royalists and to give military subsidies to any country willing to fight France.

The negotiations for peace between 1796 and 1802 revealed the basic differences between Pitt and Grenville. Both mildly supported the peace negotiations in 1796 at Paris and more earnestly in 1797 at Lille, when naval mutinies, Irish revolts, Austrian defeats, financial difficulties, and Catherine II's death had clearly weakened Britain's negotiating position, but neither of them was willing to return Britain's most lucrative conquests: Cape Colony, Trinidad, and Ceylon. The greatest difference was Grenville's demand for additional colonial acquisitions for Britain and compensations for its allies. The Directory's rejection of British terms after the 18 Fructidor coup was more disappointing to Pitt than Grenville who became increasingly convinced that "an honorable war was better than a dishonorable peace" (Adams, p. 53) and that only a Bourbon restoration would ensure the security of Britain. For these same reasons, Grenville and Pitt disagreed over the peace of Amiens. The undaunted, skeptical Grenville violently opposed its terms, which he considered nationally humiliating, whereas the more pragmatic, optimistic Pitt thought them reasonable, even honorable.

In 1801 when Pitt and Grenville tried to enfranchise the Irish Catholics against the strong objections of George III, they resigned. Within a year the cousins had parted company. In 1806 Grenville formed his own government, the Ministry of All the Talents, in which the leading proponent of peace, C. J. Fox, served under the leading antagonist of the Revolution, Grenville. This short-lived ministry fell over the same issue of Irish Catholic emancipation but not until it had accomplished one major achievement: abolition of the slave trade. Thereafter Grenville disengaged more and more from parliamentary affairs but continued to write political tracts in his retirement at Dropmore. Liberal in most domestic issues (slave trade, Catholic emancipation, free trade, capital punishments), he remained unbending and tenacious in his opposition to Napoleonic France.

E. D. Adams, *The Influence of Grenville on Pitt's Foreign Policy, 1787-1798* (Washington, D.C., 1904); R. P. T.-N. Grenville, Duke of Buckingham and Chandos, *Memoirs of the Court and Cabinets of George the Third*, 4 vols. (London, 1853-55); Grenville MSS, British Library, Add. MSS 58855-59494; Hist. MSS Comm., *The Report on the Manuscripts of J. B. Fortescue, Esq., Preserved at Dropmore*, 10 vols. (London, 1892-1927).

H. V. Evans

Related entries: ANNEXATION; COUP OF 18 FRUCTIDOR YEAR V; FIRST COALITION; PITT; TREATY OF BASEL.

GRETRY, ANDRE (1741–1813), operatic composer, master of the *opéra comique*. See MUSIC.

GUADET, MARGUERITE-ELIE (1755-94), a leader of the Girondin party. Born in Saint-Emilion, educated in Bordeaux and Paris, Guadet became known in Bordeaux as a resourceful, well-informed advocate. After 1789 he served in the departmental administration as presiding criminal judge in Bordeaux and as a Girondin deputy to the Legislative Assembly (1791–92), where he became a noted orator. Though probably republican, he was alarmed by the crisis of July 1792, and, with P.-V. Vergniaud, attempted to negotiate with the king. He disliked J.-P. Marat and M. Robespierre and distrusted the influence of Paris; on 30 August 1792 he moved the abolition of the Revolutionary Commune.

Reelected to the Convention, he was actively anti-Parisian and anti-Montagnard, using his oratorical talent for personal attacks on his opponents. In the king's trial, he made a major speech for a referendum and supported the J.-B. Mailhe amendment and a reprieve. The revelation of his and Vergniaud's correspondence with the king (3 January 1793) confirmed Montagnard prejudices, but he served on the Committee of General Defense from 1 January until 6 April. He continuously opposed Parisian radicalism, voted for J.-P. Marat's impeachment, and in May proposed that the Convention's *suppléants* should move to Bourges to replace the Convention. After the events of 2 June, he left Paris for Caen. Later he hid for some months in Saint-Emilion before being discovered and guillotined in Bordeaux without trial as an outlaw.

A. Kuscinski, *Dictionnaire des conventionnels* (Paris, 1916–20); B. Melchior-Bonnet, *Les Girondins* (Paris, 1969); M. J. Sydenham, *The Girondins* (London, 1961).

A. Patrick

Related entry: VERGNIAUD.

GUARDS, FRENCH. See FRENCH GUARDS.

GUIBERT, JACQUES-ANTOINE-HIPPOLYTE DE (1743-90), military writer. Guibert was born in Montauban in 1743, the son of a French army captain who ultimately attained the rank of lieutenant general for distinguished services in the War of the Austrian Succession and the Seven Years War. Young Guibert spent hours with his father discussing, diagraming, and demonstrating tactical maneuvers even before he entered the army as a lieutenant in 1756. He distinguished himself at Rossbach and later served on the staff of the duc de Broglie, who came to take an active interest in his career. At the end of the war, Guibert returned home to resume his theoretical studies and to work with his father, now employed by the minister of war to work on revising drill regulations. In 1769 Guibert accompanied the expeditionary corps to Corsica where, as a staff officer, he gained valuable experience in training and later commanding a Corsican legion. In 1773 he spent six months visiting the principal battlefields of central Europe and studying the Prussian army, and in 1775 he was called to the War Ministry to devote the next two years to military organization. He served for the next ten years as a regimental commander, but to his dismay his regiment was not among those sent to North America, nor was he elected to represent his district assembly at the Estates General in 1789. He died in 1790.

Guibert was one of the most important and influential military writers of the eighteenth century. His most famous work, *Essai général de tactique* (1772), established his reputation as a military writer overnight and gave access to the most celebrated salons. (In 1775 Guibert married Mademoiselle Boutinon de Courcelles, and he had conspicuous success with "the reigning Queen of the salons," J. de Lespinasse.) Translated into all major languages and even into Persian, the *Essai général de tactique* won praise from Frederick the Great, the prince de Ligne, and Napoleon. In 1777 Guibert wrote *Observations sur la constitution militaire et politique des armées de s.m. Prussienne*, a perceptive analysis of the spirit and the tactics of the Prussian army under Frederick. And in 1779 appeared his *Défense du système de guerre moderne*, in which Guibert vigorously defended his tactical ideas, many of which subsequently marched into the *Ordinance of 1791*, which became the basis for French tactics in the cycle of wars that soon followed.

Simplicity and mobility dominated Guibert's thought. He sought to simplify the manual of arms, fire training, drill movements, and evolutions, retaining only what was natural and essential. He would reduce the size of an army to manageable proportions by stressing quality rather than quantity in artillery, operating with smaller infantry battalions and cavalry squadrons, by curtailing both baggage and magazines, and by overhauling the supply system. Taking a broad view of the term *tactics*, Guibert included even the knowledge essential for the subsistence of an army. He urged increasing the marching tempo from sixty to eighty paces a minute to enhance mobility. According to Guibert, the ideal size of a field army was between 50,000 and 70,000 men, with up to one-fourth of them cavalry, depending on the terrain, and with about three guns per thousand men. This was a lower ratio of artillery than was customary, but Guibert viewed artillery as a useful and important accessory rather than an arm in itself, and he looked to improved methods of training and handling the guns to create more mobile and effective batteries.

Guibert's theories represent a synthesis of the prevailing trends in eighteenth-century military thought. While stressing firepower, he deplored the Prussian emphasis on speed of fire at the expense of accuracy. Independent firing from stationary positions was to be preferred to the succession of rolling volleys delivered by Frederick's troops as they advanced, "as if noise killed." And while advocating teaching soldiers to fence with the bayonet, Guibert at the same time rejected those who contended that the musket with bayonet was essentially a shock weapon to be used in formations in depth rather than the linear formations made popular by the success of the Prussians. Guibert's system made use of either formation, according to circumstances. In open country he preferred the three-rank line in order to capitalize on improved firepower; in attacking posts or entrenchments, he advocated a combination of columns and line or a series of small columns linked with skirmishers to cover the intervals. This meant that infantry was also to be adept at light infantry tactics, while all cavalry should function essentially as light cavalry although continuing to employ shock tactics. Guibert devised new and simpler ways to form column into line and vice-versa, and if he did not invent the concept of the permanent infantry division, he advocated breaking armies up into divisions so that they could advance by several roads and yet remain close enough to support each other.

Guibert also represents an important transition from the *ancien régime* to the age of Napoleon. He was among the first to grasp the relationship between an army and the society it served—hence the need to formulate national tactics—and to appreciate the citizen soldier, although his last work suggests some back-peddling on this issue, in large measure because the American Revolution convinced him that an army composed of militia was no match for a professional army if the latter was competently led. As a *philosophe*, Guibert tried to apply the test of a reason to military practices and institutions, dreaming of the day perhaps when France would experience a national regeneration transforming subjects into citizens who shared interests and a common vision of the future, and when wars would be waged in pursuit of national objectives and no longer to satisfy the whim of a sovereign. Guibert understood the difference between limited and unlimited war, and his writings seemed to anticipate the changes in warfare that shortly would be unleashed by the French Revolution and harnessed by Napoleon. If he failed to foresee the growth in the size of armies, the unprecedented quantities of artillery, and the full implications of a people's war, the spirit that saturated Guibert's writings made him ideally suited for the armies of the First Republic and Napoleon.

E. Carrias, *La pensée militaire française* (Paris, n.d.); J. Colin, *L'infanterie au XVIIIe siècle: la tactique* (Paris, 1907); J. A. H. de Guibert, *Ecrits militaires 1772-1790* (Paris, 1977), and *Essai général de tactique*, 2 vols. (Liège, 1775); R. S. Quimby, *The Background of Napoleonic Warfare* (New York, 1957); S. Wilkinson, *The French Army before Napoleon* (Oxford, 1915).

J. Luvaas

Related entries: BONAPARTE, N.; BROGLIE.

GUILLOTINE, mechanical device introduced during the Revolution for decapitating those condemned to death. This instrument consists of two tall posts surmounted by a cross beam. The posts are grooved so as to allow a slanted blade, heavily weighted at the top, to be raised to the cross beam by a cord. When released, the heavy blade drops swiftly and forcefully on the neck of the victim who is held in place horizontally on a plank with his or her head protruding from stocks. A modern version was used in France until 1982.

It is paradoxical that this machine, which is associated in the minds of many people with one of the most gruesome aspects of the Revolution, was in fact seen by its proponents as a contribution to human progress. Since it was a carefully designed device, tested before its use, it was an example of the applied science of the age. It was also intended to be much quicker and less painful than earlier methods of execution, such as breaking the person on the wheel. Moreover, since those condemned would all be executed by the same machine, whereas decapitation had been previously reserved for the privileged classes, it represented the new equality under the law. It thus stood for three major ideals of the Enlightenment and the Revolution: technology, humanitarianism, and egalitarianism.

It was also paradoxical that a death-dealing machine is the principal, and most often the only, contribution attributed to J.-I. Guillotin (1738-1814). Guillotin was a professor of anatomy, physiology, and pathology in the University of Paris. Under the Old Regime, he had repeatedly taken up causes that he considered to be in the public interest. In 1788 he had been one of the first to call for doubling the Third Estate for the coming assembly of the Estates General. Subsequently he had been elected as a deputy for the city of Paris. In the Constituent Assembly, he was a member of the Committee on Mendicity and Public Health and wrote an important report on the teaching and practice of medicine. In October and again in December 1789, he proposed that all persons found guilty of a capital offense be put to death in the same way: decapitation by a simple machine. It was this proposal that eventually linked his name to the lethal device.

Although Guillotin had proposed a machine for decapitation, his role in its development was limited. Exactly what kind of machine he had in mind is not known. The record does not reveal whether he submitted a precise plan for such a machine. One thing is clear: he invented nothing. There were a number of prototypes available. Various mechanisms similar to the guillotine had been used in Ireland, England, Scotland, Germany, Italy, and southern France, about which he may have heard. In any case, his proposal was not approved at once. When decapitation was finally adopted in June 1791, he took no part in the debate. Moreover, it was not until March 1792, under the Legislative Assembly, that it was decreed that such decapitation be carried out by means of a machine.

The expert whom the Legislative Assembly consulted about the design of the machine was not Dr. Guillotin but another doctor, A. Louis, secretary of the Academy of Surgery, who used his knowledge of anatomy to design a machine that would cut smoothly through the human neck. The first such machine was constructed by a German harpsichord maker, T. Schmit. The machine was tested first on animals and then on the corpses of paupers who had died in the hospital. It was used for the first time in April 1792 to execute a highwayman who had been kept waiting while various improvements and adjustments were made to ensure its effectiveness. Soon it became the principal means of executing political offenders.

For a time the head-chopping machine was called the Louison or Louisette because of the leading role of Dr. Louis in designing the actual working model; however, the device became forever associated with Dr. Guillotin. During the debate on his proposal in December 1789, in response to a criticism, he had emitted a remark he lived to regret; he claimed his machine could lop off a head in the blink of an eye without any pain. The Assembly had broken out laughing. By calling it *ma machine*, the kindly doctor had meant merely whatever device was finally adopted according to his suggestion, but his proposal to slice off heads in a philanthropic fashion gave rise to endless jests. In December the royalist newspaper *Actes des apôtres* published a song mockingly praising the patriotic doctor for his bright idea and christening his proposed device the "Guillotine." Thus Guillotin's name was given to the machine before it was designed.

After its use in Paris, identical guillotines were distributed to all the departments in 1792 so that a common method of execution would prevail throughout France, administrative uniformity being another ideal of the age. The new device soon became part of French popular culture. It became the theme of popular songs and vaudevilles. It was reproduced in miniature as an ornament in living rooms and as a piece of jewelry. It was used as a motif on snuffboxes and china. Children sometimes played with toy models of it, lopping off the heads of mice or birds. The authorities in Arras ordered these playthings seized lest children lose all humanitarian feelings.

Above all the guillotine became a symbol for both supporters and opponents of the Revolution. For ardent Revolutionaries, it was the people's avenger, the national axe, the republican sword, or the patriotic shortener. Some even viewed it as a sort of religious object, the holy guillotine, used in the liturgy of the Red Mass to purify the world. For counterrevolutionaries it was used to represent the excesses of the Revolution, especially the death toll of the Terror of 1793–94 in which thousands perished under the blade of the efficient machine. Right-wing artists frequently used it in their engravings to evoke revulsion. One caricature shows M. Robespierre, standing amid a forest of guillotines, about to decapitate the executioner after having all the rest of France guillotined.

A. Kershaw, *A History of the Guillotine* (London, 1965); G. Lenotre [pseud. for Louis Gosselin], *La guillotine et les exécuteurs ... pendant la Révolution* (Paris, 1914); P. Quentin-Bauchart, *Le Docteur Guillotin et la guillotine* (Paris, 1905).

J. A. Leith

Related entries: MEDICINE; TERROR, THE.

GUSTAVUS III (1746-92), king of Sweden. Strongly French in culture, Gustavus was raised on the philosophy of the Enlightenment and twice visited France. After ascending the throne in 1771, he overthrew the Swedish constitution of 1720 through a coup in 1772 that restored strong royal authority. While he carried out numerous enlightened, practical reforms, he thereafter remained sensitive to any threat of insurrection, at home or abroad. His apprehensions were further aroused by a mutiny, the Anjala Confederation, among his aristocratic officers during a war with Russia in 1788, which sought to impose constitutional limits to his power. In response, Gustavus gained the support of the non-noble estates of the Diet and early in 1789 further strengthened the royal prerogative in return for the leveling of most remaining corporate privileges in Sweden.

The French Revolution thus found Gustavus bitterly opposed to any threat to monarchical power, yet he was critical of Louis XVI's lack of resolution. From 1790 he strove constantly to organize a monarchical crusade to crush the Revolution, using Count A. von Fersen as his principal agent, but was thwarted by the indifference or antipathy of the other European courts. On 16 March 1792, he was shot by a group of his aristocratic enemies, and he died on 29 March, an intriguing mixture of crowned revolutionary and counterrevolutionary.

H. A. Barton, *Count Hans Axel von Fersen* (Boston, 1975) and "Gustav III and the Enlightenment," *Eighteenth Cent. Stud.*, 6 (1972); A. Geffroy, *Gustave III et la cour de France*, 2 vols. (Paris, 1867).

H. A. Barton

Related entries: CATHERINE II; ENLIGHTENMENT; FERSEN.

H

HEBERT, JACQUES-RENE (1757-94), member of the Paris Commune, dechristianizer, leader of the Paris *sans-culottes*. Born in Alençon in 1757, Hébert was the son of a jeweler and a mother of bourgeois background. Young Jacques lost his father at age nine, but his mother, who was some thirty years younger than her husband, lived on for another twenty years. Thus, his education was largely under her influence. She enrolled him in the Jesuit collège of Alençon where he acquired the usual education in Latin and the classics. As a young man, he became involved in a romantic affair with a young widow, leading to a trial in which he was sued for slander by a rival, lost the case, and was forced to leave for Paris in 1780. For the next decade he lived in poverty. In 1790, he began to publish the *Père Duchesne*, which became the most popular of all the Revolutionary journals. At last he had found his métier.

The popularity of *Le Père Duchesne* rested on its author's unusual talent to speak the patois of the streets and army camps. F. Brunot called Hébert the "Homère de l'ordure," but it must be remembered that the untutored masses who read his newspaper and were moved by the "great anger" or the "great joy" of Père Duchesne could hardly have been touched by polite expression or classical allusion. The journal was an accurate expression of the way the *sans-culottes* expressed themselves. Moreover, it taught them politics as seen through the eyes of the man who spoke as a Revolutionary democrat and expressed their needs and concerns. Hébert freely admitted that the journal was not written for "*des demoiselles*" of his day. Moreover, its scurrilous language expressed the frustrations and disappointments felt by the *sans-culottes* who had sacrificed so much but who had received so little in return.

Like so many others, Hébert turned his back on the constitutional monarchy and became an ardent republican after Louis' flight to Varennes. What he wanted, however, was not a bourgeois republic but a democratic one. He was indignant at the division of Frenchmen into active and passive citizens and denounced the substitution of an aristocracy of birth by one of wealth. A few weeks before the king's overthrow, Hébert was elected president of his section, Bonne-Nouvelle, then as commissioner to the insurrectionary Paris Commune that put an end to the monarchy. Shortly thereafter he was chosen elector, and in December became second substitute to P.-G. Chaumette, the *procureur* of the Paris Commune.

Although at first opposed to the execution of the king, he changed his mind under the impact of the factional struggle between the Mountain and the Girondins. As commissioner to the Temple, where the royal prisoners were confined, he informed Louis, together with D.-J. Garat and P.-M.-H. Lebrun, that he had been condemned to execution. In revealing these events to his readers, he admitted, however, that the king had shown dignity, firmness, and unshaken faith during his last moments.

From September 1792 until June 1793 he never ceased repeating that the Girondins were the "most mortal enemies" of France. His continual attacks on them led to his arrest and imprisonment by the Commission of Twelve '(24-25 May 1793), which only served to arouse a vast popular movement in the sections of Paris that freed him several days later. Unlike his colleague, Chaumette, who remained prudent on the eve of the insurrection against the Girondins, Hébert insisted boldly that the Convention had to be purged. After the *journée* of 2 June 1793, he revived the program first launched by the Commune of 10 August to establish a federation of all the communes of France under the aegis of Paris. This was an obvious challenge to the Convention and to the Committees of Public Safety and General Security. The *Affiches de la Commune* became a rival of the Convention's *Bulletin*, something the Revolutionary government did not forgive. Whatever possibility existed in grouping the communes around Paris was destroyed with the federalist revolt and the military invasion of the foreign coalition.

Unlike the *enragés* who had a specific program to solve the economic and political crisis—the maximum, prohibition of speculation and engrossment, converting the *assignat* into fiat money, and introducing direct democracy—Hébert relied on purely political measures, some bordering on abstract moral precepts. To deal with shortages and high prices he advocated "good laws, unity, and peace." Once the Constitution of 1793 was put into effect, he wrote, the economic problems faced by the *sans-culottes* would be resolved. It is possible that Hébert's desire to become a minister, after the resignation of Garat, helps to account for this appeal. Yet he supported the *journées* of 4-5 September 1793 when the *sans-culottes* were able to impose their will on the Convention for the last time. It is also conceivable that for lack of an economic solution to the profound problems faced by the *sans-culottes*, Hébert turned to dechristianization as a substitute. Nevertheless, he remained tolerant of all religions, denied that he was an atheist, and saw Jesus as the first *sans-culotte* and as "the founder of all popular societies." He always honored the deist J.-J. Rousseau, rather than the skeptic F.-M. Voltaire. In his no. 335 he wrote that "all religions are good when they inspire love of humanity, respect for the law, peace, and concord."

The bitter struggle between the Hébertists and the Dantonists led ultimately to the destruction of both factions and the temporary triumph of the Revolutionary government. The decree of 14 Frimaire (4 December 1793) ended the independence of the Paris Commune and, thereby, the political base of Hébertism. The belief that the Revolution had gone far enough held by the Dantonists, and the desire to push it further in a leftward direction by the Hébertists left little room for compromise. M. Robespierre collaborated with G.-J. Danton against Hébert for a brief time and even supported L.-C.-S. Desmoulins until the latter began to threaten the whole structure of the Revolutionary government.

After the arrest of F.-N. Vincent, C.-P. Ronsin, and S. Maillard and their release because of the mounting pressure of popular support, the Cordeliers became a focus of opposition to the Convention and its committees. Rash remarks by Hébert and J.-B. Carrier calling for a ''holy insurrection'' on 14 Ventôse (4 March 1794), coupled with the discontent of workers and *sans-culottes* suffering under shortages and the high price of necessities, laid the basis for the government's charges against Hébert and his colleagues. If the government was convinced that social peace was the only way to save the Revolution and that the factions were undermining this policy, it was only a matter of time until it struck at both sides.

The constant attacks of Hébert on the rich and his endorsement of the *loi agraire*, together with his never-ceasing demand to instruct the *sans culottes*, frightened the bourgeoisie and its adherents. The Committee of Public Safety struck at dawn of 22 Ventôse (12 March 1794) and arrested Hébert, Vincent, A.-F. Momoro, and Ronsin. Other arrests followed. The leaders of the *sans-culottes* were subjected to a campaign of slander and were linked to a foreign conspiracy. A.-Q. Fouquier-Tinville was told to amalgamate various prisoners with the Hébertists. Hébert protested vainly that he did not even know the people with whom he had allegedly plotted to overthrow the government. Nothing helped. Ronsin perhaps best appreciated the nature of the indictment. He understood the political nature of the trial and the hopelessness of any defense once opportunity for action had been lost; the best he could hope for was popular vengeance. Hébert insisted to the end that he was being persecuted for his patriotism and predicted that others would follow him since ''envy seeks its victims everywhere'' and no one was free from its poison. The Hébertists were executed on 4 Germinal Year II (24 March 1794). Four months and five days later came 9 Thermidor.

P.-J.-B. Buchez and P.-C. Roux, eds. *Histoire parlementaire de la Révolution française*, vol. 36 (Paris, 1837); L. Jacob, *Hébert le Père Duchesne, chef des sans-culottes* (Paris, 1960); *Le Père Duchesne*, 1790–1794; A. Soboul, *Les sans-culottes parisiennes en l'an II* (Paris, 1958).

M. Slavin

Related entries: ACTIVE CITIZEN; GIRONDINS; HEBERTISTS; INDULGENTS; MOMORO; MONTAGNARDS; PARIS COMMUNE; PASSIVE CITIZEN; VARENNES.

HEBERTISTS (1793-94), a loose and disunited group to the political left of the Robespierrists; their views were publicized through J.-R. Hébert's newspaper, *Le Père Duchesne*. The Hébertists made themselves the spokesmen of those particular members of the Paris *sans-culottes* who objected to the Montagnard government after 2 June 1793, believing it to have become politically, economically, and socially timid since the August 1792 deposition of Louis XVI. The *journée* of 4–5 September 1793 was not of their making, yet it was supported and used by the Hébertists. They participated in the suppression of the *enragés* with whom they had been competing for public support. They also attached themselves to the *mouvement populaire* as better leaders and as J.-P. Marat's true heirs. Their position was strong. Hébert was a member of the Revolutionary Commune; F.-N. Vincent served in the Ministry of War; C.-P. Ronsin played an active role in the *armée révolutionnaire*; and A.-F. Momoro led the radical section Marat. And since late autumn 1793 the reradicalized Cordeliers club was their meeting place.

The Hébertists were among the most ardent supporters of the dechristianizing campaign during the fall of 1793. They advocated the idea of *terreur à outrance*; moreover, the Hébertists believed in the *guerre à outrance*, the revolutionizing of Europe. They demanded the total removal of the *ci-devants* from public office, taxation of the wealthy, rigorous implementation of the maximum, provision of the necessities of life for the *menu peuple*, and democratization of the leadership cadres. Socialization tendencies, however, were as alien to them as anarchism or communist concepts.

Despite the Hébertist demands, they had no concrete program for achieving them. As lower-middle-class *simplificateurs* they attempted to use or intensify, partly for purposes of agitation, various propaganda techniques. Despite similarities, however, even after the downfall of the *enragés*, not every left-wing assault on M. Robespierre's policies—for example, those of J.-N. Billaud-Varenne, J. Fouché, S. Maréchal, and F.-N. Babeuf—can be viewed as Hébertist.

After the institutionalizing of the Revolutionary government under the leadership of the Committee of Public Safety, by virtue of the Law of 14 Frimaire (4 December 1793), the Hébertist strategy consisted of attacking the Dantonist-led right wing of the Jacobins (citras). That failing, they began attacking directly the new parliamentary group of the *endormeurs* surrounding Robespierre. These *conventionnels* accused the Hébertists of being ultrarevolutionary (ultras). In the division, citras versus ultras, the government saw a danger to its own system of centralized dictatorship. It therefore used the allegation of a proposed insurrection against it as grounds for arresting the Hébertist leaders during the night of 13-14 March 1794.

A.-Q. Fouquier-Tinville, public prosecutor of the Revolutionary Tribunal, invented the label *Hébertists* in order to denounce the popular Hébert as the leader of a conspiracy (which he was not) and make him a scapegoat. To prove this charge during the trial, Fouquier linked Hébert with several undesirable foreigners, including P.-J. Proli, J. Pereira, J. C. de Kock, and A. Cloots. On

24 March 1794, the so-called Hébertists were guillotined. P.-G. Chaumette who, as *procureur-général* of the Commune, stood between the Hébertists and the Jacobins, was executed on 13 April.

The persecution of real and alleged Hébertists was continued by the Revolutionary government during the succeeding months in an effort to weaken any potentially uncontrolled popular movement. The *armées révolutionnaires* were liquidated; the antihoarding agents were eliminated; the Hébertist Commune was purged, leading to the establishment of a Robespierrist body; and many of the sections, deprived of Hébertist leadership, became politically impotent.

After 9 Thermidor a temporary, not totally irrelevant neo-Hébertist grouping developed. By the end of 1794, however, this group had fallen apart, largely as a consequence of pressure exerted on it by the Thermidorians. A few men who were close to Hébertism were active in the Club Panthéon in 1795–96, and were in contact with the Babouvists who, according to F. M. Buonarroti, did not want to join themselves to Hébertism because of its narrow historical tradition.

R. C. Cobb, *Les armées révolutionnaires*, 2 vols. (Paris, 1961-63); A. P. Herlaut, *Autour d'Hébert* (Paris, 1958) and *Le général rouge Ronsin, 1751–1794* (Paris, 1956); L. Jacob, *Hébert le Père Duchesne, chef des sans-culottes* (Paris, 1960); W. Markov and A. Soboul, *Die Sansculotten von Paris: Dokumente zur Volksbewegung, 1793-1794* (Berlin, 1957); *Le Père Duchesne*, 1790-1794; *Procès instruit et jugé au Tribunal révolutionnaire contre J.-R. Hébert* (Paris, 1794); V. G. Revunenkov, *The Commune of Paris, 1792-1794* (in Russian) (Leningrad, 1976); A. Soboul, *Les sans-culottes parisiens en l'an II* (Paris, 1961); G. Walter, *Hébert et le Père Duchesne* (Paris, 1946).

W. Markov

Related entries: ARMEES REVOLUTIONNAIRES; DECHRISTIANIZATION; HEBERT; INDULGENTS; MOMORO; MONTAGNARDS; ROBESPIERRE, M.; SANS-CULOTTES.

HELVETIC REPUBLIC, French-sponsored regime, or satellite, in Switzerland during the Directory and Consulate, 1798-1803. Before 1789 the Swiss confederation was composed of thirteen cantons that formed small independent republics; the federal diet was merely a conference of their delegates. Certain territories were allied by treaty to these cantons: the Valais, Geneva, Mulhouse, and the bishopric of Basel. Finally, the cantons dominated some *bailliages communs*: the Valtelline, the bailiwicks (*bailliages*) of Tessin, and the Vaud, regions where Romansch, Italian, or French was spoken, whereas German was the language of most of the sovereign cantons. Switzerland was also divided by religion; most of the cantons were Protestant, but some, notably Lucerne and Fribourg, practiced Catholicism. Political institutions varied considerably from one canton to another. The smaller ones practiced a sort of direct democracy, while the larger ones (Bern, Zurich, Fribourg) were aristocratic republics dominated by a restricted number of patrician families. Everywhere a feudal regime was in effect, and it often imposed a heavy burden on the population.

The French Revolution made a profound impression in Switzerland, because for several centuries France had been the ally and virtual protector of the confederation. A number of intellectuals felt that Switzerland should be reorganized on the French model to establish greater equality among the inhabitants and to emancipate the vassal regions. Moreover, the peasants of the bishopric of Basel appealed for French troops in 1792 and proclaimed a republic, which was annexed to France a year later and became the department of Mont Terrible. The democrats of Geneva also revolted in December 1792 and "democratized" their republic. At that time, France intervened only through propaganda. In his speech of 13 November 1793, M. Robespierre declared that France wished to respect the neutrality and independence of Switzerland.

Things changed when N. Bonaparte occupied northern Italy in 1796 and the following year created the Cisalpine Republic; the shortest route from Paris to Milan passed through Geneva, the Valais, and the Simplon pass. In order to ensure passage, Switzerland had to be "democratized." Besides, this was the desire of Helvetic patriots, notably P. Ochs at Basel and F. C. Laharpe at Lausanne. During a dinner in Paris on 8 December 1797, J.-F. Reubell, Bonaparte, and Ochs decided that the confederation should be transformed into a "republic, one and indivisible" and that the "vassal regions" should become cantons equal to the others. Geneva and Mulhouse would be annexed to France. These changes would be effected by the Swiss themselves; they would simply ratify a draft constitution, copied from the French constitution of 1795 and drawn up in Paris.

The Swiss, however, did not readily accept these changes. The people of Bern did not want to recognize the independence of the Vaud. The Vaudois appealed to the French forces of General G.-M.-A. Brune, who occupied the entire Vaud on 26 January 1798, while the soldiers of A. Masséna invaded the Tessin bailiwicks and A.-H.-A. Schauenbourg's troops marched on Bern, which was conquered on 6 March. The original cantons—Zug, Uri, Unterwalden, Glaris, Appenzell, Saint-Galen, Sargens—persisted in rejecting the new constitution; they were defeated on 3 May, as were the insurgent peasants of the Valais on 17 May, and the constitution was put into effect. The republic was headed by a directory of five members, assisted by a legislative body and a senate, elected by universal male suffrage. Switzerland was divided into nineteen cantons, equal in rights and roughly equal in area. At the head of each canton was a prefect and, under his orders, subprefects. Feudalism was abolished and numerous reforms were introduced.

But the regime did not function without problems. The French commissioner, J.-J. Rapinat, carried out a coup d'état to force two directors to resign on 16 June 1798 because he believed them not well enough disposed toward France. In 1799, with the renewal of war, the Helvetic Republic became an essential theater of operations. General Masséna defeated the Russians under A. V. Suvórov in the region of Zurich on 25 and 26 September, but the occupation of more than half the territory by Austro-Russian forces had reinforced the conservatives' opposition to the centralist constitution of 1798. After Bonaparte came to power in France, centralists and federalists clashed violently for over two years. Finally, Bonaparte imposed his mediation by the act of 19 February 1803. While the confederation continued to be composed of nineteen equal cantons, each of them became practically autonomous. A federal diet was composed of delegates from the cantons but exercised only weak powers. The executive authority was confided to one of the leaders of the six director cantons. The Valais was excluded from the Helvetic Confederation and formed an independent republic, tightly controlled by France. The Helvetic Republic, one and indivisible, was dead.

Correspondance de Frédéric-César de la Harpe sous la République helvétique, publiée par J.-C. Biaudet et M.-C. Jequier, vol. 1 (Neuchatel, 1982); J. Godechot, *Les commissaires aux armées sous le Directoire* (Paris, 1938) and *La grande nation* (Paris, 1956); A. Rufer, *La Suisse et la Révolution française* (Paris, 1973).

J. Godechot

Related entries: BATTLE OF ZURICH; CISALPINE REPUBLIC; DOCTRINE OF NATURAL FRONTIERS; REUBELL; SECOND COALITION.

HERAULT DE SECHELLES, MARIE-JEAN (1759-94), member of the Committee of Public Safety. Hérault de Séchelles was born in Paris into a wealthy and distinguished noble family on 20 October 1759, two months after his father's death in battle. He grew up a spoiled child, but he had charm, intelligence, and ambition, which he put to use in a very successful legal career. In December 1777, only eighteen years old, Hérault became a royal attorney at the Châtelet. Eight years later, in July 1785, Madame de Polignac, who was his cousin and the queen's intimate friend, obtained for him royal favor and the important post of attorney-general at the Parlement of Paris. The handsome young ladies' man was now "the delightful Séchelles," renowned in the capital for his eloquence in the courtroom and his wit and learning in the salons. He was a lover of books as well as of women, and he collected 4,000 volumes, among them the original manuscript of J.-J. Rousseau's *Nouvelle Héloïse*. He wrote several minor works himself. These included a journalistic account of his interview with the naturalist Buffon, whom he regarded as the messiah of the scientific age, and *The Theory of Ambition*, a cynical yet agreeable essay on how to achieve fame.

Hérault had tasted all the sweetness that the Old Regime could offer, but his philosophical convictions led him to embrace the Revolutionary cause in 1789. He later claimed to have participated in the assault on the Bastille. His only apparent regrets were for his loss of seigneurial dues and hunting rights on his estate outside of Paris. After a brief voyage abroad, he accepted election to a judicial post in December 1790. He resigned it the following month to serve on a royal commission sent to calm discontent in Alsace (January–April 1790). He took up another judicial post on his return. His family, infuriated by his support of the Revolution, disowned and disinherited him. He later used his influence to shield them during the Terror. Many historians, like many of Hérault's own contemporaries, have suspected his sincerity and labeled him an opportunist and unprincipled hypocrite. Certainly he was given to florid rhetoric and showy political gestures, but he felt compelled to prove the patriotism and Revolutionary commitment that his noble status and wealth might otherwise have called into question.

Hérault joined the Jacobin club in April 1791, only to quit it during the crisis of June–July 1791 and help found the more moderate Feuillants. Elected by Paris to the Legislative Assembly in September 1791, he initially sat on the Right until, alarmed by the dangers of counterrevolution and dismayed by the king's incapacity, he moved to sit with the Girondins. He rejoined the Jacobin club in December. That winter he used his eloquence to advocate war, and by the summer he was a Dantonist. It was he who summoned the Assembly to declare *la patrie en danger* on 10 July 1792. The department of the Seine-et-Oise returned him to the National Convention in September 1792. His colleagues evidently held him in high regard, for they elected him once president of the Legislative Assembly (2–16 September 1792) and twice president of the National Convention (1–15 November 1792 and 8-24 August 1793).

Between December 1792 and May 1793, Hérault was on mission with three other deputies to organize the new Mont Blanc department, and he was not therefore in Paris for the trial of Louis XVI. The four men, however, did send a letter to Paris in which they condemned the king as guilty but mentioned no penalty. He was back in the capital in time to support the deputies of the Mountain at the culmination of their struggle with the Gironde. He presided over the expulsion of the Girondins from the Convention on 2 June 1793. Named to a special committee to draft a new constitution on 30 May, Hérault was the principal author of the democratic Constitution of 1793, composed in one week (3-10 June) and adopted by the Convention on 24 June but never implemented. On 5 June he entered the Committee of Public Safety in which he shared responsibility for foreign affairs with B. Barère, who did most of the real work. Hérault never got along well with the other members. His cynicism, atheism, aristocratic affectation, and rumored corruption offended many of them, M. Robespierre in particular. Thinking it wise in these circumstances to leave Paris for a while, Hérault went on mission to the Haut-Rhin department on 26 October 1793. There he followed a more or less Hébertist policy, creating a Revolutionary army and a Revolutionary tribunal and lending his support to dechristianization. Yet while he loudly proclaimed the need for drastic measures ("Terror alone can establish the Republic here"), he executed few men. His excesses, as always, were more rhetorical than real. He also carried on secret diplomacy in Switzerland in an attempt to find a compromise that would end the war. His activities ran counter to official policy, and the Committee of Public Safety recalled him under a cloud of suspicion on 11 December 1793. Five days later, even before Hérault's return, F. Bourdon de l'Oise denounced him in the Convention as a former noble who maintained suspect relations with foreigners and corrupt financiers. Hérault's self-defense on 29 December was a brilliant and effective speech. It temporarily saved him, but he thought it prudent to remain away from meetings of the

Committee of Public Safety, for his colleagues there openly suspected him of leaking secrets to the Austrians. He managed to avoid arrest until 15 March 1794. He was subsequently tried with the Dantonists on charges of conspiracy, and he accompanied them to the guillotine on 5 April 1794. He died bravely, with the haughty and detached air so characteristic of him.

A.N., F⁷ 4742 and W342, dossiers on Hérault's arrest and trial; A. de Contades, *Hérault de Séchelles* (Paris, 1978); E. Dard, *Un épicurien sous la Terreur* (Paris, 1907); L. Gaudel, "Jean-Marie Hérault de Séchelles," *Revo. française* 22 (1935); J. Robinet, "Hérault de Séchelles: Sa première mission en Alsace," *Révo. française* 12 (1892).

M. D. Sibalis

Related entries: BOURDON; CHAMP DE MARS "MASSACRE"; COMMITTEE OF PUBLIC SAFETY; CONSTITUTION OF 1793; COUNTERREVOLUTION; DECHRISTIANIZATION; FEUILLANTS; HEBERTISTS.

HOCHE, LOUIS-LAZARE (1768-97), general. On 24 June 1768, L.-L. Hoche was born in the town of Montreuil, the son of a professional soldier. Having had very little formal education, he entered the army at the age of sixteen. He was a corporal in the French Guards five years later when the Revolution began. Self-educated, intelligent, and sincere, he championed the National Assembly and the ideas of the Revolution. When his corps was disbanded in August 1789, he joined the National Guard with the grade of sergeant. After France declared war in April 1792, he was promoted to lieutenant in May and captain in August. He served at the siege of Thionville, became aide-de-camp to General A.-P.-M.Leveneur de Tillières, and served at the Battle of Neerwinden. In May 1793 Hoche was named adjutant general. However, he was arrested in the summer of 1793 and sent before a Revolutionary Tribunal. As there was a lack of evidence, he was acquitted and given command of the garrison at Dunkirk. His skillful handling of the defense of that city resulted in his promotion first to brigadier general in the fall of 1793 and then to general of division on 23 October 1794. He had risen through the ranks from lieutenant to general of division in two and a half years. Hoche was only twenty-six years old.

With his promotion to brigadier general, Hoche also received command of the Army of the Moselle. He pulled the poorly disciplined and poorly equipped army together and marched against the duke of Brunswick, then campaigning in that sector. But after three days of heavy fighting, the superior numbers of the Prussian army forced him to withdraw and regroup. In December 1793, he turned his attention to the Austrian army on the west bank of the Rhine. In a successful campaign, he drove the enemy out of Spire and Worms and back across the Rhine. This limited success merited for him command of the Army of Italy. Hardly had he taken command at Nice when he was arrested and taken to Paris and imprisoned. The general languished in prison until the Thermidorian Reaction opened the doors to political prisoners. At the end of 1794, he was given command of the Army of the Coasts of Brest with instructions to repress the insurrection in the Vendée. Hoche was both wise and moderate in his handling of the people of the west. By mid-February 1795, he had pacified most of Brittany. But on 15 July the British landed a royalist force on the Breton coast. Hoche gathered his army of 9,000 men and marched against them. He defeated them, capturing a large portion in the process, and sent the remnants fleeing back to the British ships. In recognition of this success, Hoche was given command over all of the armies in the west under the title Army of the Ocean. As a result of his moderate administration and religious toleration, he was able to proclaim the insurrection ended by mid-July 1796. He was honored by the Directory with the title Pacificator of the Vendée.

General Hoche was subsequently given command of the military expedition to Ireland that sailed from Brest on 16 December 1796. However, the fleet was scattered by a storm shortly after its departure, and the vessels arrived one at a time at Bantry Bay. When the frigate *Fraternité*, with Hoche aboard, did not arrive as scheduled, General E. Grouchy, who was second in command, refused to assume the responsibility for landing the army and returned to Brest with the expedition. When the *Fraternité* did arrive at Bantry Bay, Hoche learned from the Irish that the fleet had returned to France. There was nothing else he could do but to follow Grouchy back to Brest. Because the failure of the expedition had not been Hoche's fault, he was given command of the Army of the Sambre-et-Meuse (February 1797). He reorganized the army, crossed the Rhine, defeated the Austrians in three battles and several minor engagements, and was in the process of a very successful campaign when he received news of the armistice concluded by General N. Bonaparte and the Austrians at Leoben (April 1797).

With the end of hostilities on the Continent, Hoche's thoughts again turned to an invasion of Ireland. However, a threat to the government of the Directory in Paris caused him to turn his attention toward the capital. He was prepared to save the Directory, but General P.-F.-C. Augereau was given command of the troops in Paris on 18 Fructidor, and the crisis passed. He settled down at his headquarters in Wetzlar, where he became ill. After a brief but miserable sickness, marked by convulsions, coughing, and the spitting up of blood, Hoche died on 19 September 1797.

E. C. d'Ornano, *Hoche, sa vie, sa correspondance* (Paris, 1892); G.-A.-J. Escande, *Hoche en Irlande* (Paris, 1888); E. H. S. Jones, *An Invasion That Failed: The French Expedition to Ireland, 1796* (Oxford, 1950).

J. G. Gallaher

Related entries: BATTLE OF NEERWINDEN; COUP OF 18 FRUCTIDOR YEAR V; IRELAND; PRELIMINARIES OF LEOBEN; QUIBERON; THERMIDORIAN REACTION; VENDEE.

HOLLAND, KINGDOM OF. See BATAVIAN REPUBLIC.

HONDSCHOOTE, BATTLE OF. See BATTLE OF HONDSCHOOTE.

HOPITAL GENERAL. See PRISONS.

HOSTAGES, LAW OF. See LAW OF HOSTAGES.

HULIN, PIERRE-AUGUSTIN (1758–1841), one of the first to attack the Bastille on 14 July 1789, general under Napoleon. See BASTILLE.

I

ILLUMINATI, secret society. The founder was A. Weishaupt, professor of law at the University of Ingolstadt in Bavaria. He intended, through an organization dedicated to education and propaganda, to combat the strong influence of the clergy and especially the ex-Jesuits in Bavaria. Ironically enough, Weishaupt held the chair of canon law, reserved before their expulsion in 1773 for the Jesuits. In 1776, Weishaupt, with a few friends, launched his secret society, which he initially called the Order of Bees; he constructed an entire allegory on the theme of a hive of bees ruled benevolently and absolutely by their queen. Weishaupt had hoped to attract students into his order, but as the organization spread slowly into other Bavarian cities in the next several years, it attracted instead a membership consisting mainly of bureaucrats, clerics, and nobles. The group came to be known as the Order of Illuminati, a name suggesting both the traditional Catholic mystical enlightenment embodied in Saint Augustine and Saint Teresa of Avila and the modern enlightenment expressed by F.-M. Voltaire, P. Bayle, and G. E. Lessing. Like many other young German and Austrian Catholics of his generation, Weishaupt was especially affected by the new intellectual interchange with the Protestant north, the first in two centuries.

Freemasonry had been another important intellectual influence on Weishaupt's generation, but initially there was no direct contact between the Freemasons and the Illuminati. Only in 1781, when Weishaupt and his associates were accepted into the Munich lodge called Théodore de Bon Conseil, did the interaction become important. The Illuminati made a key convert in Baron A. von Knigge, who for many years had been trying to reform the entire Masonic system. Initiated into the Illuminati, he set to work to create for them a more elaborate system of rituals and ranks and to extend their proselytizing efforts beyond Bavaria. It was Knigge who wrote the rituals for the higher grades that expressed a militant anti-Catholicism and the belief that society would evolve over the centuries to the point at which men would no longer need kings and all would be brothers. A decade later, the Illuminati were portrayed as the agents of violent subversion, but in fact their ideas were close to those expressed by Mozart in *The Magic Flute* and Schiller in his *Ode to Joy*.

Thanks to Knigge's efforts and their new Masonic contacts, the Illuminati spread rapidly after 1781. Lodges were established in most of the major towns of southern Germany and the Rhine valley. With Joseph II's accession to the imperial throne in 1780, there were high hopes for the spread of the new ideas into the Hapsburg empire. A lodge was established in Vienna whose membership included some high government officials. At the height of their influence, however, the Illuminati could claim perhaps 1,000 members at most, 600 of them in Bavaria.

In 1782, the branch of Freemasonry called the Strict Observance held a conference at Wilhelmsbad, attended by the leading mystical and occultist Masons of Europe. Several of the Illuminati, including Knigge, were present, hoping not only to gain members for their order but also to combat the influence of "crypto-Catholicism" that they believed had permeated the Freemasons of the Strict Observance. Although the myth of an Illuminist conspiracy would later implicate the Wilhelmsbad conference in the alleged plot to overthrow existing society, in fact efforts of the Illuminati met with almost no success. The great majority of the Wilhelmsbad delegates hoped to turn Freemasonry toward an apolitical mysticism and occultism, the precise opposite of the rationalism with political overtones expressed by Weishaupt and Knigge.

The collapse of the Illuminati after 1783 was as rapid as had been its growth in the preceding few years. Even before the authorities in Bavaria, Austria, and other German states closed the lodges, the order was in serious trouble. Some members, including Knigge, had left in protest at the authoritarianism of the pedantic Weishaupt, and many patriotic Bavarian members left because of the order's efforts to woo Austrian members by a pro-Hapsburg policy.

It is clear that both the remarkable, if brief, success of the Illuminati and their demise must be seen within the context of south German developments. After a long intellectual isolation, Bavaria and Austria were open to outside influences, and in both states the rulers seemed to be interested in extending civil and religious liberties. Events in both countries soon showed that the appearance was illusory.

By 1786, the Order of the Illuminati had been entirely suppressed, yet its other history, the legend of the Illuminist plot to foment the French Revolution, had only begun. The Illuminati had themselves contributed to the mentality that could accept such a legend as fact, believing as they did that the Catholics and especially the Jesuits were plotting to dominate Freemasonry, as well as all the governments of Europe. The Jesuits proposed similarly that there was a rationalist plot to overturn religion and civil society. Some German Protestants were eager to make common cause with like-minded Catholics to maintain the hegemony of Christianity against the subversive ideas represented by groups like the Illuminati.

Between 1785 and 1787, there appeared a number of pamphlets by both Catholics and Protestants that claimed that the Illuminati were still plotting to overthrow crown and altar. Among the leading exponents of the legend were the Hanoverian pastor J. A. Starck and the Viennese professor L. A. Hoffman. With the coming of the French Revolution, published claims concerning the activities of the Illuminati extended still further. A Hamburg journal alleged that the duc d'Orléans was the ringleader of an international conspiracy that included them, and Hoffman, in his *Wiener Zeitschrift*, was perhaps the first to contend that the ideas of the Jacobins were identical with those of the Illuminati.

After the fall of the Jacobins in 1794, the attacks on their nonexistent allies, the Illuminati, achieved even wider circulation. In Germany, the continued concern for political-religious subversion produced a whole body of conservative-mystical writings that would lead to the German political romanticism of the nineteenth century. In Great Britain, an ex-Jesuit *émigré*, J. Barruel, and J. Robinson, a professor of science at the University of Edinburgh, published rather different but widely influential versions of the Illuminist-Jacobin plot. Barruel's version claimed that the Illuminati, the mystical lodges of the Freemasons, and the French encyclopedists were all part of the great plot whose climax was international Jacobinism. The five volumes of his *Mémoire pour servir à l'histoire du Jacobinisme* are filled with confusions of facts and dates and misreadings of sources, but the book nonetheless was widely read in several editions and in English, Italian, Spanish, and Russian translations. Robinson's *Proofs of a Conspiracy*, which appeared a year later in 1798, is more scholarly, although it, too, relies heavily on the works of Hoffman and the other anti-Revolutionary propagandists.

The legend of the Jacobin-Illuminati plot has provided the basic scenario for other plot theories in the nineteenth and twentieth centuries, most notably that of the Jewish plot. The names and some of the facts might be changed, but the central premise that it was even possible that an obscure collection of intellectuals could conspire to manipulate world history has been thriving in its various guises ever since the French Revolution.

J. Droz, *Le Romantisme allemand et l'état* (Paris, 1966); R. van Dühlmen, *Der Geheimbund der Illuminaten* (Stuttgart, 1977); H. Grassl, *Aufbruch der Romantik* (Munich, 1968); R. Le Forestier, *Le Franc-Maçonnerie templière et occultiste* (Paris, 1970); A. Viatte, *Les Sources occultes du Romantisme* (Paris, 1969).

C. Garrett

Related entries: ENLIGHTENMENT; FREEMASONRY; ORLEANS; VOLTAIRE.

IMPARTIALS. See SOCIETY OF 1789.

INCROYABLES. See *MERVEILLEUSES*.

INDULGENTS (latter part of 1793-April 1794), party or faction in the National Convention that favored a moderation of the emergency measures of the Revolutionary government, especially the Terror, and the return to a constitutional regime; the group was also denominated "citras" by contemporaries and came to be called "Dantonists" after its alleged leader, G.-J. Danton.

Organized political parties did not exist during the Revolution. Eighteenth-century liberals looked askance at parties. Yet loose groups were to be found in the National Convention. In the summer of 1793, France was faced with a serious crisis: military—foreign and domestic—and economic. A strong, autonomous movement of *sans-culotterie* developed. Concurrently, in the Convention the more revolutionary deputies, the Montagnards, grew in ascendancy. The liberal democratic Constitution of 1793, which they prepared, was suspended on 10 October 1793 as the Montagnard-influenced Convention groped toward the further development of a Revolutionary government. By that was meant eventually an extraconstitutional, emergency government whose aim was the victory of the Revolution and the establishment of the ideal Republic. In the process of elaborating the Revolutionary government, some Revolutionists in and outside the Convention—first the *Enragés* and then the Hébertists or ultras—seeking the support of the *sans-culottes*, wished to carry the Revolution further. On the other hand, the later Indulgents—mostly Montagnards—wished to stabilize the Revolution and limit violent measures. Attitudes frequently changed as a deputy spoke, voted, or acted one way on one occasion and in a different way on another. Personal interests and rivalries played an important role in the emerging divisions. Whenever a deputy—the future citra or ultra—did not approve of an act of the government, he might propose the beginning of the implementation of the suspended constitution, and thus the end of the provisional government.

In August 1793 the policies and statements of deputies who were to be called Indulgents are revealing. On 1 August, five days after M. Robespierre joined the Committee of Public Safety, Danton proposed to the Convention a significant increase in the power of the committee. He was supported by his associates C. Delacroix (who had served with Danton on the first committee) and J.-A. Thuriot (a member of the committee from 10 July to 20 September). Three weeks before, however, the journalist L.-C.-S. Desmoulins had opposed the concentration of power. And on 11 August, Delacroix, reversing himself, proposed measures to prepare for the election of a new legislature under the constitution. Behind the contradictory moves of these more moderate Montagnards was the search for a political method to curb the extremists.

Sans-culotte pressure for radical measures precipitated the Hébertist *journées* of 4-5 September. Concessions to *sans-culottisme* were made concurrently with an increase in the power of the Revolutionary government. Danton was able on 5 September to obtain the passage of a decree ending the permanence of the sections of Paris and permitting only two meetings a week, with a salary for those attending. Danton's policies and the interests of Robespierre and the Committee of Public Safety coincided in many respects. While *sans-culotte* support was necessary to win the war and save the Revolution, the people's government—with its Revolutionary armies, its sectional assemblies, its Revolutionary committees, and its popular societies—would prevent the establishment of a strong central government and instead lead to anarchy and the defeat of the Revolution. So long as *sans-culotterie* lasted, an alliance between Robespierre and Danton, though never complete or continuous, was inevitable.

Robespierre and the committee, nevertheless, had to perform a delicate balancing act between the forces on their left and right flanks. Military successes, such as the great victory at Wattignies on 16 October by J.-B. Jourdan and L. Carnot, combined with successes against the internal enemies, facilitated the growth of centralization and strengthened the Revolutionary government.

That fundamental trend could not be concealed by tangled domestic events. About 10 October the ex-actor and playwright P.-F. Fabre d'Eglantine, an old comrade of Danton, revealed to Robespierre and nine other selected members of the Committees of Public Safety and of General Security that there was a foreign plot involving the extremists to destroy the Republic. He named as culprits P.-J. Proly, the Belgian banker, and other foreigners, and included the ex-nobleman and member of the Great Committee, M.-J. Hérault de Séchelles. In mid-November the complicated East India Company scandal began to unravel, implicating deputies who were now acting as moderates, such as F. Chabot, C. Basire, and Fabre (though Fabre may not have been as guilty as A. Mathiez has maintained). The two committees ordered the arrest on 18 November of four deputies (including Chabot and Basire but not Fabre) and eight accomplices.

At the same time as these "conspiracies" were being discovered, the Revolutionary government was faced with a dechristianization movement sponsored mainly by the ultras. In Paris it culminated in the Festival of Reason at Notre Dame on 10 November. On 21 November at the Jacobin club, Robespierre, expressing his own profound religious feelings as well as the attitude of a statesman, bitterly condemned dechristianization and the menace of atheism. He connected the movement to the activities of the alleged foreign agents, with Proly as their leader, who were stirring up the *sans-culottes* and calling for the dissolution of the Convention. Robespierre proposed successfully that the foreign agents he named be expelled from the club. He also obtained a *scrutin épuratoire* of the Jacobins. The purge was to continue for two and one-half months.

Danton, who had been on leave at his home in Arcis-sur-Aube from mid-October until 18 November, was soon speaking in the Convention, attacking dechristianization and the ultras and repeatedly urging the concentration of power in the Committee of Public Safety. Attacked in the Jacobins on 3 December, he found a champion in Robespierre, who vouched for his patriotism. Danton, with the aid of Thuriot and F. Bourdon (de l'Oise), was instrumental in achieving the addition to the "Constitution of the Terror" (introduced by J.-N. Billaud-Varenne in the name of the committee) of national agents in the localities serving at the pleasure of the committee. The adoption of this "constitution" (4 December, 14 Frimaire) made it clear that any deviation from Revolutionary government was counterrevolutionary.

Yet citras and ultras, as they were now being called, continued to assail each other. Indulgents, like P. Philippeaux, Bourdon, and A.-C. Merlin de Thionville—all representatives on mission recalled by the Committee of Public Safety—attempted unsuccessfully in December to remove some of the members of the committee. It is probable that they were planning to replace J.-M. Collot d'Herbois or J.-N. Billaud-Varenne (both of whom had been added to the committee as a result of the September *journées*) with Danton. There is no doubt that Danton wanted France to return to a normal way of life. This tall, powerful-looking orator of the people, with his stentorian voice, speaking extemporaneously, could sway audiences. He was friendly and easy-going; he loved life and money. He had boldly led France for a time after 10 August 1792. Yet he had most probably profited financially from the Revolution. Now he was tired; he wanted to enjoy life. Around him swarmed a motley group of deputies. There is little evidence of any planning or coordination of activity among them. Nor is there any concrete evidence of Danton's providing any leadership. Indeed, Danton did not always agree with other Dantonists. The Dantonists were truly a very loose faction.

Bourdon and other deputies frequently attacked the executive council of ministers. J.-B.-N. Bouchotte, the minister of war, bore the brunt of the criticism. After all, F.-N. Vincent, his secretary general, was an ultra, and the entire office was a haven for extremists. On 17 December, Fabre, Bourdon and Philippeaux were able to have the Convention order the arrest of Vincent and C.-P. Ronsin, the commander of the central Revolutionary army. (They were released on 2 February as a result of ultra pressure on the government.) The Indulgents also urged the freeing of unjustly imprisoned patriots without success.

As Collot d'Herbois, the butcher of Lyon, J.-R. Hébert, and other extremists counterattacked the Indulgents, Robespierre at the Jacobins appealed for unity among patriots (23 December). Three days later he denounced the popular societies, which were controlled by the ultras. As the purge continued in the Jacobin club, he and Danton cooperated to dampen personal denunciations and to urge unity.

Desmoulins had begun publishing a new journal, the *Vieux Cordelier*, on 5 December. This and the second issue, both of which were read beforehand and approved by Robespierre, were essentially violent attacks on the ultras as foreign agents and their dechristianization movement as atheism. At the Jacobins on 12 December, Robespierre borrowed some of Desmoulins' language in a vehement indictment of A. Cloots, the rich German internationalist revolutionary and a prominent Hébertist. On 14 December, in the continuing purge, Robespierre, while criticizing Camille for mistakes, praised his republicanism and urged his admission. In December Robespierre did attack moderation, but his criticism was mainly reserved for the extremists.

Within a short time came Robespierre's rupture with the Indulgents. On 7 January at the Jacobins, he turned against Philippeaux and satirically criticized Camille for his opinions in the third to fifth issues of his newspaper. The next day he went beyond a denunciation of Desmoulins and Fabre to castigate the foreign factions—both ultras and citras—directed by W. Pitt and the duke of Coburg, whose aim was the dissolution of the National Convention. In his mind

Fabre was the chief conspirator. On the night of 12-13 January, Fabre was arrested.

A combination of events precipitated Robespierre's conclusion that the citras as well as the ultras were enemies of *la patrie*. Desmoulins' impolitic remarks at the Jacobins and the later issues of the *Vieux Cordelier*, which could be interpreted as antigovernment and not only antiextremist, irritated him. On 7 January in the Convention, Philippeaux had attacked Vincent, Ronsin, and Bouchotte. The Indulgent campaign seemed to be in full swing. Fabre's involvement in the East India Company scandal seemed to have become evident, and Fabre had shown that he was a citra. The recent return of Collot d'Herbois had reinvigorated the Parisian ultras. Unity had to be reestablished in the committee by finding a position in the center between the two factions and above them. Since September Robespierre had been endeavoring to comprehend the complicated domestic developments. Suddenly everything became clear. For the Incorruptible, the perfectionist, *l'homme engagé*, the true Revolutionary obsessed with the Revolution, there was but one straight path. Grafters, moderates, and extremists were all cooperating under the aegis of the coalition to dismantle the Revolutionary government and thereby abort the Revolution. Robespierre's great speech of 5 February (17 Pluviôse) to the Convention, in the name of the committee, on the principles of political morality presented the justification of the Revolutionary government and denounced both factions as traitorous.

In the meantime, Danton stopped coming to the Jacobins and made cautious speeches in the Convention to save Fabre, to defend certain victims of the Terror, or to urge the Convention not to accept unquestioningly every action of the two committees. These were not the deeds of a leader of a faction. The Hébertists, meanwhile, rang their own death knell by attempting an insurrection, which failed. On 13-14 March (23-24 Ventôse) and in the next few days, the leading Cordeliers (including Hébert, Ronsin, and Vincent) and a number of foreigners (such as Cloots and Proly) were arrested. After a brief trial, eighteen were executed on 24 March (4 Germinal). The government was ready to end *sans-culotterie*.

The trial of Fabre had not yet been held because of Robespierre's hesitation about granting Billaud-Varenne's demand that Danton and Desmoulins be liquidated along with Fabre. Robespierre was finally convinced by political and personal reasons. Billaud and Collot had to be appeased for the execution of the Hébertists in order to maintain the cohesion of the committee. Furthermore, Robespierre could not basically approve of Danton's way of life—which was not that of a true revolutionist like Robespierre himself—and his continued support of Fabre. It is probable that Robespierre had a few private meetings with Danton and possibly did not reach a final decision until the meeting of the two governing committees in the night of 29-30 March (9-10 Germinal). The committees agreed to arrest Danton, Desmoulins, Philippeaux, and Delacroix. Once Robespierre had made up his mind, he threw himself fully into the effort to destroy these enemies of the Revolution. He edited meticulously the report of

L. Saint-Just on the Dantonists and cowed the Convention on 31 March to listen in silence to the report and to vote unanimously for the trial of the four deputies. To facilitate their conviction, the committees included them in an amalgam with Fabre, Chabot, and others accused of dishonesty, alleged foreign agents, and Hérault de Séchelles. Danton's bellowing defense before the Revolutionary Tribunal was soon silenced by a decree. Found guilty on 5 April 1794 (16 Germinal Year II), the accused were guillotined the same day.

The Committee of Public Safety seemed to have gained control of the state and was winning the war. The Revolutionary government's life, however, was to be of short duration. Even though the Indulgent or Dantonist party was an unorganized, almost leaderless, and evanescent group, the trend toward indulgence was a fundamental historical force, which was to triumph after Thermidor.

C. Desmoulins, *Le Vieux Cordelier*, ed. H. Calvet (Paris, 1936); M. Eude, "Une interpretation 'non-mathiezienne' de l'affaire de la Compagnie des Indes," *Ann. hist. de la Révo. française* 244 (1981); A. Fribourg, *Discours de Danton* (Paris, 1910); N. Hampson, *Danton* (New York, 1978); A. Mathiez, *L'affaire de la Compagnie des Indes* (Paris, 1921); J. I. Shulim, "The Birth of a Revolutionary: Robespierre in Artois," *Pro. of the Cons. on Revo. Eur., 1977* (1978) and "The Birth of Robespierre as a Revolutionary: A Horneyan Psychohistorical Approach," *Am. J. of Psychoanalys.* 37 (1977).

J. I. Shulim

Related entries: ARMEES REVOLUTIONNAIRES; ATHEISM; CLOOTS; COMMITTEE OF GENERAL SECURITY; COMMITTEE OF PUBLIC SAFETY; COMPAGNIE DES INDES; DECHRISTIANIZATION; DESMOULINS; *ENRAGES*; FABRE; HEBERTISTS; HERAULT DE SECHELLES; LAW OF 14 FRIMAIRE; MONTAGNARDS; ROBESPIERRE, M.; *SCRUTIN EPURATOIRE*; SECTIONS.

INSTITUT PHILANTHROPIQUE (1796-1800), a conspiratorial organization created to undermine the Directory and prepare a Bourbon restoration. The abbé A.-C. Brottier and S. Despomelles, two members of the royalist Agency in Paris, drew up the original plan for the Institut in August 1796. Modeled after the Freemasons, the Institut was to consist of a general membership known as the friends of order, who would be recruited to combat Revolutionary extremism and support moderate candidates in elections. These members would not know of the organization's royalist goals, but an inner core of legitimate sons devoted to the Bourbons would control the Institut behind the scenes. They would not only direct its overt and legal activities but would also prepare secretly for an armed insurrection.

The actual organization of the Institut philanthropique and the recruitment of members had not proceeded very far before Brottier and several other members of the royalist Agency were arrested in February 1797. Despomelles, who had not been seized, subsequently joined forces with A.-B.-J. d'André, a former right-wing deputy in the National Assembly, who had won the support of the English for a scheme to pack the legislative councils with counterrevolutionaries and use them to restore the monarchy. André adopted the Institut idea and gave it new impetus, dispatching several agents to organize branches in the provinces in the six weeks prior to the elections of April 1797. The Institut had not been in existence long enough to exert much influence on the elections, but André expected to use it as a base for future operations. The organization was most successful where it could absorb already existing counterrevolutionary groups, as it did in the Sarthe, where the veteran *chouan* leader F.-G. Rochecot headed the local branch, and in Bordeaux, where M. Dupont-Constant, who had already formed a group to influence the elections, became the Institut's agent. In several decidedly counterrevolutionary departments, local government officials joined the organization. In theory, the Institut was to have a pyramidal structure, with members on each level knowing only their immediate superior and with agents in every urban street and rural commune, but it is unlikely that this tidy scheme was ever implemented successfully.

During the summer of 1797, André worked to expand the organization, first with the intent of using it to control the elections of 1798 and later in hope of combating the impending republican coup, which finally occurred on 18 Fructidor Year V. By then, the Institut had branches in fifty-eight departments, mostly in the south and the region around Paris; it had little support in the Vendée, where it failed to supplant indigenous royalist groups, or in the central and eastern departments. André personally supervised the southern departments, and he strongly criticized Despomelles, who took charge of the rest of the country, for his laziness. The English agent W. Wickham funded the Institut, but Louis XVIII gave it only grudging support, resenting André's policy of cooperation with former constitutional monarchists and his downplaying of insurrectional tactics.

Unknown to the organizers, the Directory had learned of the plan for the Institut as early as February 1797, when Brottier's co-conspirator T.-L.-M. Duverne de Presle had revealed it after his arrest. P. Barras obtained further details from the prince de Carency, another royalist agent, in August 1797. André's efforts to use the organization to oppose the Fructidor coup had no result; the three victorious directors published Duverne's confession to discredit their victims and link them to a broader royalist conspiracy.

The Fructidor coup disorganized the Institut's national structure. It remained active on a local level, especially in southern France, but did little beyond rescuing a few political prisoners. Leaders like the abbé de la Marre in Lyon and Dupont-Constant in Bordeaux tried to prepare an armed insurrection in the south, to occur simultaneously with a renewed rising in the Vendée and an Austro-Russian invasion from Italy, but the plan never succeeded, and only a few small armed bands ever saw real action. The Institut had no role in the actual uprisings that did take place, like the one in Toulouse in 1799, and in fact tried to prevent futile local revolts. After 18 Brumaire Year VIII, strengthened police repression and the defeat of the Second Coalition killed the organization's hopes.

The plan of the Institut philanthropique reflected royalist leaders' recognition that their movement needed a central coordinating organization, as well as their realization that an avowedly royalist movement committed to insurrection could not count on a strong following. Brottier, Despomelles, and André were naive in thinking that an effective nationwide organization could be created without the Directory's knowledge, and they were never able to overcome the local disputes that were endemic to the royalist movement. Consequently the Institut had little actual impact. It does not seem to have inspired counterrevolutionary sentiment where it did not already exist. It played only a minor role in the 1797 elections, and the grand plan for an insurrection in the south never materialized. The republican directors made good use of the Institut's plans to justify the Fructidor coup and did more than anyone else to build up the myth that it had been a substantial organization.

G. Caudriller, *L'association royaliste de l'Institut philanthropique à Bordeaux* (Paris, 1908); M. Dupont-Constant, *Essai sur l'Institut philanthropique* (Paris, 1823); W. R. Fryer, *Republic or Restoration in France? 1794-1797* (Manchester, 1965); H. Mitchell, *The Underground War against Revolutionary France* (Oxford, 1965); M. Reinhard, *Le département de la Sarthe sous le Régime directorial* (Saint-Brieuc, 1936).

J. Popkin

Related entries: ANDRE; BARRAS; *CHOUANNERIE*; COUP OF 18 FRUCTIDOR YEAR V; VENDEE.

INSURRECTION OF 1-4 PRAIRIAL YEAR III. See PRAIRIAL MARTYRS.

INTENDANTS, agents of the central administration in the French absolute monarchy. Provincial intendants were responsible for implementing royal policy and laws. Other intendants with more specialized duties were intendants of commerce and intendants of finance, who assisted the controller general in formulating economic policy, and intendants of the army and of the navy, civilians who supervised military administration. The provincial intendants, keystones in the structure of royal government, have been viewed in two ways in their relation to the Revolution, each interpretation requiring modification.

The intendants of the early eighteenth century were depicted by the duc de Saint-Simon, expressing the contempt of a peer, as men of low birth. On the eve of the Revolution, historians agree, the intendants were noble. This contrast has led to the conclusion that new men could no longer rise in the hierarchy of the royal administration (in the army, judiciary, and church as well) and that this aristocratic reaction, blocking opportunities for social mobility, created frustration among the bourgeoisie, making them hostile to the society and government of the *ancien régime*. Recent research lends support to a more nuanced interpretation, in particular for the provincial intendants.

At the beginning of the eighteenth century as well as at the end, the royal intendants were overwhelmingly noble, but they were largely drawn from families ennobled through venal office, purchase of letters patent, or living as country gentlemen on landed estates, and their ennoblement had been conferred as recently as the intendant's own lifetime or as long ago as seven or more generations. Dynasties of intendants even arose; yet more intendants had older noble origins at the beginning of the century and more were newer nobles at the end of the century, contrary to the traditional view. If the intendancies contributed to the Revolution, it was not because commoners no longer became intendants, since commoners had rarely become intendants unless they were previously ennobled, a feat possible for the well-to-do in the *ancien régime*.

A. de Tocqueville argued for the continuity of centralized administration from the *ancien régime* through the Revolution, with national agents in the Republic and prefects in the Empire reenacting the roles of royal intendants as agents of a central government. But Tocqueville gave less importance to a critical shift in attitudes and practices in the last years of the monarchy and the first years of the Revolution. A growing reaction against centralization and a greater desire for public participation in local government at this time were powerful sentiments leading Frenchmen to seek new administrative and governing institutions, promoting the onset of revolution.

The intendancies originated in the midst of internal disorders, especially during the first half of the seventeenth century when the crown was compelled to send intendants of justice, police, and finance to local regions to supervise tax collections, suppress riots, and administer royal justice. By the 1640s intendants were becoming the principal agents of royal government in the provinces. Their legal status, professional careers, and administrative role combined to make them useful instruments of the crown.

Intendancies were not purchased as private property, and intendants consequently were not irremovable, virtually autonomous, or of doubtful loyalty, as venal officers proved to be in the civil war of 1648 (the Fronde). Intendants were commissioners, appointed by the crown for a period of time and subject to removal by the crown, and thus more controllable and dependable as agents of the royal will. Their training as junior members of the Royal Council (masters of request) gave them experience in performing the king's work and made them loyal to royal interests. Ambition, the prospect of promotion to higher ranks in government as councillors of state or secretaries and ministers of state, reinforced their loyalty.

The effectiveness of intendants in expressing royal authority and enforcing the king's law led to their introduction and permanence in every province and newly acquired area in France, to a total of thirty-four in 1789. An intendant administered a *généralité*, a territory coterminous with a province (as Brittany), part of a large province (as in Normandy), or a combined unit of small provinces (as Tours). Intendants in provinces with estates (*pays d'état*) had less power since the estates carried out certain administrative tasks while the intendant's primary function was to negotiate taxes with local officials and ensure their collection for the crown. Those in provinces with no estates had a broader range of activities and greater authority.

Already during Louis XIV's reign, provincial intendants did more than impose order and collect taxes; they extended royal control over local government, gathered information about local conditions to inform the king's policymakers, and aided the commercial or manufacturing ventures, which the controller general J.-B. Colbert hoped would develop the national economy. Only with the end of Louis XIV's wars and with economic recuperation in the eighteenth century did the intendants cease to be primarily police agents; from about 1750 they became increasingly agents of reform. Intendants (the most famous being A.-R.-J. Turgot, the future controller general) encouraged and carried out programs of urban planning and rebuilding, oversaw public-works projects, especially road building, supported tax reductions in times of crisis, and introduced tax innovations to ameliorate arbitrary and unequal levies; supervised workshops for beggars, distributed poor relief, and introduced emergency work projects for the unemployed. In the last years of the monarchy, they were becoming advocates of their provinces.

Success had its reverse side. Not all intendants were active reformers, some administering in routine ways. Lack of technical means and personnel limited the power and effectiveness of all intendants to ensure that the king's policy and law were not ignored. And insufficient support or shifts in policy by the king and ministers often undermined their efforts. Above all, they never gained the attachment of the public.

Centralized administration through the intendants translated into daily practice and routine the crown's claim to absolute sovereignty, and as agents of centralization and absolutism, the intendants aroused criticism and opposition from the beginning. Their presence, authority, and activities deprived local groups of their traditional public roles or conflicted with the jurisdiction of other institutions. Sovereign court magistrates, high nobles and provincial gentlemen, venal judges and administrators, and municipal officials rebelled in 1648 against the intendants and sought their suppression. The failure of the Fronde permitted the crown to reintroduce intendants, but although opposition was silenced, it did not end.

The most beneficial reforms caused complaints, reform infringing on established privileges or introducing practices that enlarged the intendants' range of activity and authority. Appointed by the king and ministers in Versailles, intendants were viewed as strangers to the region, with little knowledge of or commitment to local needs and interests, whose functions could better be performed by local people. Thus was nurtured an outlook hostile to the intendants and the centralization they represented, favorable to forms of local control. From 1787, local control was publicly and actively sought, a goal reiterated in the *cahiers* of 1789. The authority of intendants, already seriously contested, was further weakened when riots in 1788 and 1789 forced some of them to flee from their posts. In 1790 the intendancies were abolished, and until 1793 France had decentralized administration by elected and autonomous local bodies.

P. Ardascheff, *Les intendants des provinces sous Louis XVI* (Paris, 1909); A.-M. de

Boislisle, ed., *Correspondance des contrôleurs généraux des finances avec les intendants des provinces, 1683-1715* (Paris, 1871-97); D. Dakin, *Turgot and the Ancien Régime in France* (London, 1939); H. Fréville, *L'intendance de Bretagne, 1689-1790* (Rennes, 1953); V. R. Gruder, *The Royal Provincial Intendants: A Governing Elite in Eighteenth-Century France* (Ithaca, 1968).

V. R. Gruder

Related entries: *CAHIERS DE DOLEANCES*; TOCQUEVILLE.

IRELAND. A decade before the French Revolution, Ireland had a revolution of its own—bloodless, limited, and ultimately futile. Taking advantage of the war in America, the dominant elite—the Protestant Ascendancy—extorted free trade and legislative independence from a harassed Great Britain. After 1782 the Kingdom of Ireland was, in theory, linked with its larger neighbor only by possession of a common sovereign.

The new Ireland was, however, a Protestant nation in which the Catholics (some 80 percent of the population) were excluded from civil rights. This anomaly was compounded by a corrupt and unrepresentative parliamentary system that left even many of the Protestants dissatisfied and by the continuing subservience of the Irish administration to British policies in all matters of substance. A decade of efforts by liberal-minded politicians to build on the achievements of 1782 through parliamentary reform and the removal of Catholic disabilities accomplished little against the entrenched guardians of privilege. After Britain went to war against France in 1793, frustrated activists such as T. W. Tone parted company with the moderate reformers and looked to radical solutions under the inspiration, and with the assistance, of Revolutionary France.

Irishmen had long been accustomed to look to France for support in their quarrels with England, and plans for the invasion of Ireland were regular features of Old Regime strategy. Thus, despite the novel circumstances of the Revolutionary era, the Irish and the French were old and natural allies, and there were numerous Franco-Irish descendants of refugees on hand to facilitate the new collaboration. Of these, N. Madgett in the Foreign Ministry and H. Clarke in the War Ministry were particularly active.

The Society of United Irishmen, founded in 1791 to promote denominational cooperation in the interest of political reform, now became avowedly separatist and revolutionary, aiming at the creation of an Irish republic on the French model. Negotiations to coordinate an Irish rising with a French invasion were already under way in 1794 when an informer betrayed the plan. Tone, the most dynamic of the United Irish leaders, was banished to America, while others, as yet undetected, began recruiting a secret army for the day of revolt.

Early in 1796, Tone arrived in Paris and revived discussions with the Directory. The result was a series of invasion attempts. The first, in December 1796, was thwarted by a storm at sea, and the second, in 1797, was aborted by the annihilation of the Batavian fleet at the Battle of Camperdown.

In Ireland, meanwhile, the increasing radicalization of the masses by United

Irish propaganda and the brutal repression carried out by the government had polarized the country and produced an unbearable state of tension. The society's leaders had ever greater difficulty in restraining their followers, insisting that the rising must await the coming of the French. When the five-man Directory was arrested in the spring of 1798 and its military organizer, the renegade aristocrat, Lord E. Fitzgerald, was killed resisting capture, restraint was no longer possible.

The insurrection that broke out in May 1798 was random, leaderless, and in its disorganized confusion only a pale shadow of the great national upheaval envisioned by Tone and his colleagues. After initial successes against scattered and ill-led royal forces, the poorly armed peasant bands were defeated in one district after another by hastily mustered reinforcements. By the time the long-awaited French troops arrived in late summer, the rebellion had been crushed. General J.-R. Humbert's 1,000-man force routed local militia and raised a brief revolt in the hitherto quiet western counties but was overwhelmed at Ballinamuck on 8 September.

A few weeks later, another small force was intercepted by a British naval squadron and among the prisoners was Tone. Condemned to death for treason, the leader of the United Irishmen took his own life on 19 November. With Tone's death and the execution or banishment of the surviving rebel commanders, the rising was over. Determined to safeguard its western flank against further dangers, Britain now cajoled or bribed the thoroughly frightened Ascendancy landowners into voting their autonomous parliament out of existence.

On 31 December 1800 the Kingdom of Ireland ceased to exist, and the island became a province of Britain. Like so many other kingdoms, it owed its extinction to the French Revolution. Yet it was to that same "gigantic event," as Tone called it, that Ireland owed its tradition of revolutionary, separatist nationalism through which independence was ultimately regained.

For Revolutionary France, Ireland represented a great opportunity lost. Had the United Irishmen been given timely, substantial assistance, Britain's strategic position and its ability to carry on the war against France would have collapsed. As N. Bonaparte belatedly lamented at St. Helena: "If, instead of making the expedition of Egypt, I had made that of Ireland, what would England have been today . . . and the political world?" (Las Cases, vol. 3, p. 555).

R. J. Couglan, *Napper Tandy* (Dublin, 1976); J. S. Donnelly, "Propagating the Cause of the United Irishmen," *Studies* 69 (1980); M. Elliott, *Partners in Revolution: The United Irishmen and France* (New Haven, 1982); W. D. Griffin, "The Forces of the Crown in Ireland, 1798," in G. L. Vincitorio, ed. *Crisis in the Great Republic* (New York, 1969); R. Hayes, *Ireland and Irishmen in the French Revolution* (London, 1932); E.-A.-D. de Las Cases, *Mémorial de Sainte-Hélène*, 4 vols. (Paris, 1823); R. B. McDowell, *Irish Public Opinion, 1750-1800* (London, 1944); T. Pakenham, *The Year of Liberty* (London, 1972).

W. D. Griffin

Related entries: HOCHE; TONE.

ISNARD, MAXIMIN (1751-1830), merchant and manufacturer, Girondin, deputy to the Legislative Assembly, the National Convention, and the Council of Five Hundred. Born in Grasse in 1751, Isnard was elected in 1791 to the Legislative Assembly, where he was openly critical of Louis XVI, his ministers, the royal court, and priests for their alleged treachery. He gained visibility by insisting that nonjuring priests should not only be deprived of their pensions but also be deported and punished like common criminals. After his election to the Convention (September 1792), he voted for the death of Louis XVI. A partisan of the Girondists, he was instrumental in forming the Committee of Public Safety. From 16 to 29 May 1793, Isnard served as the president of the Convention. Following J.-R. Hébert's arrest on 25 May, the Paris Commune demanded his freedom, but Isnard refused the request. This, in addition to his support for the federalist movement, prompted demands for the impeachment of Isnard and other deputies. He offered to resign from the Convention. Meanwhile, his criticism of the Commune and the Jacobins led to his being placed in the category of outlaw. After 9 Thermidor he reemerged and was reelected as a deputy from the Var (December 1794). After M. Robespierre's fall, anti-Jacobin movements surfaced, and Isnard encouraged the groups in the Var who hunted down the Jacobins. He was elected to the Council of Five Hundred in 1795 and served until 1797. After that date he disappeared from the political scene. He died in 1830.

A. Patrick, *The Men of the First French Republic* (Baltimore, 1972); M. J. Sydenham, *The First French Republic, 1792-1804* (London, 1974) and *The Girondins* (London, 1961).

N. Chaudhuri

Related entries: FEDERALISM; HEBERT; PARIS COMMUNE.

ITERATIVES REMONTRANCES. See PARLEMENTS.

J

JACOBINISM, a form of political action, an organizational structure, and a current of thought under the Revolution. In the course of the French Revolution there took place a transition from a group of adherents of the club of the Jacobins to the much broader notions of Jacobins and Jacobinism. Originally the Jacobins were simply the members of the Society of the Friends of the Constitution, which, beginning in November 1789, sat at the convent of the Jacobins in Paris. This club, which very quickly became the most important of such groups, developed out of the Breton Club, which had been a meeting place for provincial deputies since before 14 July.

Dominated from the outset by the outstanding personalities of the bourgeois Revolution, such as I.-R.-G. Le Chapelier and A. Barnave, from the very first it was something of a learned society (*société de pensée*), very restricted in its recruitment (a majority of members were deputies) and equally moderate in its objectives. Very early, however, different opinions came to light in the club where some isolated orators on the Left, such as M. Robespierre, J. Pétion, and J.-P. Brissot, began expressing their views. The most original aspect of the club from 1790 was the important network of correspondence and coordination that it was able to establish by affiliating with provincial clubs and societies within a tight framework.

Between 1790 and 1791, the club, despite its moderate origins, experienced a shift toward the Left under the dual pressure of a counterrevolutionary threat, for which rival clubs on the Right were the spokesmen, and by opposition on the Left by new kinds of popular societies, such as the Cordeliers. The Jacobins themselves welcomed newcomers. During the crisis set off by the king's flight to Varennes when the Cordeliers won over members by their campaign for the abolition of royalty, they were helped by the wave of repression that led to the secession of many members who formed a new Society of the Friends of the Constitution, which sat at the Feuillants, and the desertion of all but six deputies (among them Robespierre, the abbé Grégoire, and Pétion).

The Jacobin club managed to survive this crisis and emerged from it renovated. It enjoyed the loyalty of most of the affiliated societies in the provinces, whose numbers continued to multiply, reaching 1,000 in September 1791. It democratized its program and procedures and adopted new methods of recruitment, notably the *scrutin épuratoire*. Thus, it was able to resist the attacks of conservative monarchists who were trying to outlaw it.

At the opening of the Legislative Assembly in the autumn of 1791, although fewer deputies joined the Jacobins than the Feuillants (100 compared to 164), the club nevertheless displayed its dynamism; its sessions were made public, and it exercised constant pressure to push the constitution in a democratic direction and to keep an eye on authorities who might be under counterrevolutionary influence. This evolution increased Robespierre's influence, while the future Girondins turned more to the politics of the Assembly. Nevertheless, in the debate over war in the spring of 1792, the Jacobins supported Brissot by opting for a belligerent policy.

From April 1792 to the fall of the monarchy, the club searched for a new direction. Abandoned by the Girondins, the Jacobins were, on the other hand, deserted by the most active elements who felt there was too much mere talking. Furthermore, the Jacobins played no role in initiating the events of 10 August.

Under the Convention, the club took on a new character, and it was then that appeared the personage of the Jacobin. Henceforth the club called itself the Society of the Jacobin Friends of Liberty and Equality. Its members became what J. Michelet described in terms that are both misleading and perspicacious at the same time ''as mostly illiterate but men generally honest and disinterested.''

The increased aggressiveness of the Jacobins was evidenced in the struggle of the Mountain against the Gironde. In defending the Montagnard leaders under attack (Robespierre, J.-P. Marat, G.-J. Danton) and subsequently in passing to the attack themselves against the Girondins, the Jacobins not only took a new line but also fashioned a whole array of practices (petition, *scrutin épuratoire*, regeneration), which made them an effective instrument of the popular movement. They participated actively in preparing the Revolutionary *journées* of 31 May and 2 June 1793, which marked them as ''the grey eminence of the Convention'' and as agents of ''the despotism of Liberty'' (in the words of M. Gaston-Martin, 1945).

At the apogee of Jacobinism, in the Year II, the club capped a network of 2,000 provincial branches in France and counted some 100,000 affiliated members. In the distribution of roles and actual powers, the Parisian society discussed and prepared important measures of public safety, which were presented to the Convention. At the other end of the chain, the Committee of Public Safety invested the popular societies with control over the enforcement of governmental measures.

Reflecting and emanating from the *sans-culotte* movement, the Society of the Jacobins was sensitive to the currents that eddied around it and particularly to the strong activist current that culminated during the winter of 1793-94 in dechristianization and in the demand for increased political and economic Terror. Can one say that the Jacobins were brought under control in Frimaire Year II (December 1793), like the rest of the popular movement? The denunciation of A. Cloots, who was then club president, and of the "foreign conspiracy" (as Robespierre called it) and the victory of the Incorruptible placed the society in a position of wisdom and dominance since the great purges were prepared at the Jacobins. Yet the Jacobins, in an increasingly difficult position, reflected the contradictions of a revolution that henceforth became frozen. The club was bureaucratized at the same time as it provided personnel and cadres to the government that asked for them. But the internal tensions, although veiled for a time, flared up again, as Robespierre's enemies raised their heads. On 9 Thermidor, however, the faithful showed their weakness; they listened to Robespierre but were unable to do anything for him. On 10 Thermidor the club was closed; its reopening on 11 Thermidor, which was followed by a purge, represented only a respite. A campaign of intimidation and repression was launched against the Jacobins, and the closing of the club was demanded. Punitive expeditions by counterrevolutionaries furnished the pretext; the club was closed definitively on 23 Brumaire Year III (13 November 1794).

Thus, Jacobinism followed a very clearly delineated curve in which its hegemony corresponds to a very brief phase. Some time ago Michelet distinguished constitutional Jacobinism (represented by A. Barnave), a liberal and democratic Jacobinism (embodied by P.-V. Vergniaud), and a Jacobinism of the Robespierrist period, which was undoubtedly the most original and authentic. In turn, C. Mazauric, in a recent summary, proposed three phases: a long period of birth and maturation from 1789 to the spring of 1793 during which theory and practice were elaborated, then a brief period of political hegemony from 2 June 1793 to 9 Thermidor, and finally the third phase, which the author correctly suggests should be extended to the suppression of the Babeuf conspiracy and of the Jacobin revival of the Year VI.

Some years ago C. Brinton proposed a sociology of Jacobinism. Now out of date, it deserves to be refined in the light of new monographic studies, such as those on Toulouse and Marseille, and by a more rigorous methodology. Were the Jacobins a Revolutionary elite? Brinton estimated that members of the clubs constituted 4.2 percent of the population. Some of the current studies confirm a membership of this magnitude, but others suggest that this is considerably overestimated in the Midi. This militant minority does not differ sociologically from the group of *sans-culottes*: married in three-fourths of the cases, they were mature men (average age being forty-one to forty-two). Brinton proposed an evaluation of properties, but his system of classification is questionable. Nevertheless, while taking into consideration the necessary readjustments, one can confirm the relatively high social status of part of the membership (at first 24 percent and then, after 1792, 18 percent were members of the liberal professions, while 9 percent and later 8 percent were merchants) and the growing importance of proprietors of stores and shops (10 percent and later 17 percent were shopkeepers). The number of wage earners is weak and the abstention of the peasantry significant. While this older study does not make very clear the extent to which Jacobinism was democratized in the Year II, certain more recent works are much more explicit; for example, in Marseille the virtual elimination of the mercantile oligarchy (the number of merchants fell from 17 percent to less than 1 percent) was accompanied by a very striking increase in the number of artisans. Despite everything, in the end the Jacobins, as a group, differed from the *sans-culottes* in general insofar as they maintained a more elite social composition.

Did the originality of Jacobinism lie on the ideological level? Insofar as we can evaluate it by using discourses as collective evidence, at the beginning it appears to have been imbued with the heritage of the Enlightenment, modified to suit the times: faith in the necessity of a political revolution as the means of realizing the fundamental aims of humanity and a suspicious patriotism that demanded national unity as the essential means of Revolutionary government. Into this system the progress of the Revolution introduced major variations, notably the questioning of the legitimacy of liberalism with respect to the problem of subsistence and of the absolute character of property rights when the rich came to be suspected of oppression. Analyses of the language of Jacobinism that are currently being done should allow us to better comprehend what C. Mazauric (1975) defines as a *"fuite en avant idéologique et metaphysiquement unitariste,"* which found expression in the Cult of the Supreme Being and in the exaltation of Virtue.

Beyond doubt, it is on the level of practical politics that the special character of Jacobinism stands out most strikingly. Without returning to the point of view of some old conservative historians like A. Cochin, who saw in Jacobin techniques simply the application of a cunning Machiavellian plot, we should recognize that the Jacobins had a sense of political initiative, a tactical pragmatism that continuously put them in the center of the action and at the same time kept them in direct touch with the aspirations of the masses. In this sense, the Jacobins justified their role as an active minority, whose cohesiveness was maintained by efficient techniques, such as purges and regenerations, and whose effectiveness was maintained by an organization that was simultaneously supple and strict, as evidenced by the network of affiliated societies and extensive correspondence. This organization was put to use to disseminate instructions and suggestions, especially for the celebration of festivals, which the Jacobins frequently initiated. This is what conservative historiography has translated as "manipulation of the mob" and Michelet called the Jacobin "Inquisition," alluding to the Jacobin system of control that, in fact, constituted a considerable authority, parallel to that of the government.

Is there among all these themes a common denominator? One is tempted to find it, as Mazauric has, in the strategy of social and political alliances that had as its purpose the isolation of counterrevolutionary, aristocratic opposition. The tactic employed to unite different social groups with contradictory interests against counterrevolution helps to explain, among other things, the flight forward (*fuite en avant*), of which the Cult of the Supreme Being is the symbol.

During the period of the French Revolution, Jacobinism was not uniquely a French phenomenon but rather European in scope. In crossing frontiers, however, the term sometimes changed, if not its sense, at least its coloration. The international investigation of national Jacobinisms is well under way; groups of English, German, Belgian, Swiss, and Italian Jacobins are being analyzed, and Hungarian and Polish Jacobins are being discovered. Among these groups there are considerable differences due to political and social conditions. They manifested themselves as much in their ideology as in the sociology of their recruitment; German intellectuals, Italian bourgeois from the Mezzogiorno, and minor Polish and Magyar nobles differed significantly, one suspects, from their French counterparts.

C. Brinton, *The Jacobins* (New York, 1930); L. de Cardenal, *La province pendant la Révolution: Histoire des clubs Jacobins* (Paris, 1929); J. Castelnau, *Le Club des Jacobins* (Paris, 1948); M. Gaston-Martin, *Les Jacobins* (Paris, 1945); M. Kennedy, *The Jacobin Club of Marseilles* (Ithaca, N.Y., and London, 1973); M. T. Lagasquié, "Le personnel terroriste toulousain," *Ann. hist. de la Révo. française* 43 (1971); C. Mazauric, "Quelques voies nouvelles pour l'histoire politique de la Révolution française," *Ann. hist. de la Révo. française* 47 (1975).

M. Vovelle

Related entries: BARNAVE; BRISSOT DE WARVILLE; CLOOTS; COMMITTEE OF PUBLIC SAFETY; CORDELIERS CLUB; CULT OF THE SUPREME BEING; DECHRISTIANIZATION; FEUILLANTS; JACOBINS; *JOURNEES REVOLUTIONNAIRES*; 9 THERMIDOR YEAR II; PETION DE VILLENEUVE; ROBESPIERRE, M.; *SCRUTIN EPURATOIRE*; TERROR, THE; VARENNES.

JACOBINS, the best-known and most influential of the political clubs of the French Revolution, which also lent its name to the political ideology of Jacobinism, particularly during the height of the Revolution in the Year II (1793-94). The club had its origins in the *sociétés de pensée* of the eighteenth century where men of influence discussed current problems and the ideas of the *philosophes*. From the opening of the Estates General, patriot deputies established the custom of meeting, as the Breton Club, at the Amaury coffeehouse (today the Brasserie Muller) in Versailles. When the National Assembly was transferred to Paris in October 1789, the club was established in the convent of the Jacobins (Dominicans of the rue Saint-Jacques) on the rue Saint-Honoré, from which derives the name most commonly given to this Society of the Friends of the Constitution.

At the beginning it was composed essentially of assemblymen and comprised more than 200 deputies, who first gathered in the monks' refectory and later in the library, because the club soon admitted nondeputies, writers, scholars, publicists, and well-to-do bourgeois, who paid an entry fee and high dues. A majority of the members were partisans of a constitutional monarchy and had as their mission "to enlighten the people and warn them of their mistakes," as well as to emphasize the regulation of 8 February 1790.

Very soon similar clubs were created in provincial cities, and they requested affiliation with the Parisian society, whose rules they accepted. In July 1790 their number was put at 152, spread through all of France, while the Jacobins of Paris counted nearly 1,200 members, including the duc d'Aiguillon, the duc de Noailles, the marquis de Lafayette, A. Du Port, A. Barnave, and M. Robespierre. The club's sessions took place on Monday, Wednesday, Friday, and Sunday evenings and lasted until about 11 P.M. Tight control prohibited access to the public, but necessity required enlarging the meeting space, and on 29 May 1791 the club moved into the church, the choir and its appendages.

At the time of the king's flight, several members, including J.-P. Brissot and J.-N. Billaud-Varenne, proclaimed their republican sympathies. After the "massacre" of the Champ de Mars (17 July 1791), moderate deputies left the club and joined a new one nearby, in the former convent of the Feuillants. At this point it was feared that the Society of the Friends of the Constitution was about to dissolve; but some loyal patriots, such as Robespierre and J. Pétion, managed to gather the most ardent Parisian members around them and to rally a number of the provincial clubs. By September 1791 Jacobin unity was more solid and its influence more extensive than before. A thousand local societies obeyed the club and spread its propaganda. During the elections for the Legislative Assembly and for the Paris Commune, the Jacobins succeeded in seating their candidates. Henceforth the public was admitted to follow the debates of the "brothers and friends," who, in the light of the inexperience of the Assembly, arrogated to themselves the roles of adviser and censor, by proposing decrees, criticizing ministers, receiving petitions, and drafting addresses and circulars. Robespierre played an important part in the club and spoke approximately a hundred times between October 1791 and August 1792, but the Brissotin majority did not always follow him; for example, he was refused the opportunity to speak three times on 29 April 1792. Although the insurrection of 10 August was planned nearby, the club did not participate in it, and the September Massacres disturbed its members.

Events seemed to be passing the club by; yet once more it survived by rejuvenating itself. On 22 September it took the name Society of the Jacobin Friends of Liberty and Equality, thereby attempting to attract well-to-do *sans-culottes*, artisans, shopkeepers, and clerks. The club's principles became stricter and its action more rigorous. The Jacobin spirit triumphed during the trial of Louis XVI. Brissot and the principal Girondin deputies were excluded from the club, although they maintained a majority in the Assembly. The insurrection of 31 May 1793 ousted the latter from power to the benefit of the Montagnards; and the society henceforth became the faithful supporter of the Revolutionary government. The club officially monopolized political life, distributed "the good word," made and unmade reputations, and condemned without appeal the undecided, the suspects, the traitors, the prevaricators. Through its network of faithful, it exercised a real dictatorship over public opinion; under the label of *Jacobin*, popular opinion soon mixed together patriots, Montagnards, *sans-culottes*, and republicans.

In the Year II (1793-94) Jacobinism constituted a historical reality rather than a philosophical system. It expressed not the aspirations of a class but the spirit of the militant element among citizens from all social groups. On the political level, it was opposed to the liberalism of 1789 and sacrificed particular interests to the general interest and public safety. The great principles of liberty, equality, and fraternity were for the friends of the Revolution alone; its enemies deserved only prison or death. The Terror should be applied to the latter alone. A religious, fanatic, intransigent enthusiasm sustained the Jacobin and justified his actions. This was the despotism of Liberty. But the "brothers and friends" sometimes indulged in excesses and, especially in the provinces, involved themselves in extreme measures, dictated by the *Enragés* and encouraged by economic problems. Dechristianization and the "masquerades" of the Cult of Reason were praised. The Convention had to respond in order to preserve governmental authority; and the mother society proceeded to purge its members. The representatives on mission acted the same way in the provinces.

During the winter of 1793-94 the Hébertists and Dantonists were successively eliminated from the political scene and from local administrations. After Ventôse, however, Jacobin personnel would continue to operate, but more and more in isolation from the *sans-culottes* and the peasant masses. The anti-Christian struggle, the requisitions, and the maximum alienated the countryside. The governmental apparatus appeared an artificial construction and its excessive centralization recalled the Old Regime. Robespierre and his friends, the defenders of the Jacobin order, were charged with the excesses of the Terror, and the successive purges did not restore confidence. In Prairial and Messidor Year II problems erupted; France became frightened. In Paris the section activists were divided, and some of them would hesitate to become involved in the final test of Thermidor.

Unconscious of the danger, the Jacobin club continued its deliberations. Robespierre, who sulked against the Convention and the Committee of Public Safety, maintained the hope that he could rally public opinion from the rostrum of the Jacobins, where he spoke fourteen times in eleven sessions. But time was short and the malaise profound. On 8 Thermidor at the Jacobins, he repeated the long indictment that he had just presented at the Convention and won over his audience, which refused to listen to J.-N. Billaud-Varenne and J.-M. Collot d'Herbois, who had joined his opposition. However, the next day they triumphed in the assembly. Robespierre and his friends were executed and the club was closed. Although the Jacobins reopened on 11 Thermidor, the club was doomed. Public opinion held it responsible for everything that was wrong. At first, the Convention forbade any affiliation with it; then, after the Paris club's session on 19 Brumaire Year III, when it had been attacked by agitators, the Convention voted its definitive suppression on 22 Brumaire (12 November 1794). Some members rallied around P.-F. Tissot and F.-E.-J. Raisson in a ballroom on rue des Boucheries Saint-Germain. Soon after, the old location was demolished, and the site became what is now the Saint-Honoré market.

The Jacobin spirit, however, survived the disappearance of the club in France and abroad. Jacobinism was the moving force behind the uprisings of Germinal and Prairial of the Year III (spring 1795), behind the Panthéon club under the Directory, and behind the winds of the Carbonari during the Restoration. It reappeared in 1848 during the uprisings in France and throughout Europe. But little by little, Jacobinism, isolated from its historical context, passed away. However, there has been preserved the image of men pure, honest, and just, severe and intransigent, patriotic and democratic, who reconciled their actions with their principles, and who conceived of an ideal society, both virtuous and egalitarian. In the same way, the socialist theories of the nineteenth century were inspired by Jacobinism and the memory of the Year II.

F.-A. Aulard, *La Société des Jacobins*, 5 vols. (Paris, 1889); F.-P. Bénoit, *Les idéologies politiques modernes: Le Temps de Hegel* (Paris, 1980); M. Bouloiseau, *La République jacobine* (Paris, 1972); C. Brinton, *The Jacobins* (New York, 1930); A. Cochin, *L'esprit du jacobinisme* (Paris, 1979); M. Gaston-Martin, *Les Jacobins* (Paris, 1945); J. Godechot, *La pensée révolutionnaire, 1789-1799* (Paris, 1954).

M. Bouloiseau

Related entries: CHAMP DE MARS "MASSACRE"; CULT OF REASON; DECHRISTIANIZATION; FEUILLANTS; JACOBINISM; LAW OF THE MAXIMUM; ROBESPIERRE, M.; *SANS-CULOTTES*; TERROR, THE.

JALES, a small, rocky, wooded plain around the mouths of the Granzon and other lesser tributaries of the Chassezac River, and center of counterrevolutionary activity, 1790-96. Jalès lies near the southern extremity of the hilly lower Vivarais, which constitutes the southeast corner of the Massif Central. During 1782 and 1783, masked, armed outlaws rendered this area infamous. Victims of their assaults were chiefly merchants and legal experts of various sorts, whom the populace considered alien parasites rapaciously disrupting traditional order in an agrarian society. The Constituent Assembly permanently allocated to the department of the Ardèche this zone, part of which, by general agreement, lay within the diocese of Uzès and therefore had been part of the *sénéchaussée* of Nîmes. Located on an isolated elevation near the present Croisée de Jalès, the château of Jalès towered over the plain. This fortress had long been headquarters for a *commanderie* held by the Knights Hospitalers of Saint John and earlier by the Templars. It became the symbolic focus for a series of federative camps, which brought together militant counterrevolutionaries from many zones in the central sector of southern France.

Students sympathetic to popular counterrevolutionary movements have identified an armed assembly at Jalès during each year from 1790 to 1796, inclusive, and several thereafter. Tens of thousands drawn from all ranks in scores of villages and towns purportedly attended. Documentation is sketchy, widely scattered, and almost universally partisan, especially regarding secret projects of the organizing committees. The menace that these assemblies posed to the new order was consistently exaggerated by both participants in the meetings and authorities working to prevent the occurrence of additional camps. No solid evidence of direct intervention by paid agents of *émigré* princes survives from before 1792. However, publicity from both extremes in the local political spectrum painted all of the episodes at Jalès as key elements in a grandiose scheme—conceived by the French Bourbon court in exile—to reverse the course of the Revolution entirely. Beneath the polemic are patterns that underscore the precocious and persistent agitation against the Revolution that was common among Catholics in areas of the Midi where large neighboring communities of Calvinists seemed to benefit, at Catholics' expense, from the Revolution.

The leading agitator of militant Catholics on both sides of the boundary between the Gard and the Ardèche in August 1790 and in February 1791 appears to have been L. Bastide, *seigneur* of Malbos. While some officials accused him of complicity with the *masques armés*, others credited him with purging banditry. Along with other chiefs of the early camps at Jalès, Bastide claimed to erect a counterpoise against the conquest of power in the Gard by Protestants and their dependents, who designated themselves patriots. In particular, counterrevolutionary rhetoric stressed the urgency of responding with force to tyranny imposed by hostile civilians armed as militiamen. Bloody engagements in which patriots prevailed had climaxed at Nîmes in June 1790, during sessions of the assembly that selected the first administrators for the department of the Gard. In numerous cities and towns, shock waves emanating from this civil war reverberated in contests over public administration. This pattern became particularly evident just as the Civil Constitution of the Clergy was being implemented. The most notable instance occurred at Uzès early in 1791 during the public election of a replacement for the nonjuring bishop. After the culmination of conflict at Nîmes and again after the echo at Uzès, armed detachments of the defeated party gathered at Jalès. At each camp, commanders discussed and formally endorsed a resolution that buttressed demands for overturning the current local administration by allegations that Catholics were being persecuted. Nevertheless, some ambivalent participants subsequently insisted to patriot officials that they had valiantly risked their lives to pacify the insurgents. The most penitent among former counterrevolutionary leaders claimed to have moderated inflammatory demands that received wide publicity. The camp of February 1791 resolved to seize a territorial base by force. However, it selected as general commander the weak-willed J. Chastenier de Burac. He did not execute the plan but acquiesced rather in patriots' dominion over the Gard, even though they continued to impose serious indignities on defeated Catholics. Nevertheless, officials sent militiamen to interdict future counterrevolutionary intrigue. They arrested Bastide, who died soon after, while still in captivity.

The main force behind the third and fourth camps was C. Allier (Alliez), a priest from Chambonas, near Jalès, who had collaborated with Bastide in animating earlier camps. He was aided most notably by A. Charrier, a notary from

Nasbinals and a deputy of the Third Estate to the Constituent. Encouraged by the Bourbon princes at Coblentz, they expected intervention by the Spanish army, as well as a great domestic insurrection linking opposition to the Revolution in southern France with that in the northwest. In July 1792 Allier placed large armed contingents in the field, notably one of about 2,000 under Count François-Louis of Saillans. T. Conway, acting on behalf of the court in exile, financed this operation and was supposed to control its actions. However, regulars commanded by General L.-A. d'Albignac soon routed the insurgents, massacring many. Civilian officials sanctioned the burning and razing of the château at Jalès, of that at Banne, located in the foothills to the west, and of numerous properties in the plain between them. Yet regimes of the First Republic faced renewed hostile federations in this zone. After the guillotining of Allier, 5 September 1793, his brothers Charles and above all Dominique lent continuity to subsequent camps, in which several former nobles participated. Notable among D. Allier's lieutenants were P. de Pialety in 1794, the baron of Saint Christol in 1795, and, in 1796, the comte de Lamothe, and the marquis de Surville. The plain of Jalès served again as a rallying point for royalist conspirators in 1813 and for White Terrorists under the duc d'Angoulême in 1814 and 1815. Subsequently, it became a common destination for royalist Catholic pilgrims, but the Orleanist monarchy prevented erection there of a monument to counterrevolutionary martyrs.

Les administrateurs composant le Directoire du Département de l'Ardèche, *Conspiration de Saillans* (n.p., [1792]); S. Brugal [pseud.], *Les camps de Jalès* (Nantes, 1885); C. Jolivet, *L'agitation contre-révolutionnaire dans l'Ardèche sous le Directoire* (Lyon, 1930); P. J. Lauze de Peret, *Eclaircissemens historiques en réponse aux calomnies dont les Protestans du Gard sont l'objet: et précis des agitations et des troubles de ce département depuis 1790 jusqu'à nos jours* (Paris, 1818); M. Sonenscher, "La révolte des masques armés de 1783 en Vivarais," *Vivarais et Languedoc: 44e congrès de la Fédération Historique du Languedoc Méditerranéen et du Roussillon* (Montpellier, 1972).

J. N. Hood

Related entries: COBLENTZ; COUNTERREVOLUTION; *EMIGRES*; *SENECHAUSSEE*.

JAURES, JEAN (1859-1914), socialist historian and politician from the Tarn, who had a profound influence on the subsequent historiography of the Revolution; assassinated on 31 July 1914, just as Europe was about to embark on World War I.

In June 1898 the publisher J. Rouff proposed to J. Jaurès that he direct a socialist history of France covering the period from 1789 to 1900. Jaurès agreed to become the general editor and to do the section on the French Revolution, from the Constituent Assembly to 9 Thermidor, himself. The interest of the socialist orator in the Revolution of 1789, however, dated to a much earlier time. Since 1887, when he was doing a study of J.-J. Rousseau, he had been interested in the origins of the Revolution. After defending his thesis in philosophy in 1892, he turned again to the history of *la Grande Nation*, undoubtedly at the suggestion of C. Perroud, rector of the University of Toulouse and a specialist in Madame Roland. Thus, he began his research around 1892 and from 1897 became more and more systematic in it. In 1898 he was relieved of his parliamentary obligations and could devote himself more completely to the task that thrilled him since he could thereby teach the French and, more particularly, the proletariat how socialism had its deepest roots in the soil, in the very heart of the history of France. Appearing in volumes bound in red ox-blood leather and abundantly illustrated, the four volumes prepared by Jaurès cost 10 francs in 1902. The volume on *The Constituent* sold at the equivalent of two days' wages for an experienced railwayman or a half-week's wages for a beginning teacher.

Writing a history of the Revolution was not, for Jaurès, a distraction from the ongoing political struggle (this was in the midst of the Dreyfus affair) but rather an extension of this struggle by different means. The team that Jaurès assembled to carry out the socialist history was not what he expected. To treat the history of France for over a century in a social and socialist spirit, he would have liked the cooperation of the leaders of different socialist tendencies but did not get it. Instead of P. Brousse, J. Allemane, J. Guesde, or E. Vaillant, he would have at his side G. Deville, L. Herr, C. Andler, J. Labusquière, and L. Dubreuilh. For the research on the part of the history for which he was responsible, he had the assistance of young *Normaliens*, but most of the work and all of the editing he did himself.

His research was sometimes interrupted by political combat; but he obstinately and scrupulously went back to it. He read his predecessors, A. Thiers, J. Michelet, L. Blanc, and H. Taine, but also kept current with the latest scholarship; he was familiar with the works of P. Sagnac, I.-V. Loutchisky, F. Rouvière, A. de Charmasse, A. Lichtenberger, P. Langevin, and, of course, F.-A. Aulard, whose *Political History of the Revolution* appeared in 1901. He dug through the library of the Chamber of Deputies, which included the Portiez de l'Oise Collection, whose volumes he read three or four times a week until late in the evening. He scrupulously researched the Archives parlementaires and the newspapers of the period. At the Archives Nationales, he ordered the documents in series F^{10}, F^{11}, and F^{12} that dealt with the economy of France, surveys on the prices of necessities, and the maximum. In the provinces he devoted his short vacations to visiting the archives of the Tarn or of Lyon.

He investigated not only works that had been published long before but also documents that had been largely or entirely ignored until then. His approach was also new, in that it led him to become interested not only in history seen from above, from the rostrum of the assemblies, but also in history seen from below. In the course of his economic research, his constant concern was to understand man and man in society, and alongside the bourgeois, whom he discovered there, he was constantly running across peasants or the popular classes of the cities, people of the fourth estate, as they were already called in 1789. Thus, in the end he created a history that in the words of the historian M. Rebérioux (1966) was "triply new."

It was new, first of all, in its scope. His history of the Revolution was not dependent only on the history of the popular masses of Paris or on that of the Revolutionary government. Jaurès listened to and then made his readers hear the rumors and the cries of violence that came from the other major cities, Bordeaux, Nantes, Marseille, Lyon and also from the villages. He integrated local studies, already published, with the great movement that was shaking all of France.

He went beyond the national level. Although he ignored Russia and paid little attention to Italy, he frequently dealt with Switzerland, Germany, and England, without neglecting the French colonies. Above all, he showed the spread and the limits of democratic ideas.

His history was novel also in the time span encompassed. He knew that the Revolution could not be restricted to rigid dates: July 1789, 9 Thermidor, 18 Brumaire. He wrote, "We shall consider the French Revolution as a massive and wonderfully fruitful phenomenon; but it is not in our eyes a definitive phenomenon, the history of which will subsequently only unfold its endless consequences. The French Revolution indirectly prepared for the coming of the proletariat. It realized the essential conditions of socialism, democracy and capitalism. But it was, in its essence, the political advent of the bourgeois class."

He searched among certain Revolutionaries, who always remained in the shadow of power, for the germs of socialist ideas: the abbé Dolivier, F.-J. Lange, whom he viewed (without doubt, incorrectly) as a predecessor of C. Fourier, and G. Babeuf who fascinated him. Of Babeuf, Jaurès correctly noted, "With him communism ceases to be a doctrine found only in books; it enters into the life of History; it becomes tied to the very evolution of democracy" (*Histoire socialiste*).

Finally, Jaurès' work is new because of the primacy accorded economic and social history. Certainly, before him, A. Barnave, F. Guizot, and A. de Tocqueville had put the study of social classes at the heart of their interpretations. Jaurès, however, gave this approach even more meticulous attention, with the desire of scrutinizing the fate of the entire people and with the constant attempt—and here he is clearly Marxist—of continuously relating economic analysis to social conflicts.

The Revolution was the child of misery, Michelet had claimed; Jaurès added, also the child of prosperity. It was prosperity that, over the long term, produced the middle class and its accession to power. Jaurès placed the bourgeoisie at the heart of the Revolution without, however, forgetting the anticapitalist demands of peasants and the urban little people.

The *Socialist History* of Jaurès, thus, is filled with new directions, which historians of the twentieth century would pursue. The course Jaurès indicated was also a fertile one because he was the first, from 1903, to make an effort to collect, classify, and publish archival documents relative to the economic life of the Revolution. The commission that he established for this purpose remains a historical workshop, bringing together researchers, from Paris to the provinces, from the provinces to foreign countries.

Thus, from the centennial to the bicentennial celebration of the French Revolution and beyond, Jaurès remains a dominant influence on the history of the Revolution.

V. Auriol, *Souvenirs de Jean Jaurès* (Paris, 1945); M. Dommanget, "Jaurès, historien de la Révolution française," *La pensée socialiste devant la Révolution française* (Paris, 1966); H. Goldberg, *The Life of Jean Jaurès* (Madison, Wis., 1962); J. Jaurès, *L'histoire socialiste de la Révolution française*, 4 vols. (Paris, 1901-2); M. Rebérioux, "Jaurès et la Révolution française," *La pensée socialiste devant la Révolution française* (Paris, 1966).

J.-P. Bertaud

Related entries: MATHIEZ; SOBOUL.

JAY, JOHN (1745-1829), U.S. statesman, minister plenipotentiary to Spain; secretary of foreign affairs under the Articles of Confederation, first chief justice of the U.S. Supreme Court. See JAY TREATY.

JAY TREATY (19 November 1794), an agreement that temporarily adjusted a series of disputes between the United States and Great Britain and led to a worsening of Franco-American relations. The Jay Treaty arose out of Anglo-American disputes that stemmed from the Peace Treaty of 1783, from subsequent commercial relations, and especially from problems created by the outbreak of war between France and England on 1 February 1793.

In the United States, the Jeffersonian-agrarian-Republican faction viewed the war as an opportunity to exact concessions from England by a strong stand on neutral rights. The Hamiltonian-Federalist group, representing the northern, urban, shipping interests, was determined to avoid a war with Great Britain, which it felt would destroy American commerce and undermine A. Hamilton's recently established fiscal system. Although the Hamiltonian view prevailed and President G. Washington issued a neutrality proclamation, England and the United States differed sharply over the issue of neutral rights. The British order in council on 6 November 1793 (rescinded in January 1794), which authorized the seizure of all neutral ships bound to and from French colonies, resulted in the capture of over 250 American vessels and brought the two nations to the brink of war.

At this critical juncture, Hamilton and the Federalists persuaded Washington to send J. Jay, chief justice of the Supreme Court, to England as an envoy extraordinary to resolve the points of conflict between the two countries. The controversial treaty was signed on 18 November 1794. Under its terms, England agreed to and did evacuate the six northwestern frontier posts stipulated in the Peace Treaty of 1783. The American government guaranteed the payment of American private pre-Revolutionary debts to English creditors, which in 1802 were fixed at 600,000 pounds. The treaty provided for the establishment of a commission to fix the amount of damages that had arisen from the seizure of each nation's ships by the other party ($10,345,200 was subsequently awarded to the United States and $143,428 to England). Two boundary commissions were established to determine the frontier in the northwest and the boundary line of the Saint Croix River in the northeast (only the latter was successful). The treaty also provided that American ships of less than seventy tons burthen could trade with the British West Indies. In return the United States agreed not to raise the tonnage duties on English vessels for a period of twelve years. The British made no concessions whatsoever on the shipping rights of neutrals. A disappointed Washington reluctantly submitted the treaty to the Senate, which, on 24 June 1795, after acrimonious debate, voted twenty to ten for ratification. Most contemporary historians are inclined to agree with Jay's assertion that the terms were the best possible under the circumstances; the Jay Treaty did preserve for a time peace between the United States and England.

The Jay Treaty also had a negative effect on Franco-American relations. The French government denounced it as an infamous betrayal and stated in July 1796 that, as a result, the treaties of 1778 were altered and suspended. In an attempt to restore normal relations, President Washington sent C. Pinckney to France as the American minister. But the Directory refused to receive him and forced Pinckney to flee the country under threat of arrest. In March 1797, the French government issued a decree that in essence authorized the seizure of American vessels carrying British goods. Fuel was added to the fire with the XYZ affair in which agents of C.-M. Talleyrand, French minister for foreign affairs, demanded a bribe from a commission sent by President J. Adams to resolve Franco-American problems. This incident, together with the seizure of American ships, resulted in a spirited though undeclared naval war between the two countries that lasted from 1798 to 1800. The war was brought to an end with the Convention of 1800 in which Napoleon agreed to the abrogation of the Alliance of 1778 in exchange for the payment of French spoliation claims amounting to approximately $20 million.

A.N., AF III, Carton 56; A. H. Bowman, "The Struggle for Neutrality: A History of the Diplomatic Relations Between the United States and France, 1790-1801" (Ph.D. dissertation, Columbia University, 1954); J. A. Combs, *The Jay Treaty: Political Battleground of the Founding Fathers* (Berkeley, 1970); T. M. Iiams, *Peacemaking from Vergennes to Napoleon: French Foreign Relations in the Revolutionary Era, 1774-1814* (Huntington, N.Y., 1979).

D. M. Epstein

Related entries: JEFFERSON; TALLEYRAND; XYZ AFFAIR.

JEANBON SAINT-ANDRE, ANDRE. See SAINT-ANDRE.

JEFFERSON, THOMAS (1743-1826), U.S. minister to France, U.S. secretary of state, president of the United States. Thomas Jefferson replaced Benjamin Franklin as minister to France in May 1785. He had arrived as American peace commissioner ten months before, celebrated as a passionate exponent of American republicanism. He did not confuse conditions and events in France with his own country's practices and achievements, however, and he revealed none of the ardor for a democratic society later attributed to him in American politics. His greatest achievement as minister was his negotiation of America's first consular convention, which he signed with Foreign Minister A.-M. comte de Montmorin in November 1788. By eliminating many of the extraterritorial features of the 1778 Treaty of Amity and Commerce, particularly those pertaining to the privileges, powers, and immunities of consuls, this agreement reduced substantially America's earlier political dependence on France.

Until the convening of the Assembly of Notables in February 1787, Jefferson took little interest in French internal politics. Convinced that a representative democracy was beyond the reach of the French, he anticipated only limited reforms and generally was more satisfied with a cautious course of events than were the republicans and moderate royalists who befriended him. He embraced the Assembly's call for provincial assemblies and a convening of the Estates General as effective steps toward constitutional government. Privately, he sought to restrain such friends as the marquis de Lafayette from provoking a conservative reaction by urging more fundamental changes. It was Jefferson's lack of confidence in France's capacity to absorb political innovations that prompted him, despite his hatred of England, to advise Lafayette and others to look for constitutional solutions in the English rather than the American model of government.

By May 1789, Jefferson favored the Estates General meeting in two houses similar to the English Parliament. Should that occur and should that body meet regularly, issue a bill of rights, and provide the king with a civil list, he believed it would accomplish most of what was then possible. Frustrated by the deadlock in the Estates by early June, he drew up a Charter of Rights and circulated it privately. In proposing annual meetings of the Estates General with power to levy taxes and approve appropriations, the elimination of aristocratic financial privileges, the broadening of personal liberties, and the easing of the king's financial burdens through, among other means, a grant of money, Jefferson's constitution provided little more than the king's program offered on 23 June. It reflected Jefferson's hope that the aristocracy could trade more equitable fiscal policies for constitutional concessions touching both human rights and class privileges.

Never did Jefferson envisage the French achieving legal, social, or political equality. He did hail the Third Estate's proclamation of a National Assembly on 17 June and applauded that body's subsequent adoption of a Declaration of Rights. Yet he remained apprehensive that the legislature would pursue innovations too ambitious for French political realities. He left France in October 1789, content that the Revolution had attained a reasonable conclusion with the achievement of a limited monarchy, supervised by a National Assembly, dominated by the aristocracy.

With Jefferson's appointment as secretary of state in February 1790, his passion deepened for promoting France as a counterbalance to British commercial and political strength in American affairs. Privately he attempted to capitalize on American sympathy for changes in France both to enhance the position of his Republican party and to reduce the power of the Federalists, whom he believed were wedded to English interests and monarchical forms. Publicly he encouraged amicable relations and greater commercial ties with France. Despite continuing French reluctance to expand trade with the United States, Jefferson counseled unavailingly that France be exempted from the Tonnage Act of 1789, which imposed duties on all foreign ships equally.

In 1792, Jefferson's complacency toward France's limited monarchy yielded to enthusiasm for French republicanism, a change triggered by the outbreak of war in April between France and the Austro-Prussian coalition. The success of the Revolution in France now seemed to him in jeopardy and, with it, the security of America's own republican experiment. So fearful was he of the defeat of the Revolution and the diminution of America's republican aspirations as a result of that likelihood that he chose now to exult the Girondists and even to accept the view that their foreign policy was essentially defensive in nature.

Jefferson urged recognition of the new French leadership and acknowledgment of the continuing validity of the 1778 Treaty of Alliance. He maintained that the United States must accord recognition of any government "which is formed by the will of the nation substantially declared," a view that remained basic to American foreign policy until W. Wilson's administration. By arguing that no revocation of the treaty had occurred through the change of governments in France, he wished to guarantee American war materiel for France. That America could help France more as a neutral than as a belligerent seemed clear to him. He had no intention of seeing America dragged into the European conflict even after France's declaration of war against England in February 1793.

By April 1793, American leaders understood that America must remain neutral, but it remained uncertain under what circumstances neutrality would be established. Jefferson advocated a statement from Congress and maneuvered to employ any announcement of his country's neutrality to wrest concessions from both England and France but was frustrated in each instance. Even after President Washington proclaimed American neutrality without first squeezing concessions from either belligerent, Jefferson looked to salvage advantages for France, maintaining that should England continue to prohibit shipping to France in American vessels, America could retaliate by denying the British access to American markets. Such a diplomatic stance would at once be consistent with American neutrality, aid France, and diminish British economic influence in the United States.

Jefferson's task was complicated when, at this point, the Girondists sent E.-C. Genêt to America as minister. Genêt was charged with enlisting American military help, with holding Americans to the Treaty of Alliance (which offered French privateers advantages in American waters and guaranteed the integrity of the French West Indies), and with fomenting insurrections in the British and Spanish North American possessions. Jefferson's quest for neutrality was genuine, but his deep attachment to the French Revolution and his appreciation of its importance for American political developments colored his response to Genêt. He did little to discourage Genêt's plans to incite insurrections in Spanish Louisiana, for instance, going so far as to provide the French adventurer, A. Michaux, a letter of introduction to the governor of Kentucky.

Jefferson's handling of Genêt was at best inept. He led the Frenchman to believe that the American people supported French stratagems even as he maneuvered, as secretary of state, to deny France rights to dispose of naval prizes in American ports or to have privateers armed in American waters. Still, it was only after Genêt's activities had become insufferable even to heretofore pro-French Americans and the secretary of the treasury, Hamilton, had initiated moves on 12 July to have Genêt recalled, that Jefferson repudiated the Frenchman and his actions. When Jefferson resigned his post in December 1793, he could take comfort that his foreign policy had been successful and that the Republican party (in his eyes, along with the French, the torchbearers of world republicanism and enlightenment) had not been irreparably damaged either by Genêt or his own shortcomings.

As vice-president after 1797, Jefferson condemned the removal of J. Monroe as minister to France and resisted Federalist efforts to use the XYZ affair to exacerbate Franco-American relations and to damage the Republican party. Jefferson's championing of French interests had failed by 1799 to produce the results he had nourished for his party or his country, but between his retirement as secretary of state and that date he continued to support every effort, official and unofficial, to lessen tension between the two countries.

The Convention of 1800 ended America's quasi-war with France, but it was the collapse of the Directory in November 1799 that freed Jefferson from his earlier emotional attachment to France. No pretense could be made that N. Bonaparte's Consulate represented principles and visions that he had associated with the Revolution or with his own country's republicanism. Thus, the Convention that negated former treaties between the two countries elicited no protests from Jefferson.

Jefferson employed his inaugural address as president in March 1801 to issue a solemn warning against entangling alliances and to proclaim peace America's passion. He was attracted to Bonaparte's willingness to expand rights for non-belligerents—a policy shift provoked by French need to lure neutral navies into a League of Armed Neutrality against England—yet he recognized that American sovereignty was threatened by the transfer in October 1802 of Louisiana from a weak Spain to a powerful France. Despite constitutional reservations regarding his actions, Jefferson moved to purchase New Orleans. It was his threat to align with England and perhaps to participate in a joint Anglo-American attack against Louisiana if France failed to conclude the sale, coupled with France's problems in the West Indies and Europe, that eventually forced Bonaparte to approve the sale of all French Louisiana. It was Jefferson's crowning achievement as president.

Jefferson's policy of neutrality during the European conflict initially enabled

American merchants to dominate markets heretofore controlled by the English and forced France to open its West Indian colonies to American shipping. By 1805, however, both England and France were harassing American carriers bound for the other's ports. It was England's naked contempt for American rights and Jefferson's own appreciation that England represented the greater threat to American interests, as well as his commitment to peaceful responses, that explain Jefferson's employment of the embargo in December 1807. He was not unaware that American policy struck more forcefully at England and thus worked to Bonaparte's advantage, but he hoped it would encourage France to aid the United States in obtaining Florida from Spain. By the time Jefferson left the presidency in March 1809, the embargo had created grave economic hardships in America while achieving few of his foreign policy aims. Despite this failure, he had kept America out of European wars, a goal he had pursued single-mindedly as secretary of state and as president.

S. F. Bemis, "Thomas Jefferson," in *American Secretaries of State and Their Diplomacy*, vol. 2 (New York, 1927); A. H. Bowman, *The Struggle for Neutrality: Franco-American Diplomacy during the Federalist Era* (Knoxville, 1974); J. Boyd et al., eds. *The Papers of Thomas Jefferson*, vols. 7-20 (Princeton, 1950-); L. S. Kaplan, *Jefferson and France: An Essay on Politics and Political Ideas* (New Haven, 1967); D. Malone, *Jefferson and His Time*, vols. 2-6 (Boston, 1948-1981); R. R. Palmer, "The Dubious Democrat: Thomas Jefferson in Bourbon France," *Pol. Sci. Q.* 72 (1957); M. D. Peterson, "Thomas Jefferson and Commercial Policy, 1783-1793," *Wm. and Mary Q.*, 3d ser., 22 (1965).

G. S. Rowe

Related entries: ASSEMBLY OF NOTABLES; GENET; GIRONDINS; JAY TREATY; XYZ AFFAIR.

JEMAPPES, BATTLE OF. See BATTLE OF JEMAPPES.

JESUS, COMPANIES OF. See COMPANIES OF JESUS.

JEUNESSE DOREE, well-to-do young men who constituted the core of reactionary militants during the Year III. Although this sort of reactionary youth was active in many towns, the Parisian groups acquired a national political significance and the term most usually designates the militants of the capital. There is no evidence to suggest much collusion between activists in different cities, although young men from Paris were active at Lyon and Marseille, and vice-versa. Antiradical militancy among wealthy youths was not a new phenomenon in either Paris or the provinces. They formed conservative militias during the municipal struggles of 1789 in centers such as Lyon and Marseille; they created disturbances at Paris in 1793 over recruitment and fought in southern federalist uprisings in the same year. Indeed, there was considerable continuity in personnel between the earlier years and the Year III. However, it was only in the latter period that they achieved sustained action and political influence.

Two features distinguish the Parisian *jeunesse* from that of the southeast, the other area of their most extensive activity. In the southeast, they often appear as extensions of traditional, pre-Revolutionary youth groups, but at Paris they seem unrelated to traditional perceptions; southerners included murder among their anti-Jacobin pursuits, whereas (according to their memorialist C. Lacretelle) the Parisians refused to have recourse to it. In all other respects, reactionary youth shared common characteristics.

The Parisian *jeunesse* numbered 2,000 to 3,000 at most. Drawn from the western and center-west sections, they were predominantly lawyers', merchants', and bankers' clerks and employees in government offices. Subject to military service, they either had real or false tickets of leave and exemptions or else were in protected employment. They had usually either been in prison during the Terror or were related to people who had been executed, arrested, or had emigrated. Their meeting places were cafés, especially the Café de Chartres. They identified themselves by extravagant clothes, affected speech, and great expenditure. They played a role somewhat analogous to that of the *sans-culottes* in 1793 as the major extraparliamentary pressure group of the period. Their action falls into three fairly distinct phases: before Germinal, the Germinal and Prairial days, and the period leading to the Vendémiaire Year IV uprising.

In early Year III, they were instrumental in breaking up what remained of the radical organization. They initiated a campaign of personal assaults that continued for the rest of the year and fueled the moderate conquest of the sections. Their first major success was the closure of the Jacobins, since their riotous assault on the club brought the Convention to decree its closure on 22 Brumaire (12 November). In Pluviôse, their campaign developed further with attacks on the busts of J.-P. Marat. The propaganda exercise was reinforced by riotous scenes in the theaters to impose plays and songs with a political message to their taste. The arrest of G. Babeuf, the closure of the clubs in the Lazowski and Quinze-Vingts sections, and the removal of Marat from the Panthéon on 20-21 Pluviôse (8-9 February 1795) must be seen as results of their pressure. In Ventôse, they attacked the Montagnard J.-B. d'Armonville and jeered others. Their pressure in the public galleries of the Convention contributed to the arrest of J.-N. Billaud-Varenne, J.-M. Collot d'Herbois, B. Barère, and M.-G. Vadier on 12 Ventôse (2 March).

The de facto repression of Jacobinism before the Germinal rising was largely the work of the *jeunesse* in defiance of governmental reticence. They presented a series of faits accomplis in the escalation of reaction by the harassment of individual Jacobins, by an assault on Jacobin organizations and symbols, and by agitation in the Convention galleries. Their activity aggravated the insurrectionary temper of the populace leading to the Germinal uprising. Collisions with the youth preceded it, and one of the demands in both the Germinal and Prairial *journées* was for the repression of the *jeunesse*. Government favor to the *jeunesse* grew in proportion to the acuity of the popular threat. The unreliability of the National Guards in many sections and the unwillingness of bourgeois to serve in others made them an attractive auxiliary in a confrontation with democratic forces. Thus, on 11 Germinal (31 March), the Committee of General Security called them to defend the Convention the next day. Their contribution to the defense was negligible. Their role in the Prairial days was more prominent. Although brushed aside by the crowd on 1 Prairial (20 May), it was they who were entrusted with breaking up groups in the city on 2 Prairial. After a period of disfavor on 3 Prairial, they were armed and formally organized. On 4 Prairial, they marched into the faubourg Saint-Antoine, only to be forced to retreat ignominiously. However, their performance in the Prairial crisis gives the true measure of their potential force. The effective repression had been undertaken by regular troops and properly organized National Guards from some bourgeois sections. Quarrelsome, anarchic, and self-indulgent, the youth could not cope with large-scale armed clashes. This was verified in the royalist Vendémiaire rising in Paris.

The relationship between the *jeunesse* and the government had always been ambiguous. Certainly during the early months, they were applauded by reactionary elements in the Convention, particularly turncoat Montagnards like J.-L. Tallien and L.-M.-S. Fréron who used this pressure to support their maneuvers. Indeed, Fréron's *L'orateur du peuple* aired their views and gave them directives, while his pamphlet *Invitation à la jeunesse parisienne* (23 Nivôse, 12 January) urged them to intensify their militancy. Contemporaries had good reason, then, to call them "Fréron's youth." Nonetheless, the Committee of General Security in particular (despite the membership of their friend J.-S. Rovère) never much liked their behavior. It tried to dampen the reactionary offensive in the sections in the winter of 1794-95; it arrested a group of them during the theater disturbances of Pluviôse, even though it eventually gave way and banned the play they disliked; more were arrested in a drive against speculators in late Floréal; in the middle of the Prairial days, it disarmed them momentarily (3 Prairial). It was the popular threat, stimulated indeed by themselves, which gave the *jeunesse* leverage; the crushing defeat of the popular movement in Prairial brought the inherent tension between government and youth to the surface.

The conflict arose partly over an attempt in late Prairial to resolve the price problem by detaining speculators, who included elements of the youth. The principal reason, however, lay in their increasingly explicit royalism. Self-interest alone was enough to unite the mass of the Convention against royalism, and the defeat of the democratic offensive relieved them of the need to conciliate the *jeunesse*. Even Fréron soon turned against his youth. In Messidor and Thermidor, the Committee of General Security, increasingly sure of the republicanism of the troops (by definition largely hostile to the deserters and shirkers in the *jeunesse*), began to release Jacobins as potential support against the progress of royalism. The rupture became overt at the end of Messidor when, after renewed trouble in the theaters, a riotous demonstration was dispersed by cavalry, the Café de Chartres was closed, and some eighty youths arrested.

By alienating bourgeois opinion with its attempted self-perpetuation in the Two-thirds Law, the Convention gave the *jeunesse* the chance to contend with it. Their activity in the primary assemblies was instrumental in obtaining the massive rejection of this law in the plebiscite in Paris and presaged a confrontation. In the days leading up to 13 Vendémiaire (5 October), youth violence was met by government measures to enforce departure for military service and the rearming of disarmed terrorists. However, although hostile middle-class opinion was bound to be alarmed further by such tactics, it was equally dismayed by the disorder and royalism of the *jeunesse*. In the event, the rising of 13 Vendémiaire was predominantly a clash between this youth and regular troops, which could not fail to mark the final destruction of the *jeunesse* as a political force. The organized youth of the southeast was soon also disrupted by the delegates of the Directory, notably Fréron.

G. Duval, *Souvenirs thermidoriens* (Paris, 1844); F. Gendron, *La jeunesse dorée* (Québec, 1979); C. Lacretelle, *Dix années d'epreuves pendant la Révolution* (Paris, 1842); C. Lucas, "Violence thermidorienne et société traditionnelle," *Cah. d'Hist.* 24 (1979).

C. Lucas

Related entries: BABEUF; *JOURNEES REVOLUTIONNAIRES*; *SANS-CU-LOTTES*; TALLIEN; 13 VENDEMIAIRE YEAR IV; TWO-THIRDS LAW.

JEWS. On the eve of the French Revolution, there were two kinds of Jewish population in France. In the southeastern corner of the country, in the regions of Bordeaux and Bayonne, there were some 3,500 Sephardim, who had been arriving since about 1500 from across the borders of both Spain and Portugal. The first such settlers had come as Marranos, as crypto-Jews, but by the middle of the eighteenth century, the Jewish identity of this community was increasingly known, and by the end of the century, it began to be recognized in legal acts. By 1776, when the French crown issued its last *lettres patentes* in favor of Sephardic Jews, this community had succeeded in establishing its right to live as an avowedly Jewish merchant guild anywhere within the authority of the Parlement of Bordeaux. Their leading families, led by the Gradis clan, engaged in international trade and lived like other *grands bourgeoises* of Bordeaux. Among the Sephardim, there were already deists and unbelievers.

The Sephardim were the only Jews who had any kind of legal existence in the older France, the territories from which Jews had been expelled in 1390. The far larger Jewish presence of perhaps some 30,000 Ashkenazim, Yiddish-speaking Central European Jews, was on the eastern border of France, in Alsace, Lorraine, and the city of Metz. These Jews had been added to the population of France by conquest following the wars of the seventeenth and eighteenth centuries involving these territories. Never added formally to the French state, these lands were administered at the end of the Old Regime as border territories by the Ministry of War, and the French crown simply replaced their former rulers and accepted the maintenance of the older political structure, which, in many of these jurisdictions, included the right of some Jews to live and trade there. These Ashkenazim were far more foreign than the Sephardim, for they were only geographically in Western Europe, but culturally, aside from local variations, they were indistinguishable from the Jews of Central and Eastern Europe. They made their livings by dealing in cattle and in many kinds of petty trade and in small-scale money lending to the peasants. This embroiled them in frequent conflict with the non-Jewish element in the local population.

The issue of the Jews became a matter of some consequence in the two decades immediately preceding the French Revolution. All of the major thinkers of the Enlightenment were involved in discussing biblical religion, to its discredit, and they were thus inevitably confronting the ancient Jews, the source of the Bible. These enemies of fanaticism sympathized with the Jews as the object of hatred of Christians and especially of the Inquisition, but they also found the source of such fanaticism in the Bible. A major argument among the men of the Enlightenment was concerned with the question of the character of the Jews. F.-M. Voltaire held that they had an ineradicably different character, which few could transcend, even in an unfanatical, open society. More moderate thinkers such as the marquis de Mirabeau (the younger) and the abbé Grégoire, held that no community had an innate character, that Jews, like all other people, had been created by their circumstances, and that once the negative circumstances of persecution changed, the Jews would improve.

The stage was thus set for the notion that what was required to make the Jews better was some form of social engineering. The last act of the drama of pre-Revolution discussion of the Jewish question took place in 1784. The Royal Society of Arts and Sciences in Metz announced an essay contest on the question of what means would be required to make the Jews happy and useful. The first prize was eventually won by the abbé Grégoire with an essay that argued mainly for improved economic conditions, approaching equality of opportunity. The government itself acted twice that same year on the Jewish question. In January, a decree was issued forbidding the levying of the body tax on Jews, for, in the language of the decree, this was a humiliation that equated human beings with animals. On the other hand, in July 1784, a much more comprehensive decree was issued, to cover the Jews in Alsace, who numbered about two-thirds of the entire Jewish population of the eastern provinces. This act provided some increased opportunities for rich Jews in banking and large-scale commerce and gave them freedom to create factories for textiles, iron, glass, and pottery, but the poor Jews, the overwhelming majority, were made more miserable. Henceforth, no marriage could be contracted without royal permission, and the traditional Jewish pursuits, the trades in grain, cattle, and money lending, were further restricted. Worst of all, a census was ordered in preparation for the expulsion of all those Jews (and there were many) who could not prove their legal right to live in the province.

These new restrictions were fought, and the debate on the Jewish question continued through the last years of the *ancien régime*. As late as 1788, one of the royal ministers, C. de Malesherbes, was at the center of consultations with the leaders of both the Sephardim and the Ashkenazim looking for new legislation for the Jews. Nothing came of this initiative, for the discussions were soon overtaken by the events of the Revolution.

Jews did not receive equality automatically at the dawn of the Revolution. The Declaration of the Rights of Man at the National Assembly, adopted on 27 August 1789, was immediately interpreted as not applicable to the Jews. Their rights were debated separately for the first time in a three-day session from 21 to 24 December 1789 inconclusively. It was clear to the proponents of the emancipation of the Jews that they had no majority within the chamber. A month later, on 28 January 1790, a very limited decree was enacted giving equal rights to Spanish and Portuguese Jews and to those from Avignon. C.-M. Talleyrand advanced the argument that those Jews had already assimilated to the rest of France. The question of the unassimilated Ashkenazim in eastern France was held in abeyance for the next two years, and despite repeated debates, a majority could not be mustered for their emancipation. Such a decree was passed on 27 September 1791, in the closing days of the National Assembly, in order, as the proponents argued, to complete the work of the Revolution. By then even actors, hangmen, and Moslems had been given equality. It would hardly do to exclude only the Jews. Nonetheless, the next day, the Assembly passed a decree of exception, placing the debts that were owed to Jews in eastern France under government supervision. Anti-Jewish opinion maintained that equality for the Jews would simply give them an opportunity to increase their usury. Jews refused to comply with this act and believed, quite correctly, that it contradicted their emancipation.

The battle of opinions over the emancipation of Jews was not confined to the traditional lines. To be sure, some clerics, led by Bishop de la Fare of Nancy, said that Jews were on religious grounds an alien people, but this was an argument that became less and less effective at the high point of the Revolutionary fervor.

The most important and effective arguments were advanced by left-wing thinkers, most notably J.-F. Reubell, a Jacobin representing Alsace. He insisted that Alsace needed to be defended "against those cruel hordes of Africans who have infested my region" (Hertzberg, p. 356). A grant of equality to Jews would give them greater scope to increase their supposed economic control over the poor in eastern France, and it would thus be a counterrevolutionary act. There had, indeed, been mob outbreaks against the Alsatian Jews during the summer of 1789, and the Jews of Metz had formally requested protection from the National Assembly.

Prevailing opinion in eastern France was anti-Jewish, despite the moderate Société des amis de la constitution in Strasbourg, which was much influenced by the Cerferre family, the greatest Jewish magnates of eastern France, who had taken the lead in the preceding two decades in the battle for increased Jewish rights. The policy of the Société was that the Jews ought to be given economic opportunity to enter "productive occupation," and thus the enmity toward Jews, no longer in petty money lending with the peasants, would end.

With the granting of the final decree of emancipation on 27 September 1791, the old tensions and the older life in eastern France did not end automatically. Although religious bodies had been declared voluntarist, the structure of the Jewish community remained intact. There were some rebellions and dissociations by village Jewish communities, especially around Metz, from the central authority of the larger community; the villages refused to pay for the upkeep of the central Jewish authority in Metz and to be held responsible for the large debt that had been incurred in the course of the eighteenth century. A few Jews entered schools of general education, and one or two even began to make their way toward the professions, but this trend was insignificant in the Revolutionary era. It began to be of some importance, though hardly yet anything near a majority form, in the era of Napoleon.

In the early days of the Revolution, occasional Jews were, with some difficulty, permitted to serve in the armed forces. Nonetheless, the older life, including the older economy, remained relatively intact. Jews did suffer during the period of the Terror, when synagogues were shut and their goods confiscated, but the Jewish institutions were not attacked with any perceptively greater venom than those of the other religions. When the Terror ended, the synagogues were reopened in their older forms. Those who attended religious services continued to be mostly middlemen or peddlers. Very few Jews had begun to work in factories or own land—that is, to devote themselves to primary production.

The older leadership continued to dominate in the Jewish community of the 1790s, but the situation had changed somewhat as the result of the Revolution. In southern France in 1793-94, a club that had been formed by a group of Jewish Jacobins took over the civil government of Saint-Esprit, the largely Jewish suburb of Bayonne. A few individuals in all of the several types of Jewish communities participated in the religion of Reason. There were some cases of mixed marriage, but very few. The personal status of Jews remained a confused matter for some French courts, who still continued to recognize Jewish law as the sole authority on such matters as marriage.

If during the time of the Terror the Jews were attacked by the Left, their problems during the Thermidorian Reaction were the reverse. The central government ordered the protection of Jews against incitement in eastern France, but their enemies continued to attack them for supposedly being in league with the remnants of the Jacobins. On the whole, Thermidor was regarded by Jews as a positive era, for religious persecution had ended. More important, the new rulers made no change in the legal status of Jews; the emancipation remained, in law, intact.

On the other hand, the economic conflict in eastern France remained and so did their orthodox religious tradition, which by its nature enjoined considerable apartness from everyone else. The question of the reform of the Jews and, for that matter, the reorganization of their community in such fashion as to serve the purposes of the central government, remained unsolved. It was to be dealt with in the next era by Napoleon.

In the first debates about the Jewish question, in the opening days of the

Revolution, Comte S. de Clermont-Tonnerre, a liberal noble from Paris, said on 28 September 1789 that the Jews should be emancipated totally as individuals but that they could not be granted anything as a group; "there cannot be a nation within a nation," he asserted. He went further to say that the Jews had a choice to make: accept assimilation into the French majority for their equality or leave in a body and go to Palestine. The question remained to haunt the relationship of Jews to the majority society in the Revolutionary era and beyond, both in France and elsewhere. The Revolution granted legal equality, supposedly undifferentiated, to individuals. However, at the high point of its fervor, it proposed the religion of Reason and *civisme* as the appropriate new faith. Even as the Revolution came to terms with Christianity, the religion of the overwhelming majority, it did not know what to do with the striking difference of Jews, both in their economic pursuits and in their religious outlook. For that matter, the Jews themselves became more divided and uncertain in their response to the new era. They wanted equality, but most were not eager to surrender their Jewishness, at least all of it, on the altar of the new freedom.

F. Delpeche, "La Révolution et l'Empire," *Histoire des Juifs en France*, ed. B. Blumenkranz (Toulouse, 1972); A. Hertzberg, *The French Enlightenment and the Jews* (New York, 1968); Z. Szajkowski, *Jews and the French Revolutions of 1789, 1830, and 1848* (New York, 1970).

A. Hertzberg

Related entries: CLERMONT-TONNERRE; DECLARATION OF THE RIGHTS OF MAN AND THE CITIZEN; GREGOIRE; MALESHERBES; REUBELL; TERROR, THE; THERMIDORIAN REACTION; VOLTAIRE.

JOSEPH II (1741-1790), archduke of Austria, king of Hungary, Holy Roman Emperor (1765-1790). Joseph was the oldest son of Maria Theresa with whom he reigned as coregent from 1765 to 1780. His sister Marie Antoinette (1755-93), married to Louis XVI, became queen of France. Joseph became the boldest enlightened European despot of the eighteenth century. In 1781 he issued the Edict of Tolerance, which removed most of the discriminatory measures against Protestants. Subsequently, most restrictions against Jews were repealed and many monasteries closed. Between 1781 and 1785, he abolished serfdom in most Hapsburg territories. Personal feudal services were converted into money payments, however, a measure that caused peasant discontent. Joseph also centralized the administration of his lands, made the use of the German language mandatory, and introduced tax and penal reform. His reforms aroused much opposition, and toward the end of his reign many measures were repealed. Opposition was especially intense in Hungary and Belgium. In the Netherlands territories, a revolt broke out in November 1789, which was ended in 1790-91.

Joseph's foreign policy was equally unsuccessful. He renounced the Barrier Treaty of 1715 with the Dutch Republic and demanded free passage through the Scheldt. The Dutch Republic and France successfully opposed this demand. He failed to effect an exchange of his Belgian territory for Bavaria because of German opposition led by Frederick the Great of Prussia (1740-86). His involvement in another war against Turkey (1788-91) produced no dividends.

T. C. W. Blanning, *Joseph II and Enlightened Despotism* (London, 1970); S. K. Padover, *The Revolutionary Emperor Joseph II* (New ed., Hamden, Conn., 1967).

G. D. Homan

Related entries: BELGIUM; ENLIGHTENMENT,THE.

JOSEPHINE, COMTESSE DE BEAUHARNAIS (1763-1814), born Marie-Josephe-Rose de Tascher de la Pagerie; first wife of Napoleon Bonaparte and later empress. Josephine was born on 23 June 1763 in Martinique, the daughter of a sugar planter whose aristocratic family had come from France in 1726. She was modestly educated in the convent of the Dames de la Providence at Fort Royal in Martinique, which at that time had little in the way of true society or culture. At the age of sixteen, she was taken to France by her father for an arranged marriage (December 1779) to Alexandre, vicomte de Beauharnais, son of a former governor of Martinique whom she had known as a child. They had two children: Eugène, born in 1781, eventually viceroy of Italy and grand duke of Leuchtenberg, and Hortense, born in 1783, who married Napoleon's brother Louis and became queen of Holland.

Josephine's marriage proved extremely troubled, her husband leaving her for long periods of time, so that in March 1785 she obtained a legal separation, living as best she could on restricted funds. Between 1788 and 1790, she paid her only visit to Martinique.

During the Revolution, Josephine and her husband became partially reconciled. Beauharnais was elected to the Estates General as representative of the nobility of Blois and soon accepted the Revolution, giving up his title. In July 1793, when hostility to former aristocrats was mounting, he resigned his post as commander of the Army of the Rhine. Under the Terror, he was arrested in March 1794, Josephine joining him in prison a month later. He was quickly tried and guillotined in July; probably only the fall of M. Robespierre kept her from a similar fate. Through the favor of J.-L. Tallien, she was released in August.

Josephine soon became a member of the fashionably reckless society of the Directory, a friend of T. Tallien and Madame Récamier, the reigning beauties. By common recognition, she was one of the many mistresses of P. Barras, the most powerful of the directors. In the autumn of 1795, she met General N. Bonaparte, soon to be made commander in chief of the Army of Italy. Six years her junior, he fell deeply in love with her, as his letters indicate. They were married in a civil ceremony on 9 March 1796, with Barras and Tallien attending. Two days later, Bonaparte left Josephine to assume his Italian command.

Evidence indicates that Josephine continued the heedless life of the preceding years, notably with H. Charles, a foppish young captain of hussars. Bonaparte became aware of this, threatening once to have Charles shot, and although a reconciliation of a sort was effected when she at last joined him in Italy, the troubles erupted again while he was absent in Egypt during 1798 and 1799. A final, tearful reconciliation ensued when Bonaparte returned to Paris in October 1799.

After the coup of Brumaire, Josephine assumed her place as mistress of the Tuileries, playing her role with unique grace, but she found it possible to help many of her aristocratic friends now seeking to be stricken from the lists of *émigrés*. Although never popular with members of the Bonaparte family, she led a life of comfortable accommodation with her husband. A church marriage ceremony privately performed on the eve of her coronation as empress in December 1804 was intended to make the civil marriage of 1796 secure. Despite this, Napoleon divorced her in 1810, claiming the need for an heir, and married the young Marie-Louise, daughter of the Austrian emperor. Josephine retired to Malmaison, where she lived quietly until her death on 29 May 1814. She was buried in the nearby parish church of Rueil.

The estate, or château, of Malmaison, eight miles west of Paris, is inseparably linked with Josephine. She bought this badly rundown seigneurial property in April 1799 for a relatively modest price. Enormous sums were spent on its restoration and furnishings. The emperor found it a happy retreat from the pressures of politics and war, and Josephine indulged to the full her growing interest in all the arts, as well as in its gardens. Botanical specimens, birds, and animals were obtained from all parts of the world. Neglected during the nineteenth century, Malmaison, superbly restored today, is Josephine's chief memorial. She is the only Frenchwoman to have become empress of France.

E. J. Knapton, *Empress Josephine* (Cambridge, Mass., 1963); F. Masson, *Joséphine de Beauharnais* (Paris, 1899), *Madame Bonaparte* (Paris, 1920), *Joséphine impératrice et reine* (Paris, 1899), and *Joséphine répudiée* (Paris, 1900); J. Savant, *Napoléon et Joséphine. Première édition intégrale, avec de nombreux inédits, des lettres de Napoléon à Joséphine* (Paris, 1955).

E. J. Knapton

Related entries: BARRAS; BONAPARTE, N.; CABARRUS, J.-M.-I.-T.; COUP OF 18 BRUMAIRE; *MERVEILLEUSES*; RECAMIER; TALLIEN.

JOUBERT, BARTHELEMI-CATHERINE (1769-99), general. Born at Pont-de-Vaux in Burgundy on 15 August 1769, Joubert received a fine education and attended law school at Dijon in 1789. Two years later, he joined the army with the rank of sergeant. In the early years of the war, he served in campaigns on the Rhine and in Italy. Joubert was promoted to the rank of colonel on the battlefield of Loano and took an active part in N. Bonaparte's first Italian campaign (1796-97). At the battles of Lodi, Montenatte, Castiglione, and Rivoli, he displayed courage and leadership. He led the advance guard during the difficult march into the Tyrol, and on the conclusion of peace (1797), he was given the privilege of escorting the captured enemy flags to Paris and presenting them to the Directory. In 1798 General Joubert commanded the French army in Holland but resigned his command under questionable circumstances. His services were desired by members of the Directory to assist in the overthrow of the government and the establishment of the Consulate. To enhance his military prestige, he was given command of the Army of Italy in 1799. While attempting to rally his troops and move them to the attack, he was shot in the chest and killed. General Bonaparte, recently returned from Egypt, was then given the command of the troops of Paris, originally meant for Joubert, and became First Consul.

A. H. de Jomini, *Histoire des guerres de la Révolution*, vol. 15 (Paris, 1820-24); J. de la Lande, *Sur le général Joubert* (Paris, 1799); G. Six, *Les généraux de la Révolution et de l'Empire* (Paris, 1947).

J. G. Gallaher

Related entries: BATTLE OF LODI; BONAPARTE, N.; DIRECTORY.

JOURDAN, JEAN-BAPTISTE (1762-1833), general, politician, marshal of the Empire. Born at Limoges on 29 April 1762, the son of a surgeon, Jourdan worked for some time as a clerk in the silk trade until 1778 when he enlisted in the Regiment of Auxerrois, with which he campaigned in America and participated in the siege of Savannah. Returning to France in 1782, he was discharged two years later and established himself as a haberdasher at Limoges, where he married in 1788. While a captain in the National Guard of this city, he enrolled as a volunteer and was elected lieutenant colonel of the second battalion of the Volunteers of the Haute-Vienne on 9 October 1791.

While serving in the Army of the North, he took part in the battles of Jemappes and Neerwinden. Promoted to general of brigade and subsequently general of division, he commanded the center of the French army at Hondschoote, where he was wounded. As commander in chief of the Army of the North, he defeated the duke of Cobourg at the Battle of Wattignies (15 and 16 October). Dismissed in January 1794, he was recalled to command the Army of the Moselle on 10 March, and later the army assembled on the Sambre with which he won the famous Battle of Fleurus on 26 June. After a series of military successes that led him from Namur to Coblentz and to Dusseldorf, he left this command to assume that of the Army of the Sambre-et-Meuse, which he led in 1795 and 1796. During this time he also experienced failure, for he was defeated at Wurzbourg on 3 September 1796.

Elected deputy to the Council of Five Hundred from the Haute-Vienne, starting in April 1797 he began his political career, which was marked by the drawing up of the law on conscription that bears his name and would regulate military service in France until 1814. All Frenchmen on reaching the age of twenty had to be inscribed on army recruitment records and remain there until the age of twenty-five. Naval conscripts and married men were exempt. Since it was assumed that each class would furnish more men than were required, only the youngest members of each class would actually depart.

Having resigned from his position as deputy on 14 October 1798, he received command of the Army of Mainz the next day. Defeated at Stockach on 25 March 1799, he left the army for reasons of health on 3 April and was reelected deputy for the Haute-Vienne to the Five Hundred on 13 April. In Brumaire (9-10

November 1799) he tried to oppose the coup d'état and was excluded from being a national representative. N. Bonaparte did not, however, hold this against him and named him inspector general of infantry and cavalry in 1800, then ambassador to the Cisalpine Republic, general administrator of Piedmont, member of the Council of State, general in chief of the Army of Italy, and finally marshal of the Empire on 19 May 1804.

After his appointment as governor of Naples, King Joseph took a liking to him and brought him in his suite to Spain. As commander of the Fourth Corps of the Army of Spain, he participated in the Battle of Talavera on 28 July 1809 and won that of Almonacid on 11 August. Vexed by the lack of support from the other marshals, he returned to France in October 1809 and retired to his estate of Le Coudray in the Seine-et-Oise. He retook service in Spain where he was defeated at Vittoria on 21 June 1813. Placed on the retirement list in August, he became the ranking commander of the Fourteenth and Fifteenth military divisions. He rallied to Louis XVIII, but during the Hundred Days Napoleon, nevertheless, confided the command of Besançon to him. After Waterloo, he again supported the Bourbon regime. He refused to take his seat as president of the Council of War that was to judge Marshal M. Ney.

As a peer of France, he defended public liberties before the upper house, and during the Revolution of 1830 he held, briefly, the portfolio of foreign affairs and, subsequently, command of the Invalides. He died at Paris on 23 November 1833. He is the author of *Opérations de l'armée du Danube* and *Mémoires pour servir à l'histoire de la campagne de 1796*.

R. Valentin, *Le Maréchal Jourdan* (Paris, 1936).

J.-P. Bertaud

Related entries: BATTLE OF FLEURUS; BATTLE OF JEMAPPES; BATTLE OF NEERWINDEN; CISALPINE REPUBLIC; JOURDAN LAW.

JOURDAN LAW, legislation enacted 19 Fructidor Year VI (5 September 1798) establishing military conscription. Except for the brief period following the Peace of Amiens (1802), France was continually at war from 1792 to 1814. During this time the several French governments had at their disposal what remained of the *ancien régime* army and the battalions of volunteers. Beginning with the Year II, however, desertion from the ranks became rampant, and the armies of the Republic suffered severely from a shortage of manpower. By the end of the Year VI, this acute problem was resolved by the Directory. The celebrated general, J.-B. Jourdan, was then a member of the Council of Five Hundred, and on his recommendation, the Directory adopted the important law on conscription (the word itself being new). This Law of 19 Fructidor Year VI (5 September 1798) definitively organized recruitment for the army.

In the event of a national emergency, all citizens were eligible for military service of unlimited duration. Outside of this, the army would recruit volunteers who were to enlist for four years, subject to two-year renewals. Conscription would be imposed if voluntary enlistments were insufficient to fill the ranks, and all Frenchmen between twenty and twenty-five years of age were to be registered and divided into five classes. Municipal and departmental authorities were to establish lists of young men subject to the draft.

This law was first applied for the campaign of the Year VIII (1799). The coalitions raised against France necessitated constant levies of manpower for France, leading the Consulate and, later, the Empire, to apply the Jourdan law rigorously. With some modifications in detail, this law remained throughout the nineteenth century as the fundamental basis for the recruiting of the French army.

E. Lavisse, ed., *Histoire de France contemporaine*, vol. 1, *La Révolution, 1789-1792* by P. Sagnac (Paris, 1920); R. Legrand, *Le recrutement des armées et les désertions* (Abbeville, 1957).

R. Legrand

Related entries: AMALGAM, THE; JOURDAN.

JOURNAL DE LA REPUBLIQUE FRANCAISE. See *AMI DU PEUPLE, L'.*

JOURNEE DES TUILES (Day of the Tiles). See DAUPHINE.

JOURNEES REVOLUTIONNAIRES, relatively brief events in the course of the Revolution, circumscribed in place and time and marked by an intense popular mobilization, at the end of which a crowd, generally armed, exercised a direct pressure on the legal, constituted authorities to force them to intensify, modify, or reverse the course of their policy. The Great Fear and the periodic jacqueries that affected the French countryside between 1788 and 1793, which took their own peculiar forms within a diffuse movement engulfing the vastness of rural France, clearly bore a certain resemblance (in a political sense) to the insurrectional *journées* that affected urban centers. In spite of this, here the use of the term is restricted to urban insurrections; furthermore, even this limitation by itself is inadequate.

Grenoble in 1788, Bordeaux in 1789, Lyon in 1792, Rouen in 1792, Marseille in 1793, and so on, all witnessed events that could be described as Revolutionary *journées*. However, this description is generally reserved for insurrectional movements in Paris, and despite the importance of other movements—sometimes considerable—there is reluctance to treat every urban uprising as a *journée*. The reason is that in Paris pressure from the streets, supported by the deployment of armed men possessing artillery, was able, within limits, to influence in a lasting and profound way the opinion of the constituted authorities and force them to follow the desires that had been manifested. In the provinces, this was never possible over the long term. The political and cultural centralization of France based in its great capital and the political maturity of its people, inscribed in a centuries-old tradition, made Paris and its 600,000 inhabitants the arbiter and the interpreter of the nation and its public opinion. In 1789 the high degree of unity in the French nation and the leadership exercised by the capital, where (either in the city itself or at nearby Versailles) most of the great political and cultural institutions were located, quickly made every Parisian event a movement of national significance. From 1789 to 1795, then, Revolutionary *journées* were simply insurrectional *journées* for which Paris was the scene. A *journée* was a Parisian uprising that usually was a success or was considered a victory by those who endorsed it.

Revolutionary *journées*, thus conceived, were not very numerous; I count eight critical episodes that culminated in Revolutionary *journées*, six of which resulted in important successes and two of which met with defeat. The events of 14 July 1789 led to the fall of the Bastille and forced Louis XVI and the court to renounce their plans and allow the National Constituent Assembly to impose its authority over the nation. The days of 5 and 6 October 1789, which were set in motion by S.-M. Maillard and led to completion by the marquis de Lafayette and the Parisian National Guard, the market women, and the people of the faubourgs, forced the king to reside in Paris and promulgate, at last, the Revolutionary measures of that summer. Although something less than a *journée*, 20 June 1792 was a formidable manifestation of patriotic anxieties and democratic demands, which was clumsily exploited by the Brissotin ministers. On 10 August 1792, which was even more than a second revolution that established democracy (as A. Mathiez and G. Lefebvre viewed it), Paris witnessed, along with the capture of the Tuileries and the abolition of royalty, the expression of a great national movement confirming the Revolution that had begun in 1789; this was accomplished as a result of a Parisian *journée* with the support of the *fédérés* who had assembled in the capital and who fully engaged in the insurrection. On 31 May and 2 June 1793 the National Guard, commanded by F. Hanriot, and the sections by their violent insurrection imposed the removal of the Girondin deputies from the National Convention. The *journée* of 4 and 5 September 1793 had an extremely popular—even worker—character; socioeconomic demands were expressed with particular force. In the midst of the Thermidorian Reaction, the *journées* of 12 Germinal and 1 Prairial Year III failed in their attempt to impose taxation and regulation, along with the implementation of the Constitution of 1793, but they are important because they marked the end of the armed popular movement in Paris until July 1830 and the last attempt on the part of the streets to dictate political conduct to the legal authorities. The attempted reactionary coup of 13 Vendémiaire Year IV, which had as its aim channeling discontent to the advantage of a royalist maneuver, was comparable to a Revolutionary *journée* only in a formal sense; by its nature, it was the opposite of the classic *journées* of the Revolution during its ascendant phase, when it was establishing new values and institutions that increased the role of the people in political life.

The primary characteristic of successful insurrectional *journées* was that they had results. In a forceful and lasting way, these events reoriented social and political struggles in a direction that favored popular aspirations, without their being completely satisfied however. Also, with the exception of 10 August 1792, whose republican objective conformed to the desires of the political elite, all the *journées* resulted merely in a new compromise between the established (or re-structured) powers and the streets. But this never led to the abolition of representative authority or to the abolition of pressure from the faubourgs, at least until May 1795. Thus is revealed the essentially political nature of these confrontations, whose function, as well as whose essence, was never anything beyond the development of a balance of power between the Revolution in its popular dimension and the Revolution in its liberal, bourgeois dimension, both, in different ways, engaged in the same common process of abolishing the old social regime.

To distinguish a model of a popular, Revolutionary *journée*, one must first evoke the context of all the insurrections: fear, fear of death, fear of famine, fear of aggression, all concrete fears, alone capable of driving away paralyzing and divisive anxiety. Among these various fears, however, the dominant ones in Paris and other cities were fear of a plot (which was murderous) and fear of scarcity (which was destructive). The most common Revolutionary *journée*, then, had a dual origin that marked it as a major popular uprising stirred up by the effects of crises. First of all, there was the economic crisis, as studied by E. Labrousse; this is a crisis of popular underconsumption and, as a consequence, unemployment in urban manufacturing. On the other hand, there was also a political crisis, reducible to planned treason, ascribed to aristocrats in general, to the "black party," to evil advisers, to corrupt ministers. G. Lefebvre has shown how in the popular mentality the association between the famine pact and the idea of an aristocratic plot formed an imaginary but logical link, which legitimized popular intervention and provided a moral force in the struggle against monopolies and high prices, against reactionary maneuvers and attempts to compromise with the Right. It was nourished by the ancient tradition of distrusting the rich and the capitalists, the mentality of the little people, artisans and shop-keepers, and of the dependent and small consumers who spent from a third to three-fourths of their resources to buy bread (according to G. Rudé). As for the aristocratic plot emanating from the alcoves or the salons, concluded in the palaces or the châteaux, organized underground or in fortresses, its evocation was specific to the French Revolution and the threat of counterrevolution supported by foreign intervention. In 1789, however, urban fear derived its militant expression and its effectiveness from the attitude that intimately associated fear of famine with fear of an aristocratic plot; thus, B. de Launay, the governor of the Bastille, and L.-B.-F. Bertier de Sauvigny, the intendant of Paris, were expiatory victims, the first for having ordered the firing on the crowd on 14 July and the second for being responsible for the inadequate provisioning of the capital. Fear, then, changed into a defensive reaction—gaining the support of armed men, stripping armories, tearing pikes from the iron fences of gardens, leveling cannon; people organized at the sound of the tocsin, at the beating of drums, at the insistent noise of a fusillade (as on 10 August). Popular processions took over the city, overflowed into the highways and squares where festivals and commemorations were held; this led to the appropriation of the apparatus of the bourgeois city by the people, as happened on the place de Grève on 4 and 5 September 1793. This also led to the undermining of the sacred character of the seats of power by the faubourgs, such as the invasion of the Tuileries on 20 June and of the meeting hall of the Convention in Prairial. The exercise of a punitive will and the move to creative political action were among the results of the insurrectional victory. The punitive will expressed a kind of transition from the original fear to the exorcism of ever-recurring evils, that is, fear and oppression; but beginning in 1789, it also conveyed the recognition by the people of the faubourgs of their own strength: "This feeling of collective strength that imposes a collective mentality on the undecided at the same time encourages all those present to take the offensive against the political or social authority that is resisting them" (Lefebvre, 1954). Such was very much the case in 1792 during the uprising of 10 August, in 1793 when the will of the Convention was forced to bend in the month of June and later in September, and even in the Year III.

The crowds that gathered were made up of *sans-culottes*. To them were added women—housewives, market women, working women, single women—and also some children. The total number of people who assembled together certainly never numbered over 100,000 (according to M. Reinhard), perhaps 150,000 if one included the armed men of the National Guard. On 14 July the crowd seized 30,000 muskets from the armory of the Invalides, but the crowd did not exceed 80,000 people; the same is true of 20 June. On 10 August Parisians from the sections were joined by 80,000 *fédérés*. On 2 June 1793, 80,000 of the 116,452 National Guardsmen responded to Hanriot's orders but they were supported by huge columns of unarmed *sans-culottes*, women, and children. This *journée* was in no way a spontaneous uprising; it resulted from an organization that depended on the initiative of the political structures of the Parisian *sans-culottes* and Revolutionary democracy: the battalions of the National Guard, the companies of cannoneers, the sections with their permanent agencies, the clubs or popular societies, and finally the sectional societies. But an entire sociological structure contributed to popular mobilization. The socioprofessional structures of Parisian artisans and shopkeepers, which arose from the old corporate system, already facilitated the effective assembling of Parisians at the time of the League, in the sixteenth century; the same arrangement played its role between 1789 and 1795. The masters of each trade, the genuine leaders in their neighborhoods, exercised a political authority over the journeymen and small producers comparable to their economic and professional influence. Their refusal to participate was a severe blow to the plans of the Babouvists and made the insurrection of the people, which they planned, fail. From 1789 to 1795, however, their participation in *journées* was at the same time the guarantee of their success and the assurance that a compromise would be found. In contrast, their reduced role in September 1793 is explained by the increasing demands for higher wages, and their weak role in the insurrections of the Year III partly explains the disorganized behavior of the great anarchical and fraternal demonstrations.

The ideological universe of the *sans-culottes* expressed itself in the *journée*;

and, moreover, the ideological stimulus contributed to its success. First of all, there was a passion for egalitarianism. Beginning in 1792, everything that appeared to endanger the right to existence, such as the possession of property beyond the scope of physical needs, was automatically suspect. This egalitarian ideology, however, was accompanied by a strong sense of community, including family, profession, and neighborhood, that was expressed by the ideal of direct democracy, exercised without any intermediary and recognized in the famous right to insurrection proclaimed by the Constitution of 1793.

Symbolic elements gave structure to the insurrectional movement. The pike expressed the personal involvement of the poor *sectionnaire* in the struggle. The cannon, a modern weapon, was the expression of the common man since it extolled a metal product created by men who worked with their hands. To destroy objects that represented religious fanaticism or aristocracy had a redeeming value. To undermine the reactionary threat by transforming the red flag of martial law into the symbol of popular insurrection was important as a wager on the future. To the powdered wig, the knee breeches, and buckled shoes were opposed the virtues of straight hair, trousers, and wooden sabots; to the words of those who "talked fancy" was opposed the sturdy language of the *sans-culottes*; the spoken word was judged superior to the written, which was academic. Insurrection in the popular *journée* expressed the emergence, in the forefront of the Parisian scene, of a popular culture and of a scale of values, ordinarily repressed and more and more effectively repressed in cities like Paris since the seventeenth century. Was this the revenge of the repressed?

The historical function of the Revolutionary *journée* in the process of the Revolution was to check compromises with the Right while pushing the Revolutionary bourgeoisie further in the direction of liberal politics—and in 1793, even social democracy. Radical politicians from the Revolutionary bourgeoisie accepted, even encouraged, a popular insurrectional movement, with which they never completely identified, even on 10 August, even on 14 July. They needed, at the same time, the cooperation of the people of Paris and their armed rebellion to overcome the political forces of the Old Regime, but they hoped to establish a new state that would be a bourgeois state, a class state. After 1793, in the Year III, the *journée* became superfluous, even dangerous, for the Revolution was searching for a level of stability between political democracy and a bourgeois republic. It became necessary to repress and disarm the celebrated faubourgs of Saint-Antoine and Saint-Marcel from which came the forces that had been so admired from 1789 to 1793; popular heroism and sacrifice would no longer be qualities praised in official literature. In the end, the Parisian *journée* was historically effective only as long as Paris exemplified national exigencies, which were acceptable to the country when they were transmitted by the thousand canals through all of France. The significance of the Revolutionary *journée* can be understood only in reference to its national, patriotic, and social background and to the reality of the bourgeois and democratic Revolution.

Identified as a fundamental development, as a result of the exaltation of 14

July 1789, the national holiday of France, the *journée* is responsible for a long-lived myth in the contemporary history of the country, transmitted by neo-Babouvism: that of the Long Night, at the end of which the dominant elites, in the face of the united people, were suddenly convinced they must do good or lose their leadership and undertook the building of a just society and a harmonious state that would lead man beyond "the ancient order of things" (in the words of K. Marx).

R. M. Andrews, "Reflexion sur la conjuration des Egaux," *Ann.: Econ., soc., civ.* 29 (1974); J. Delumeau, *La peur en occident (XVI-XVIIIe siècles)* (Paris, 1978); C. E. Labrousse, *La crise de l'économie française à la fin de l'Ancien Régime et au début de la Révolution* (Paris, 1944); G. Lefebvre, "Foules révolutionnaires" in *Etudes sur la Révolution française* (Paris, 1954); A. Mathiez, *Le 10 Août* (Paris, 1934); C. Mazauric, *Textes choisis de Babeuf*, 2d ed. (Paris, 1976); M. Ozouf, *La fête révolutionnaire (1789-1799)* (Paris, 1976); M. Reinhard, *La chute de la Royauté* (Paris, 1969); G. Rudé, *The Crowd in the French Revolution* (Oxford, 1959); A. Soboul, *Les sans-culottes parisiens en l'an II*, 2d ed. (Paris, 1962); E. Tarlé, *Germinal et Prairial* (in French) (Moscow, 1960); K. Tønnesson, *La défaite des sans-culottes: mouvement populaire et réaction bourgeoise en l'an III* (Paris, 1959).

C. Mazauric

Related entries: BASTILLE; GREAT FEAR; OCTOBER DAYS; THERMIDORIAN REACTION; 13 VENDEMIAIRE YEAR IV.

JULIEN (of Toulouse), JEAN (1760-1828), *conventionnel* and regicide. Julien was born in Nîmes in 1760 and before the Revolution established himself as a Protestant minister in Toulouse. He allied with the patriots from the beginning of the Revolution, served first as a departmental administrator in the Haute-Garonne, and then in September 1792 was elected to the National Convention. He voted for the death sentence in the king's trial and in all matters took the side of the Montagnards. Julien was sent on mission by the Convention to Orléans in May 1793 and then was elected to the Committee of General Security.

In the Convention he was known for his zealous persecution of opponents, but before long, leading Jacobins began to suspect him of collusion with army suppliers, speculators, and aristocrats. He was removed from the committee in September 1793, and his papers were seized for investigation. Julien went into hiding on hearing that his arrest had been ordered. After Thermidor, the Convention suspended its decree against him, and Julien actively participated in Paris politics under the Directory. After N. Bonaparte's coup d'état, he fled to Turin where he made his living as a lawyer. He returned to France after the restoration of Louis XVIII and died there in obscurity.

A. Mathiez, "Un deputé d'affaires sous la Terreur: Julien (de Toulouse)," in *Etudes Robespierristes: La corruption parlementaire sous la Terreur* (Paris, 1927).

L. A. Hunt

Related entries: COMMITTEE OF GENERAL SECURITY; COMPAGNIE DES INDES; COUP OF 18 BRUMAIRE; 9 THERMIDOR YEAR II.

JULLIEN (of Paris), MARC-ANTOINE (1775-1848), Jacobin politician and journalist. The son of the *conventionnel* Marc-Antoine Jullien (of the Drôme), Jullien was an ardent Jacobin from his youth. He entered government service in 1792. During the Year II (1793-94) he served as commissioner to the Army of the Pyrenees, as an agent of the Committee of Public Safety in some maritime ports and in the Vendée, and helped supervise the *levée en masse*. He sent some of his reports directly to M. Robespierre, who was very close to him and who referred to Jullien in his diary as one of the *patriotes ayant des talents*. It was at Jullien's instigation that the proconsul Carrier was recalled from Nantes for his role in the massacre of prisoners there, and in 1794 he unmasked the abuses perpetrated at Bordeaux by the representatives on mission C.-A. Ysabeau and J.-L. Tallien.

Immediately after 9 Thermidor Jullien was arrested for belonging to Robespierre's entourage. While in the Plessis Prison during the autumn of 1795 he became acquainted with G. Babeuf, F. M. Buonarroti, and their friends; and after their release—a result of the amnesty of Vendémiaire—he maintained some contact with them. Jullien, however, disagreed with Babouvist tactics; he advocated some sort of deal with the Left within the Directory and strongly criticized Babeuf in his newspaper, *L'Orateur plébéien*. Despite this, in 1796 Jullien was arrested along with the Equals, but was saved from criminal prosecution due to the intervention of his influential father.

Jullien then appealed to N. Bonaparte, who was in Italy, and was made chief editor of the *Courrier de l'armée d'Italie*. After the coup of 18 Fructidor, along with J.-B. Drouet, R. Lindet, J.-N. Pache, and P.-A. Antonelle, he was occupied with preparing leftist candidacies for the elections of the Year VI. In 1798 illness prevented him from accompanying Bonaparte to Egypt. He joined General J.-E. Championnet in his offensive into Naples and played a prominent role in the declaration of the Parthenopean Republic there. Jullien became secretary-general of the newly installed government and supported reforms in the interests of the peasants and *lazzaroni*. In 1799, however, he was recalled, together with Championnet, by the French government.

After hesitating briefly, Jullien joined the Brumairians in late 1799, arguing that Bonaparte needed the support of republicans, who had no alternative but to support him. Nevertheless, he disapproved of Bonaparte's Italian policy and antidemocratic tendencies. Consequently, he was relieved of all public responsibilities except his office in the Intendancy of the Army. In 1813 he was in contact with J.-H. Pestalozzi and Mme. de Staël and, for this, was again arrested. He attempted to return to politics after 1815 but did not succeed.

V. M. Daline, "Marc-Antoine Jullien après le neuf thermidor," *Ann. hist. de la Révo. française*, 36, 37, 38 (1964, 1965, 1966); P. Gascard, *L'ombre de Robespierre: Marc-Antoine Jullien* (Paris, 1979); H. Goetz, *Marc-Antoine Jullien de Paris: Der geistige Werdegang eines Revolutionärs* (Berlin, 1954).

V. M. Daline

Related entries: CARRIER; COMMITTEE OF PUBLIC SAFETY; CONSPIR-
ACY OF EQUALS; COUP OF 18 BRUMAIRE; COUP OF 18 FRUCTIDOR;
LEVEE EN MASSE; 9 THERMIDOR YEAR II; NOYADES DE NANTES;
TALLIEN; YSABEAU.

JUSSIEU, ANTOINE-LAURENT DE (1748-1836), professor at the Paris Museum of Natural History, organized its botanical collection. See SCIENCE.

JUSTICE. The ultimate objective of securing justice persisted from the absolute
monarchy to the Revolutionary Republic. The continuity was not merely abstract
but included many aspects of the practical working of the courts. With these
continuities, however, the system of justice exhibited major contrasts between
the Old Regime and the successive new regimes.

In principle, during the Old Regime, justice emanated from the king. His
council regularly held a type of session that was judicial and was known as the
conseil des parties. Below it were the thirteen parlements with more than 1,000
magistrates in all. Below them were the *bailliages* with a total of about 2,700
magistrates. Below them were the local royal courts, *prévôtés*, and equivalents
variously named. In all these courts, the king appointed the judges and the
attorney for the public interest (*procureur du roi*); he appointed only those who
had property rights. The royal hierarchy was part of the ordinary system of courts
in which most disputes between private persons and most prosecutions were
tried and if necessary appealed. Equally part of the ordinary system were thousands of seigneurs' courts. In one of these, the seigneur owned the court; he
appointed the judge(s) and the attorney for the public interest (*procureur fiscal*).
Some seigneurial courts had power to hear appeals and so resembled royal
bailliages. Most seigneurial courts were local, and most local courts were seigneurial. Although seigneurial courts no longer possessed the political power they
had had in medieval times, they continued to be important in common people's
lives.

Beside the ordinary system of courts, there stood the special tribunals with
distinctive subject matter. The Grand Conseil, formerly part of the king's council,
was one. The *chambres des comptes* judged the accuracy and honesty of the
official accountants who managed crown funds and royal domain lands. The
cours des aides were courts of appeal in tax cases decided in first instance by
collectors who used judicial powers and forms of procedure. The lakes, streams,
and woodlands were governed by their own code and tribunals. So was military
law. So were coinage, admiralty law, and commercial law. As a whole, the
court structure was intelligible but very complex.

The gradual creation of an extremely elaborate structure of courts had been
in the interest of those who wanted to become judges and of those litigants who
would benefit from the judges' expert knowledge, or their celerity of decision,
or elaborate and time-consuming procedural formalities. Both the producers and
the consumers of judicial decisions wanted a wide choice of types of tribunal.

Royal power had taken advantage of these circumstances by selling property rights in the judicial offices and by creating offices in order to sell them. The holders of judicial offices had won from the king various privileges: the right to resell to potential incumbents and to bequeath the offices, exemption from many taxes, and, in the highest courts, ennoblement after sufficiently long service and the power for a judicial company to exclude non-nobles. The court structure was permeated by ownership of office and the motives to which it gave rise.

On 4 August 1789, the National Assembly voted to establish a new judicial system and made clear two of its basic principles: it was to be purely public, and it was to be uniform everywhere in the kingdom and for all social classes. Existing seigneurs' courts were abolished and were even treated as usurpations surviving from the feudal past; no indemnity was provided to compensate for their abolition (article 4). Ownership of judicial offices was marked for abolition, too, but existing office-holders were treated as purchasers entitled to reimbursement (article 7). Uniformity followed generally from the abolition of all the special privileges of provinces and local communities. In particular it was enacted that ancestry would be irrelevant to eligibility for office.

Basic principles are also in the Declaration of Rights, but mainly for the executive and the legislature. The Declaration says nothing of habeas corpus, of a right to refrain from giving evidence against oneself, or of trial by a jury of one's peers. A presumption of innocence is mentioned, but only as the basis for a prohibition of torture or unnecessary rigor in the treatment of arrested persons. The Declaration limits punishments to those that are "strictly and obviously necessary," legally applied in accordance with a law promulgated prior to the offense. The Law of 10 October 1789 created additional rights of accused persons, abolishing interrogation under oath and providing for arraignment within twenty-four hours after arrest, advice of counsel throughout investigation and trial, and public judgment.

The enactments of 1789 strengthened accused persons' rights to humane treatment and fair trial but wrought no change in civil procedure or in the substantive law to be applied by the courts. In the administration of justice, therefore, the Revolution meant at first a strong new assertion of public authority as against privilege, together with the promise of reform to make the court system simpler.

The reformed organization was outlined in the Law of 16 August 1790, supplemented by later laws. The guiding intention was to minimize the number of lawsuits and to keep decision making accessible and untechnical. The law began with the statement that "arbitration is the most reasonable way to end disputes between citizens." It made this method available in every type of case to any person capable of acting at law and required it in intrafamily disputes. It also provided for easy enforcement and limited appeals of arbitrators' decisions.

The local magistrate was now to be a justice of the peace, who was not required to have legal training or experience. He was elected for a two-year term by the active citizens, from among those paying an annual direct tax at least ten times the amount of the local daily wage for common labor. One justice of the peace was elected in every canton (there were 4,720 in 1792) and at least one in every town (there were about 700 towns of 2,000 or more inhabitants). In each municipality, whatever its size, four active citizens were elected to sit as *assesseurs* counseling the justice of the peace. He had a wide civil jurisdiction: damage to fields and harvests, trespass, landlords' or tenants' demands for repairs or indemnities, enforcement of contracts between employers and workmen or domestics, torts such as insults and assaults, and small claims involving movable property. The justice of the peace and his *assesseurs* served as the bureau of peace and conciliation for their town or canton, except in the chief town of a district where the town council appointed the bureau members. The bureau of peace was to attempt mediation in every dispute. A certificate that it had been attempted was necessary for a plaintiff filing a lawsuit. Laws of 1791 also gave the justice of the peace a role in criminal justice. He issued or declined to issue arrest warrants in serious cases. He headed a three-man police tribunal that tried misdemeanors such as mendicity, vagabondage, petty theft, offenses against morals, and even negligent homicide.

The professional judges had to have law degrees and five years' experience. They were elected by the electors. Every court also had a commissioner appointed by the king to represent the public interest and to see to the carrying out of judgments. Each district had a civil court of five judges. It tried all civil cases except those assigned to justices of the peace and commercial tribunals. It was also the court of appeal for decisions by justices of the peace in its territory and for decisions by neighboring civil courts. Each department had a criminal court. The public prosecutor and the chief judge were elected; three other judges were assigned by turns from the civil courts in the department. In all, there were about 2,850 judges in the new civil and criminal courts.

The top-heaviness of the Old Regime judiciary disappeared. No equivalent took the place of the parlements. The tribunal of cassation, with forty-two elected judges, was organized in 1791. It had power to determine whether judges below had contravened the law or committed procedural errors and, if so, to quash and remand. The national high court, established in 1791 at Orléans, had 4 judges and a jury of 24 men drawn at random from the 166 veniremen chosen nationwide by the electors. It was to try cases involving crimes against the state or the constitution and prosecuted on indictments by the legislature.

Throughout the Revolutionary decade, politicians and lawyers spoke of the need to draw up new codes of law and procedure. Geographic diversity of laws seemed incompatible with the idea of one national citizenship. The ordinances of 1667 on procedure in civil cases and 1670 on procedure in criminal cases were unenlightened. A new code of criminal penalties was adopted 25 September 1791, but then the movement for reform and codification of law and procedure came to a standstill until 1800.

Ordinary judicial institutions were scarcely affected by the monarchy's downfall, but elections under the Republic brought in many new judges and justices of the peace in November 1792. Hesitant attempts began to prosecute counterrevolutionary crime, with the creation of the Tribunal of 17 August which, however, was abolished 29 November 1792. Later, under a Convention decree of 11 January 1794, the departmental criminal courts were allowed to judge *révolutionnairement* if specifically authorized by a representative on mission. On the whole, however, Revolutionary justice was administered by special courts and commissions.

The Constitution of the Year III (1795) abolished the districts and established one civil court in each department. This reduced the number of judges by about 1,000 and caused a growing backlog of cases awaiting trial. The Directory began filling vacant judgeships by appointment in 1795, and the proportion of appointed judges increased. The trend was toward the scenes depicted by H. Daumier, but extensive reorganization was to begin only in 1800.

J. Bourdon, *La réforme judiciaire de l'an VIII*, vol. 1 (Rodez, 1941); S. Clemencet, et al., *Guide des recherches dans les fonds judiciaires de l'ancien régime* (Paris, 1958); J. Godechot, *Les institutions de la France sous la Révolution et l'Empire*, 2d ed. (Paris, 1968); J. F. Traer, ''From Reform to Revolution: The Critical Century in the Development of the French Legal System'' *J. of Mod. Hist.* 49 (1977).

P. Dawson

Related entries: ACTIVE CITIZEN; *BAILLIAGE*; DECLARATION OF THE RIGHTS OF MAN AND OF THE CITIZEN; PARLEMENTS; PASSIVE CITIZEN; REVOLUTIONARY TRIBUNAL; TERROR, THE.

K

KAUNITZ, WENZEL ANTON, PRINCE VON (1711-94), Austrian foreign minister during the early years of the Revolution. Kaunitz was born in Vienna on 11 February 1711, the son of a Moravian count. He was originally destined for the church, but the death of an older brother gave him the opportunity to study law and prepare for service in the Hapsburg diplomatic corps.

He served first at Turin, then as chief minister to the governor of the Austrian Netherlands. In 1748 he represented Austria at the Aix-la-Chapelle peace congress. In 1749 he called for a major change in Hapsburg foreign policy. Prussia, he argued, had become Vienna's most dangerous enemy; moreover, Austria could expect little help from its traditional allies, England and Holland, against Prussia. Therefore Austria should form an anti-Prussian coalition with Russia and France. As ambassador to France from 1750 to 1753 and afterward as state chancellor, Kaunitz worked to secure an alliance with the Hapsburg's age-old enemy. His diplomatic revolution was finally achieved and set the stage for the Seven Years War.

After 1763, Kaunitz followed a more cautious policy designed to expand Austrian territory and power without undue risks. Austria successfully gained a substantial portion of Poland in 1772 but failed to obtain Bavaria or engineer the Belgian-Bavarian exchange. An alliance with Russia for a war against the Ottoman Empire led to a serious confrontation with England and Prussia during the first years of the French Revolution.

Kaunitz neither liked nor understood the Revolution but agreed with his emperor, Leopold II, that a war with France was undesirable. Austria was deeply involved in the eastern crisis, trouble was brewing in Poland, and Vienna preferred to try to keep France as an ally rather than add it to the list of real and potential enemies. Leopold and Kaunitz therefore devised a policy of threat and intimidation designed to frighten French radicals, strengthen the moderates, and keep Louis XVI on his throne. Austrian policy was successful until late 1791, when the political balance in France shifted and many individuals and factions sought a foreign war in order to gain power at home. Moreover, Leopold's death brought to the throne an emperor who desired to use force against the Revolution. By this time, the aging Kaunitz had lost power to others; he kept his titles but had little or no influence on Austrian policy. He died in 1794.

A. Beer, *Die orientalische Politik Oesterreichs seit 1774* (Prague, 1883); J. H. Clapham, *The Causes of the War of 1792* (Cambridge, 1899); A. Sorel, *L'Europe et la Révolution française*, 8 vols. (Paris, 1885-1904).

S. T. Ross

Related entries: DECLARATION OF PILLNITZ; LEOPOLD II.

KELLERMANN, FRANCOIS-CHRISTOPHE DE (1735-1820), general. Kellermann led a long and honored life as a soldier. His family traced its origins back to Saxony, but in the seventeenth century it had settled in Strasbourg. After securing commercial wealth, the family was ennobled. The future general was born 28 May 1735. He began his military career at age fifteen as a cadet with the Lowendhal Regiment; subsequently he rose up the ladder of promotion and emerged from the Seven Years War as a captain. In 1765 he served Louis XV on a secret mission to Poland. The year 1770 saw Kellermann return to Poland with C.-J.-H. Vioménil as a volunteer. There he fought and trained Polish cavalry forces. On his return to France in 1772 he was promoted to lieutenant colonel. In 1784 he reached brigadier, and in 1788 he became a *maréchal de camp* (major general).

In 1789 he threw in his lot with the Revolution and became a partisan of the new ideals, although he was not basically a political man. He was a soldier above all, and before long he was called on to play a soldier's role. A great many *émigrés* had banded together just across the Rhine, and a threatened government appointed Kellermann commander in Alsace in 1791. There Kellermann's Revolutionary sympathies led him to encourage his men to attend the meetings of political societies. March 1792 brought with it his promotion to lieutenant general. The outbreak of war found him still in Alsace where his meager forces were christened the *Armée de la Sarre*. Kellermann's troops were soon attached to the *Armée du Rhin*, under the command of A.-L. duc de Biron. Kellermann occupied his troops in training during the spring and summer. And when the government recognized that Marshal N. Luckner was unequal to leading the *Armée du Centre*, headquartered at Metz, Kellermann replaced him. Kellermann stepped in on 2 September. This change in command set the stage for Kellermann's greatest part in the drama of the Revolution.

Invading Prussian troops led by the duke of Brunswick had taken Verdun the day that Kellermann assumed command of the *Centre*. Kellermann set his army into motion on 4 September to intercept the advancing Prussians. To the north, C. Dumouriez was doing the same with the *Armée du nord*. Dumouriez delayed the enemy until Kellermann was able to unite his army with Dumouriez' battalions at Sainte-Menehould on 19 September. The armies took up a position a few miles west of Sainte-Menehould at Valmy, where Brunswick encountered them on 20 September. Dumouriez stood in reserve to Kellermann's army that day of victory. Tactically the battle was little more than a stand-off at long range, but it was one of the decisive battles of history. No other service in Kellermann's career would come close to equaling what he did that day.

After Brunswick began his retreat, Kellermann's *Centre* did not press the pursuit; instead the French harried the Prussians across the border. During A.-P. Custine's expedition along the Rhine, Kellermann was ordered to drive up the Sarre to Trier with the *Centre*, rechristened the *Armée de la Moselle*. He balked at this offensive and had only assembled troops for it when he was removed from command in early November, as a result of Custine's complaints and accusations. Kellermann traveled to Paris where he appeared before the Executive Council and exonerated himself. He then received command of the *Armée des Alpes* and joined his new army in December. His troubles with the Paris government were far from over, however. The Committee of Public Safety recalled him to Paris in early 1793 to answer further accusations by Custine, but again he was cleared. Kellermann was then given command over both the *Armée des Alpes* and the *Armée d'Italie* on 21 May 1793. Not long after he returned to his command, Lyon revolted against the central government, and Kellermann received orders to besiege the rebellious city. He undertook this task with no great enthusiasm. In order to marshal troops for the siege, he had to strip the frontier; his fears that the Austrians and Piedmontese might attempt an incursion were realized in August and September. These threats had to be met while the siege had to be maintained. Concentrating on the siege, the representatives on mission could excuse Kellermann from Lyon only for four-day periods, when he would race to the front, make arrangements, and then return to the siege. Especially during the first days of October, Kellermann demonstrated considerable skill in driving off the attacking forces. The Committee of Public Safety was still dissatisfied with Kellermann, however. In mid-September, it made a move to replace him, but he remained until Lyon fell on 9 October. Two days later the committee ordered his arrest for having betrayed the Republic. Taken to Paris, he was imprisoned in the Abbaye for thirteen months before his acquittal on 8 November 1794. He had narrowly escaped trial several times before, when the verdict would almost certainly not have been as kind. His reputation as the victor of Valmy probably saved him.

Finally restored to rank in January 1795, he once again received command of the *Armée des Alpes* and the *Armée d'Italie* in March. Appraising the situation astutely, he considered the latter as the crucial force and delegated responsibility for the *Alpes* to subordinates. The *Armée d'Italie* was small and suffered from an extreme shortage of supplies. Yielding ground when the Austrian offensive began, Kellermann's activities kept the *Armée d'Italie* from disintegrating. He fought off the Austrian advance tenaciously during the summer, often surmounting great difficulties as he played for time. Peace with Spain in July 1795 allowed the transfer of thousands of troops who had been holding the Pyrenees' line. But before Kellermann's patient preparation allowed him to take the offensive, the *Armée d'Italie* was given to General B.-L.-J. Schérer. Kellermann left on 30 September. Now restricted to the secondary *Armée des Alpes*, Kellermann assisted General N. Bonaparte's offensive in 1796 by engaging the enemy along his own front. But Bonaparte's startling advance soon cleared the front of the *Armée des Alpes* and relegated it to a depot for the victorious *Armée d'Italie*.

Kellermann left the *Armée des Alpes* in the spring of 1797; he never again commanded a combat army at the front. After 18 Brumaire, Bonaparte honored Kellermann with a seat in the Senate, where Kellermann rose to be president. In 1804 the emperor made Kellermann one of four honorary marshals created that year. Four years later, the old soldier was raised to the title of duc de Valmy. Napoleon thought that Kellermann lacked the qualities necessary for great command, but the emperor used him to command reserve armies in 1805-7, 1808, 1809, 1810, and 1812-13. When he commanded forces in Spain during 1808, he once again briefly led his men against enemy troops.

In 1814, Kellermann made his peace with the Restoration and sat with the liberal nobles in the Chamber of Peers. He died at age eighty-five on 23 September 1820.

A. M. Chuquet, *Les guerres de la Révolution*, vol. 2 (Paris, 1899); R. W. Phipps, *The Armies of the First French Republic and the Rise of the Marshals of Napoleon the First*, 5 vols. (London, 1926-39).

J. A. Lynn

Related entries: BATTLE OF VALMY; BIRON; BRUNSWICK; COMMITTEE OF PUBLIC SAFETY; COUP OF 18 BRUMAIRE; CUSTINE; DUMOURIEZ; FEDERALISM; LYON; PRISONS.

KERALIO, LOUISE DE (1758-1822), editor of the *Mercure National*. See *MERCURE NATIONAL*.

KLEBER, JEAN-BAPTISTE (1753-1800), general. Kléber was born at Strasbourg on 9 March 1753 and trained as an architect in Paris. After practicing this profession several years, he enrolled in a military school at Munich. He entered the Kaunitz regiment and later served in the armies of several German states. He returned to Alsace (1785) where he became the inspector of public fortifications and directed the construction of several public and private buildings. In July 1789 he joined the National Guard at Belfort. He first served in the Army of the Vosges as a lieutenant colonel, but soon he was given responsibility for the exterior defenses of Mainz and was named *adjutant général chef de brigade*. Besieged by the enemy from April until July, he was ultimately forced to surrender the city (23 July 1793). He was recalled to the National Convention, where he successfully defended his actions at Mainz.

Hence, he was promoted to general of brigade and assigned to the advanced guard of the Army of La Rochelle (12 August 1793) operating in the Vendée. He served against the Vendéans, captured Cholet, and played an active role in crushing the royalists at Le Mans (12-13 December) and Savenay (22-23 December). Kléber was soon confirmed as general of division (January 1794) and assigned to the Army of the North (May 1794). Serving under General J. Jourdan, he commanded the left wing of the army with distinction at the Battle of Fleurus. He was then given command of a division of the Army of the Sambre and Meuse commanded by Jourdan, and during the invasion of Germany he demonstrated the qualities of a first-rate tactician and commander (1795-96). However, after Kléber complained of what he regarded as Jourdan's indecision and inability, he attempted to resign his command several times between August and February (1797), until it was finally accepted.

He returned to Strasbourg, but he was ordered to the Army of Egypt under the command of N. Bonaparte. Although wounded in the attack on Alexandria (2 July 1798) Kléber took an active part in Napoleon's Syrian campaign. He served at the battles of El-Arish, Jaffa, Saint Jean d'Acre, and Mount Tabor. When Napoleon returned to France (20 August 1799) Kléber was named commander in chief. He negotiated the Treaty of El-Arish with Admiral Sir S. Smith (24 January 1800), only to have it rejected by the English government. He overwhelmed the Turkish army at Heliopolis (23 March 1800) and crushed the revolt in Cairo (21 April 1800), but his career was cut short when on 14 June 1800 he was assassinated by a young Moslem fanatic, Sulieman el Halepi. Kléber was one of the most competent of the republican generals. Although disagreements with his superiors sometimes caused him personal difficulties, he was a tactician of the first order and a highly dedicated patriot.

A.-A. Ernouf, *Le général Kléber: Mayence et Vendée, Allemagne, expédition d'Egypte* (Paris, 1870); H. de Font-Reauly, *Le général Kléber* (Limoges, 1891); J. Lucas-Dubreton, *Kléber, 1753-1800* (Paris, 1937).

D. D. Horward

Related entries: BATTLE OF FLEURUS, EGYPTIAN EXPEDITION; JOURDAN; MENOU; VENDÉE.

KOSCIUSZKO, ANDRZEJ TADEUSZ BONAWENTURA (1746-1817), Polish national hero and military leader, who established his reputation in the American Revolution, led the unsuccessful Polish insurrection of 1794, and remained thereafter the chief symbol of Polish freedom and independence. Descended from a noble family of modest fortune, T. Kościuszko was born on 4 February 1746 at Mereczowszczyzna (Volhynia) to L. T. and T. (née Radomska) Kościuszko. A student of the Piarists at Lubieszów, he left school at the age of fourteen because of family financial difficulties following his father's death (in 1758). In 1765, with A. Czartoryski's support, he was admitted to the Military School recently created by King Stanislas Augustus. After completing one year of studies, he remained at the school as an instructor.

In 1769 Kościuszko, who had been promoted to captain in the meantime, left for France at the suggestion of Czartoryski in order to study military architecture, artillery, tactics, civilian architecture, drawing and painting. His sojourn in France was financed partly by his family and partly by a subsidy accorded by the king. Kościuszko stayed in France four years, during which time he completed his education, while becoming acquainted with the intellectual currents that were prevalent in France on the eve of the Revolution.

In 1774 Kościuszko returned to Poland. He fell in love with L. Sosnowska, but her father, the voivode of Smolensk and constable of Lithuania, refused him her hand. Kościuszko tried to carry the young lady off but failed. Fearing the vengeance of her father, he left Poland in October 1775, going first to Saxony and then to France, where he enlisted as a volunteer in the American army.

He embarked for America in June 1776. After arriving in Philadelphia, in cooperation with the French engineer R. de l'Isle, he drew up a plan for the fortification of Billingsport to protect the seat of Congress against the British fleet. Between 1776 and 1782, he was appointed colonel of engineers, served in the Saratoga campaign (1777), and became the commandant of the corps of engineers (1780). During the following two years, he saw service in South Carolina, where he distinguished himself several times in battle and as an engineer. Admitted to the Society of the Cincinnati, he was promoted to the rank of brigadier general on 13 October 1783, and Congress congratulated him on his achievements.

In the summer of 1784 Kościuszko left the United States and returned to Poland, where he established himself on his estate (Siechnowicze). The resolution of the Polish Diet on 20 October 1788 to increase the size of the army provided him with the opportunity of resuming military service. Appointed general, he participated in the war against Russia in 1792; the Battle of Dubienka (17 August 1792), the fiercest of the campaign, won him further recognition. On 26 August 1792 the Legislative Assembly made him a citizen of Revolutionary France. After the armistice with Russia, Kościuszko refused to continue serving and emigrated, a decision that reinforced the prestige and moral authority that he already enjoyed in Poland and abroad.

In the first months of 1793, Kościuszko made *démarches* at Paris to obtain French aid for the Polish insurrection that was being prepared but obtained no definite promises, and in August he went to Leipzig where the political life of Polish emigration was concentrated. The expected leader of the insurrection, he postponed launching it because he considered the preparations insufficient. This decision appeared to be a mistake; changes in the disposition of Polish troops and the arrest of conspirators at Warsaw weakened the chances of the insurrection. Under the pressure of events, Kościuszko decided to proclaim the insurrection in March 1794. On 24 March he publicly took the oath at Cracow, while assuming dictatorial power and supreme command of the army. His strategy and policy during the insurrection were determined by the requirements of the war. Above all, he strained to mobilize all national energies against the aggressors, and to attain this end, he was ready to compromise, depending sometimes on the left wing (the Jacobins) and sometimes on the right wing of the insurrection. Leaving the question of the country's future political regime open, Kościuszko appointed the Supreme National Council, a collegial organ, divided into eight sections, which fulfilled the functions of a government. Kościuszko's manifesto of 7 May 1794 suppressed serfdom, reduced statute labor, and forbade the eviction of peasants by lords. These measures, which aimed at winning the peasant masses to the struggle for national liberation, in practice were often sabotaged by the nobles and only partially achieved their purpose. To mitigate the numerical inferiority of his army and inspired by his American experience and that of Revolutionary France, Kościuszko used new tactics that allowed him to employ units composed of peasants who were inadequately trained and not properly armed. He was thus able to gain a tactical victory over the Russian army at Rocławice on 4 April and successfully defend Warsaw against Russian and Prussian forces. On 10 October he lost the battle of Maciejowice against a Russian corps. Wounded, he was captured by the enemy. The insurrection, deprived of its leader, lasted only a few more weeks and then collapsed.

Confined at Saint Petersburg, Kościuszko was freed only after the death of Catherine II (November 1796). He went to the United States by way of Sweden and England. On 18 August 1797 he arrived in Philadelphia, where he was welcomed by an enthusiastic crowd. The following year (May 1798) he departed for France. He refused to accept command of the Polish legions formed in Italy because he did not want to be dependent on a foreign government. Since the Poles struggling for their independence considered him their spiritual leader, however, he represented Polish interests to the French government and intervened in affairs concerning the legions.

Initially connected with the moderate wing of the *émigrés*, he soon drew closer to the republican group. His relations with General N. Bonaparte were cool, and after the coup d'état of 18 Brumaire, Kościuszko became his opponent since he considered him the "grave-digger of the Republic." Under Kościuszko's inspiration, in 1800 J. Pawlikowski published the tract *Can the Poles Reconquer Their Independence?* which defended the thesis that the nation could liberate itself without foreign assistance and that the struggle for liberty should be tied to social reforms, especially the manumission of the peasants. During this time, he also prepared a treatise on artillery tactics, published in New York and London in 1809 as *Manoeuvres of Horse Artillery*.

On the eve of the campaign of 1806, Napoleon wanted to make sure of his cooperation, but the conditions required by Kościuszko—restoration of the Polish state with its former frontiers and with a constitution modeled on that of England—were deemed inadmissible. Kościuszko therefore stayed in France. After the fall of the Napoleonic empire, Czar Alexander tried to obtain his return to Poland, which would have been of symbolic value, but again Kościuszko posed conditions concerning the eastern frontier of the Kingdom of Poland along with social and political reforms. Seeing no likelihood of realizing his demands, Kościuszko decided to establish himself in Switzerland. He passed the last years of his life in Soleure, where he died on 15 October 1817.

Kościuszko is without doubt the most popular national hero of Poland. His legend has inspired works of art and literature, and interpreted in diverse ways, it has been used for propaganda by different political currents in Poland.

M. Haiman, *Kosciuszko in the American Revolution* (New York, 1943) and *Kosciuszko: Leader and Exile* (New York, 1946); S. Herbst, "Tadeusz Kościuszko" in *Polski Sołwnik Biograficzny (Polish Biographical Dictionary)*, vol. 14 (Wroclaw, 1968-69); J. Johns, *Kosciuszko: A Biographical Study with a Historical Background of the Times* (Detroit, 1965); T. Kościuszko, *Pisma (Writings)*, ed. H. Mościcki (Warsaw, 1947); K. Sreniowska, *Kościuszko, bohater narodowy. Opinie wspołczesnych i potomnych (Kościuszko, National Hero: The Opinions of Contemporaries and Posterity)* (Warsaw, 1973).

M. Senkowska-Gluck

Related entry: POLAND.